SPEECHES,

ADDRESSES AND LETTERS

ON

INDUSTRIAL AND FINANCIAL QUESTIONS.

TO WHICH IS ADDED

AN INTRODUCTION, TOGETHER WITH COPIOUS NOTES AND AN INDEX.

BY

WILLIAM D. KELLEY, M. C.

PHILADELPHIA:
HENRY CAREY BAIRD,
INDUSTRIAL PUBLISHER,
406 WALNUT STREET.
1872.

S. A. George & Co., Stereotypers.
Collins, Printer.

TO

THE GREAT MASTER OF ECONOMIC SCIENCE,

THE PROFOUND THINKER,

AND THE

CAREFUL OBSERVER OF SOCIAL PHENOMENA,

MY

VENERABLE FRIEND AND TEACHER,

HENRY C. CAREY,

THIS VOLUME IS WITH GRATEFUL AFFECTION

INSCRIBED BY THE

AUTHOR.

PHILADA., Nov. 1, 1871.

INTRODUCTION.

In offering this volume to the public it is proper to state that I make no pretension to a critical knowledge of literature or rhetoric, and that, when preparing the papers it contains, I did not suppose they would ever be collected for republication. They are expressions of opinion called forth by occasions; and, as the reader will observe, not unfrequently in the excitement of current debate in the National House of Representatives, or in response to invitations to address popular assemblies under circumstances that precluded the possibility of reducing them to writing in advance of their delivery. It is proper also to say that I am not wholly responsible for their publication in book form, inasmuch as they have been collected and annotated in deference to the judgment and wishes of citizens of different sections of the country, who, though strangers to each other and engaged in pursuits involving apparently conflicting interests, agreed in persuading me that by this labor I might render a service to those of my countrymen who are engaged in farming or who depend on their labor for the means of supporting their children while giving them that measure of education without which no American citizen should be permitted to attain maturity.

While I regret some expressions in the colloquial portions of the Congressional speeches, and would have omitted them could it have been done without impairing the argument, I find no reason to question the soundness of my positions. The theory that labor—the productive exercise of the skill and muscular power of men who are responsible for the faithful and intelligent performance of civic and other duties—is merely a raw material, and that that nation which pays least for it is wisest and best governed, is inadmissible in a democracy; and when we shall determine to starve the bodies and minds of our operatives in order that we may successfully compete in common markets with the productions of the under-paid and poorly-fed peasants of Europe and the paupers of England, we shall assail the foundations of a government which rests upon the intelligence and integrity of its people. To defend our country against this result, is the office of a protective tariff, and for this duty it alone is sufficient.

This was not always my belief. My youthful judgment was captivated by the plausible but sophistical generalities by which cosmopolitanism or free trade is advocated, and my faith in them remained unshaken till events involving the prostration of our domestic industry, and the credit not only of cities and States, but of the nation, demonstrated the insufficiency or falsity of my long and dearly cherished theories. In 1847, I had seen with gratification the protective tariff of 1842 succeeded by the revenue or free trade tariff of 1846. To promote this change, I had labored not only with zeal and industry, but with undoubting faith that experience would prove its beneficence. A number of remarkable circumstances conspired to promote the success of the experiment. The potato rot was creating an unprecedented foreign demand for our breadstuffs. It was then ravaging the fields of England and the continent, having already devastated the fields, and more than decimated the people of Ireland, who, to escape starvation, were fleeing *en masse* to this country. The gold fields of Australia and California had just been discovered, and promised, by increasing the circulating medium of the world, and concentrating many thousands of emigrants, who would engage in mining, in countries without agriculture or manufactures, to create great markets for our productions of every kind, thus increasing our trade and quickening every department of industry. Beyond all this, however, and, as I afterwards came to understand, as a result of the condemned protective tariff, in conjunction with recent improvements in our naval architecture, our commercial marine was growing rapidly, our ship builders were prosperous, and our ship owners were receiving as compensation for extra speed a shilling a chest in advance of English freights for carrying tea from Hong Kong or Canton to London. Each of these circumstances was a good augury for the success of a tariff for revenue only. Going into effect under such favorable conditions, it must, I believed, procure for our farmers cheap foreign fabrics and wares, and secure a constantly increasing market for the productions of their farms; and by enlarging our share in the carrying trade of the world compel the rapid construction of ships and steamers, whose employment would increase our receipts of coin and immigrants. Trade being so nearly free, we must in a few years see the ships of all nations coming to New York for assorted cargoes, and our commercial metropolis would then become the financial centre of the world, in which international balances would be settled. That these were but a small part of the great results my theories promised will appear to any one who will refer to the annual reports of the then Secretary of the Treasury, Robert J. Walker, who was not more sanguine than I, and whose statements of the general prosperity that would flow from a revenue tariff were as positive and rose-tinted as those with which Messrs. Atkinson and Wells now beguile their followers.

Were we early revenue reformers worshippers at false shrines, or did the sequel approve our faith? History answers these questions with emphasis. It needed but a decade to demonstrate the folly of attempting to create a market for our increasing agricultural productions, and to develop our mining and manufacturing resources by the application of the beautiful abstractions disseminated by Free Trade Leagues. It was just ten years after the substitution of the revenue tariff of 1846 for the protective tariff of 1842, that the general bankruptcy of the American people was announced by the almost simultaneous failure of the Ohio Life and Trust Company, and the Bank of Pennsylvania, and the suspension of specie payments by almost every bank in the country. In that brief period, our steamers had been supplanted by foreign lines, and our clipper ships driven from the sea, or restricted to carrying between our Atlantic and Pacific ports. At the close of that brief term, the ship-yards of Maine were almost as idle as they are now when railroads traverse the country in all directions and compete with ships in carrying even such bulky commodities as sugar, cotton, and leaf tobacco;* and while the families of thousands of unemployed workmen in our great cities were in want of food, Illinois farmers found in corn, for which there was no market, the cheapest fuel they could obtain, though their fields were underlaid by an inexhaustible deposit of coal that is almost co-extensive with the State. Capital invested in factories, furnaces, forges, rolling mills and machinery was idle and unproductive, and there was but a limited home market for cotton or wool. Taking advantage of this condition of affairs, foreign dealers put their prices down sufficiently to bankrupt the cotton States, to induce many of our farmers to give up sheep raising, and to constrain many thousand immigrants who could not find employment to return to their native countries. 1847 had been a good year for farmers, mechanics, miners and merchants; but 1857 was a good year for sheriffs,

* See figures from the report of Mr. Nimmo, Chief of Tonnage Division, in note, page 431.

constables and marshals, though few were purchasers at their sales except mortgagees, judgment creditors, and capitalists who were able to pay cash at nominal prices for unproductive establishments, and hold them till happier circumstances should restore their value.

Not one of the glowing predictions of Political Economy had been fulfilled, and the surprise with which I contemplated the contrast presented by the condition of the country with what it had been at the close of the last period of protection, amounted to amazement. Nor did my cherished theories enable me to ascertain the cause of the sudden and general paralysis, or suggest a remedy for it. Yet I could not abandon them, for, as their ablest recent American champion, Mr. Edward Atkinson, of Boston, in his article in the *Atlantic Monthly* for October, says of the details of the Revenue Reform budget, they were "simple, sensible, and right." Was not each one a truism that might be expressed as a maxim—an indisputable proposition—the mere statement of which established its verity? To prove that they were not responsible for the prostration of our industries, the want of a market for our breadstuffs, and the widespread bankruptcy that prevailed, required the enunciation of but one of them: CUSTOMS DUTIES ARE TAXES.* No one can dispute this proposition, for the people pay them, and the Government collects them, and not only may but should raise its entire revenue through them. Surely nobody could have the temerity to assert that an industrious and prosperous people could be reduced to idleness and bankruptcy by the repeal or reduction of taxes, and thus charge this national disaster to free trade and the *doctrinaires* who had kindly taught us Political Economy, and induced us to abandon the protective system. The case was clear. Yet, strange to say, perfect as the demonstration seemed to be, I was forced by the condition of the country to doubt and ask myself whether, in some occult way, the reduction of the rate of duties might not have had something to do with producing it. The results promised by the teachers of my cherished science, and those attained by experiment, were irreconcilable, and I was constrained to ask myself whether it might not be possible that Political Economy was not an exact—an absolute—science, the laws of which were equally applicable to all nations, without regard to the conditions and requirements of the people, or the extent, variety or degree of the development of their resources? It was easier to harbor this doubt than to believe the alternative, which was, that the Almighty had not put

* See Dr. Bushnell, in note, pages 317, 318.

production, commerce and trade in the United States under the government of universal and immutable laws, but had left them to the control of chance. This conclusion being inadmissible, there was nothing left but to waive the further consideration of the subject, or to withdraw my theories from the dazzling light of abstract reason, and examine them under the shade of present experience.

It is a cardinal maxim among the adherents of free trade that TWO MARKETS IN WHICH TO BUY AND SELL ARE BETTER THAN ONE, and I could not dispute it; but when in the progress of my re-examination, I announced it to an intelligent protectionist as indisputable, he admitted that it was so. "But," said he, "where is the evidence that free trade is the road to two markets for the United States?" In endeavoring to answer this question satisfactorily to myself it became apparent that I had evaded the real point at issue. Both parties to the controversy agree that two markets are better than one. But the protectionists say, "Do not risk the loss or diminution of the home market afforded by our people when fully employed and well paid, by attempting to secure another, in a direction where success will be, to say the least, exceedingly doubtful;" the free traders saying, "Court foreign trade by all means, and as you are sure of the home market, you will thus secure two." Which are right? To determine this, we must ascertain whether trade between nations is reciprocal or nearly so.* To settle this question, I made a thorough and searching appeal to the trade statistics of our own and other countries, and ascertained that the amount of our productions consumed by the manufacturing nations of Europe has in no degree, in any year, depended upon the amount of their productions consumed by us; but on the contrary, that they never took an equal amount, and frequently, when we were taking most from them, took least of everything but cotton, which they could not obtain elsewhere, from us. Thus it had often occurred that when our store-houses were being gorged with productions of the underpaid workmen of England, she, taking gold and silver from us, had gone to Prussia, Germany, Austria, Turkey, and France, who bought but little from her, and the chief diet of whose laboring people consisted of rye bread, potatoes and garlic, for her breadstuffs. This examination further showed that the amount of breadstuffs England will ever take from us is measured by the slight deficiency she may expect to experience after having exhausted the markets of those lower priced

* See extract from Kirk's Social Politics, in note, page 186.

countries, whose people are subjects, and whose wages mark the minimum on which families may subsist. When Æsop's stupid dog snapped at the shadow in the water he lost his bone; and the investigation convinced me that the attempt to secure a second market by reducing our customs duties had destroyed our home market, but opened no other for any of our productions except gold and silver, and State and corporate bonds. It had given England, with her low rates of wages and interest, two markets in which to sell, and by destroying our home market for grain, an additional one in which to buy; but had deprived us of the one on which, under an adequate system of protection, we could always depend, as has been shown by the uniform general prosperity that has prevailed since the Morrill tariff of 1861 went into effect. Thus it appeared that the fallacy was not in the abstract proposition which neither party disputed, but in the assumption that free trade would insure us two markets.

Kindred to the foregoing proposition, and equally undeniable as an abstract truth, seemed this other: YOU SHOULD BUY WHERE YOU CAN BUY CHEAPEST.* Yet we had been doing this for ten years, and were bankrupt. This condition of affairs could not, it seemed to me, be the result of reduced rates of duties, and the payment of reduced prices for what we had consumed. What process of reasoning could show these facts to be related as cause and effect? England could sell us railroad bars to lay over our wide stretches of limestone country, and our immense fields of coal and iron, at lower prices than, in the undeveloped condition of our resources, and with our higher priced labor and money, we could produce them; and we had bought our supply from her. With her accumulated capital, machinery, skilled labor, and her lower wages, she could also spin and weave cotton and wool, and make the cloth into garments cheaper than our countrymen could, and we had bought from her our clothes, or the cloth from which to cut them. So, too, she could sell us chemicals, prepared drugs, pig-iron, raw steel, and an immense number of other commodities for less money than we could produce them; and we had gone to her markets and bought them where we could buy them cheapest. Meanwhile, we had mined hundreds of millions of dollars worth of gold and silver; had raised unprecedented crops of cotton, tobacco, and breadstuffs; had produced immense supplies of naval stores and other exportable commodities; and had, withal, issued hundreds of millions of interest-bearing bonds, by which our future productions and those of our posterity

---

* See Dr. Bushnell, in notes, pages 285 and 354.

were mortgaged. Yet, strange to tell, in spite of the lower duties paid on our imports, and the lower than American prices at which we had procured our supplies, we had not gold and silver enough to serve as a basis for a redeemable currency, and being, in many instances, unable to pay the interest on our bonds were sued and sold out by our English friends, to whom our gold, silver, and bonds had gone. We were, however, rich in one class of commodities—the productions of the farm. Of these the people of the Western States had a superabundance. It was, however, unfortunately, not possible to make them available, as our English creditors would not take them even in payment of debts unless we would, after paying for their transportation to the sea-board, let them have them at the low prices at which they could obtain like articles which had been produced by the ill-fed peasants of Russia, Prussia, Austria, Hungary, and Turkey. Than to do this it was better for farmers in the extreme West to let their crops perish on the field.

Our condition was anomalous. There was no element of wealth, or of the conveniences of life that could be produced by a reasonable amount of labor outside of the tropics of which we did not possess greater stores in the form of raw materials than any other nation; and of the productions of the farm our supply was so superabundant that some of us were, as I have said, using corn for fuel; yet, our manufacturing operatives were poor and unemployed, our farmers were unable to pay for past purchases or fresh supplies, and our merchants and banks, involved in the common fate, were unable to meet their obligations. Did this strange experience prove that it is not best to buy where you can buy cheapest? No. But it did prove that money-price is not the test of cheapness; and that we buy more cheaply, though the nominal price of each commodity be higher when we buy what we consume of those who will buy what we produce at fair prices, than we do when we buy at lower prices for cash, or on credit, and permit our productions to perish for the want of a market. Thus did deductions from unquestionable and present experience demonstrate the fallacy of the system of "established principles," which I had cherished as a sufficient economic creed.

The terrible ordeal through which the working classes of England are now passing, is constraining her statesmen and scholars to bring the prevailing system of Political Economy to the test of experience, and one of these scholars has been bold enough to deny not only the policy, but the morality of the proposition I have just considered. Mr. David Syme, in a well-considered and powerful article on the "Method of Po-

B

litical Economy," in the *Westminster Review* for July, 1871, which has come under my notice since the foregoing was written, says:

"A close investigation will, indeed, lead to the conclusion that the spirit of the moral law is incompatible with the modern economic doctrine of buying in the cheapest, and selling in the dearest market. For a scrupulous sense of duty will often compel a man to act contrary to his own personal interests. Such a man will conduct himself in his business relations on the strictest principles of honor and fair dealing. He will refuse to take an advantage when the law may permit it, when, by so doing, he might prejudice the interests of others. He will not take all he can get, and give as little as he can; but he will give as much as he can afford, and take only what is fair and equitable. This is not Utopianism, but the true spirit of the moral law.

"If, moreover, we consider man in the social state, we shall find that the individual is bound to recognize the interests of others as well as his own. He cannot, even if he would, be guided in his social relations by an exclusive regard for his own interests. In seeking his own advantage he must be careful to do nothing that might in any way be injurious to his neighbor. He must not sell a spurious article for a genuine one, nor a deleterious compound for a wholesome one. He must not use false labels or unjust weights. . . . . Economic science recognizes the existence of the social state, and the social state presupposes the existence of the social virtues—honor, honesty, and a regard for the feelings and rights of others."

It was not easy to abandon opinions I had cherished through so many years, and in which my faith had been so implicit, but it was still more difficult to accept the opposite system, that of protection, which I had so often denounced as false, selfish, and exclusive. Nor did I do this hastily: more than two years had been devoted to the writings of the ablest advocates of both systems, and still I halted between them. Meanwhile, it became apparent to me, not only that Political Economy was not a science, but that it was impossible to frame a system of abstract economic propositions which would be universally applicable and beneficent; and, further, that the same principles could not be applied beneficially to England and the United States. The conditions of the two nations are not the same, but are in striking contrast. England is a small island, but the United States embraces almost the entire available territory of a continent. The former is burdened by an excess of population, and vexed by the question as to how she shall dispose of the excess; but our great need is industrious people, and with us the question is how can we increase immigration. She has to import food for half her people, and her foreign trade is to her what seed-time and harvest are to the countries from which she procures the breadstuffs she requires but cannot produce; but were they on our soil, we could feed ten times the number of her whole people; and even while I write, the merchants of Minnesota, Iowa, and other northwestern States are suffering financial embarrassment because the farmers they supply cannot find a market for their crops. She is dependent on foreign countries for most of the raw materials she consumes; but we have within our limits exhaustless stores of every variety not dependent upon tropical heat for their production. Her resources are ascertained and developed; but ours await development, and in regions, any one of which is larger than all western Europe, including the British Islands, await definite ascertainment. Her population is compacted within narrow limits, and her railroads are completed and paid for; but our people are settled sparsely over half a continent, and most of our system of roads, for which the capital is yet to be produced, is to be constructed. The charges for transportation within her circumscribed and populous limits are very light; but over our extended and thinly-settled country they are necessarily heavy. Her factories were erected and supplied with machinery while she maintained the most rigid system of protection the world has ever seen; but ours are to be built as experiments in the face of threatened free trade which would involve a more unequal competition than any against which she defended hers by protective duties and absolute prohibitions. Her average rate of interest is 3 per cent. per annum; but ours is never less than 6 per cent. per annum, and in large sections of the country is often 3 percent. per month. The great body of her laborers, even since the recent extension of the suffrage, are *subjects* without civic duties; but ours are *citizens*, and liable to such duties. She pays the daily wages of her workmen with shillings; but we pay ours with dollars worth four shillings each, and give many classes of them more dollars than she does shillings: It is, therefore, impossible that the same economic polity can be applied with equal advantage to countries whose condition presents so many and such important contrasts.

Ten years under a tariff which levied the lowest rates of duties consistent with the purpose of raising by imports the amount of revenue required by the current expenses of the government, sufficed to destroy the industries and credit of the American people. The immense advantages England possesses in manufactures and trade have enabled her to withstand the untoward influence of free trade for a longer period than we were able to; but at the end of a quarter of a century it has become apparent that even the mistress of the seas and the work-shop of the world cannot, at less cost than the loss of national prestige and threatened revolution, throw her ports open to unrestricted competition. The effect on England of the abandonment of the protective system does not exhibit itself in wide-spread bankruptcy as it did with us. The enormous accumulations of capital held by her privileged classes have prevented this. It is, however, observable in the disappearance of the small farmer, and of the small work-shop that in more prosperous times would have expanded into a factory; in the concentration of land and machinery in the hands of a constantly diminishing number of persons; and in the rapidly increasing destitution, idleness, intemperance, and despair of her laboring classes.*

In the course of his admirable sermon before the University of Oxford, December 20th, 1868, Rev. Brooke Lambert said: "The severance between the rich and the poor is to me an even sadder thing than the wretched state of the labor market. I can fancy a remedy possible for the one, I can foresee no remedy for the other. The gap between them seems widening every day, as trade and land fall into the hands of large capitalists, who absorb all smaller concerns, all smaller holdings." And *Blackwood's Magazine* for April, 1870, in an article entitled "The State, the Poor, and the Country," says: "The lamentable depression of trade, and consequent want of employment which have recently prevailed, have now reached a most serious magnitude in many of the larger towns, and most of all in London and its far-spreading suburbs. The intensity of the distress in the metropolitan districts has not been equalled in recent times. And the break-down of our Poor-law system, despite all efforts of voluntary associations, has been appalling in its results. Not a week passes without several cases of 'deaths from starvation,' duly attested by the verdict of coroners' inquests, where the medical and other evidence reveals an amount of unaided wretchedness and starvation, which one would suppose impossible in a civilized country. Men, women and children dying from sheer famine in the heart of the wealthiest city in the world!"

The extracts from the works of Sir John Byles, Sir Edward Sullivan, Professor Kirk, Messrs. Grant, Patterson, Smith, Hoyle, and other recent British writers, which will be found in notes throughout this volume, more than con-

* See extracts from Grant's Home Politics, in note, pages 31, 32; and Sir Edward Sullivan's Protection to Native Industry, pages 194, 195.

firm this statement. Sir Edward Sullivan admonishes the governing classes that if they do not wish to reduce England to the condition of a manufacturing country without workshops or skilled workmen, they must protect native industry sufficiently to restore the home market for cotton fabrics, which has fallen off 35 per cent., by reason of the fact that the enforced idleness of masses of the working people has deprived them of the ability to consume this indispensable element of comfortable attire; and Mr. Hoyle produces from official statistics the figures to prove the startling statement.

Nor can the British Government longer close its eyes to this distress and continue to assert that THE LAW OF SUPPLY AND DEMAND is the heaven-appointed and all-sufficient regulator of societary movements. It is even now feebly attempting to regulate both supply and demand by its own action. To this end Earl Granville, Foreign Secretary, as early as the 14th of April, 1870, addressed a circular dispatch to the Governors of British Colonies, from which I take the following paragraph:

"The distress prevailing among the laboring classes in many parts of the United Kingdom has directed public attention to the question of Emigration as a means of relief. It has been urged on Her Majesty's Government that while there are in this country large numbers of well-conducted, industrious laborers, for whom no employment can be found, there exists in most of the colonies a more extensive demand for labor than the laboring class on the spot can supply. The result of emigration would, therefore, it is said, be equally advantageous to the emigrant and the colonies—to the former, by placing him in a position to earn an independence; to the latter, by supplying a want that retards their progress and prosperity. Under the circumstances, Her Majesty's Government is anxious to be furnished with your opinion as to the prospects which the colony under your government holds out to emigrants, both of the agricultural and the artisan class.

. . . .

"The points on which we should be specially desirous of receiving information are: the classes of laborers whose labor is most in demand in the colony under your government; the numbers for whom employment could be found; the probable wages they would earn; whether married men with families could obtain wages to enable them to support their families, and house accommodation for their shelter; what assistance or facilities would be provided to pass the emigrants to the districts where their labor is in demand; and whether any pecuniary assistance would be granted either toward their passages, or toward providing depots and subsistence on their first arrival, or toward sending them up to the country."

That England will soon so far modify her revenue system as to re-adopt many of the distinctive features of the Protective System, I confidently predict. Not that I credit her privileged classes with quick or enlarged sympathy with the laboring classes, but because I know that they have always had sufficient tact to avert popular outbreak by timely concession. And though I remember how the people of Ireland and Orissa were permitted to starve, I still believe that the consumers of England will consent to pay duties on such goods as compete with English labor in the home market, and relieve from taxation the tea, coffee, sugar, currants, raisins, tobacco, and spirits of the laboring classes, rather than incur the risk of widespread famine in London, Lancashire, and other great industrial centres of the country. But, were they capable of the fatuity of withholding their consent, the question has passed from their decision. Their last concession to the popular will, the extension of the suffrage, makes this one inevitable. The article in *Blackwood*, already referred to, thus defines the position of the question:

"A new power has been introduced into our political system, new forces are at work within the pale of the Constitution. The Government has become National in the fullest sense of the word; and with the change a new breath of life is stirring society. New views are rapidly forming; new hopes and aspirations are entering into the heart of the masses. The rule of the middle classes established by the Reform Bill of 1832, has come to an end; and the doctrines which regulated the legislation of that period are now being tested and considered from a different, indeed opposite point of view.

"For nearly forty years the prime object of our legislation has been the interests of the Consumers; *now*, we shall soon have the masses advocating their own interests as Producers. What is more, the State has now become simply the nation itself, acting through a chosen body of administrators; and it is easy to discern that under the new *régime* the Government will be called upon to adopt a very different policy in domestic affairs from that represented by the principle of the Whigs and *doctrinaires*, which has been paramount since 1832. That principle well suited the interests of the wealthy and comparatively fortunate classes, who needed no help from the State, yet who got all they asked for, by the abolition of all custom duties which shackled their business. But will that principle keep its ground now that the weaker classes also have a voice in the Government?

Will they not maintain that they, as an integral part of the nation, have a claim to be fully considered in the policy of the Government; and that, if they can point out any system of governmental action which will benefit them, without doing injustice to the rest of the community, no *doctrinaire* limitations upon the actions of the State shall be allowed to stand in the way? The maxims of the Liberals, which have been predominant since 1832, will be thrown into the crucible and tried anew. Already in vague murmurs, which ere long will become distinct and earnest speech, the masses are beginning to say that the principles which have been in vogue during the rule of the middle classes will not suit them. 'Our interests,' they say, 'are those of Producers, not of Consumers.

"'We also are poor, and you are wealthy; we are weak, and you are strong; with us employment is a far more precarious thing than it is with you, and we have but small earnings to fall back upon when out of work. State help, though not needful to the middle classes, is needed at times by us; and we shall never rest contented until that principle is acknowledged and properly applied.'"

The government cannot long refuse to listen to this demand, which no longer comes from the laboring classes alone, but is enforced by many such writers as those to whom I am indebted for many of my most instructive notes, and now by *Blackwood*, the *Quarterly Reviews*, and other great organs of opinion. That school of political economists who propound free trade as the result of their system is finding less favor with the thinkers of England than heretofore. They discover that it is not producing the results it promised, but other and very different ones, and are demanding that it be tested by the inductive system, and proven by the facts of experience. It has become clear to many of them that under its influence the working people are not prosperous or contented; that the home market for some of their great staples diminishes steadily; and that in spite of Government assurances that British trade increases, it is stationary, if not absolutely diminishing. Discarding statements prepared by skilful statistical jugglers like Mr. Wells, our late Commissioner of Revenue, they are comparing and analyzing results for themselves, and have thus detected the fraudulent practices by which they have been deceived. The last trick British statistics have been made to play was by her Majesty's Commissioners of Customs, who, to prove the steady increase of trade, proclaimed with much triumph that the exports during 1870 were 11 per cent. greater than they were in 1868. This cheering result, which, isolated from the general facts to which it is related, is true, is made to prove the steady increase of trade by a device that would do no discredit to the cunning and audacity of our great statistical manipulator. This is the process by which it is done. The French army moved toward the German frontier about the 15th of July, 1870, and at the close of the year the war was at its height, promising not only to be of long duration, but threatening to involve all Europe. It caused a general suspension of the industries of France and Germany, whose wares and fabrics were crowding those of England out of so many markets, or the employment of their operatives in the production of arms and munitions of war. It also gave England an immense market for these. But what was, perhaps, more important than all this, it caused the withdrawal of the commercial marine of those countries from the ocean, and gave the ships and shops of England a monopoly of the carrying and foreign trade of the world. Her trade could not fail to be exceptionally large that year, as owing to the war having extended far into it, and been prolonged by the folly of the *Commune* it will be this year. The Commissioners of Customs prove the virtues of free trade by contrasting the exports of this exceptional year with those of 1868, in which they were lower than they have been since 1865. The following official figures will suffice to show that the exports from Great Britain for the last four years, including 1870, which was so exceptionally large, have on the average been less than during 1866 by the considerable sum of more than $6,700,000 per annum:

1866.	Total value of British Exports...............	£188,917,536
1867.	" " "	181,183,971
1868.	" " "	179,463,644
1869.	" " "	189,953,957
1870.	" " "	199,649,938

The reader who will add the value of the four years, '67–70, and divide the result by four, and compare the figures thus obtained with the total exports of 1866, will ascertain precisely how rapidly and steadily the trade of Great Britain increases.

Mr. Syme, in the course of his article in the *Westminster Review*, to which I have referred, says: "Political Economy exhibits no sign of progressiveness. Instead of discoveries, of which we have had none of any consequence since Adam Smith's time, we have had endless disputation and setting up of dogmas. Whatever progress may have been made in other sciences during the last century, there has been none in this. The most elementary principles are still matters of dispute. The doctrine of free trade, for instance, which is looked upon as the crowning triumph of Political Economy, is still very far from being universally recognized. Even in England, after twenty years' trial under most favorable circumstances, free trade has been put upon its defence. We make no progress, and from the very nature of our method of investigation, we can make none. The Political Economist observes phenomena with a foregone conclusion as to their cause. His method, in fact, is the method of the savage. The phenomena of nature, the thunder, the lightning, or the earthquake, strike the savage with awe and wonder; but he only looks within himself for an explanation of these phenomena. To him, therefore, the forces of nature are only the efforts of beings like himself, great and powerful, no doubt, but with good and evil propensities, and subject to every human caprice. Like the Political Economist, he works within the vicious circle of his own feelings, and he cannot comprehend, any more than the savage, how he can discover the laws which regulate the phenomena which he sees around him. The savage would reduce the Divine mind to the dimensions of the human; the Political Economist would reduce the human mind to the dimensions of his ideal.

"Our conclusion is, that the inductive method is alone applicable to the investigation of economic science, and that we shall never be able to make any solid progress so long as we continue to follow the *à priori* method—a method which has not aided, but clogged and fettered us in the pursuit of truth, and which is utterly alien to the spirit of modern scientific inquiry."

For the edification of those who may be incredulous as to free trade being on its defence in England, Mr. Syme refers to Professor Bonamy Price's arraignment of it in the *Contemporary Review* of February, 1871.*

The *London Quarterly Review* for July [1871], contains a spirited article on "Economical Fallacies and Labor Utopias," in which it handles with great freedom "the school of political economists now in the ascendant." The date at which it was published proves that the author could not have seen the article entitled "Free Trade—Revenue Reform," in our *Atlantic* for October, yet he says: "There is an utopianism which counts its chickens before they are hatched, nay, cackles over chickens it expects to hatch from eggs that are addled." Referring to Mr. John Stuart Mill, who, had the *Atlantic's* article been anonymous, might, from the freedom with which it disposes of existing relations and interests, well have been suspected of its authorship, the *Quarterly* proceeds to say:

"If Mr. Mill, the recognized leader of that school, is to be designated as an economical 'enthusiast,' or perhaps more

* See also remarks of Sir John Byles and Mr. R. H. Patterson, in notes, pages 199 and 200; and also of Sir Edward Sullivan, in note, pages 378, 379.

properly as the founder and propagator of economical enthusiasm, he has earned that designation more by the excessive exercise of the dialectical than of the imaginative faculty, and does not so much body forth to himself the forms of things unknown, as suggest to his disciples revolutions, unrealized even in imagination, of all existing relations between classes and sexes, as *logically* admissible, and not to be set aside as practically chimerical without actual experiment. His enthusiasm is the speculative passion of starting ever fresh game in the wide field of abstract social possibilities—philosophically indifferent to all objections drawn from the actual conditions of men, women, or things in the concrete. Mr. Mill would be very capable, like Condorcet, of deriving from the doctrine of human perfectibility the inference that there was no demonstrable reason why the duration of human life might not be prolonged indefinitely by discoveries (hereafter to be made) in hygiene. And to all objections drawn from universal human experience of the growth and decay of vital power within a limited period, it would be quite in the character of his mind and temper to reply calmly that the life of man, like the genius of woman, had not hitherto been developed under such conditions as to draw out its capabilities to the full extent. Like Condorcet, too, while dealing perturbation all around him, Mr. Mill is imperturbable, and might be described as *he* was, as '*un mouton en rage—un Volcan couvert de neige!*' "

It was the opinion of the great Bonaparte, that Political Economy would grind empires to powder, though they were made of adamant. The British Government is proving the excellence of his judgment, and schoolmen and theorists are industriously laboring to induce the American people to confirm it by even a grander illustration. This pretended science which, Mr. Mill says, "necessarily reasons from assumptions, and not from facts," is sedulously and devoutly taught at Yale, and most of our leading colleges. It is fortunate that the intimate relations of many of the students with the industries and people of the country render the scholasticisms of their teachers harmless; and in parting from them, they sometimes throw back upon them the terrible results of experience, as their reply to the weary chapters of deductions from assumptions with which they have been tortured. How boldly and aptly, yet respectfully this may be done, was shown by Mr. Orville Justus Bliss, of Chicago, at Yale's last commencement. A leading scholar of his class, he had been selected to deliver the Valedictory, in the course of which he said:

"A cry for relief has gone forth, and refuses to be hushed

We cannot always ignore these men. Neither can we forever satisfy them by quoting Adam Smith. Suppose some wise individual should stand with a copy of 'The Wealth of Nations' in his hand before a mob of London bread-rioters, and begin to read the chapter on wages; would they all go off rejoicing in the beauties of the science, and convinced that they were happy? Political Economy has had ample trial in England. A mill agent recently said, 'I regard my work people just as I regard my machinery. So long as they can do my work for what I choose to pay them, I keep them, getting out of them all I can. When my machines get old and useless, I reject them, and get new; and these people are part of my machinery.' Is not that a sufficiently rigorous application of the law of demand and supply? And it describes the whole factory system in England, up to the time when the agitators took it in hand. What it has done for England, I need not repeat. Suffice it to say, that Political Economy, as a solution of this question, is a disastrous failure."

And again: "The poor cannot help themselves. They are tied hand and foot with an enslaving destitution. We say: 'It is a free country; let every one make of himself as much as he can.' We challenge one and all to an unbounded competition. But to these people the seeming fairness is mockery. It rivals the brave boy who first takes a good long start, and then turns around and offers to race with you to the next corner. The child of the laborer may lift himself from his degradation, and become a power for good. But there must be some measure of intelligence, to serve as a basis upon which to build. They must be made to feel that society is their friend, not an enemy, whose prosperity is their defeat. What, then, is the laying of a cable, or the spanning of a continent? What beauty do they find in literature, what exaltation in science—I had almost said, what solace in religion? Not in the name of an endangered society, imminent as its peril is; not in the interests of great money-wielders, plainly as those interests point to educated labor, do I plead the cause of these people; but because they are part of our common humanity, and have a right to partake of our common, intellectual, æsthetic, and social delight."

I have said that I believe England will soon readopt many of the distinctive principles of the protective system. Unless *we* determine otherwise, she must do this soon. Her newly enfranchised producers will demand it, and the action of her colonies will impart vehemence to the demand. Protection is a settled principle with the governments of Victoria, New South Wales, Queensland, and other Australian colonies. Speaking of this, together with the fact that they are establishing Customs Unions on the principle of the Zollverein, Charles Wentworth Dilke, in his *Greater Britain*, says: "It is a common doctrine in the colonies of England that a nation cannot be called 'independent' if it has to cry out to another for supplies of necessaries; that true national existence is first attained when the country becomes capable of supplying to its own citizens those goods without which they cannot exist in the state of comfort they have already reached. Political is apt to follow on commercial dependency, they say." After a somewhat glowing portrayal of the moral beauty of cosmopolitanism or free trade, Mr. Dilke, recurring to the colonies, says: "On the other hand, it may be argued that if every State consults the good of its own citizens, we shall, by the action of all nations, obtain the desired happiness of the whole world, and this with rapidity, from the reason that every country understands its own interests better than it does those of its neighbor. As a rule, the colonists hold that they should not protect themselves against the sister colonies, but only against the outer world; and while I was in Melbourne an arrangement was made with respect to the border trade between Victoria and New South Wales; but this is at present (1868) the only step that has been taken toward inter-colonial Free Trade."

The British Government cannot, without our consent, maintain its present revenue system for five years more. But we may enable it to postpone the change a few years longer, inasmuch as by maintaining our workshops in England rather than in the United States, we can soothe popular discontent by giving employment to her hundreds of thousands of unemployed workers. This would also not only increase her foreign trade, but by enabling those who are now idle and requiring support to earn wages and purchase supplies, would, till we should again reach bankruptcy, revive her home market.* To repeal or reduce our protective duties, while our people are burdened by the annual levy of more than $100,000,000 of internal taxes, is the only method by which the languishing trade and industry of England can be materially invigorated under her present free trade revenue system.† Should the American people conclude that cheap goods for cash constitute the chief end of men and nations, and that their interests will be best served by having

* See extract from Ryland's *Iron Trade Circular*, in note, page 405.

† See extract from *Our National Resources, and how they are Wasted*, by Wm. Hoyle, page 103.

their ores smelted, and their pig-iron, railroad bars, Bessemer and cast-steel, chemicals, cotton and woolen goods, and other wares and fabrics, made in foreign lands by people whose food is raised by the ill-fed peasants of Russia, Prussia, Austria, and Turkey, the discontented artisans of England will probably be pacified, and the emigration of her skilled workmen to this country be arrested for a decade. What the farmers of the Mississippi Valley would do with their crops meanwhile, is a question worthy of their consideration.

But I may remark that it was the consideration of the question, Where shall the farmers of America find a steady and remunerative market for their crops? that confirmed my adherence to protection. The circumstances were these: In 1859, during the period of doubt heretofore referred to, I sought the privilege of renewing a neglected intimacy with Henry C. Carey, to whom I have since gone, and never in vain, when troubled by doubt on any economic question. Hitherto, our intercourse had been that of earnest adherents of conflicting systems, but henceforth it was to be that of friends in council, or rather of teacher and pupil. I already recognized the fact that with their surplus capital, immense sums of which are invested in our bonds and those of other nations which pay as high rates of interest as we do, it was always possible for English manufacturers, in every department of production, to combine, and by selling their goods, for a season or two, in this one of their many markets, at rates slightly below their actual cost, to destroy their American rivals, whose capital was not often adequate to the demands of their business, and who, when compelled to borrow, were subject to high rates of interest.* And I also knew that the workingmen of this country could not maintain homes and rear and educate families on such wages as those of other countries were compelled to receive. But the question that gave me difficulty was (for such I mistakenly supposed must be a result of protection), why should the farmer be taxed to defend the manufacturer and his employees against such conspiracies, and this inevitable, though fatal, competition? This apparent conflict of interest it was at which I halted, and the service Mr. Carey rendered me was that of showing me that no such conflict existed; but that, on the contrary, the prosperity of the American farmer did then, and always must, depend on the steady employment of the American miner, artisan, and laborer, at such wages as would enable them and their families to be free consumers of the productions of the field, the orchard, and the dairy. With the clear

* See extract from Report of Parliamentary Commission, in note, page 328.

perception of this truth, that, at least in the United States, the prosperity of the farmer is dependent on that of the manufacturer, and the prosperity of the manufacturer equally dependent on that of the farmer; and that, in so far there was no conflict, but an absolute harmony of interests between them, I became a protectionist. My last doubt had been removed, for I now saw that the Protective System was not chargeable with the selfish exclusiveness I had ascribed to it, but was, in fact, the truest and most beneficent cosmopolitanism; nay, more, that it was essential to the enjoyment of absolutely free trade by the American people.

Let me hastily demonstrate the truth of these propositions. Trade is most free when there is an active and remunerative demand for all the commodities that can be produced; and this is when the people are so generally employed in remunerative pursuits that the number steadily increases of those who, by their earnings, can, while supplying themselves and families with the average necessaries and conveniences provided by modern civilization, accumulate sufficient capital to enable them to change their business, or vicinage, as inclination, health, or circumstances may dictate. In other words, trade is most free when the greatest number of people are able to buy or sell, to work or rest, to spend money in travel, or for a coveted luxury—or to deposit the amount required for this in a savings bank, or purchase therewith an interest-bearing bond. The authors from whose works most of the notes by which I have enforced the doctrines of my addresses and letters have been taken, prove that the number of the people of England, Ireland, Scotland, and Wales who enjoy these conditions, is steadily diminishing; that there are more than a million inhabitants of these countries who are vagrants, and more than another million who are paupers; and that this is not because they were born to pauperism and vagrancy, but because, at least in a large majority of cases, they cannot get work whereby they may earn the means of independent subsistence.* As freedom from customs duties does not establish free trade, it has not enabled them to sell or buy freely. On the other hand, the farmers of Minnesota, Iowa, Nebraska, Kansas, Missouri, and Arkansas find that there is such a surplus of food in the world that their trade is greatly restricted. Having all raised grain and live stock, there is no chance for commerce between them, and though we are importing vastly more foreign goods than ever before, they can-

---

* See statements of Grant, Sullivan, Kirk, Hoyle, R. Dudley Baxter, Smith, and Patterson, in notes, pages 24–5, 195–7, 267–9, 338–9, and 422.

not find a market for their productions at prices that will reimburse the cost of production. These States abound in the ores of iron, copper, lead, zinc, nickel, and other metals, and in fuel and water-power. They all raise wool, some of them cotton, and Arkansas is a natural silk field, in every quarter of which the mulberry tree is indigenous; but these exhaustless stores of the elements of wealth, and the forces whereby they may be utilized, have been neglected. Had they been largely appropriated, there would be no glut in the grain markets of these States. Trade throughout their limits would be both free and active. Many of the vagrants and paupers of England have the skill to mine and smelt ores; to convert them into wares; to spin wool, cotton, and silk—weave them into fabrics, and color them with exquisite skill and taste. Can we not, in lieu of homesteads, offer such of their skilled countrymen as still have the ability to come, steady work at such generous wages as will tempt a million or two of them —miners, smelters, engineers, machinists, spinners, weavers, dyers, and other classes of artisans—to come and open the mines of those States, build and work furnaces, forges, rolling-mills, and factories? This would not only give their farmers free trade, but by building up towns, and requiring local railroads, quadruple the price of every acre they own.* This can only be done by putting Protection on the foundation of a settled policy, for who will invest capital in mines, mills, or furnaces to stand idle while we go abroad for our wares and fabrics? Or why should intelligent artisans come here to be idle, or work for such wages as they can earn at home? The farmer should have a liberal price for his grain, but to live well and enjoy free trade he must let others live, not grudging the laborer generous wages for his work, or withholding from enterprise and capital just guarantees of a fair return for their efforts at developing the resources of a new country. Could a million of English people, the adults being, not farmers but miners, smelters, machinists, engine builders, spinners, weavers, dyers, and artisans generally, be induced to settle in the States I have named, and pursue their respective callings, the glut in the grain market would soon disappear, and the freest trade would prevail between them and the farmers. By the pre-emption and homestead laws, we are tempting agricultural immigrants to come by tens of thousands annually to increase our production of grain and live stock. Protection to high wages is needed to bring other classes. The homestead on which nothing marketable can be raised will prove but a poor boon to the

* See notes, pages 202 and 360–1.

immigrant. And by promoting the immigration of artisans, we should render to the impoverished masses of England the highest service. By making prosperous American citizens of a million of them, we should improve the chances in life of those who remained behind. The prosperity that would result from the infusion of such an immigration into even the remotely interior States I have named, would quicken the trade of England; for a prosperous people always consume freely, irrespective of the money price of commodities. They will not only satisfy their wants, but gratify their desires; and our importations are always largest when, under protective duties, our labor and machinery are most fully employed. The present is a striking illustration of this fact.

The existing tariff is highly protective. With a larger free list of raw materials than ever before, the rate of duty averages, I believe, about 40 per cent.; yet, our imports are vastly in excess of any former year. How are we to account for this paradox? Thus: We are prosperous, and a prosperous people will gratify their desires. The value of our foreign imports during the last fiscal year was nearly 22 per cent. greater than those of any preceding one. In the year ending June 30th, 1866, they amounted to $444,811,066, but did not attain this magnitude again till that which ended with June, 1871, during which they exceeded it by nearly $100,000,000, having been $541,493,776. This increased importation of foreign goods surprises no intelligent protectionist. It but confirms his theory that protection is the pathway to free trade: that a well protected and generous home market is the only basis on which extended foreign trade can be maintained.* When, as is the case at present, customs duties are so adjusted as to countervail the lower rates of wages and interest prevailing in competing countries, increased importations do not come as they would under free trade, to undermine and destroy our industries, but to supplement them. Our productive power increases more rapidly than our imports, and we are producing each year a greater percentage of our total consumption. But rapid as is the increase of our productive power, such is our general prosperity that our ability to purchase and consume tasks it to its utmost in all departments save that of farming. This is shown by the fact that in those departments in which our production has increased most steadily and rapidly, the home demand is so active and remunerative that it saves us from sending so many of our goods as we did in less prosperous seasons to foreign markets for sale in competition

---

* See note, page 10.

with the cheaper goods of Germany and England. If readers desire proof that such is the case, they will find it on page 125, of the July number of the *North American Review*, where Mr. Wells enumerates a number of articles of which we export less than we did in 1860, and points to that fact as evidence of declining prosperity. Every reader will recognize the fact that our production of each of the articles named by him has increased in a ratio exceeding that of our increase of population, and see that the circumstance from which the writer cunningly suggests our failing condition, is pregnant proof of our increased prosperity, our power to purchase and consume more than ever before. I may remark, in passing, that this is but a fair illustration of the unscrupulous ingenuity that has characterized the writings of Mr. Wells since his return from England.

Without free access to our markets, England cannot find employment for her people or capital; but as our tariff, by defending the home market, invites enterprise, her capital and people can find profitable employment in developing our resources, and both are coming.* Thus reinforced, we are producing such a proportion of our own wares and fabrics, including those consumed by the cotton planters and tobacco growers of the South, that we can afford to receive in luxuries, or such necessaries as we need in excess of our capacity to produce, part of the proceeds of those special agricultural supplies which Europe takes from us because they cannot be obtained elsewhere. This must be the solution of the paradox, for while augmenting our imports so largely, we are producing not only vastly more iron, steel, lead, copper, zinc, and the infinite variety of utilities into which they may be converted; of cotton, woollen, silk, and flax goods; of chemicals, clocks, watches, jewelry, and works of art, than ever before; but of "dwelling-houses, cooking-stoves, furnaces, pumps, carriages, harnesses, tin-ware, agricultural tools, books, hats, clothing, wheat, flour, cheese, steamboats, cars, locomotives, bricks, coal oil, fire engines, furniture, marble-work, mattresses, printing-presses, wooden-ware, newspapers," and a thousand other things, which, it is falsely said, "cannot be imported to any great extent, under any circumstances," and the production of which gives "to the farmer by far the largest market for his produce." So great indeed is the prosperity of all classes, save those farmers who have gone beyond the reach of a market, that Mr. Atkinson, in his onslaught on Protection in the *Atlantic Monthly*, is constrained to acknowledge that: "At the present time this country is so vigorous, and production so great, that a vicious currency and an enormous tariff simply

* See note from Kirk, page 389.

appear to create uneasiness, but do not seriously impede prosperity."

To have withheld such an admission, damaging as it is to the author's argument, would have been still more damaging. It gives an aspect of fairness and candor to an article that is essentially ingenious and disengenuous; and had it not been made, each intelligent reader would recall the prosperous condition of the country as a sufficient reply to his suggestions: For our general prosperity is not known and felt by ourselves only, but by the British people and government. The Commissioners of Customs state that the amount of the manufactures of Great Britain, taken by the United States during 1870, was £28,335,394, adding that this is "the largest sum ever reached in any year, with the exception of the very prosperous year of 1866, when the values were £28,499,514, and exceeding the value of the exports of 1860, the year before the American war, by six millions, or nearly 31 per cent." It is not unworthy of note that the only year in which our British imports exceeded those of last year was one of extreme protection, and that in each they exceeded by more than 31 per cent. those of the last year of free trade, or a revenue tariff. A leading English journal, overlooking the fact that the amount had ever been exceeded, says: "The United States have long been the best customers the British manufacturers have had throughout the world, and last year their pre-eminence is more marked than ever."

Thus does current experience attest the mutual dependence of the American farmer and manufacturer, and prove that for them the protective system is the only road to really Free Trade. That at so late a day, as it did, it should have required Mr. Carey to convince me of these truths, illustrates the almost absolute dominion long cherished abstractions obtain over the minds of men; for no fact in our history is established by more abounding proof than the dependence of our farmers on a home market capable of consuming more than 90 per cent. of the annual crop of the country. It is proven anew by each year's experience, and strikingly illustrated by the statistics and general results of each of the alternating periods of Protective and Revenue Tariffs. A thorough examination of these results will, I am persuaded, convince any candid mind that a rigid system of Protection must, for many years, be the paramount political necessity of the farmers of the United States.

But, waiving historical or statistical proof, I propose to test the correctness of this proposition by existing facts. The price of grain is not satisfactory to our farmers, and, as I have more than once suggested, is not sufficient to cover the cost of production and transportation to the seaboard of the crops of the trans-Mississippi States. Is this the result of an unusually fruitful year? By no means. For the yield per acre throughout the country has been considerably below the general average. It is because too large a proportion of our people are engaged in producing grain, and have, in a year in which the foreign demand is exceptionally large, produced it in excess of the world's demand. The leaders of the corn market of England watch the progress of the crops of the Continent as closely as they do those of the British Islands, inasmuch as they usually draw thence from 90 to 95 per cent. of the annual deficiency. And their advices for this year are as follows, as I learn from one of their organs, published September 11th: "The great deficiency in the area under wheat on the Continent (in France and Germany), as reported by us in May last, could not fail to show a very large falling off in their crop as compared with 1868 and 1869, and hence, instead of being liberal exporters of grain as formerly, they will require to import freely during the year. Our late advices from Russia confirm previous estimates in regard to their crops, viz.: that their surplus of wheat will be 10 per cent. less than last year." If, under these circumstances, there be no market for our crop, when and where may we expect to find one? Certainly the near future does not promise a European one; for the war between France and Germany has terminated, and the peasants of both of those countries are preparing their fields for the production of the usual amount of grain for the English market in 1872. Nor is the remoter prospect more promising. The increase of the population of Europe is scarcely appreciable. But her capitalists adopt improved methods of production, and the rapid extension of her railroad system is bringing her interior grain fields into cheaper and more rapid communication with her capitals and seaports. Under these circumstances, to anticipate a steady and remunerative trans-Atlantic market for our grain would be absurd. And what is the outlook at home? For the farmers of the remote interior it is even more gloomy. Our laws offer sublime inducements to the peasantry of the world to come and increase our production of grain. To every one who will do this, they offer with citizenship and free schools a farm without money and without price; and constantly increasing tens of thousands of them are accepting the offer annually. I do not think it would be an exaggeration to place the number of new farms that will be prepared for crops this year, in the six States I have heretofore named, at one hundred thousand. Who are to consume their productions?

Says Professor Kirk, in his admirable essays on "Social

Politics in Great Britain and Ireland:" "There are above 70,000 souls in the east end of London who must emigrate speedily or die. . . . . Above 25,000 of these are workmen more or less skilled in engineer and shipbuilding occupations. These are not shepherds, nor are they ploughmen, nor will they ever be to any great extent one or the other. They are mechanics, and will be so go where they may. In the vast hives of industry in Lancashire there are a greater number who must emigrate or die. . . . . Not one is either pastoral or agricultural, and few are likely ever to be either."

Some of these, he tells, are able to get off "to Massachusetts to find full occupation in cotton." Charity is sending others, and the Government transporting as many as it can to its North American provinces. Can we not prove our cosmopolitanism, and our desire that all men may trade freely, by giving 150,000 skilled workmen of London and Lancashire the guarantee of steady work at generous wages, and so open a way for the employment of those who, for the want of passage money, must otherwise die, as *Blackwood* says, "from sheer famine in the heart of the wealthiest city of the world?" What a market would they and their families create for farm products in all their varieties, and how immensely and rapidly would the application of their skill and industry to our undeveloped resources increase the general wealth of the country!

Let the report of our high wages, *with assurances that these shall be protected by law*, be made in all the great industrial centres of Great Britain, France, Belgium, and Germany, as the freedom of our public lands has been in the pastoral and agricultural districts, and our farmers will not long want a market. But this involves the maintenance of a rigid and generous system of Protection. In the addresses and letters, which compose this volume, the reader will find little else than the application of the principles here enunciated to questions of policy as they have arisen since the suppression of the rebellion.

In advocating such a system of Protection as would enable our miners and manufacturers to pay wages sufficiently liberal to induce skilled workmen to immigrate and enable them to become liberal consumers, I have believed that I was asserting and defending the right of the American farmer to a market—a remunerative market—for his crops. Should this volume convince any number of my countrymen of the correctness of these views, it will vindicate the judgment of those who persuaded me to prepare it for publication, and gratify the most ardent wish of

THE AUTHOR.

PHILADELPHIA,
November 1*st*, 1871.

CONTENTS.

CONTENTS.

SPEECHES AND LETTERS

ON

INDUSTRIAL AND FINANCIAL QUESTIONS.

PROTECTION TO AMERICAN LABOR.

SPEECH DELIVERED IN THE HOUSE OF REPRESENTATIVES, JANUARY 31ST, 1866.

THE House being in the Committee of the Whole on the state of the Union—

Mr. Kelley said:

Mr. Chairman—The eloquent gentleman from Indiana, [Mr. VOORHEES,] whose voice during the war was so potent in the councils of the Democratic party, and who has borne so prominent a part on this floor in resisting all the legislation by which the rebellion was to be, and has been crushed, in the course of his recent defense of the President's message and policy lauded him as a champion of free trade. He said the President had struck "a manly and honest blow" at the protection afforded by the tariff to the varied industries of the country, and cited this brief extract from his message in proof of his assertion:

"Now, in their turn, the property and income of the country should bear their just proportion of the burden of taxation, while in our impost system, through means of which increased vitality is incidentally imparted to all the industrial interests of the nation, the duties should be so adjusted as to fall most heavily on articles of luxury, leaving the necessaries of life as free from taxation as the absolute wants of the Government, economically administered, will justify."

Entertaining, sir, the views I do, and which I propose to submit to the committee, I had found in that portion of the President's message the expression of a desire to foster the industry, develop the resources, and increase the wealth and power of the country. Till the gentleman called my attention to the fact, I had not observed that

Mr. Johnson's expression was enigmatical and susceptible of at least a double construction. I will not, however, detain the committee by endeavoring to ascertain the President's meaning, which time will disclose; but without abandoning the hope that my apprehension of his words is correct, will proceed, in a general way, to demonstrate that the gentleman's views as to how we may best equalize and increase the wealth of the people of the United States are erroneous. In the course of his remarks he said:

"We have *two* great interests in this country, one of which has prostrated the other. The past four years of suffering and war has been the opportune harvest of the manufacturer. The looms and machine shops of New England and the iron furnaces of Pennsylvania have been more prolific of wealth to their owners than the most dazzling gold mines of the earth."

Again:

"The present law of tariff is being rapidly understood. It is no longer a deception, but rather a well-defined and clearly recognized outrage. The agricultural labor of the land is driven to the counters of the most gigantic monopoly ever before sanctioned by law. From its exorbitant demands there is no escape. The European manufacturer is forbidden our ports of trade for fear he might sell his goods at cheaper rates and thus relieve the burdens of the consumers.* We have declared by law that there is but one market into which our citizens shall go to make their purchases, and we have left it to the owners of the market to fix their own prices. The bare statement of such a principle foreshadows at once the consequences which flow from it. One class of citizens, and by far the largest and most useful, is placed at the mercy, for the necessaries as well as luxuries of life, of the fostered, favored, and protected class to whose aid the whole power of the Government is given."

And again:

"Free trade with all the markets of the world is the true theory of government."

Sir, as I proceed, it will, I think, appear that we have more than "two great interests," and that protection such as can only be afforded by a tariff is required by them all;

---

*Experience has demonstrated the absurdity of this theoretical conclusion. The tariff of 1857 was a free trade tariff. The duties it fixed were lower than had prevailed since the 1st of July, 1812, yet the importation of foreign goods under it in 1858-59 and '60 averaged but $327,849,178. The tariff which Mr. Voorhees denounced was confessedly protective; the duties it levied were about treble those imposed by the law of 1857, and higher than had ever been levied before, yet the importation of foreign goods during the years 1866-67-68 and '69, when the people of the Southern States were too much impoverished by the war to construct railroads or indulge in foreign luxuries, averaged $416,920,364. (*See the official table appended to speech of March 25th,* 1870.)

that they are interwoven with such exquisite harmony that no one of them can suffer alone; and that to destroy any one is to impair the vital power of all.

Gruff old Samuel Johnson said in substance that, when he contemplated the many diseases to which human life is a prey and the countless means for its destruction, he wondered that anybody lived to maturity; and when, on the other hand, he beheld the infinitude of specifics offered for every form of disease, he was led to wonder that people ever died. And the thought recurs to me as I contemplate the condition of our country from either of two stand points—that of the despondent patriot and him who conceals his determined treason under expressions of acquiescent loyalty, or that of the cheerful patriot who knows something of our unmeasured resources. Regarding our debt, which set forth in figures seems so crushing, and our pension lists, which, embracing more names than did the muster rolls of the contending armies at Waterloo, announce the fearful amount of infirmity, widowhood, and orphanage for which we are bound to provide; remembering how the ruling powers of other nations hate us; looking at the immense extent and resources of the British dominions on our north, and considering how sedulously the imperial Government has pursued the design of uniting those dominions and constructing such governmental works as would "render Canada accessible to her Majesty's forces at all seasons of the year, as well upon grounds peculiar to Canada as from considerations affecting the interests of the other colonies and of the whole empire;" remembering, again, the Monroe doctrine, and the fact that he who occupies the throne of Mexico is, though an Austrian, the creature of the ambitious man whose will is law to France; and, in view of these facts, considering the internal condition of our country, with nearly a million square miles of our territory desolated by four years of stubborn war, and with its people divided into three classes, distrusting and hating each other—four millions of them born as things for a market and strangers to the enjoyment of any human right; six or eight millions more poor and ignorant nearly as they, and unused and averse to labor, less hopeful, and tending each year more nearly to dependence on the rifle, the net, and the line; and the remaining class, less numerous than either of the others, but possessing all the wealth and culture, acknowledging themselves a conquered people, but with rare exceptions proving by all their acts that they are unconverted, and that they hate the Union, its Constitution, and the people who maintained the unity of the one and the sovereignty of the other as intensely as they did when they began the unholiest war of history; regarding, I say these facts, the disguised traitor may still hope for the accomplishment of his purpose, and the despondent patriot may well despair.

On the other hand, he who contemplates our geographical position, which makes us, on the one ocean, business neighbors to seven hundred and fifty millions of the people of Asia, and on the other to two hundred and fifty millions of the busy people of Europe, our vast agricultural resources, our unestimated mineral wealth, the magnitude of our rivers, and the natural wealth of the country they drain, the capacity of our people for enterprise, their ingenuity, and persistence, and who withal comprehends the laws of political economy and social science, and believes that a free and educated people will give practical effect to great truths, smiles with derision upon him who sees danger to our country in the complicated facts suggested.

I have before me, sir, the yellowed pages of a pamphlet, printed in London in 1677, which contains a panacea for all our ills, the suggestions of which, illustrated by the experience of our own and other nations, will, if applied to our resources, bring permanent peace and prosperity to our country, elevate the freedman into the prosperous and intelligent citizen, bless the master spirits of the South with wealth beyond their past imaginings, and give them, as steady competitors in the race of life, "the mean whites," as they designate their poor neighbors; will reconstruct their broken railroads and canals, rebuild their ruined cities, towns, and villages, and make their barren and wasted fields bloom and blossom as those of the fairest portions of the North, of Belgium, Germany, France, or England.

This quaint old pamphlet was written by "Andrew Yarrinton, Gentleman," and is entitled, "England's Improvement by Sea and Land. How to outdo the Dutch without Fighting, to pay Debts without Moneys, to set at Work all the Poor of England with the Growth of our own Lands." It disposes very effectually of the gentleman's proposition that free trade "is the true theory of government."

When Andrew Yarrinton wrote, the Dutch were disputing the supremacy of the seas with England, and she was exporting raw materials and buying manufactured articles; and one object of his pamphlet was to relieve the English people from the taunt of the Dutch that they "sold their whole skins for a sixpence, and bought back the tails for a shilling"—a commercial policy which the American people, with rare and brief exceptions, have steadily pursued. To Yarrinton and Sir George Downing, author of the Navigation Act, an American by birth, and a member of the first graduating class of Harvard college, England, in my judgment, owes more of her wealth and power than to any other two men, however illustrious their names may be in her history. Before they influenced her counsels Holland was mistress of the sea. But the Navigation Act and the employment of her people on the growth of her lands, transferred the scepter to England. The purpose of Downing's bill as declared in its preamble, was "to keep his Majesty's subjects in the plantations in a firmer dependence," to "increase English shipping," and to insure "the vent of English woolens and other manufactures and commodities." What Yarrinton and Downing taught their country we can practice for the benefit of ours. And as England outdid the Dutch without fighting, so can we outdo her by the arts of peace, and enforce the Monroe doctrine against the world without firing a gun; and, vast as is our indebtedness, strangers will come and cast their lot with us and liquidate it if we so legislate as "to set at work all the poor of" the United States "with the growth of our own lands." They will bring with them arts and industries, and implements with which we are not familiar; will open new quarries, mines, and ore banks; will build new furnaces, forges, mills, and workshops; will revive wasted lands and open new fields. and by creating a home market will enable the farmer to practice skillful and remunerative husbandry, and will create American commerce by enabling our merchants to supply ships with assorted cargoes of American goods.

THE ONE WANT OF OUR COUNTRY.

Sir, the pressing want of our country is men. We need not sigh for additional territory. We need go to no foreign nation for any product of agriculture. Abundant as are our ascertained stores of gold, silver, coal, iron, copper, zinc, lead, cinnabar, kaolin, petroleum, and the infinite number of substances man has utilized, the extent of our mineral wealth is unmeasured and unimagined. And our ocean-bound coasts, the immense inland seas that bound us on the north, the land-locked Gulf that laves our southern shores, and our grand rivers, impel us to commercial enterprise, and proclaim the one great want of our country to be men. Labor alone can make these unparalleled resources available; and when by securing to industry its just reward we shall develop and attract hither from other lands a supply of labor that will make the march of our conquest over the elements of our wealth steadily progressive, our debt, though expressed by the numerals required to tell it now, will shrink into comparative insignificance, and the Powers which by treachery and disregard of international law during the last four years would have destroyed us, will assume relatively Lilliputian proportions.

These are not new thoughts. So long ago as 1689, Locke, in his Essay on Civil Government, said:

"Let any one consider what the difference is between an acre of land planted with tobacco or sugar, sown with wheat or barley, and an acre of the same land lying in common, without any husbandry upon it; and he will find the improvement of labor makes the far greater part of the value. I think it will be but a very modest computation to say that of the products of the earth useful to the life of a man, nine tenths are the effects of labor. Nay, if we will rightly consider things as they come to our use, and cast up the several expenses about them—what in them is purely owing to nature, and what to labor—we shall find that in most of them ninety-nine hundredths are wholly to be put on the account of labor. There cannot be a clearer demonstration of anything than several nations of the Americans are of this, who are rich in land and poor in all the comforts of life; whom nature having furnished as rich as any other people with the materials of plenty, that is a fruitful soil, apt to produce in abundance what might serve for food, raiment, and delight, yet for want of improving it by labor have not one hundreth part of the conveniences we enjoy."

But to make labor fully available it must be steadily employed and generously rewarded, and to secure these results the employments of a country must be largely diversified. A nation whose territory is broad and remote from dense populations cannot, by pursuing commerce and agriculture alone, prosper or endure. This is the decree of nature. Land, as well as man, requires rest and food;

and a purely agricultural and commercial nation can afford neither of these. The social history of the world verifies this proposition. To make a nation prosperous remunerative employment must be accessible to all its people; and to that end industry must be so diversified that he who has not the strength for agricultural or other labor requiring muscle may make his feeble sinews available in some gentler employment. Agriculture and commerce afford few stimulants to inventive genius; diversified industry offers many. Childhood in a purely agricultural community is wasted in idleness, as are the winter months of robust men, and to realize the truth of the maxim that time is money, the varied industry of a country should offer employment to all for all seasons of the year, that each day may be made to earn its own subsistence. And herein is illustrated the harmony of interests, for where diversity of employment is successfully promoted, agriculture finds its readiest markets and earns its richest rewards: for within accessible distance from the city or town the farmer has a market for those perishable productions which will not bear extended transportation, but the cultivation of which, in alternation with white or hard crops, strengthens and enriches his land. But of this hereafter.

WHY THE SOUTH DEMANDED FREE TRADE.

Unhappily, sir, it has not been the policy of those who have governed our country to permit, much less to encourage, such needed diversification of employment and productions. I have before me an imperial octavo volume embracing more than nine hundred pages, and illustrated with the likenesses of many distinguished southern statesmen and teachers. It is entitled "Cotton is King, and Pro-Slavery Arguments, comprising the Writings of Hammond, Harper, Christie, Stringfellow, Hodge, Bledsoe, and Cartwright on this Important Subject, by E. N. Elliott, LL. D., President of Planters' College, Mississippi, with an Essay on Slavery in the Light of International Law, by the Editor." This volume, so valuable to the future historian, bears the imprint of Prichard, Abbott & Loomis, Augusta, Georgia, 1860. And the title page announces that it was "published and sold exclusively by subscription." When this work was published, the establishment of the southern confederacy was, doubtless, a foregone conclusion in the minds of its publishers and their patrons;

there was, therefore, no further reason for the southern leaders disguising the purposes they had had in view while, in the name of the Democratic party, governing our country. I refer to it in order that these distinguished writers may, for themselves, declare the aims and motives that governed them. The objects they proposed to attain are thus expressed under the head of "Economical Relations of Slavery:"

"The opposition to the protective tariff by the South arose from two causes; the first openly avowed at the time, and the second clearly deducible from the policy it pursued; the one to secure the foreign market for its cotton, the other to obtain a bountiful supply of provisions at cheap rates." . . . . "But they could not monopolize the market unless they could obtain a cheap supply of food and clothing for their negroes, and raise their cotton at such reduced prices as to undersell their rivals. *A manufacturing population, with its mechanical coadjutors in the midst of the provision growers, on a scale such as the protective policy contemplated, it was conceived would create a permanent market for their products and enhance the price; whereas if this manufacturing could be prevented, and a system of free trade be adopted, the South would constitute the principal provision market of the country, and the fertile lands of the North supply the cheap food demanded for its slaves.*

Again:

"By the protective policy, the planters expected to have the cost of both provisions and clothing increased, and their ability to monopolize the foreign markets diminished in a corresponding degree. *If they could establish free trade, it would insure the American market to foreign manufacturers, secure the foreign markets for their leading staples, repress home manufactures, force a large number of northern men into agriculture, multiply the growth and diminish the price of provisions, feed and clothe their slaves at lower rates,* produce their cotton for a third or fourth of former prices, rival all other countries in its cultivation, monopolize the trade in the article throughout the whole of Europe, and build up a commerce that would make us the ruler of the seas."

Again:

"The markets in the Southwest, now so important, were then quite limited. As the protective system, coupled with the contemplated internal improvements, if successfully accomplished, *would inevitably tend to enhance the price of agricultural products, while the free-trade, anti-internal-improvement policy would as certainly reduce their value,* the two systems were long considered so antagonistic that the success of the one must sound the knell of the other. Indeed, so fully was Ohio impressed with the necessity of promoting manufactures that all capital thus employed was for many years entirely exempt from taxation.

"*It was in vain that the friends of protection appealed to the fact that the duties levied on foreign goods did not necessarily enhance the cost to the consumer; that the competition among the home manu-*

facturers and between them and foreigners had greatly reduced the price of nearly every article properly protected; that foreign manufacturers always had, and always would, advance their prices according to our dependence upon them; that domestic competition was the only safety the country had against foreign imposition; that it was necessary we should become our own manufacturers in a fair degree to render ourselves independent of other nations in time of war as well as to guard against the vacillations in foreign legislation; that the South would be vastly the gainer by having the market for its products at its own doors and avoiding the cost of their transit across the Atlantic; that, in the event of the repression, or want of proper expansion, of our manufactures by the adoption of the free-trade system, the imports of foreign goods to meet the public wants would soon exceed the ability of the people to pay, and inevitably involve the country in bankruptcy. Southern politicians remained inflexible and refused to accept any policy except free trade and the utter abandonment of the principle of protection. Whether they were jealous of the greater prosperity of the North and desirous to cripple its energies, or whether they were truly fearful of bankrupting the South, we shall not wait to inquire."

The author doubtless felt that it would be sacrilegious to inquire too curiously into the motives of the ministers of a monarch so absolute as King Cotton, but we, who do not live in the fear of his majesty, may freely, and not without advantage, consider the questions propounded.

And again, in connection with the assertion that with slave labor they could not become manufacturers, and must therefore remain at the mercy of the North, both as to food and clothing, unless the European markets should be retained, the writer says southern statesmen saw that—

" *Combinations of capitalists, whether engaged in manufacturing wool, cotton, or iron, would draw off labor from the cultivation of the soil, and cause large bodies of the producers to become consumers,* and that roads and canals, connecting the West with the East, were effectual means of bringing the agricultural and manufacturing classes into closer proximity, to the serious injury of the planters."

These honest and fearless exponents of the free trade of which the gentleman from Indiana says the President is an advocate, seem to have considered the chief end of man, that is, of all American men, save slave-holding planters, to be to produce cheap food for slaves; and in this book, so remarkable for its frankness, we find a quotation from a speech made by one of them, which runs as follows:

" *We must prevent the increase of manufactories, force the surplus labor into agriculture, promote the cultivation of our unimproved western lands, until provisions are so multiplied and reduced in price that the slave can be fed so cheaply as to enable us to grow our sugar at three cents a pound.* Then, without protective duties, we can rival Cuba in the production of that staple and drive her from our markets."

RESULTS OF FREE TRADE.

By the persistent and domineering pursuit of these ends by the South, and the unhallowed spirit of compromise which always controlled the North, the manufactures of the country were destroyed; and the West (for great railway thoroughfares had not then been constructed) having been reduced to dependence on the South for her market, consented to her own ruin. It may be that having deprived herself of any other market, her poverty and not her will consented; but the story of her seduction and ruin is thus happily told in "Cotton is King:"

"The West which had long looked to the East for a market had its attention now turned to the South, the most certain and convenient market for the sale of its products; the planters affording to the farmers the market they had in vain sought from the manufacturers. In the meantime steamboat navigation was acquiring perfection on the western rivers, the great natural outlets for western produce, and became a means of communication between the Northwest and the Southwest, as well as with the trade and commerce of the Atlantic cities. This gave an impulse to industry and enterprise west of the Alleghanies unparalleled in the history of the country. While then the bounds of slave labor were extending from Virginia, the Carolinas, and Georgia, westward over Tennessee, Alabama, Mississippi, and Arkansas, the area of free labor was enlarging with equal rapidity in the Northwest, Ohio, Indiana, Illinois, and Michigan. Thus within these provision and cotton regions were the forests cleared away or the prairies broken up simultaneously by those two antagonistic forces. Opponents no longer, they were harmonized by the fusion of their interests, the connecting link between them being the steamboat. Thus also was a *tripartite alliance* formed, *by which the western farmer, the southern planter, and the English manufacturer became united in a common bond of interest*, the whole giving their support to the doctrine of free trade."

With this unnatural alliance the work seemed to be completed, and in verification of the theories of the northern leaders of the Democratic party who, like the gentleman from Indiana, took their opinions from the southern planters, the commerce of our country should have rapidly expanded, and Great Britain furnished a market for all our surplus grain. But what were the results? The laboring people of the manufacturing States were soon without employment and living upon past earnings. The deposit lines in our savings banks ran down; the banks of discount and deposit lost their specie; merchants made small sales, or sold on long and uncertain credits; and sagacious men saw that bankruptcy impended over all. The ruined people of the North and East were unable to pay for the products of the South or West. Large numbers of them, abandoning the callings to which they had been trained, and in the pursuit of which while providing amply for the support of their families they could have accumulated capital and added to the national wealth and power, became unskilful farmers on mortgaged land in the distant West. England, no longer simply mistress of the sea, but the commercial mistress of the world, seeking customers who could pay for what they purchased, bought her grain from the Baltic, from Egypt, or wherever she could buy it cheapest or with greatest convenience; and the western farmer, having supplied the coarse provisions that were required as cheap food for the slaves, and their two hundred and fifty thousand masters, saw his wheat rot in the field, and consumed his corn as fuel.

But what was the effect of this free-trade alliance upon the interests of the planters? Did it enlarge their markets, increase the price of their staple, and by a golden harvest to them, seem to compensate for the universal ruin in which it had involved the people of the North? We shall see. Had cotton manufactures in this country been fostered, the manufacturers of England and America would have been competitors in the cotton market, and, as competition among buyers ever does, would have maintained the price of that commodity. But the mad pursuit of cheap food for slaves had destroyed competition for the planters' product. Their policy had given England a monopoly of the market for cotton. They had made England, to whose ports the fabricants of Europe went for their supply, their only customer; and she, having accumulated capital which yielded but small interest, while they were needy debtors compelled to borrow, found herself in a condition to control the price of their commodity. Perceiving the vast relative importance of a continued supply of cheap cotton to an immediate return of interest on the capital involved in one year's supply, the English merchants accumulated cotton to an extent that enabled them to decline further immediate purchases from those who were always in debt to their factors, and whose necessities in the absence of any other market would soon compel them to sell at any price. And the author from whom I have quoted so extensively gives us, on page 72 of the volume, the legitimate result of the folly of the chief American party to the *tripartite alliance* in favor of free trade, when he says:

"Cotton, up to the date when this controversy had been fairly commenced, had been worth, in the English market, an average price of from 29 7-10 to 48 4-10 cents per pound; but at this period a wide-spread and ruinous depression occured, cotton in 1826 having fallen in England as low as 11 9-10 to 18 9-10 cents per pound."

Thus had free trade, the reign of which the Democratic party is endeavoring to restore, accomplished its mission in the United States. Commerce, manufactures, and agriculture, involving the merchant, artisan, farmer, and planter, were all prostrate and at the mercy of the capitalists of Great Britain, whose selfishness is only equaled by that of the class whose arrogance and unreasoning will had thus subjected the entire people of our country to their control.

EFFECT OF FREE TRADE ON THE POOR WHITES OF THE SOUTH.

Mr. Chairman, having ascertained the result of the planters' free-trade policy upon their own interests and those of the people of the North, let us contemplate the condition of the masses of the people of the cotton States. I will not detain you by any reference to that of the slaves and free people of color. Other occasions will be more fitting for that. But on nearly one million of square miles of territory which the planters regarded as their exclusive domain, were some six or eight million people designated as "poor" or "mean whites," to whom were accorded all the rights of citizenship, and I will inquire whether their interests had been promoted by this policy? Let us, in contemplating their condition for a few moments, do it, not from our stand-point, but through the eyes of southern men.

Mr. Tarver, of Missouri, in the course of a paper on Domestic Manufactures in the South and West, published in 1847, says:

"The free population of the South may be divided into two classes —the slaveholder and the non-slaveholder. I am not aware that the relative numbers of these two classes have ever been ascertained in any of the States, but I am satisfied that the non-slaveholders far outnumber the slaveholders—perhaps by three to one. In the more southern portion of this region, the non-slaveholders possess, generally, but very small means, and the land which they possess is almost universally poor, and so sterile that a scanty subsistence is all that can be derived from its cultivation; and the more fertile soil, being in the possession of the slaveholder, must ever remain out of the power of those who have none.

"This state of things is a great drawback, and bears heavily upon and depresses the moral energies of the poorer classes. . . . . The acquisition of a respectable position in the scale of wealth appears so difficult, that they decline the hopeless pursuit, and many of them settle down into habits of idleness, and become the almost passive subjects of all its consequences. And I lament to say that I have observed of late years that an evident deterioration is taking place in this part of the population, the younger portion of it being less educated, less industrious, and in every point of view less respectable, than their ancestors."

Governor Hammond, addressing the South Carolina Institute in 1850, spoke of this portion of the people of the South when he said:

"They obtain a precarious subsistence by occasional jobs, by hunting, by fishing, by plundering fields or folds, and too often by what is in its effects far worse—trading with slaves, and seducing them to plunder for their benefit."

William Gregg, Esq., addressing the same Institute in 1851, said:

"From the best estimate that I have been able to make, I put down the white people, who ought to work, and who do not, or who are so employed as to be wholly unproductive to the State, at one hundred and twenty-five thousand. . . . . By this it appears that but one-fifth of the present poor whites of our State would be necessary to operate one million spindles. . . . . I have long been under the impression, and every day's experience has strengthened my convictions, that the evils exist in the wholly neglected condition of this class of persons. Any man who is an observer of things could hardly pass through our country without being struck with the fact that all the capital, enterprise, and intelligence is employed in directing slave labor; and the consequence is that a large portion of our poor white people are wholly neglected, and are suffered to while away their existence in a state but one step in advance of the Indian of the forest."

Hon. J. H. Lumpkin, of Georgia, in a paper on the Industrial Regeneration of the South, published in 1852, in advocacy of the establishment of manufactures which had been attempted in Georgia, but which had been resisted on the ground that they would become hot-beds of crime and endanger the safety of slavery, said:

"It is objected that these manufacturing establishments will become the hot-beds of crime. . . . . But I am by no means ready to concede that our poor, degraded, half-fed, half-clothed, and ignorant population—without Sabbath schools or any other kind of instruction, mental or moral, or without any just appreciation of character—will be injured by giving them employment which will bring them under the oversight of employers who will inspire them with self-respect by taking an interest in their welfare."

Down to that time free trade had certainly done but little to bless the poor white people of the South. Nor does it seem from recent descriptions, and from our observation of them in military prisons and hospitals, to have materially benefited them down to the present day. J. R. Gilmore, Esq., "Edmund Kirke," in his discourse on the social and political characteristics of the southern whites, before the Jersey City Literary Association, estimated the number known as the "mean whites" at over four millions, and described them as "herding together in sparse communities and gleaning a sorry subsistence from hunting, fishing, and poaching, in the mountain districts of Virginia, upper Georgia, Alabama, Mississippi, and in the sand hills of North Carolina and the barrens of Tennessee, and throughout the rest of the South; as hovering around the borders of large plantations, quartering themselves upon the 'chivalry,' stealing the deer from their forests and the hams from their smoke-houses." He said they were tolerated by the planters for the two hundred thousand votes they gave for slavery and the mad theories of the planters, and added, "They are far below the slaves in morals and civilization; are indolent, shiftless, thieving, lying; given to whisky-drinking, snuff-dipping, clay-eating, incest, and all manner of social vices. Not one in a thousand of them can read; not one in ten thousand can write;" and that he "had met many who had never seen a book or newspaper, and some who had never heard of a Bible or a spelling-book."

Mr. B. C. Truman, an accredited correspondent of the New York Times, in a letter to that journal, dated Montgomery, Alabama, October 23, 1865, said:

"There is a class of beings in all the southern States known as poor whites. The little monosyllabic adjective does not give the faintest idea of these things with bodies and souls. How under the heavens they live is a question for the philanthropist, if indeed that paragon of benevolence has ever visited the region in which they exist—the 'homes' of the poor whites. In a visit to Spanish Fort a few days ago, in company with a naval officer, we stopped at the 'shebang' of one of this species. Most of these poor whites are natives. The individual whom we called upon, however, was a Scandinavian, but had lived in the place we found him for thirty years. For a long time he made his living by manufacturing turpentine; but the trees ran out years ago, and since then he has lived upon what he has raised, buying nothing but sugar and coffee, for which he traded chickens and eggs. His wife was of the regular mold, lean and long, with seven little children by her side, and a pipe in her mouth. I told her I was a newspaper correspondent, and she did not know what that was. I endeavored to explain, and found that she did not know what a newspaper was, *and yet she resides within twenty miles of Mobile.* The husband could not read or write his name, but could drink like a fish. Both husband and wife had on wooden shoes, while the children exhibited no feet covering except what nature had provided for them.

"Throughout the southern portion of Alabama, upon both sides of the river, is what is known as the 'piney woods country.' It is one of the most barren sections I have ever seen. Neither corn nor cotton will grow to any extent. Sweet potatoes are the chief product, and this vegetable and bacon, and a little corn bread, form the bill of fare morning, noon, and night all the year round. These people are scattered all through these piney woods, and live in log huts which in a way protect them from the tempestuous weather and violent storms of wind and rain which howl through this barren waste during certain periods of the year. Oh, how I pity these poor beings who have been the recipients of uncounted woes and unheard-of sufferings during the long, long years of African slavery!"

Dixon, the traveling correspondent of the Boston Daily Advertiser, whose admirable letters prove him to be a keen observer and faithful reporter, writing from Fort Valley, Georgia, November 15th, said:

"Whether the North Carolina 'dirt-eater,' or the South Carolina 'sand-hiller,' or the Georgia 'cracker,' is lowest in the scale of human existence would be difficult to say. The ordinary plantation negro seemed to me, when I first saw him in any numbers, at the very bottom of not only probabilities, but also possibilities, so far as they affect human relations; but these specimens of the white race must be credited with having reached a yet lower depth of squalid and beastly wretchedness. However poor or ignorant or unclean or improvident he may be, I never yet found a negro who had not at least a vague desire for a better condition, an undefined longing for something called freedom, a shrewd instinct of self-preservation. These three ideas, or, let me say, shadows of ideas, do not make the creature a man, but they lift him out of the bounds of brutedom. The Georgia 'cracker,' as I have seen him since leaving Milledgeville, seems to me to lack not only all that the negro does, but also even the desire for a better condition, and the vague longing for an enlargement of his liberties and his rights. I walked out into the country back of Albany and Andersonville, when at those places, and into the country back of Fort Valley this morning; and on each occasion I fell in with three or four of these 'cracker' families. Such filthy poverty, such foul ignorance, such idiotic imbecility, such bestial instincts, such groveling desires, such mean longings, you would question my veracity as a man if I were to paint the pictures I have seen! Moreover, no trick of words can make plain the scene in and around one of these habitations; no fertility of language can embody the simple facts for a northern mind; and the case is one in which even seeing itself is scarcely believing. Time and effort will lead the negro up to intelligent manhood; but I almost doubt if it will be possible to ever lift this 'white trash' into respectability."

Sir, is not the gentleman from Indiana mistaken in asserting that free trade "is the true theory of government," and can a policy which produces such results as these writers have depicted be wise? Can we rely on it to pay the interest on our debt, to meet the pensions we owe to those who have been disabled in our service, or to the widows and children, or aged and dependent parents of those who have laid down their lives in our cause? Such free trade as he advocates can produce but one result; and that is bankruptcy, personal, corporate, State, and national. It is against the laws of nature and the providence of God. It involves as a necessary consequence idleness for one half the year to all, and for all the year to many of our people who would find adequate and remunerative employment under a system of diversified industry.

HOW ENGLAND ESTABLISHED HER SUPREMACY.

The propositions I enunciate are not deduced from our experience alone. All history affirms them. Other nations have tried free trade and ever with the same result. England, the workshop of the world and mistress of the seas as she proclaims herself, tried it, and from the time of Alfred to that of Edward the Confessor, sold her skins for a sixpence, and bought back the tails for a shilling, by exchanging her unwrought wool for Dutch and Flemish clothing; and the question as to how population might be prevented from exceeding the ability of the land to feed the people perplexed her rulers throughout the long period.*

* Believing herself to be strong enough she has renewed the experiment, and at the end of a quarter of a century of free trade, finds herself agitated as never before by the question; "How shall we feed our people?" Daniel Grant says: "No man doubts the broad fact that we cannot feed ourselves. It has been accepted by Parliamentary Committees, made the plea for large Inclosure Acts, and it caused the repeal of the Corn Laws; equally as little can it be doubted that this condition is ever on the increase, for it is shown by the Registrar General's returns, and the ever-increasing competition for work. Day by day the tell-tale of our population mounts higher, and its results are to be found in the increasing requirements for foreign food. But at great Manchester meetings men tabulate out this enormous increase, and appeal to it as an evidence of the value of free trade; whilst the facts are that our imports of food have only the one meaning, viz: we import that food which we cannot produce for ourselves. The re-

Even so late as the thirty-sixth year of Elizabeth's reign a law was enacted against "the erecting and maintaining of cottages," which, after reciting that "great inconveniences have been found by experience to grow by erecting and building of great numbers and multitudes of cottages which are daily more and more increased in many parts of this realm," enacts that no such tenement shall be erected unless four acres of land be attached to it. And Charles I., in 1630, issued a proclamation "against building houses on new foundations in London or Westminster, or within three miles of the city or king's palaces." This proclamation also forbade the receiving of inmates in the houses which would multiply the inhabitants to such an excessive number that they could neither be governed nor fed. The population of England has quadrupled since then, and her modern capitalists, regarding labor as raw material, maintain a supply of laborers in sufficient excess of the demand to cheapen it to the lowest point, to which end the British islands raise for annual exportation, a quarter of a million of people, feeding them in their unproductive infancy and childhood.

The change has been wrought by the diversification of her industry, which has been accomplished by so legislating as to set at work all the poor of England with the growth of her own lands; and the spectacle which Ireland presents, of years of famine, and an industrious people whose attachment to their native land is intense, fleeing by millions from the homes of their childhood and the graves of their ancestors, is the result of that one-sided free trade which England, since the Union, has forced upon her, by which her woolen, worsted, silk, cotton, and linen factories have been destroyed. Protected by her

---

lation that food thus bears to our population makes itself felt in a variety of ways; it changes the character of our pauperism, the conditions of our destitution, and the price of food itself; it also enforces the importance of our export trade and the danger of foreign competition. All these circumstances, so apparently remote, are linked together by the one tie, that our land cannot feed our people.

"With respect to the first point, the state of our pauperism, it is so changed that it no longer represents its original elements. The first poor-law was based on the idea that paupers were the idle and the worthless, and to such a labor test was the natural limitation of help; but to-day men seek work and cannot find it, enforced idleness saps energy, and thus it is they sink slowly down to pauperism. The same may be said of destitution with even greater force; that silent, hopeless, broken misery, which is too powerless to create work, too feeble to force it, and too proud to beg—that poverty which sinks, suffers, and dies; that destitution of all others the most fearful, and the most real, also springs from over-population."—*Home Politics, by Daniel Grant, page* 169. *London,* 1870.

legislation of 1783, these and other branches of diversified industry were prosperous and her people contented at the date of the Union. But English free trade having done its work nothing is now of so little value in Ireland as an able-bodied laborer with a good appetite. Let him who would understand the causes of the miseries of the Irish people and the depopulation of Ireland read the thirteenth chapter of Henry C. Carey's Slave Trade, Domestic and Foreign. It is a brief story, but pregnant with instruction upon the point under consideration.

I cannot tell, sir, when England first determined to abandon dependence on the production and exportation of raw materials, but find by reference to McCallagh's Industrial History, page 74, that in 1337 she passed an Act imposing

> "A duty of forty shillings per sack on all wool exported by native merchants and sixty shillings on all exported by foreigners. The next year a Parliament was held at Westminster that went still further in the same direction, enacting that no wool of English growth should be transported beyond seas, and that all cloth-workers should be received, from whatever parts they should come, and fit places should be assigned them with divers liberties and privileges, and that they should have a certain allowance from the king until they might be in a way of living by their trade."

While England remained a purely agricultural country her capitalists encountered the difficulties which those of the South have to overcome, and Wade, in his History of the Middle and Working Classes, page 31, says:

> "In the year 1376 we have evidence of a strong disposition to vagrancy among laborers, in a complaint of the House of Commons that masters are obliged to give their servants high wages to prevent their running away; that many of the runaways turned beggars and lived idle lives in cities and boroughs, although they have sufficient bodily strength to gain a livelihood if willing to work, and that the chief part turned out sturdy rogues, infesting the kingdom with frequent robberies."

There are those who utter such complaints in our days, and especially deplore the fact that they "are compelled to give their servants high wages to prevent their running away." At a meeting of the planters of Marlboro' district, South Carolina, the proceedings of which I find reported at length, and properly attested, in the Charleston Daily News of December 9th, the following, with many like resolutions, were adopted:

"*Resolved,* That, if inconsistent with the views of the authorities to remove the military, we express the opinion that the plan of the military to compel the freedman to contract with his former owner, when desired by the latter, is wise, prudent, and absolutely necessary.

"*Resolved,* That we, the planters of the district, pledge ourselves not to contract with any freedman unless he can produce a certificate of regular discharge from his former owner.

"*Resolved,* That under no circumstances whatsoever will we rent land to any freedmen, nor will we permit them to live on our premises as employés.

"*Resolved,* That no system can be devised for the present which can *secure success* where the discipline and management of the freedman is entirely taken out of the hands of the planter, and we invoke the authorities to recognize this fact, which cannot but be apparent to them.

"*Resolved,* That we request the military to cease the habit of making negroes act as couriers, sheriffs, and constables, to serve writs and notices upon planters—a system so destructive to good order and discipline."

It is evident that neither the thunders of Gillmore's "swamp angel," nor the howl of her ponderous shells, had sufficed to awaken these somnolent gentlemen to consciousness of the fact that the fourteenth century had passed in the Palmetto State.

Englishmen in those early days exhibited the same elements of character as the negroes of our days, showing that however the complexion of races may differ, the impulses and yearnings of humanity are the same in all times and among the children of all climes. Each man embraces the elements of perfect manhood and the germ of every human faculty and emotion; and the Africo-American, in his new-found freedom, desires, as did the English laborer of the fourteenth century, to work for whom he pleases, at what he feels he can do best, and in the field which will give him the amplest reward.

Slight as the stimulants applied to British manufacturing industry by parliamentary protection had then been, they caused the land-holders to manifest as much anxiety for despotic control over the laboring people as do the pardoned rebels of the South; and Wade tells us that the complaints of the Commons in 1406 furnish evidence of the competition which had commenced between rural and manufacturing industry at that day, and that—

"To avoid the statutes passed some years before for compelling those who had been brought up to the plow till they were twelve years of age to continue in husbandry all their lives, agricultural laborers had recourse to the expedient of sending their children into cities and boroughs, and binding them apprentices when they were under that age; and that further, in order to counteract this, it was enacted that no person, unless possessed of land of a rental of twenty shillings a year should bind children of any age apprentices to any trade or mystery within a city, but that the children should be brought up in the occupation of their parents, or other business suited to their conditions."

But even in those dark days the British Government seems to have been more enlightened than they who claim the right to legislate for the Southern States, or Brevet Brigadier General Fullerton, late Commissioner of the Freedmen's Bureau at New Orleans; for it provided that such children were nevertheless to be allowed to be sent to a school in any part of the kingdom; which their proposed legislation and his arbitrary orders for the government of the laboring people of Louisiana would effectually prohibit.

These stupid parliamentary restrictions on the freedom of laborers were not to edure forever, and the progress of England in the development of her resources has been marked by a constantly-growing system of protection, not always judicious, sometimes infringing the rights of the subject, but tending constantly to build up the power of the kingdom, increase the material comfort of the subject, and give her ascendency over the nations of the world.

In 1727, Dean Swift, appealing to the Irish people in behalf of Ireland, said:

"One cause of a country's thriving is the industry of the people in working up all their native commodities to the last; another, the conveniency of safe ports and havens to carry out their goods, as *much* manufactured, and bring those of others as *little* manufactured, as the nature of mutual commerce will allow; another, the disposition of the people of the country to wear their own manufactures and import as little clothing, furniture, food, or drink as they can conveniently live without."

These were not abstract notions with him, for by that time England had become thoroughly protective in her policy, and was increasing in population, wealth, and power; while Ireland, though not wholly disregarding the necessity of protecting her own workmen and developing her resources, exhibited a tendency to be governed by that plausible but shallowest of economical sophisms which teaches that it is wise, regardless of all other circumstances and conditions, to buy where we can buy for least money and sell where we can sell for most, and was sinking in the scale of national consideration. How protective England had become, is illustrated by the fact that from having for many centuries exchanged her raw wool for manufactured cloths, she had in 1660 prohibited the exportation of *unmanufactured* wool. This prohibition continued till 1825. And to protect her silk manufacturers, from 1765 to 1826, she prohibited the importation of silk goods manufactured in other countries, and confirmed the parliamentary prohibition by a reservation in the treaty of commerce concluded with France in 1786. She also prohibited the export of tools and machines used in various branches of manufactures. In 1696 she prohibited by special act of Parliament the exportation of Lee's stocking-frame—a machine invented nearly a century before. She also prohibited by various acts the exportation of certain machinery used in woolen, silk, cotton, and linen manufactures. Such favor did protection to English labor find that her laws prohibiting exportation were made to embrace presses or dies for iron buttons, engines for covering whips, tools for punching glass; in fact, anything for which it was thought worth while on the part of any class of manufacturers or mechanics to seek protection at the hands of Parliament by securing Englishmen a monopoly of the implements required for the production of their goods.

And when, in 1824, a commission, created to inquire into the expediency of repealing these prohibitions, reported generally in favor of the repeal, it was unable to recommend their unconditional abrogation, but qualified the suggestion by recommending that the Privy Council should continue to exercise their discretion in permitting the exportation of such tools and machinery then prohibited as might appear to them not likely to be prejudicial to the trade or manufactures of the United Kingdom, "because it is possible that circumstances may exist which may render a prohibition to export certain tools and machines used in some particular manufactures expedient." To justify even this conditional repeal the commission set forth the advantages England had derived from the protection of her infant or feeble industries in the following language:

"Placed beyond all comparison at the head of civilization as regards manufacturing skill, *with capital far more ample than is possessed by any other people*, with cheap and inexhaustible supplies of iron and fuel, and with institutions every way favorable to the development of the industry and ingenuity of her citizens, she must always be able at least to maintain her superiority of position where circumstances are in other respects equal, and be ready to turn to the utmost advantage every improvement which may reach her in common with her less powerful rivals."

It was not, we perceive, until by adequate protection to her labor she had kept the balance of trade in her favor long enough to make capital so abundant as to secure a steady and ample supply of money at low rates of interest; and by setting all her people to work on the growth of her lands had trained artisans and accumulated an abundance of superior machinery, which had paid for itself by profits on its use, that England was willing to admit the labor of the world to compete with that employed in her varied industries.

Nor had she resorted to these devices alone in her progress to this assured position, for an English writer, Porter, in his history of the Progress of the Nation, says:

"Previous to 1825, the jealousy of our Legislature in regard to the progress of foreign manufactures was extended so far as to interfere even with the natural right of working artisans to transfer their industry to countries where it could be most profitably exerted. Any man who had acquired a practical knowledge of manufacturing processes was thereby rendered a prisoner in his own country, and not only might the arm of the law be interposed to prevent his quitting his native shores, but heavy penalties were imposed on all persons who should abet the expatriation of one of our artisans."

ENGLAND PREACHES BUT DOES NOT PRACTICE FREE TRADE.

These, however, were not the most effective means by which England has protected her capital and augmented her power. While prohibiting the exportation of tools and machines, and restraining her skilled workmen from emigrating, she was, from so early as 1337, as we have already seen, encouraging by special grants and privileges the artisans of other countries to bring the implements of their industry and employ them within her limits. Her policy is unchanged. The free trade she proclaims is theoretical and plausible, but to some extent false and delusive.*

* England's enormous annual subsidies to Steamship Companies are part of an ingenious system of protection by which she hopes to maintain a monopoly of ship building and the carrying trade. She thus pays part of the freight on

The world hailed her admission of foreign grain free as a step toward really reciprocal free trade. Her statesmen, however, saw in it a master-stroke by which her manufacturing supremacy would be maintained. Sir Robert Peel knew that the manufactures of England were the source of her power; that cheap food for her laborers was an element of cheap production; and believed that so long as other nations would employ her to manufacture their raw materials it was immaterial whether she raised any grain, and that every acre of her arable land not required to raise vegetables and fruits which do not bear transportation, might be appropriated to sheep walks and pasturage, and, through her diversified industry she would draw from the prairies of the United States, the banks of the Nile, and the shores of the Baltic a supply of food far more generous than the insular dimensions of England could possibly yield.

Her policy is to undersell all others. To do this she must depress the wages of labor, and to accomplish this she must provide her laboring people at the lowest possible prices with the simple and coarse fare on which her low wages compel them to live. To have retained the duties on grain would have been, in so far, to tax raw materials, as we do,* but she is too astute for that. She wants cheap food for her slaves as the southern planters did for theirs, and seeks to get it as they did by forcing British free trade on the American people. She is the foe of the working-men of every country, and impairs their wages by depressing those of the men upon whose toil her own power depends.† She protects the capital of

---

foreign raw materials used by her manufacturers, and the fabrics and wares they export. These subsidies amounted last year, as was stated by the Chancellor of the Exchequer in his speech of April 20th, 1871, when presenting to Parliament his budget for this year, to £1,225,000, or over $6,000,000.

* The Act of July 14th, 1870, reduced the duty on tea and coffee and transferred to the free list many varieties of raw material which we cannot yet produce; and I hope that Congress will, during the next session, make tea and coffee free. The harmless stimulants taken morning and evening by the farmer and laborer should not be taxed.

† Let us for a moment think what are the conditions of our poor to-day. *Apart from the question of our agricultural population, whose almost hopeless lot is best told by the simple fact, that in many places the luxury of meat is comparatively unknown;* apart from the questions of special emergency, such as the cotton famine, or the East End Emigration Society, which has been brought into existence for the purpose of relieving the great mass of destitution and poverty in

England as I wish to protect the labor, ingenuity, and enterprise of the American people. Her aim is to be the workshop of the world, and to bind the people of all other lands to the rude employments of unskilled agriculture.

Her agricultural interests resisted the repeal of the corn laws. To admit grain duty free it was said would ruin the farmers and lessen the market and taxable value of the land of the kingdom. But experience demonstrated the laws of social science and proved the harmony of interests by increasing the agricultural products of England in a ratio equal to the increased amount of her import of raw material and food for her land and people.

FREE TRADE EXHAUSTS LAND AND IMPOVERISHES FARMERS.

I have said, sir, that a nation cannot prosper by foreign trade and agriculture alone; and our bitter experience of wasted lands and oft-recurring bankruptcy, contrasted with the steadily increasing affluence of the agriculturists of England, confirms the fact. Let us examine this question. We boast ourselves an agricultural people, and are content to look to nations beyond the seas for the fabrics we consume and a market for our products. Not having a home market we cannot diversify our crops, but must confine ourselves to the production of those commodities

---

that neighborhood; apart from all such special and exceptional cases, we have the general sense of depression and want everywhere spread around us. It is not necessary to dwell on the scenes of human misery, where wholesale suicides or cruel murders mark the profound despair of those who lay trembling on the confines of want. It is equally unnecessary to recall those verdicts that appear time after time at coroner's inquests under the simple but expressive phraseology —"Death from Starvation." It is not necessary to recall these things, because the newspaper press of the country drives these truths home without stint and without compromise; but it may be important to remember that the individual cases, which thus come to the surface, are known only by accident, and that the great mass of misery that suffers and dies,—dies and tells no tale. Occasionally and by accident the curtain is drawn on one side, and we see into the midst of the life of poverty that surrounds us; and we then know by the glance thus afforded us, what the general life must be; wasted by poverty, decimated by fever, shattered by want; and it thus rises before us, in the full force of its appeal to that sense of human sympathy which is common to us all. But the general acceptance of the positions here stated will be aided by a few facts. Let us see what the barometer of pauperism has to tell us. Our pauper population in 1866, was 920,344; in 1867, 958,824; in 1868, 1,034,823; and the number is still increasing; yet these numbers show that our pauper population has increased 114,479 persons in two years, or at the rate of more than 1000 per week.—*Home Politics, by Daniel Grant, p. 3. London, 1870.*

which will keep long and will bear transportation. Wheat, corn, pork, cotton, rice, tobacco, and hemp are our great staples, and our crops, omitting those produced within a radius around the large cities, narrowing as they diminish in importance, decrease from year to year, while those of England, stimulated and varied by a home market, increase so wonderfully that science pauses before declaring that she has yet ascertained the measure of wealth a single well-fed acre under scientific culture will yield. The virgin soil of America gives back to the farmer at least thirty bushels of wheat to the acre; and in his early crops he does not fear the Hessian fly, the midge, weevil, or any insect-destroyer of grain. In the old wheat-growing States remote from cities, the same amount of labor bestowed upon an acre is rewarded by but seven or at best ten bushels, and the farmer regards himself as lucky whose fields are not visited once in three years by some of the deadly foes to wheat—the insects that live and swarm upon the diseased juices of feeble grain, the offspring of famished soil. The most carefully-prepared tables I have been able to find give twelve bushels or less as the average wheat crop per acre of America.

In England the fields are enriched by the bones, woolen rags, and other nutritious manures which we export; the grain crop is followed by a green crop, or those vegetables, the tops of which absorb from the atmosphere and return to the earth the aliment abstracted by cereals; and the amount of labor which, when England was a purely agricultural country, drew but from twelve to fifteen bushels of wheat from an acre, is now rewarded by from thirty-eight to forty-three bushels, or the equivalent thereof in roots for the sustenance of man and beast. Under our exhausting process of extorting from famished fields the last elements of the white crop, and our exportation of fertilizers and manures, our very fruit crop is disappearing. The diseased trees of the orchard, the apple, the pear, the plum, blossom and bring forth fruit, and the borer, the curculio, and others of the insect tribe that are sent to scourge us into good husbandry, revel in it, and it falls before maturity as if to give some subsistence to the starved stem that gave it its sickly life. This is no fancy sketch. In endeavoring to sell in the dearest money markets and buy where we can buy for least money, we have sold the very life of our acres and mortgaged ourselves to a class of middle-men, mostly foreigners, who take the results of our industry as the price of carrying our products to market and bringing us the few and inferior commodities—the tails—we receive in return for our skins. Our life is an inevitable game of cross purposes. Ambitious of commercial importance we produce only raw materials and can have no commerce, but must enhance the maritime power of our rival by employing her ships, sailors, and merchants to do our carrying; and while eager to keep down our steadily-increasing foreign indebtedness we ship our least bulky but most potent manures in the same British vessels that carry away our cotton, corn, and gold. The real balance of trade is ever against us, and our debts—commercial, corporate, and State—are ever increasing. Let us mine gold and silver never so fast, we can keep none of it. Our suspensions of specie payments are periodical. England maintains the balance of trade as steadily in her favor; and her statisticians calculate that her annual accumulation of capital has attained the enormous dimensions of £50,000,000 or $250,000,000. Her limits offer no investments for this annual increase, and the managers of the railroads that carry our crops over our own soil to the sea-board for shipment extort exorbitant freights to enable them to pay interest on bonds sold at low rates to foreign holders, or pay large dividends to British capitalists who, in default of other investments offering profits equally great, have taken the stock. Without manufactures we can have neither foreign trade nor commercial marine; for a purely agricultural people, depending on foreign nations for a limited market, have nothing with which to freight vessels to the general markets of the world, and no assorted commodities to exchange for those that would enrich the country and build up upon the sea-board commercial emporiums with native citizens and American interests.

But, sir, let us look a little more closely at the effect on the land of the country of the mad theories propounded by the gentleman from Indiana. Professor Henry gave it as his opinion, some years ago, (and I believe it to be true to-day,) that there was more wealth invested in our soil in fertilizing matter at the moment this country was discovered by Columbus than there is at present above the surface in improvements and all other investments. Ohio, justly proud of her comparatively superior American agriculture, was admonished by John H. Klippart, Esq., corresponding secretary of her State Board of Agriculture in 1860, that her staple crop, wheat, was annually decreasing in its yield per acre; that in less than fifty years the average product was reduced from thirty to less than fifteen bushels per acre, and that unless her farmers turned their attention, and that very soon, to the renovation of their wheat lands, even Ohio would soon be one of the non-wheat-producing States. During the first five years of the last decade her corn crop averaged $36\frac{31}{100}$ bushels to the acre, while during the last five years of the decade its average had fallen to $32\frac{95}{100}$. It matters little, practically, whether a man sell his acres or sell only their vital principles. It would have been better, could we have done it, that we had exported our acres in all their breadth and depth than to have extracted from them as we have, and exported or burned as fuel their productive power. We should then have seen that that market in which goods can be bought for the least money is not always the cheapest, and realized how fearful a price we were paying for the tails of the skins we had sold so recklessly.

I have referred to Ohio as an example, not because her case is exceptional, but because if it be exceptional it is in favor of her better than average American husbandry.

The South has been less desolated by war than by long continued unreciprocal free trade with England. The ravages of war can soon be repaired. Houses, canals, and railroads can soon be rebuilt. Villages, as unimportant as those of the South, (and in this I embrace her cities all other than New Orleans,) are things of very rapid growth in countries where men are free to exercise their skill or enterprise, and industry is well rewarded. But who shall restore her waste lands? War was not the demon that blasted them; it was the free trade that England imposes on semi-civilized nations; it was the desire to create a monopoly of the cotton and sugar trade; it was the belief that a poor and ambitious people whose expenditures anticipated their annual crop could be victorious in a commercial contest with a wealthy people whose diversified industries gave them the control of all markets, and whose accumulations of capital enabled them to choose their own time and place for purchasing. I will not describe what I have seen in the South, or take the reports brought by northern men. Let southern men describe the condition of their plantations.

A southern journal, which is quoted by Carey in his Social Science, but of which the name is not given, says:

"An Alabama planter says that cotton has destroyed more than earthquakes or volcanic eruptions. Witness the red hills of Georgia and South Carolina, which have produced cotton till the last dying gasp of the soil forbade any further attempt at cultivation; and the land, turned out to nature, reminds the traveler, as he views the dilapidated condition of the country, of the ruins of ancient Greece."

Dr. Daniel Lee, in his Progress of Agriculture, in the United States Patent Office Report for 1852, says:

"Cotton culture presents one feature which we respectfully commend to the earnest consideration of southern statesmen and planters, and that is the constantly increasing deterioration of the soil devoted mainly to the production of this important crop. Already this evil has attained a fearful magnitude; and under the present common practice it grows a little faster than the increase of cotton bales at the South. Who can say when or where this ever-augmenting exhaustion of the natural resources of the cotton-growing States is to end, short of their ruin?"

De Bow, in his Resources of the South, published in 1852, says:

"The native soil of middle Georgia is a rich argillaceous loam, resting on a firm clay foundation. In some of the richer counties nearly all the lands have been cut down and appropriated to tillage; a large maximum of which have been worn out, leaving a desolate picture for the traveler to behold—decaying tenements, red old hills, stripped of their native growth and virgin soil, and washed into deep gullies, with here and there patches of Bermuda grass and stunted pine shrubs, struggling for a scanty subsistence on what was once one of the richest soils of America."

Governor Hammond, in an address before the South Carolina Institute in 1849, after presenting the same class of facts, said:

"These are not mere paper calculations, or the gloomy speculations of a brooding fancy. They are illustrated and sustained by facts, current facts of our own day, within the knowledge of every one of us. The process of impoverishment has been visibly and palpably going on step by step with the decline in the price of cotton."

Clement C. Clay, of Alabama, speaking in the United States Senate, said:

"I can show you, with sorrow, in the older portions of Alabama, in my native county of Madison, the sad memorials of the artless and exhausting culture of cotton. Our small planters, after taking the cream off their lands, unable to restore them by rest, manures, or otherwise, are going further West and South in search of other virgin lands, which they may and will despoil and impoverish in like manner. . . . . In traversing that county, one will discover numerous farm-houses, once the abode of industrious and intelligent freemen, now occupied by slaves, or tenantless, deserted, and dilapidated; he will observe fields, once fertile, now unfenced, abandoned, and covered with those evil harbingers, foxtail and broomsedge; he will see the moss growing on the moldering walls of once thrifty villages, and will find 'one only master grasp the whole domain' that once furnished happy homes for a dozen white families. Indeed a country in its infancy, where fifty years ago scarce a forest tree had been felled by the axe of the pioneer, is already exhibiting the painful signs of senility and decay apparent in Virginia and the Carolinas."

Dr. Lee, in the paper to which I have already referred, says:

"Of the land cultivated in this country, one hundred million acres are damaged to the extent of three dollars per acre per annum, or, in other words, a complete restitution of the elements of crops removed each year cannot be made short of an expense of $300,000,000."

FREE TRADE KEEPS US IN SUBJECTION TO ENGLAND'S COLONIAL POLICY.

Sir, this is a melancholy picture to contemplate—a country wasted in its youth, and its people impoverished in the midst of abounding natural riches. And, sir, what adds to its sombre character is the fact that it is not accidental—that it is not the result of Providence, save as Providence permits some men to trifle with their rights and interests, and others to take advantage of their wickedness, weakness, or folly. It is the work of man; it is the result of design; it has been brought about as the end sought to be obtained by the sagacious and far-seeing legislators who have guided the counsels of Great Britain and their allies, the free trade leaders of the Democratic party of our country. The laws by which these melancholy results were produced are demonstrable, and have long been well understood. They are the golden rule as administered by selfish and perfidious England to young or feeble nations and her own colonies. They were understood by Locke when he prepared his essay on Civil Government. Dean Swift, as I have shown, expounded them when he endeavored to inspire the people of Ireland with wisdom and save to that unhappy country a future.

They were understood by Andrew Gee when he published his work on Trade in 1750, and among other illustrations of his clear apprehension of them said:

"Manufactures in our American colonies should be discouraged, prohibited. . . . . We ought always to keep a watchful eye over our colonies, *to restrain them from setting up any of the manufactures which are carried on in Great Britain;* and any such attempts should be crushed at the beginning. . . . . Our colonies are much in the same state as Ireland was in when they began the woolen manufactory, *and as their numbers increase, will fall upon manufactures for clothing themselves, if due care be not taken to find employment for them* in raising such productions as may enable them to furnish themselves with all the necessaries from us. . . . . As they will have the providing rough materials to themselves, so shall we have the manufacturing of them. If encouragement be given for raising hemp, flax, etc., doubtless they will soon begin to manufacture, *if not prevented.* Therefore, *to stop the progress of any such manufacture,* it is proposed that no weaver have liberty to set up any looms, without first registering at an office, kept for that purpose. . . . . That all slitting-mills, and engines for drawing wire or weaving stockings, *be put down.* . . . . *That all negroes be prohibited from weaving either linen or woolen, or spinning or combing wool, or working at any manufacture of iron,* further than making it into pig or bar iron. That they also be *prohibited* from manufacturing *hats, stockings, or leather of any kind.* This limitation will not abridge the planters of any liberty they now enjoy; on the contrary, it will then turn their industry to promoting and raising those rough materials. . . . . If we examine into the circumstances of the inhabitants of our plantations, and our own, it will appear that *not one-fourth of their product redounds to their own profit, for, out of all that comes here, they only carry back clothing and other accommodations for their families,* all of which is of the merchandise and manufacture of this kingdom. . . . . All these advantages we receive by the plantations, *besides the mortgages on the planters' estates and the high interest they pay us, which is very considerable.*" *

I think, sir, that I have shown by the extracts I have made from that remarkable book, "Cotton is King," that the men of the South understood the laws of trade (certain as that of gravitation) well enough to comprehend the fact that free trade must ultimately destroy the varied interests of the North. They may not, mad with ambition as they were, have seen that the operation of the laws whose penalties they were inflicting upon others would involve them in common destruction; but that they understood the fatal operation of free trade upon the great interests of the country is apparent in every chapter of the essay from which I have quoted.

---

* See quotations from Thomas Jefferson in Speech on Centennial Celebration, Jan. 10, 1871, *supra.*

I know not, sir, whether the gentleman from Indiana has studied the laws of social science, but they have been thoroughly comprehended by the statesmen of England, and furnish the key alike to her diplomacy and legislation. Illustrative of this is the case of Portugal. In the latter part of the seventeenth century she had established manufactures of woolen goods, which were thriving, adding to the comfort and prosperity of her people, and to her own respectability and power. They, however, needed protection against the hostile capital and more fully developed industry of England, and in 1684 the Government, discovering the advantages it derived from these manufactures, resolved to protect them by prohibiting the importation of foreign fabrics of the kind. Thenceforward their increase was so rapid as to attract the attention of British capitalists, who determined upon their destruction. This was not to be accomplished at once; but, evading the technical language of the law, they manufactured articles under the names and of descriptions not precisely covered by the act of prohibition, which would supply their places, and threw them in great abundance into the Portuguese markets.* The effect upon the industry of the country was soon felt, and the Government gave its

* This device has been practiced upon during the two past years to the great detriment of the public revenue and of the American wool grower and manufacturer, by invoicing woolen and worsted goods as manufactures of cow and calf hair. Mr. James Dobson, in a letter which appears in the New York Daily Bulletin of January 26th, 1871, says: "In the first place, I would say that these so-called 'calf hair cloakings' are not made from the materials the importers say they are, but in place of being made from cow or calf hair are only so in part—the balance being wool; and some goods that have been so classified contain nothing but wool. Out of two hundred and eighty-five invoices that had passed, between July 1st to Nov. 7th, 1870, under the assumption of being calf hair, there were seventy invoices of curled Astrachans which, if properly and honestly invoiced, would have paid duty as manufactures of worsted goods. Samples of these goods can be seen in the Appraiser's Office in New York, if they have not been destroyed since Nov. 7th, 1870. If they have, then I can produce certified samples by the Deputy-Appraiser who passed them. About twenty specimens of the poorer quality of these so-called calf hair goods were submitted by the Treasury Department for microscopic examination, for the purpose of detecting whether any wool was contained in them, and in every instance wool was discovered, some specimens contained seventy per cent. wool, while others had variable proportions. You can find this report in the Treasury Department at Washington. You can also find it embodied in the Department letters, of Dec. 7th and 8th, 1870, to the Collector of the Port of New York. Again, your correspondent says that the assumption that one house in Huddersfield had sent nine-tenths of these goods to the United States, is groundless, like the rest of my statements. All I have to say to this is that I here quoted a portion of the American Consul's letter written to the Collector of New York, calling his attention to the frauds that were being daily perpetrated on the revenue of the country. The letter bears date September 17th, 1870, a copy of which is on file both in New York

attention to the matter, and prohibited the introduction of these "serges and druggets." But British capitalists were as determined that their fabrics should clothe the people of Portugal as they have since been that we should consume their cotton, woolen, steel, iron, and other goods; and what they had been unable to accomplish by the mere force of capital or by skilful evasions of Portuguese laws, they at last achieved by diplomacy. Portugal failing to perceive that England could not produce Portuguese wines, as she cannot produce American cotton, hemp, rice, tobacco, and grain, listened to the words of such diplomacy as induced us to enter into the Canadian reciprocity treaty, and subjected the energy, ingenuity, and industry of her people to the control of the Government and capitalists of England; the inducement to this step, artfully put forward by Great Britain, was that the wines of Portugal should be admitted into Great Britain at a duty one-third less than that imposed on wines imported from other countries. The effect of this treaty on the industry of Portugal is narrated by an English writer, who says:

"Before the treaty our woolen cloths, cloth serges, and cloth druggets were prohibited in Portugal. They had set up fabrics there for making cloth, and proceeded with very good success, and we might justly apprehend they would have gone on to erect other fabrics until at last they had served themselves with every species of woolen manufactures. The treaty takes off all prohibitions and obliges Portugal to admit forever all our woolen manufactures. Their own fabrics by this were perfectly ruined, and we exported £100,000 value in the single article of cloths the very year after the treaty.

"The court [of Portugal] was pestered with remonstrances from their manufacturers when the prohibition was taken off pursuant to Mr. Methuen's treaty. But the thing was passed, the treaty was ratified, and their looms were all ruined."--*British Merchantmen*, vol. 3, p. 253.

In the spirit of the diplomacy of Methuen was the par-

---

and Philadelphia, also at the Treasury Department at Washington, and is a public document. He says:

"'My attention having been drawn to the fact that certain manufacturers of this district have refused to give calf-hair certificates to the goods sold this firm in question, because they knew them to be false and did not wish to perjure themselves for the sake of gain, however the impression gained ground that the sworn certificate was only a matter of form. I was led to infer that this house in question must be the house who had so misled the manufacturer, and the developments have reached such a form that I feel it incumbent on me to call the attention of the revenue officers at New York to all the invoices of this firm, which have passed through this agency.'"

liamentary eloquence of Henry, now Lord Brougham, in 1815. Having described the effect of the peace of 1814, which bound continental Europe to the use of British manufactures, and produced an excessive exportation of British goods in that direction, he said:

"The peace of America has produced somewhat of the same effect, though I am very far from placing the vast exports which it occasioned upon the same footing with those to the European market the year before, both because ultimately the Americans will pay, which the exhausted state of the Continent renders very unlikely, and *because it was well worth while to incur a loss upon the first exportation in order by the glut to stifle in the cradle those rising manufactures in the United States which the war has forced into existence* contrary to the natural course of things."

Though I should not pause here, I cannot abstain from asking the gentleman from Indiana whether he is ready to permit "British capitalists" to glut our markets and stifle in the cradle the rising manufactures which the late war has called into existence? In further proof that they will do so, and if we do not protect them, throw the workmen engaged in our furnaces, forges, factories and workshops out of employment, let me add that the commission appointed under the provisions of the act of 5th and 6th Victoria, chapter ninety-nine, showed how well it understood that the supremacy of Great Britain depends on the maintenance, at whatever cost, of her manufacturing supremacy. In its report to Parliament in 1854 it said:

"I believe that the laboring classes generally, in the manufacturing districts of this country, and especially in the iron and coal districts, are very little aware of the extent to which they are often indebted for their being employed at all to *the immense losses which their employers voluntarily incur in bad times, in order to destroy foreign competition, and to gain and keep possession of foreign markets.* Authentic instances are well known of employers having in such times carried on their work at a loss amounting in the aggregate to three or four hundred thousand pounds in the course of three or four years. If the efforts of those who encourage the combinations to restrict the amount of labor, and to produce strikes, were to be successful for any length of time, *the great accumulations of capital could no longer be made which enable a few of the most wealthy capitalists to overwhelm all foreign competition in times of great depression,* and thus to clear the way for the whole trade to step in when prices revive, and to carry on a great business before foreign capital can again accumulate to such an extent as to be able to establish a competition in prices with any chance of success. *The large capitals of this country are the great instruments of warfare against the competing capitalists of foreign countries,* and are the most essential instruments now remaining by which our manufacturing supremacy can be maintained; the other elements—cheap labor, abundance of raw materials, means of communication, and skilled labor—being rapidly in process of being realized."

FRANCE, ENGLAND, PRUSSIA, SHODDY

Nor, sir, have other nations failed to discover that social life is not subject to chance, or to enforce what are now termed the laws of social science. Indeed, the more sagacious and powerful nations have been compelled in self-defence to do what we—grand as are the dimensions and resources of our country—must do or be forever dependent and subject to ever more frequently-recurring periods of bankruptcy, private, corporate, State and national.

Carlyle's brilliant word-painting depicts the horrors that flowed from contempt for the value of labor in France, and the historian of the rebellion just crushed will portray those which flowed from our disregard of the rights of the laboring people of our country. Had Louis XIV. appreciated the value and national power of the skilled industry of France, he would not have revoked the edict of Nantes; commenting upon which, Hume says:

"Above half a million of the most useful and industrious subjects deserted France, and exported, together with immense sums of money, those arts and manufactures which had chiefly tended to enrich that country. . . . Near fifty thousand refugees passed over into England."

Since the days of Colbert, however, with the exception of a brief term during which she adherred to the stipulations of a "reciprocity treaty," into which England inveigled her, France has protected her industry by prohibitory acts, by bounties or concessions, and by high protective duties. Her present astute ruler and the British Government have recently attempted to dazzle and mislead other nations with theories of free trade which neither was willing to carry into operation; but the tariff act prepared by M. Chevalier, after conference with Mr. Cobden, who, in his desire to improve the condition of the laboring classes of England by securing them cheap food, was led to adopt all the fallacies of the school of free traders, is perhaps the most scientifically protective revenue law ever devised.

France permits none of her raw material, which is not absolutely in excess of her demand for food or fabrics, to be exported; nor will she admit into her ports any article that may come in competition with her industry without requiring it to pay her and her people adequate compensation for the injury such admission may inflict. A recent illustration of this is before us. The free-trade papers are announcing that France has determined to admit raw whalebone free of duty. They cannot, however, tell us, that she has consented to admit foreign hops on the same terms; for while inviting cargoes of whalebone to her ports, she has rejected an application for the free admission of hops. She welcomes the product of the American whaler, for whalebone enters into an infinite number of her manufactures. She has no domestic source from which she can derive the article; and the duty upon it as upon any raw material, was a tax upon her manufacturers, or a bounty to their rivals. She therefore remits the duty for the same reason that she taxes hops. She produces much wine, and but little beer; and her own soil and labor furnish her with an adequate supply of hops for all uses within her limits. To admit them would be to injure her agriculturists, and perchance, to stimulate an appetite for a beverage that might injure the market for French wines. We ship in the same vessel our wheat, and the bones, rags, and other refuse matter which would, were our own industry broadly diversified, after application to many purposes of use and pleasure, restore to the earth the elements extracted from it by the tons of wheat which they accompany to foreign markets. These France, England, and Germany guard most sedulously; and in a pamphlet now before me, entitled "The History of the Shoddy Trade, its Rise, Progress, and Present Position," published in London in 1860, I find that in England:

"Materials regarded at one time as almost worthless, are converted, by the improved processes of manual labor and machinery, into valuable elements of textile manufactures. The seams or refuse of rags are used after lying to rot, for the purpose of manuring arable land, particularly the hop grounds of Kent and adjacent counties, and are also made into flock partially for bedding and stuffing uses. They are, moreover, (which seems strange indeed), manufactured into a chemical substance, namely, prussiate of potash, a valuable agent in dyeing. Shoddy dust, too, which is the dirt emitted from rags and shoddy in their processes, is useful as tillage in like manner with the waste which falls under scribbling-engines. *The latter is saturated with oil, in which consists, mainly, the fertilizing property. Waste is of more value than dust for farming purposes, the former having been generally about double the price of the latter; but dust has of late increased in value so as to be well nigh equal to waste. A large quantity of these materials is annually sent from this district (the West Riding of York) into Kent and other counties to till the soil.* Shoddy dust is useful in other respects than as tillage. It is now even carefully preserved in separate colors and applied in the manufacture of flock paper-hangings, which are the best description of this article. Not a single thing belonging to the rag and shoddy system is valueless or useless. There are no accumulations or mountains of debris to take up room or disfigure the landscape; all, good, bad, and indifferent, are beneficially appropriated."

Of these valuable materials this little work shows that America furnishes England more than any other nation, and that in point of quality her woolen rags are the best, even better than those derived from the city of London; that so largely are we the consumers of the cloths manufactured in greater or less part from our own refuse matter, that a commercial crisis in this country affects every manufacturer in the shoddy districts; and that the most calamitous eras in the history of the generally thriving towns depending on this manufacture were the years immediately following 1837 and 1857, when their industry was entirely suspended by the destruction of the American market.

France, less lavish of her wealth and more careful of the welfare of her people than we, sedulously guards such elements of wealth and comfort. How sedulously, will appear from the following extract from the little work I have just quoted:

"As to rags, we have not been able to import any from France, *on account of their having been prohibited as an article of export;* but according to the treaty of commerce just concluded between France and England [that arranged between Chevalier and Cobden], the former has engaged to remove the prohibition, *but reserves the privilege of imposing a heavy duty on rags shipped thence to this country.* The amount of duty has not been fixed yet, we believe; but there are fears on our part that it will be such as to preclude either paper or woolen rags being brought over to any material extent."

The fear expressed by the writer was well founded. Shrewd men played at an intricate game when that treaty was made; and while France consented far enough to give a text upon which she and England might preach free trade to the other nations of the world, she reserved to herself the amplest power to maintain the most perfect defensive warfare between her interests and those of aggressive England.*

Prior to 1844, England herself subjected rag-wool, that is, shoddy-wool prepared from rags by any other nation, to a duty of a half-penny per pound; but when other nations refused to sell her their rags in bulk, the prepared or rag-wool became the nearest approach she could obtain in adequate supply to that species of raw material, and she abolished the duty which, light as it was, favored the industry of her rivals.

Nor is Prussia behind France and England in this matter, for the same pamphlet tells me that at Berlin there are a number of manufactories of rag-wool, several of which have been established by enterprising Englishmen from the shoddy towns of Dewsbury and Batley.

"These factories," says the writer, "produce both shoddy and mungo, and appear to be successful undertakings. The principal reason why our countrymen prosecute this business at Berlin and other places in Prussia *is because that Government levies a heavy duty on the exportation of rags, and permits shoddy, the manufactured article, to go out free*, thus affording facilities for an export trade in rag-wool not extended to rags."

Insignificant as the territory of Prussia is in comparison with ours, the Government has found it well to insist upon Englishmen, who wish to work the raw materials of the country, coming with capital and machinery to furnish employment to its men, women, and children with the growth of the land, and to supply agricultural stimulants and a market for farm products within its limits, rather than repeat the unsuccessful experiment of clothing the people in foreign goods by selling their raw material at a price fixed by a distant customer, and buying it back in cloth at prices fixed by the same party. Will the American people never learn this simple lesson?

SECRET OF BONAPARTE'S POWER.

The first Napoleon said, and his words cannot be too often repeated in a republican country, a majority of whose people are dependent on their labor:

"In feudal times there was one kind of property—land; but there has grown up another—industry. They are alike entitled to the protection and defense of the Government."

---

* The French were merely throwing dirt in our eyes when they reduced their *ad valorem* duties from 50 or 30 to 15 per cent. on articles that would be equally as well prohibited by an *ad valorem* duty of 5 per cent.; or in changing total prohibition for a 30 per cent. *ad valorem* duty on articles that could not be sold at a profit, even if admitted without any duty at all; yet this is actually what is done.—*Sullivan: Protection to Native Industry. London*, 1870. Am. Ed. p. 65.

And how did he attempt to protect and defend what was and ever will be almost the only property and dependence of the majority of the people—their skill and industry? Let us learn from Chaptal, his Minister of the Interior, who, in his work on the Industry of France, says:

"A sound legislation on the subject of duties on imports is the true safeguard of agriculture and manufacturing industry. It countervails the disadvantages under which our manufactures labor from the condition of the price of workmanship or fuel. It shields the rising arts by prohibitions, thus preserving them from the rivalship of foreigners until they arrive at complete perfection. It tends to establish the national independence, and enriches the country by useful labor, which, as I have repeatedly said, is the principal source of wealth. . . . . It has been almost everywhere found that rising manufactures are unable to struggle against establishments cemented by time, nourished by numerous capitals, with a credit established by continued success, and conducted by numbers of experienced and skilful artists. We have been forced to have recourse to prohibition to ward off the competition of foreign productions. . . . . I go further: even at the present time, when these various species of industry are in a flourishing state, when there is nothing to desire with regard to the price or quality of our productions, a duty of but fifteen per cent., which would open the door to the competition of foreign fabrics, would shake to their foundations all the establishments which exist in France. Our stores would in a few days be crowded with foreign merchandise, *which would be sold at any price in order to extinguish our industry.* Our manufactories would be devoted to idleness through the impossibility of the proprietors making the same sacrifices as foreigners; and we should behold the same scenes as followed the treaty of commerce of 1786, although it was concluded on the basis of fifteen per cent. . . . .

"Cotton yarn forms the raw material of our numerous laces and calicoes. If we freely open our ports to this material, which has undergone but a single operation, behold the infallible results. One hundred million livres at present production would be destroyed for the spinning manufactures of France, because it is invested in buildings, utensils, and machinery, constructed for this purpose alone; two hundred thousand persons would be deprived of employment; eighteen millions of manual labor would be lost to France, and our commerce would be deprived of one of its principal resources, which consists in the transportation of cotton and wool from Asia and America to France.

"Let it not be presumed that I deceive myself. I am well acquainted with the state of our cotton spinning and that of the two neighboring countries. In France, it is true, manual labor is cheap, but on the other side more extensive establishments, supported by large capitals, afford advantages against which it is impossible for us as yet to struggle. To this must be added that the English spinning machinery has been in use for sixty years, that the proprietors are indemnified for all the expenses of their first establishment, that the profits have been converted into new capitals, whereas ours are of recent formation, and the interest of the first investment ought for a long time to be computed in all the calculations of the profits of the manufactory. The English manufacturer, reimbursed for his first investment, and possessing a large capital, *is able to make sacrifices to overwhelm and level us*, whereas the French manufacturer is destitute of defense unless protected by the tariff."

Chaptal understood as thoroughly as Brougham that England had the power, and that it was her constant policy to "stifle the infant manufactures" of other nations "in the cradle." His language is as applicable to our interests now as it was to those of France when uttered; and we can find no other safeguard for our agricultural and commercial interests than such sound legislation on the subject of duties on imports as protected the infant but rising manufactures of France.

I cannot abstain, sir, from submitting to your consideration in this connection a brief specimen of vigorous condensation from the instructive address of John L. Hayes, Esq., before the National Association of Wool Manufacturers:

"No sooner had the First Consul, Bonaparte, grasped with a firm hand the reins of state, than he resolved to develop upon the French soil all the elements of wealth concealed within its bosom. He wished to appropriate for France all sciences, arts, and industries. Made a member of the Institute, he uttered this noble sentiment: 'The true power of the French Republic should consist, above all, in its not allowing a single new idea to exist which it does not make its own.' To learn the necessities and resources of the nation, he called upon savans, painters, and artisans to adorn with their productions the vast hall of the Louvre. From this epoch a new career was opened to the industry of France, which found its most magnificent protector in the chief of the State. Napoleon said: 'Spain has twenty-five million merinos; I wish France to have a hundred millions.' To effect this, among other administrative aids, he established sixty additional sheep-folds to those of Rambouillet, where agriculturists could obtain the use of Spanish rams without expense. By the continental blockade he closed France and the greater part of Europe against English importations; and the manufacturers of France were pushed to their utmost to supply, not only their domestic, but European consumption. They had to replace, by imitating them, the English commodities to which the people had been so long accustomed. The old routines of manufacturing were abandoned, and the reign of the Emperor became, in all the industrial arts, one long series of discoveries and progress. Napoleon saw that the conquest of the industry of England was no less important than the destruction of its fleets and armies. He appealed to patriotism, as well as science and the arts, to aid him in his strife with the modern Carthage. Visiting the establishment for printing calicoes of the celebrated Oberhampf, Napoleon said to him, as he saw the perfection of the fabrics: 'We are both of us carrying on a war with England; but I think that yours, after all, is the best.' 'These words,' says M. Randoing, 'so flattering and so just, were repeated from one end of France to the other; they so inflamed the imaginations of the people that the meanest artisan, believing himself called upon to be the auxiliary of the great man, had but one thought, the ruin of England.' "

WHAT PROTECTION HAS DONE FOR GERMANY.

Before the establishment of the Zoll-Verein, which occurred in 1835, Germany exported raw materials. Having sold her skins for a six-pence, she bought back what few tails she could at any price. Her laboring people were poor, and, as is now the case in Ireland, in such excess of her ability to feed and clothe them, that she was ever ready to sell a contingent to any party that might be engaged in war, and, if need be, to swell the ranks of both contending armies. In the absence of protective duties, there was nothing of so little value to her as an able-bodied German peasant. But the establishment of that Customs-Union has changed all this. It protects her industry, and as a consequence she imports raw materials from America and all other countries that adhere to her ancient semi-barbarous policy, and exports her grain and wool condensed into broadcloth and the multiform products of well-protected industry. The annual crop derived from her soil increases per acre steadily as that of England, and in about the ratio of the diminution of ours. Wise laws have here again demonstrated the truth that there is a harmony between the varied interests of the people of a country, and that by a wide and universal diversification of employments the welfare of each and all is advanced.

Forty years ago England had not perfected her protective system so far as to admit all raw materials free of duty, and Germany sold her thirty million pounds of raw wool, upon which she collected a duty of twelve cents a pound, part of which, when manufactured into low grades of cloth, she sold at immense profits in Germany. But thirty years of protection have changed all this. Germany now raises over one hundred million pounds of wool, and imports very considerable quantities; and having compacted her grain and wool into fine cloths, she exports them to all parts of the world. When the Zoll-Verein was formed, says Henry C. Carey :*

* *Slave Trade, Domestic and Foreign, p.* 310. This invaluable work does not, as its title implies, relate specially or mainly to chattel slavery. It is the illustration of the correctness of Mr. Carey's opinions drawn from the history and condition of many countries. If it be true that "history is philosophy teaching by example," its author should take a high place among historians. Carey's Slave Trade, Domestic and Foreign, should receive the consideration of every candid student of social science, and no library is complete in this department without it.

"The total import of raw cotton and cotton yarn was about three hundred thousand cwts; but so rapid was the extension of the manufacture that in less than six years it had doubled; and so cheaply were cotton goods supplied that a large export trade had already arisen. In 1845, when the Union was but ten years old, the import of cotton and yarn had reached a million of hundred weights, and since that time there has been a large increase. The iron manufacture also grew so rapidly that whereas, in 1834, the consumption had been only eleven pounds per head; in 1847 it had risen to twenty-five pounds, having thus more than doubled; and with each step in this direction, the people were obtaining better machinery for cultivating the land and for converting its raw products into manufactured ones."*

WASHINGTON, JEFFERSON, AND JACKSON.

In what strange contrast with this policy, so fruitful of blessings, has been that which we have pursued, and of which the gentleman from Indiana claims President Johnson as an adherent. Opposed to privileged classes we have legislated in the interests of but one class, and that an oligarchy; proclaiming "the greatest good of the greatest number" as our supreme desire, we have so legislated as to impair the value of labor, the only property of a majority of our people; vaunting our national independence, we have so legislated as to prevent our escape from a condition of commercial, manufacturing, and financial dependence; and while justly proud of our general intelligence, we have so legislated as to justify the manufacturing and commercial nations of the world in classing us among the semi-barbarous governments, whose people, rich in natural wealth, have not the capacity to mould and transmute raw materials into articles of utility, comfort, and refinement, and in ranking the people of the United States, in their estimation, with those of Turkey, Portugal, Ireland, and the mixed races of Central and South America. The fathers of the country were, in this matter, wiser than their children. They had suffered from the rigid enforcement by Great Britain of Andrew Gee's suggestion to "keep a watchful eye over our colonies, and restrain them from setting up any of the manufactures which are carried on in Great Britain;" and they knew that if the nation they had founded was to be powerful, and its people prosperous, they must be relieved from that policy by the only means possible—the adherence to those defensive laws which

* The largest and most successful iron and steel establishment in the world is not in England. It is Krupp's, at Essen, Prussia. Its protected wares compete with those of England in every country.

would protect an infant against the aggressions of a giant. The Constitution was adopted in 1787; President Washington was inaugurated in 1789, and in his address of the 8th of January, 1790, said:

"The safety and interest of the people require that they should promote such manufactures as tend to render them independent of others for essential, particularly for military supplies."

And on the 15th of the same month, Congress resolved—

"That it be referred to the Secretary of the Treasury to propose and report to this House a proper plan or plans conformably to the recommendations of the President in his speech to both Houses of Congress, for the encouragement and promotion of such manufactures as will tend to render the United States independent of other nations for essential, particularly for military supplies."

And in 1791 Congress adopted an Act for imposing duties on imports, the preamble of which contains the following language:

"Whereas it is necessary for the support of the Government, for the discharge of the debts of the United States, *and the encouragement and protection of manufactures*, that duties be laid on goods, wares, and merchandise imported."

In a communication five years later than this, Washington said:

"Congress have repeatedly directed their attention to the encouragement of manufactures. The object is of too much importance not to insure a continuance of these efforts in every way which shall appear eligible."

And Mr. Jefferson, in his message of 1802, said that—

"To cultivate peace, maintain commerce and navigation, to foster our fisheries, and protect manufactures adapted to our circumstances, etc., are the land-marks by which to guide ourselves in all our relations."

These expressions are inconsistent with the opinions adverse to the policy of fostering manufacturers in this country embodied by Jefferson in his Notes on Virginia in 1785; but he was not one of those fools who hold it a weakness to change an opinion, even under the discipline of experience; and in a letter to Mr. Benjamin Austin, dated January 9, 1816, when the subject of a protective tariff was agitated by the people and was about to be brought to the attention of Congress, said in support of his matured judgment:

"You tell me I am quoted by those who wish to continue our dependence on England for manufactures. There was a time when I might have been so quoted with more candor . . . . We have since experienced what we did not then believe, that there exists both profligacy and power enough to exclude us from the field of interchange with other nations—that to be independent for the comforts of life, we must fabricate them ourselves. *We must now place the manufacturer by the side of the agriculturist.* . . . He, therefore, who is now against domestic manufactures must be for reducing us either to dependence on that foreign nation, or to be clothed in skins and to live like wild beasts in dens and caverns. I am proud to say that I am not one of these. *Experience has taught me that manufactures are now as necessary to our independence as to our comfort;* and if those who quote me as of a different opinion will keep pace with me *in purchasing nothing foreign where an equivalent of domestic fabric can be obtained, without any regard to difference of price,* it will not be our fault if we do not have a supply at home equal to our demand, and wrest that weapon of distress from the hand which has so long wantonly violated it."

General Jackson's oft-quoted letter to Dr. Coleman, of North Carolina, was about eight years later than that of Mr. Jefferson, and nothing that he ever wrote illustrates more admirably his strong common sense and devotion to the rights and interests of all the people of the Union which he so resolutely defended. Writing to one of that class who have been pleased to call themselves "planters," to distinguish them from the "hard-fisted farmers" of the North, upon whose interests they were then waging war, that they might secure cheap food for their slaves, he said:

"I will ask, what is the real situation of the agriculturist? Where has the American farmer a market for his surplus products? Except for cotton, he has neither a foreign nor a home market. Does not this clearly prove, when there is no market, either at home or abroad, that there is too much labor employed in agriculture, and that the channels of labor should be multiplied? Common sense points out at once the remedy. Draw from agriculture the superabundant labor; employ it in mechanism and manufactures, thereby creating a home market for your breadstuffs, and distributing labor to a most profitable account; and benefits to the country will result. Take from agriculture in the United States six hundred thousand men, women, and children, and you at once give a home market for more breadstuffs than all Europe now furnishes us. In short, sir, we have been too long subject to the policy of the British merchants. It is time we should become a little more Americanized, and instead of feeding the paupers and laborers of Europe, feed our own; or else, in a short time, by continuing our present policy, we shall all be paupers ourselves."

MAN CANNOT COMPROMISE PRINCIPLES.

Mr. Chairman, why have we not regarded the teachings of history, the monitions of the fathers, the oft-recurring and bitter experience of the past? Why have we been content, to find the mass of artisans and artificers of the country, at intervals of from seven to ten years, without employment, drawing from the savings bank their hoarded earnings, seeing the little homes, under the roofs of which they had hoped in ripe age to die, passing under the sheriff's hammer; and to see the forge, the furnace, the mill, and the workshop idle, and changing hands by forced sale oftentimes at less than a fourth, and sometimes at but a tithe of their original cost? Why have we been content to see the crop of the farmer rot in the field, while the laboring people of the cities were gnawed by hunger, and causing doubts of the stability of republican institutions by threatening, and in at least one instance absolutely perpetrating, bread riots? Why has our march of emigration been a march of desolation, and the son of him who emigrated to Ohio as the far West, finding his labor unrewarded by the famished land, been constrained to cry "Westward ho!" and go to contend with the trials and deprivations of frontier life, and found a new State still more remote from markets?

And why was it, sir, that when those who would overthrow our Government fired upon the flag, that, with our unequaled ingenuity, our sheep walks of limitless extent, our boundless water power, and our measureless stores of coal and iron, we were unable to provide adequate clothing and arms for the seventy-five thousand men summoned to our defense? There is but one answer to all these questions. We suffered all these ills because we had disregarded the laws I am endeavoring to illustrate and other fundamental truths in which, on every public occasion, we proclaim our belief; had endeavored to maintain in this free and busy age an anachronism, involving the denial of all rights, and the repression of the native ability of the laborers of one half of our country; and had endeavored to prove the solecism that slavery is an essential element of free institutions, and adds to the power of a country contending for supremacy with nations that are using every expedient to animate the industry, ingenuity, and enterprise of their people. By oppressing others we enfeebled and degraded ourselves. Slavery has its laws, and they are irreconcilable with those which quicken industry and develop material power. Time will not permit, nor is this the occasion for their discussion. It is enough for the present to say that they do not tolerate intelligent or requited labor. They were understood and enforced by the slave-owning oligarchy, and were submitted to by the masses of the people, whose artfully fostered pride of race deluded them into the belief that the inequalities of caste were consistent with the democracy of a professedly Christian republic. At last the delusion is dispelled, and with it go the cruel necessities by which those who, being freemen, were, under the compromises of the Constitution, enslaved by the inherent laws of slavery; and our country having corrected the solecism and banished the anachronism, may now enter upon a career of competition with the most advanced nations of the world. The vast and varied attractions the United States present to the hopeful, the enterprising, ingenious and skilled workmen of the world, are the means by which we may enfeeble all rival Powers, while building up our own, and augmenting the prosperity of our rapidly-increasing people. Slavery being dead, let us entomb with it its twin barbarism, British free trade. Henceforth our legislation may well be directed to advancing the greatest good not only of the greatest number, but the unquestioned good of all; and in this it will stand in strange contrast with its purposes and policy in the past. To show how wide that contrast will be, let me turn again to *King Cotton*. On page 96 of this royal volume I find it written:

> "At the date of the passage of the Nebraska bill, the multiplication of provisions by their more extended cultivation, was the only measure left that could produce a reduction of prices and meet the wants of the planters. *The Canadian reciprocity treaty, since secured, will bring the products of the British North American colonies, free of duty, into competition with those of the United States when prices with us rule high.*"

This was not written by an English hand.

Our forges, furnaces, and factories were unprofitable capital. Coal, ore, and limestone lay undisturbed in the places of their original deposit, and mechanics of skill and energy went begging for employment. Yet an American writer rejoiced that the means had been secured by which the farmers of the country could be made to suffer with the afflicted multitude. With that want of patriotism which has long characterized the leaders of the Democratic party, he exulted over the subjection of the agricultural interests of his country to those of British North America by that misnamed reciprocity treaty with Canada which southern influence had forced upon us, and lauded it as the sure means by which the farmer should be driven to a still greater distance from all other markets than that afforded by the few hundred thousand men who regarded no interests but their own, and believed that these could only be promoted by procuring still cheaper food for their millions of slaves.

But listen to him again. On page 123 I find the following:

> "From what has been said, the dullest intellect cannot fail now to perceive the *rationale* of the Kansas-Nebraska movement. The political influence which these Territories will give to the South will be of the first importance to perfect its arrangement for future slavery extension, whether by division of the larger States and Territories now secured to the institution, its extension into territory hitherto considered free, or the acquisition of new territory to be devoted to the system, so as to preserve the balance of power in Congress. *When this is done, Kansas and Nebraska, like Kentucky and Missouri, will be of little consequence to slaveholders compared with the cheap and constant supply of provisions they can yield. Nothing, therefore, will so exactly coincide with southern interests as a rapid emigration of freemen into these new Territories. White free labor, doubly productive over slave labor in grain-growing, must be multiplied within their limits, that the cost of provisions may be reduced, and the extension of slavery and the growth of cotton suffer no interruption.* The present efforts to plant them with slavery are indispensable to produce sufficient excitement to fill them speedily with a free population; and if this whole movement has been a southern scheme to cheapen provisions and increase the ratio of the production of sugar and cotton, as it most unquestionably will do, it surpasses the statesmanlike strategy which forced the people into an acquiescence in the annexation of Texas. And should the anti-slavery voters succeed in gaining the political ascendency in these Territories, and bring them as free States triumphantly into the Union, *what can they do but turn in as all the rest of the western States have done, and help to feed slaves*, or those who manufacture or sell the products of the labor of slaves?"

These paragraphs show that the slaveholders achieved what an examination of the topography of the country might have led them to regard as a last grand triumph. Their system held undisputed sway; and let me ask whether, had they been content to live under the Government that existed, it could have prospered long? Two interests alone were to be pursued: the growing of grain in the North and West, and the growing of cotton, sugar, rice, tobacco, and hemp in the South. In the light of the extracts, showing the rapid exhaustion of our soil by the exportation of its products, which I presented in the earlier part of my remarks, and of the experience of every farmer and planter, will it be asserted that this system of culture could long have continued? Science could have calculated the years of its possible duration with almost perfect accuracy. When, under such a system, could the earth have rest for recuperation? And whence could come the stimulants to restore its wasted energies? The system omitted these essential conditions of prosperity, and thereby provided for its own decline. The scheme was an impracticable one, which though it might have served as a temporary expedient, could not endure, for it was in conflict with the laws of Providence.

It may be that an indistinct perception of this drove the oligarchy to the madness of war; for all now admit that there was not, in the election of Mr. Lincoln, or the purposes of the Republican party, anything to justify their attempt to destroy the Union by war. But be this as it may, the war did but hasten, by a few years, the inevitable termination of their persistent folly and crime. The commercial crisis of 1860, following so closely upon that of 1857, and repeating, as both did so minutely, in all their details, the disastrous and wide-spread incidents of 1837 and 1840, would in themselves have constrained the people to demand such legislation as would promote and secure a diversification of our industries, the development of our resources, and the laying of foundations for a widely-extended commerce. The American people had become too numerous, too enlightened, too energetic, and had endured too many of these commercial crises to have been willing longer to submit their fortunes and destinies to the control of the few arrogant theorists, whose views were so narrow and whose fancied interests were so diametrically opposed to those of all the rest of their countrymen.

THEN AND NOW.

Sir, let us contemplate for a moment our condition when the champions of slavery and free trade fired on the flag of the country. April, 1861, found us unable to clothe our soldiers or furnish them with implements and munitions of war. When the President called for seventy-five thousand troops, and that number of the flower of our countrymen promptly responded, they were clad, not in our blue alone, but in gray, the chosen color of our enemy, in black, in red, or any other color, because we had not the proper material with which to clothe them. We had not the quality of iron from which to fashion a gun barrel, nor could we make it. We had not blankets to shield our men from rain or frost, in camp or bivouac; and as the people regarded the base character of the articles with which our army was provided, many of which had been made from American rags in the shoddy towns of Yorkshire, they raised a universal cry of "fraud" against both public officers and contractors. Our mills, forges, furnaces, and factories stood still. The frugal laborer was living upon the earnings of past years. Commerce, having dwindled from the expiration of the protective tariff of 1842, had ceased to animate our ports. The crops of the West stood ungathered in the fields, and the bankruptcy of 1857, from which we had not yet recovered, had returned to sweep away the few who had withstood the surge.

But the case is altered now. Necessity has compelled us to do what reason and experience long ago suggested. The fact that we determined to pay in gold the interest on our bonds and to obtain the required bullion by collecting the duties on imports in coin, has done much to animate and diversify our industry. This fact and the general results of the war*—for the duties we lay on raw materials and our internal taxes more than counterbalance the protection afforded to many branches of industry by our tariff laws—have enabled us to recover from our prostration and started us in a career of prosperity and progress; and if wisdom guide our legislation, the waste lands of which I have read will soon be reinvigorated; the ancient village will be absorbed in the expanding city; new towns will mark the plain and river bank; and where the mean white and the negro have loitered listlessly through the months, diversified and well-paid industry, quickening their energies and expanding their desires, will employ all their hours, and enable each to carve his way as an American citizen should do in a career that will afford him pleasure or profit. The gentleman from Indiana may desire to recall the idleness and misery of 1860, but I cannot believe that he is justified in intimating that President Johnson sympathizes with him in this respect.

* The most immediate and beneficent of which was the volume of currency created by the issue of greenbacks.

VIRGINIA.

General Frank P. Blair, jr., intent upon neutralizing any service he may have rendered the country during the war, having gathered about him the representative men of the eighty thousand disfranchised traitors of Missouri with whom he now affiliates, recently charged, as does the gentleman from Indiana, that the Republican party of the country is under the control of men whose object is to aggrandize New England, and by a protective tariff tax the agricultural interests of the country for the benefit of a few wealthy manufacturers, and that the resistance offered to the admission of representatives of the conquered but unregenerated people of the South by Congress is the result of this purpose. How false this is he well knows; for every member of the family in the councils of which he bears so distinguished a part, and which always speaks as a unit, may be shown, by their published utterances, to understand that protection to American industry is essential to the prosperity of the agricultural interests of the country. Adequate protection to American industry, its defense against the assaults of the accumulated capital, machinery, cheap labor, and skill of foreign countries, is of less importance to the middle and New England States than to any other portion of the country. The wasted South most needs it; and next to the South, the Northwest, rich in all the elements of manufacturing greatness, and poor only from her want of local markets, which the diversification of her industry and developement of her multifarious resources would create.

Sir, Virginia is not a New England State; nor do her people delight in being called Yankees, though they will hereafter be as proud as we are of our national cognomen. But no portion of our country, unless it be General Blair's own Missouri, with her boundless stores of varied mineral wealth, would be so blessed by setting all its poor at work upon the growth of its own lands as Virginia. A discriminating writer, who in August last traversed a large portion of the gold region of the State, in company with three eminent mineralogists, in the course of an article in the December number of Harper's Magazine, says:

"To give any adequate description of the mineral wealth which Virginia contains, would be not only to minutely describe every rod of her entire length, embracing hundreds of miles, but to enumerate almost every mineral of value hitherto known among mankind. It is not in gold alone that she abounds—but, scattered in profusion over almost her entire surface are to be found iron, copper, silver, tin, tellurium, lead, platinum, cinnabar, plumbago, manganese, asbestos, kaolin, slate, clay, coal, roofing slate of the greatest durability, marbles of the rarest beauty, soap stone, sulphur, hone-stone, equal to the best Turkey, gypsum, lime, copperas, blue stone, grind stone, cobalt, emery, and a variety of other materials that we have hitherto been compelled to import or to do without. Indeed, it may be said, without exaggeration, that in the single State of Virginia, in the most singular juxtaposition of what might be considered geologically incongruous materials, is to be found an almost exhaustless fund of God-given treasures, more than enough to pay off our whole national debt, and only awaiting the magic touch of capital and enterprise to drag them to light for the benefit of man."

Of what avail have these boundless deposits of multiform riches been to the people of Virginia, and what have the Democratic party, slavery, and British free trade done for their most fortunately situated and devoted adherents? The aristocracy of Virginia have withheld from the laborer his hire, and the native fertility of their land has wasted away. They have traded in human muscles as a source of power, and laboring men have shunned their inviting climate; and their water power, exceeding in one year the muscular power that all the slaves found in the United States at the taking of the last census could put forth in a lifetime, has flowed idly to the sea, often through forests so wide that it could "hear no sound save its own dashing." And the State, from having at the close of the last century been the first in point of population and political power, fell, in sixty years, as is shown by the census of 1860, to be the fifth in population, and to rank the equal of free young Indiana in the fifth class in political power.

The laws of Providence are inflexible, and it could not be otherwise. Despising labor, the Heaven-appointed condition on which alone man shall eat bread, she tended year by year toward poverty and want, and though she raised millions of laboring people of every shade of human complexion, the sweat of their brows enriched not her fields but those of other states. Like Germany before the establishment of the Zoll-Verein, and Ireland since the Union, she raised little else than labouring people for exportation. If he who fails to provide for his family be worse than an infidel, what shall be said of the legislation that drives the heirs to so goodly a heritage as the lands of Virginia forth in want and ignorance to dwell among strangers?

The Republicans of New England and the Middle States would make all her people comfortable, happy, and intelligent, in the homes of their fathers. We of Pennsylvania will welcome them to generous rivalry in every branch of industry to which we have devoted ourselves. In this age of iron, fire is force, and Virginia is underlaid by the purest fuel. If she wishes to leave her rich gold and silver mines in all their wealth to posterity, let her rival us in contributing to the needed supply of iron and steel for the exhausted South. Her kaolin is equal to any in England, and why will she not lessen our dependence on that country by building up an American Staffordshire, and embodying in porcelain the conceptions of American art? And as the product of the quarries of New Jersey and northeastern Pennsylvania have driven British roofing and school slates from our northern market, why will she not send hers to every market in the South? The country would be none the less powerful or respectable if every child in that section, however black, were expert in the use of the slate and pencil, or if their now squalid homes were embellished, as are those of many of the working people of the North, by ornate brackets, shelves, mantles, pier slabs, and table, bureau, and wash-stand tops of what everybody but the connoisseur and expert mistakes for porcelain, mosaic, or Spanish, Egyptian, red and green Pyreneese, verd-antique, Siennese, porphyry, brocatel, or other marbles, but which are produced at little cost from the slate of Lehigh county.

PENNSYLVANIA CHALLENGES GENEROUS COMPETITION.

Is it said, sir, that Pennsylvania seeks to obtain a monopoly of the American iron market? Why, then, does she ask you to so legislate that capital shall find its advantage, and the laborer become rich, in working the unmeasured iron and coal-beds of her near neighbors, Maryland, Virginia, West Virginia, Kentucky, and Tennessee? England can no longer supply herself with charcoal pig-iron. She has not the fuel. Her forests have yielded to the demand for pasturage and sheep walks. She is in this respect dependent on foreign countries, and buys such pig metal as raw material where she can get it best and cheapest, from Sweden, Norway, Russia, or Nova Scotia, all of which are in the same isothermal zone, in which are found underlying forests which yield an average of fifty cords per acre, the inexhaustible beds of better than Swedish ore of the Marquette region of Michigan and Wisconsin. And, gentlemen of the Northwest, I ask you whether patriotic Pennsylvania manifests a disposition to tax you for her advantage when she challenges your competition, and implores you to help her to outdo England without fighting and enrich yourselves by setting unemployed laborers at work with the growth of your own lands? The Bessemer or pneumatic converter is coming largely into use, and the exigencies of the war and the incidental protection it has given our industry have created manufactories of American steel; and in each of these facts you have a guarantee of steady increase in the demand for your unrivaled product, and of the profits of the railroad companies, which will carry away your commodities and return with people to build the cities your expanding iron and steel works must create. A few figures will verify these assertions. Dr. Robert H. Lamborn, than whom there is no more careful statistician, tells us that—

> "By comparing the production of this region with that of other iron districts, it will be found that it produced in 1864 more pig metal than Connecticut or Massachusetts in the same year, and sixty per cent. more than New York in 1850. Reckoning ore and metal together, the mines of Marquette threw into consumption in 1864 154,905 tons of metal, or three-fifths as much as the total pig-iron production of the United States, according to the census returns of 1850, *and one-eighth of all the pig-iron produced by the United States in* 1864."

In view of these gratifying facts, can it be possible that the people of the Northwest are anxious for an early renewal of the "*tripartite* alliance formed by the Western farmer, the Southern planter, and the English manufacturer," so exultantly referred to in "Cotton is King," by which the furnaces producing all this metal shall be closed, and their proprietors and the laborers they employ reduced to bankruptcy, as those of Ohio and Pennsylvania have so often been by British free trade?

If, gentlemen of Missouri, Pennsylvania is seeking a monopoly, why do her people labor to persuade you to produce at the base of Iron mountain and Pilot Knob the utilities to the creation of which they devote their capital and industry? No, our efforts are not selfish. We wish to raise the prostrate South and give her an onward and upward career, and to secure to the American laborer wages so liberal that the report thereof shall invite to our shores the skilled and enterprising workmen of every craft and country. By employing all our people with the growth of our own lands we can create an urgent demand for labor, and thereby solve the most difficult problem before the country; for when labor is in quick demand its value will be regarded and the rights of the laborer protected.

By no other means can the exhausted South be restored, or the work of her recuperation be commenced. Who will emigrate to the recently insurgent States? Vast and varied and peculiar as are their natural resources, will capital, proverbially timid as it is, fly to a region characterized by turbulence and lawlessness, or enterprise to a land in which labor is regarded as the disgraceful office of a subject race, and where legislation is employed to repress the intellect and suppress the aspirations of the laboring people for a higher and better life? Sir, there is not a Northern State that does not outbid them for emigrants and offer superior inducements to the capitalist and those that are infinitely more attractive to him who has but his labor and that of his family to sell. Pennsylvania needs a million laborers. She can feed and clothe and house them all should they come to her in the current year. We want them to gather and refine petroleum, to construct and manage railroads, to conduct our internal carrying trade, to build factories, forges, furnaces, founderies, and the towns they will beget; to quarry slate, zinc, coal, iron, marble, and the thousand other elements of wealth condensed within the limits of our State. Inert as these natural elements of wealth are, they are of no available value; but the quickening touch of labor will transmute them all to gold; and energy, enterprise, and capital in the hands of men whose earlier years were passed in manual labor, are holding out to industry the richest bribes to induce it to come and help pay our national debt and increase our country's power by enriching themselves and us. But, sir, we offer higher inducements than wages in dollars and cents. Our equal laws, recognizing the fact that the children of a State are its jewels, put a school-house near every laboring man's dwelling, and as a reward for his industry, and to increase the power of the State, secure to each child coming into it the keys of all knowledge in the mastery of the English language, the art of writing, and at least the elementary rules of arithmetic. And in the neighborhood of every hamlet the church spire points the way from earth to heaven. Before the altar employer and workman meet as equals, and in the same class in the Sunday-school their children learn practical lessons of Christian equality.

A SUGGESTION AND EXAMPLE TO THE SOUTH.

These are conditions that the South cannot yet offer to the emigrant from our fields or those of Europe. If she would prosper she must Americanize her system of life, abandon her contempt for labor, and her habits of violence and disregard of law. She must learn to respect man as man, and stimulate his exertions by quickening his intellect, expanding and chastening his desires, and insuring him a just reward for whatever he shall put forth in the way of industry, ingenuity, or enterprise. She can only create the elements of her new and great future by developing the resources now at her command, the chief of which she will find to be her apt and docile laboring people. Her present purpose seems to be not to do this, but to enter on a new career of oppression. Her dream is still of dominion over large plantations and imbruited laborers. Let her abandon the problem, "How can I *make* my laborers work?" and occupy herself upon the gentler one, "How can I *induce* these people by whom I am surrounded to enrich themselves and me?" and she will begin to learn how rich and powerful she is. When she shall have accomplished thus much, when her laborers are freely paid and her common schools offer shelter and culture to the laborer's child, she may successfully appeal to those who can elsewhere find wages, security, and equal chances in life to come and cast their lot with her. She should hasten the coming of that day. In common with us, she is burdened by the debt of $3,000,000,000 in which she has involved us. Let her remember that she, too, has coal, iron, lead, copper, zinc, silver and gold, cinnabar, tellurium, and all the elements of manufacturing and commercial power which characterize so abundantly every section of our country; that she has broad land which will not be fully worked when every man and woman within its limits may say, with truth, "I am indeed an American citizen, and have, by my well-requited voluntary labor, earned the bread my dear family has this day eaten." And she will find that she has added vastly to her wealth when the field hand shall have been transformed into a skilled workman; when he who, under the lash, has lazily hoed cotton or corn, under the stimulus of liberal wages, converts ore and coal into rails, cannon, or anchors, or into any of the thousand minor fabrics from the fish-hook and the sail or packing needle to the heavy and complicated lock advertised in the catalogue of one concern, that of Russell & Erwin, of New Britain, in Connecticut—a State producing so little iron as to be scarcely remembered when enumerating the iron-producing Commonwealths of the country. This concern, I am informed, sold but $30,000 worth of goods in the first year of its operations, and $3,000,000 worth during the last year. Meanwhile it has concentrated in the village enlivened by its works a thriving and highly-educated population, and has converted unskilled laborers into mechanics and accomplished mechanicians, though their hands were no nimbler or their minds more comprehensive or versatile than those of the laborers to be found in the devastated South, whose extermination or expatriation seems to be within the purview of those who assert their right to control the policy of that section.

It is not for the rich, the comparatively few who have accumulated capital, that we demand protection. We ask it in the name of the millions who live by toil, whose dependence is on their skill and ability to labor, and whose labor creates the wealth of the country. To what fearful competition they are subjected when by withholding protection we leave them undefended against the assaults of British capital, is aptly set forth by Daniel J. Morrell, Esq., in his admirable letter to the secretary of the American Iron and Steel Association. He says:

"That portion of the price of a ton of *imported* iron which stands for the wages of labor, represents *coarse food, mean raiment, and worse lodging, political nullity, enforced ignorance, serfdom in a single occupation, with a prospect of eventual relief from the parish.*

"That portion of the price of a ton of American iron which stands for the wages of labor, *represents fresh and wholesome food, good raiment, the homestead, unlimited freedom of movement and change of occupation, intelligent support of all the machinery of municipal, State and national Government, with a prospect of comfortable old age, at last dividing its substance with blessings among prosperous children.*

"Thus it is easy to see why imported iron may be cheap and American iron dear; for the latter, in addition to its other burdens, pays an extraordinary tax to freedom and enlightenment, which are assuredly deserving of protection."

Mr. Morrell evidently does not agree with the magnates of the South in their opinion that the way to make a State great and powerful is to oppress and degrade its working people.

WE CAN PAY OUR DEBTS "WITHOUT MONEYS."

I have never been able to believe that a national debt is a national blessing. I have seen how good might be interwoven with or educed from evil, or how a great evil might, under certain conditions, be turned to good account; but beyond this, I have never been able to regard debt, individual or national, as a blessing. It may be that, as in the inscrutable providence of God it required nearly five years of war to extirpate the national crime of slavery, and anguish and grief found their way to nearly every hearth-side in the country before we would recognize the manhood of the race we had so long oppressed, it was also necessary that we should be involved in a debt of unparalleled magnitude, that we might be compelled to avail ourselves of the wealth that lies so freely around us, and by opening markets for well-rewarded industry, make our land, what in theory it has ever been, the refuge of the oppressed of all climes. England, if supreme selfishness be consistent with sagacity, has been eminently sagacious in preventing us from becoming a manufacturing people; for with our enterprise, our ingenuity, our freer institutions, the extent of our country, the cheapness of our land, the diversity of our resources, the grandeur of our seas, lakes, and rivers, we should long ago have been able to offer her best workmen such inducements as would have brought them by millions to help bear our burdens and fight our battles. We can thus raise the standard of British and continental wages, and protect American workmen against ill-paid competition. This we must do if we mean to maintain the national honor. The fields now under culture, the houses now existing, the mines now being worked, the men we now employ, cannot pay our debt. To meet its annual interest by taxing our present population and developed resources would be to continue an ever-enduring burden.

The principal of the debt must be paid; but as it was contracted for posterity its extinguishment should not impoverish those who sustained the burdens of the war. I am not anxious to reduce the total of our debt, and would, in this respect, follow the example of England, and as its amount has been fixed would not for the present trouble myself about its aggregate except to prevent its increase. My anxiety is that the taxes it involves shall be as little oppressive as possible, and be so adjusted that, while defending our industry against foreign assault, they may add nothing to the cost of those necessaries of life which we cannot produce, and for which we must therefore look to other lands. The raw materials entering into our manufactures, which we are yet unable to produce, but on which we unwisely impose duties, I would put into the free list with tea, coffee and other such purely foreign essentials of life, and would impose duties on commodities that compete with American productions, so as to protect every feeble or infant branch of industry and quicken those that are robust. I would thus cheapen the elements of life, and enable those whose capital is embarked in any branch of production to offer such wages to the skilled workmen of all lands as would steadily and rapidly increase our numbers, and, as is always the case in the neighborhood of growing cities or towns of considerable extent, increase the return for farm labor; this policy would open new mines and quarries, build new furnaces, forges and factories, and rapidly increase the taxable property and taxable inhabitants of the country. Would the South accept this theory and enter heartily upon its execution, she would pay more than now seems her share of the debt and feel herself blessed in the ability to do it. Her climate is more genial than ours; her soil may be restored to its original fertility; her rivers are broad, and her harbors good; and above all, hers is the monopoly of the fields for rice, cane sugar, and cotton. Let us pursue for twenty years the sound national policy of protection, and we will double our population and more than quadruple our capital and reduce our indebtedness *per capita* and per acre to little more than a nominal sum. Thus each man can "without moneys" pay the bulk of his portion of the debt by blessing others with the ability to bear an honorable burden.

How protection, by animating, diversifying, and rewarding industry, will pay our debt is well shown by the experience of the last five years. And though we do not owe that experience to sagacious legislation, but, as I have said, to the exigencies of the war, it should guide our future steps. The disparity between gold and paper has added to the duties imposed on foreign products, and enabled our manufacturers to enter upon a career of prosperity such as they have never enjoyed, save for a brief period, under the tariffs of 1824 and 1828, and again for four years under that of 1842, a prosperity in which the farmers are sharing abundantly, as is shown by the fact that they are now out of debt, though most of their farms were mortgaged five years ago. When the war began we could not, as I have said, make the iron for a gun-barrel; we can now export better gun-barrels than we can import. We then made no steel, and had to rely on foreign countries for material for steel cannon and those steel-pointed shot by which alone we can pierce the five-and-a-half inch iron-clads with which we must contend in future warfare. Many of our regiments that came first to the capital came in rags, though every garment on their backs was new, and many of them of freshly imported cloth. But, sir, no army in the world was ever so substantially clothed and armed as that which for two days passed in review before the President of the United States and the Lieutenant General after having conquered the rebellion, and which, when disbanded, was clad in the product of American spindles and looms, and armed with weapons of American materials and construction.

It is said that ten years ago "a piece of Lake Superior iron ore was a curiosity to most of our practical metallurgists." In 1855 the first ore was shipped from Marquette county. How rapid the enlargement of the trade has been is shown by the following statement:

In 1855 there were exported	1,445	tons.
1856	11,594	"
1857	26,184	"
1858	31,135	"
1859	65,679	"
1860	116,948	"
1861	45,430	"
1862	115,720	"
1863	185,275	"
1864	235,123	"

The production of charcoal pig iron in that region, we are told by Dr. Lamborn, commenced at the Pioneer works near the Jackson mine in 1858. Those works were the pioneers of a great army, and already the Collinsville, the Forrestville, the Morgan, and the Greenwood furnaces are in profitable operation. The production of charcoal iron in that county has been as follows:

In 1858 there were exported	1,627	tons.
1859	7,258	"
1860	5,660	"
1861	7,970	"
1862	8,590	"
1863	8,908	"
1864	13,832	"

And though we produced no steel in 1860, a table constructed from information furnished by the report of the Commissioner of Internal Revenue for the year ending June 30, 1864, shows that the Government had in that year derived $391,141 39 of internal revenue from the steel made and manufactured in the United States during that year.

Time will not permit me to indicate the many new branches of industry which have sprung up, or the vast extension and improvement of those which, under our old free trade system, had found an insecure footing and were enduring a sickly existence. I may, however, venture on a few remarks upon this head. California is not a New England or an eastern State; she has perhaps been less affected by the war than any other State, unless it be Oregon; and I find that, though she raised in 1859 but 2,378,000 pounds of wool, she raised in 1863, 7,600,000, and in 1864, 8,000,000 pounds. She is, we are assured by her papers, realizing the advantage of bringing the producer and consumer together; and though during the last year she shipped to New York some 7,500,000 pounds of wool, she is showing that her people understand the importance of saving the double transportation they would otherwise pay on those of their own products they might consume—that for carrying the raw material to the factory, and that for bringing the fabrics back again. I find in one of her papers the following statement:

"CALIFORNIA WOOLEN MILLS.—The Pioneer Mill, at Black Point, California, has thirty-one looms at work now, consumes annually 1,200,000 pounds of wool, employs 220 laborers, pays out $100,000 yearly in wages, uses a capital of $500,000, and runs fifty-two sewing machines. About one-fourth of the wool purchased is used in making blankets, the importation of which has now entirely ceased, the home production having taken entire possession of the market.

Nearly half the production is flannel, which is gradually crowding the imported article out of the market. About one-third of the wool consumed at this mill is made into tweeds and cassimeres, which is mostly made up into clothing in San Francisco. Broadcloth is not made there in quantity, because of the scarcity of pure Merino wool. The Pioneer and Mission Mills together consume about 2,400,000 pounds of wool, employ about 450 laborers and $1,000,000 of capital, and pay out $200,000 in wages annually."

Well done, California. Your tweeds and cassimeres and blankets will crowd foreign articles not out of your own State alone, but out of the markets of the Pacific slope. You will soon need machinists to construct your sewing-machines and make the tools for those who do such work. Land around your cities will grow in value; and those who own it need not compete with farmers so distant from market as to limit them to the production of grain alone. Hay, potatoes, turnips, and all other roots for the sustenance of man and beast, and fruits for the table, may engage their attention and give them ample reward for their labor.

Oregon has also felt the quickening influence of the times. She paid to the internal revenue department, during 1864, taxes on the manufacture of $128,620 67 of woolen cloth.

THE PEOPLE OF THE PRAIRIES NEED A PROTECTIVE TARIFF.

The people of the prairies, next to those of the desolated South, are interested in the creation and maintenance of diversified industry. While they depend on grain-growing, and that commerce which Engllsh free trade permits the producers of raw materials to enjoy, cities will be founded and grow at points on the lakes and rivers; but none of these even can be great cities without manufactures. Here and there a concentration of railroads may also create a first-class town or an inferior city; but the rest of their wide country will be but sparsely populated by an agricultural community, and dotted at wide distances apart by beautiful villages such as now gratify the eye of the traveler through the West.

The prairie States have within them the elements of innumerable profitable industries. The western farmer clears his new land by girdling and burning the primitive forests. The wood is not without value, and condensed as it might be, it would bear transportation to a market.

Constituents of mine have been for two years engaged in erecting works which cover over fifteen acres of land for the production of paper pulp from wood. There now lie around their vast buildings thirty-five thousand cords of wood; and in a few days they hope to put their works in operation. For awhile they ran part of their machinery and produced to their entire satisfaction and that of the trade pulp which, intermingled with five per cent. or less of that produced from cotton rags, furnished admirable printing paper.

Now, the corn husks—ay, and the corn with the husks—of the farmers of the West, go to waste, or find no better use than supplying them with fuel during the winter. The following article, clipped from the New York Evening Post of November 25, invites them to experiment and learn whether they act more wisely in wasting this material than the southern planters, who feared the establishment of American manufactures, did in failing to utilize their cotton seed, which, if we may accept De Bow's authority, would have produced from $100,000,000 to $120,000,000 per annum if converted into oil and oil cake:

"At a recent meeting of the Institute of Technology in Boston, Mr. Bond made a statement of results recently attained in this country and in Europe in the manufacture of paper from corn husks. Experiments upon this material have been in progress in Bohemia since 1854, but have not reached a satisfactory result until within the last two or three years. In the successful processes lately adopted the husks were boiled in an alkaline mixture, after which there remained a quantity of fiber mixed with gluten. The gluten was extracted by pressure, forming a nutritious article like 'oil cake,' and then the fiber was subjected to other processes in which it produced the real paper 'stock' or 'pulp,' and left a fiber which has been made into strong and serviceable cloth. The husks yield forty per cent. of useful material; ten per cent. of fiber; eleven per cent. gluten, and nineteen per cent. of paper stock. This paper stock is equal to that made from the best linen rags. Allowing the profit of thirty-eight per cent. to the manufacturer, the different articles can be produced for six cents per pound for fiber, one and a half cent for gluten, and four cents for paper stock."

Were this branch of manufactures well established on the prairies, the press of the West would give up its denunciations of the paper makers of the country as conspirators, monopolists, and extortioners, and cease to publish such paragraphs as the following, clipped from a recent number of the Galena (Illinois) Gazette:

"We understand that many of the people of Warren and other towns in the east part of the county are using corn for fuel. We had a conversation with an intelligent gentleman who has been burning it, and who considers it much cheaper than wood. Ears of corn can be bought for ten cents per bushel by measure, and seventy bushels, worth seven dollars, will measure a cord."

Could the people of Illinois bring themselves to believe that they are capable of doing any other labor than raising raw material, they would bring into use cheaper fuel than corn or wood at seven dollars a cord. Their lands are underlaid by lead, zinc, copper, and iron; and would they determine to bring their metals into market *as much manufactured* as their skill and supply of labor will permit, they would, by creating a demand for fuel, compel the development of the magnificent deposits of bituminous coal by which nearly the whole State is underlaid. Let them be admonished before it is too late that the fertility of their soil, exuberant as it is, is not exhaustless.

But, inviting as is this branch of my subject, I must leave it with the remark that, ignorant as we are of the extent of our mineral deposits, we are more ignorant of the uses to which may be applied many elements of life with which within a limited range of purposes we are quite familiar; and that, varied and wide as are the expanding opportunities to achieve usefulness and wealth, he who embarks his capital or enterprise in such as will yield the most golden results will not be more benefited by the introduction of new branches of manufacture than the owners of land, who will find in the markets of the village and the refuse of the factory the means of following the methods of English husbandry, succeeding the exhausting white crop by a green one, and giving to the soil each year more of the elements of fertility than the crop abstracts from it; and who, having a market at their doors, will save the transportation which now makes a yard of Manchester cloth worth many bushels of wheat in Kansas, and a bushel of Kansas wheat worth many yards of the same cloth in Manchester. Under free trade transporters, factors, and commission men absorbed what would have been the joint profit of the American manufacturer and the grain-grower, had the producer and the consumer been side by side or in reasonable proximity to each other.

DOMESTIC COMMERCE IS MORE PROFITABLE THAN FOREIGN.

There is other commerce than that between foreign nations. France and England lie nearer to each other than New Jersey and Ohio, or than Indiana and Missouri. Commerce between New England and the Pacific slope takes place at the end of longer voyages than that between New and Old England. A quick market and active capital make prosperous commerce. Interest on borrowed capital is often a fatal parasite, and a nimble sixpence is always better than a sluggish shilling. Commerce is the traffic in or transfer of commodities. It should reward two capitals or industries—those of the producer of each commodity; and where trade is reciprocal, and really free, each man selling or buying because he wishes to do so, it does reward both. It is, therefore, apparent, that if we consume American fabrics, as well as home-grown food, these two profits, and a third, (two of which now accrue to foreigners, one absolutely and the other in great part,) would remain in the country. These are the profits on the production of raw material, on its manufacture, and too often on its double transportation. But trade between a country in which capital is abundant, and the machinery of which, having paid for itself in profits already realized, is cheap, as is the case in England, and a new, or in these respects poor country, as is ours, is never reciprocal; for the party with capital and machinery fixes the terms on which it both buys and sells.

In addition to keeping both profits on our commerce at home and doing our own carrying, the diversification of our industry will insure markets for all our products, and render the destruction of any one of the leading interests of the country by a foreign commercial Power an impossibility. By securing the home market to our industry, and giving security to the investment of capital in furnaces, forges, mills, railroads, factories, founderies, and workshops, we can steadily enlarge the tide of immigration. Men will flow into all parts of our country—some to find remunerative employment at labor in which they are skilled; some, finding that land, mineral wealth, water-power, and commercial advantages are open to all in an eminent degree, will come in pursuit of enterprises of moment, and each new settlement, and each new branch of industry established, around which thousands of people may settle, will be a new market for the general products of our skill and industry: so that we shall not only become independent of Great Britain in so far as not to depend on her for that which is essential to our comfort or welfare, but independent in having a population whose productions will be so diverse that though the seas that roll around us were, as Jefferson once wished them, "seas of fire," our commercial, manufacturing, and agricultural employments could go on undisturbed by what was happening in other lands. When we shall have attained this condition of affairs we will build ships and have foreign commerce, for we will have that to carry away which, being manufactured, will contain in packages of little bulk our raw material, food, mechanical skill, and the labor of our machinery; and in exchange we will get whatever raw material we do not produce, and the ability to retain the basis of a sound currency which England and France, by the free trade they preach but do not practice, now draw from us and other countries in the position we so humbly occupy of producers of raw material, and whose people lack the foresight or the ability to supply themselves with clothing and the means of elegant life.

WHAT CONGRESS SHOULD DO.

Mr. Chairman, it is not my purpose to propose at this time any specific modifications of our tariff or internal revenue laws. They operate most unfortunately upon several leading interests of the country. But I have confidence in the gentlemen composing the Committee of Ways and Means, and the suggestive report of the United States Revenue Commission is now before us. The responsibility will justly rest on Congress, if with such aids we fail to correct those incongruities in our laws which have prostrated several important branches of manufactures.

I may, however, remark that I am opposed to prohibitions or prohibitory duties, but will gladly unite in imposing on foreign manufactured commodities such discriminating duties as will defend our industries from overwhelming assaults at the hands of the selfish capitalists who see that Britain's power depends on Britain's manufacturing supremacy, and are ever ready to expend a portion of their surplus capital in the overthrow of the rising industries of other nations. Judicious legislation on this subject will, by inviting hither her skilled workmen and sturdy yeomen, so strengthen us and enfeeble England that she will not make railways and other improvements for military purposes in Canada, for she will see that, when Canada shall be made the base of military operations against the United States, her American dominions will pass promptly into our possession.

WE ARE STILL IN COLONIAL BONDAGE TO ENGLAND.

I find, sir, in a journal upon which I am in the habit of relying, in an article on the British exports of iron and steel, the statement that during the seven months terminating July 31, 1865, the United States purchased more than one third of the railroad and bar iron exported by England. While we were thus adding to the wealth and power of England, by purchasing one third of her entire export of railroad and bar iron, one of her "men-of-war," commanded by an American traitor, was destroying our unarmed whalers engaged in the peaceful pursuits of their dangerous trade, and our furnaces, forges, and rolling-mills were idle, or but partially employed. The internal taxes levied directly and indirectly on a ton of American railroad iron are heavier than the duty imposed on a ton of foreign rails by our tariff, and at this time most of the furnaces and rolling-mills of our country are suspended. The Pennsylvania iron works at Danville, in that State, make both pig and railroad iron. The invested capital of the company is $1,500,000. When in full operation it employs twelve hundred men, upon whom not less than five thousand women and children depend. The works are adapted to the production of both pig iron and rails. They cannot, however, produce an adequate supply of iron for the rolling-mills, and the company are annual purchasers of pig iron. Their capacity is twenty-seven thousand tons of pig iron and thirty-three thousand tons of rails. Their actual production in the last two years was but as follows:

In 1864,	Pig iron	17,154	tons.
	Rails	22,512	"
In 1865,	Pig iron	14,758	"
	Rails	15,956	"

The Rough and Ready rolling-mill, in the same town, is capable of producing about twelve thousand tons of rails per annum. Its proprietors purchase their pig iron. Its production during the two last years has been in the exact proportion to its capacity as that of the Pennsylvania works. The difficulty with both is that our internal taxes so far more than counter-balance the protection afforded by our tariff that when gold ranges at less than forty, British iron masters can undersell either in our own markets. Our laws instead of protecting American labor, thus discriminate against it and in favor of that of England. The duties and internal taxes on iron evidently need revising. The interest is depressed, not only in Pennsylvania, but in every part of the country. During the latter part of the seven months referred to, four rolling-mills in southeastern Ohio, with a capacity of sixteen thousand tons of rails per annum, were idle, and the blast furnaces in the region which can produce one hundred and thirty-five thousand tons of charcoal pig metal, produced in 1865 but fort-five thousand.

Of the twenty furnaces on and near the Alleghany river, in Pennsylvania, only eight were in blast at the close of the year. I am told there are nine blast furnaces in Missouri capable of producing about forty-five thousand tons, and that but three are now in operation. But one of the four blast furnaces near Detroit was in operation in December. The twenty-five rolling-mills of Pittsburg were, I am informed, then running but quarter-time, and the production of bloom iron in the counties of New York bordering on Lake Champlain was in 1865 but about one third of that of 1864. Let me ask, sir, whether Congress is faithful to the laboring men of the country when it deprives them of the opportunity to enrich themselves and the country by expending their labor on the growth of our own lands?

From the same journal I also learn that, during the same seven months, the United States imported more than one-half of the unwrought steel exported from Great Britain, while a very carefully prepared list of the steel-works of the country, showing the kinds of steel made, the product for the last year, and the capacity of each, shows that the product during the last year was but eighteen thousand four hundred and fifteen tons, though the capacity of the works is forty-two thousand one hundred tons. It thus appears that we could have made of the growth of our own lands, and by the employment of our own people, every ton of rails, bar iron, and unwrought steel we imported during that period. Will the gentleman from Indiana say that it would not have been wise to withhold this patronage from our treacherous rival and bestow it upon our toiling countrymen?

The western farmer and the railroad man say, "Let me buy iron and steel cheap; it is my right to buy where I can buy for least money;" and their Representative, complying with their wishes, refuses to put an adequate duty upon iron and steel. May it not be pertinent to remind these gentlemen that the manufacturers of the iron and steel they import live in houses built of British timber and British stone, and furnished with British furniture; that they are taught, so far as they are educated, by English teachers; attended in sickness by English doctors; clothed and shod by English artisans; and that their wages are expended in confirming British supremacy by augmenting British industry and British commerce; that they are fed with wheat gathered on the banks of the Nile and the Baltic, or wherever England can buy it cheapest; and that General Jackson's assertion, that to transfer six hundred thousand men from agricultural to manufacturing employments would give us a greater market for our agricultural products than all Europe now supplies, is as true now as it was when first uttered. And that, if we import the men to make the iron and steel we will need for 1866, 1867, and 1868, the implements with which they will dig the limestone and ore, and mine the coal, will be of American production; the food they will eat will be grown on American soil; the timber of the houses they will occupy will be cut from American forests; the stones with which it will mingle will be quarried from American quarries; and the tailor, shoemaker, and hatter, the teacher, preacher, and doctor, and all others whose services they will require, and whose presence will augment the population of the village, the town, or the city will be Americans, and depend for their supplies on American labor. And may I not ask whether the farmers of the country, in being relieved from colonial dependence, and having a steady market thus brought to their door—a market in which wheat from the banks of the Nile and the shores of the Baltic will never compete with and cheapen theirs—would not, though they paid more dollars per ton, find that they were buying their iron and steel cheaper if they gave fewer bushels of wheat for it, and less frequently consumed their surplus crops as fuel or permitted them to rot in the field? He does not buy most cheaply who pays least money for the articles he gets, but he who gives the least percentage of his day's, month's or year's labor in exchange for a given commodity; and tested by this standard, the cheapest market in which iron and steel can be bought for American purposes will be found in the protected market of America.

PROTECTION CHEAPENS GOODS.

But protection begets competition and invariably cheapens the money value of commodities. This is not mere theory; it is fact established by the experience of all nations that have protected their industry. Washington's Secretary of the Treasury understood this as perfectly as the adept in social science understands it to-day. Every nation that ever protected its industry improved the quality and lessened the price of its productions; and no people, while not protecting their manufactures, have ever been able to hold a fair position among the commercial nations of the world, because they could not compete in cheapness with protected industries. While Holland protected her industry more adequately than England, she sold her cheap goods in that country and maintained her supremacy on the seas. It was then that the Dutch raised the ire of Andrew Yarrinton by taunting Englishmen with their want of skill, and England with her want of civilization, in selling her raw products at the price others would give, and buying back part of them when manufactured at the price at which others would sell. But when England perfected her protective system, her superior advantages in coal and iron gave her commercial supremacy, by enabling her to cheapen articles she had believed herself unable to produce, and to employ British ships in carrying English fabrics to mere growers of raw material in every part of the world.

France, as I have shown, protects her industry, and her silks, laces, cloths, cassimeres, and products of iron and steel hold their place in the markets of the world in spite of England's larger commercial marine and more abundant supply of coal and iron. Has protection increased the price of anything but labor in Germany? Before the establishment of the Zoll-Verein or Customs-Union she exported nothing but raw materials, and was only too happy, as I have shown, to send with these her peasantry either for war or civic purposes; but under the influence of protection the value of man has risen in Germany, and that of German products fallen in the markets of the world, till her cloths and the multifarious products of her diversified industry compete with those of England and France in the markets of the United States, and other nations whose people devote themselves to the production of raw materials. Even Russia, with her thirty millions of recently freed serfs, who enter upon the duties of freemen without disturbance, because the wise Emperor who enfranchised them had secured employment and wages for each by protecting the industry of all, is now entering into the general markets of the world in competition with France, Germany, Belgium, and England. But we enter no foreign market with productions which attest our wealth, skill, genius, or enterprise; and the prices of what we do export—grain, coarse provisions, and whisky—depend on such contingencies as drought, excessive rain, the potato rot, or other widespread calamity for a transatlantic market. When good crops prevail in Europe there is no market there for us. Consistent with the experience of other nations has been our own. Under the tariffs of 1824 and 1828 the prices of all those commodities in the production of which our people engaged to any extent fell rapidly. When the tariff of 1842 went into effect our country was flooded with British hardware of every variety, from a tenpenny nail to a circular saw, and from table cutlery to butt hinges, thumb latches, etc. But when 1847 came round, four years of adequate protection had so stimulated the skill and ingenuity of Americans, and had brought from Great Britain so many skilled workmen, that our own market, at least, was ours for an infinite variety of ironware, and we have held it in many departments of the business from that day to this, no nation having been able to undersell us in our own streets. If, sir, we are now paying too high for iron and steel-ware, we are but suffering the penalty of our folly. Had we continued the protection afforded by the tariff of 1842, or modified it from time to time as branches of business and the condition of the market required, by transferring the duties that had defended and advanced a branch of industry to articles needing greater protection, we would now be producing an adequate supply of cheap iron for our own use, and competing with France and England in the markets of Mexico and Central and South America. We are thus, I say, paying the penalty of our own folly in having destroyed our industry and rendered the investment of capital in manufacturing enterprises insecure. Let but the capitalists of the country know that Congress will so revise the duties on railroad iron as to give it adequate protection over the taxation its production encounters under the law for raising internal revenue, and competition will spring up all over the country and make from the growth of our own lands cheaper and better iron or steel rails than we can import.

How can it be otherwise? Do not the people of Michigan and Wisconsin wish to develop their resources and make them available? Are the people of Missouri insensible to the advantages which would flow from deriving income from the conversion of their mountains of ore into rails, machinery, and hardware? Will not the people of Tennessee allow the descendants of the colored men who worked his furnaces and gave Cave Johnson his majority in his first contest for Congress, and others like them, to enrich that devastated State by working her mines and bringing her forges and furnaces again into profitable use? And why may not the whir of the rolling-mill be heard throughout Kentucky, Tennessee, Virginia, Georgia, and other Southern States which are heavily underlaid with iron? There will be quick demand for the yield of all if we determine to develop the wealth of our whole country, and interlace its parts, as we should, with railroads. By excluding from our markets one-third of the annual export of railroad and bar iron from England we will bring hither the men who make it. Why should we, with the capacity established in five years —for when the war began and furnished its incidental protection, the manufacture of steel was unknown in our country—why should we, who in five years have created facilities for manufacturing about fifty thousand tons of steel per annum, buy from England one-half of her entire export of unwrought steel? Rather let us enfeeble her and strengthen our country by bringing hither the men who make it.* The iron of the States I have named,

* How effectively the diversification of our industries and the better wages protective duties enable us to pay for labor is doing this, is thus shown by Professor

and I may say of almost every State of the Union, would give us steel as pure and tenacious as England can make. The establishment of this branch of trade would lead to immense internal commerce, and reward our railroads with business that would flow both ways in all seasons of the year. The ores of the Marquette region will be in request in every iron-producing State, as those of Sweden, Norway, Russia, and Nova Scotia are in France and England.

WHY AN EXPORT DUTY SHOULD BE LAID ON COTTON.

Mr. Chairman, permit me, in drawing to a conclusion, to repeat that we need not resort to the prohibitions which have been practiced by other countries. Our natural advantages and those which spring from our personal free-

---

Kirk of Edinburgh. His figures also prove that British emigrants are no longer chiefly agricultural laborers, but skilled artisans. He says:

"So long as there is inhabitable surface on the earth not yet occupied, it is probable we shall have emigration. This abstract thought, however, has very little to do with the actual facts of emigration as it now goes on. It is, as we have seen, a great delusion for men to think that our emigrants are going away from us because there is no room for them in their native land. It is a still greater delusion to imagine that it is a relief to those who remain behind to be quit of those who go. If our readers will give us a little careful attention, we may be able to make the truth clear as to our situation in this important matter.

"In 1815, the total emigration from the United Kingdom was 2081—in 1866, it had risen to 204,882. That is such an increase as may well arrest the attention of all who feel interested in their country. There were higher years than 1866; but these had to do with the gold fever, and need not be taken into account in our present paper. In 1852, for example, the number of emigrants rose to 368,764; but 87,881 of these went to Australia and New Zealand. It is to the steady flow of nearly 200,000 persons a year, as reached from the small beginning—2081 in 1815—that it is interesting to turn attention.

"And yet it is far more interesting to consider the destination of these emigrants. The number from 1815 gives a grand total of 6,106,392 persons, and of these no less than 5,044,809 went to North America. Large as the Australian and New Zealand exodus has been, it had reached only 929,181 in 1866; that is, it had not reached one million when the American had gone beyond five. It is important, too, to notice that by far the largest number of our emigrants to America go to the United States. In 1866, those to the 'colonies' were 13,255, while to the States they reached the high number of 161,000. It is therefore very clear that it is with America we have specially to do in considering the bearings of this vast and growing emigration. The States of America *are not now a new country*. They begin to have all the characteristics of an old established nation, especially in their northern and eastern portions. New England is a well peopled region of the world; and, to as great an extent as Old England, it may be regarded as a manufacturing country, and certainly not a land remaining to be occupied. An emigration from Britain to these States is not a going forth to subdue the wilds of the earth's surface, but to increase the population of large manufacturing centres.

"This leads us, however, to notice further, the nationality of the emigrants going from us. Up to 1847, the emigration was from Ireland in a very much larger proportion than from the rest of the Empire. During the following eight years the flow from Ireland became comparatively low, though it still keeps up to a high rate. The emigration from Scotland was next in importance to that

dom, are sufficient to relieve us from all difficulty on this point. There is, however, one of our agricultural productions upon which, did the Constitution permit, I would lay an export duty; and that is cotton. And I hope the Constitution will be so amended as to permit it; for though for years—for the life of more than a generation—the country was ruled in the interest of slavery, to the destruction of the interests and rights of our free laborers, by the pretended apprehension that if American cotton were not cheapened rival fields would be developed, the delusion has been dispelled, and all men know that ours are the only available cotton fields of the world. For five years we maintained along the coast of the cotton States a

---

of Ireland, when the extent of our population is taken into account. England, with six times as many people as Scotland, sent but few emigrants till of late years. The Irish emigration was so great, that in 1851 the census revealed a deficiency in the population amounting to 2,555,720. That is, had Ireland had no emigration in the ten years previous to 1851, she would have had 2,555,720 more than were actually in the island. In 1861, there had been a positive decrease of 751,251, instead of an increase of a much larger figure, and it is anticipated that there will be a still more important decrease in 1871. In 1851, but more so in 1861, Scotland was found to be affected in a somewhat similar way, though not to the extent of producing an actual decrease in the number of people. Instead of an increase of twelve or thirteen per cent., as was in former decades, there was only one of six per cent. from 1851 to 1861. The rate of increase in England and Wales had not been sensibly affected. Now the chief stream of emigration is flowing from England. In the first or winter quarter of the year 1869 the emigration was 2702 Scotch, 9800 Irish, and 11,100 English. It need not be told any one who thinks and reads at all on the subject that it is now in England almost exclusively we have excitement in connection with emigration. And we may assuredly calculate that the census of 1871, and far more fully that of 1881, if matters go on as now, will reveal a decrease in the population south of the Tweed.

"What is the great relation in which these three kingdoms stand to each other and mankind? Ireland is agricultural and pastoral; so is Scotland to a great extent; England is the workshop for these and for the world. There is a small manufacturing power in Ireland, a much greater in Scotland, but by far the greatest of all in England. This explains how emigration did not set in on England or on Scotland, as it has done on Ireland. It also explains why it did not till now affect England as it has affected Scotland. A pastoral people are the first to emigrate in the course of nature. An agricultural people are the next in order. From a land like this a manufacturing people would never emigrate if matters were right. The climate and mineral store of this country are such that no other country can at present compete with it in manufacturing power, if the natural course of things were followed. Even our shepherds have an immense advantage at home, and our farmers have a still greater advantage, but our manufacturers have so great facilities as can scarcely at present be equalled. It is, consequently, matter of extreme interest when we find that England is emigrating. It introduces us to the mining, mechanical, and manufacturing character of our emigrants now. *There are above 70,000 souls in the east end of London who must emigrate speedily or die.* They are being shipped off as fast as charity and Government can transport them to North America. Above 25,000 of these are workmen more or less skilled in engineer and shipbuilding occupations. These are not shepherds, nor are they ploughmen, nor will they ever be to any great extent one or the other. They are mechanics, and will be so go where they may. *In the vast hives of industry in Lancashire there*

blockade such as never was attempted before. The people of those States planted no cotton and burned much of what they had produced, and did all that madness or ingenuity could suggest to develop rival fields if any existed; and what is the result? Necessity constrained the temporary use of Indian cotton, and Calcutta became so rich that her *ryots* put silver tires around their cart wheels. But when the power of our armies had reopened the cotton fields of the South, when it became known that freedmen were working upon the Sea Islands, and that our Government was again to possess the cotton region of the South, there came a fearful revulsion in India, and all men acknowledged that God had given the United States a monopoly of the available cotton fields of the earth.* Upon that one production we should put an export duty,

---

are a greater number who must emigrate or die. These are getting off as fast as they possibly can to Massachusetts to find full occupation in cotton. Not one is either pastoral or agricultural, and few are likely ever to be either. Irishmen and Scotchmen can be anything, but not so Englishmen, and they will not need to be anything in the world but what they have been. Their skill is too valuable to be sent to the backwoods when abundance of rough hands are there already, and skilled men are needed to make a great country fit to manufacture for itself. Till within the last four years our emigrants were chiefly pastoral and agricultural, *now they are chiefly mining, mechanical, and manufacturing.* It is to this that we feel it of such importance to call attention. Our position as a nation depends to a great extent, upon our usefulness to the world in a mechanical and manufacturing line. Commerce has its being in the fact that one nation is so situated that it excels in one thing, while another excels in another. It is in the exchange of produce that all trade lies, and such exchange clearly depends on the excelling we have mentioned. If this nation loses its excellence in manufacturing power, it loses its only possible share in the exchange of the world, and its commerce dies.

"We must also look at the effect of emigration on the character of the population left behind. How do the Emigration Commissioners account for the vast deficiencies in the population of Ireland? More than two millions and a half of deficiency was double the emigration, but it was accounted for by the fact that the *young men and women* had gone off to such a degree that marriages and births had fallen off sufficiently to account for all. 'The proportion of persons between the ages of twenty and thirty-five,' in the ordinary settled course of society, is about twenty-five per cent.—that proportion among emigrants is above fifty-two per cent. This is not the only matter of consideration at this point. Miss Rye, in a letter to the *Times*, some months since, said: 'I will not, I dare not, spend my time in passing bad people from one port to another.' And 'bad people' cannot, as a rule, pass themselves; they have generally no inclination to do so. No doubt bad enough people go, but that is not the rule. We dare not now send our criminals abroad, nor dare we send our paupers, nor should we be allowed to send any class unfit to support themselves. *It is the best of our mechanical and manufacturing hands that are now going, and they are leaving the proportion of those who burden society largely increased.'"—Kirk: Social Politics in Great Britain and Ireland,* page 112. London and Glasgow, 1870.

* An export duty of 2 cents a pound on unmanufactured cotton, coupled with the free export of yarns and fabrics, would soon transfer the capital, skill, and machinery of Lancashire to our cotton growing States, in most of which exhaustless water-power runs to waste.

and the result would be that the men of the cotton States, no longer dependent on England for a market for their bulky raw material, would, with their cheaper fabrics, drive her cotton goods from the markets of the world. Though I would not, by legislation, prohibit the export of the elements of any branch of manufacture or machinery, I will endeavor to retain in the country many of the elements of manufactures that now go abroad, by making them more valuable in this country than in any other, and by impressing upon the American people the conviction, so long ago inculcated upon the people of Ireland by Dean Swift, that to enrich themselves they must

> "Carry out *their own goods as much manufactured* and bring in *those of others as little manufactured* as the nature of mutual commerce will allow."

To gratify our patriotic desires we need not resort to prohibitory duties. We can nationalize our policy by relieving from duty tea, coffee, and every raw material which we do not produce, but which enters into our manufactures or arts.* I would give the wool-growers protection, but would stimulate the manufacture of carpets and increase the demand for American wool by admitting free of duty those low grades which we do not produce; and would lay light duties on those articles in the manufacture of which machinery has been perfected and large capitals have been accumulated, especially where the original cost of the machinery has been returned in profits; and would make them heavier and heaviest upon those branches of

---

* American production, furnishing all National power, is to the country, its commerce, and trade, on a large scale, what the water-wheel and the steam engine are to mills and machinery on a small one—the prime mover. In the absence of this great National prime mover, as it may be called, all motion, nay, even the life of the body politic itself must cease. As all of the people of the country must ultimately, directly or indirectly, live off of or from this production, so must all taxes, National, State, and local, be finally drawn from American producers, unless some portion of our taxation can be levied upon foreigners who seek our markets, and enjoy the advantages and profits thereof.

Such being the case, it follows that the American producer has a right to demand that his Government shall levy duties on foreign imports, and in so doing shall levy them, first and foremost upon those commodities the like of which *are produced* in this country, for the following reasons:

First. Because such commodities come in direct competition with the productions of American producers who are obliged to pay National, State, and local taxes; and to grant privileges to foreigners which are and must be withheld from ourselves would be a manifest and gross injustice on the part of the Government to its own people.

Second. Inasmuch as these commodities are such as are produced in this country, foreigners may be made to pay the duties thereon, as, having American competitors with whom they must compete, these duties must first be paid by them before they can place themselves in a position for such competition. If

industry which are most feeble but give assurance of ultimate success. When we do this our country will cease to be a mere agglomeration of sections, and we will be a national people, homogeneous in our interests by reason of their immense diversity.

Such, sir, is my plan for enforcing the Monroe doctrine, acquiring Canada, paying the national debt, and by relieving the South of its embarrassment, recementing the shattered Union. The poor whites must be weaned from the rifle, net, and line, by the inducements of well-rewarded labor. Their idle wives and children may thus be brought to habits of order, method, and industry, and in a few years we shall cease to remember that in this nineteenth century, and under our republican Government, there were for several decades millions of people tending rapidly to barbarism. The same inducements will disclose, even to the eye of prejudice, the manhood of the freed man, and that kindly relation between the employer and his employé which exists throughout the busy North and East will spring up in the South. Oppressed and degraded as he has been, the colored man will find that there are fields open to his enterprise, and a useful and honorable career possible to him, and will prove that, like other men, he loves property and has the energy to acquire it, the ability to retain it, and the thrift to make it advantageous to himself, his neighbors, and his country.

Let us then measure our resources by experiment and open them to the enterprise of the world; and the question whether we owe three hundred or three thousand millions will, ten years hence, be one of trifling import-

---

not made to pay these particular duties, there are no other taxes which they can, by any possibility, be made to pay in selling in our markets; and the heavily taxed American has an absolute right to demand that, enjoying the advantages and profits of these markets, foreigners shall take with them some of the many drawbacks and disadvantages which he himself is obliged to bear.

Third. Because if these duties are in whole or in part levied upon productions the like of which we do not ourselves produce, and must or will have, they must ultimately and inevitably fall upon the shoulders of American producers, thus causing them to be again taxed, indeed almost encompassing them by a network of taxation, escape from which is impossible.

Hence we develop the grand and immutable principle: *That the moral right of the Government to levy duties on articles the like of which are not produced in this country, only commences when it has exhausted all the means of collecting duties on such articles as are produced in the country, or until it has reached a full measure of the burdens imposed upon American producers and still finds itself in need of revenue. Then, and then only, may it, consistently with the rights of American producers, resort to other sources of taxation, including duties on the importation of commodities the like of which are not produced in the country.—The Rights of American Producers.* By Henry Carey Baird, Philadelphia, 1870.

ance; and, as Andrew Yarrinton showed the people of England how to "outdo the Dutch without fighting," we will find that peace hath her victories for us also; Canada will come to us like ripe fruit falling into the hands of the farmer; and if Maximilian remain in Mexico, it will be as the citizen of a republic and an adherent of the Monroe doctrine.

TRADE WITH BRITISH AMERICA.

SPEECH DELIVERED IN THE HOUSE OF REPRESENTATIVES, MARCH 7, 1866.

THE House, as in Committee of the Whole on the state of the Union, having under consideration the bill (H. R. No. 337) regulating trade with the British North American possessions—

Mr. Kelley said:

Mr. Chairman: If I had made my remarks yesterday afternoon, I should have added another to the many illustrations I have given this session of the mistake made by the gentleman from Illinois [Mr. Wentworth] when he said I never took less than an hour when I got the floor, for I am quite sure that twenty minutes would then have sufficed me. But I have had a night in which to examine the provisions of this bill and to reflect upon them, and I shall probably ask the attention of the House for a longer period this morning.

I would have been satisfied yesterday with the amendment proposed by the distinguished gentleman from Maryland [Mr. F. Thomas] with one or two others. To-day, however, this will not satisfy me. Sir, the bill should be rejected. It is false in principle and in detail, and will materially diminish the revenues of the country by suspending several important branches of our industry. As I conned its sections I became doubtful of its origin; whether it was of British or American conception. There are many of its features which constrain me to think that it is of foreign and not of American origin. I point, gentlemen, to the ninth section. Its authors seem to have been oblivious to the fact that we are still living under democratic-republican institutions, and have not yet fallen under a dictatorship. The ninth section confides the regulation of all the commerce that may grow up between the United States and the British Provinces to the absolute and unrestricted control of the President. Let me astound gentlemen who have not examined the bill by reading that portion of the section to which I refer:

"SEC. 9. *And be it further enacted*, That the President is hereby authorized to terminate or suspend the provisions of this act, or any section or sections thereof, and as to the whole or part of the British North American colonies, by giving public notice of such termination or suspension, whenever in his opinion it may appear just and proper, etc."

Sir, such power may be exercised by the Emperor of Russia in regard to the commerce of his empire; but such power, regulating the trade of this country according to his caprice, has never been confided to the President of the United States, or will be while the American people remain free.

Mr. Rogers. Will the gentleman allow me to ask him a question?

Mr. Kelley. I would rather not now. The gentleman knows my time is limited.

Mr. Rogers. I wanted to ask the gentleman from Pennsylvania if this bill gives the President any more power than was proposed to be given to him by the Freedmen's Bureau bill?

Mr. Kelley. I have no time for side issues now. I will answer that question some time when my distinguished friend has the floor and kindly yields to me. [Laughter.]

Sir, this bill is of a piece with others now pending before the House. It is like the loan bill, which proposes to contract the business of the country to the narrow dimensions it filled before the war, and to give the Secretary of the Treasury, while he has an average balance of $40,000,000 lying on deposit in the banks, the power to control the currency of the country by contracting or expanding it at his will. It is also in this respect like the postal bill, which, as an inducement to the people to buy their envelopes from Government employés or contractors, proposes to give one free of cost to every man who buys a postage stamp.

Sir, when I regard these features of the bill, I feel that its paternity may have been American, that it may have emanated from the Administration. But when I consider its provisions in reference to trade, and see how well they are calculated to prostrate many of the leading interests of the country; the advantages it secures to foreign commodities which compete with the productions of our laboring people; how it stimulates the development of the resources of the British Provinces, and induces emigration to them, while it restricts the development of our resources, and is calculated to divert immigration from our shores; when I see all this, I say, I feel that the Canadian ministry must have concocted this bill.

Mr. Conkling. I would like to ask the gentleman from Pennsylvania a question pertinent to what he is now saying.

Mr. Kelley. I would rather not yield now, having just declined to yield to the gentleman from New Jersey [Mr. Rogers].

I know, Mr. Chairman, how hard it is to break away from habit, to escape from established usage; and I remember that for more than ten years, under the fraudulently named reciprocity treaty, we have had our habits, usages, and modes of thought controlled by the infamous provisions of that treaty; and it may be that this influence has controlled the committee that presented the bill. But, sir, nothing is more certain than that had we never had that treaty we never would have had this bill; it is its legitimate offspring, and embodies many of the worst vices of its parent.

Sir, what was that treaty? It was conceived in iniquity and executed in sin. It was one of the master-strokes of policy of the sagacious and recklessly ambitious men who had even then determined to destroy our country. Its object was to enfeeble and impoverish the North, and to strengthen the Provinces of our most powerful enemy, which bound the whole line of our northern frontier. It was the result of a deliberate conspiracy, the first object of which was to give the American market to foreign manufacturers, by destroying every leading branch of American manufactures; and the second was, when they had attained the first, to prostrate the grain-growers and provision-producers of the West and North, and thus reduce the impoverished North to subjection to the slaveholding oligarchy of the South. Its ultimate purpose was to produce bankruptcy and discord in the North, that they might more easily accomplish their then purpose, which they expressed by open war in April 1861.

In order that gentlemen may see that I speak by the record, I send to the Clerk's desk a volume bearing the imprint of Prichard, Abbott, & Loomis, Augusta, Georgia, 1860, and entitled "Cotton is King, and Pro-Slavery Arguments, comprising the Writings of Hammond, Harper,

Christie, Stringfellow, Hodge, Bledsoe, and Cartwright, on this Important Subject, by E. N. Elliott, LL.D., president of Planters' College, Mississippi, with an Essay on Slavery in the Light of International Law, by the Editor."

Let one of these distinguished men inform the country whether I am correct in what I now say.

The Clerk read, as follows:

"Thus also was a *tripartite alliance* formed by which the western farmer, the southern planter, and the English manufacturer became united in a common bond of interest, the whole giving their support to the doctrine of free trade.

"This active commerce between the West and South soon caused a rivalry in the East, that pushed forward improvements by States or corporations, to gain a share in the western trade. These improvements, as completed, gave to the West a choice of markets, so that its farmers could elect whether to feed the slave who grows the cotton or the operatives who are engaged in its manufacture. But this rivalry did more. The competition for western products enhanced their price and stimulated their more extended cultivation. This required an enlargement of the markets, and the extension of slavery became essential to western prosperity.

"We have not reached the end of the alliance between the western farmer and southern planter. The emigration which has been filling Iowa and Minnesota, and is now rolling like a flood into Kansas and Nebraska, is but a repetition of what has occurred in the other western States and Territories. Agricultural pursuits are highly remunerative; and tens of thousands of men of moderate means or of no means are cheered along to where none forbids them land to till.

"For the last few years public improvements have called for vastly more than the usual share of labor and augmented the consumption of provisions. The foreign demand added to this has increased their price beyond what the planter can afford to pay. For many years free labor and slave labor maintained an even race in their western progress. Of late the freemen have begun to lag behind, while slavery has advanced by several degrees of longitude. Free labor must be made to keep pace with it. There is an urgent necessity for this. The demand for cotton is increasing in a ratio greater than can be supplied by the American planters, unless by a corresponding increased production. This increasing demand must be met, or its cultivation will be facilitated elsewhere, and the monopoly of the planter in the European markets be interrupted. This can only be effected by concentrating the greatest possible number of slaves upon the cotton plantations. Hence they must be supplied with provisions.

"This is the present aspect of the provision question, as it regards slavery extension. Prices are approximating the maximum point, beyond which our provisions cannot be fed to slaves, unless there is a corresponding increase in the price of cotton. Such a result was not anticipated by Southern statesmen when they had succeeded in overthrowing the protective policy, destroying the United States Bank, and establishing the sub-Treasury system. And why has this occurred? The mines of California prevented both the free-trade tariff (the tariff of 1846, under which our exports are now made, approximates the free-trade principles very closely) and the sub-Treasury scheme from exhausting the country of the precious metals, extinguishing the circulation of bank notes, and reducing the prices of agricultural products to the specie value. At the date of the passage of the Nebraska bill, the multiplication of provisions by their more extended cultivation was the only measure left that could produce a reduction of prices and meet the wants of the planters. The Canadian reciprocity treaty, since secured, will bring the products of the British North American colonies, free of duty, into competition with those of the United States when prices with us rule high, and tend to diminish their cost."

Mr. Kelley. Mr. Chairman, as the bill before the House has, in my judgment, all the vices of that treaty, I shall propose the following as a substitute for it.

The Clerk read, as follows:

"Strike out all after the enacting clause and insert as follows:

"That from and after the 17th of March, 1866, there shall be levied, collected, and paid on all articles imported from her Britannic Majesty's possessions in North America, that is to say, from Canada, New Brunswick, Nova Scotia, Newfoundland, Prince Edward's Island, and the several islands thereunto adjacent, Hudson's Bay Territory, British Columbia, and Vancouver's Island, the same duties and rates of duties which are now imposed by law on like articles imported from other foreign countries."

Mr. Kelley. I am not prepared to say that my substitute contains all the provisions it should; that it may not be amended with advantage; but I do say that it is infinitely preferable, for every leading interest of the country, to the bill now under consideration.

Why should we have a special tariff law for the British Provinces? What have they done to win our love? Why should we sacrifice our interests to protect or advance theirs?

The gentleman from Vermont [Mr. Morrill] said in the course of his remarks that we should not base our action on hatred or fear. I do not propose to base any of my acts in this House upon any of the passions. I mean to be governed by cool judgment.

But, sir, I remember that when we were in a death grapple with our insane brethren of the South, the people of these Provinces smote us first on one cheek and then on the other; and I know, sir, if we were prepared to forgive them seven times seventy, their transgressions against us had exceeded that number before they organized a raiding party and sent it into the gentleman's own State to rob the banks and murder the citizens who attempted to defend them. Backed as they are by the power of England, they are our most dangerous enemies, because they are our nearest; and I do not find it laid down even in the Christian code of morals that we shall injure ourselves and impoverish our families and country to benefit those who would have disseminated poison among us, who would have burned our cities and towns, and who did all that the devilish ingenuity of the madmen of the South could suggest to injure us and destroy our country.

They are foreigners to our soil, and let us regard them as we do the people of other countries, as friends in peace and enemies in war. Let us legislate for them, as the substitute I have submitted proposes to do, precisely as we do for the rest of mankind. I can understand, sir, in the light of the invaluable book from which I have had an extract read, and to which I have so often referred in previous discussions, why every provision of the so-called reciprocity treaty was adverse to our country. Both parties to it meant mischief to us. But I cannot understand why a bill should be reported by the Committee of Ways and Means containing so many of its worst features, and which if adopted, would inevitably strike down several of the principal or leading interests of our country. It might well be entitled a bill to destroy the fisheries, salt-works, and lumber trade of the country, and to prevent the working of bituminous coal-beds within the limits of the United States, east of the summit of the Alleghanies. Should it become a law it will ruin all these great branches of industry.

The gentleman from Vermont, in introducing the bill, said with great plausibility—more plausibility than candor, I am sorry to say:

> "Coal is a raw material, and for every ton of iron made at least three tons of bituminous or two of anthracite coal are consumed. It is the motive power of railroads and steamboats as well as of manufacturing establishments. We tax iron and all other manufactures when produced and sold, and we tax railroads and steamboats on their business. Can we not afford to have our coal free? It is, too, an article of universal consumption, required in our rigorous climate in large quantities by those unable to clothe themselves in heavy and abundant woolens or thick and costly furs; by the poor as well as the rich. There are hardly more reasons for a tax

on coal than upon firewood. In addition to this, our own coal-fields are unsurpassed in extent and quality by any in the world.

"But our export to the Canadas of coal from Ohio, Virginia, and Pennsylvania bids fair to equal in amount all that we bring from the Provinces; the value of our exports in 1864 being $555,332, and that of our imports $883,805. So that under any circumstances here is one article which approaches the idea of reciprocity, and an interchange effects economy in long lines of freight, relieving ourselves as well as others from positive loss."

Carlyle tells us that nothing lies like figures, although the general proposition is that figures never lie; and the statement just quoted is as plausibly delusive as a statement each of the propositions of which is in itself true can be.

Sir, is chalk cheese, or cheese chalk? In speaking about bituminous and anthracite coal we speak of two distinct articles, as unlike as cheese and chalk. This bill does not in any way, or by any possibility, affect either advantageously or disadvantageously the anthracite coal trade and interests of the country.

Canada must have our anthracite coal. She has none of it, nor can she obtain it elsewhere. Our Pennsylvania anthracite coal-fields are a God-given monopoly, as are the long-staple cotton-fields of the South. Our anthracite interest asks no protection. Indeed, were it constitutional to impose an export duty you might put a light one on anthracite coal, and the Canadas would still buy it from us. The $555,332 worth of coal exported under the treaty in 1864 was anthracite, and in fact, therefore, has no part in a discussion relating as this does to the bituminous coal interests of the country. The article bears the name of coal, and there is no other reason why it should be named in connection with this bill.

From what fields, and to what provincial ports, have we exported bituminous coal from Ohio? I ask the well-informed gentlemen who compose the Ohio delegation to tell me if there be one line of steamers, or any other kind of boats, employed in carrying Ohio coal to the British Provinces. Why, sir, they could not sell it at the wharf in any provincial town for its cost. Virginia coal go to the British Provinces! It cannot, in the nature of things, have gone there save as a curiosity for mineralogical cabinets. It never went there as an article of commerce.

The gist of the gentleman's argument is that we need cheap coal. Why, then, does he not propose to take the duty of a dollar and a quarter per ton off British coal, so that we may have it still cheaper? Where is his logic?

Mr. Morrill. Does the gentleman desire an answer?

Mr. Kelley. Yes, sir.

Mr. Morrill. Mr. Chairman, in relation to this subject of coal, I confess that I am not clear that it is proper to protect it at all. I do believe that it is one of those articles that cannot be increased by protection, and if it is so, the whole foundation of the doctrine drops out, in my judgment.* I think, as I stated in the extracts which the gentleman has just read, that it is so nearly allied to firewood that it deserves perhaps no protection.

And while I am up allow me to ask the gentleman if he has any statistics to show that this coal that goes to Canada is not bituminous coal. Do they not use it there for the purpose of making gas? Or do they use anthracite coal throughout the Provinces for making gas? I ask for information.

Mr. Kelley. I will answer the question of the gentleman. Some small quantity of Ohio coal may have gone there for experiment in gas making, or occasionally a vessel may have carried it as ballast to some western town. It is not a recognized article of commerce, and there is neither an organized company for the sale or carrying of bituminous coal from Ohio, Virginia, or Pennsylvania, to the Canadas. I admit that there may be special cargoes shipped for gas companies in some extreme western parts of Canada, but that does not touch the argument. But while I admit the fact, for the argument's sake, I must say that I do not believe it, for I do not see how it can be true.

---

* The fallacy of the theory that coal "is one of those articles that cannot be increased by protection," is evident from the rapid increase in the production of bituminous coal for consumption upon the Atlantic seaboard, which has been accompanied by a marked decline in price of the imported article since the duty of $1.25 per ton upon it was revived by the expiration of the Reciprocity Treaty in March, 1866:

Year.	Home Production of Bituminous Coal for consumption on the Atlantic Seaboard.	Price of Pictou (N. S.) Coal delivered in Boston, duty paid.	Rate of Duty.
1863	1,656,852	$ 7.40	Free
1864	1,711,798	10.40	Free
1865	1,989,247	9.60	Free
1866	2,482,932	8.54	$1.25
1867	2,788,103	8.10	1.25
1868	3,308,655	8.16	1.25
1869	4,233,980	7.78	1.25
1870	4,168,476	6.60	1.25

The gentleman from Vermont says the production of coal cannot be increased. Allow me to say that I am speaking for no Pennsylvania interest to-day. I am speaking for poor, wasted, war trampled Virginia, for Maryland, West Virginia, Kentucky, Tennessee, and Missouri, Georgia, and all the southern States. They all need our fostering care, and have inexhaustible beds of bituminous coal that ought to be productive. I am not willing that the rebellious people of the South shall become my political master or equal in the councils of the nation until they are politically regenerated. But I desire to develop their natural resources, to induce capitalists, laborers, and men of enterprise to go and settle among them, and build up industrious and peaceful Commonwealths in the hearts of whose people loyalty to the Union shall dwell. It is in these interests that I speak. The bituminous coal interest of eastern Pennsylvania is comparatively unimportant; but we have the only paying bituminous coal company east of the summit of the Alleghany mountains. Thirty odd millions of capital have already been invested outside of my State in this branch of the coal trade. Thirty millions more have been invested in railroads to convey the coal from the mines to market, and though it is all unproductive, or nearly so, the owners do not abandon it as lost.

They hope that Congress, impelled by a sense of justice, or the pride of American citizenship, will protect them against the assaults of British capital and ill-paid labor. They have waited in hope for the day when the infamous treaty which blasted their prospects should be annulled and they be permitted to enjoy equal chances with foreigners in our own markets. Give them but an even chance, burdened as they are by our war taxes, and all these dead millions will become productive. I challenge any member of the House to name another bituminous coal company than the Westmoreland Company that has paid or earned a dividend in the last three years on the eastern slope of the mountains. Give them protection equal to the taxes, direct and incidental, which you impose upon them, and you will find that instead of the product of 1867 being but two million tons, as it was last year, its increase will show that we can produce ninety-five million tons, as England did in that same year. Our fields are broader and richer than hers and those of Nova Scotia combined. They are scattered from the mountain above the clouds, on the brows of which Hooker and his brave comrades fought, eastward, northward, southward and westward all over the country. Give our miners but that measure of protection, which, under the weight of taxation they bear, will secure an equal chance in our markets, and they will give you an adequate supply of coal, and in two or three years domestic competition, while it will by patronizing your railroads and carrying companies have filled your Treasury and enabled you to reduce your scale of taxation, will bring down the price of coal in all our markets.

Pennsylvania, I repeat, has no special interest in this question. Her interest is that the general prosperity of the country shall be promoted. We want you manufacturers of New England to clothe the men who dig and handle our coal; we want you men of the Northwest to feed the men who dig and handle our coal; and Pennsylvania will rejoice in her share of the general prosperity which will then bless our country.

Sir, I turn to the fortieth page of the letter of the Secretary of the Treasury, embodying the report of the revenue commissioners, and find that in the fiscal year 1865 there were imported, under the reciprocity treaty, 13,025,432 bushels, being 465,194 tons of bituminous coal, free of duty, from the British Provinces. There were imported in the same year, paying a duty of $1 25 a ton, 6,131,608 bushels, being 218,986 tons, from England. There were exported of domestic production, which, as I have said, was all or nearly all anthracite, 3,708,264 bushels, and there were exported of foreign production 25,536 bushels, making nearly 1000 tons.

Sir, will it be said that the vast coal-beds of this country cannot supply our wants, and that we cannot increase our production? Or will any gentleman say that a duty of fifty cents is enough to protect these embarrassed but important interests? I ask gentlemen to mark the fact, that though 465,194 tons came in under the reciprocity treaty, free of duty, from her Provinces, England was still able to send in, and pay $1 25 duty per ton, the enormous amount of 218,986 tons. Is it not apparent from these facts that we will bankrupt every bituminous coal company in the country if we pass this bill?

Do gentlemen say our demands in this behalf are exorbitant, or ask why our coal cannot be sold cheaply as that of England and the Provinces? I answer them in part by another question, which is, do they wish the American miner to toil for the wages given to laborers in English collieries? Sir, the heartlessness of the capitalists of England was never more fully exposed than by the report of the parliamentary commission appointed to inquire into the condition of the mining population of the country.* England's shame is nowhere written in broader or darker colors than in that report, and I will not permit myself to believe that any member of this House is anxious that we should emulate that page of her history.

Our better wages for labor and our heavy war taxes answer the suggestion thrown out. How much England and her American Provinces did to protract and aggravate the war is known to all, and I am not willing they should derive advantage from their treachery. On this subject I quote a few lines of a letter from an intelligent coal operator:

> "It is almost impossible to compute precisely the amount of revenue that Government reaps from a ton of bituminous coal, but the fairest way to get at it will be to take the cost of putting the article on board a vessel before the war, (or in 1860,) $3 50 per ton, as compared with the present cost, seven dollars per ton, making an increase in the actual cost of $3 50 per ton. This increase is in the main occasioned by the taxes which have been levied in order to support the Government, (which we pay cheerfully;) and they touch every article of provisions and repairs about the mines and railroads, as well as the two and a half per cent. upon the gross rate of transportation and five per cent. upon the net earnings of the carrying companies, which, when all summed together, amount to very nearly if not quite three dollars per ton."

Sir, we are in a transition age; and here I reply further to the remark of the gentleman from Vermont that coal ought not to be protected. We are in a transition age in more senses than one. We are passing from war to peace and from the age of iron to the age of steel. In a few years, if we foster our industry, steel will supplant iron in almost all the uses to which it is now applied. Sir, coal and iron are the muscles of modern civilization; and fire—ignited coal—is the material force that is impelling us onward and upward. Had the southern States had equal mastery with us of these elements, I doubt whether we would yet have made conquest over them. I query

* "Though England is deafened with spinning-wheels, her people have not clothes; though she is black with digging of fuel, they die of cold; and though she has sold her soul for grain, they die of hunger."—*Ruskin.*

whether the result might not have been otherwise than it was. What were Vulcan and the Cyclops to an American mechanic handling a steam engine or a trip-hammer? We live in a new age. Old mythologies and traditions serve but to hamper us. We must adapt ourselves to the agencies by which we are surrounded and the exigencies in which we are involved.

Sir, when the consular wreath first graced the brow of Napoleon he had only conquered Italy, which in the somewhat boastful language of the historian, extended "from the Alps to the Papal dominions." And what had he done? Why, sir, all that Italy which he had conquered, could it be lifted bodily, could be set down comfortably within the limits of the State of Maine or of South Carolina. He had never then commanded so many men as Burnside marched through the city of Washington when taking his single corps to swell the grand army of Lieutenant General Grant in the Wilderness. How was it that we could move such masses of men, fight this war over the broadest theatre of international or civil war known to history, and conclude it in little more than four years? It was because we used coal and iron as our muscles, and fire—ignited coal—as our force. These gave us New Orleans, and battered down Fort Fisher. And I may add that, had there been a well-stocked railroad from Moscow to the Rhine, Napoleon's retreat would have been marked by fewer horrors, and the history of the nineteenth century would not probably have read as it does.

And if the chairman of the Committee of Ways and Means desires to secure us a respectable position among the nations, he will not strike down, disparage, or neglect the coal and iron interests of the country, to subserve any interest of his State, or section. They are the primordial elements of our greatness, and should be cherished above all others. Look at their power. Behold a woman with an iron machine moving noiselessly before her; it is impelled by coal and iron fashioned into an engine, and is doing more work in one day than one hundred such women could have done in a week one century ago. Or see yonder pallid little girl attending such a machine; she will produce results in one day that would have taxed the industry of her grandmother for years. The power of these delicate people is not superhuman; it is coal and iron that produce these more than magical results.

The gentleman doubts whether the production of coal can or should be stimulated, and is willing we should depend on our most powerful and our nearest enemies for this elemental substance. The country will not respond to such purblind patriotism. And the passage of this bill will reduce us to such abject dependence.

In eleven months of 1865—I do not go back to 1864, but take the first eleven months of 1865, of last year—sixty-six per cent. of the bituminous coal consumed in the States east of Pennsylvania was mined by the laborers of Britain or of the British Provinces. Let me prove this. The amount of bituminous coal received at Boston and New York from the British Provinces, free of duty, to the 1st of December, 1865, was 392,158 tons. The amount of English coal received at the same points during the same period, which paid a tax of $1 25 per ton, was 103,723; total foreign coal, 495,891 tons. The amount of coal produced in the United States, delivered during the same period at the same points, was but 287,874 tons; balance in favor of foreign coal, 208, 874 tons—one coal company in the British Provinces declaring dividends of one hundred and seventy-five per cent. in a year, and but one of the hundreds of companies in our country being able to declare a dividend of one per cent., making a contrast so unfavorable to us that many of our enterprising people, as was shown yesterday by the gentleman from Maryland, [Mr. F. Thomas,] abandoned their country and embarked their capital in the coal regions of Nova Scotia. Can we strengthen our country by exporting enterprise, industry, and capital?

And is it not marvelous that such an exhibit against us can be made, in view of the facts that our bituminous coal-fields are so much broader and richer than those of England and Nova Scotia combined, and that we depend for the support of our Government and its credit upon taxes derived in great part from the forge, the furnace, the foundery, the railroad, the machine shop, the coal-bed, and iron mine? Are gentlemen willing to perpetuate the malign influence that has produced a state of facts so disparaging to our intelligence, patriotism, and interests? No; I believe they will agree with me that the time has arrived when we should develop our own resources, foster American labor, and guard our own interests. One effect of the reciprocity treaty has been to send to Canada one million five hundred thousand immigrants who, but for the advantages it gave the Provinces over us, would have swelled our population. Let us now, by taking care of our own people, induce them to come and share our burdens and blessings.*

Sir, I have said that I would not legislate with reference to the Provinces under the influence of fear or hate. It would indeed be unwise, for these people will yet be our countrymen. When British free trade, by preventing the people of the British Provinces from diversifying their industries, shall have impoverished their soil and repelled immigration from their shores; when that system of trade which keeps those upon whom it is inflicted at hard labor in the production of white crops, has impoverished their fields as it has those of our old States, and reduced them to oft-recurring bankruptcy, as it inevitably must; and when adequate protection to our labor shall have developed our boundless resources, and generous wages invited to our shores the skilled laborers of the world, the contrast between our condition and that of the people of the Provinces will impel them to unite their destiny with ours, and I will be ready to greet them cordially as compatriots.

Sir, what do we get in return for the immeasurable degradation proposed by this bill? Why, sir, we get the right to navigate the St. Lawrence and to patronize the canals and railroads of Canada, and the right to cut lumber —mark you, "the right to cut lumber or timber of any kind on that portion of the American territory in the State of Maine watered by the river St. John and its tributaries, and when floated down that river to the sea to ship the same to the United States from the Province of New Brunswick without any export duty or other duty." I take it, sir, that these rights will not be long withheld from us, even if we determine to give the American miner a fair field in which to compete with those of England and her Provinces.

Let me pause for a moment to say to the gentleman that his statement of the amount of coal imported and exported is more plausible than candid in a respect not yet noticed. It is appraised at *ad valorem* prices, which are specie prices in the land from which it is exported; while ours is calculated at currency prices. This fact must

* Since the repeal of the Reciprocity Treaty, there has been a large annual immigration of Canadians to the United States.

be borne in mind in making the calculations of relative quantities.

But to resume and conclude. Sir, to get these rights we give precisely the same rights in larger degree and with greater advantage to the British colonists. We will therefore get them without this bill. I do not wish to acquire them by force. I am anxious to see them granted reciprocally by our country and the Provinces; but not as this bill does it.

It can be done by treaty or by act of Congress; but be that as it may, do not let us agree to destroy the fisheries of New England, the salt-works of West Virginia, Michigan, and Louisiana, the lumber business of the Northwest and of Maine, and the bituminous coal-works of the whole country, as the price of the privilege of yielding more specifically and in kind than we get.

No, sir; let us maintain our rights, our interests, and our country's dignity. Let us go on our way as though there were no British Provinces; and the mere action of British legislation, constraining their people, as I have already said, to unrequited agricultural labor, will make them sigh for our prosperity. And then we shall find that the American Constitution is as elastic as it is grand and enduring. It has expanded to embrace immense tracts of territory. Our flag has swept from the limits of the original thirteen States to the Pacific, and southward to the Rio Grande; and, sir, when the people of Canada shall, as they will if we protect our labor, ask to unite their destinies with ours, the world will receive additional proof that when Providence impelled our fathers to the creation of our Government, it gave them the wisdom to bless us with a Constitution which is the fit canopy of a continent, and will yet crown one.

HOW AND WHEN OUR WAR DEBT CAN BE PAID.

SPEECH DELIVERED IN THE HOUSE OF REPRESENTATIVES, JANUARY 3, 1867.

The House being in the Committee of the Whole on the state of the Union—

Mr. Kelley said:

Mr. Chairman: Within an hour of the opening of the present session I introduced the following resolution, which was adopted without dissent:

"That the Committee of Ways and Means be instructed to inquire into the expediency of immediately repealing the provisions of the internal revenue law whereby a tax of five per cent. is imposed on the products of the mechanical and manufacturing industry of the country."

On the succeeding Monday, having in the meantime examined the report of the Secretary of the Treasury, I submitted the following:

"*Resolved.* That the proposition that the war debt of the country should be extinguished by the generation that contracted it is not sanctioned by sound principles of national economy, and does not meet the approval of this House."

I hoped that this resolution would also receive the immediate assent of the House, but it was thought proper to refer it to the Committee of Ways and Means. I am, however, not without an assured hope that with the sanction of that committee it will at an early day meet the approval of the House and relieve the country from the profound anxiety and depression created by the unprecedented propositions of the Secretary. With these resolutions in view I propose, Mr. Chairman, to detain the committee for a little while by an examination of that budget of inaptitudes, incongruities, and *non sequiturs*—the report of the Secretary of the Treasury.

This report is indeed a noticeable document. It abounds in phrases and propositions of doubtful meaning; its abstract propositions, many of which as mere abstractions are true, and should be considered by the founder of a new and independent community, are not only inapplicable to, but are contravened by the inexorable peculiarities of our condition; its abounding facts do not sustain but with emphasis gainsay the conclusions they are marshaled to support; and the means by which it proposes to return to specie payments and extinguish the national debt within given periods would, by virtue of laws as fixed as that of gravitation, produce bankruptcy, individual, corporate, State, and national, and postpone the permanent resumption of specie payments for a quarter of a century. There is nothing in this report to gratify one's national pride. As we read it we seek excuses for its author, and hope we may be able to say for him that he confided its preparation to a subordinate who dealt unfairly by him. It may, however, be that Mr. McCulloch, like an oarsman, rowed one way and looked another, and was too modest to announce his real purpose. He may have improved the occasion to repair a neglect in the education of the people; for Rev. Mr. Nasby tells us that the Secretary was present at the Cabinet meeting convened to consider the "onparallelled loosenin uv the Nashnel-Union-Johnson-Dimekratic party in the various States wich held elections on the 9th uv October last," and that he attributed it "to the limited knowledge the masses hed uv 'Ingeany bankin.'" But, be this as it may, I am sure the country will sustain the assertion that whatever commendation the report may deserve or receive from "Ingeany" or other bankers, it is marked by no suggestion adapted to the existing exigencies of our country.

The Secretary's wisdom is that of a man owning a thousand fertile acres, who by the aid of a loan on mortgage had fenced them in and built barns and all requisite outbuildings, and gathered live stock and the many implements by which genius has lightened the labors and increased the profits of the farmer, and who withal had able-bodied sons to share his labors, and was by aid of these accumulating a fund with which in a few years he could extinguish his indebtedness; but who when a fire consumed his barns and implements and choice stock, would not use his savings to renew his stock and implements, but though his creditor was not anxious for his money, would sell his interest-bearing bonds and hand over the proceeds, his working capital, as part payment of the mortgage debt.

He who under such circumstances would come to such a conclusion and execute it, would find but little sympathy among his neighbors. Eager as they might be to repair his losses, they would not be likely to make him county treasurer or confide the township funds to his administration. They would probably deem him inadequate to the management of his own property, and feel that their neighborhood was well rid of one who could thus stupidly sacrifice his resources and doom his sons to idleness or to earn laborers' wages on the land of strangers. Yet, disavowing all disposition to exaggeration or caricature, I present such an one as the prototype of our Finance Minister, as he discloses himself in this report.

Witness the exultation with which he announces that during the brief period of fourteen months, namely, from August 31st, 1865, to October 31st, 1866, the principal of our debt was reduced $206,379,565.71. I wonder whether in his exultation Mr. McCulloch remembered that this immense sum of more than $206,000,000 had been added to the cost and market price of the product of but fourteen months of American labor, and that by its addition to the cost and price of our home productions those of the underpaid labor of Europe had been given the advantage over the American laborer, in our own markets and those of the world. I wonder whether in his pride he perceived that he was announcing the needless abstraction of more than two hundred and six millions of active working capital from the business men of this country, many of whom were struggling to maintain infant industries which had been called into existence by the war and needed the fostering care of the Government to give them prosperity and permanence. Unfamiliar as he appears to be with the laws of social science and the history of their development, it is possible that he did not know the advantage he was giving to British monopoly over competing American enterprise and industry by recommending the continuance of the excessive taxation which enabled him to pay those hundreds of millions. England is the foe of the laborer in every land. To maintain her monopoly she must undersell other nations in their own markets, and to effect this must depress the wages of labor to the lowest possible point and use shoddy or other base material whenever it can be done without immediate detection. Her capitalists are, we are assured, accumulating £100,000,000 or $500,000,000 surplus capital per annum; and for more than a century it has been their policy to apply a portion of this surplus to the destruction of the industries of other nations by underselling them, though for a time it involved loss on certain kinds of goods. We have often been the victims of this unscrupulous policy, and if the suggestions of the Secretary prevail it will again prostrate us.

The war of 1812 developed our productive power very considerably; but in two years after the war closed the capitalists of England, by the express advice of her leading statesmen, and in pursuance of a deliberate combination, swept our young manufactures out of existence. In the course of a speech in Parliament in 1815, Henry Brougham, exulting over our wide-spread bankruptcy, said:

> "It is well worth while to incur a loss upon the first exportation, in order by the glut to stifle in the cradle those rising manufactures in the United States which the war has forced into existence."

History, so far as that chapter is concerned, is repeating itself, and our market is glutted with British woolen goods which until our factories shall discharge their work-people and suspend operations will be sold at less than cost. The assessment of extraordinary taxes for the extinguishment of the war debt while such a contest is waging will make the victory of our enemy an easy one.* The policy is suicidal, and will prove fatal to our revenues by paraly-

* English manufacturers are beginning to discover that the internal taxes to which free trade subjects them, operate as a bonus to their foreign competitors. Wm. Hoyle, a cotton manufacturer, recently published a work entitled, *Our National Resources, and How they are Wasted*. It ran quickly to a fourth edition, on the 88th page of which I find the following:

"I have often heard it stated, and there is considerable truth in the statement, that, owing to the heavy local taxation in Manchester, and other large towns, spinners and manufacturers find it impossible to compete with country mills, where the taxation is lighter; and hence it is observed that, whilst no new mills are being built in Manchester, old ones are being stopped, and the trade is gradually shifting to more lightly taxed regions.

"What is true of different districts in the same country, is equally true of different countries; the rates which a manufacturer has to pay must come out of trade profits, which makes the production of goods more expensive; and, consequently, other things being equal, if a large mill is taxed at the rate of £500 per annum in this country, but only £100 on the Continent, the Continental manufacturer has the advantage of £400 per annum over his English competitor.'

zing the productive power of the country and diminishing the ability of the people to consume either dutiable or taxable commodities. This is not the language of declamation. It has high official sanction, among which is that of the revenue commission appointed by the Secretary himself, as appears by the following extract embodied in the last annual report of the secretary of the National Association of Wool-Growers.

Before presenting this extract I should remark that the tax on manufactures has been reduced from six to five per cent. since the preparation of the official reports to which it refers:

"The internal revenue tax paid in the year 1865 upon 'woolen fabrics and all manufactures of wool' amounted to $7,947,094, being 3.79 per cent. upon the whole of the internal revenue collected. How heavily this tax bears upon our manufactures is shown by facts presented in the report of the secretary of the State of Massachusetts upon the industrial statistics of the State for the year 1865. The capital invested in woolens proper is shown to have been $14,775,830, and the value of the woolen product to have been $48,430,671. Six per cent. upon the latter sum, the amount of the revenue tax, is $2,905,846, being 19.66 per cent, or in round numbers 20 per cent. upon the capital invested in woolens. This tax has been paid cheerfully under the impulses of patriotism. But it cannot be borne long. In the language of one of the special reports of the revenue commission, 'It has no parallel, probably, in the fiscal regulations of any civilized nation. It would utterly destroy in ten years two-thirds of the various kinds of production subject to its operations.'"

Gentlemen will not fail to observe how perfectly the views of the commission are supported by the facts above cited in relation to the woolen manufacturers of Massachusetts. But I recur to the report of the commission:

"A very large proportion of the manufacturing establishments in the United States sell products yearly to two or three times the amount of their invested capital; and in many departments of production their sales yearly amount to more than three times the cost of their establishments. If the capital invested be $100,000 the sales may amount to two or three hundred thousand dollars, and the tax on that business will range from twelve to eighteen thousand dollars; that is, from twelve to eighteen per cent. on the cost of the manufacturing establishment."

And again:

"In every point of view in which it is presented it seems clear that the six per cent. tax upon manufactures will destroy productive power in a increasing progression; that it will in a few years, if not removed, furnish a sad monument to perpetuate the memory of a great mistake."

The Secretary's time and attention have probably been so absorbed by his offical guillotine that he has not been able to examine the reports submitted to him by the revenue commission. I will, in the hope of bringing them to his attention, add to the foregoing the following brief extract from their preliminary report of last year, submitted to him by Mr. Commissioner Wells:

"The remedy, therefore, for the difficulties above pointed out and illustrated, save in a few striking instances which have probably resulted from oversight in the framing of the law, must, in the opinion of the commission, be sought for in such a revision of the present internal revenue system as will look to an entire exemption of the manufacturing industry of the United States from all direct taxation (distilled and fermented liquors, tobacco, and possibly a few other articles excepted). This the commissioners are unhesitatingly prepared to recommend." *

These grave considerations, though specially reported to him by his own agents, do not seem to have attracted the attention of Mr. McCulloch; for while exulting over the rapid payment of the debt, without seeming to detect the cause of the popular emotion, he says:

"Nothing in our history has created so much surprise, both at home and abroad, as the reduction of our national debt. The wonder excited by the rapidity with which it was created is exceeded by the admiration of the resolution of the tax-payers themselves that it shall be speedily extinguished."

It is true, Mr. Chairman, that surprise and wonder agitate the practical men of the country. These emotions are not, however, excited by the fact that we were able to bear extraordinary taxation while the development of our

---

* While in England Mr. Wells saw reason to abandon this view. His last report as Special Commissioner of Revenue was made in December 1869. Our internal taxes abstracted from the people that year $185,235,867. Did he recommend their exemption from this grievous burden, or any considerable portion of it? Let him speak for himself. While admitting that the surplus of the preceding year had been $124,000,000, and that of the current year would be much larger, he said:

"Allowing, then, for the extreme possible loss under incomes, the amount of taxation above proposed to be remitted to the people, *in consideration of the present large and increasing surplus of receipts over expenditures,* would be in the neighborhood of $26,000,000."

He would retain not only $150,000,000, or 175,000,000 of internal taxes, but proposed in connection therewith a schedule of tariff by which not less than $82,500,000 should be raised from tea, coffee and other imported articles of food and drink. By what potent logic had he been persuaded to abandon often-expressed opinions, and assert that the true way to stimulate development was to paralyze industry by excessive taxation on the food of the laborer and the productions of his toil?

boundless productive power was stimulated by the exigencies of the war, and our own market was secured to our own producers by the difference between our lawful currency and gold, in which payment of duties on imports was required. The taxes under which those hundreds of millions accumulated were assessed while war was raging and for war purposes, and could have been borne as long as the conditions I have indicated were maintained. Wise men know this, and that the war terminated abruptly and earlier than was expected, and do not hold the Secretary accountable for the results of this contingency. No matter what sacrifices it involved, the people would have cheerfully borne them rather than yield the questions put at issue by the war. But these questions have been happily settled by war's arbitrament. Peace is restored, our currency approximates the specie standard, and it is discovered that by aid of our inordinate internal taxes foreign manufacturers are monopolizing our home market. Our publishers buy their paper and print and bind their books in England or Belgium; our umbrella-makers have transferred their workshops to English towns; our woolen and worsted mills are closed or closing, and the laborers in these branches are not only wasting their capital, which consists in their skill and industry, but drawing from the savings-banks or selling the Government bonds in which they had invested their small accumulations to maintain their families during the winter; and our enlarged importations of foreign goods are swelling the balance of trade against us and preparing us for general bankruptcy. The surprise of which Mr. McCulloch speaks is excited by the fact that in view of this condition of things the Secretary of the Treasury should urge the maintenance of extraordinary taxes sufficient to enable him to apply not less than $50,000,000 per annum to the extinguishment of our debt by the rapid absorption of the only portion of it which bears no interest.* Wonder amounting almost to awe does possess our people, but it is excited as was that of the unsophisticated sailor who, in the midst of an exhibition of magical illusions, was blown into the air by the accidental explosion of powder, and in his damaged condition wondered what would come next in the order of exercises.

* Mr. McCulloch's proposition was to maintain all existing taxes in order to contract the currency by cancelling $50,000,000 of greenbacks annually.

That the tax-payers have resolved that the principal of our debt "shall be speedily extinguished" I deny. They regard the attempt as Quixotic, as destructive of our industrial interests, and beneficial only to money-lenders, speculators in Government securities, and foreign manufacturers. Sir, if the Secretary is accessible to the voice of remonstrance he must by this time be satisfied that there is no tax-payer in the country who is not engaged in importing foreign goods or shaving notes, or who, having bought bonds at low rates in a depreciated currency, hopes to have them redeemed at an early day in specie, who does not dissent from the assessment of extraordinary taxes for the extinguishment by the generation which created it, of a debt, the security of which is undoubted and which was incurred for the benefit of posterity. The opinion of the people on this question is modestly expressed by the editor of the ablest and most instructive of our industrial journals, the Iron Age. He says:

"We are glad to see that a resolution for the entire removal of the manufacturers' tax of five per cent. has been introduced, and hope it will be adopted. As an independent proposition, outside of any other amendment of the tax or tariff laws, this will commend itself to the good sense of the country as one so manifestly just that we should expect there would be a very general expression of public feeling in its favor. All classes can heartily unite in this effort to untrammel the industry of the country and to cheapen production. The free-trader and protectionist can at least here agree; the workman is quite as directly interested in this matter as the employer, for the effect of the tax is only to restrict the demand for the products of his labor. As a war necessity we cheerfully accepted this burden which the manufacturers of the country have borne with such uncomplaining loyalty; but now that the necessity is past, and that the national exchequer is in such a condition that it can easily and safely dispense with the revenue it produced, we think we are entitled, on behalf of manufacturers and their workmen, to demand its repeal. England, with all her load of taxes, has no such impost as this; her uniform policy is in every way possible to cheapen the production of her wares, and in the unequal contest which we are called to wage with her it is in the last degree unwise to put ourselves under this additional and unnecessary disability."

Sir, this generation embraces the widows, orphans, and maimed soldiers of the contending parties in a civil war, each of which parties had armies numbering more than a million men in the field. They at least are in no condition to welcome excessive taxation, especially those of the South, who are without even the poor pittance we give ours as pensions. The folly of the dull farmer I have supposed—a case of stupidity scarcely probable, though possible within the range of human dullness—is the wisdom by which the Secretary proposes to guide the finances of this country and extricate them from embarrassments which in this report he depicts as almost overwhelming. Let us hear him. He says that—

"He has been clear in his convictions that specie payments are not to be restored by an accumulation of coin in the Treasury to be paid out at a future day in the redemption of Government obligations; but rather by quickened industry, increased production, and lower prices, which can alone make the United States what they ought to be—a creditor and not a debtor nation."

And as if to illustrate his want of sincerity, or the confusion of his ideas, proceeds to speak of "certain branches of industry that are now languishing under the burdens which have been imposed on them;" and to tell us that though "the people of the United States are naturally a commercial and maritime people, fond of adventure—bold, enterprising, persistent"—

"The disagreeable fact must be admitted, that, with unequaled facilities for obtaining the materials, and with acknowledged skill in ship-building, with thousands of miles of sea-coast, indented with the finest harbors in the world, with surplus products that require in their exportation a large and increasing tonnage, we can neither profitably build ships nor successfully compete with English ships in the transportation of our own productions. Twenty years ago it was anticipated that ere this the United States would be the first maritime Power in the world. Contrary to our anticipations, our foreign commerce has declined nearly fifty per cent. within the last six years."

And as if to impress us more profoundly with our present inability to bear excessive taxation, he sets forth the following statistics:

"The tonnage of American vessels engaged in the foreign carrying trade which entered United States ports was—

	Tons.
In 1860	5,921,285
In 1865	2,943,661
In 1866	3,372,060

"The tonnage of such vessels which were cleared from the United States was—

	Tons.
In 1860	6.165,924
In 1865	3,025,134
In 1866	3,383,176

"The tonnage of foreign vessels which entered our ports was—

	Tons.
In 1860	2,353,911
In 1865	3,216,967
In 1866	4,410,424

"The tonnage of foreign vessels which were cleared was—

	Tons.
In 1860	2,624,005
In 1865	3,595,123
In 1866	4,438,384"

While admitting that something of the diminution of our shipping must be attributed to the effects of the war, the Secretary, as if to prove that high taxes have been more destructive than war, says:

"The scarcity of American vessels ought to have produced, and but for a redundant currency and high taxes would have produced, activity in our ship-yards and a rapid increase of tonnage; but this has not been the case. The prices of labor and materials are so high that ship-building cannot be made profitable in the United States, and many of our ship-yards are being practically transferred to the British Provinces. It is only a few years since American ships were sought after on account of their superiority and cheapness; and large numbers of vessels were built in Maine and other States on foreign account or sold to foreigners, while at the same time our own mercantile marine was being rapidly increased. . . . . . . It is an important truth that vessels can be built very much cheaper in the British Provinces than in Maine. Nay, further, that timber can be taken from Virginia to the Provinces, and from these Provinces to England, and there made into ships which can be sold at a profit; while the same kind of vessels can only be built in New England at a loss by the most skilful and economical builders. . . . .

"The same causes—a redundant currency and high taxes—that prevent ship-building tend to prevent the building of houses and even of manufactories. So high are prices of every description that men hesitate to build dwellings as fast as they are required, and thus rents are so advanced as to be oppressive to lessees, and the healthy growth of towns and cities is retarded. So it is in regard to manufactories. Mills which were built before the war can be run profitably, but so expensive are labor and materials that new mills cannot be erected and put into operation with any prospect of fair returns upon the investment unless upon the expectation that taxes will remain as they are and prices be sustained, if they are not advanced. The same causes are injuriously affecting agriculture and other interests which it is not necessary to particularize. It is everywhere observed that existing high prices are not only oppressing the masses of the people, but are seriously checking the development, growth, and prosperity of the country."

What remedies does our sagacious Secretary propose for the evils he so truthfully depicts? One, and apparently in his judgment the most efficacious, is that which I have been considering, namely, to add not less than four or five million dollars per month to the price of American products by taxing them to that amount for the express purpose of extinguishing so much of our national debt! If gentlemen doubt my statement I beg them to give the report an attentive reading. This mad policy pervades all its suggestions. Nor is it to be temporary. It is to be the fixed policy of the Government, and he says our debt which, according to his statement, was on the 31st of October last $2,551,424,121.20, "can be paid by the generation that created it."

Sir, if my suspicion that the preparation of the Secretary's report was committed to a treacherous subordinate be correct, gentlemen will be able to estimate the wantonness of that person's cruelty by the fact that in further illustration of the absurdity of its leading proposition he proceeds to tell us that "between the years 1848 and the 1st of July, 1860, the product of the gold and silver mines of the United States was about $1,100,000,000," but that "it is not probable that the amount of gold and silver now in the United States is very much larger than it was eighteen years ago." And as if to give greater effect to what, were it not gravely trifling with the prosperity of the American people, might be regarded as a huge joke, adds the fact that beside exporting all our bullion we have, in exchange for perishable foreign commodities which we might have fabricated from our own raw materials, given to foreign capitalists, who now hold them, interest-bearing evidences of debt to the amount of $600,000,000, as follows:

United States bonds	$350,000,000
State and municipal bonds	150,000,000
Railroad and other stocks and bonds	100,000,000
Total	$600,000,000

Nor does he yet stay his hand in presenting reasons why we should not adopt his proposition, for he informs us that the reports of the custom-houses show that though we exported specie during the fiscal year which ended June 30th, 1866, to the amount of $82,643,374, the balance of trade, as shown by those reports, was still against us in gold values $8,009,577. And with a measure of candor for which I award him full credit adds:

"But these figures, taken from the reports of the custom-houses, do not present the whole truth. For many years there has been a systematic undervaluation of foreign merchandise imported into the United States, and large amounts have been smuggled into the country along our extended sea-coasts and frontiers. To make up for undervaluations and smuggling, and for cost of transportation paid to foreign shipowners, twenty per cent. at least should be added to the imports, which would make the balance for the past year against the United States nearly $100,000,000. It is evident that the balances have been largely against the United States for some years past, whatever may have been the custom-house returns."

Mr. Chairman, I confess my ignorance of "Ingeany bankin'," and will proclaim my gratitude to any of its disciples who will so far admit me to its mysteries as to enable me to reconcile the Secretary's premises and conclusions.

Meanwhile I ask who but he, unless it be bankers and shavers of notes, importers of foreign goods, and holders of our bonds who desire to get two dollars for every one they invested in them, who but these does not see in this fearful array of evidences of our tendency to universal bankruptcy a necessity for developing our productive power by diminishing the internal taxes of the country to the lowest possible amount consistent with an economical administration of the Government? And who except the classes just enumerated does not see that by continuing the course we are pursuing we are retarding the permanent resumption of specie payments and postponing the day when we shall be able to enter judiciously upon the extinguishment of our debt?

Mr. McCulloch does not seem to perceive that this fearful array of facts is but so many concurrent items of evidence that notwithstanding our freedom, enterprise, and energy, and our infinitely diverse, easily-accessible, and inexhaustible stores of natural wealth, our extended sea-coast, fine harbors, broad lakes, and far-rolling rivers, which invite us to manufacturing and maritime effort and preëminence, we are but a mere commercial dependency. Like all other debtors we are at the mercy of our creditors. Though richer in natural resources than all of them combined, the continuance of our prosperity is dependent upon the caprices or necessities of England and the nations of Europe, which, by protecting their industry and importing only raw material or commodities but slightly wrought and exporting products as much manufactured as possible, practice economies unknown to us, and by diversifying their industry provide remunerative employment for all their people.

Manufactures and agriculture are each the handmaid of the other, and the successful practice of both is a prerequisite to profitable and sustained commerce. That seaboard nation which most diversifies its productions and best protects its skilled labor against unequal competition will ever be foremost in the race for commerce.

No, sir; the Secretary does not see the proper application of the facts he cites, and while dilating upon them illustrates his profound ignorance of the progress social science has made by reiterating trite maxims from English handbooks of political economy to prove that international trade-balances are settled with gold and silver and that the flow of specie "indicates the condition and results of trade between different nations." In the light of these laws I point him and the country to the fact that the trade between us and foreign nations has carried them our cotton and wool, our beef, pork, grain and other staples, and $1,100,000,000 of our bullion with $600,000,000 of our bonds to pay for wines, silks, laces, cloths, etc., which have been consumed, and iron rails to stretch across the coal and iron beds which underlie our country from the Atlantic coast to the Pacific and from the lakes to the Gulf, and ask them if the facts do not indicate bankruptcy as the "result" if the present and past "condition" of that trade be maintained? And whether, when as now we are compelled to look to internal taxes for the bulk of our receipts, when duties on foreign imports could under no possible system provide us with adequate income, it would not be well as a pure question of revenue to so adjust our taxes as to relieve American labor and land from every possible exaction, and by every possible device stimulate the development of our productive power and the immigration of skilled laborers into the country? Thus, and thus alone, can we check the flow of specie and bonds to Europe and retain among us as capital the production of our gold and silver mines with which to redeem the $600,000,000 of bonds now held by foreigners. This the Secretary professes to desire, but how the imposition of extraordinary taxes upon our industry to the amount of $50,000,000 per annum is to promote it he has not condescended to inform us.

The scheme of the Secretary is as unprecedented as it is unwise. It is without a single historical example. The first Federal debt was funded in 1791, and for sixteen years no effort was made to reduce it. In 1807 the receipts of the Government from ordinary sources were in excess of current expenses, and the surplus was applied to the debt. This easy and natural process of extinguishment continued until 1812. The average rate of payment per annum from 1807 to 1812 was about $6,000,000, and at the breaking out of the war with Great Britain the debt had been reduced from $75,000,000 to $45,000,000. It was swollen by that war to $127,000,000; but no extraordinary taxes were imposed for its redemption. The revenues of the Government were derived from ordinary sources, and such balances as remained after paying current expenses were applied to its absorption. No statesman of either period proposed to cripple industry and retard the development of the country by the imposition of extraordinary taxes as a means of extinguishing its debt. They wisely stimulated both by imposing higher duties upon foreign importations, and under the avowedly protective tariffs of 1824 and 1828 paid it off. Such a spectacle had never been witnessed before, for no other nation had ever liquidated its entire debt.

The American people will rather follow the successful example of the statesmen of those days and foster our industry, than accept the crotchets of our present Secretary of the Treasury and cripple labor and diminish production by extraordinary taxation. They freely lent their substance to the Government and hold more than eighty per cent. of our national securities, and none of them are demanding payment. Nor need we be specially anxious about that part of our bonds that are held in Europe. They who hold them bought them as investments or as matter of speculation. As investments they pay better interest than the holders can elsewhere obtain with equal security, and we are not required to prostrate our industry by a vain attempt to hasten the day on which foreign speculators shall realize anticipated profits. England has never been guilty of such stupidity. When the Napoleonic wars closed, the governing class of England held her bonds, and like the money-changers and "Ingeany" bankers of our country clamored for the resumption of specie payments that they might get par for the bonds which they had bought during those wars at such prices as our own sold for and in paper as irredeemable and depreciated as ours has been. By this operation they would have made an average of one hundred per cent. on their investments. But governing class as they were, it was not until seven years after the close of the war that the statesmen who controlled the financial affairs of Great Britain attempted the experiment of resumption, or till the suspension had endured for well nigh a quarter of a century. And only within a few years—I think I may say within the present decade—has England made serious effort to reduce the principal of her debt, nor has she yet imposed an extraordinary tax for the purpose. Her statesmen knew that her population was increasing and her productive power in process of rapid development, and they know that so long as the interest is ready at maturity and the creditors of the nation see that its taxes are diminishing and its population and resources increasing, they will regard the investment as safe.

Thus has England, while permitting her debt to increase, by showing her steady ability to diminish the taxes upon her people and provide for interest and current expenditures, been able to reduce the interest on her debt from war rates to the low rates at which she now holds it; and that debt which by its immense volume seemed to overshadow her whole future, is now not in the proportion of ten per cent. per man, per dollar, and per acre to what it was at the date of the treaty of Paris. So will it be with us if we shun the nostrums of the Secretary of the Treasury. The estimated wealth of the loyal States at this time is $17,-428,000,000, and their annual product is at least $4,685,-000,000. But thirty years hence, if the progress of our growth is not retarded by financial charlatanism, the wealth of those States will be $90,000,000,000, and the annual product not less than $23,000,000,000, and the now prostrate but naturally richer South will then rival the people of the North in prosperity and tax-paying power.

Let me, Mr. Chairman, as it is due to the Secretary I should, say, that he does not rest this urgent demand for the speedy extinguishment of the debt upon principles of social science or national economy. In this matter his head yields to his heart. He is guided by a sentiment. He prides himself upon his magnanimity, and would ruin the industry of the North and retard the development of our country for a century if need be rather than wound the sensibilities of our "erring southern brethren." Thus, after indulging in some trite reflections upon the evil of public debt in general, he tells us that—

"To the perpetuation of the existing debt of the United States there are also, it may be proper to remark, serious objections growing out of the circumstances under which it was created. Although incurred in a great struggle for the preservation of the Government, and therefore especially sacred in its character, its burdens are to be shared by those to whom it is a reminder of humiliation and defeat. It is exceedingly desirable that this, with other causes of heart-burnings and alienation, should be removed as rapidly as possible, and that all should disappear with the present generation, so that there may be nothing in the future to prevent that unity and good feeling between the sections which are necessary for true national prosperity."

To others than the Secretary it is known that the country is no longer divided into hostile sections. That which made the South sectional was slavery and pride of caste. Slavery, thank God, has been forever abolished, and pride of caste is vanishing. Yes, sir, the decree, sustained by a majority of nearly half a million of the voters of the northern States and enduring as the fiat of Heaven, that pride of caste must disappear from American politics has gone forth. Henceforth he who breathes the air of our country, let his color or fatherland be what or where it may, may by his own volition invest himself with the attributes of American citizenship. Every one born on the soil is a citizen, and our naturalization laws are henceforth of universal application.

I fear the southern people after reading the Secretary's report will regard him rather as a man of sentiment than of affairs. They may applaud the delicacy of his sensibilities, but while doing so will probably wish that a well-informed statesman presided over his Department. Destructive to northern interests as the attempt to provide for the payment of our debt by extraordinary taxes on this generation would be, the southern people are less able than we to endure the mad experiment. Among them are, as I have said, the widows, orphans, and maimed soldiers of their armies, whose poverty is not relieved even by the pittance we give as pensions to the same classes; their industrial system has been overthrown and is not yet reorganized; their cities and towns by their dilapidation tell how their trade and commerce have suffered, and their lands to a great extent lie waste; their banks, insurance companies, and other moneyed institutions have gone into liquidation; their railroads are in ruins and almost bare of rolling-stock; and they are making daily appeals to the people of the North, whose presence among them the baser sort of Southerners will not permit, for capital with which to open and work mines of gold, silver, copper, lead, iron, and coal, in which their land abounds. Scourged by the results of their own folly they are awakening to a knowledge of the value of their possessions, and are proposing to make them available. They desire if they can obtain the requisite capital to locate the factory near the cotton-field and the forge and furnace near the mine and ore bed.

A brief extract or two from southern papers of very recent date will show how cruel Mr. McCulloch is to those to whom he wishes to be so kind. Says the Petersburg, Va., Index:

"The variety of schemes devised for the relief of that numerous and unfortunate class of persons who are now laboring under pecuniary embarrassment evinces the necessity, as well as the difficulty, of providing an adequate remedy for the mischief sought to be prevented. A further extension of the stay law, a total or partial repudiation of private indebtedness, and the exemption of specified property from involuntary alienation are some of the expedients now brought forward to meet the pressing exigencies of the occasion."

The Nationalist, Mobile, Alabama, says:

"Reliable planters from Mississippi say that not one half dozen, on an average, in each county in that State, can pay their debts. Large tracts of valuable land are selling at nominal rates.

And the Richmond, Va., Times says

"If the tide of immigration continues to flow by us, and we make no energetic and intelligent effort to secure it, taxation will speedily devour what little the war left, and a few years hence when the pine, the persimmon, and the sassafras have made a wilderness of many a broad and once fertile field, some inauspicious day the tax-gatherer or the sheriff will hang out his red flag over the ruins of the old family mansion, and then, alas for the paternal acres, and the dear, sacred old homes of our boyhood! for everything, even the dear old graveyard, where repose the honored dust of our forefathers and the bones of many a noble 'soldier son' and fair daughter, will pass into the hands of some codfish-eating Puritan from Boston or Nantucket."

How incapable the people of North Carolina are of enduring extraordinary taxation is shown by reference to facts which occurred anterior to the war by a writer in the Newbern Times of September 8. After saying with truth that "the old North State is inferior to none of her sisters in the combined advantages of situation, climate, agricultural and mineral riches," he proceeds to make the following exhibit:

"In 1860 North Carolina ranked as twelfth among the States, containing a population of 992,622, of whom 331,059 were slaves. The free population are distributed according to places of birth, as follows:

Born in North Carolina	634,220
Born in other southern States	21,446
Born in northern States	2,399
Born in foreign countries	3,299
Born at sea and not classified	201

"While North Carolina was thus receiving from without her limits about twenty-seven thousand immigrants, she sent as emigrants to other States no less than 272,606 of her free-born offspring who are scattered throughout the western and southwestern States, of whom Tennessee received 55,000, Georgia 29,000, Indiana 27,000, Alabama 23,000, Arkansas 18,000.

"She was ninth among the States in her contribution to the population of the Union; seventh in contributing to the population of other States; behind all, save little Delaware and South Carolina, which ranks last of all, in the reception of citizens from other States.

"Of the vast foreign immigration, numbering upward of four millions, which has built up the manufactures and the internal improvements of the northern and western States, she received only about three thousand, standing in that respect behind every State in the Union and behind three of the Territories."

But how capable the future people of North Carolina will be is well shown by the editor of the Old North State, published at Salisbury. In an article entitled "The Future of North Carolina," he says:

"The questions present themselves, how is all this to be done, and can the Government promote the great object by a proper policy? We shall endeavor to answer these questions to the best of our poor ability.

"The abolition of slavery has, in our opinion, changed the destiny of the State. The negro cannot be entirely relied upon as a laborer, and he must be assisted by, or his place be supplied with white laborers sooner or later. These, except in a small portion of the State, cannot be profitably employed in agricultural pursuits until other interests are brought prominently forward and partially developed. This cannot be done without an influx of capital from abroad.

"The greatest of these interests, and those which we shall notice on this occasion, are the mining and manufacturing interests. It is perfectly useless for us to speak of the vast mineral wealth of North Carolina; it is known to all the world to be inferior to that of no country on the globe, both in quantity, quality, and variety of minerals, but we may have no capital to render them available.

"And to the capitalist who desires to engage in manufacturing, no country in the world presents more inducements than North Carolina. Her water-power is unsurpassed. As a general thing steam is useless in the State for manufacturing purposes; for the face of the country is intersected by water courses such as abound in few other lands. If we look at the map we shall see that there is a perfect net-work of streams, showing that it is one of the best watered portions of the earth, and the structure of the country is such that every one of these streams can be made to drive machinery. All this magnificent provision of nature has thus far been permitted to waste, in a great measure at least.

"It is scarcely necessary to refer to these facilities more in detail. Every reader knows the vast capacity of our larger rivers for these purposes. That of the Roanoke, the Neuse, the Haw, the Deep, the Main Yadkin, the South Yadkin, the Little Yadkin, the Catawba, and other rivers of the State for driving machinery, is scarcely equaled by any in the world, while we have many other smaller streams of very great capacity.

"And when all this water power is turned to account for manufacturing purposes, as it will be at no great distance of time, when we have thousands of furnaces in full blast turning the ores from the bowels of the earth into the richest marketable commodities, and when our vast deposits of coal shall be used for these and other purposes for which nature intended them, what a country we will have! What vast amounts of wealth must then flow into our laps. Our State will then be dotted over with the most flourishing manufacturing towns and villages and our now barren fields will teem with the richest verdure.

"This must necessarily be so. We stated at the outset that until the mining and manufacturing interests were at least partially developed imported white labor could not be profitably employed in agricultural pursuits. But when these interests become to be a power in the State the thing changes. All the thousands, if not the hundreds of thousands, of factory operatives and miners must find a support, and the result will be that vast home markets will be created. The soil will be heavily taxed for their sustenance and consequently vast improvements will be made in our system of agriculture—and nothing needs improvement more.* But we will not pursue this line of remark further—we have presented the general outlines and we leave it to the imagination of our readers to fill up the picture. In the course of time the farms of our State will rival those of the Dutch Pennsylvanians; our lands will become equally productive, while our system of internal improvements will become equal to theirs."

More gladly, sir, than the people of the North will

* Dreading such an influx of immigrants, the democratic members of Congress from North Carolina voted with the free trade representatives of New York city against protective duties.

those of the South welcome release from every dollar of taxation from which sagacity can exempt them. And I assure the Secretary that the people of no part of the country have shared so largely as those of the South the surprise and wonder to which he alludes.

Mr. McCulloch truly says:

"We have but touched the surface of our resources; the great mines of our national wealth are yet to be developed."

This is specially true as to the southern portion of our country, and in the name of the impoverished people of that section I ask, is it well to tax a generation the surface of whose resources has not been touched by the transmuting hand of labor, and the mines of whose wealth are yet to be developed, in order to pay the principal of a mortgage the holder of which neither needs nor desires his money? and would not wisdom or state craft suggest the propriety of enabling the owners of these mines of wealth to accumulate capital with which to work them and by the magic touch of labor to convert them into current gold? The taxing process must continue our exhausting dependence on foreign nations, while the developing process would make us as free commercially as we are politically, and enable us, by our example of liberal wages and freedom from their exhausting hours of toil, to influence the commercial and manufacturing usages of European States, as our political example is influencing their political and social institutions.

The Secretary, however, has other prescriptions than that of excessive taxation by which to restore the country. In his opening paragraphs he says:

"With proper economy in all the Departments of the Government, the debt can be paid by the generation that created it, if wise and equal revenue laws shall be enacted and continued by Congress, and these laws are faithfully enforced by the officers charged with their execution."

Again, he tells us that he "has mainly directed his attention to measures looking to an increase of efficiency in

---

* Mr. McCulloch's Fort Wayne speech, in which he promised to bring about a resumption of specie payments in two years by contracting the currency, cost the American people hundreds of millions. The mere announcement paralysed enterprise. No new projects were undertaken till Congress prohibited further contraction, and many that were in process of construction were suspended or abandoned. Practical men everywhere saw that the result of his policy would be bankruptcy and not resumption.

the collection of revenues, to the conversion of interest-bearing notes into five-twenty bonds, and to a reduction of the public debt." Efficiency in the collection of revenues, forsooth! "The faithful enforcement of laws by the officers charged with their execution!" These are brave words to fall from the lips of one whose faithless exercise of official functions in this very matter has during the past year cost the Government more than $50,-000,000. Brave words, indeed, are these from one who in a wicked attempt to subvert the popular will by the corrupt use of official patronage has removed hundreds of well-tried, capable and experienced officers of the revenue and customs departments and substituted for them men deficient alike in capacity, experience, and character. There is not a congressional district in the country whose people are not grieving over the fact that the Secretary of the Treasury, who embodies these fine phrases in his report, has wantonly and wickedly aggravated the onerous taxation under which they groan. Let who else will speak of the necessity of a faithful administration and due enforcement of the revenue laws, for which every patriot will pray, becoming modesty would constrain the Secretary of the Treasury to avoid the topic. This is a matter on which Congress should take early action, and if it means that the customs and internal revenue laws shall be faithfully and impartially enforced it must see that another than the author of the report I am considering shall have the selection of officers for their enforcement.

Some of the Secretary's suggestions are embodied in distinct—no, not in distinct, but in numerical propositions. To one of these I invite the attention of the committee. It is as follows:

"2. That the duties upon imported commodities should correspond and harmonize with the taxes upon home productions, and that these duties should not be so high as to be prohibitory, nor to build up home monopolies, nor to prevent that free exchange of commodities which is the life of commerce. Nor, on the other hand, should they be so low as to seriously impair the revenues, nor to subject the home manufacturers, burdened with heavy internal taxes, to a competition with cheaper labor and larger capital which they may be unable to sustain."

"There's wisdom for you!" I venture to assert that Jack Bunsby never uttered a more characteristic proposition than that; and all will agree that since the celebrated Kane letter of James K. Polk our political literature has embodied no utterance more shrewdly Delphic.

This ingeniously inexpressive proposition is not the Secretary's only allusion to "home monopolies." He seems to hold them in special dread; and it is to be deeply regretted that he has not indicated the arguments by which his apprehensions are sustained, as they are not to be found in the works of the disciples of any school of political economy or social science.

The teachers of free trade do not agree with him in believing that high duties "build up home monopolies." They assert that protection secures undue profits to certain branches of production and tempts capitalists to ruin themselves by so overdoing the business as to glut the market and compel them to sell their goods at small profits or at a loss. Their theory proceeds upon the want of judgment in capitalists and business men—but by asserting that high duties beget undue domestic competition denies that they promote local monopolies.

Nor does Mr. McCulloch agree with the school of protectionists, for they say that assured protection against unequal competition gives capitalists confidence and induces them to open mines and build furnaces, forges, and factories, whereby constant employment and ample wages are secured to the otherwise idle people of the country. This theory proceeds on the assumption that the American manufacturer is competent to measure the contingencies of our own markets and of the course of foreign trade, but is not competent to resist the gigantic efforts which were commended by Lord Brougham, and one of which is now making by the Crœsus-like capitalists of England "to stifle in the cradle those rising manufactures in the United States which the war has forced into existence."

Our present condition resembles very closely that of the States of Europe at the close of Napoleon's wars, and the following passage from the admirable address of John L. Hayes, Esq., entitled, "The Fleece and the Loom," embodies illustrations of fixed laws applicable enough to our condition to dispel even the Secretary's dread of "home monopolies:"

"What would have been the future industrial condition of continental Europe if at the time when peace restored the nations to labor the textile manufactures had been left to their own free course and no legislation had intervened to regulate their progress? Can there be any doubt that they would have become the exclusive occupation of England? Alone in the possession of steam power and machinery; alone provided with ships and means of transport; alone endowed, through her stable legislation, with capital to vivify her natural wealth, she had absolute command of the markets of the Continent. The question was presented to the continental nations whether they should accept the cheap tissues of England, or at some sacrifices repel them, to appropriate to themselves the labor and profit of their production. The latter course was successively adopted, with some modifications, by each of the continental nations; and with what results to their own wealth and the industrial progress and comfort of the world? Instead of a single workshop Europe has the workshops of France, Russia, Austria, Prussia, Belgium, Sweden, Denmark, Spain, each clothing its own people with substantial fabrics; each developing its own creative genius and peculiar resources; each contributing to substitute the excellence of competition for the mediocrity of monopoly; each adding to the progress of the arts and the wealth and comfort of mankind." *

The fifth of the Secretary's propositions is "the rehabilitation of the States recently in insurrection." Referring to the conquered territories, which notwithstanding the President's usurpations await the action of the law-making power for reconstruction, Mr. McCulloch says:

"Embracing as they do one-third part of the richest lands of the country, and producing articles of great value for home use and for exportation to other countries, their position with regard to the General Government cannot remain unsettled, and their industrial pursuits cannot continue to be seriously disturbed, without causing such a diminution of the production of their great staples as must necessarily affect our revenues, and render still more unsatisfactory than they now are our trade relations with Europe. . . . . . . There will be no real prosperity in these States, and consequently no real prosperity in one-third part of the United States, until all possess again equal privileges under the Constitution."

If it be true, as it undoubtedly is, that "one-third part of the richest lands of the country" are by reason of temporary causes not producing "articles of great value for home use and for exportation to other countries," would it not seem to suggest the idea that this unhappy state of affairs should be permitted to pass away and these lands be made productive before they should be burdened with taxes not demanded by imperious necessity? And the question whether before these lands shall be able to bear taxation for that purpose the people of the North, whose

* Why may not the Carolinas compete with New England in cotton goods, and Alabama and Missouri with Pennsylvania in iron and steel

sacrifices during the war saved the integrity of the Union, should be called upon to extinguish the debt created by the crimes of the possessors of this broad and rich territory? The people of the northern States have certainly arrived at this conclusion, and I have shown that schooled by suffering the people of the South, while antagonizing them on many points, agree with them in this.

Pursuing this branch of his subject, Mr. McCulloch asks, "Can the nation be regarded as in a healthy condition when the industry of so large a portion of it is deranged?" And the people, North and South, answer "No; and in our enfeebled condition we pray you not to rob us of our working capital in order to extinguish a debt which was contracted for the benefit of mankind and future ages."

He asks again, "And can the labor question at the South be settled as long as the political status of the South is unsettled?" And the country answers, "Yes, there is no inseparable connection between the labor question and the political status of the conquered territories;" and adds that the "political status" of the South cannot be settled until its rebellious leaders discover that the loyal people of the country are able to defend its institutions against the usurpations of Andrew Johnson, and accepting the constitutional amendments already adopted and which are in process of adoption by three-fourths of the States which now constitute the Union, submit to Congress constitutions republican in form upon which the people shall have set the seal of their approval. The people of the loyal North cannot restore those of the conquered territories to their "political status." We can only consent to their restoration when they shall be willing that it shall take place on terms which will render the future peace of the country secure, and for this we are and have been ready. The leaders of the South, not we, are the dog in the manger. It is they who, by refusing to abandon the dogmas that evoked the war and the oligarchic institutions that sustained it, resist the influx of the tide of immigration that would fertilize their lands and republicanize their institutions.

The imminent want of the people of the South is not "political status." That would not enable them to settle the "labor question." What they want is capital and currency and a willingness to permit loyal men, whether white or black, native or foreign, to dwell among them, and by their labor quicken into commercial value the boundless and varied natural wealth of the land they occupy, but which they will neither work themselves nor permit others to work in peace and safety. When in obedience to a healthy national sentiment or the promptings of their own interests they shall make capital secure, opinion free, and give peaceful scope to enterprise within their borders, the immense deposits which profitless to their owners now lie in bank, because under the hammering process of the Secretary of the Treasury judicious men are afraid to embark in new enterprises, will be transferred to the South to develop her productive and taxable power, and make her populous and prosperous beyond the wildest dream of the visionary theorists who involved her in a war as causeless as it was disastrous.

Mr. Chairman, time will not permit me to answer all the Secretary's interrogatories or examine each of his propositions.

But his friends may complain that I have not alluded to that which they regard as his chief specific. It is set forth in the second of another series of propositions as follows: "a curtailment of the currency to the amount required by legitimate and healthful trade." On this point, though not condescending to indicate what amount of currency is in his judgment required by "legitimate and healthful trade" in the present abnormal condition of the country, the Secretary is peculiarly coherent and luminous. He is clearly a disciple of Dr. Sangrado. He recognizes the circulating medium as the life-blood of commerce, and as Sangrado attempted to restore his patients by withdrawing blood and injecting warm water into their veins, he proposes to assist extraordinary taxation in the work of rehabilitating the southern States, whose great want is currency and working capital, and in invigorating the languishing interests of the North by contracting the currency, and especially by withdrawing that portion which is of equal and unquestioned value in every part of the country—the United States notes, commonly called "greenbacks." He says:

"He regards a redundant legal-tender currency as the prime cause of our financial difficulties and a curtailment thereof indispensable to an increase of labor and a reduction of prices to an augmentation of exports and a diminution of imports, which alone will place the trade between the United States and other nations on an equal and satisfactory footing."

And that—

"He is of opinion that the national banks should be sustained, and that the paper circulation of the country should be reduced, not by compelling them to retire their notes, but by the withdrawal of the United States notes."

Mr. Chairman, had I been properly instructed in the mysteries of "Ingeany bankin'" I might be able to comprehend and appreciate these suggestions; but in the blindness of my ignorance I cannot see what there is to commend his theory to the Finance Minister of our country. The greenbacks are, it is true, part of our debt, and must therefore at some day be redeemed; but they are the only part of our immense debt which bears no interest; and while there are outstanding, as the Secretary's statement of December 1st, 1866, shows, $147,387,140 of compound-interest notes which are currency and used as such by the national banks, and $699,933,750 of three-years' notes bearing seven and three-tenths per cent. interest, all of which were purchased in a greatly depreciated currency, I cannot comprehend the philosophy which proposes to let the interest on these run, while absorbing a non-interest-bearing loan which the people cherish as furnishing the best currency for our immense domestic commerce they have ever had.

The experiment if attempted as a means of hastening specie payments will prove a failure, but not a harmless one. It will be fatal to the prospects of a majority of the business men of this generation and strip the frugal laboring people of the country of the small but hard-earned sums they have deposited in savings banks or invested in Government securities. It will make money scarce and employment uncertain. Its object is to reduce the amount of that which in every part of our country and for the hundreds of thousands of millions of dollars of domestic trade is money, and to increase its purchasing power; and by thus unsettling values to paralyze trade, suspend production, and deprive industry of employment. It will make the money of the rich man more valuable and deprive the poor man of his entire capital, the value of his labor, by depriving him of employment. Its first effect will be to increase the rate of interest and diminish the rate of wages, and its final effect wide-spread bankruptcy and a more protracted suspension of specie payments. Anxious as the people are to relieve the country of the evils entailed upon it by the war, and willing as they have proven themselves to endure any privations or sacrifices required by the exigencies of the country, they will not consent to an experiment involving such terrible consequences for the purpose of paying the "Ingeany" and other banks which hold and use as part of their reserve our compound-interest notes, two dollars for every one they invested in this interest-bearing portion of our "lawful money." Much as banks, bankers, and speculators in Government securities may approve this policy, the people earnestly and indignantly protest against it.

Does Mr. McCulloch forget that the compound-interest-bearing notes are part of the "legal tender currency" against which he declaims, and that by absorbing them he will be contracting the currency and reducing the volume of interest that is compounding against the Government? The banks are required, those of certain cities, to maintain a reserve of "lawful money" equal to twenty-five per cent. of their circulation and deposits, and all others a like reserve of fifteen per cent., and as he well knows they have absorbed and hold not greenbacks, but compound interest notes as that reserve. He should keep his non-interest-bearing notes afloat till these are redeemed. They will mature in 1867 and 1868, and by redeeming them he will contract the currency at the rate of $6,000,000 per month and relieve the Government of one of its most exhausting interest accounts. By this process he will keep five-twenties above par, promote the conversion into them of seven-thirties, and reduce the interest on that portion of our debt from seven and three-tenths to six per cent. But by his process of contracting the volume of greenbacks and imposing extraordinary taxes on our industry he will delay the redemption of the one and the conversion of the other, and may deprive us of the ability to redeem either the seven-thirties or compound-interest notes at maturity.

The people do not regard greenbacks and the notes of national banks with equal favor, but have a well-grounded preference for the former. They know that the ultimate redemption of the bank notes is secured by deposits of Government securities and the maintenance of a reserve of greenbacks; and as the substance is more solid than its shadow, they prefer that which secures to that which requires to be secured. Several national banks have failed; and though the ultimate redemption of the notes was secured, there was no provision for their immediate redemption, and the laboring people who held them had to sell them at great loss to "Ingeany" or other bankers, who could afford to hold them till the Government was ready to redeem them. Having sustained no such losses by greenbacks they naturally prefer them. Adequate as these reasons are for the popular preference, there are others which I will state, in the language of the Secretary's report.

Mr. Hooper, of Massachussetts. If I understand the gentleman from Pennsylvania, he asserts that when national banks fail their notes cease to circulate. Has the gentleman ever heard of any such an instance? The Government is still responsible when the bank fails, and these notes are redeemed when presented at the Treasury. I understand they circulate, therefore, as well after as before the suspension of the bank. It may be remembered that the Treasurer of the United States was recently somewhat criticised by the press for his statement that the national bank notes were better after the bank failed than before.

Mr. Kelley. I have recognized the ultimate responsibility of the Government for them, but I know that traders in money take advantage of all contingencies, and I have known laboring men to sell to brokers the notes of a broken national bank at considerable loss. The announcement that a bank has failed depreciates the notes in the market, for the people, especially laboring people, who are not as familiar as the gentleman from Massachusetts with all the minute provisions of the law by which the ultimate redemption of these notes is secured; and when a bank fails those poor people, who cannot carry them to the Treasury for redemption, are compelled to sell them at a heavy loss. But, as I was proceeding to show, the Secretary of the Treasury more than sustains my position on this point, for he deliberately argues that legislation is required "to make them throughout the United States a par circulation." He says:

"The solvency of the notes of national banks is secured by a deposit of bonds with the Treasurer at Washington; but as the banks are scattered throughout the country, and many of them are in places difficult of access, a redemption of their notes at their respective counters is not all that is required to make them throughout the United States a par circulation. It is true that the notes of all national banks are receivable for all public dues, except duties upon imports, and must be paid by the Treasurer in case the banks which issued are unable to redeem them; but it will not be claimed that the notes of banks, although perfectly solvent, but situated in interior towns, are practically as valuable as the notes of banks in the sea-board cities."

These depreciatory remarks are not applicable to greenbacks. They are of equal value throughout the country, and the people cherish them for this reason more than from the fact that they are the evidence of a patriotic loan made by the people to the Government without interest. Had Mr. McCulloch suggested that the national bank notes, for holding bonds to secure which we pay the banks $18,000,-000 per annum, should be supplanted by greenbacks, and that a sum equal to the interest on the bonds should be applied to the creation of a sinking fund for the redemption of the national debt, the people would have applauded his wisdom and patriotism, and not questioned his motives as they are now constrained to.

Had such been the Secretary's suggestion he might have omitted this one of his propositions, namely, to compel "the national banks to redeem their notes at the Atlantic cities, or, what would be better, at a single city," which, in plain language, is a recommendation that we increase the power and profits of the banks of New York by compelling every national bank outside of that city to deposit a portion of its funds with them. The gambling tendencies of the New York speculators in stocks and provisions need no such stimulant as this; and recent experience has shown that leading banks of that city are managed more recklessly than any others in the country, and would therefore be an unsafe depository for so large a trust. Less than a month ago the Secretary tested their management by calling upon them for a small portion of the Government deposits, which were mistakenly supposed to be represented by a reserve of greenbacks in their vaults, and produced a perturbation in prices throughout the country by which fortunes were lost and won. He has not given the facts to the country, but it is known in well-informed circles that some of them were compelled to ask for a "brief extension" because they were unable to pay the Government drafts. Practical men may therefore be excused for speaking of the proposal of such remedies as charlatanism.

Mr. Chairman, as I have said, the Secretary has not ventured to indicate what in his judgment, in the present condition of the country, is the amount of currency "required by legitimate and healthful trade." That condition is abnormal, though not entirely peculiar, and certainly not unprecedented. By unwise and unpatriotic legislation, which was dictated by the magnates of the South, millions of our poor people were doomed to the simplest and least remunerative forms of agricultural labor, or to enforced idleness, in which they were tending to barbarism, while our raw materials were being wrought into fabrics for our use in the workshops of transatlantic nations, and we had thus been drained of specie and had become largely a debtor nation before the war began. Those same magnates plunged us into a war of unprecedented proportions, which we were unable to maintain with a specie or convertible currency. In the hour of our need we discerned the fact that ours is one of the two countries to which, in the language of Gortschakoff, the enlightened prince who is guiding the destinies of the other, "God has given such conditions of existence that their grand internal life is enough for them," and determined that until the war and its consequences should have passed away we would give the world an example of our ability and self-reliance, and use a currency based, not on the international standard, gold and silver, but on our faith in the resources of our country and the integrity of its Government. We thus furnished the Government $3,000,000,000 with which to create, arm, feed, clothe, and pay our Army and Navy.

How this prompt supply of money quickened industry and developed the productive power of the country I need not pause to say. I will, however, remind the committee that though it was "irredeemable legal-tender currency," it restored the credit of the nation, which had been unable to borrow $5,000,000 at twelve per cent., and lifted the people from the bankruptcy of 1857 to a degree of prosperity unequaled in our history. From 1857 to 1861 the rate of interest was high and that of wages low, and neither capital nor labor could find profitable and permanent employment. But with a safe, though perhaps somewhat redundant, currency, by the use of which our people were compelled to look to our own workshops for supplies, prosperity, in the midst of war, succeeded the adversity of contracted and stagnant peace with magic speed. And if we now adopt a tariff that will protect our industry as faithfully as did the difference between our paper and gold, in which we required the duties on foreign imports to be paid during the war, we will soon discover that there is ample and profitable employment for all the currency authorized by law; and that if we resolutely refuse to increase its volume it will approximate the standard of convertibility more rapidly by the development of the productive power of the country and the diversification of employment for the people than it can by the process of contraction at any rate. Protection and development will insure a prosperous future; but rapid contraction will reproduce the stagnation, bankruptcy, and suffering of 1837 and 1857.

The question presented to the mind of practical statesmen is not what would be the best currency if we were founding a new community, or how far we might with advantage add paper to a purely metallic currency, but is, what under existing conditions do the true interests of the country require. And on this question I again take issue with the Secretary of the Treasury and deny that the country will find in a rapid or material contraction of its currency, or in extraordinary taxation, a remedy for any of the evils that afflict it. If, as some of his friends have done, the Secretary should point me to the high prices which many articles command, or to the immense deposits which, unproductive to their owners, are enhancing the present profits and future liabilities of the banks, I will reply to him, as I have to them, that these are not proofs of the redundancy of the currency, but of his mistaken policy and inveterate mismanagement.

Though the use of these immense deposits is lost to their cautious proprietors, the money does not lie idle in the vaults of banks; it is lent on call in large sums to adventurers, who by its use enhance the price of such commodities as they can monopolize or control. Those who could make their own capital productive are afraid to use it, and reckless gamblers riot in its use. Yes, sir, the Secretary's policy is calculated to diminish production and stimulate speculation, which symptoms have been the twin precursors of all our commercial crises and eras of bankruptcy. Under his fatal policy—

"The native hue of resolution
Is sicklied o'er with the pale cast of thought;
And enterprises of great pith and moment,
With this regard, their currents turn awry,
And lose the name of action."

The sagacious but prudent owners of these deposits grieve that the money with which they would gladly open coal mines and ore banks, and build forges and furnaces and factories, and import skilled laborers from Europe to increase and diversify our productions, enlarge our home market, and swell the revenues of the Government, lies dead and profitless to them. They justly charge their loss and that of the country to Mr. McCulloch, who, from his Fort Wayne speech forward, has lost no opportunity, official or unofficial, to warn the energetic men of the country against embarking in any new enterprises or accumulating any considerable stock of goods, or otherwise enlarging their arrangements for the future; and who, in his last utterance—the report which I am considering—notifies them of the near approach of the fatal collapse by assuring them that though the banks are without specie, the balance of trade vastly against us, and the Treasury has nearly one billion dollars of temporary loan to provide for, he is "confident that specie payments may be resumed by the time our interest-bearing notes are retired, which must be done in less than two years, and probably will be in a much shorter period."

What the effect of an effort at early resumption under such circumstances would be every experienced business man in the country knows. They know that it can by any possibility be but a spasmodic movement, which will literally vomit forth from the country the little gold and silver left in it. They know that it will bankrupt individuals, corporations, States, and, alas, it may be, the national Government itself. The avowed object of the Secretary in contracting the currency is to increase the purchasing power of money; and they know that the rapid decline in prices pending this mad experiment will sweep away the garnered capital of those manufacturers whose stock, exclusive of buildings and machinery, largely exceeds their working capital, that mechanical and manufacturing production must be wholly suspended till the blighting tornado shall have spent its power, and that while it rages the receipts of the Internal Revenue Bureau must fall to zero.*

But, sir, if by thus returning to the wretchedness of 1857 and 1837 we could resume specie payments, how long could we maintain them? The Secretary tells us that $350,000,000 of our bonds are held abroad. The average rate at which they were bought, when gold for long periods was above two hundred per cent., was less than fifty cents on the dollar, nor was that small amount paid in specie; for he also tells us that—

"The opinion that the country has been benefited by the exportation of its securities is founded upon the supposition that we have received real capital in exchange for them. This supposition is to a large extent unfounded. Our bonds have gone abroad to pay for goods which without them might not have been purchased. Not only have we exported the surplus products of our mines and our fields, with no small amount of our manufactures, but a large amount of securities also, to pay for the articles which we have purchased from other countries. That these purchases have been stimulated and increased by the facility of paying for them in bonds can hardly be doubted. Our importations of goods have been increased by nearly the amount of the bonds which have been exported. Not one dollar in five of the amount of the five-twenties now held in England and upon the Continent has been returned to the United States in the form of real capital. But if this were not a true statement of the case, the fact exists, as has been already stated, that some three hundred and fifty millions of Government bonds—not to mention State and railroad bonds and other securities—are in the hands of the citizens of other countries, which may be returned at any time for sale in the United States, and which being so held may seriously embarrass our efforts to return to specie payments."

---

* The following figures, from the financial column of the papers of July 3d, furnish pregnant proof of the criminal charlatanism of those who advocate a resumption of specie payments, while the interest account and balance of trade are sufficiently against us to justify these figures.

"The exports from New York of gold and silver coin and bullion for the fiscal year 1870–71 are as follows:

July	$16,922,451	January	$2,149,211
August	10,587,040	February	4,022,066
September	4,618,850	March	7,569,880
October	2,416,356	April	9,593,029
November	4,896,257	May	9,615,698
December	1,950,879	June	*9,265,460

Total, fiscal year 1871	$93,566,219
Foreign specie imported	9,591,731
Net outgo from New York	$83,974,488

The clearances of gold and silver on Saturday, July 1, not included in above, but coming into the new fiscal year, were $3,125,797."—*The Press*, July 4, 1871.

* Unofficial.

Thus by Mr. McCulloch's own statement it appears that our bonds were bought at half their nominal value and paid for in commercial products which should have been created by our own industry from our own raw material by setting "our unemployed and poor people at work on the growth of our own lands;" and if we may believe the Secretary's statement to which I have referred, a large portion of these commodities were brought into the country in fraud of our revenue laws by "undervaluations and smuggling." For what purpose, let me ask, were those bonds bought by their foreign holders? How long will they be held? When and under what contingencies are they likely to be returned to this country? And in this connection a more pregnant question still: what effect would be produced by the early return to specie payments threatened by the Secretary of the Treasury?

That I may do Mr. McCulloch no injustice, I answer these momentous questions in the language of his report:

> "A large portion of these bonds have been bought on speculation, and will be likely to be returned whenever financial troubles in the countries in which they are held shall make it necessary for the holders to realize upon them, or whenever satisfactory profits can be made by returning them, which will be when they nearly approach their par value in coin."

Here at least he is right. Those bonds, having been bought at half the value expressed on their face, will be returned "when they nearly approach their par value in coin," and that will be when we resume specie payments. But as Mr. McCulloch has failed to pursue this operation to its inevitable result, the committee will pardon me for attempting the duty, though in doing so I may deepen the shades in the melancholy picture of our future which I have presented.

When the foreigners who bought our bonds on speculation perceive that by returning them they can convert them into gold and double their investment, they will assuredly avail themselves of the literally golden opportunity. Questions as to how they can reinvest the proceeds advantageously need not deter them. They know how limited our stock of specie is, how heavy is the balance of trade against us, and consequently that by selling their bonds in our markets they would compel us to suspend specie payments again. Nor are they strangers to the fact that during that suspension they would be able to repurchase their bonds for half the gold received for them. Thus the experiment of the Secretary would inevitably terminate in the impoverishment of the people and the disgrace of the country by a renewed and more protracted suspension of specie payments.

Mr. Chairman, neither the Secretary of the Treasury nor Congress know whether our currency is in excess of the amount required by legitimate and healthful trade, or if it be, how long it will remain so if undisturbed by legislation. Nor can we settle these points by an appeal to experience, for many of our conditions are novel. That would be a curious and instructive calculation which would show the country the precise demand for currency created by the operation of the Bureau of Internal Revenue, or by the enlargement of the Army and Navy and clerical force of the Government.

Under the discipline of Providence the southern people will, before many years glide away, consent to permit their fields to be tilled, their mines to be worked, and their cities to be rebuilt and expanded; and who can tell the amount of currency that will then be required by the four million enfranchised slaves and the millions of poor whites, who did not in the past, but are henceforth to earn wages and buy and sell commodities, or for handling the crops and mineral productions of the South? Since we last adjourned the iron horse has crossed Nebraska on one of the routes to the Pacific, and his snort has been heard in the neighborhood of Fort Riley on another; and during the last year three hundred thousand industrious people, who had been fed and clothed through unproductive childhood at the cost of other nations, came and cast their lot among us to till our fields, smelt our ores, work our metals, and manage our spindles and looms; and I cannot guess what amount of currency these energetic people and the westward-marching column of our civilization will require. But, sir, of one thing I am certain, and it is that had the Secretary of the Treasury not destroyed all sense of security in the future, the demand for currency to purchase, especially in the South, mineral and other lands and develop their productive power would have prevented the accumulation of the immense deposits which now lie paralyzed in bank or are loaned on call to speculators in the necessaries of life. We unsettled values and made or scattered fortunes by the rapid expansion of the currency; and the people implore us to avoid another violent change fraught with like consequences, and to stay the work of contraction till we shall have ascertained, at least proximately, the amount of currency required by healthy and legitimate trade.

Mr. Chairman, the Secretary of the Treasury is not a philosopher—

"A primrose by a river's brim
A yellow primrose is to him;"

And the thing that has been is, in his belief, the thing that shall be forever. Neither his experience as an "Ingeany" banker nor his official connection with the Government has disclosed to him the real relation of currency in detail or in volume to the business of a community. Throughout his report he assumes that the currency is redundant, and ascribes to its alleged redundancy consequences which are directly attributable to another cause, but remotely connected with the question of the amount of currency. I refer to the prevailing and traditional vice in our banking system, that of building credits upon credit, of banking on deposits, or of lending money by a bank to one man because it owes a like amount to another who has intrusted his funds to it for safe-keeping and convenience. To this vice in our banking system, which Mr. McCulloch has done much to aggravate by leaving stupendous balances of the public funds in favored banks, is to be ascribed nearly all the evils he mistakenly attributes to a "redundant legal-tender currency." If the corporations and private bankers of the country were prohibited from lending on call the deposits intrusted to them or from using them in discounting paper, doubling the volume of currency would not produce a material advance in the price of commodities in general. This vice in our banking system, this banking on deposits or lending that which the banks owe, and to calls for the payment of which they are constantly liable, aggravates from four hundred to one thousand fold every modification of our currency, whether it be by contraction or expansion.

Neither the price of gold nor of other commodities is regulated nor materially influenced by the amount of currency; nor is the difference between gold and our currency evidence that the latter is inflated. If the Secretary controverts these propositions, I will remind him that gold commanded a premium of 185 in 1864, and ask him to let us know how much he had contracted the currency before it went down to 25, as it did in June, 1865; and again, how much he expanded the currency to put the premium on gold up again to 50, at about which figure it stood so long before dropping to 29 and ascending again to its present price. During all these fluctuations the volume of currency was not essentially modified. What a commentary these facts are upon the theories of the Secretary and his costly but vaunted attempts "to keep the business of the country as steady as possible." On this point he says:

> "He has regarded a steady market as of more importance to the people of the country than the saving of a few million dollars in the way of interest."

And elsewhere, that—

> "The Secretary has also deemed it to be his duty to use such means within his control as were, in his judgment, best calculated to keep the business of the country as steady as possible, while conducted on the uncertain basis of an irredeemable currency. To accomplish this he has thought it necessary to hold a handsome reserve of coin in the Treasury."

But, sir, assuming that the volume of currency does not regulate prices, and that apart from the often fatal vice in our banking system to which I have alluded it has but little influence on them, I appeal from the judgment of Mr. McCulloch to that of the people, and ask whether, if the volume of currency regulated prices, it would not affect every species of property equally or nearly so?

If prices are regulated by the volume of currency, how is it that American wool is as cheap in the Philadelphia market now as it was before the war? How is it that corn is unusually low and wheat is commanding a higher price than ever before in the history of our country? How is it that during the last month one variety of cotton goods, those known as brown or unbleached goods, advanced twenty per cent., or two cents per yard, and another variety, bleached goods, declined twenty per cent., or from five to seven cents per yard? How is it that mess pork commands but about half last year's prices, while the decline in beef has been little more than nominal? And how is it that in 1865, with gold at 25, Lehigh coal commanded at the shipping point from five to six dollars per ton, and in 1866, with gold ranging from 32 to 40, the same qualities of coal at the same points will not bring three dollars to three dollars and a quarter per ton?

But I will not weary the committee with further illustrations of the absurdity of the Secretary's postulate. It is, however, proper that before leaving this point for the present I should admit that a violent and sudden contraction of the currency at a time when the loans of our banks are extended by lending their deposits, does work an inevitable and often ruinous reduction of prices. It is thus: under the influence of contraction depositors draw upon their reserve, and the banks to meet the demand call upon their debtors, and they to protect their credit must sell, no matter at what sacrifice, at such prices as they can get. I need not follow the movement to its consequences. A tight money market, by causing a few failures, has more than once begotten panic and wide-spread bankruptcy, and would now extinguish the revenues of the Government. Had the Secretary of the Treasury ascribed the fluctuations in business and the inordinate prices at which many of the necessaries of life are held to their real cause, our habit of banking on accumulated credits, and not pressed the purpose of contracting the currency, the country would not be depressed as it is. Threatened contraction has hung like the sword of Damocles over the heads of our producing classes.

Let me ask, what is currency and what is its function? Currency is that which a people have agreed to accept and use as money. It is the medium by which the small transactions of daily life are settled. Its sphere is that of personal use and retail trade. Except in the final settlements between banks and their customers, it is not commonly used in large transactions. We carry currency upon our persons to meet current demands. You find it in the till of the retail dealer and the hands of workmen, who, when currency is abundant, are paid in it, and not in orders on stores at which they are compelled to select articles from a small stock of inferior goods and pay high prices as they do when currency is scarce. It is possible that Mr. McCulloch does not know that the abundance of currency has redeemed our laboring people from the exhausting taxation inflicted upon them by the order system and payment in the depreciated paper of distant and unknown banks. Currency in its legitimate use has no wider sphere than I have indicated. Like all other blessings, it may be perverted, as it is when it accumulates as deposits in banks and is used as the basis of large loans to adventurous speculators. In the heavy operations of business currency finds no place. These are settled by checks, drafts, and bills of exchange. Before the war currency was scarce, and the deficiency was supplied by the promissory notes of individuals who, by endorsing the notes of those who bought from them or those of their factors or commission merchants, became debtors to the amount due them from others. It is said that when the war began the amount represented by the promissory notes of individuals was more than $2,000,000,000: but now the supply of currency is adequate, few men take such notes, and none propose to give them but the people of the South, who have no currency. The contraction of the currency insisted upon by Mr. McCulloch would revive the credit system, with its orders, for work people, and its periodical returns of wide-spread bankruptcy to the community at large.

I do not think the Secretary is entirely ignorant of the simple truths I have been enunciating. It would be pleasant to know that he is, for it is not agreeable to be constrained to doubt the motives of one to whom we have given our confidence. But in view of the communication made by Mr. Nasby, and the fact that the Secretary's theories, if carried into execution, will promote speculation, I cannot help thinking that he regards banking and stock operations as the interests to which all others should be subordinated. He recommends the withdrawal of the greenbacks that the national banks may supply the circulating medium of the country, and he wishes each national bank to be compelled to deposit in one of the Atlantic cities a sufficient amount of its capital to justify the redemption of its notes at that point. The Atlantic city to which he points is the great centre of banking and speculation, and compliance with these suggestions would aggravate the speculative power of New York by the proportion such deposits would bear to its general fund. His theories are in perfect accord with his practice, for I find that he is in the habit of furnishing the banks, and through them speculators, an average loan of about twenty-five million dollars. Thus by an official statement which lies before me it appears that the Government balances in the hands of the national banks was—

June 1, 1866	$26,335,725.59
July 1, 1866	34,124,171.21
August 1, 1866	36,931,415.22
September 1, 1866	32,590,274.58
October 1, 1866	30,976,979.85

I am, however, informed officially that there was during those months a liability to draft on these balances distributed through not less than three months amounting in all to $14,000,000 by coupons *in transitu* or in the hands of the holders; so that the banks could with safety lend on call during the whole period $25,000,000 to those engaged in speculating in food and increasing its price. Had $20,000,000 of the sum been applied to the absorption of seven-thirties or compound-interest notes speculation would have been less rife, our interest account would have been materially diminished, and a slight approximation have been made towards specie payments and the ultimate redemption of the public debt. Doubtless, Mr. McCulloch's desire "to keep the business of the country as steady as possible" alone prevented this happy consummation.

Sir, it is within our memory that the establishment of the sub-Treasury—the divorcement of the public Treasury from the banks and banking system of the country—overthrew the administration and party that inaugurated it; but it is also remembered that so beneficent were its operations that no succeeding administration of any party dared assail it. It had not been in operation a year till it had vindicated its wisdom in the estimation of every judicious business man. Nor would it probably ever have been interfered with in time of peace. The great convulsion which threatened to divide our country interrupted its action, which should forthwith be restored. It acted as a regulator, a natural regulator, of the trade of the country. When importations ran to excess and unduly increased the public revenues, it withdrew from circulation and locked up a portion of the currency, and by the stringency thus created admonished banks and business men to pause; and when, having given an early check to rash operations and diminished the current revenues of the country, it gently, as by a process of nature, restored vigor to the circulation by the fact that its payments were in excess of its receipts, as its receipts had just been in excess of its payments. As a safeguard for the public funds, if for no other reason, the Secretary should have recommended its full restoration, for during the entire period of its existence, as far as I know, the Government did not lose by any of its officers as much as it did recently by the failure of the Merchants' National Bank of Washington alone. It was a safe depository for the public money, as well as a healthful influence in the business operations of the country. Had the Secretary suggested that it would answer as well for a mixed currency as it did for the era of specie payments, and recommended its immediate reëstablishment he would have done much to give steadiness to the business of the country, diminish speculative prices, quicken production, and increase the revenue of the country. And I trust that Congress before it rises will pass a law prohibiting the deposit of any portion of the Government funds in any bank, or, in other words, divorce the Treasury from the banks by reorganizing the sub-Treasury.

It was, perhaps, too much to hope for such a recommendation from the Secretary. He enjoys the control he now exercises over the business of the country, and would not willingly surrender it. But for the maintenance of an average deposit of more than $30,000,000 could the National-Union-Johnson party have extorted from the banks —perhaps not directly as corporations, but from their stockholders and officers, to be accounted for in the item of incidental expenses—the large contributions which the newspapers told us certain banks were forced to make in aid of the recent effort of the President and the Secretary of the Treasury to subvert the popular will? But this was but an occasional incident, probably never to occur again; for I believe that the future can produce to our country no second Andrew Johnson, or that should it contain within its womb another like unto him he will be unable to find creatures to sacrifice their own convictions and the interests of the country for the poor privilege of unworthily filling high places in a great Government. That of which I speak is the influence these deposits, coupled with his exclusive control of the gold in the Treasury, averaging about one hundred million dollars, which he complacently calls a "handsome reserve of coin in the Treasury," give the Secretary over the business of the country.

Under the action of the sub-Treasury, as I have shown, a payment of money by the Government relieved a stringent money market; but how is it now? When the Secretary of the Treasury is sacrificing such immense amounts of interest in order to give steadiness to business, the Government deposits are loaned by the banks on notes of short date or on call; and if the current revenues of the Government be in excess of its current expenses, as they have been throughout his administration, its deposits accumulate, and swell the volume of such loans. The receipts of the Government thus aggravate the tendency to undue expansion; and what is the effect when it is required to use any considerable amount of its deposits? It is this: the Secretary notifies the banks that he is about to call for ten or twenty million dollars; and the banks, not knowing which of their debtors will be ready and who may be utterly unable to pay, notify not alone borrowers of the precise amount demanded by the Secretary, but holders of five, six, or ten times the amount. Thus that which should give relief to the market becomes an exaggerated cause of contraction, and the payment of $10,000,000 by the Government is made to interfere with business operations to the amount of $100,000,000. We have all observed this and know that instead of being a natural operation, the effects of which should be felt beneficially, each payment of any considerable sum of money by the Government, after a long line of deposits has accumulated, produces a perturbation through all commercial circles. The payment of but $15,000,000 in the early part of last month came near producing a national panic and damaged the credit of leading banks. This system gives the Secretary despotic control over the markets of the country, and his favorites may have ascertained practically, as did Voltaire, who was given to stock speculations, that "it is a good thing to have a friend at court" through whom they may learn when it is well to sell, because things have reached their highest price, as Government is about doing that which should establish confidence, but which, owing to the Secretary's efforts to insure steadiness to business, will produce consternation if not panic and a general decline in prices; and when it is well to buy, because it suits the convenience of the Government to make another large and long loan to the banks. Such a power over the business of the country should be vested in no man; and I challenge the world to point to any fact in the official career of the present Finance Minister of the country which would induce any judicious man to vest it in him. There certainly is nothing in the suggestions of the report which I am considering to indicate that he is a safe depository for so useless, so wide-spread, and so dangerous a power.

But, Mr. Chairman, I am admonished that I should hasten to a conclusion. I must, however, beg the committee to bear with me while I examine briefly another of Mr. McCulloch's suggestions. It is offered as a specific remedy, because it is said it will diminish the rate of interest on our loans and protect us against the direful contingency of the bonds bought on speculation at depreciated rates coming home to exhaust our specie within a month of the day on which we are, by the magical agencies suggested by Mr. McCulloch, to resume specie payments within two years. It is characterized by the candor and wisdom which pervade his other suggestions. To a shrewd man of mere practical business habits, one not skilled in the mysteries of "Ingeany bankin'," it might seem to be somewhat impracticable; and the country regards it with humiliation and disgust. It is this: that after having carried on the war without an appeal to foreign nations or capitalists and without their sympathy; after having by our patriotic sacrifices put our credit so high that the people of Europe have voluntarily come and carried away, with great profit to themselves, $350,000,000 of our bonds; that now, when peace is restored, and when we again possess the custom-houses, post offices, forts, and arsenals of the country, and when our taxes are not divided between our Treasury and that of a hostile confederacy, but all flow to our own, we shall issue "bonds payable in not over twenty years and bearing interest at the rate of not over five per cent., payable in England or Germany, to an amount sufficient to absorb the six per cent. bonds now held in Europe and to meet the demand there for actual and permanent investment."

If this scheme were practicable, I for one would spurn it. With their pirate ships on every sea, their ship-yards and factories busy in fabricating implements of war for our enemies, and in the face of their hatred, with self-reliance, of which posterity will be proud, we marched steadily on to conquest and final victory. And now, in the hour of our triumph, or in the calm season which should succeed so grand and successful an exhibition of power, with a continent abounding in raw material for the profitable employment of every art, trade, and mystery known to ingenious man beneath our feet; with India decimated by famine, Europe disturbed by wars and rumors of war, Ireland in incipient rebellion; and when we offer to the people of Europe established peace, political equality, public schools, a free church, and briefer hours of labor with better wages than those known to the artisans of any other country, this suggestion is as degrading as it is inopportune. Sir, nothing but some such folly as this official proclamation, as it would be regarded by the people of Europe, that our struggle exhausted us, and that with victory came premature decrepitude, can prevent us from compelling the nations of the world, by the tide of skilled workmèn that will flow from their shores to ours, to follow our example and give those who produce their wealth culture, leisure, and the consciousness of free manhood. In such an hour and in view of such a prospect I am sure that Congress will not degrade the country by asking the money-changers of Europe to lighten its burdens or help us bear them.

But the scheme is hopelessly impracticable. Mr. McCulloch may see advantages in it which others fail to detect. It would serve, I doubt not, by what he calls "the trifling commissions to the agents through whom the exchanges might be made," to found a great American banking-house in London with continental branches, and might bless the country with the hope of large gratuities from some future George Peabody whom the Secretary would designate as the agent for making transfers and paying interest; but it would not accomplish the purpose its author suggests. With such knowledge of human nature as we possess let us consider the proposition. Those who hold our bonds bought them either as an investment or on speculation, and the interest upon them ranges from six to seven and three-tenths per cent. Is it probable that those who bought them as an investment will change them before maturity for bonds bearing but five or four and a half per cent.? Or will those who bought them as a matter of speculation, in view of the Secretary's assurance that in less than two years we will resume specie payments and enable them to convert them into gold at par, hasten to make such a conversion? When the leopard shall change his spots, the vulture protect the dove, and hungry mice abstain from eating unguarded crackers and cheese, I will be prepared to regard the Secretary's proposition as practicable.

Nor need we grieve that it is not practicable. Our destiny is written. Unwise legislation or such reckless maladministration as now prevails may retard it, but it will be achieved. It is written in the sublime doctrine of human equality, which gives vitality and stability to our institutions, and more perceptibly though not more enduringly in the geographical position, the continental proportions, and the unequaled resources of our country. Bounded by both oceans, with a larger area than all the nations of Europe, including Great Britain, which lie between the same distant parallels of latitude that mark our limits, and embracing mineral, agricultural, manufacturing, and commercial resources greater than they combined possess, the United States must be the foremost, richest, and most powerful nation of the world. However blind our Finance Minister may be to this fact, others perceive it, and our affairs will yet be administered in accordance with the sublime assertion of Gortschakoff, who, in an utterance to which I have already referred, when speaking of Russia and our country, said: "God has given to the two countries such conditions of existence that their grand internal life is enough for them."

Yes, the capitalists of Europe will yet be eager to lend us money as cheaply as they now loan it to England; but it will be when, by the conversion of our now profitless raw material into fabrics, by the skill and industry of our now unemployed citizens and the millions of industrious people who are coming to us from abroad, we manufacture more than we consume, and by rivalling England, France and other continental nations in tropical markets, and those of other non-manufacturing regions, shall have turned the balance of trade in our favor. Then Americans will be able to compete with foreigners in bidding for our loans; and in exchange for cotton, tobacco, and other staples, our bonds will be returned to us instead of woolen goods and various other textile and metallic fabrics, which we now receive but ought to manufacture for ourselves. But foreign capitalists will not take bonds from us at four and a half or five per cent. in exchange for those which pay six per cent., while the balance of trade is against us to the amount of $100,000,000 per annum, and with compound-interest and seven-thirty notes afloat to the amount of nearly $1,000,000,000, we with more than Gascon vanity promise the almost immediate return to specie payments.

THE SOUTH—ITS RESOURCES AND WANTS.

ADDRESS DELIVERED AT NEW ORLEANS,

MAY 11TH, 1867—AS REPORTED IN THE NEW ORLEANS REPUBLICAN.

Fellow-Citizens of Louisiana: In response to the invitation of your Governor and the Mayor of this beautiful city, I am here to counsel with you as to the best interests of our country. Let me, however, first congratulate you upon your enfranchisement, and thank the loyal men among you, without regard to race or color, who during the late struggle braved the dangers of battle in defence of the old flag, or quietly remained true to it amid the dangers which surrounded you, for the part you took in my enfranchisement. Having addressed a large and enthusiastic audience in Memphis on Tuesday night, and, standing in the midst of this brilliant scene in the city of New Orleans, I am at last able to proclaim that I am a free man in my native land, and may traverse its wide extent, carrying with me my conscience and convictions without fear of personal violence. This was impossible before the war. The institutions of the South were not cosmopolitan. Her *peculiar* system of labor not only controlled but contracted her civilization.

Disregarding the practice and precepts of the founders of our Government, and ignoring the admonitions of experience, the South turned a deaf ear to reason, refused to listen to remonstrance, and finally punished dissent from her judgment as a crime deserving outlawry and death. Attempting in a progressive age, and in a land of vast and varied resources, peopled by a generation more enterprising than any that had preceded it, to maintain a system which was "peculiar," and incapable of modification, save by absolute overthrow, she arrayed against her all the forces of civilization. No poet ever sang the charms of slavery. No limner ever embodied its beauties on canvas. No orator ever descanted upon its blessings; and though dumb dogs that could not bark proclaimed from many a pulpit the duty of servants to obey their masters as the sum and substance of the gospel, the voice of Christianity bade conscientious men do unto others as they would have others do unto them—be eyes to the blind and feet to the lame—and the cries of the wronged against those who withheld from the laborer his hire, ascended incessantly to the ears of the Lord of Sabaoth.

To this attempt on the part of the people of the South to isolate themselves, to exclude from their broad and fertile territory the advancing civilization of the age, may be ascribed the terrible war through which we have just passed. It made them intensely sectional, while the steady development of the North was demonstrating to its more rapidly increasing millions the beneficence of nationality. It created a separate and antagonistic system of civilization. The North welcomed all classes of emigrants from all lands. She made herself familiar with the inventions and discoveries of the day, and applied them to purposes of utility. She challenged the freest discussion of all topics and all systems. She provided liberally for the education of all her people, including the unhappy few to whom, in deference to Southern demands, she denied the full rights of citizenship. But the South, wrapt in its delusion, repulsed emigration—rejected all science and literature that controverted the divinity of slavery, and the justice and economy of unrequited toil. She denied to her laborers education, and consequently could not avail herself of, and was indifferent to the scientific and mechanical progress of the age. Thus, while the breach between the two sections was widening, the disparity in power between them was constantly increasing. Contrast, my friends, the development of the two sections; behold the great cities of the North. New York, with its environs, which are really, though not municipally, part of it, already exceeds Paris in wealth, splendor, trade, and population. London and Paris are the only trans-atlantic cities which exceed Philadelphia in these respects. Boston, Cincinnati, Chicago, and other cities, each exceed New Orleans in population. Yet New Orleans, past which the waters of sixty thousand miles of rivers flow, is the greatest city of the South.

Let me illustrate this point familiarly. The railroads connecting New York with Philadelphia, and Memphis with Grenada, Mississippi, differ in length less than ten miles. They are each a link in a great thoroughfare North and South. Over the former eight passenger trains pass daily each way; each train is made up of several cars. Over the latter one train of two cars passes daily. The fare from New York to Philadelphia is $3; but from Memphis to Grenada it is $8. The time required to make the journey from New York to Philadelphia is less than four hours, while it takes six and a half hours to pass between Memphis and Grenada. The land along the route, in New Jersey and Pennsylvania, for agricultural purposes, is worth from $250 to $400 per acre; that along the other can be bought from $3 to $20!

These contrasts are not accidental or arbitrary. They illustrate great principles—sleepless laws of social life.

When the sages of '76 proclaimed that all men are born equal, and invested by nature with the right to life, liberty, and the pursuit of happiness, they uttered the law that was to fashion the institutions of America, and shape the civilization of her people. They were ever true to that law. They controlled the States at the time they framed the Constitution of the United States; and then every free man, without regard to color, was a voter in every State, except South Carolina; and while the Executive Government remained in their hands, and their personal influence controlled the legislation of the country, the free colored man was not denied the right of suffrage under any Territorial Government. Though South Carolina had steadily demanded his exclusion from 1778, in the convention for framing articles of Confederation, it was not until 1812 that she succeeded in inserting the word *white* in a law establishing a Territorial Government. That word appears for the first time in the law establishing the Territory of Missouri, which was enacted in that year.

The little monosyllable white, embodied in that law, was the germ of the war through which we have just passed. It involved an attempt to stay the course of American civilization—it was in conflict with its essential law—the great truth to which I have alluded, and involved strife between the spirit of liberty and the impulse of the masses on one hand, and the grasping selfishness of an oligarchy and the wrongs of slavery on the other. From that time to this our country has not been free from agitation; and while the institutions of the North have been more and more republicanized by the spirit of democracy, the written law of the land, yielding to the reactionary spirit which won its first triumph in the Missouri contest, has been controlled by the spirit of slavery, and been marked by a total disregard of the vital principle of our Government. Our Government rests on two great sentiments—personal liberty and territorial unity; and any law which restrained personal liberty, or engendered or fostered sectional interest, was a necessary cause of discord and strife. When, therefore, yielding to Southern persuasion or dictation, the North consented to deprive the free colored man of suffrage in the Territories; and when, under the same influence, State after State, throughout the free North, made color a test of citizenship, until out of New England, citizens of African descent were everywhere disfranchised, they who made these concessions were not, as they be lieved, cementing the Union, but making war inevitable Nations are not the creatures of chance. God's providence embraces the American continent. His judgment is its final law. And these abandonments of the principles upon which our Government was based—which had been reverently accepted by our forefathers as in harmony with His will—did not pass without His notice. Has He not repealed all these reactionary statutes, and by His breath wiped out these modern improvements of State constitutions? From the firing on Sumter to the surrender of the armies of Lee and Johnston, He was teaching us, by the terrible baptism of battle and blood, how infinite is His power and justice, and how easily He can make the folly and madness of man to praise Him. Had the South been national and truly democratic as the North, and had her legislation been progressive, slavery would have gradually disappeared, and the colored population of the country have been absorbed into its citizenship without a crisis, and almost without special notice. But that was not to be. By an inscrutable law, all great blessings come to us through suffering. Blood has been the price of freedom to every nation. For it is the same with nations in this respect as with individuals. Who can tell the agony that is requited when the mother first beholds a smile play over the face of her sleeping infant? It is to the garden and the cross that we go, in sorrow and humility, for our highest hopes and most enduring promises, and amid the tumult and tortures of the battle-field, the horrors of the wreck upon the maddened ocean, or the wearying sufferings of the feverish bed, we pass from the cares of life to the beatitude of eternity. And, as Americans, we may look back on years of war, we may count the dead of the contending armies at nearly one million, and behold the fairest and most fertile regions of our smiling country, your own lovely South, scarred and desolated by war, and rejoice that the agony which was to purchase our country's great blessing is over. Henceforth it shall be the boast of every American that though his country embraces all climates, from the summer breezes that ever linger over your broad Gulf to the wintry winds that howl the requiem of gallant navies as they sweep over the mighty lakes of the North, its atmosphere is so pure that no slave can breathe it and remain in bondage. [Immense applause.]

Let me not be misunderstood: I charge this war not upon the South alone. It is, perhaps, more largely due to the unprincipled men in the North, who should have met the issue at the threshold, and settled the question while it was susceptible of legislative control,' than to the men of the South, who, prompted by the short-sighted demands of present interest, insisted upon concessions which sagacious men of principle would not have accorded. Let me illustrate: No statesman had denied that slavery in the Territories was the subject of Congressional legislation until John C. Calhoun introduced into the Senate, on the 19th of February, 1847, three resolutions, embodying mere abstract propositions, the last of which was as follows:

> "That the enactment of any law which should, directly or by its effects, deprive the citizens of any State of this Union from emigrating with their property into any of the Territories of the United States, will make such discrimination, and would, therefore, be a violation of the Constitution and the rights of the States from which such citizens emigrate, and in derogation of that perfect equality which belongs to them as members of this Union, and would tend directly to subvert the Union itself."

The object of these resolutions was to extend slavery over the almost boundless territory then belonging to the United States. So repugnant was the proposition to the members of the Senate, largely Democratic, and with no Republican member in it, that Mr. Calhoun did not dare press his resolutions to a vote.

In May, 1848, the Democratic party met in convention

at Baltimore, and Mr. Yancey, Calhoun's great disciple, submitted the following:

> "*Resolved*, That the doctrine of non-interference with the rights of property of any portion of this Confederation, be it in the States or Territories, by any other than the parties introduced in them, is the true Republican doctrine recognized by this body."

There were 282 members in that convention. The South was fully represented. But so novel and dangerous was this doctrine then considered that every delegate from the North and most of those from the South united in demanding a direct vote upon the question, that they might send to the people of the country an expression of their abhorrence of the new and dangerous dogma. But about one in every eight delegates was then prepared to sustain it, the vote upon it being 36 for and 246 against. But behold the sequel: In less than twelve years the unprincipled men who governed the Democratic party brought on the fierce struggles in Kansas, by accepting the doctrine they had thus promptly spurned, and persuading the Southern people that the North had abandoned the faith of the Fathers, and was in reckless disregard of the restraints of the Constitution robbing them of their rights. Impelled by ambition, and seeking wealth through the intrigues of a corrupt political era, they encouraged you to prepare for war. They assured you that if you would strike for your supposed rights they would stand by you on the battle-field, as they had done in caucuses, conventions, and on the floor of Congress.

I have seen a copy of a letter from one of them who had once filled the Presidential chair, saying to you, through one of your leaders, that if you seceded there would be no war; or that if there were it would be co-extensive with the country, and blood would flow in every village, town, and city of the North.

How little Franklin Pierce knew the real spirit of the people among whom he lived! How ignorant was he of the fact that the world is under moral government! Were his pledges kept? In what city of the North did blood flow? Between the citizens of which Northern States was there armed collision; and from which of the Northern States did men swarm to swell the ranks of the Confederate armies? As the echo of the guns fired upon the flag over Sumter reverberated through the glens and valleys of the

North and swept over the broad prairies of the distant Northwest, these same false and unprincipled friends of the South, in obedience to the demands of popular sentiment, flung to the breeze, at their dwellings and places of business, the resplendent flag of the Union; and, with Fernando Wood at their head, made themselves prominent in the work of recruiting and organizing troops for your subjugation. How did they aid you? The whole North gave you two soldiers whose names are known—Gustavus W. Smith and Mansfield Lovell! Can any of you name a third? [Shouts of "no, no."] I'll tell you what they did give you, though. They gave you what the little girl, who was asked to contribute the value of the sugar she used to the missionary cause, gave. She replied, "No, grandpa, I don't think I can do that; but I'll tell you what I will do. I'll give the cause my prayers." [Laughter.] They gave your cause their prayers, and, as if fearing they might prove effective, hastened to meet their neighbors and swear they had done no such thing! [Immense cheering.] A hopeless minority in Congress throughout the war, unable to influence, much less to control a single act of legislation, they made speeches for distribution through the South, as if to encourage you in your hopeless struggle, so that when it ended you should be utterly exhausted. In so far, history will hold the North—especially the Democratic party of the North—responsible for the war.

Still, the million of graves, in which sleep the best and bravest of both sections, are chargeable to the South. It withdrew the questions involved from the forum of diplomacy and legislation, and submitted them to war's last dread arbitrament. To prepare the way for this, its controlling spirits had kept the mass of the people in profound and degrading ignorance. Each State having received large grants of land for educational purposes, none of them had provided schools for the people. The laws of each State prohibited, by penal statutes, the education of the slave population. This was inevitable. Intelligence and culture are incompatible with slavery; the penalty God attaches to the crime of holding a brother in bondage is that he who is so held shall be of little value to him who holds him; and sluggish indolence is, like ignorance, the inevitable law of slavery. The absence of schools, the want of diversified fields of employment, degraded the non-slaveholding whites of the South, and the most enterprising of them left the land of their birth to find happier homes. Thus the South, whose great need was population to develop her vast and varied resources, and build up cities, towns, and villages along her great lines of transit, and thus increase the value of her lands and diminish the cost of travel and transportation, was constantly expelling her own children. Nor did she welcome emigration. The German, the Irishman, the Englishman, and the Scotchman quit the scenes of their childhood and the graves of their fathers in pursuit of liberty and a higher degree of physical comfort than is accorded the laboring man in those lands. In their native homes they learn that in the North there is political equality for all, and that every fair day's work done by man, woman, or child, is assured by the law of the land a fair day's wages; and that westward, to the last frontier, there is no village, however small, in which the free school is not open to every child. Thus attracted, they have come to the North and West by millions. The immigration last year numbered more than 300,000, and added a sum greater than the total of our national debt to the wealth of the people whose numbers they swelled. I found this morning that I had with me by accident, a copy of an address made to my neighbors, October 3d, 1856, from which, if it be only to show you that I teach no new doctrine, I beg leave to submit a brief extract:

"I have another set of illustrations to give you, and I now speak not of slaves, but of the free white men of the South. Men love their homes; the place of their birth; the institutions under which they pass happy childhood, prosperous youth, and enter into a successful career of manhood. There are thirteen millions of Northen men from whom emigrants might go, while there are but six millions of free people in the South, yet the census of 1850 found 609,371 persons who were born in the slave States living in the free States, while only 206,638 persons born in the free States were living in the slave States. Yes, my fellow-citizens, in 1850 there were 609,371 men and women of Southern birth living in the Northern States; they had fled from the blessings of labor owned by capital. But you may say, 'they had come to the cities to engage in commerce; had come to pursue the arts in Philadelphia, New York, Boston; had come to find employment in all the various pursuits of our great cities.' Let us see, therefore, how many people born in the planting States had emigrated into two States of the North—Indiana and Illinois—in which there are no great cities; in which you may say there are no universities; in which the arts have scarcely been developed; in which commerce has scarcely a footing; which are two of the young grazing and grain-growing

States of the North.* In 1850 there were in those two States 47,026 who had emigrated from North Carolina, 8,231 from South Carolina, 2102 from Georgia, 45,037 from Tennessee, 1730 from Alabama, 777 from Mississippi, 701 from Louisiana, 107 from Texas, 44 from Florida; making the total of those who had left these nine planting States to go to those two agricultural and grazing States, 105,755."

Do you reproach me and others of the North that we did not in those days come and lay these arguments before you? Ah, my friends, you forget the terrible despotism you had established over yourselves. The fact that I entertained the opinions I am expressing made the climate south of the Potomac and Ohio so insalubrious for me that I did not dare breathe it for an hour. When you raised the cry of abolitionist against a Northern man, beings, with hearts as unrelenting as the blood-hound, pursued him to his death. Not only did you prohibit men who would have gladly sat with you at your hearthside and taken sweet counsel with you, from entering your beautiful region, but, through the arts of your politicians and the demagoguery of the Democratic leaders of the North, you hunted them to their very homes. While delivering the very address from which I have read to you, a shower of eggs was hurled at me by pro-slavery Democrats; and my only consolation was to thank God that the American Eagle laid fresh eggs at that season of the year. [Great laughter and applause.] Nor was this conduct ascribable to individuals only. The State of South Carolina seized from the deck of their vessels colored citizens of other States who chanced to enter the ports of that State, and incarcerating them as felons, made them chargeable with costs and jail fees, and in default of the payment of these, sold them and their posterity as slaves. And when, what Southern men called the Sovereign State of Massachusetts, sent one of her ablest and most venerable lawyers to raise the question of law arising out of this conduct, before a South Carolina court, the people of Charleston—not the roughs, but those who could do such an act with highest courtesy—the very pinks of the chivalry of that city, gave that distinguished man and the accomplished daughter that accompanied him the option of departure from the city in twenty-four hours or tar and feathers and jolly rides on rails. Again, it is known to

* It must be remembered that these remarks were made in 1856, and are wholly inapplicable to those progressive States now.

all the North, though perhaps you may not be aware of the fact, that the State of Georgia, by solemn act of her Legislature approved by the Governor, and to be found among her printed laws—offered a reward of five or twenty thousand dollars, I forget which, for the body, dead or alive, of a citizen of Massachusetts, who had never entered that State, or been so far South as the capital of his country; but who had had the temerity to publish, through the columns of his own paper, his disbelief in the divinity of slavery, and an assertion of the right of every woman to the possession of the body of every living child that had cost her the pangs of maternity. You treated difference of opinion as the most heinous of crimes; and from each and all of the Southern States, native citizens, and some of them men of just distinction, were driven by threats of popular violence. Such was the case with the Grimkes, of South Carolina; Underwood, of Virginia; and Helper and Professor Hedrick, of North Carolina. Why did we not come and reason with you? Do you forget that you would not receive nor permit your neighbors to receive, through the post-office, any papers or periodical that did not pander to your prejudices? The receipt through the post-office of the *Liberator*, the *Anti-Slavery Standard*, the *Independent*, the New York *Tribune*, or any leading Republican paper, by one of your neighbors, branded him as an Abolitionist, and rendered his life insecure among you. The North would gladly have discussed the question. It opened its public halls to your orators, and its people swarmed to hear them. It received your papers, and its conscientious people were amazed at the infatuation which was driving the two sections headlong into war. But I come not to bandy crimination or recrimination with you. There is "ample room and verge enough" for that between you and the leaders of the Democracy of the North. But for myself and the Republican party, I say: shake not your gory locks at us, for you cannot say we did it. You spurned our counsels; and though we would gladly have embraced you as brothers, you refused to listen to our fraternal prayers.

Happily, these things belong to the past. Having endured the agony of four years of war, conducted with unequalled valor, and on a scale of unequalled magnitude, we rise as a new nation, to perfect the continental temple of freedom and equality, the foundations of which were so wisely laid by our forefathers. From those foundations we have removed the only two faulty stones—those on which were inscribed the fatal words, *Compromise* and *Slavery*. In all this broad land no man now owns his brother man. [Sensation.] You, men of color—you citizens of Louisiana, who wear the livery of Afric's burnished sun—give thanks unto God that he has turned and overturned, until the humblest of you stands erect in the majesty of free manhood, the equal of your fellow man before the laws of your country, as you are before the beneficent Father of all.

He guided the pen of Abraham Lincoln while writing the proclamation of emancipation. [Great enthusiasm and applause.] And they who enacted the civil rights bill and the military bill, to secure the enforcement of its provisions, went reverently to Him for counsel, and recognized His sovereign presence as in their midst. The charter of your freedom is from Him. Freedom is His last, best blessing to you. Maintain it by sleepless vigilance, and by any requisite sacrifice; for in surrendering it you will be alike recreant to man and God. See to it, that a common school system, broad enough as is that of the North, to embrace every child born in the Commonwealth, or brought into it by emigration, is established by the constitution soon to be framed for your State. See to it, that the press is free; and be tolerant of opinion, for by the collision of opinion is the truth elicited. Welcome among you the people of every clime and nation; and remember that the prosperity of the State is but the aggregate prosperity of the individual citizens thereof. Will you not do this? [We will, yes, yes.] I know you will. And as this assurance thrills me, I behold a vision grander than that of Columbus; for I know that behind the islands that interrupted his Western voyage to the Indies lies a broad continent, sweeping from the rock-bound coast of the storm-lashed Atlantic to the golden shores of the sleeping Pacific. [Applause.] And that from the Rio Grande to the perpetual snows of Mount Hood, it is inhabited by one people, who, though differing in origin, are homogeneous in language, thought and sentiment; and who, though the citizens of many States, each having its own constitution, recognize as supreme one government, and that the freest yet devised by man. [Applause.] I cannot better illustrate the value of this unity than by pointing to the future of your own beautiful city. It is the entrepôt for the commerce of the Gulf, the trade of which proceeds under our bright flag. The river that winds around you carries to the sea the waters of sixty thousand miles of river course. The valley it drains will sustain a population of five hundred millions of people. They will be free, intelligent, enterprising, and given to commerce; and your city will be the centre of their great commercial exchanges. [Applause.] But as I look through the vista of a brief future, the glories of the great cities of antiquity fade away, and Florence, Venice and Genoa, recur to me as but so many distant villages. Not Paris or London will be your equal; for behind each of them lies a territory less in extent and resources than any one of a score of American States; while behind New Orleans lie the resources—agricultural, mineral and manufacturing—of a territory broader and richer than all Europe, and a people destined at no distant day to be more numerous than the people of Europe. And when those days shall come, loyal men of Louisiana, the name of Abraham Lincoln will be uttered with reverence by every lip, and all men will give thanks to God that He so ordered His providence as to establish political equality throughout the enduring Union of American States. [Tremendous applause followed this eloquent reference to the man whom all in the audience delight to hear spoken of.] My colored friends, permit me to thank you for the enthusiasm with which you greeted my advent among you. If at any time I have suffered for you, you have abundantly rewarded me by this exhibition of your generous appreciation. Permit me now to address a few remarks more especially to those who have not known as you, the woes of slavery or the consequences of disfranchisement under popular government. My white fellow-citizens, let me say to you that you are charged with a duty grander than is often confided to a generation of men. You are to unite with those whom through life you have been taught to despise as an inferior race, in organizing a party in Louisiana in harmony with the great Republican party of the North. That party is based on, vivified and cemented by two sentiments, love for the Union, and devotion to human freedom. Its whole creed may be summed up in the phrase, perfect and indestructible unity of the States, with the perpetual maintenance of the largest liberty of the individual citizen, consistent with the general welfare. If you fail to give full scope and power to either of these sentiments, you will in so far fall short of the due performance of your mission. Justice is blind, and knows no color; and justice is the law of the Republican party. In enfranchising our fellow citizens of African descent we must accept them as entitled to all the rights, privileges, and amenities of citizenship. We must not give a mere intellectual assent to the propositions on which we base our action; but accept them as animating and controlling sentiments. Rights not guaranteed by daily practice are not secured. Established habit is the only sure safeguard of personal liberty in our land. The Constitution of the United States has always guaranteed to every citizen the rights, privileges, and immunities of citizenship to the citizens of each State in the several States; but when, before this war, was I, or men who hold opinions in common with me, safe in attempting to exercise that constitutional right in any slave State? As I have shown you, dominant sentiment may override constitutional and legal provisions. Rest not, therefore, your experiment upon the embodiment in constitution or law of abstract principles; but see to it that they are embodied practically in the organization of primary caucus and convention, and ultimate organization of parish, city, and State. If you rise to the prompt accomplishment of this great work the day of strife will have passed, and the American sword may be beaten into a ploughshare. A homogeneous people, *bound together by the immense diversity of their varied interests,* by the most unrestrained personal intercourse and the freest interchange of thought through a free press, will find no issues that legislation or diplomacy may not settle. And a nation that, in its infancy, put into the field, and kept there for four years, during which the bloodiest and best-contested battles of history were fought, armies each numbering more than a million of men, need fear no foreign war. [Applause.] The prestige of this war is at the back of our European diplomacy, and if we listen to the voice of reason in our demands, American questions will be matters of easy and speedy solution by the courts of Europe. Let us, then, not grieve over the past, but bating no jot of heart or hope move onward in our great work, and the struggling millions of Europe will find encouragement in our labors, and innumerable posterity will rise to revere our country's flag, and call those who fell martyrs in its maintenance, and those who through the civil strife completed their work, blessed among men. [Long and continued applause.]

ADDRESS AT MONTGOMERY, ALABAMA.

MAY, 16TH, 1867, AS REPORTED IN THE MONTGOMERY SENTINEL.

I HAVE not come into your State, fellow-citizens of Alabama, for the purpose of fomenting discord between classes or races, or States or sections, but in the hope that possibly by some poor service I may heal the wounds of my bleeding country, and promote the welfare of all her citizens. We have gone through a war unparalleled in history by the breadth of its theatre, the number and valor of its armies, and the results of which in the long future of our country are destined to be more beneficent than those of any other war. While we rejoice that it is over, and deplore the fact that it could not have been averted, we have the satisfaction of knowing that the sufferings attendant upon it mark the birth of a new and grander nation than the world has yet seen. I know not why it is, nor can philosophers divine, that Providence has decreed that all our great blessings shall be purchased by suffering. As I remarked the other evening in New Orleans, a mother only can tell the pains and agonizing doubts that are requited by the first smiles which play over the face of her sleeping infant. It is through the storm of battle, the horrors of shipwreck upon the tempest-tossed ocean, or the weary pains of protracted sickness, that we pass from the woes of life to the bliss of immortality; and we go to the garden, the agony and the cross, for our highest and most enduring hopes. Let us, therefore, hope that in this war we have gone through the throes of the birth of a new and nobler nation.

I have travelled from my distant home as far South as New Orleans, and thence hither, and from the time that I passed the Ohio I have been constantly and painfully impressed with the difference between the country and the condition of the people South of that river and the Potomac, and those to the North of them. The results are apparent. But the causes of the contrast lie deeper than you think. You ascribe them to the war, but they existed before the war began. Nature has been more profusely lavish of her gifts to you throughout the whole broad South than to us. You have natural wealth in infinite abundance and variety; but much of our land is sterile, and throughout the North man has to toil for every dollar he gets. Our labor is more diversified and is gentler than that of your mere laborers in the field; and in spite of your greater natural wealth our people are richer than yours, are better educated, and enjoy more of the conveniences, comforts, and luxuries of life than have ever been accessible to the people of the South.

Alabama has more natural wealth than all the New England States together. Alabama abounds in iron, while New England is without any, save a little bed of ore on the borders of Connecticut and Massachusetts, so small that it would scarcely be noticed amid the broad veins of heaven-enriched Alabama. She has no coal, while coal and limestone in immense deposits lie in close proximity to your beds of iron ore. New England can grow but little wheat, corn or rye. So thin and sterile is the soil of Massachusetts in many places that her people sow rye, not for the grain but the straw, to manufacture into hats and other articles; and so wide apart do the stalks grow, that at the proper season children find employment in plucking them stalk by stalk, and laying them down perfectly straight, that those who are to work them into fabrics may have them at their greatest length. In my own dear Pennsylvania, it will be late in August before the wheat is ripe, but yours in favored parts of the State is now ready for the sickle.

But ample and diversified as are the agricultural resources of Alabama, she has deemed it wise to devote herself to one single crop, (cotton,) and depend on other States for corn, hay, and other products of the soil. This was the great error of her people; for that State is richest, most prosperous, and independent that can supply all its wants within its own borders, and by the diversity of its productions provide remunerative employment for all its people. You should do this in Alabama. Every vegetable grown in the North can be successfully produced upon some of the beautiful hillsides of your extensive State. Do you doubt this, and say, as one of your citizens said to me, that you cannot raise root plants because of their tendency to run to woody fibre? I tell you that this is because your culture is artless, and because you continuously raise crops that exhaust the soil and make no return to it in manures containing the elements you abstract.

Invoke the aid of experience and science, and give to your land sufficient and appropriate food before you deny to a State so broad and varied in its topography and climate any measure of productive power. But to return to the contrast between your State and New England. She has no copper, lead, or gold, while nature has given them all to Alabama with lavish hand. I have been surprised in the last hour by discovering, through the kindness of your Governor, your capacity to supply the country with sulphur. Many of you probably do not know, indeed, I apprehend that few of the best informed of you know, how primary an element of our life this is. A philosophic statesman has said that the best test of the advance of a people in civilization was to be found in the quantity of crude brimstone consumed *per capita* by its people. It enters into our chemicals, our cloths of all descriptions, and almost every department of science and the mechanic arts; and if you but develop your resources in that behalf, you will bring within your limits millions of dollars which we now send abroad every year for its purchase.

But who knows what the resources of Alabama are? They have not been tested by experience or explored by science. When interrogated as to them by strangers, you tell them that you have the everglades or piney woods, the broad, rich cotton belt, the wheat growing region to the north of us, and north of it again, but still within your limits, pasture and cattle lands in the hill country. Inadequate as this statement of your resources is, when you shall be able to proclaim it in connection with the fact that you have established a generous system of free schools, and secured by law fair wages for labor, millions of toiling men will come to dwell among you and alleviate the burdens that now oppress you.

But how do you use these advantages? You have failed to avail yourselves of them, or to permit others to do so. Believe me, citizens of Alabama, when I say that I have not come to triumph in your depression, and do not wish to wound your sensibilities; but have come as a brother to reason with his brethren upon subjects in which they have an equal interest. The whole country is ours. It is yours and mine, and will belong to our posterity. Go with me to my cold and distant home, and you will not only find the stars that render that flag above you so resplendent as the symbol of your country's power, but gazing above the flag, in the darkness of the night, you will discover that the stars with which you are familiar here will look down upon you there and tell you that you are still at home.

It is, therefore, in the interest of our country that I speak, when I ask you how you use the advantages with which nature has so bounteoulsy provided you? and tell you that you have impoverished yourselves by treating them with contempt.

We turn our coal and iron to most profitable account. You permit yours to slumber in their native earth. Availing ourselves of their power, one man with us does the work of a hundred with you. One little girl, tending a machine in a factory, will spin or weave more cotton in a day than one of your women will in a year by the ancient method of the wheel and the hand-loom still in use among you. You have not deemed your mineral wealth worthy of consideration. In your devotion to your peculiar system of labor you have forgotten that iron and coal are the most potent agents of modern civilization. Mere muscular power has become a thing of secondary consideration. Iron is the muscles of modern civilization, and coal, ignited coal—fire—is the nervous force that animates it.

What is it that drags the long train of heavily-freighted cars, hour after hour, and day after day, at a speed greater than that of the fleetest horse? Is it not iron fashioned into a locomotive? It was these rejected elements of your greatness that expanded my native city, a mere village in my childhood, into a city of 700,000 prosperous inhabitants. In some of our workshops from 1500 to 2000 hands find employment, none of whom do heavy, muscular labor. We throw that species of labor on iron and coal. A little girl or woman watches a machine simply to see that no loose thread mars the smoothness of the fabric, and so earns good wages. Thus we provide for the widows and orphan daughters of our soldiers. In the heavier workshops massive blooms are converted into finest plate or bar iron by the trip-hammer or rolling-mill, which steam operates, and men or boys do but guide. Few of you have ever seen a trip-hammer at work. In its full force it will flatten at a single blow a rounded mass of heated iron; but its power may be so controlled that it will crack and yet not break an egg.

We strive to develop and convert to immediate profit our coal and iron beds by connecting our city and great thoroughfare railroads with roads from every pit's mouth, and have thus tempted from England, Scotland, Wales, and the iron districts of Belgium and Germany, the most skilful of their miners and workmen in metals.

Will you notice how this has enriched others than the parties directly concerned? Lands within the corporate limits of Philadelphia, which twenty years ago were under the plow are now selling as town lots, at from seven thousand to twenty thousand dollars per acre, and others at from sixty thousand to a hundred thousand dollars per acre, and are covered by palatial residences or stores, crowded with stocks of goods gathered from every quarter of the globe.

While we thus add to our wealth we cheapen the conveniences and comforts of life. Let me illustrate this by some facts drawn from other States. The railroads from New York to Philadelphia, and from Memphis to Grenada, Miss., are both links in great lines running from North to South. They differ in length but a few miles, being one precisely, and the other nearly a hundred miles. Over that between Philadelphia and New York eight trains pass each way daily; over the other but one. From Memphis to Grenada the time is six hours and a half; between the other points it is less than four hours. From Philadelphia to New York the fare is three dollars, and we complain of it as extortionate; but on the other road it is eight dollars. The traveller in either of the Nothern cities, anxious to reach the other, need not wait over three hours at any time. At Memphis or Grenada he may be compelled to wait nearly twenty-four hours. In view of these facts may I not ask whether I do wrong in suggesting that there is something in our experience worthy of your study and adoption?*

* The Philadelphia citizen of 1870 travels five miles for 6¼ cents over the safest and smoothest roads of our surprising modern civilization. Of these magnificent city thoroughfares there are one hundred and seventy-five miles in

In Philadelphia, almost every temperate and industrious laboring man is the owner of the house in which his family dwells. He may still owe part of the purchase money, and if so, he has an additional incentive to industry and economy. Young people who do not own, rent, each family a separate tenement, and he is regarded as a bad citizen who builds a working man's home and does not provide it with a bathroom, into which hot and cold water are introduced. This is deemed essential to cleanliness and health. In view of the assemblage by which I am surrounded, can I give offence by remarking that there is a vast difference between the comforts enjoyed by your laboring people and ours?

My native State—indeed, I may say, the whole North, from Maine to Kansas—is divided into districts, not congressional, not senatorial, not legislative, not judicial, but *school* districts; and every man throughout each State is taxed in proportion to his wealth, to build schools, furnish books, and pay teachers, so that every child, however poor, that is brought into the State, may receive a good elementary education; and we expect the bright apprentice boy of to-day to become the master of an establishment larger and more perfect than that in which he acquires his trade. We hold all places of honor or profit open to all our people, and thus stimulate every boy and man to give the State the best results of his industry, enterprise, or genius. Thus we draw from, or rather create upon even the sterile soil of New England, products that bring us in return the best results of the industry of all other people; and more cloth, more writing, printing, and wall paper, and greater varieties of well-prepared food, are consumed by our people *per capita*, than by those of any other section of our own or any other country in the world.

How are we to account for this difference? I behold around me a laboring population, not only poor but desti-

---

Philadelphia alone, over which last year nearly sixty-five millions of passengers were transported.

The cost of these city railroads was six millions of dollars; their annual receipts are three millions eight hundred thousand; they run daily thirty thousand miles over our streets; *they employ four thousand horses, which consume eleven thousand tons of hay and twenty million pounds of grain.* There are now three hundred and fifty miles of paved streets in Philadelphia.—*Address of Col. J. W. Forney*, July 4th, 1871.

The working people are the chief patrons of these roads, and thus furnish our farmers with markets for horses, hay and oats, which they would not enjoy if under free trade our wares were made in foreign countries.

tute; almost homeless, and untutored in all but the simplest arts of life. Tempting as are your boundless resources and genial climate, no emigrants come to settle in your midst. You have built no great city, New Orleans being the largest city of the South. Your cities would be only first class towns or villages in the North. You have no New York, Philadelphia, Brooklyn, Boston, Baltimore, Cincinnati, St. Louis or Chicago. Yet, north of the Potomac and Ohio are no such boundless and diversified stores of wealth as you possess. You have the choice cotton fields of the world; the rice, cane-sugar, hemp and tobacco fields of the United States are yours; and on some of your hillsides, or in your smiling valleys you may grow every plant or find every mineral that is native to the country east of the Rocky Mountains. How, my fellow-citizens, shall we account for the poverty and depression of the South, and the general and growing prosperity of the North? We can only do it by turning from nature to society. Our prosperity is the result of our development of *man*, by giving him a fair field for the exercise of all his energy and talents; and you lag behind because your system repressed man's energies, restrained his enterprise, and contracted the field of his usefulness. This must be the cause, for in all other respects our policy has been the same. The same flag represented our country's power and beneficence. In all other respects our institutions were the same. The same legislative, executive and judicial organization, the same division of the State into counties, townships, cities and boroughs. The one difference was that we knew at the North what you failed to perceive —that the boy who could read and write was worth more than one of equal strength and age who could not; and that the boy who saw before him the chance for wealth or distinction would strive to attain one or the other, and by study, industry and economy, endeavor to gather capital with which to labor for himself rather than for another. Having provided for the education of all their children, the people of the Northern States made ample provision to secure a fair day's wages for every fair day's work that might be done by man or woman.

But you may say this would affect only the people in cities. This is your mistake, and has been to you a fatal delusion. The landholder whose estate has been absorbed by a growing town or city has often received more for a little building lot than his whole estate had cost him; and he who had invested the earnings of years in a poor home in the suburbs has been enriched by the city growing beyond him, and its increasing commerce or manufactures giving value to his lot. Thus, too, are our farmers enriched. I know not what land is worth in a circle of ten miles around your beautiful city. I doubt whether forty or fifty dollars would be too low an estimate, but you would not buy land in the North as near as large a city, with such wonderful capabilities, for less than hundreds of dollars. So it would be here, would you connect your city with the neighboring coal and iron districts, and build furnaces, forges, rolling mills, machine shops, and factories, and availing yourselves of the magnificent water power at Wetumka, spin and weave your own cotton, and create an Alabama Lowell or Manchester. You would then learn what your rich lands are capable of.

Nobody can estimate the agricultural value of the stimulants created by great towns and the refuse of factories. You have grown cotton until you have extracted the very life from the lighter soils of your States. As I passed through Mississippi I saw wide stretches of land so exhausted by cotton that they would not produce fibrous roots enough to prevent the soil from washing away. Soil was gone, and the wash had left little mounds, that, in the light of the setting sun, looked like red tongues of fire rising from the earth to avenge its wrongs.

Throughout the North crops are alternated, and in the neighborhood of cities, or even of new manufacturing towns, fields that had been exhausted by injudicious culture until they yielded but ten or twelve bushels of wheat to the acre, have been reinvigorated, and now yield thirty bushels, as they did in their primitive condition. Make Montgomery a great city, and you will add to the wealth of every man within a circuit of a hundred miles. Let it be your ambition to raise a fair amount of cotton, but let it also be your desire to supply the States bounding the gulf with corn, and to send it and your cotton hence behind locomotives and over rails of your own construction.

Do not tell me that you have not laborers intelligent enough to assist you in this great work. I saw yesterday in your freedmen's schools abundant evidence of the incorrectness of this statement. I am very familiar with the public schools of the North, but I was profoundly astonished by what I saw among the younger pupils of the freedmen's schools of this city, and say without reservation that I never saw in any school pupils of equal age whose attainments and general intelligence exceeded those of two, a boy and girl, one six and the other seven years old, who I examined yesterday. I doubted the fairness of the exhibition, and believed that they had been specially prepared for it, but taking the examination into my own hands, and testing them in spelling, reading, geography, and other branches, was not only convinced of the honesty of the public exhibition, but amazed at the proficiency of the children. Tell me not that the race from which they spring is wanting in intellect or adaptation, or that their little hands will not one day be competent to the most delicate or ingenious labor. Yes, gentlemen, you have competent laborers at hand for the wide diversification of your pursuits. To demonstrate this, you have but to give poor people, regardless of color, a fair field and generous inducements. I reiterate that I am endeavoring to wound none of your susceptibilities in speaking thus pointedly to you. I am simply laboring to induce you to enter into generous competition with us at the North. If you will, you may be blessed beyond us as much as we are beyond any other people.

I speak the more freely because I once shared your prejudices, but I long since came to know that we can only be happy as we accord to every other man, however humble he may be, every right that we demand from others for ourselves; and I seek in vain for any other cause for the disparity between the two sections than our respect for man's rights, and your contempt for man as *man*. Let me then implore you to enter earnestly upon the work of reconstructing your State upon the plan provided by Congress. Let not freedom and equality be forced upon you by others. Accept the inevitable and find in it a good providence.

Some of you may ask, as others have done, whether the military bill is a finality. *That, the controlling minds of the South must determine.* It was so meant by Congress, if it was fairly accepted by the South. No further congressional legislation touching the South will be had, unless by a spirit of resistance on the part of the Southern people its necessity is made manifest.*

*Andrew Johnson's determination to nullify the reconstruction acts had not then been disclosed.

I am gratified in being able to report that I have found generally throughout the South a generous spirit, a readiness to acknowledge the right of all to travel freely, and to discuss with frankness and candor the issues of the day; and though in some quarters a different spirit prevails, I believe that in five years the South will be more liberal than the North has been.

Now a word to you, my colored fellow-citizens: you are free, and it is your duty, every one of you who can find employment, to labor, and to practice temperance and economy. If there be among you one able-bodied man who can find employment at wages, who wastes his time in idleness, he is committing a crime against himself and his race. Freedom means the assured right of a man to earn his livelihood, and to manage his affairs as he may deem best. I cannot better illustrate what liberty is than by a little incident that happened one day while I was walking with a friend, his arm resting in mine. He suddenly withdrew it, and I turned to discover why he had done so. There lay upon its back upon the ground a broad, green-backed insect, which the boys in our section call the gold bug, kicking upward for the ground. Working the end of his walking-cane under it, he gave it a toss, and it lit on its feet. "Now go, poor devil," said he; "hoe your own row; you have just as good a chance as any other bug of your kind."

Liberty is to each of you the assurance that the Government will secure to every one of you the right to hoe his own row with as good a chance as any other bug of his kind. Do you ask me what is your kind? It is MANKIND. I hold that there is but one race of men, and if there be two, then one of two things is certain: that this Southern sun plays the deuce with the African's complexion, or there are large numbers of ex-slaves in the freedmen's schools that are not there by virtue of African descent.

Freedom establishes the fact that a good man is better than a bad one; that a wise man is better than a fool; that a learned man is better than one who is content to pass his life in ignorance; that an active man will win the race and take the prize from an indolent one. If you have a dollar, freedom will secure it to you; and if you acquire land, freedom will protect you in its enjoyment and possession. You have not always had the right to protect your wife, but freedom not only gives that right, but makes it your duty to do it, to deal tenderly with her in all things, and to put over her head the roof of your own home. Freedom requires you to see to it that your children occupy seats in the public schools, so that their chances in life may be better than yours, and by any amount of toil you can endure, to contribute in taxes your share of the common charge.

Some of you may desire to travel and to emigrate, but the great mass of you are to pass your lives here in Alabama, and freedom requires you to live in peace with your neighbors, for you now have common interests. By industry, sobriety, the improvement of your minds, and care and culture of your children, you will command the confidence and esteem of those among whom you dwell. God made you free. You did not win your freedom, nor did we give it to you. God guided the course of battles, and controlled events so that when the war closed every man of you was as free as his white brother. You are now involved in the duties of citizenship, and must look to it well that you so perform your duties as to maintain that freedom for yourselves and all other men within the broad limits of your country.

Many of you, I am told, are skillful mechanics, carpenters, bricklayers, house-wrights, shoemakers, tailors, or are skilled in other mechanical branches. See to it, those of you who are capable of engaging in business for yourselves, that you do not spend your lives in laboring for wages. You cannot all be employers and master workmen, but some of you can, and the number of such will increase if you are industrious and thrifty. Most of you have been bred to plantation or farm work. Let the aim of such be to acquire land, put up a dwelling and procure adequate stock to work your acres. The homestead law offers lots of eighty acres to each and every one of you, but I am told that the land offices are so few and distant, and the expense of travel and clearing the land is so great, that you cannot avail yourselves of its privileges ; but Congress will remedy this at its next session, for it is its purpose to secure if possible a homestead for every family that desires to till the soil. Thus every one of you may aim at a manly and honorable independence in life, and a vigorous struggle in the pursuit of such aim will not fail to secure you the sympathy of all good men.

Addressing the white citizens, Mr. Kelley continued:

I do not come to the South as the agent of any faction or party, but, in conclusion, I must say something of the principles of the Republican party, because I believe that the welfare of our country is bound up with the success of that party for some years to come. The North, in which that party prevails, is intensely national. The South, in which it had no recognized existence or adherents, was on the other hand intensely sectional; its people, priding themselves on the sovereignty of the States, and looking to them rather than to the General Government for the maintenance of their rights. The Republican party is inspired by two grand sentiments; the first, national unity, and the second, individual liberty. It believes, as did Thomas Jefferson, that every man is endowed by nature with the right to life, liberty, and the pursuit of happiness. It holds with him that all men are born equal; not equal in stature, or color, or intelligence, but with equal rights before the laws of State and country, as they are equal before the judgment-seat of Him who is the common father. It is not, as has often been alleged, the purpose of that party to overthrow the constitution or invade the rights of States, but to promote the welfare of all, and to cement the Union by watching over the general and external interests of every State.

Let me illustrate this. Under the State rights doctrine there could be no general levee system for the Mississippi river, and the result is that the rich low lands bordering that river and its tributaries, from Tennessee to the Gulf, are overflowed, and their owners and laborers driven from their occupancy. Under the State rights system, Tennessee, Mississippi, Louisiana and Arkansas each had separate levee regulations; and some of these States again remitted the duty of keeping the levees in order to the counties in which they lay. Thus it happened that negligence on the part of a country or State north of others which constructed proper levees, often causes the ruin of those whose levees would have protected them from danger. The Republicans regard the Mississippi river as a great national highway, that should be under the charge of the General Government, and desire that its banks shall be guarded by a general system of levees, of which the National Government shall have the care and responsibility.

In illustration of the Republican party's love of liberty, I point to the homestead law, by which it would convert the largest possible number of the people of the country into independent landholders. Thus it is pledged to maintain the equality of every man before the laws; to secure the largest liberty to individuals consistent with the public welfare, and to preserve an indivisible Union from the Gulf to the northern boundary, and from ocean to ocean.

Had the statesmen of the South, when slavery was overthrown and the armies of the Confederacy surrendered, accepted the situation cordially, and legislated for man as *man*, Congress would not probably have interfered with their local legislation. But when State after State enacted Vagrant Laws and Apprentice Laws, by which slavery was to be perpetuated under a new guise, and, failing to provide for the education of the people, they denounced as "school marms" and "nigger teachers" and persecuted the noble women who, sacrificing everything else but Christian duty, hastened here to prepare the ignorant freedmen for the proper enjoyment of the new condition upon which they were entering, Congress found a high duty devolved upon it, and did not shrink from its performance. Believing that a Democratic Republic can exist securely only so long as the equal rights of all are guarded and maintained, it exhibited its willingness to exercise its amplest powers in this behalf.

The people of the North want peace and amity to pervade the whole land, but they feel that these blessings, with general prosperity, can only be assured when all shall acknowledge that the protection of the liberty of the citizens is the highest duty of the Government.

Citizens of Montgomery, I thank you for the courtesy and attention with which you have listened to me. You have heard the remarks I intended to make to the citizens of Mobile; and though some of you may deem them insulting and incendiary, you will hardly say, as the people of that city did, that I ought to be shot for attempting to utter them.

ADDRESS AT PHILADELPHIA, PENNA.

DELIVERED JUNE 17TH, 1867, REPORTED FOR THE INQUIRER.

My Friends, Neighbors, and Constituents: I am profoundly grateful for this demonstration of your affectionate interest. I never knew how sacred that word home, so felicitously uttered by Mr. Pierson, was, until during my recent absence from you. When cowering before more than a hundred bullets, or while my body was shielded from them by those of two negroes, who perilled their lives to save mine, I realized how dear were home, kindred, and friends. I left you at the invitation of the Governor of Louisiana and the Mayor of New Orleans to visit that distant State and city, hoping that I might serve our distracted country, and eager to view that nearly one-half of our country, from which, by reason of my love of personal liberty, I had so long been excluded. I did not dream of danger. Others spoke of it, but I scoffed at the idea. I went, bearing no hatred to any man; but believing that the truths which for the last eleven years I have been in the habit of proclaiming to you would be specially useful to the people of that section, I gladly availed myself of the opportunity of uttering them kindly and courteously in their midst; and, my friends, throughout my extended excursion I was received with all the kindness and courtesy the people were able to bestow upon me, save in one city. I therefore beg you not to charge the murderous spirit of the Mobile mob to the Southern people at large. [Applause.] That outrage was due more largely to Andrew Johnson, the reactionary President of the United States, than even to the municipal authorities of Mobile or the mob they should have held in subjection. The chief promoter of that murderous riot was a recreant Northerner, who had been sent to that city by the Pesident as assessor of internal revenue, Colonel Mann, formerly of Michigan, who owns the Mobile *Times*. That paper had, in advance of my arrival, excited the passions of the Southern people against me, and in an article on the day preceding my arrival, every allegation in which Colonel Mann admitted, in the presence of two gentlemen now present, to be wholly false and unfounded, had inflamed the passions of the Irish citizens of Mobile against me. But not to detain you with the details of that sanguinary scene, let me say that the outbreak was provoked by no indiscreet word of mine. It had been planned before I went to the meeting, if not before I arrived in Mobile, and the man immediately behind me would have been shot through the head, as he was, and another not five feet from me would have been murdered, as he was, at the preconcerted signal had I been reading the Litany or the Lord's Prayer. I am told it has been sneeringly said that I got under a table. I have never been a soldier or sought reputation at the cannon's mouth, and very freely admit that, when bullets were whizzing by and pattering against the wall behind me, I would have thanked Almighty God for a bullet-proof table under which to creep.

In Memphis, the people of which I addressed before going to New Orleans, the elegant opera house was crowded. My audience represented every shade of complexion and political opinion. In many instances, at least, so well-known citizens of Memphis assured me, the late rebel soldier, who had met our army on many a field, and the enfranchised slave, sat side by side, and when I closed my extended address, my name and those of our city and State were heartily cheered.

Had I been in some signal respect the nation's benefactor, I could not have been more honored in New Orleans than I was during my four days' stay in that gay and beautiful city. After I had addressed ten thousand of her people in Lafayette Square, I was generously entertained by (among others) a former citizen of Philadelphia, three of whose sons had served and one fallen in the Confederate army. From many such I received thanks for the frankness and courtesy of my speech.

Leaving Mobile on a Government boat, which, I may remark, was provided for me not at my request, but because Gen. Sheppard, the post commandant, concurred in the judgment of the Union men of Mobile, that my friends and I would encounter insult, if not outrage, on the regular boat for Tensas, where we must take the cars, I proceeded to Montgomery. In that city, the picturesque site of which strikingly resembles that of Washington, we occupied rooms in the hotel from which the order to fire on Fort Sumter had gone forth, from the balcony of which the Confederate Declaration of Independence had first been read to the public, and on the balcony of which Stephen A. Douglas had been pelted with eggs in 1860. Though pursued by the malignant falsehoods of the Mobile papers, I felt as safe and spoke as frankly in Montgomery as I now do at the threshold of my home.

I addressed the citizens from the rear of the Capitol. The meeting numbered about three thousand people, white and colored, whose political opinions were quite as diverse as their complexions. Nothing disturbed the harmony of the meeting; and at its close I was not only cheered, but leading citizens grouped about me and pressed me to visit other sections of the State and address the people. Conspicuous among these was Judge Walker, chief justice, who was also chief justice of the Confederate State of Alabama.

To comply with this request was impossible, and we started next morning for Atlanta, Ga., a beautiful and prosperous city, which, by its sudden rise from its ashes exceeds the fabled Phœnix. It is rapidly fulfilling its destiny, and becoming a great railroad and commercial centre. We arrived there toward the close of a bright Sunday afternoon, and were received at the depot by a committee of prominent citizens, and thousands of colored people, in their clean gay Sunday attire. The next morning we visited the Storr's school for freedmen, and, large as is my familiarity with the schools of the North, I am free to say that I have rarely seen a classified school superior to this. In the afternoon I addressed a meeting resembling that at Montgomery in numbers, character, and good order. The same generous expressions followed my remarks, and among the pleasant things said by the many who gathered around me was an offer by the Quartermaster General of the Confederate State of Georgia to pay my expenses if I would remain in the State and address the people of every county.

My engagements in North Carolina required my early departure, and we left the next morning. On arriving at Augusta, Ga., we were met by Mayor Blodgett, and at the Planters' House, to which he conducted us, were waited upon by large numbers of citizens. I shall always regret that my engagements precluded the possibility of my complying with their urgent request to remain and address the citizens. Had I been able to do so, it would have deprived the Conservative papers of the stupid story they are circulating that General Pope had admonished me to speak no more in Georgia.

In North Carolina I spoke at Charlotte, Concord, Salisbury, and Greensboro, and my reception in each case was as cordial as at Memphis or New Orleans, but less demonstrative, because the cities were smaller. I came thence to Danville, Virginia, where I made my closing address to a very large assemblage of citizens. Thus, you will see, my friends, that I crossed Kentucky, Tennessee, Mississippi, Louisiana, and leaving the last-named State by Lake Pontchartrain and the Gulf, for Alabama, came thence through Georgia, South Carolina, North Carolina, and Virginia, on the homeward trip, and must have seen something of the South.

I now know from observation and intercourse something of its people, and I but say to you what I said to each of my audiences, large or small, in school-room, or from public platform, that the whole people will soon regard the terrible war through which we have just passed as the throes and agony of the birth of a new, holier, and more blessed nation than the world has yet known. [Great applause.]

I saw during my trip a country upon which the Almighty has with most lavish hand bestowed His richest material gifts. It is gorged with every mineral. I have scarcely been in a State that does not abound in coal, iron, copper, and lead, and have travelled over a region of country richly underlaid with gold-bearing quartz. Let me speak specially of North Carolina, because, as is equally true of Virginia, poverty has driven hundreds of thousands of her native citizens into exile. My friends, North Carolina is the most beautiful and richest portion of God's earth upon which my vision or feet have ever rested. You know that she produces cotton, rice, indigo, tar, pitch, turpentine, and superior timber. You know that her soil and climate are adapted to the cereals, wheat, corn, rye, buckwheat, and oats. But you probably do not know that that State, long known as the Rip Van Winkle of the Union, from which more than fifty thousand free white people have fled to the two States of Indiana and Illinois, is the land of wine and honey, the apple and peach, the fig and pomegranate, all of which I saw prospering in open field and under the most artless culture. Its native vines made the fortune of Longworth, who carried cuttings thence. The wine-producing vineyards of Western Pennsylvania, around the base and on the islands of Lake Erie, and those scattered through Missouri, are from the cuttings taken from the native vines of North Carolina. The Catawba, the Lincoln, the Isabella, and richer than all the Scuppernong, of which, as it has not yet been successfully transplanted, Eastern North Carolina has the monopoly. There it grows spontaneously as a weed.

The woods and hill-sides teem with the richest honey-bearing flowers, and the bees invite you to put up but a rude box, that they may reward your kindness with the sweetest treasure. There is not a vegetable we produce that will not thrive in North Carolina, and under these abounding stores of agricultural wealth, a belt, ranging from forty to one hundred miles wide across the entire State, is so richly underlaid with gold that a person with a common frying pan may wash the sands of many of the rivulets and make from one to three dollars per day. My friends, as I travelled from day to day through this native wealth and beauty I saw how sin had driven man out of Paradise, for never had I seen such poverty as I found in North Carolina, save in South Carolina, Alabama, and Mississippi, where people are starving in the midst of nature's richest bounties.

You cannot comprehend and credit this statement. I tell you it is true. I could not credit it myself. It was long before observation enabled me fully to comprehend it. Go with me to Mississippi. I will take you to Hernando. Once Hernando was an important railroad town and station. There are scattered around it a few large old mansions, abandoned and going to ruin. It was once the centre of a great cotton-growing region, but now, as far as the eye could range from the platform of the car, we saw nothing but sedge grass, a surface weed, or the red subsoil, washed and cut by countless gullies, till under the bright sun it looked like a myriad flames of red fire, blazing up from the earth.

The owners of that once rich land had planted it each successive year with cotton, till they extracted from it every agricultural element, and those fibrous roots with which nature mats the soil and protects it from washing. In response to a question as to the extent of the desolation we beheld, a fellow-traveller, a Mississippian, said, "It is pretty wide. There is not a plantation within some miles of the station on which a family could make a living," and he added, "the soil was always light, and when the rain began to wash it, it made quick work of it." Skilful culture would not only have saved that wide region from desolation, but added to its wealth-producing power.

Come with me again, my friends, to South Carolina, and behold a mother, a delicate looking white woman, who, having "roped" herself to a plow, is striving to drag it through the earth, while her son apparently about eleven years old, endeavors to guide it, that they may open a furrow in which to deposit the few seeds Northern charity has sent them. You cannot imagine such a scene. But I assure you that I could detain you for hours by illustrations but little less striking than these of the terrible results of devoting an entire people to the production of a few bulky agricultural products. I wish you to remark that I have not spoken of the negroes of the South, but of the poor non-slaveholding whites, "the low downs," as I often heard them called.

What would we in Pennsylvania, with our manifold diversification of pursuits, think if the owner of a farm of one hundred acres should apply to the Government for rations to support his family? Yet it is not a novel or unnatural sight at the South. Lieutenant Colonel J. R. Edie, of the 8th infantry, is post commandant at Salisbury, N. C., and administers the affairs of the Bureau of Refugees and Freedmen within his command. I recognized in him not only a gallant son of Pennsylvania, but an old personal friend. It happened to be ration day, which occurs, I believe, once a fortnight, and with my companions I gladly accepted his invitation to his office, that we might observe the character and necessities of the applicants. They must have numbered hundreds, a large preponderance of whom were whites. Many of them had walked more than fifteen miles to procure a little corn and bacon.

As one lean, pale woman advanced and gave her name, the Colonel said: "You have been here before, and I think you own land." "Yes, sir," said she; "I own a little." "How much?" asked he. "About a hundred acres." "How much of it is cleared?" "The butt end of it." "Well then, why did you not plant it?" "All that is cleared is planted." "What, then, brings you for rations?" "Want, Colonel; I must have something for the children to eat till the corn ripens. I can't make it ripen till the season comes." [A voice—"They are too lazy to work!"] No, my friend, they are not too lazy to work. They are willing to work. They need guidance and instruction. I told them in my public addresses that in their primitive way they work harder than we. ["They are too lazy to work."] No, my friend, I understand them better than you. You would deem it pretty hard work to walk fifteen or twenty miles for a few pecks of corn and pounds of bacon, and carry them on your shoulder to your distant home.

The woman of whom I was speaking was not probably a lazy woman. She knew nothing of our agricultural implements or methods, but was doubtless regarded by her neighbors as an adept in Southern agriculture. Like her neighbors, whose lands would not produce cotton, or who did not own laborers to cultivate and pick it, she had planted her exhausted acres with corn, and when that single crop failed the country was famine-stricken, as Ireland was when rot assailed the potato. Yet we had eaten, the day before, at Concord, but thirty miles distant, at the hospitable table of Mr. McDonald, an old Pennsylvanian, but long a citizen of North Carolina, a variety of delicious vegetables, among which were potatoes as mealy as can be grown on our virgin hill sides.

The people of whom I speak had been taught to believe that cotton was the one thing to the production of which the South should devote herself, and that corn, as food for "mules and niggers," might, with propriety, be raised when cotton could not. A former Southern leader said to me: "We bought niggers and mules to raise cotton, and raised cotton to buy niggers and mules," and I good humoredly replied, "Yes, and your continuous culture of cotton having eaten up your land, your negroes and mules were about to eat you when you began the war." [Laughter and applause.] Thus it came that destitution and despair brood over the sunny South, while its unequaled water-power runs to waste, and its widely-diffused and inexhaustible mines of gold, silver, copper, lead, iron, etc., etc., and coal to work them, lie undisturbed where nature deposited them.

There are in North Carolina, as the census shows, 47,000 white adults who cannot read, and in Virginia 74,000. These figures, I apprehend, indicate the general condition of the South in this respect. In their ignorance the masses have been swayed to their ruin by the wealthy and ambitious men who dwell among them. They will gladly enrich themselves by adopting our methods and pursuits when they come to understand them. When I told them that they worked harder than we, and at more exhausting labor; that we lifted the toil that bowed them from the shoulders of man and devolved it upon coal and iron, and that without swinging the heavy scythe we made machinery mow and reap our fields, many of them looked incredulous. To sustain my point I invited their attention to what they had all seen, that ingeniously contrived mass of iron, a locomotive, and begged them to note how it would, when animated by a little water from one of their brooks, and a little coal from one of their abounding beds, under the guidance of a single man, move, at a speed greater than that of the race horse, masses of freight which their mules and negroes could not move.

You ask what are the chances of improving these people? The great difficulty in the way is their indifference to or contempt for education. In this they contrast most strangely with the freedmen and their children.

The white people seemed to be indifferent to education; but at Memphis, New Orleans, Montgomery, Atlanta, the four cities of North Carolina, and Danville, Virginia, we visited freedmen's schools, and I do but state the simple truth when I say that if we do not establish schools, and contrive some means to induce the white people of the South to educate their children, the colored people will, in five years, be their superiors intellectually.

By day the freedmen's schools are crowded with children from five years upward, and at night, after their day's work is over, with men and women. The story of one black man was this, That he had come into the school, and asked whether he could stay there until he could get an education. He was asked in return who would support him. "I will support myself while I stay," said he. "I got a little piece of land, and made a good 'crap,' and sold it well; I have come for an education while my brother works the land on shares. I want to stay here until I can get an education." He will get an education, for he is the first scholar in one of the finest classified schools I ever saw.

Another remarkable thing in these schools is the large proportion of white pupils found in them. This, doubtless, surprises you, after what I have just said. That is because you have not visited the cities of the South, and suppose that the question of the color of a person depends on prismatic rays, pigments, or chemical combinations. That is a delusion. Throughout the South the color of a human being is not a question of science, but of tradition; and the teachers of one freedmen's school, in which there was no pupil that had not been a slave, assured us that quite twenty-five per cent. of the scholars would be recognized as white people in any part of the North. This gives you the key to the abandonment by the Southern leaders of the narrow dogma that slavery was the true position of the *negro* and their assertion of the broad doctrine that slavery is the true position of the *laborer*. This occurred about 1847, and I remember inviting the attention of such of you as then heard me to it, on the 16th of September, 1856, in my address at Spring Garden Hall. Promiscuous intercourse had expelled the blood of Africa from the veins of so many of their slaves that they were compelled to take this position or fail to cover by their logic their most valuable property.

But you ask, "What is the spirit and temper of the Southern people?" There is, doubtless, a great deal of sullen discontent. The time has not yet come when it would be safe to withdraw the military. This would be unsafe. Not but that there are large portions of the South that are well regulated and orderly, without any troops within fifty or a hundred miles of them. I have referred to Danville. The nearest post to that town at which troops were stationed was seventy-three miles, and yet order prevails there and in the vicinity as perfectly as at the large stations. Intelligent people all over the South are welcoming intercourse with the North, are subscribing to Northern Republican, agricultural, and religious newspapers, and are, in a political sense, asking earnestly and prayerfully, "What must we do to be saved?"

The colored people understand themselves and the questions at issue thoroughly. They need no Northern missionaries among them. If the North will educate them that is all they want, to free them from the shackles of ignorance. The political work there will be better done by themselves than through Northern visitors. They have among them orators that would surprise those who assert the intellectual inferiority of the race. L. S. Berry, of Alabama, who did but know his letters when the war ended, is said to be one of the most remarkable orators in the United States; and it is claimed that, if he makes a tour through the North, he will rival Fred. Douglass, with all his scholarship and foreign travel.

In North Carolina a colored man named Harris has the reputation of being one of the ablest popular orators in the State. James Simms, the brother of Thomas Simms, the slave who was taken from Boston in triumph, is said to be gifted with the power of declamation and invective almost beyond any living American orator; and the people in every town in which we were entertained did not fail to bring to our notice men who were slaves two years ago, and whom they now cheerfully recognize as their political equals. One gentleman, speaking of a shoemaker, said to me: "We always knew he had better sense than his master, though he was a learned judge."

Some of you have heard me called a "negro worshipper." If that phrase is intended to characterise one who appreciated the intellect and character of the Africo-American people, it was misapplied to me. I freely admit that I had done the race gross injustice by my highest estimate, and a few years will demonstrate the fact to all unprejudiced minds.

Poor and ignorant as they were when they escaped from slavery, they are rapidly acquiring property. In this good work members of the Society of Friends are aiding them most judiciously by purchasing land in large tracts and selling it to them in small quantities at cost, and on time. I saw places nicely improved on the last payment for which seven years had been given, but which two years had served to free from indebtedness. They have neither eaten nor wasted the seeds sent them by Northern benevolence or the Agricultural Department, but around each freedman's home where these have gone is a vegetable garden, such as we observe in our rides in this vicinity. They are an improving people, and will, by their industry, enterprise and thrift, regenerate the South.

My friends, some of you, tired of city life, may think of emigrating. To such, I say, put not a thousand or fifteen hundred miles between your families and their old homes by going to the distant West or Northwest. There is a more genial climate and a country as rich and beautiful within a few hundred miles of your home, where you can buy agricultural and mineral lands at from two to five dollars an acre; in which you can buy land contiguous to towns destined, under the influence of freedom, soon to be large cities, whose railroad connections are already established, at from five to fifteen dollars an acre. In this region your skill as machinists will be of immense value. Many of the rich gold and copper mines of North Carolina have already passed into the possession of Northern men, and are being worked by the most approved machinery.

As experience demonstrates their richness, this field will become largely productive of wealth and employment. But the rivers of the South furnish boundless water-power, much of which washes beds of iron, coal and limestone. I have visited Lewiston, Me., Nashua and Manchester, N. H., and Lowell and Lawrence, Mass., and I assure you that a single stream in each of the States of Alabama, Georgia, South Carolina, and North Carolina, furnishes power vastly in excess of that required to move the machinery of these cities. Much of the cotton crop will yet be spun and woven by this power, near the fields on which it is grown. To enterprising and ingenious emigrants I say, go to the rich and fertile, but exhausted South.

What is required to regenerate the South is subsoil ploughs, phosphates, agricultural implements generally, a large increase of horses, mules and horned cattle, a steadily increasing supply of steam engines and machinery, and such manufacturing machinery as can be moved by water-power. These, with a comparatively small amount of cash capital, and a few earnest men to teach others their use and value, would in a few years make the South bloom like a garden, and develop a population as loyal as was that of any Northern State during the war. [Applause.] The interests of Northern capitalists require them to supply these potent agents at the earliest practicable day.

But, my laboring friends, when I advise you to move South, understand me to couple it with the suggestion that you go in little colonies, say of ten or twenty families. Carry with you your Northern habits. Arrange for the regular receipt of the papers and magazines for which you now subscribe, and let one of your number be at least capable of conducting a fair country school. In this way you will regenerate the neighborhood into which you go, and preserve your children from the ignorance which prevails. A single man or family going there would unconsciously lapse into the habits which prevail. Again, let me say, do not think of going to work for wages. There is little demand as yet for skilled labor, and unskilled labor is in terrible excess of the existing demand.

The colored hands in the tobacco factories of Danville, Va., can earn about nine dollars per week; but in one of the towns of North Carolina we saw girls and women, who in a Philadelphia factory would receive from four to six dollars per week, working long days in a tobacco factory for twenty-five cents a day. One of the applicants to Colonel Edie for rations stated, and established the fact, that her husband worked in a sawmill for thirty cents a day; and the best laborers in their vicinity, without distinction of color, are employed in the rich gold mines of the latter State at one dollar per day.

In this picture of helpless destitution I am not portraying the effects of war. No; the fruitful seeds of this misery were brought from Africa in slave ships. It was not the war that reduced Norfolk from the first commercial port of the Union to the position of an inconsiderable town without foreign commerce. The war did not convert the rich and beautiful land around Hernando into an arid waste. The war did not drive the once proud occupants from those long-abandoned mansions, whose columns and architraves are now so dilapidated, or from those villages of huts, about which the poisonous vine has for years twined its beautiful but fatal embrace.

Said one who for years recognized Mr. Calhoun as his inspired leader, but now has but little hope for the South: "We have sacrificed our country to cotton, mules, and niggers, and if you regenerate it, its prosperity will be our lasting reproach. They were most happy who fell in the war, before the delusion was quite dispelled." Said another: "Why did not the North and South understand each other? I believed that I was fighting for the prosperity of my country; but some months' imprisonment in one of your forts and a plentiful supply of your newspapers satisfied me that I was fighting against every cherished desire of my heart."

The South must be regenerated, and we of the North must do it. There are, however, many there who will aid us in the work, but we must plan and guide it. Let our statesmen traverse the South, and, as occasion offers, speak frankly, bating no jot or breath of their opinions, but uttering them courteously; and if any of you has a friend in any one of the States, send him your paper daily after you have read it. What they need is to understand us, our habits and purposes. When in my several addresses I told them—not the colored people, or the "low downs," but the wealthier portion of my audiences—that, masters as they had been of thousands of acres and hundreds of slaves, they had never been able to provide themselves and families with many of the best results of wealth which enter into the daily life of a Philadelphia workingman, they would look skeptical; but after I had described our neat two-story houses with four rooms each, and the outer kitchen and bath-room supplied with hot water from the range, and lighted throughout with gas, and of the large, well-ventilated school-house for the children, near home; the public library or institute near by; the choice among churches of all denominations, the cheap daily newspaper, and other things familiar to you all—most of them would admit the correctness of my proposition. We can thus teach them much, and the time has come when many of those who were recently our foes are willing to hear us and co-operate with us in any good work for the poor among whom they dwell.

Let us, then, my friends, while manfully defending all that is good in our opinions or institutions, endeavor to forget the past and strive to improve the future. Yesterday is gone, no man knows whither, but to-morrow is before us, with its inevitable duties and its possible blessings or calamities. Let each man labor within the limits prescribed by good conscience, to promote his own welfare and that of his family, for so all will be blessed. In the development of the agricultural, mineral, and manufacturing resources of the country, work, and wages will be secured to all, and ample opportunity for daring enterprise afforded to the most restless.

Then will sneering Europe discover that the Union is not only indivisible and indestructible—[applause]—but that the atmosphere of our country, from Alaska, as Mr. Sumner calls our newly-acquired possessions, to the Rio Grande, is so pure that no slave can breathe it. [Applause and cheers.]

Again thanking you, my friends and neighbors, for this manifestation of your personal regard, I pray that God's best blessing may follow you to your homes.

AMERICAN INDUSTRY AND FINANCE.

SPEECH DELIVERED AT THE MUSIC HALL, MILWAUKEE, SEPTEMBER 24, 1867. REPORTED FOR THE DAILY SENTINEL, AND REVISED BY THE AUTHOR.

Ladies and Gentlemen: The United States should be the first commercial power of the world. But she is not. She is the chief commercial dependency of Great Britain. With her extended sea-coast, her unlimited agricultural capacity, and as yet unexplored mineral resources, she should be the leading manufacturing nation of the world; and that nation which manufactures more than it consumes of articles of general use universally leads in commerce. But no nation that has contented itself with producing bulky raw material has ever attained commercial dignity. History names no such one. We are not in the position we should be—the leader of the civilization of the world—because this has been our policy, and we have preferred that England should spin and weave our cotton and wool, should fashion coal, limestone, and iron ore into implements for our use, and rails to lay over our limestone beds, ore banks, and coal mines. We are truly enough her best customer; and are tending toward bankruptcy and increasing our foreign indebtedness by exporting national, State. and corporation bonds in exchange for consumable commodities, for the production of which we have abundant raw materials. Last year, if we may accept the statement of Secretary McCullough, we imported $100,000,000 more than we exported, including our entire production of gold. This year, down to the report of September 4, I find by the custom-house statistics that our importations at New York are $171,178,058, and our exports only $124,978,938. England pats us on the head and says, "Good boy; you are not only our favorite son, though you did tear away from the apron-strings, but we are ready to call you our brother, sister, or uncle, as you please, so long as you maintain the profitable commercial relations now existing between us. You buy from us more than any of our colonies or other people. But for you our balance-sheet would last year have made a sad exhibit. Our export trade in cotton goods fell off about $5,000,000; our exports of silk goods fell off nearly $1,000,000; and but for the increase in the American demand for iron, our iron trade would have fallen off in a larger degree than these." True it is, that we thus buy from her from choice, and that she buys cotton and tobacco from us because she cannot buy them anywhere else. She buys from us nothing that she can get from other nations.* A theory is abroad that she largely consumes the cereals of the West. It is false, and I was infinitely shocked, the other night, at hearing Rev. Newman Hall, in the midst of the most pious ejaculations, exclaim that half the wheat eaten in England is raised in the Western States of America; and when on the succeeding evening I addressed the people of Springfield, I corrected his statement and apologized for it, saying that he had entered a field with which he was not familiar. But in reading the report of the speech he made at St. Louis, while I was thus defending his veracity in Springfield, I find that he not only reiterated the assertion, but added: "I have made a calculation, and ascertained that a loaf made of your flour can be bought cheaper in England than here in Missouri." My friends that statement is demonstrably false. No such fact can be ascertained by calculation. Bread is not as cheap in England as in Missouri. Nor has England ever bought from the United States one-half of one per cent. of her wheat.

In the first place she raises about eighty per cent. of her own wheat. That leaves but twenty per cent. to divide

---

* Take, for example, that of the United States and France as most striking. In 1868, we imported from the United States no less than £8,892,394, in gold and silver, and we sent out only £112,519. As a contrast to this we sent to France, £9,011,394, and brought home only £1,325,487. The balance of trade, so far as gold and silver could show it, was £8,779,875 in our favor with the American States, and £7,685,907 against us with France. How was this? The United States took the produce of our industry to that extent expressed by the sum stated over and above what they sent us chiefly in useful produce for the masses of our people. But the money passed at once into the hands of those to whom France sends her silks and wines, and (over and above the value of a vast amount of goods of a substantial character) it was spent in luxury. Our large export to France might have brought over a vast supply to feed the hungry and clothe the naked; but the power over it was in hands whose wishes and tastes gave it a different destination. We sent to France, in value, £12,862,668, chiefly useful articles, besides the balance in money we have stated, and we got back, almost exclusively in articles of luxury, £33,033,401.—*Social Politics, Kirk.*

among the other nations of the world. Of the deficit she obtains, as nearly as can be calculated from her statistics, from sixty-eight to seventy per cent. from Russia and Prussia. She obtains largely more from France than she does from the United States. She obtains twice as much from poor, sick Turkey as she does from the broad United States of America, and yet this emissary of the Free-trade League is under the guise of religion reiterating this infamously false statement to the people of the entire West.

You may ask what this has to do with American industry and finance, announced for discussion this evening? I think you will find as we proceed that it is relevant. I think you will agree with me that if Illinois will develop that wonderful coal bed she has underlying 35,000 square miles of her territory; if Indiana will develop that part of the same bed, containing 15,000 square miles; and Missouri, Kansas, and Iowa bring into use a small portion of the seventy odd thousand square miles that underlie them; that if you will work the iron ore and limestone of Wisconsin, and Illinois will bring into play that great condensation of the elements of iron that underlies the southern tiers of her counties; if Missouri will develop her beds of tin, and bring her copper mines into rivalry with those of Michigan and Wisconsin, we can withdraw from England much of the trade on which she lives, and thus without striking a blow overthrow that enemy which, during our recent struggle, drove our commerce from the sea, by hoisting the flag of the Confederacy on British ships, armed with British men and weapons. [Applause.]

Some of you are Irishmen; others are the descendants of Irishmen. If you would see the green and beautiful old fatherland free, and Irishmen counted as men, and equal to any English lord on election day, you should strive to develop our resources, and regenerate Ireland by reducing the wealth and power of England. [Applause.]

Mr. Hall pleads for England's supremacy, and I for the commercial independence of the United States, and this allusion to him has something to do with what I have to say. I am here begging an audience, as I have done elsewhere in the West, to permit me to utter a warning which relates to the interest of our broad country, and which specially touches the interests of the people of Wisconsin. I have recently travelled over seven of the disrupted Southern States. I saw much, and learned more through intercourse with the people, and still more from a large correspondence that grew out of my visit, and from many pamphlets and newspapers since sent me by citizens of the South.

The rebellion and its suppression have rendered an entire revolution in the industries of America inevitable. No State in the Union is more directly interested in this change than Wisconsin, and yet few of your wisest and most far-seeing men seem to have learned the fact. They still think that the South was an agricultural country. Why, gentlemen, do agricultural countries go abroad to buy food for man and beast? I thought they raised it. Yet, true it is, that before the war, the West and Northwest fed the South. Your wheat, corn, beef, bacon, and hay went to the Southern States for a market. I do not speak specially of the productions of your own State, but of the States of the West and Northwest.

You have no adequate foreign market! France, England, and Belgium, in the three years preceding the breaking out of the war, purchased annually—the three nations combined—but ten millions of agricultural products from the United States—including wool, lumber, pork, wheat, flour, and corn. But $10,000,000! That was not an adequate market for the productions of the West; and yet it was all the manufacturing nations of Europe purchased. Your best foreign customers were the non-manufacturing countries south of the Gulf of Mexico, and Central and South America, whose people took about $30,000,000 of your productions in each of the years referred to, or three times as much as all transatlantic nations. The market on which you relied was in the South, and the cities and manufacturing districts of the Eastern States. Pennsylvania is a great wheat-growing State, but she cannot supply the demands of her people, and half her miners and operatives are fed from your fields. This Eastern market is still yours, but you are no longer to feed the people of the Southern States. Nor is that all. Hereafter you are to encounter Southern provision growers in the markets of the East—in the southern part of this hemisphere, and the small market open to you in Europe—and to compete with them after they shall have taken the cream off. If you do not diversify your productions, you will soon be ready to cry to the Lord to send drought or excessive rain to destroy crops, and enable you to sell your wheat, corn, and cattle. You will feel that a curse has fallen on you if this year's generous crops shall be vouchsafed next year. You may say this is strange talk. Gentlemen, I recently travelled between twelve and fourteen hundred miles by railroad, from New Orleans to Baltimore—between corn and cotton, cotton and corn, and if I were under oath, I could not say which I saw most of—cotton or corn. Where the land had been cultivated, and the crop gathered, the stubble of wheat remained. Where I saw other crops than cotton or corn growing, as I did in northern North Carolina and Virginia, it was wheat—the great staple of Wisconsin. During the three days I passed in St. Louis last week, I saw corn from Mississippi and Alabama being delivered from steamers, instead of being shipped thence to Mississippi and Alabama, as it used to be; and I also saw a drove that would have gratified the eye of any cattle-fancier, of long-horned Texas cattle, driven through the streets of St. Louis, which looked to me amazingly like the South feeding the North, at least to some extent. From Nashville they are shipping corn and wheat to Ohio, Indiana, and the Eastern States. The corn crop of Indiana, and even most of Ohio, has been blighted. But, you may say, I am an unskilful observer. Will you, therefore, pardon me for reading a brief extract from a well-considered official statement? The Confederate Legislature of Louisiana instructed the Governor to select some competent gentleman to make a survey of the mineral, manufacturing, and agricultural resources of Louisiana, and report to the Legislature. Allen, the Confederate Governor, selected for that duty Hon. John B. Robertson, a man of marked ability and great breadth of study. I hold his report in my hand. Pardon me while I read you a brief extract:

"Wheat with us should be planted in September, October, or November. It is a beautiful season for preparing the ground. It may then be reaped in the last half of April and May, a time usually selected for making brick, on account of its fair weather. The daily quotations show that Southern flour, raised in Missouri, Tennessee, and Virginia, brings from three to five dollars more per barrel than the best New York Genesee flour. Louisiana and Texas flour is far superior to the Tennessee, Virginia, or Missouri, owing to the superior dryness, and the fact that it contains more gluten, and does not ferment so easily. Southern flour makes better dough and maccaroni than Northern or Western flour; it is better adapted for transportation over the sea, and keeps better in the tropics. It is therefore the flour that is sought after for Brazil, Central America, Mexico, and the West India markets, which are at our doors. A barrel of strictly Southern flour will make twenty pounds more bread than Illinois flour, because, being so much drier, it takes up more water in making up. In addition to this vast superiority of our grain, we have other advantages over the Western States in grain growing. Our climate advances the crop so rapidly that we can cut our wheat six weeks before a scythe is put into the fields of Illinois; and being so near the Gulf, we avoid the delays in shipping and the long transportation, the cost of which consumes nearly one-half of the product of the West. These advantages, the superior quality of the flour, the earlier harvest, and the cheap and easy shipment, enable us absolutely to forestall the West in the foreign demand, which is now about 40,000,000 of bushels annually, and is rapidly increasing; and also in the Atlantic seaboard trade. Massachusetts, it is calculated, raises not more than one month's supply of flour for her vast population. New York not six months' supply for her population, and the other Atlantic States in like proportion. This vast deficit is now supplied by the Western States, and the trade has enriched the West, and has built railroads in every direction to carry towards the East the gold-producing grain. We can, if we choose, have a monopoly of this immense trade, and the time may not be far distant when, in the dispensation of Providence, the West, which contributed so largely to the uprooting of our servile system and the destruction of our property, will find that she has forced us into a rivalry against which she cannot compete, and that she will have to draw not only her supplies of cotton, sugar, and rice, but even her breadstuffs from the South.

"A close estimate of all the expenses, in raising a crop of wheat or barley, or a crop of cane or cotton, placed in juxtaposition, would show largely in favor of the grain crop. In raising the grain, the full force need be hired and fed no longer time than two or three months of the year, while in the other crops they must be hired and fed for twelve months.

"Vast numbers of freedmen could be hired for one or two months at the time for liberal day wages. This system is in conformity with their ideas and notions of work; they reluctantly contract for a year. Rye, barley, and buckwheat have been tried in Louisiana. Barley and buckwheat are both natives of a Southern climate, and flourish remarkably well here. In Texas, during the past year, the papers state that eighty-five bushels of barley were made to the acre in Central Texas; sixty bushels could easily be made here, and as it is superior to the Northern barley for brewing, the fourteen breweries of New Orleans would alone consume vast quantities of it. Barley, as compared with corn, is a better food for stock, particularly work stock, as it is muscle-producing, and does not heat the system like the oil or fat-producing property of corn, and while it produces three times as much to the acre of grain, the stock consumes all the straw. A hand can cultivate much more ground in barley than corn, and it needs no work after planting. Grain growing would not only be profitable to the planter, but it would build up New Orleans, and make her the greatest city on the continent.

"What New Orleans lacks is summer trade; her business has been heretofore compressed into six or eight months. After the cotton and sugar crops were received and disposed of, the merchants and tradesmen had nothing to do. Most of them went north with their families, leaving New Orleans a prey to epidemics, when a small portion of the very money which they had earned in New Orleans, and were spending so lavishly abroad, would have perfected sanitary measures, which would have protected those from the epidemics. During this season of inactivity nearly all branches of business are suspended; the merchant must, however, pay house rent, insurance, clerk's hire, and other incidental expenses; must lose interest on his investments, and have his goods and wares damaged by rust, dust, moth, and mould. If the cultivation of grain were begun and encouraged around New Orleans, grain would pour in during the month of May, and the summer months, and would fill up this fatal hiatus in our trade.

"The merchant would be compelled to reside here in summer as well as winter, and he would be forced on his own account to lend his time and money towards building up the city, and improving its health.

"Every branch of business would be kept up then throughout the whole year, and our own steamships would supply the countries south of us with provisions, and we should not as now be compelled to import coffee by way of Cincinnati. Northern and European emigrants knowing that our grain growing was more profitable than at the North, and that they could grow grain without working during the summer months in that sun they have been wrongfully taught to dread, would flock to our lands; and of course, where provisions and all other necessaries of life would be cheap, manufactures would necessarily spring up to work up the raw materials so abundant there. I have thus lengthily urged the cultivation of the cereals, because I find so little is known among the most intelligent as to the capabilities of our State in this respect, and because, too, I think that therein lies the true secret of recuperation and permanent prosperity for our people. It is a business which all classes of agriculturists may profitably engage in, from the poor farmer of the pine hills to the rich planter of the coast. It is a business in which every landholder, lessee, laborer, mechanic, manufacturer, tradesman, merchant, ship-owner, and, indeed, every citizen is deeply interested, as it is a question of large profits and cheap bread, and the State of Louisiana and the United States have a deep concern in it, as large owners of land in the State. I have placed grain first in the list of productions, for, looking to the future, I am sure that grain will become our leading staple, and that New Orleans is destined to become the leading grain market in the world." *

---

* The following Associated Press dispatch is strikingly confirmatory of my prediction:

"NEW ORLEANS, July 1st, 1871.—The Cotton Exchange Committee on statistics and information made reports upon the growing cotton and grain crop, with dates from the 15th to the 20th of June. The following is the summary:

"MISSISSIPPI.—*Cotton.*—Reduction of acreage 20 to 25 per cent., with an average of half to three-quarters the yield of last year per acre. *Corn.*—Acreage increased 25 to 40 per cent. The latest reports indicate a short yield per acre.

"LOUISIANA.—*Cotton.*—Reduction of acreage 10 to 12 per cent. Crop three weeks backward. Considerably injured, especially in the low lands, by rain and lice. *Corn.*—Nearly sufficient for home consumption planted.

"ARKANSAS.—*Cotton.*—Reduction of acreage 25 to 33 per cent., with propor-

In support of these views I have with me, but am not going to detain you with extracts from it, an address made at the close of the agricultural, mechanical, and industrial fair in New Orleans, by Wm. M. Burwell, of Virginia, in which the Southern people are urged, as they are by Mr. Robertson, to divide their lands and to remember that the South has three seasons; that wheat matures in the spring; that corn matures at midsummer; and that cotton is a fall crop; and advised to take advantage of all the seasons. These gentlemen agree, as do a score of writers whose communications I have with me, in urging the people to put not more than one-tenth of their land in cotton, and the remainder in grass and diversified crops of food. They tell them that the South abounds in seaports, that the grain of every part of the South can be got to market in bulk in vessels, in which a bushel of wheat may be carried twenty-three thousand miles—from San Francisco to Liverpool—cheaper than it can be carried from Minnesota or Kansas to New York over railroads; and that as theirs is the early season they can avenge themselves upon the West and North by pre-occupying the markets. These are not pleasant tidings to bring to a people prosperous as are those of the West, and so identified with their present pursuits that they will yield or modify them reluctantly.

My fellow-citizens, notwithstanding these unpleasant auguries, the future of the West was never so bright as it is to-day. The cloud that overshadows your prospect is but the mist that lingers over a mountain stream. The sun is rising yonder and will dispel it, and you will then see the beauty of the golden valley! Yes, the rebellion

---

tionate increase in grain. Prospects generally good, except in the southern portion of the State, where not more than half of last year's yield per acre is anticipated. The grain crop is very promising.

"TEXAS.—Information mostly from the northeast portion of the State. *Cotton.*—Reduction of acreage 25 to 33 per cent., with a corresponding increase in grain. Cotton two weeks backward, though with a favorable season an average crop per acre is expected.

"ALABAMA.—*Cotton.*—Reduction of acreage 10 to 20 per cent. Crop three weeks backward. The average production per acre will be less than last year. *Grain.*—Increased acreage 20 to 30 per cent. Fair prospect.

"GEORGIA.—Cotton accounts meagre, embracing the west centre and centre of the State, and thence northeast. Decrease of acreage 20 to 33⅓ per cent., in the northeast, and 15 in other sections heard from. Condition unpromising; half to three-quarters per acre of last year's yield expected. *Grain.*—Corresponding increase of acreage. Prospect unpromising.

"TENNESSEE.—Information confined to the western part of the State. *Cotton.*—Decrease of acreage 5 to 12½ per cent., with prospects of an average yield per acre. *Grain.*—Considerable increase of acreage. Prospects good."

struck the shackles from the industries and enterprises of the West, and has opened to them a glorious and profitable career. If any of you have the Chicago *Republican* or Chicago *Journal* of to-day, you will find in the course of an address I delivered at Springfield, extracts with which I do not care to detain you now, proving most irrefutably from the highest Southern authorities, that in order that she might have the monopoly of the supply of cotton, and England the monopoly of manufacturing it, the South insisted on such congressional action as would forever prevent the development of the vast and infinitely varied resources of the West. I take the liberty of inviting your attention to those extracts, and ask you to consider them as part of this address.* These shackles have been stricken off. The powers that ruled us were the monopoly that has made a hell of Ireland, and of India! The monopoly that so long as we were colonial, prohibited the establishment of a rolling-mill, a slitting-mill or iron-works in our country! The monopoly that has reduced a million of English workmen to pauperism, and swelled the poor-tax of Scotland from one dollar to $4.50 during the brief reign of Victoria. For every dollar paid to maintain the poor of Scotland in the last year of the reign of William IV., $4.50 was required in 1865. The manufacturing power of England was one conspiring monopoly, and the other was that which sold men, women, and children on the auction block throughout the South. These two monopolies were co-conspirators against the people of the West, and I refer you to the authorities, as you will find them in the *Republican* and *Journal* of to-day. That powerful combination fell with slavery, and the day dawns when the West shall be more crowded with immigrants than ever before, and when in parts of every State there will be a market near the farmer's door for his productions. You will not then fear to raise too much. I propose to show you how to increase your power, to raise more wheat than you have ever raised on your virgin soil, and feed more cattle per acre than ever fed before upon your broad prairies and rolling lands, while creating a market for it all.

And now is the time for this great work. England is in her decadence! Nay, she is in a rapid decline, what

* See extracts from "Cotton is King."

doctors would call the "galloping consumption."* [Laughter.] I speak advisedly, and I have yet to give you some facts by which to sustain my conclusions. She is a wonderful nation, and her story shows, as does our own last six years of history, that the hand of Providence is ever guiding the affairs of nations by immutable laws She has taught the world what may be done by legislative protection to labor. Look at her—a little speck in yonder ocean! Not so large as Wisconsin—not so large as Pennsylvania, and yet she has been the mistress of the seas, and her morning drum, even to this day, may be heard at any hour encircling the world. She achieved her preëminence by a well-devised system of protection, by which she employed all her own people on her own soil and materials. She protected the laborers engaged in working the coal, iron, copper, tin, and whatever lay in the mines, or could be dug from the hills, or be grown upon the soil of England. She gave employment to all her people, and stimulated their industry and energy in developing her resources. She used to be laughed at by the Dutch—when

---

*We are told that our manufacturing industries, far from being ruined, are prosperous. It is true they are not yet ruined, but many are more depressed than they have ever before been. Very many of them are sick—very sick; far more so than those unacquainted with them have any idea of, and a few years more of such depression will see many of them *in extremis*. There are many who argue that our manufacturers would at once give up manufacturing if it did not pay; and no doubt it is a very natural assumption, that if a manufacturer continues his business it is a proof he is making money by it; but it is very often the case that he continues to manufacture only because he cannot afford to stop. They little know how many manufacturers continue to struggle on in business merely because they do not know how to get out of it. A man with twenty, thirty, fifty, or a hundred thousand pounds sunk in works and machinery cannot give up business without ruin. The causes that diminish the demand for his produce diminish also the value of his plant; his capital and interest are imperilled at the same time and by the same cause. It is not to be expected, it is not in the nature of Englishmen, that he should at once throw up the sponge, and declare himself beat; he will continue to tread the mill though he gets nothing for it; he will struggle on for years, losing steadily, perhaps, but yet hopeful of a change. Millions of manufacturing capital are in that condition in England at present. Capitalists continue to employ their capital in manufacturing industries because it is already invested in them; but in many cases it is earning no profit, and in others diminishing year by year.

It takes some time to scatter the wealth of England. The growth of half a century of industrial success is not kicked over in a day. Moreover, it is only now, only within the last three years, that the foreign producers have acquired the skill and capital and machinery that enables them really to press us out of our own markets. The shadow has been coming over us for many years, but it is only just now we are beginning to feel the substance; their progress corresponds with our decline. A great manufacturing nation like England does not suddenly collapse and give place to another; her industries are slowly, bit by bit, replaced by those of other countries; the process is gradual, and we are undergoing it at present. The difference between England and her young manu-

Van Trump, the representative of little Holland, then the mistress of the sea, carried his broom at the masthead—for selling raw materials and buying manufactured goods. The Dutch said, "England sold her skins for sixpence, and bought back the tail—dressed—for a shilling." [Laughter.] But she got over that. She welcomed industrious emigrants from every land. If they introduced a new industry, she gave, by special order or legislation, protection to that industry until it should take firm hold on English soil. She legislated in favor of her own ships. The foreign article brought in English bottom came into her ports under differential duties lower than those on the same article coming in on the same day in foreign bottoms. She thus stimulated the building of English ships, and created a great English Navy, and had she protected her colonies as she did the people of England, would have been the great benefactor of the world. But when she gained a colony, she looked only for the raw material she could get from it, and the manufactured articles she could sell its people. Her policy was to ex-

---

facturing rivals is simple, but alarming. France, Austria, Prussia, Belgium, Switzerland, have increased their export trade and their home consumption; England has increased her export trade, but her home consumption has fallen away, in the matter of cotton alone, 35 per cent. in three years!

In the present condition of manufacturing industries it is foolish to tell the operative class to attribute the prosperity to Free Trade; they are not prosperous; it is a mockery to tell them to thank God for a full stomach, when they are empty! they are *not* well off; never has starvation, pauperism, crime, discontent, been so plentiful in the manufacturing districts—never since England has been a manufacturing country has *every* industry great or small been so completely depressed, never has work been so impossible to find, never have the means and savings of the working classes been at so low an ebb.

We have had periods when some two or three of the great industries were depressed, but health still remained in a number of small ones: now the depression is universal; the only industry in the country that is really flourishing is that of the machine makers, turning out spinning and weaving machinery for foreign countries! many of these works are going night and day.

Now many persons doubt this distress, deny it altogether, and appeal to the Board of Trade returns and to the dicta of certain retired manufacturers, who, having invested the wealth acquired in former years, and being released from the anxieties and dangers of declining trade, can now, without danger, afford to indulge their commercial theories without injuring their pockets.

The manufacturing districts are depressed as they never have been before, and any one who will visit them may see by evidence that cannot lie, by smokeless chimneys, by closed shops, by crowded poorhouses and glutted jails, by crowds of squalid idlers, that the distress is real. Take the one simple fact that the consumption of cotton goods in England has fallen off 35 per cent. in three years! Can any fact afford stronger proof of the poverty and depression of our operative classes? Cotton constitutes the greater proportion of the clothing of the lower orders; when, therefore, the consumption of cotton falls away it is proof positive that the working classes are taking less clothing.—*Sullivan's Protection to Native Industry*. London, 1870. Am. Ed., p. 17.

port products as much manufactured as possible, and import the products of other nations as little manufactured as possible, so as to stimulate her own industries. We have been told that if we did not buy her manufactures she would not buy our grain; yet from Prussia and Russia each, the most protected nations on the continent except Belgium, she gets eight times as much grain as she does from us. From France, the next highest protected country, she gets largely more than she does from us, and Mecklenburg and Turkey each furnish her more than we do. Her policy is to buy cheap and sell dear! She buys little of America, for she can get goods cheaper from countries whose wages are lower; but she sells more to America than any other country, for she finds the people fools enough to buy whatever is dear, rather than make it for fear of creating a monopoly. [Laughter.] So, she has illustrated the wisdom of setting the people of a State or country at work upon the productions of their own soil; giving employment to every person, at all seasons of the year, bringing the producers and consumers side by side, and getting manufactured articles without great cost of transportation.

But she has recently given a new illustration of the law by which the power of nations is developed. She found herself short of food, and Cobden and other noble men engaged in the work of giving the working people cheap food. But they carried their theories too far. They opened their markets for manufactured goods to competition with the world. The wise legislation that had made her the most powerful nation of the world was repealed. What is the result? A little over twenty years has elapsed, and England is "sick unto death," and can never recover without going through the process of a revolution.* I have told you that her export of cotton goods

* The small farmer gives way to the mere ploughman; and capitalists, few in number, command the soil. This gives rise to a very remarkable state of things. The Irish farmers, with their families, are driven off from their farms, and come over to Scotland in shoals to press their labor on our capitalist farmers. They are fast taking the place of the Scotch peasantry, while these are driven into the towns, or altogether off the country. Again, our Scotchmen are crowding in upon English labor and competing with that, both in the country and in the towns. The Irish are cheaper than the Scotch, and the Scotch are cheaper than the English; and without knowing why, the working masses are being shoved off in thousands to save them from death.—*Social Politics, Kirk.*

These things must be laid to heart, for (as we have said more than once) emigration cannot help us out of the difficulty which these bring, and must keep

had fallen off five millions of dollars last year; that her exportation of English manufactured silk goods fell off one million of dollars. She exported comparatively little British-made paper. Her "free trade" is uprooting her feebler industries and converting her skilled workmen into paupers. Seventeen silk manufactories made the town of Macclesfield prosperous when that treaty was signed. Of those seventeen but one exists, and it is working up its raw material, and the proprietor is buying no more. The English silk maker cannot compete with the low wages of France, and the still lower wages of Belgium. The paper trade was next attacked. It was one of the few industries left to Ireland, and it has been extirpated, and in the tables of the exports of Great Britain for last year you will find the bulk of her exports were of Belgian paper. Her books are printed in Belgium. I bought to-day in Mr. Strickland's store, a book to carry home to my little child—it bears the imprint of a London house—the paper in it is Belgian, the printing is Belgian, and the binding is Belgian. And what a sad story is connected with this change in her trade. I refer you to the files of your own paper for three weeks, for I have read it everywhere as I travelled, that five thousand compositors, the most skilled in England, are out of employment and going upon the poor rates. The *London News* describes it as a pitiable scene; those skilled and intelligent workmen gathering daily at the Trade Rooms to the number of three hundred, and remaining there all day in the hope that some of them may be called to fill the place of a sick or absent workman. And the *News* remarks that it is painful to record that such calls do not average two a day. During last winter, the same paper

upon us so long as the present system goes on. The cause must be arrested, or the effect will continue to grow upon us. As we shall more fully show, when we come properly to the point, the men who emigrate are the very hands by whose industry we have been kept so long from the state of collapse, which has at length come. The men and women they leave behind are the comparatively helpless, whose energy is not even sufficient to stave off pauperism from themselves, and who cannot possibly wage a successful war with a system which drains off every possible penny, and thing, to be devoured in luxury.—*Ibid.*

Men who can make and unmake the legislature will not die in favor of deer, merely because it so happens that a selfish hand has the landholder's hold of the soil by technical right. The people of this country need not, and we think they will not, resort to any other means by which to redistribute the surface so that all shall have space enough on which to live, than such as will inevitably follow the suppression of unfair modes of dealing between class and class in the community.—*Ibid.*

states that five thousand of the best shipbuilders in England, too proud to receive charity, went to breaking stones in default of other employment. One after another of the more feeble industries are going; and at last England, the land of coal and limestone and iron, finds herself crowded out of foreign markets and will be crowded out of her own, even in the iron trade. So frightened have the governing English people begun to feel, that the iron masters selected two men of great ability, H. Herries Creed and Walter Williams, Jr., to travel on the continent and inquire into the cause of the diminution of the English iron trade. They returned and published a book called "Handicraftsmen and Capitalists," and I purpose to detain you briefly by reading an extract from this remarkable work:

"We are in presence of a real danger while these people are looking at one of which there is only a shadow, and that, as we believe, a shadow created by imagination, and not that of an existence. We are face to face now, at this moment, with the greatest obstruction that British industry has ever been checked by, and unless we can remove it, and remove it promptly, the supremacy which we have held in production and manufacture will be transferred to wiser and harder working nations. The civil war of America and the political condition of Germany have stayed the progress of those countries, and have checked the advancing foot that was treading on our heels. We have again widened the before narrowing distance between us, and we again hold our own in the production of textile fabrics and many other industries. But in the meantime Belgium, which has enjoyed even to a greater extent than ourselves the advantage of being a neutral Power, and France, whose great hoarded wealth and hitherto insufficiently appreciated powers of production have been receiving rapid as well as continuous development from the application of the wonderful administrative ability of her Emperor, have been steadily overhauling us at a pace increasing daily. And they have been doing this most remarkably in the very industry in which, above all others, we ought to have been able to set competition at defiance. In cotton we were dependent upon another nation for the raw material. In the case of iron every description of raw material required in aid of its manufacture is the produce of our own soil. It is under our feet; and yet, with all this advantage—with the additional advantage, too, as we are told, of possessing the best and most advanced skilled workmen in the world—Belgium and France have been thrusting us out of foreign markets to an extent which the public will hardly credit, and of which the trade itself is scarcely aware. . . . . . .

"A like state of things obtains in Spain. There, again, England is thrust aside, defeated by Belgium and by France. We cannot compete with their producers either in price or continuousness and certainty of supply. Nor is this all. Even at home, even within our own boundaries, these industrious and pushing people are challenging our supremacy, and that not infrequently with success. In bar iron, in rails, in engines for agricultural purposes, and even in locomotives for railways, they have lately been obtaining orders even in our own market here at home.

How and why is this? How is it that our position in so great an industry has been slipping from under us? It is a question of grave import, and these are facts calculated to create great anxiety, not only to the capital which embraces in its operations eighteen English counties, besides the Scotch, Welsh, and Irish districts, but to a large population of special habits and industrial skill, dependent upon the maintenances of our mines and our ironworks in full activity and progressive development. To these latter the question we have asked is of far greater moment than it is or can be to either the state or the capitalist. The State may lose, and yet exist, and carry on with loss more or less; the capitalist may be compelled to make a sacrifice in converting his fixed capital into movable, but he can carry that diminished capital and his undiminished reputation and administrative ability to Belgium, to France, to Spain, or to Russian Poland. There, in any and all of those countries, he will find great coal fields of excellent yield, upon or near which he can establish iron works, where, with the appliances that his capital can command, and his administrative experience manage, he will, with the aid of native labor, cheerfully furnished at a comparatively nominal rate, far outstrip the hampered efforts of his country, seize for himself that profit of which a large proportion would have been public property, and leave the discontented and combative artisans of England a burden to their country and a difficulty to themselves. To the artisan of Great Britain, to the unionists of her manufacturing districts, this question is of the extremest importance. Their life or death hangs upon its prompt solution. Transfer of themselves is simply an impossiblity. Foreign nations have a superabundance of labor with which, untrammelled as they are by legislative restrictions, they can, with the aid of the improved processes obtained by them from us, proceed independently and triumphantly in the path upon which they have entered so promisingly, and which, unless we can cross it, must conduct them to monopoly."

Sagacious Englishmen are discovering that free trade is not likely to prove so pleasant to England as they thought it would.* There are thirty Prussian locomotives running

* Whoever contemplates, on the one hand, the enormous powers of production in the United Kingdom, and on the other, the misery which nevertheless grinds down masses of the population, will necessarily conclude that the circumstances which ensure or promote the creation and due distribution of wealth, are yet unknown or mistaken. He will see the science which assumes to teach these things, discredited, helpless, and utterly at fault. There must be something fearfully wrong or essentially deficient in the prevailing system: there must necessarily be some *error in theory*. No adequate practical measures of relief can be devised till it is discovered.—*Sir John Byles, in preface to 9th edition of Sophisms of Free Trade.* Manchester, 1870.

The claptrap of leaving everything to "supply and demand" of heartless Political Economy (so called, but not the true thing) has had its day. The first want of mankind is the means of subsistence; but what does this "law" of supply and demand do here? What is at present reckoned the correct view of

over the Northwestern Railroad of Great Britain. English goods are too dear for Englishmen, but we buy them, and pay the cost of transportation from Manchester to the seacoast, across the Atlantic to New York, and thence to our Western frontiers. We could do a great deal better than that if we would do as France and Belgium and Prussia do—set our own people to work upon our own vast and varied materials. You have iron in grand abundance. You have peat as cheap as coal to make it. You have the coal of Illinois and Iowa lying near to the respective boundaries of your State. You have copper, zinc, lead—all that you want is energy and enterprise, and determination to see to it, that your representatives will look to your interests, and you can build American rolling-mills, such as I examined this afternoon at Bayview, in every section of your State. You can go to England, and lift out of want and pauperism the skilled workmen of that country who are hungering in poverty, and who would thank you to the latest day of their lives for making them independent workingmen, and free American citizens. [Applause.] Among the disastrous effects of free trade on the interests of the working people of England last year, it is reported by Sir Roderick Murchison, that in Cornwall and Devonshire three hundred copper and tin mines were closed. Three hundred mines closed in order that 70,000 tons of cheap ore might be imported from Chili and other South American States. What effect had the closing of these mines on the miners

---

State economy? Is it to provide work for the poor, the honest, and the willing? Not at all. That is not the Political Economy (falsely so called) which is the idolatry of English politicians. It is for the state to stand aloof when widespread distress prevails, and to give no help until the unemployed have sunk to the rank of paupers, when they are handed over to the humiliation and demoralization of the Poorhouse, and the tender mercies of the local bodies so frequently misnamed "guardians."—*The State, the Poor, and the Country.* By R. H. Patterson. Edinburgh and London, 1870.

The weak point of Political Economy has hitherto been that, by many of its teachers, the financial test has in all cases been made absolute. The immediate production of wealth has frequently been made the sole object of the science: overlooking the fact, not only that the amount of wealth in a community is far from being an absolute test of national well-being, but also that many an expenditure upon the improvement of the moral and intellectual condition of the people, howsoever unproductive in the first instance, or it may be for many years, transmutes itself into a positive financial gain in the end, besides from the first conducing to the increased contentment and good order of the community.—*Ibid.*

But such Political Economy is not only heartless, but eminently short-sighted. It disregards two grand elements of the question,—the element of the future, and also the question of social well-being.—*Ibid.*

whose only estate was their skill and industry? But seven thousand of them were able to emigrate, for English wages do not enable the miner to own a home, or lay up money by which to carry a family to a distant country; and there are more than seven thousand, yes, three times seven thousand of them reduced to want, and swelling the list of paupers, who now number more than a million in England alone. I will not talk of Ireland, and have already alluded to Scotland in this connection. But on the last day of last March there were dependent on the poor rates of England 993,000 people—one out of every fourteen, and the number is steadily increasing. Bring these poor people here, pay their passage, and let them dig into your iron beds, and your limestone, and your peat beds. Let them work your copper, zinc, and lead mines, and you will find that your State will increase in power, and population, and wealth, and that your markets will not depend on long lines of transportation. This will be doing a work of humanity. It will be doing God's work—taking care of His poor. Yes, it will be robbing the tyrant of the world of the power to ever again interfere in our family quarrels and destroy our commerce. [Applause.] I find at Bayview a beautiful rolling-mill not yet completed. It has I am told already added about 1000 to the inhabitants of Milwaukee. If it be extended and the wages of those who are to work in it be protected by an adequate tariff, there will be furnaces and forges added to it, and apparatus for digging peat, pressing and consuming it. There will be commerce landing at your broad new pier. It will be crowded with iron from the Marquette region and coal from Pennsylvania, Iowa, and Illinois. Vessels will be going there, taking old rails to be re-rolled, and carrying away rails that have been made, or rolled; and I predict that under the energy that presides over this new industry, Bayview will in five years be one of the greatest commercial points of Milwaukee. If you do not crush out the enterprise, in order that England can enjoy your markets, this point will grow in population to five or ten, probably fifteen or twenty thousand people during the next decade. Depend upon it, this one industry will gather around it laboring people, skilled mechanics, iron workers, machine makers, and the merchant, the teacher, the physician, the preacher, and all the elements that you find in a prosperous village.* This is the way we have changed Philadelphia from a sprawling city of one hundred and twenty thousand when I first knew it, to a city of seven hundred thousand inhabitants. We have gone into all lands, gathered skilled workmen, however poor, and put them at work upon our soil or mineral productions. There are establishments in my district, employing 2500 hands, almost every one a head of a family, with which he lives in a home that he owns, and calls no man lord on this earth! [Applause.] But, citizens of Wisconsin, I have not come to you to-night to plead for the iron interests of Pennsylvania, nor for the manufacturers of the East, but to plead with you—with your cheaper food and more abundant resources—to enrich yourselves by rivalling them in gaining the profits which are derived from any branch of

---

* How fully my predictions have been anticipated is shown by the following letter, which, though not intended for publication, I cannot withhold:

OFFICE OF THE MILWAUKEE IRON COMPANY,
MILWAUKEE, *Feb. 21st*, 1871.

HON. WM. D. KELLEY,

Dear Sir:—I just happened to think that you visited our city in 1867 shortly before our mill for re-rolling went into operation. That was the beginning of the iron industry of this State. I recollect that you prophesied things concerning the future business of our company, which seemed almost fabulous even to me. I am writing this, merely to tell you how near you came to the truth, as I know you are interested in these things.

In 1868 we made 8000 tons of rails and employed 150 men. The business then was confined to re-rolling. In 1870 we made over 16,000 tons of rails. This month we started a new puddling mill, which more than doubles our puddling capacity. The capacity of the works is now 30,000 tons of rails per annum, and that quantity we hope to make in 1871. We started our No. 1 Blast Furnace in April, 1870. No. 2 Furnace will start in about a month. These furnaces are second to none on the continent of America, and can easily make 30,000 tons of pig iron per annum. We have an inexhaustible supply of the finest ore within fifty miles of us, from which we draw most of our material. We use also Lake Superior ore. We now employ 700 men in our works. The works have already far outgrown your prophecy, and there is every reason to believe that they are yet in their infancy. Bessemer steel works are now contemplated, and will doubtless be built.

The iron interest of the West is rapidly growing in importance. As these manufacturing centres grow, people who have heretofore been blind on the subject are beginning to see that Protection *means something*. The land on which our works stand, was bought in 1866 for $100 per acre. A large and thriving village has grown up, and land within a radius of half a mile of our works now sells for $1000 per acre. Fully nine-tenths of our men are from Europe, many of them brought here directly by us, and *because* these works were built. This iron interest so rapidly developing has changed the sentiments of the people of this city. You would have a larger audience now, could you again talk to them of Protection. I hope the time will soon come, when we may see you *here;* we of the West believe there is to be a *fight* on this subject. You who are known as the champion of the cause must come to us. You will not be told that "you are working only for the Pennsylvania iron interest." That interest is now a national one.

Yours very respectfully,
JAS. J. HAGERMAN.

business in which they engage, and thus establish a sure market for the provisions you will still grow, but which your former customers no longer require.

More specially than this, my fellow-citizens, I come to urge you to engage in another branch of agriculture. I saw, as I travelled through the South, not only that it was growing grain, and raising pork and beef, but that it was raising but little sugar; that it was soon to look to the great West for sugar. Wisconsin will yet make sugar for Louisiana.

As others have done, you laugh at this as a sensational proposition. Believe me, it is a practical suggestion, if what can be done in Sweden, and Poland, and Russia; in France, Austria, and Prussia, can be done in America. Last year we sent eighty million of dollars across the Atlantic for sugar and molasses. Had the people of the Northwest listened to the warning of Dr. Schrœder, of Bloomington, Illinois, nearly twelve years ago, who then begged them to engage in raising beets and making sugar, every dollar of that eighty millions would have remained in the country. The limited sugar fields of the South cannot provide for the constantly increasing consumption, and you can make beautiful sugar cheaper in the West than the coarse sugar of Cuba can be produced, and can thereby add to your crops of wheat, and hay, and oats, and to your capacity to raise sheep and cattle. What has been the experience of France, and all the countries I have named, would be your experience, and is being realized by certain enterprising men of Illinois.

Do you know that by devoting your land to beets one year out of three you can raise more grain or hay than you can by continuous crops of hay or grain? You can if you will grow the beet and manufacture sugar. The secret is this: The beet requires deep ploughing. It must be covered by the earth at maturity. If any part of it escapes from the earth it is damaged, and the beet will not command a fair price, and is only fit to be fed to cattle; therefore sugar-beet culture requires deep ploughing. It requires either new land, like that through which I have been travelling in the West, or rich manure. It should have manure for the second year, at any rate; but in the first year good crops may be grown in the fresh lands of the prairie. In old land it requires for its first crop rich manure; but to get a double crop of wheat the next year you will require no manure; you have but to break the surface and put in the seed. The next year too go through the same process of treating the surface and putting in your wheat, and your crop will be double, or nearly so, and in the two years you will have got more than by three consecutive crops with usual culture. In the meanwhile, you will have sold your beets, and, at ordinary prices, a larger profit will be derived than if you had sold grain, wheat, or hay. The beets are pressed, the juice is taken for sugar, and the pulp which remains you can buy again as a capital substitute for hay. It is the custom in Europe that, when a farmer sells his beets, he contracts to purchase back such amount as he may want of the pulp to feed to his cattle and sheep; it fattens them like oil cake.

Thus this industry, hitherto neglected by Americans, furnishes both animal and vegetable manures for its own promotion, and there is a great increase in the agricultural and cattle growing quality of the districts in which it is practised. One of the arrondissements of France, in which, when Napoleon I. started beet culture by offering a liberal system of bounties for relative degrees of success, the farmers could feed but 700 head of cattle, reported 11,500 head of cattle, and better crops of hay and all the cereals, when Napoleon III. and his Empress visited it, in 1865. The beet root on the one hand, and free trade in England on the other, have changed the relation to animal food of the Englishman and Frenchman. The English formerly called the French Johnny Crapeau, "the man that lives on frogs," and used to make fun of his thin broth. Yet so largely has the production of cattle been increased by beet culture in France that she exports beef and wheat to England, and the proportion of Frenchmen who eat beef or mutton is steadily increasing, while the proportion of British people who eat beef or mutton is diminishing. Enlightened Frenchmen ascribe this change to the beet-root culture. This wonderfully beneficent industry is the child of protection. In 1812-13-14, Napoleon found the coast of Europe blockaded. His people could get no sugar. The price went up to from 93 cents to $1.00 per pound, American money, and the people clamored for it. Napoleon did not send out vessels laden with gold or bonds to run the blockade and bring in sugar, but determined to make France so independent that they might blockade the coast and Frenchmen could still enjoy the necessaries of life. He had read of experiments in making beet-root sugar. He consulted the best chemists, and the most experienced agriculturists; and satisfied that France could produce her own sugar, he ordered 100,000 acres of land to be planted in beets at the expense of the Empire. He appointed a competent man to superintend it. He also offered an immense reward to the chemist or practical mechanic who would extract most sugar from a ton of beets, and another to him who should obtain the largest amount of beets from an acre of land. Then to interest the whole people, he offered two classes of premiums: one to those who should raise not less than a given number of tons of beets from an acre, and the other to those who should succeed in extracting not less than a given amount of sugar from a ton of beets. Thus he engaged the mind and skill of France in the great experiment of supplying her with sugar. And he attained his object. But, by and by, the blockade was lifted, and Great Britain undertook to destroy the new industry by supplying France with cheap cane sugar from her colonies. Napoleon said No! He not only protected the industry he had created by high duties, but for a time prohibited the importation of sugar, that the people who had engaged in trying to supply him and the nation with the means of subsistence while engaged in war, should be protected until their industry was fully established. When that was done, the prohibition was removed, but adequate duties were levied to protect the trade.

On this point let me read you a brief extract from E. B. Grant's admirable work on beet-root sugar:

"The price of beet-root sugar in April, 1866, was four and three-fourth cents per pound.

"The preceding table shows that the price of sugar has constantly fallen since 1816. Yet production has steadily increased. It will be seen that the price of sugars, exclusive of duties, was in 1816 about three times greater than at present. But this does not fully give an idea of the difference in the state of things existing then and now.

"From 1816 to 1833 beet sugars were protected by a duty on foreign sugars varying from five to eight cents per pound.

"From 1840 to 1860 they were protected by a duty of from one to three and a half cents per pound on foreign sugar.

"From 1860 to the present time, not only has there been no protection as against foreign sugars, but sugars of the French colonies have had an advantage over all others of nearly half a cent per pound.

"In addition to constantly diminishing price, with steadily decreasing protection, wages have doubled, and it is to increased skill alone that the beet-sugar manufacture owes its present existence."

Yes, beet-root sugar is the child of protection, and I beg you to notice how munificently it is repaying those who fostered it in its hours of weakness. I have here Grant's book, to which I wish every one of you in the wealthy State of Wisconsin had access. I quote from it again:

"It is the constant effort of the French sugar manufacturer at the present day to induce the Government to reduce the duties and imposts on sugar, feeling that the reduction in the price consequent upon such action would increase consumption. He does not ask protection against the manufacturers of cane sugar in any part of the world; for although the industry is entirely the creation of the protective policy, yet under it so great an amount of skill has been acquired, and the cost of manufacture has been so reduced, that he is now able to compete upon equal terms with the whole world.

"In France the impost is laid upon the sugar produced; in Belgium it was formerly laid upon the juice expressed from the beet, but at present it is upon the sugar, as in France; in Germany upon the beets; in Austria upon the sugar produced, or upon an agreed estimate of the capacity of the mill; in Russia upon the hydraulic presses. It varies in the different countries from forty to eighty-five dollars per ton."

The *Journal des Fabricante de Sucre*, says:

"But even if the duties on foreign sugars should be abolished, the advantage would be on the side of the beet sugar manufacturer, who will probably have less need of protection than the Louisiana planter.

"The people of the Northern States will not long defer the cultivation of a plant which contains so much sugar that it will soon teach them to forget that which was formerly produced upon the banks of the Mississippi. As to the competition of Cuban and Brazilian sugars, they have no more cause to fear it than have the beet sugar makers of France and Germany, where the economical conditions are far less favorable than those of the Northern and Western States.

"The beet-sugar industry has been of vast benefit to Europe, notwithstanding the high protective policy to which it owes its existence, and which, as a matter of course, was pursued for a time at the expense of the public, which paid higher for sugar than it would otherwise have done; yet there is no question that the sugars have been cheaper throughout the world for the past fifteen years than they would have been had the industry not existed.

"Formerly the production of sugar was a monopoly, confined to the tropics, where its possession, combined with the cheapness of land and the system of slavery, fostered in planters and manufacturers an extravagant, shiftless, and costly method of manufacture.

"The vast improvements that science has brought to bear on the chemistry and mechanics of beet sugar production in Europe have awakened the planters and manufacturers of the tropics to the necessity for progress if they desire to retain their supremacy.

"Almost all the improvements made in cane sugar manufacture in the last fifteen years owe their origin to the beet sugar establishments of France and Germany.

"The effects produced upon agriculture in Europe by the cultivation of beets for sugar and alcohol have been astounding, and the importance of the interest is now everywhere acknowledged.

"In the cane sugar countries upon the territory surrounding a sugar establishment no crop is to be seen but the cane, while cattle and sheep are few. In the sugar districts of Europe, on the contrary, the fields in the vicinity of a sugar manufactory are covered with the greatest diversity of crops, among which are beets, wheat, rye, oats, barley, corn, rape, flax, tobacco, and all the cultivated grasses. Every field is cultivated close up to the roadside, and the stables are filled with fine cattle, sheep, horses, and swine. No farmer needs to be told which system is the best and most enduring."

Thus, my fellow-citizens, this feeble child, created by protection, fostered by prohibition, and sustained by a protective tariff, now pays from $40 to $85 a ton taxes to the Government. It gives the people sugar such as I hold in my hand—the product of the soil of Illinois, as beautiful loaf sugar as I ever saw, and which you will be able to buy, not for twenty cents a pound, the price you now pay, but for four cents, when you learn to depend on your own resources and withdraw your patronage from England, Spain and their colonies. Thus, protection wisely administered, always proves a boon to the consumer.

Let me give you another striking illustration of this important and inflexible truth. During the war the Central Railroad of Pennsylvania and the Philadelphia, Wilmington, and Baltimore Companies needed a few steel rails. They sent an agent to *England* to buy them at the cheapest rate. He could not get them for less than $150 in gold per ton, which, as gold was at $2.40, made every ton of that railroad steel, duties included, cost over $400, in currency. The officers of these and other companies determined to build a steel rail manufactory, and relieve our transporters of such exactions. The city of Harrisburg tendered them twenty-five acres of ground on which to put it. They imported a thousand steel makers and their families from England, put up their machinery, and made a batch of rails. They then concluded to go on manufacturing, and the company, every one of which was an officer of a railroad company, who owned a large amount of stock, agreed between the stockholders of the railroad companies and the managers of the steelworks, what would be a fair price, so as to give the holders of the steel works a fair profit, and the railroad companies in which they were interested steel rails at a fair price. One hundred and thirty dollars currency was fixed as the price. The news went to England in the next steamer, that they were making steel rails in Pennsylvania at $130 currency per ton. Until the mail brought replies to these communications, for there was no telegraph then, the English agents still asked $150 in gold. But the day the next English mail came in, every English agent was offering steel rails at $120 currency. [Laughter.] The establishment of one steel factory created this vast difference in prices. Now, mark you, when English monopolists found that their American markets were gone, the leading steel makers of England, the "Butchers," came over and bought a property which lies, part in my district and part in the Fifth, and are building immense steel works, with British capital, and will bring another thousand steel workers and their families to add to the strength and power of our country, and eat, not one-half of one per cent. of Western grain, but feed wholly on provisions grown on the soil of America. [Applause.]

I believe firmly in the protective policy. I would protect every industry that cannot certainly be developed without it, and would withdraw protection as soon as it was able and strong enough to stand competition with the lower wages of other countries. But what I am now here specially for is to ask that the people of the West, in common with those of all other sections of the country, will demand the repeal of those internal taxes, which burden our industry, and give old step-mother England an advantage in our markets. We can raise money enough without these taxes on our industry. Why should we hurry to pay our debt? England has not hurried to pay hers, and her credit has not suffered. She provides by taxing a few articles a sufficient sum annually to pay her current expenses, pay the interest on her debt, and to show that she could cut down her debt if she wanted to. We can raise from taxes on whisky, tobacco, and malt liquors, and by seeing to it that the taxes are collected (applause), money enough—the tariff standing as it is—to pay the interest on the debt and to meet the current expenses of the Government, and lay by a few millions annually for payment on the principal of the debt.

We have paid in the last two years over two hundred and forty million of dollars of the principal of the debt. In other words, we have added $240,000,000 to the price of American-made goods, and given foreign goods that advantage over them in our market; and I come to urge the West to join with the East in demanding that our taxes may be simplified and reduced, that industry may be relieved, and to appeal to an enterprising people to bless themselves by lifting millions of the poor, oppressed, degraded, but skilful, and would-be industrious laboring people of Great Britain out of pauperism into the life, and light, and glory of free American Republicanism.

CONTRACTION THE ROAD TO BANKRUPTCY: NOT TO RESUMPTION.

SPEECH DELIVERED IN THE HOUSE OF REPRESENTATIVES, JANUARY 18TH, 1868.

The House being in the Committee of the Whole on the state of the Union—

Mr. Kelley said:

Mr. Chairman: War is not an unmitigated evil. It calls into action the worst of human passions and the highest of human virtues. It contrasts the spirit that conceived and gloated over the horrors of Libby, Belle Isle, and Andersonville, by the uncomplaining patriotism and fortitude with which those horrors were endured. It may be called the science of destruction, yet it develops the germs of future prosperity, evokes wealth from unrecognized sources, and frequently leaves communities, which for the time it seems to have decimated and desolated, richer than they were in the peaceful seasons which preceded it. This is not often true of mere dynastic wars, but of such as involve a question between forms of government, or are waged for the transfer of territory from an oppressive to a liberal government, it is almost an invariable consequence.

The unparalleled struggle through which we have gone was of the latter class, and illustrates most forcibly the truth that in God's providence, so often inscrutable, war has its purposes. We mourn hundreds of thousands of the prematurely dead, among whom were the bravest, best, and most beautiful of the circles in which they moved. The maimed soldier meets us at every turn in the bustling highway, and the widows of those who fell for our country have not yet laid aside their weeds or their tender children lost the memory of the lineaments of him they loved, and who, but for his patriotism, might have lived to shield them from the ills they endure in poverty and orphanage. They suffer, but the people in whose cause they suffer were richer, more powerful, and consequently abler to endure additional taxation, on the 19th of April, 1865, when Johnston surrendered, than they were on the 14th of April, 1861, when the guns of the rebellion opened on Fort Sumter.

Mr. Chairman, I venture the assertion, and doubt not that history will demonstrate its correctness, that the war for the suppression of the rebellion developed a productive power in the country more than equal to the indebtedness, national, State, and municipal, incurred in its support and for the payment of bounties and pensions. And when gentlemen speak of securing the results of the war I ask them to regard this fact, and to see to it that it, as well as the purely political results of the struggle, be secured, in order that those who survive its victims may share its happier consequences. The policy which had with rare and brief intervals controlled the legislation of the country from its foundation to the opening of the rebellion was not calculated to develop the resources or improve the condition of the laboring people of the country. It did not aim at these results. It was conceived and enforced by those whose interests were peculiar and adverse to the general prosperity. Under the ancient *régime* the legislative power of the country resided for more than sixty years in a Democratic congressional caucus, the preponderance in which of the slaveholders of the South was almost, if not absolutely without intermission. Controlling the caucus of the dominant party, they controlled the legislation of Congress, and except in the brief periods from 1825 to 1833 and from 1843 to 1847 the policy of the caucus was to prevent the diversification of employments, impair the demand for, and so diminish the wages of, free labor, and by compelling the masses to engage in the production of provisions to so cheapen them as to make it to the advantage of the slave-owner to produce nothing but leading staples, and depend upon the farmers of the North for cheap food for themselves, their animals, and slaves. It was their aim to make mechanical labor unprofitable and degrading, that they might be able to discourage immigration by contrasting the condition of the well-fed slave with that of the laborer of the North, who in freedom should by the exercise of his skill be able to obtain but a precarious support for himself and family. I do not make this arraignment. History presents it.

That remarkable southern book, "Cotton is King," is but an elaboration of it running through well-nigh a thousand finely-printed pages; and in his remarkable address at the close of the grand fair of the Mechanics and Agricultural Fair Association of Louisiana, held in the city of New Orleans, November, 1866, one of the ablest writers and most cogent thinkers of the South, Wm. M. Burwell, Esq., in their behalf, pleaded guilty to it when, in stating "such points of southern opinion and policy as bear upon the causes of subjugation," he thus enumerated them:

"1. That the Federal Government had no right to administer any duties save those which were written down in its charter.

"2. That staple culture by slave labor was the most honorable, the most virtuous, and the most military system of State polity.

"3. That commerce, the mechanic arts, and the banking system were incompatible with the social safety of the slave States, and tended to disparage the high standard of virtue, courage, intellect, and patriotism which accompanied the pursuits of agriculture and the institution of slavery.

"4. That great cities were great sores, aggregations of people an evil, immigrant numbers and capital not desirable, and works of internal commerce only to be allowed where they were built at the private cost of those who used them. The ocean was regarded as a 'scene of strife,' and it was thought our ships and workshops should be stationed beyond the Atlantic."

Concise as these propositions are, they present a comprehensive statement of the policy of the leaders of the Democratic party. They were foes to commerce and the mechanic arts, and, in view of the extent of our country, its boundless, varied, and equally-distributed natural resources succeeded to a degree that is almost incredible in stationing "our ships and workshops beyond the Atlantic." In the southern theory of society the free laboring man had no place; its philosophy gave him no consideration. It regarded him as a nuisance, an interloper, who had no place in a well regulated State. In its ideal republic there were to be two classes of people only: the wealthy producers of agricultural staples and the slaves they owned, and upon the sweat of whose brows and by the sale of whose offspring they should live.

But so great were our natural advantages, so ingenious our people, and so largely was American industry and inventive power protected by our patent laws, that in spite of legislation, which produced commercial crises with almost regular periodicity, the manufacturing interests of the North had come to be very considerable. We, however, still remained a commercial dependency of England, and were, indeed, her principal and most profitable dependency; and, sir, notwithstanding the enormous development of our productive power during the war, we continue to be such, as is shown by the official statement of the exports from the United Kingdom to the various countries of the world during the first half of the last two years. In introducing this table the compiler remarks that there has been a considerable falling off in our American trade during the last year, owing chiefly to the prohibitory tariff and the scanty harvest of 1866. It appears that the exports from the United Kingdom to her two greatest dependencies in the periods designated were:

	1866.	1867.
To India	£9,406,838	£10,135,920
To the United States	15,228,220	11,951,179

India stands, in the exhibit from which I obtain these figures, at the head of the list of England's colonial customers, and the United States heads the column of foreign dependents.

Sir, it would weary the committee were I to bring to its attention the many illustrations that occur to my mind of the wondrous increase of our productive power during the war, but I beg you to bear with me while I submit a few of them. The war, endeavor to disguise it as we may, was an irrepressible conflict between two systems of labor, one of which regarded the laborer as a thing to be owned, and the other of which recognized his manhood, kindled his hope, and quickened his aspirations by opening to him the avenues to all public honors, and sought to secure him, however humble he might be, such wages for his work as would enable him to shelter, care for, and give culture to his family. The triumph of freedom over slavery in this contest was of inestimable pecuniary value. But at the beginning of the war we were unable to clothe our soldiers and sailors or provide them with arms and ammunition of our own production. Most of the men who responded to President Lincoln's first requisition for troops, though newly equipped, were in rags when they reached the capital. Our "boys in blue," after a few days' exposure to alternate rain and sun, were surprised to find themselves wearing red coats, and looking rather like English than American soldiers. The prospect of war had flooded the country with what Carlyle calls "cheap and nasty" British fabrics, the warp and woof of which were shoddy, and the indigo blue of which had been derived from logwood.

We had neither the wool in which to clothe them nor the spindles and looms to fashion it into cloth. Nor were we capable of producing iron fit for gun-barrels or cannon; yet when at the close of the war the armies marched on successive days through Pennsylvania avenue, more than one hundred and eighty thousand strong, they were clad as substantially—I think I may say with truth more comfortably and substantially—than had ever been a great army returning from the fields of its conquest at the close of a protracted war. They then wore the wool of America, spun by American spindles and woven in American looms; and I was assured about that time by the Secretary of War and gentlemen connected with the ordnance department that their choicest arms were of native production, and that we could manufacture better gun-barrel iron than we could import.

Every railroad company whose line runs north and south was then suffering depression, if not actual embarrassment. Their condition was not improving but deteriorating, notwithstanding the fact that communities in the same latitude can and should produce the same commodities, and that the natural course of inter-State and international trade is across and not along parallels of latitude. The Democratic policy of stationing "our ships and workshops beyond the Atlantic" contravened these natural laws, and by compelling the people of the North and South to make their commercial exchanges beyond the Atlantic instead of in our own country, had deprived the roads from north to south of business adequate to their maintenance. They were single-track roads, and a number of them had fallen into such dangerous dilapidation as to cause them to be regarded as "man-traps" and "dead-falls." Yet such was the healthful influence of active business and prompt pay in the irredeemable notes of a somewhat expanded currency that many of them, while reducing or extinguishing their indebtedness, renewed and doubled their tracks during the war, and all of them procured adequate motive power and rolling stock for any amount of business, public or private, that might offer.

At the beginning of the war the iron of Lake Superior

was not an article of general commerce, but at its close the Marquette region was furnishing one-eighth of the entire production of the country. In 1861 we were dependent on foreign factories for steel; but under the impulse of the war we are manufacturing ordinary and Bessemer steel in such quantities and of such superior quality as to justify the hope that a few years will enable us to compete in the markets of Central and South America with the nations on which we have hitherto depended. At the beginning of the war the great western coal basin had not been tested experimentally. Intelligent gentlemen from Indiana, Illinois, Missouri, Iowa, and Kansas spoke of the wonderful coal deposit which underlies their respective States as a matter of belief or theory; but now every railroad through those States has either provided itself or is devising means to procure cars adapted to the transportation of that cheap and convenient fuel. Brazil, Indiana, was then an obscure and inconsiderable railroad station, but now, as the centre of an iron and coal producing district, its population is increasing with greater rapidity than that of any town in the State, and trains of cars laden with coal leave it daily for the iron mountain of Missouri, to supply the furnaces and forges of that vicinity with fuel, and return from the iron mountain to Brazil freighted with ore to be smelted and wrought in the midst of coal beds which experience has proven to be an inexhaustible deposit of almost pure carbon. Active demand and prompt payment in irredeemable greenbacks have elicited the demonstration at both points, that in Indiana and Missouri are natural deposits that will, if properly developed, before the close of another generation, dwarf the relative importance of England, Wales, or Belgium as coal, iron, and steel producing centres.

Thus did the country respond to the necessities of the Government, and thus did the demand for industry created by the war and prompt pay by the Government for all that it bought from its citizens, in irredeemable but well-secured greenbacks though it was, enable the people to respond promptly and amply to its calls for men, money, and materials. Our progress was not, as already appears, confined to the military direction, but other branches of industry were also quickened into life. At the beginning of the war the West made no zinc or brass or clocks or watches, and she depended on foreign nations for sugar and molasses. But now the zinc of Illinois and the copper of Michigan, smelted by native fuel, is furnishing the West with merchant brass that is preferred to foreign by engravers. The town of Elgin, Illinois, which rivals the most beautiful New England villages, and which produces watches equal to the best productions of any nation, has sprung up since Sumter was fired on; and in Austin, a suburb of Chicago, not yet three years old, they make clocks, the brass, the glass, the enamel, the steel, and the frames of which, whether simple or ornate, are all of native production, and into which no particle of material enters that has ever been on salt water or paid duty at a custom-house. The inhabitants of the town of Chatsworth, Illinois, did not number two hundred at the close of 1863; they now number nearly two thousand people, who use in their intercourse fourteen of the dialects of Europe, and are producing this year nearly one thousand tons of sugar from beet roots, and an amount of molasses that will pay each laborer good wages, and for the coal consumed by the whole community; and not only did we prove ourselves able to clothe our army and improve the material, texture, and durability of its clothing, but we increased the variety and improved our woolen fabrics for private wear so much that we are able to enter the list with the most successful woolen manufacturing nations. But, sir, that we did during the war add to our productive power and realized wealth more than the principal of our debt is to my mind demonstrated by the fact that though the taxes upon our industry, trade, income, and the earnings of our corporations, were heavier than now by hundreds per cent., they were, after the first year of the war, or from the time that green-backs relieved the want of adequate currency, paid cheerfully, because they were paid from monthly or annual profits. Our people were steadily increasing in wealth, every exchange of property between them was for mutual advantage, and by increasing their wealth they added to the taxable resources of the country. The able report of the special Commissioner of the Revenue, D. A. Wells, Esq., thus corroborates this view:

"As has been already shown, the national expenditures, exclusive of appropriations for the redemption of the public debt and for interest, attained during the five years from 1861 to 1866 the extraordinary average of over seven hundred and twelve million dollars per annum, to which must also be addded the great increase during the same period of State and local expenditures. Now, while by far the largest portion of the money represented by this expenditure was borrowed, it must nevertheless be borne in mind that the average annual money statement for the years specified is in a great degree, if not entirely, the measure of the labor annually furnished to the Government in the form of commodities or services rendered in the Army or Navy, for the war in the main was conducted by means of the services of the soldiers rendered at the time, and by means of the food, clothing, and material of war raised or made during the period of hostilities, and for which money or an acknowledgment of indebtedness was given. It therefore appears that during the years from 1861 to 1866 labor and commodities were continually withdrawn from the productive employments of peace to the destructive occupations of war, and that the measure of this unproductive diversion was in excess of $712,000,000 per annum, and yet during the continuance of all this drain the northern and Pacific States did not cease to make a real progress in the creation of substantial wealth. Thus the aggregate of the northern crops, measured in bulk and quantity, and not in money, did not decrease, but increased; the area of territory placed under cultivation was continually enlarged; railroads continued to be built, mines to be opened, and mills, stores, and dwellings to be erected."

As if to emphasize this statement, the Commissioner adds the following foot note:

"It is not believed that any great amount of northern capital accumulated prior to the war was used or destroyed during the war, but that the service and commodities used were mainly the product of the time." *

Mr. Chairman, so immensely had ready demand, the rapid circulation of commodities, and prompt pay in greenbacks stimulated our industry that the amount of American productions—agricultural, mineral, scientific, or mechanical—that had been devoted to the work of destruction are thus shown to have been in excess of the requirements for civil life in a season of prosperity, and certainly in increasing excess of the production of former years.

But, sir, the war has ended; we are again at peace; the jurisdiction of the Government extends over the whole country. Twelve million producers and consumers have been brought within our jurisdiction by the extinguishment of the confederate government, under whose laws they had lived and to whose treasury they had paid tribute during the war, and the Commissioner in this connection submits this question, to which I propose, briefly as I can, to reply. He asks:

* It should be noted that this was said by Mr. Wells before his official visit to England, during which his opinions underwent a radical change.

"If a portion of the country could contribute of its surplus labor and capital an annual value of $21 07 *per capita* for destructive purposes, will it not be easy for the whole country, with its labor and capital restored to productive employments, to contribute $8 73 *per capita* for the payment of interest, expenses, and the reduction of the debt?"

This diminished rate of taxation, the Commissioner tells us, will not only provide for an annual expenditure of $140,000,000 for ordinary expenses, $130,000,000 for interest on the public debt, but $50,000,000 annually for the reduction of the principal of the debt.

Mr. Chairman, whether the people can bear this rate of taxation, reduced as it is, will depend upon our legislation. Had Congress one year ago, when I urged it to that course, repealed the taxes that have not only burdened all but prostrated many of the industries of the country during the past year, and withheld from the Secretary of the Treasury the power to contract the currency, I believe there would be no doubt on this question. My views on this point are the results of much deliberation, and have undergone no recent change. Experience has but made that history which for the two last years I have uttered to the House as prediction. When addressing the House on January 31, 1866, I said:

"England, if supreme selfishness be consistent with sagacity, has been eminently sagacious in preventing us from becoming a manufacturing people; for with our enterprise, our ingenuity, our freer institutions, the extent of our country, the cheapness of our land, the diversity of our resources, the grandeur of our seas, lakes, and rivers, we should long ago have been able to offer her best workmen such inducements as would have brought them by millions to help bear our burdens and fight our battles. We can thus raise the standard of British and continental wages and protect American workmen against ill-paid competition. This we must do if we mean to maintain the national honor. The fields now under culture, the houses now existing, the mines now being worked, the men we now employ, cannot pay our debt. To meet its annual interest by taxing our present population and developed resources would be to continue an ever-enduring burden.

"The principal of the debt must be paid; but as it was contracted for posterity its extinguishment should not impoverish those who sustained the burdens of the war. I am not anxious to reduce the total of our debt, and would, in this respect, follow the example of England, and as its amount has been fixed would not for the present trouble myself about its aggregate, except to prevent its increase. My anxiety is that the taxes it involves shall be as little oppressive as possible, and be so adjusted that, while defending our industry against foreign assault, they may add nothing to the cost of those necessaries of life which we cannot produce, and for which we must therefore look to other lands. The raw materials entering into our manufactures, which we are yet unable to produce, but on which we unwisely impose duties, I would put into the free list with tea, coffee, and other such purely foreign essentials of life, and would impose duties on commodities that compete with American productions, so as to protect every feeble or infant branch of industry and quicken those that are robust. I would thus cheapen the elements of life and enable those whose capital is embarked in any branch of production to offer such wages to the skilled workmen of all lands as would steadily and rapidly increase our numbers, and, as is always the case in the neighborhood of growing cities or towns of considerable extent, increase the return for farm labor; this policy would open new mines and quarries, build new furnaces, forges, and factories, and rapidly increase the taxable property and inhabitants of the country. Would the south accept this theory and enter heartily upon its execution, she would pay more than now seems her share of the debt and feel herself blessed in the ability to do it. Her climate is more genial than ours; her soil may be restored to its original fertility; her rivers are broad and her harbors good; and, above all, hers is the monopoly of the fields for rice, cane sugar, and cotton. Let us pursue for twenty years the sound national policy of protection, and we will double our population and more than quadruple our capital, and reduce our indebtedness *per capita* and per acre to little more than a nominal sum. Thus each man can 'without moneys' pay the bulk of his portion of the debt by blessing others with the ability to bear an honorable burden."

Confirmed in the correctness of these views by subsequent observation and reflection, at the final session of the Thirty-Ninth Congress I introduced a resolution instructing the Committee of Ways and Means—

"To inquire into the expediency of immediately repealing the provisions of the internal revenue law whereby a tax of five per cent. is imposed on the mechanical and manufacturing industry of the country."

And on the earliest day the rules would permit I offered another resolution declaring—

"That the proposition that the war debt of the country should be extinguished by the generation that contracted it is not sanctioned by sound principles of national economy and does not meet the approval of this House."

On the 3d of January, 1867, in addressing the House in opposition to the views of the Secretary of the Treasury in favor of the maintenance of extraordinary taxes, contraction of the currency, and resumption of specie payments within two years from the date of his Fort Wayne speech, or his annual report, and the extinguishment of not less than $100,000,000 of the principal of the debt annually, I said:

"Peace is restored, our currency approximates the specie standard, and it is discovered that by aid of our inordinate internal taxes foreign manufacturers are monopolizing our home market. Our publishers buy their paper and print and bind their books in England or Belgium; our umbrella-makers have transferred their workshops to English towns; our woolen and worsted mills are closed or closing, and the laborers in these branches are not only wasting their capital, which consists in their skill and industry, but drawing from the savings banks or selling the Government bonds in which they had invested their small accumulations to maintain their families during the winter; and our enlarged importations of foreign goods are swelling the balance of trade against us and preparing us for general bankruptcy."

And again:

"The experiment, if attempted as a means of hastening specie payments, will prove a failure, but not a harmless one. It will be fatal to the prospects of a majority of the business men of this generation, and strip the frugal laboring people of the country of the small but hard-earned sums they have deposited in savings banks or invested in Government securities. It will make money scarce and employment uncertain. Its object is to reduce the amount of that which in every part of our country and for the hundreds of thousands of millions of dollars of domestic trade is money and to increase its purchasing power; and by unsettling values it will paralyze trade, suspend production, and deprive industry of employment. It will make the money of the rich man more valuable and deprive the poor man of his entire capital, the value of his labor, by depriving him of employment. Its first effect will be to increase the rate of interest and diminish the rate of wages, and its final effect widespread bankruptcy and a more protracted suspension of specie payments."

Sir, these predictions were not only not heeded but were denounced as the vagaries of a mere theorist by gentlemen whose position made their voices potential; and I remember that when the productions of the handloom weavers of the country had been freed from taxation by the votes of both Houses the committee of conference upon the disagreeing votes of the two Houses on the tax bill, seizing the fact that the Senate and House had differed as to the use of a verb, restored the provision providing for the tax, and the chairman of the committee in each House proclaimed the possibility of the exemption of these comparatively unimportant productions producing a deficit in the revenue. Some reduction in the scale of taxation was made by the bill to which I refer, and it is well for the country that it was. Large as it was, it would have been better had every direct tax upon our industry been removed. Nor would the revenue of the Government have suffered from the change, for we collected during the year 1866–67 $143,904,880 more than was required for payment of interest on the public debt and current expenses. These inordinate exactions determined the line between profit and loss on many branches of industry and diminished our productions by paralyzing or suppressing such branches. Without the $67,778,082.-70, the amount derived from direct taxes on manufactures other than spirits, malt liquors, and tobacco in its various forms, we would have been able to extinguish more than seventy-five million dollars of the principal of the debt.

Permit me to say, if I may use a homely figure, that by attempting to collect such heavy taxes while contracting the currency, we lighted our candle at both ends. The loom and the spindle, no longer able to yield profit to their proprietor, stand idle; the fires are extinguished in forge and furnace, and the rolling-mill does not send forth its hum of cheerful and profitable industry. On one day of last month eighteen hundred operatives in the glass factories of Pittsburg were deprived of the poor privilege of earning wages by honest toil at the trade in which they were skilled. The establishments in which they worked are closed. In the absence of productive employment for men or machinery the small holders of bonds are selling them to save themselves from bankruptcy if they are proprietors of establishments, or to feed themselves and families in involuntary idleness if they are laborers whose hard-earned savings have been loaned to the Government in its exigency. Look where we may, to any section of the country, we hear of "shrinkage" in the value of manufactured goods, of reduction of wages, or of the hours of labor, of factories running on part time, or closed or to be closed. I present no jaundiced or partisan view of the case, for the gentleman who submitted to this House the report of the committee of conference to which I have alluded, and who resisted proposed reductions of taxes with such persuasive ability, [Mr. Morrill, of Vermont,] in a recent discussion in the Senate on the repeal of the cotton tax, said:

"It may be said that the South are clamoring for the repeal of the tax on cotton. Is there any less clamor in the West or the North or the East for a repeal of taxation? I deny it. I say there is as much urgency for a relief from taxation in the North, the East, and the West as in the South. Look at the industries that are at the present moment unusually depressed. Take, for instance, the entire woolen interest. There is not an establishment that is not losing money to-day. Take the wool-grower; not a pound of wool raised last year that will bring within ten cents per pound of its cost. Take the cotton interest; the whole circle of manufactures are in no better circumstances. Look at the value of their stocks; for instance, take the Bates manufacturing stock of Maine, worth two years ago one hundred and sixty cents on the dollar, now there are more sellers than buyers at one hundred. Take the Lyman mills on the Connecticut, worth two years ago ninety-eight to one hundred, now selling at sixty-nine or less; and so I might go on almost through the whole list. They all suffer. Take the West—Ohio, Illinois, or Iowa—look at their hog crop. Why, if they had given away all their hogs, or if they had slaughtered them a year ago and thrown them away, they would have been better off to-day. They have absolutely lost their hog crop by feeding out grain to them, which unfed would have brought more than all their pork."

Mr. Chairman, accepting the business of the oldest and best-managed savings bank for the receipt of small deposits in Philadelphia as a good index to the condition of the laboring class of the country, I have obtained a statement of the number and amount of drafts made by the depositors whose whole deposit is under one hundred dollars, and of the whole number of drafts of depositors for the month of December of the years 1865, 1866, and 1867, and the total amount drawn in each year. It is as follows:

Months.	Year.	Total deposit under $100.	Whole number of payments.	Amount withdrawn.
Dec........	1865	846	1,186	99,603 10
Dec........	1866	811	1,174	104,430 95
Dec........	1867	1,128	1,596	144,205 70

To gentlemen used to large business transactions the movement of the small sums enumerated in this exhibit may not seem important, but they tell a story of bankruptcy as grievous to the victim whose hours of toil were solaced by the reflection that he was by his small deposits garnering a trifling capital for his children or a shelter for his age as is one which is telegraphed to the press of every section of the country by reason of the large amount involved. Nay, more than that, these drafts upon the small accumulations of years of toil tell a story of practical agrarianism and confiscation that would shock gentlemen if it applied to the bonds or land of the wealthy. The attempt to force a resumption of specie payments by contracting a volume of currency which was actively, legitimately, and profitably employed, is as dishonest as it is unwise. The object and effect of such a movement is to increase the purchasing power, the value of the rich man's hoarded or invested dollars, and its projectors pause not, though they discover that it robs millions of laborers of their whole estate. The laborer's income is derived from the exercise of his thews and sinews and the skill of his cunning right hand. These are his estate—these and his little savings—and of these millions are being robbed by the mad attempt of the Secretary of the Treasury to bring about specie payments while the balance of trade is heavily against us, and our gold-bearing bonds are so largely held by foreigners that resumption would in less than thirty days induce the return of bonds enough to drain us of specie and make us feel the curse of absentee-ism as distinctly as Ireland ever felt it. Were our bonds held at home, or were commercial exchanges greatly in our favor, we might maintain a forced resumption; but with our bonds abroad, and the balance of trade heavily against us, we could not maintain it a month. And if Congress does not restrain Mr. McCulloch from persisting in the attempt he will unsettle the value of every species of property, curtail the productive power of the country, bankrupt men of enterprise, and rob millions of laboring people of their whole estate.

But permit me to inquire what effect this experiment will have on the public revenues? Can an honest bankrupt contribute much to the exchequer of his country? Are those who are conducting business at a loss apt to make large contributions to the fund derived from income tax? And are unemployed laborers who have drawn and consumed their last dollar in a condition to buy dutiable or taxable commodities? No, sir; as the number in each of these classes increases the public revenue diminishes; and in view of the facts I have hastily presented I am prepared to say that with full employment, even though prices had continued as high as they were during the war, which I maintain was impossible under the influence of our increasing activity and productive power, the people could better pay the taxes they then endured, heavy as they were, than they can with a contracting currency, low prices, and but partial or no employment for men and machinery, pay the greatly diminished rate suggested by the Commissioner.

Mr. Chairman, two policies were open to us at the close of the war. We have tried one, and the results are but too painfully apparent; the other is still open to us. It is true we cannot repair the losses already endured, but we can check the downward tendency, quicken industry, and give a new impulse to the productive power of the country. It was open to us to diminish the depreciation in the rate of wages by diminishing taxes and furnishing as we had done during the war, a sound circulating medium adequate in volume for the rapid exchange of commodities among our own people, and thus secure employment to our laborers with fair wages for their work; or, on the other hand, we could by imposing taxes not demanded by our exigencies and contracting the currency impair confidence, force sales, palsy enterprise, reduce wages, and deprive the laborer of a market for the only commodity he has to sell—his industry.

Gentlemen will say there can for the present be no employment because the markets are overstocked, and there is what political economists often speak of, "a glut in the market." Sir, the time has never been when the markets of the world were glutted. When that event shall come, every home will be well furnished, and every human being well clothed. A superabundance of the necessaries of life cannot exist while the urgent wants of millions cannot be supplied. Our markets are not glutted. The stock of goods of every kind in the hands of merchants is unusually low, and there are unemployed people in the country who need them all and who would gladly labor for the means to purchase them all. The wretch that shivers in a cheerless home without food, fuel, or adequate clothing; she who, ill-fed herself, shares her last crust with her hungry children; and they who in the midst of winter are deprived of the privilege of toiling, and as their goods are thrown rudely into the street realize a landlord's power when rent is in arrear, do not believe that the market is glutted. Nor is it. The disease from which we suffer is not glut or plethora. Its seat is in the functions of circulation. It is congestion produced by a financial tourniquet applied by a charlatan. That phrase "glut in the market" involves a perversion of terms, and is used to express the fact that the masses are from some cause unable to consume their usual supply of the comforts or necessaries of life.* It does not, as it implies, express the fact that there is an over supply of commodities essential to the comfort of man, but that there is financial derangement. It is a convenient phrase for the theorist, a veil used to conceal a fact the occurrence of which should admonish every statesman that there is something wrong in the prevailing practice of government.

The author of the next treatise on popular fallacies should make "glut in the market" the subject of a leading chapter; for they who use the phrase invariably confound terms and designate the consequence as the cause. Thus the *Irish Republic*, in the course of a generally able article in its issue of January 4th, says:

> "From all parts of Massachusetts and Connecticut we have been receiving, during the past six weeks, the very unwelcome intelligence that mill-owners and manufacturers were either contracting their producing operations or suspending them altogether. Running half or quarter time appears to be the order of the day; while not unfrequently the engine fires are blown out and the machinery left to rust in idleness. The cause is obvious. There is little or no demand for goods. The consequences are what we have already stated. The hands of hundreds of thousands of honest workmen are idle, and their children are ill-fed and ill-clad under the biting blasts of a North American winter."

Let me point out the fallacy of this statement. Fires

* There are other means of producing an apparent glut in the market than by suddenly contracting the currency of a busy and prosperous people. The working men of England in a blind effort to improve their condition, have limited the amount of production, and thereby glutted their market as effectually as Mr. McCulloch would have glutted ours had Congress not prohibited further contraction. In "Social Politics" Prof. Kirk says:

"It may not be out of place here to notice that there is a burden of no small magnitude left behind among the working men in their own state of mind on social matters. Many of them actually think the less they work the better! And they insist that no man shall do more than a very limited amount of work if they can prevent him! They insist that no one shall learn to work beyond a very limited number! They and their children are actually dying in hundreds for want of houses to live in, and yet they think that the fewer houses they build the better! They are miserably clad, and yet they think the fewer clothes they make the better! They are in semi-starvation because of high prices, and yet they actually think that the higher they can make the cost of production, the better for them!"

"Production is yet so far below the wants of men; in other words, there are yet so many starving and ill-clad, ill-housed thousands in the world, that 'over-production' is ridiculous."—*Ibid.*

are blown out and machinery left to rust in idleness, not because there is no demand for goods, but because throughout the South and West there is no circulating medium with which to effect exchanges; and the policy of the Secretary of the Treasury with the cry of the creditor class for resumption have destroyed confidence in individual credit. The proposition should be stated thus:

> "There is little or no demand for goods. The cause is obvious: it is that the hands of hundreds of thousands of honest workmen are idle, and their children ill-fed and ill-clad, because mill-owners and manufacturers have been compelled to contract their operations and withhold from laborers employment and wages with which they would be able to purchase the products of the farmer and manufacturer."

The general theory I am advancing is not new, and is one that should never be disregarded by those who legislate for the people of a republic. The social evils we are enduring, the bankruptcy that is overtaking so many men of enterprise, the want and enforced idleness that prevail so largely among our laboring classes, are due to two causes:—excessive internal taxation, and the curtailment of our currency at a time when the numbers and activities of our people were rapidly increasing. The Secretary of the Treasury and his adherents are responsible for this general prostration of credit and business. They talk of the honor of the country, and the necessity of maintaining it by making the paper dollar equal to the gold dollar, and of hastening the day when our bonds shall be paid in gold. The means to which they resort will not produce the results they desire, but will defeat them. Nor are those who resist them hostile to the bondholder. They aim to secure the laborer the possession and just fruits of his hard inheritance, and by the rapid development of the boundless resources of the country and the restoration of general prosperity to enable the Government to meet the utmost of its obligations with honor at maturity. The contest is between the creditor and the debtor class—the men of investments and the men of enterprise; and during all such contests the laboring classes are inevitable sufferers.

The issue thus raised is as old as civilization. And now, as always heretofore, the creditor class is the aggressor. Alison, in his "History of Europe" from the fall of Napoleon to the accession of his nephew, says:

"Whoever has studied with attention the structure or tendencies of society, either as they are portrayed in the annals of ancient story or exist in the complicated relations of men around us, must have become aware that the greatest evils which in the later stages of national progress come to afflict mankind, arose from the undue influence and paramount importance of realized riches. That the rich in the later stages of national progress are constantly getting richer and the poor poorer is a common observation, which has been repeated in every age, from the days of Solon to those of Sir Robert Peel; and many of the greatest changes which have occurred in the world—in particular the fall of the Roman empire—may be distinctly traced to the long-continued operation of this pernicious tendency. . . . . For the evils complained of arose from the unavoidable result of a stationary currency, coexisting with a rapid increase in the numbers and transactions of mankind; and these were only aggravated by every addition made to the energies and productive powers of society."

Again, he says:

"But if an increase in the numbers and industry of man coexists with a diminution in the circulating medium by which their transactions are carried on, the most serious evils await society, and the whole relations of its different classes to each other will be speedily changed; and it is in that state of things that the saying proves true that the rich are every day growing richer and the poor poorer."—*Alison's History of Europe*, 1815 to 1852, chapter 1.

As Sir Archibald Alison was not gifted with more than human prescience he could not have foreseen the condition of our country in the years that are passing. If, therefore, he described it, he did so by declaring a general law. That he did portray our condition with nice discrimination no one can controvert. Let us see how exact a compliance the contraction policy is producing with all the conditions the conjunction of which he tells us must produce the most serious evils to society.

The close of the war found us with a currency expanded somewhat beyond the amount to which we had been used before the rebellion, but with everybody in the North well employed. Men of character were able to borrow money at moderate rates of interest, and were everywhere engaging in new enterprises that were not merely speculative, but calculated to add to individual and national wealth. Labor was in demand at fair wages. It is true that food was high, for a great war had raged through a series of years, and been succeeded by years of drought or excessive rain, during which the fields had not yielded their usual crops. This no legislation could have averted;

but in spite of it the people at large were prosperous and confident that a fruitful year would adjust the cost of food to the prices of other commodities. From ten to twelve millions of our people, occupying more than six hundred thousand square miles of our most fertile territory, which abounds in water-power and varied mineral resources, were almost without currency. Their whole capital, other than lands and houses, railroads and canals, had been invested in confederate loans or otherwise exhausted. Their banks and insurance companies were bankrupt. They had cotton, tobacco, naval stores, and the fields from which to produce these and all other agricultural commodities. They had laborers skilled in their arts of cultivation, and willing to toil for wages unreasonably low, but they had no currency, no circulating medium with which to make commercial or other exchanges of property or to pay their laborers.

At the same time an unusual stream of emigration was flowing to us from transatlantic countries. Enterprise was pushing rapidly westward, and towns and cities were rising where, when the war began, the buffalo had roamed over unbroken prairies. With these additions to our population and to the area over which it was to circulate what was there to indicate the propriety of a curtailment of the medium by which transactions between man and man and community and community were to be carried on? For myself I was unable to see any, and protested against the mad theories of the Secretary of the Treasury and his disciples. In the course of my remarks on the 3d of January, 1867, to which I have alluded, I said:

"Neither the Secretary of the Treasury nor Congress know whether our currency is in excess of the amount required by legitimate and healthful trade, or if it be, how long it will remain so if undisturbed by legislation. Nor can we settle these points by an appeal to experience, for many of our conditions are novel. That would be a curious and instructive calculation which would show the country the precise demand for currency created by the operation of the Bureau of Internal Revenue, or by the enlargement of the Army and Navy and clerical force of the Government.

"Under the discipline of Providence the southern people will, before many years glide away, consent to permit their fields to be tilled, their mines to be worked, and their cities to be rebuilt and expanded; and who can tell the amount of currency that will then be required by the four million enfranchised slaves and the millions of poor whites, who did not in the past, but are henceforth to earn wages and buy and sell commodities, or for handling the crops and mineral productions of the South? Since we last adjourned the iron horse has crossed Nebraska on one of the routes to the Pacific, and his snort has been heard in the neighborhood of Fort Riley on another; and during the last year three hundred thousand industrious people, who had been fed and clothed through unproductive childhood at the cost of other nations, came and cast their lot among us to till our fields, smelt our ores, work our metals, and manage our spindles and looms; and I cannot guess what amount of currency these energetic people and the westward-marching column of our civilization will require. But, sir, of one thing I am certain, which is that had the Secretary of the Treasury not destroyed all sense of security in the future, the demand for currency to purchase, especially in the South, mineral and other lands, and develop their productive power, would have prevented the acumulation of the immense deposits which now lie paralyzed in bank or are loaned on call to speculators in the necessaries of life. We unsettled values and made or scattered fortunes by the rapid expansion of the currency; and the people implore us to avoid another violent change fraught with like consequences, and to stay the work of contraction till we shall have ascertained, at least proximately, the amount of currency required by healthy and legitimate trade."

But, Mr. Chairman, gentlemen ask, do you not wish to return to specie payments? I answer, yes; but not by the way of bankruptcy and repudiation; and that way leads contraction in the midst of an increase such as never existed before in the numbers of men and fields for their activity. Return to specie payments! Are we doing it? No, sir. The difference between the greenback and gold dollar widens with each month. And while a greenback dollar will buy less gold it will purchase much more of any other commodity than it would a year ago. The rate of interest demanded for loans in the West and South is so inordinate that it has suspended enterprise and must exhaust the resources of any man who attempts to pay it; and while the laboring people are idle the capital which should furnish them employment may be borrowed from the banks of Boston or New York, in whose vaults the bulk of our currency has accumulated, by those who have gold or United States bonds to offer as security, at four per cent. per annum. Contraction has destroyed confidence. The possessors of "realized riches" have no faith in spindles and looms that are producing goods for a falling market, or forges and furnaces the productions of which must be sold at a loss, and invest their funds in Government bonds, or let them lie on deposit till they can buy, at a small percentage of their value, mills, factories, mines, and other valuable properties, when bankruptcy shall cause them to be exposed at public or judicial sale. Sir, we are not on the road to resumption, and will not be till we restore confidence and quicken industry by repealing needless taxes which are giving foreign manufacturers an advantage in our market, and deprive the Secretary of the Treasury of his power to contract the currency and tamper with the market value of every species of property by secret operations in gold and the credit of the country.

Mr. Chairman, the Secretary and his adherents will assume to find a response to the suggestions I have made in the facts set forth by the Special Commissioner of Revenue in his valuable report showing that the income of the country from either internal revenue or customs has not fallen off during the last two years. The Commissioner's statements are indisputable, and I thank him for the industry, patience, and care he has exhibited in procuring and digesting the materials for his report. But, sir, there is a fact that deprives this response of anything like conclusive power. It is not alluded to by Mr. Wells, because it touched no point he assumed to discuss. Let me state it. The revenues of the country from 1860 to 1865 were derived from the loyal States. During that time the confederate States did not contribute to our public revenue, and Maryland, Kentucky, Tennessee, and Missouri were ravaged by war. To find a reply to my argument in the Commissioner's report it should show not only that our revenues during the last fiscal year have exceeded those of 1864 and 1865 in the ratio of our ordinary growth and progress, but also how largely the ten States now being reconstructed, with Missouri, Tennessee, Kentucky, and Maryland, when freed from the tramp of war, were able contribute to the resources of the country. To this fact the Commissioner does not allude. No, sir; it requires the contributions made by the people of the insurgent and border slave States during the last fiscal year to furnish the Commissioner with the gratifying figures he presents to the country and its creditors. A fair statement of the account would contain the amount received from the southern States as a credit and be debited with the amount lost by the paralysis of industry and the productive power of the North.. Were the account thus stated it would be apparent to all that, notwithstanding the addition of fifty per cent. to the taxable population, the current revenue derived by the Government was not increased, but simply steadily maintained.

Gentlemen may say that the South has yielded but little internal revenue besides that derived from the cotton tax, and I freely admit that she has not contributed so largely as we might well have hoped; but I affirm that her contributions would have been much greater had our policy been wiser. It has affected that section of the country more potently for evil than it has the North. Our society was not disorganized and our industrial force was admirably arranged and producing its best results, yet we are suffering derangement and paralysis. Wide sections of the South had been ravaged by war, and, as I have already said, its financial institutions and the accumulated capital of its citizens not invested in lands and buildings had been absorbed by the confederate loan or consumed in the war; but by judicious treatment its recuperation should have been so rapid as to have been the marvel of the world. That the natural resources of the South are greater than those of the North is undeniable. She is capable of producing every agricultural product that can be grown in our climate. Her mineral resources are greater and more varied than ours; she lies near the sea and abounds in navigable rivers, affording cheap water transportation to seaports for the greater portion of her productions, and to her belongs the monopoly of the production of cotton, fine tobacco, rice, and naval stores, and, until now that we are availing ourselves of the beet, of the sugar fields of the country also. Immense bodies of land, as fertile as any in the country, and which has never felt the pressure of the plowshare, are to be found in every southern State. Louisiana alone has sixty thousand such acres which will yield cotton or sugar, wheat or corn. Marvellous as was the increase of the productive power of the loyal States during the war, that of the southern States almost equalled it. Gentlemen will not forget that her Merrimac had sunk the Cumberland before our first monitor was ready to measure power with her. Great Britain supplied her with much of her munitions of war, but the unmechanical South overwhelmed us with surprise by the large share of these she produced for herself. Great Britain again, in defiance of our admirable blockade, clothed many of the confederate soldiers, but the spindles and looms of the constantly-increasing factories of the

South were each year supplying a larger percentage of cloths for civic and military wear. She had depended on New England for boots and shoes, but she found that she could tan her own hides, and people were found to make boots and shoes. Thomasville, North Carolina, is the Lynn, though not the only shoe manufacturing town of the South. Without detaining the committee by details of the improvement and extension of her railroad system, I will mention the fact that though Virginia and North Carolina had never been able to build a road from Danville to Greensboro', whereby a central through route from North to South would have been completed, that road was built in the first year of the war. This increased the value of every foot of a chain of roads extending from Richmond to New Orleans, which now carries a large portion of freight passing between the eastern States of the North and the South and Southwest.

But, sir, without elaborating the point, let me state in general terms that the value of the lands of the South were trebled by the recognition of facts which the war compelled the southern people to recognize, namely: that they could raise their own food, and that they had advantages over those on whom they had hitherto depended for food for man and beast in the markets of the eastern States, Central and South America, the West India Islands, and Europe. As cotton and sugar had been the only crop of the greater portion of their country the people had come to believe that they had but one harvest season—that in which those crops were gathered and prepared for market. But when the armies of the confederacy had to be fed from the fields within its lines they discovered that they had three harvest seasons—the spring for wheat and grasses, summer for corn, and autumn for cotton and sugar. And in this very year many a broad acre, after having yielded its golden harvest of wheat, will have the stubble turned under and be planted in corn that will mature before the frost threatens it. The necessities of the war also taught them the value of deep plowing, fertilizers, and of keeping procreative stock for the work for which they had kept only mules in the past. As an illustration of the value of these discoveries, let me say that it is within my knowledge that Mr. McDonald, of Concord, North Carolina, in order to settle the question of the value of deep plowing and the application of phosphates in the production of cotton, tried two experiments on fields which together embraced one hundred acres of land that had ever been regarded as too poor for cotton land. Wishing to make the experiment for public as well as private advantage, Mr. McDonald took the opinion of the planters of his section of the State as to the possibility of making cotton on such land, and found no man among his neighbors or visitors who believed that it would return him the value of the seed with which he would plant it. But with a heavy old-fashioned Pennsylvania plow he broke the land and turned in a given amount of super-phosphate to the acre, and lo, when the season came for gathering cotton he had the demonstration that the poorest land in Cabarras county had been made to yield the finest crop of cotton ever raised within her limits, and which many of her citizens pronounce the finest ever raised in North Carolina. The many intelligent planters who observed this experiment now know that by the aid of proper implements and adequate stimulants to the soil their fields may be made to yield a hundred per cent. more cotton than they ever have yielded, and that with but fifty per cent. of the labor hitherto applied.

But, as I have before said, the people of this wonderfully endowed section of our country were without a circulating medium. This was their paramount necessity. For the want of it all their interests were suffering. The Special Commissioner of Revenue suggests that our condition is such that "soothing and sustaining" treatment rather than the "heroic" is most likely to promote and hasten our recovery, and I beg leave to inquire whether his suggestion is not much more applicable to them. Inordinate taxes have borne more heavily upon the people of the South than upon us, and contraction has operated with still more aggravated severity upon them, as whatever redundancy there may have been in our currency at the close of the war would have been absorbed by the inviting fields of enterprise offered by the South, and would have gone there to quicken her resources and enable her people to consume dutiable goods and those from which internal revenue is collected by the sale of stamps. That the productive power the war developed in the South has been suppressed by lack of currency, and that by contraction we are abstracting from her people the little they had, is becoming apparent to every observant man. We find evidence of it in every paper that comes from the South. The *Standard,* (Raleigh, North Carolina,) of the 4th instant, says:

"Everything seems to have fallen in price except breadstuffs and meats, which maintain former prices on account of their scarcity. Judgments are passed, execution sales are common, the bankrupt law is taking hold of estate after estate, property of all kinds is rapidly falling in price, lands are changing hands and will soon be knocked off for a mere song; and there is no prospect, so far as we can see, that this condition of things will speedily improve. One of the first effects will be to greatly restrict if not abolish the credit system. Every step, no matter how painful or how much to be deplored, is in that direction. Credit is based on confidence between man and man, and where there is no confidence there can be no credit. The end will be that a large majority of our people will find it impossible to meet their obligations, and must have indulgence in some way, or the hard earnings of many years will be sacrificed under the sheriff's hammer or in courts of bankruptcy."

And a correspondent of the New York *Tribune*, writing from Hinesville, Liberty county, Georgia, last month, says:

"A sale has taken place at this county seat that so well marks the extreme depression in the money market that I send you the particulars: Colonel Quarterman, of this county, deceased, and his executor, Judge Featter, was compelled to close the estate. The property was advertised, as required by law, and on last court day it was sold. A handsome residence at Walthourville, with ten acres attached, out-houses, and all the necessary appendages of a first-class planter's residence, was sold for $60. The purchaser was the agent of the Freedmen's Bureau. His plantation, four hundred and fifty acres of prime land, brought $150; sold to a Mr. Fraser. Sixty-six acres of other land near Walthourville brought three dollars; purchaser, Mr. W. D. Bacon. *These were all bona fide sales. It was court day, and a large concourse of people were present. The most of them were large property owners, but really had not five dollars in their pockets, and in consequence would not bid, as the sales were for cash.* In Montgomery, Alabama, lots on Market street near the capitol, well located, 50 feet by 110 feet, averaged but $250 each. The Welsh residence on Perry street, two-story dwelling houses, including four lots, sold for $3500; Dr. Robert M. Williams was the purchaser. The same property in better times would not have brought less than $10,000. The Loftin place, near Montgomery, containing one thousand acres, was recently rented at auction for forty cents an acre. The same lands rented the present year for three dollars an acre."

It is proper that I should admit that something of this depression is due to the resistance leading men of the South present to her constitutional restoration to the Union and the hostility the baser sort of her people exhibit toward northern settlers: yet there are wide sections of the country into which northern men may go and find themselves welcomed as benefactors if they go to engage in any industrial pursuit; and it must also be admitted that under our present scale of taxation and with the Secretary of the Treasury constantly threatening contraction and able to execute his threat, that capital will not engage in any new enterprise either North or South.

Commissioner Wells is right in prescribing "soothing and sustaining" rather than "heroic" treatment for our diseased body-politic; and if the capitalists of the country do not wish to swell the cry of repudiation till it shall become the shibboleth of a party, they had better abate their demand for the further contraction of the currency and consent to the repeal of taxes that are proving the correctness of Dean Swift's proposition that "We can double the taxes and diminish the income one-half." The rapid development of the wondrous resources of our country and recuperation of the South will, under happier conditions, soon swell the volume of our exports beyond that of our imports, and enable us to recall our bonds from abroad in exchange for commodities, and resume specie payments without grinding into bankruptcy or beggary the men of enterprise and laborers of the country. In refutation of the favorite theory of the contractionists that the price of gold regulates the price of domestic productions I pause to refer to the fact that the difference between gold and greenbacks widens daily, yet the purchasing power of a greenback is now for almost every article of home production twice what it was when the bulk of our bonds were subscribed for, and is increasing coevally with a steady rise in the price of gold. The suit of clothes in which I stand, and which I know to have been woven from pure Ohio wool, was bought for forty dollars in greenbacks; not from what is called a slop-shop, but from the merchant tailors who have made my clothes for years. In 1864 it would have cost twice that sum. Many styles of cotton goods which were commanding an advance of four hundred per cent. at that time are now selling at prices less than those they brought before the war. If any gentleman be disposed to dispute the increased general purchasing power of greenbacks, irrespective of the price of gold, I recommend him to examine pages 42, 43, and 44 of the Report of the Special Commissioner of Revenue. He will there find abundant evidence of the fact.

Had Congress at the close of the war hastened to relieve the country of the taxes against which I am protesting, and while avoiding any expansion of the currency proteced its volume from diminution, and assured the people that no essential change in its volume should be made until the business of the country had adjusted itself to the conditions of peace, production would have advanced and our bonds would have been returning to us in the pockets of emigrants or in settlement of a favorable balance of trade, and millions of people North and South, who are to-day eating bread they have not earned, would have been busily employed and adding to the nation's wealth by earning each day more than they consume. A gradual decline in prices was inevitable, but it would not have destroyed confidence and suspended production, and with immensely increased production, both agricultural and manufacturing, there would have been no cry of a "glut in the market." The people of the South, whose agricultural stock and implements, furniture and apparel, were exhausted during the war, would have been supplying their wants by the sale of the results of their industry. Under the influence of northern capital and enterprise water-power that now runs to waste through cotton fields would have been moving spindles and looms. Forges, furnaces, and rolling-mills such as those the war developed at Chattanooga, Atlanta, Lynchburg, and other points, would be in profitable operation, and by supplying merchantable iron diminishing our dependence upon England and keeping down that balance of trade which with the interest on our bonds held abroad must prevent the resumption of specie payments as long as we continue the "heroic" treatment of sacrificing all other interests in order to give increased value to the hoarded wealth of the possessors of "realized riches." An increasing demand for skilled labor in the South would also be a powerful agent in the work of reconstruction and the redemption of the country from financial embarrassment.

Mr. Chairman, Bishop Kingsley, in one of his admirable letters from Europe, from Sweden, I think, stated that there were ten million industrious people in Europe eager to leave their fatherlands, cross the Atlantic, and identify themselves with us. This statement seemed to bear the aspect of exaggeration, but is confirmed by the judgment of every judicious traveler with whom I have conversed.

We have room for them all; we need them all, and could give them "ample room and verge enough" in which to live prosperously could the navies of the world bring them all to us in a single year. We need them on our vine and pasture lands and our grain-fields; in our forests, our mines, and our ore-beds. We want the industrial secrets and experience they possess, but which have not been introduced into our country. We need them to guide our magnificent water-powers running to waste, and so harness them that they shall labor for us as they speed their way to the sea. But would they better their condition to come to us at this time? I fear not. Most of them can live where they are, and are used to the ills they suffer; but could they hope to prosper as strangers in a strange land, in which there is not adequate employment for the native workingman; in which that most powerful of productive agents, the steam-engine, is idle and powerless, and machinery is decaying in inaction, because the Government arbitrarily interferes with a volume of currency to which all values had adjusted themselves, and which as a medium of exchanges in internal trade was enhancing the wealth and power of the nation in a ratio unprecedented in its history or the history of the world?

Sir, it is in the power of Congress, by reanimating the industry and restoring the confidence of the country before the sun of May shall have fitted the fields of the North for the plow, to prepare a welcome for all these people who may be able to come to us. I have indicated the principal measures by which this is to be done. There are other measures suggested to which I would gladly allude, but for the discussion of which the future will offer more fitting occasions. I have no fear for the distant future. There is nothing in our condition to justify a dread of repudiation. We are not poor and exhausted, but are richer than we or any other people ever were. I have shown that the country was richer at the close of the war by a newly created productive power far more than equal to the entire indebtedness created by the war. I have pointed to the fact that the South, now the home of freedom, will under its inspiration be no longer a burden upon the exchequer of the country for her postal system and other Government service, as she has hitherto been, but will contribute as liberally to its income as the most prosperous portions of the North have done or will do. Contraction of the currency and excessive taxation have temporarily diminished our productive power, and may produce a period of most unhealthy agitation, but the strife waging in our midst is, as I have shown, the offspring of the natural desire of the possessors of riches to expedite and increase their profits. But we are not here to legislate for them beyond the protection of their just rights. Our charge is far nobler than that; it is the welfare of a great, intelligent and enterprising people. Justice to all will injure none, and by laboring to promote the welfare of the poor and lowly we will do most to protect the property and guaranty the rights of those whose estates are largest. Were it in our power and within the scope of our functions to organize a system of coöperation, or by any other means to harmonize the conflict between labor and capital—employer and employed—it would confer the highest blessing upon our country and give stability to every interest. There is, could we but discover it, a solution of that difficult question, and let us hope that with our vast wealth, our immense bodies of public land, the intelligence and enterprise of our people, we may solve the difficult problem, and by the happy condition of our people compel the rulers of the Old World to follow our example and guaranty to every citizen of their countries the right to exercise every privilege and prerogative of a free man.

INTERNAL REVENUE.

Speech Delivered in the House of Representatives, June 1, 1868.

The House being in Committee of the Whole on the state of the Union, and having under consideration the bill (H. R. No. 1060) to reduce into one act and to amend the laws relating to internal taxes—

Mr. Kelley said:

Mr. Chairman: I would be unwilling to trouble the committee upon this most important bill without more special preparation than I have been able to make, were it possible for me to remain in the city and participate in the discussion at a later day. But the condition of my health requires that I should seek repose in the quiet of my home. I must therefore avail myself of the present opportunity to offer some general suggestions, the pertinence and importance of which will, I hope, justify the seeming temerity of following the elaborate and well-digested remarks of the able chairman of the Committee of Ways and Means in an *extempore* discussion of the general character of the bill.

First, permit me to thank the Committee of Ways and Means for the method and industry exhibited in the preparation of this bill. They have done a great work for the country in reducing to order and system the internal revenue laws. And I hope that before Congress rises their bill will, with such amendments as the Committee of the Whole and the House may determine to make, be adopted. It will be a great relief to the industry and enterprise of the country, and produce a great improvement in the morals of the people. Our law is now in such a condition that it is a fountain of demoralization. The revenue service is becoming discreditable, and honorable men dislike to admit that they belong to it. Many of the taxes it imposes are worse than injudicious; and that on distilled spirits has been demonstrated to be not only excessive but unnatural. It is not only not adapted to the condition of our country, which is too broad for the surveillance of a metropolitan police, but is in entire disregard of the infirmities of average human nature. The wisest prayer uttered by men is that they may not be led into temptation! But our Government has overwhelmed its agents by subjecting them to the almost irresistible temptations the whisky ring is able to present under existing laws.

Few well-informed men will assert that much less than one hundred million gallons of whisky have been distilled in this country during the last year. The legal tax on this amount would be $200,000,000. Yet our receipts have been only about thirteen million dollars, as we have just been told by the chairman of the Committee of Ways and Means, [Mr. Schenck,] to whom I tender my thanks for his able exposition of the provisions of the bill and the condition of the internal revenue service. Last year more than twenty-nine million dollars were collected from whisky—this year, less than one half of that sum, and by the collection of this insignificant amount we have enabled swindlers to extract from the honest consumers of the country not less than $100,000,000.

And yet those to whom the execution of the laws for the collection of this tax is confided are sealed and bound by oaths at all points, and there is not one of our revenue officers who has connived at any part of this immense and wide-spread robbery of the Government, who has not clothed his soul with perjury as with a garment. We cannot impose restraints, and couple them with temptations which average men cannot resist, and enforce our restraints by law, one whit more than we can by our statutes reverse the laws of gravitation. And experience proves that in this matter of a tax of two dollars per gallon on whisky we have undertaken an experiment not more plausible than that of regulating gravitation or the course of the stars by statute.

Sir, our legislation has diverted the production of distilled spirits from its natural locality—the grain-fields of the West and the Southwest—and concentrated it in the cities of the sea-board. The chairman of the Committee of Ways and Means tells us that the frauds are chiefly perpetrated in Philadelphia and Chicago. I hope they are; for I am told by the Commissioner of Internal Revenue that one house in Philadelphia has, within the knowledge of the Department, sold more whisky than the aggregate amount for which the Government has received tax in the whole State of Pennsylvania; but, differing from the chairman of the committee, he said that in this bad eminence Philadelphia is overshadowed by New York. Sir, it is affirmed by common rumor that one of the New York agents of the Revenue Bureau, whose name has recently become distinguished in another connection, has saved from his inadequate salary more than two million of well-invested dollars in the brief period of about two years.

Our legislation has not only transferred the seat of the manufacture of whisky and high wines, but it has changed the substances from which they are produced. The whisky of America is no longer distilled from the grain of our fields, but we import, we buy with gold from foreign lands, the material with which to make an inferior article; and the money which should go West for grain or spirits is carried in foreign bottoms, paying freight to foreign ship-owners, to buy foreign material from which to make that which, under a reasonable rate of tax, would be made in Illinois, Wisconsin, Kansas, and the other grain-growing States.

More than this, sir; our legislation on this subject has changed the *personnel* of the whole trade. Go into whichever of the cities you please, and you will no longer find the names of the old-established distillers and rectifiers, or if you find their names you will also find that the *personnel* of the establishment has changed; and it has come to pass that a business requiring large capital and broad premises is in the hands of strangers, men who are unknown to their neighbors, and many of whom, as I was assured within a fortnight by a distinguished officer of the revenue department, would be engaged in burglary or highway robbery, or expiating such crimes in penitentiaries, but that they find it safer and vastly more profitable to deal in illicit whisky and swindle the Government and honest tradesmen. Let gentlemen consult their constituents and ask who have taken the places of the honorable men who years ago added to the wealth of the community by their industry and integrity in the distilling and rectifying business. Few gentlemen will, I apprehend, be willing to exhibit the names and aliases of the men now engaged in either trade in their respective districts and endorse the list as a roll of honor. Victims of black mailing and illicit but protected competition, honorable men have abandoned or are preparing to abandon the business.

By defying the limitations of human nature we have also reversed the course of the carrying trade in this matter, and instead of whisky coming over the railroads from the West—whisky made from grain and within proper limits nutritious—your roads are freighted westward with whisky distilled from molasses, and bound to kill at forty rods. Were whisky used only as a beverage, I would not deplore this fact; but it is largely consumed in the arts of general production. And what effect is this having upon the general industry of the country? It is closing manufactures of chemicals, establishments for the production of perfumery, the manufacture of varnish, and a large number of other articles. It is diminishing the general production of the country, and lessening the wages of large classes of skilled laboring people. Sir, there is within my district one chemical works which has been largely engaged in the production among others of alcoholic drugs, such as chloroform, and using alcohol as a solvent for ingredients in other drugs, such as quinine. From a small beginning the gentlemen conducting this establishment had increased their consumption of alcohol to about one hundred and forty thousand gallons per annum. But being conscientious men, who are unwilling to violate the laws, though they might do so with impunity, and who abide by their pledge to the Philadelphia Drug Exchange to consume no alcohol that has not paid its tax, their consumption has been reduced to fifteen thousand gallons per annum, and their skilled workmen are being scattered or earning the poor wages of unskilled laborers in employments to which they are unused. But, sir, this is not all the harm done the community in this connection, for men who scruple not to make contracts with fraudulent distillers are stocking the market with inferior drugs, and substitutes for the purer articles my constituents formerly produced are being imported in foreign bottoms and paid for in gold, together with freight to foreign ship-owners on the inferior commodity.

The people of the Northwest, it seems to me, are specially interested in this question. They will find that they cannot afford to expel from their inland section of the country any branch of manufactures. They need the opportunity to export their grain concentrated in the form of whisky, high wines, or other manufactures.* I am no Cassandra and they will not believe me, but I tell them they are entering upon a competition that will exclude them from the markets of the world, if they depend upon the export of their grain in bulk as food or mere raw material. Do you mark, gentlemen of Missouri, Illinois, and Wisconsin, that California is loud in the expression of her gratitude for the fact that one hundred and thirty vessels have been added to the fleet for carrying her grain to New York and transatlantic ports? They can send grain in bulk twenty-three thousand miles to the seaboard of New England or Old England at less cost for transportation than you can send yours to the seaboard by rail. Oregon is groaning under her crop of wheat, and her people are fearing that means for its transportation to market may not be at hand. But this distant competition is not what you have most cause to dread. The South, no longer your customer for food for man and beast, looms up your competitor. Her advantages over you are manifold as they are manifest. She lies between you and the ocean. Her grain fields are upon the banks of navigable rivers which flow to the Gulf or the ocean, and at or near the mouth of each is a seaport. From Norfolk around to Galveston, Texas, the grain of the farmers of the several States may be floated to the sea-board upon rafts and there find shipping. England and western Europe are not the countries to which we chiefly export grain and flour. Our chief markets for these are Central and South America, and the islands to which the southern States are neighbors; and I tell you that if the people of the far Northwest do not take heed, and by diversifying their industry convert their raw materials into more compact productions, the day is not three years distant when their crops will waste

* It costs a bushel of wheat to carry a bushel from Minnesota or Kansas to New York or Boston for shipment or consumption. One bushel of corn will not pay the freight on another. But if the grain be concentrated into alcohol, four bushels will pay the transportation on from sixteen to twenty. If shipped as grain, that is the end of it to the farmer; but if it be distilled he not only reduces the cost of transportation, but raises a crop of hogs, and has manure with which to replenish his acres exhausted by successive crops of corn or wheat. Before the tax was put on whisky we exported immense quantities of alcohol, to the great advantage of farmers. Now we scarcely export any. The repeal of the tax on spirits would revive this branch of our foreign commerce.

in the fields for the want of a market to which they will pay the cost of transportation.*

These may seem to be idle statements. But you, gentlemen from the upper Mississippi and the Missouri, know that arrangements are making for carrying your grain in barges to New Orleans for shipment thence. The rivers of the South are never ice bound as yours are through a long winter. Sir, the ablest pamphlet upon the resources of this country I have read in many years is that from the pen of Hon. John B. Robertson, of Louisiana, who tells the people of that State that on four million acres of her soil which are yet unbroken by the plow experiment has demonstrated the fact that sixty bushels of wheat to the acre may be raised—sixty bushels of southern wheat that will bear transportation through the tropics, as spring-sown northern wheat will not. Gentlemen laugh and shake their heads; but when I tell them that six hundred bushels of sweet potatoes to the acre is in that region not more than a fair average crop, they may imagine that the land is somewhat more fertile than that they have been accustomed to manage. Seven hundred bushels of that esculent are frequently produced from an acre. But if each acre will yield but twenty bushels of wheat near a seaport, the competition will be disastrous to the grain-grower of the remote interior. But, sir, I have wandered into a digression, but shall esteem myself fortunate in having rendered the country a service if some few gentlemen note and ponder the facts I have suggested. To return to the subject—I say to gentlemen that they need the distillery and rectifying establishment, that whisky, high wines, lard and oil, rather than grain in bulk, shall seek a market from their region. It will be better for all if we of the East consume your productions than it can be if your constituents are to continue to consume whisky distilled in enlarged tea and coffee-pots in cellars and garrets from imported molasses.

Entertaining the views I have expressed, I rejoiced to hear the chairman of the Committee of Ways and Means announce the fact that the tax of two dollars had been but

---

* The recent Franco-German war and the reduction of the California wheat crop fifty per cent. by drought, have probably prevented the fulfilment of this prediction; but they have not sufficed to put up the price of grain. War and drought are not adequate guarantees for a steady market for the grain crops of this country; nothing but a wide diversification of the industries of the West will avert the ruin of the grain-growers of that section.

nominally retained, and express the hope that the House would not sustain it. But, Mr. Chairman, he proposes in the name of the committee that the tax shall be fixed at seventy-five cents. It is an immense reduction, but it does not go quite low enough to check the fraud or to restore this important trade to its natural channels. While sick at my home last week, I took the liberty of inviting to my bedside some of the best distillers and chemists of Philadelphia; separately and apart as they came I interrogated them as to the cost of molasses whisky and the point at which the tax might safely be placed; and there was unanimity among them in saying that at seventy-five cents molasses whisky could in the hands of men with some capital, incur the risks of the law, and make a fair profit. The reduction would doubtless diminish the production of whisky from molasses and thus reduce the price of molasses to such a point as to enable skilful men to operate with the certainty of large gains. They also agreed that at sixty cents the ground would be debatable, but if Congress wanted to shut molasses whiskey out from competition and to contend only with such fraud as might be effected at regular distilleries, and rectifying establishments, the tax should be put at the maximum of fifty cents; and that every cent below that until it reached twenty-five would be a guard to the revenue, an additional guard thrown round the revenue and a diminution of the temptation which the Government is now offering for perjury, conspiracy, and fraud. I hope, therefore, the tax will be reduced to at most fifty cents; and if I am able to be in my seat and find my vote will be effective in bringing it to forty cents, I shall cast it with the belief that while the change will save the revenues of the Government, it will also save the morals of the people by diminishing the temptations to which they are subjected.

I desire to say, Mr. Chairman, that when I feared that two dollars might be adhered to by the committee as the tax, and that the industries of the country would be assessed $200,000,000 in order that the infamous "whisky ring" might continue to riot in fat living and amass colossal fortunes, and that the Government, except in special taxes, as provided for in the bill, would receive no more revenue from this source than it has been getting, I was of the opinion that the rates proposed in the bill were inordinate. The estimates, as we get them from the present

Secretary of the Treasury, have always been vastly in excess of expenditures, and vastly below the actual receipts of revenue. The Secretary's estimates have not been candid. Under the pretence of a desire to extinguish the principal of the debt it has seemed to be his policy to reduce the rewards of labor and prevent the development of the natural wealth of the country. Misled by his false estimates, at fault hundreds of millions of dollars each year, we have burdened the industry and restrained the progress of the country. I am unwilling to be longer thus deluded by this systematic misrepresentation. For my own part I am determined to vote for the lowest possible amount of taxation that will provide with certainty for the payment of the current expenses of the Government and the interest on the public debt.

I find in the report of the Special Commissioner of Revenue, Mr. Wells, made in January, 1868, a passage which I shall read as illustrative of the truth of my assertion and the correctness of my theory:

"That the United States is the only one of the leading nations of the world which is at present materially diminishing its debt and reducing its taxes; and the only one, moreover, which offers any substantial evidence of its ability to pay its debt within any definite period, or even anticipates the probability of any such occurrence. In proof of which we submit the following statements and statistics:

"The figures already presented demonstrate that the United States, from the 31st of August, 1865, to the 31st October, 1867, substantially reduced its liabilities by the sum of over two hundred and sixty-six million dollars, or at an average rate of over ten millions per month for the whole included period; and that during the year ending June 30, 1867, taxation was reduced by law to an estimated amount of from eighty to one hunded million dollars per annum."

Sir, the Commissioner also informs us that our revenues do not diminish proportionately with the reduction of taxation.

After presenting a tabular statement of the revenues of the Government for the years 1866 and 1867, he says:

"A comparison of the figures above presented indicates a falling off in the receipts of internal revenue for the fiscal year 1867, as compared with those of 1866, $44,986,509. Such a falling off, however, is apparent and not real, as will be evident when the great reduction of internal revenue taxes, made by Congress during the last fiscal year, is taken into the account. To what extent this reduction has actually amounted cannot be precisely stated, but the taxes abated or repealed at the first session of the Thirty-Ninth Congress were estimated as sufficient to occasion an annual loss of revenue, taking the returns of the preceding fiscal year as a precedent, of about sixty million dollars; while the further abatement at the second session of the same Congress was likewise estimated, including the reduction of the income tax, at from thirty to forty million dollars. It would, therefore, have been nothing but reasonable to infer that the revenues for the last fiscal year (1866-67) would have fallen short of the aggregate of the preceding year (1865-66) by an amount equal to the reduction of the taxes, the effect of which was fully experienced during the period referred to; which reduction may be prudently estimated at from sixty to seventy million dollars. In addition to this, it should be remembered that the last fiscal year in the United States was a year of great commercial and mercantile depression—a year in which the crops in all sections of the country were much below an average, and in which manufacturing operations were extensively interfered with by disagreements between employers and their operatives; and yet, notwithstanding all this, the internal revenue did not fall off to an extent commensurate with the amount of taxes abated or repealed; but, on the contrary, exhibited a comparative net gain of from fifteen to twenty-five million dollars."

Sir, this is not miraculous or even wonderful, for our country is expanding in resources and taxable population beyond the degree in which any country or people ever before expanded. Six hundred miles, said the gentleman from New York, [Mr. Brooks,] into the Indian territory your Pacific railroad now runs. Yes, sir; in the midst of what but last year were plains and hills, to which civilization was a stranger, is now the flourishing city of Cheyenne, with its tax-paying population thriving and prospering, and along the whole six hundred miles of that road beyond the infant city of Omaha are people who, two years ago, were citizens of other lands or among the landless laborers of this country, who this year in their new and independent homes, will contribute to the revenues of the country through the various departments of the internal tax law and by the generous consumption of dutiable goods.

"Three-fifths of all other persons," is the language with which the Constitution refers to four million of our people—those four millions who hitherto lived without the use of money, and were habitually clad in such garments as are given the pauper and prisoner, where these unfortunates receive least sympathy—to-day walk erect in manhood and womanhood. They handle money which their labor earns. They occupy homes. Many thousands of them own lands, and standing up under their own vine and figtree acknowledging no man as master, and asking no man to supply their wants, they contribute to the revenues of the Government. Four million additional consumers of taxable and dutiable goods. They are using the matches which pay the Government a penny a box; and no longer going barefoot they contribute to the income of the Government when they buy the blacking with which to polish their boots. And, sir, there are another four million dwelling among them, the poor whites of the South, who were as innocent as they of matches and blacking, and imported silks or ribbons, but by consuming which they now, or soon will, contribute to the support of the Government which has enfranchised them also.

Three hundred thousand immigrants a year are coming in steady flowing streams to swell the taxable resources of the country! Eight million of people elevated from a condition little above that of the brute into tax-paying and dutiable goods-consuming people! And can we in view of these facts estimate the future from data furnished by the past? No, sir, we cannot from any one year calculate the resources of the country in the next, unless we impose upon our industry such burdens as will prevent its profitable employment, check immigration, and restrain the development of our wondrously varied resources.

Three years ago the vast coal-beds of the West, underlying an area of one hundred and twenty-six thousand square miles; embracing a part of Kentucky, five thousand miles; a part of Indiana, fifteen thousand; the greater part of Illinois, thirty-five thousand; and stretching under the Mississippi river and underlying nearly the whole State of Missouri and a large part of Kansas, together with that other wonderful coal formation additional to those to which I have referred, and separated from them by a narrow rocky strata, which underlies nearly the whole State of Iowa, were scarcely recognized except at Covington, Kentucky, as among the material resources of the country.* But the ore of Iron Mountain, in Missouri, as I have here-

* As an illustration of the power for varied industries these vast deposits of coal offer to the West, I may mention the fact that three tons of coal driving a steam-engine represent the labor power of a man for his lifetime. Richard Garsed, Esq., of Frankford, Pa., manufactures, in every day of ten hours, 33,000 *miles* of cotton thread—obtaining from *seven tons* of coal the necessary power. Supposing it possible for such quality of thread to be made by hand, it would require the labor of 70,000 women during the same time to accomplish this work.

tofore suggested to the House, is now carried on trains to the interior of Indiana, where, by the use of native coal, purer than has been known on the other side of the Atlantic, purer than I had ever seen before, it is being converted into every form of utility to which iron may be applied, and supplying the West with better and cheaper iron and steel than it has hitherto been able to purchase; and the train that brings the rich ore to Indiana carries back to Missouri coal superior even to that of the Big Muddy, thus demonstrating the possibility of building up at either point an iron and steel industry before which those of England, France, Belgium, and even Prussia, justly famous as is her Krupp, will sink into comparative insignificance. The true policy of this country, in view of its vast resources, and of the rapid and steady aggregation and exaltation of its people, is to reduce internal taxation to the minimum, to relieve its industry and its resources from every burden possible, to see to it that all just demands on the Government are amply provided for, and to leave the principal of the debt to be liquidated when the people of the South shall have recovered from the ravages of war, and when, enlightened by experience, the Northwest shall have adjusted itself to the competition it is to endure from the grain-growing capacity of the South, and the determination of her people to revenge themselves so far as they can upon their conquerors by growing it and monopolizing the markets open to American grain. I hope, therefore, that though I may be absent during the consideration of this bill, others will see to it that every tax which touches the industry of the country or annoys the people by its impertinent exaction, that can with safety be reduced, will be.

And in this connnection I turn to schedule A, which imposes a tax upon a $300 carriage, upon a gold watch, upon the piano you have provided for your daughter; and which requires citizens to account for the spoons and forks in use in their houses, whether given to them as wedding presents or preserved as a slight memorial of the fact that they had remote ancestors.

A Member. It is not taxed unless kept for use.

Mr. Kelley. When it comes into use it becomes taxable. After the baby is born the pap-spoon is taxable, until then it may, as a present, escape the tax collector's inquisition. The whole amount of taxes collected under schedule A during the last year, when it yielded more than ever before, was $2,116,000. Now, the chairman of the committee has shown you that under his bill at the very lowest possible estimate you are to have a surplus of $46,000,-000. Hitherto you were to have no surplus, and you raised an excess of $120,000,000 each year. Start out with aiming at $46,000,000 of surplus, and during the year with the incoming tide of prosperity you will find that you have needlessly assessed $146,000,000 of taxes. I will not enumerate the provisions of the section to which I refer. You will find them embraced in section one hundred and sixteen, on page 171.

I have been told by collectors of internal revenue that more penalties are incurred by neglect of the tax on gold watches than on any other article. More persons are made to feel that your laws inflict unjust penalties by this tax than by any other. I have heard of an instance of a conscientious widow who, learning subsequent to the day on which it should have been paid, that there was such a tax, went and reported that she had five daughters, each of whom had a gold watch, and had a special penalty in addition to the tax imposed on each by reason of her conscientiousness. The taxes are frequently collected in a manner to make the law as odious as possible; and if a Republican, or the wife or daughter of a Republican complains, the answer is, "My party is not responsible for it; we did not make the law. Why do you not get the Republicans to remedy the annoyance of which you complain?" And I trust the Republican majority in this Congress will remove all these almost fruitless but annoying taxes. Sir, all the objects named in schedule A have in no one year paid one per cent. of the revenue; they have never reached more than eight-tenths of one per cent. of the income of the Government. In the report of the Commissioner of Internal Revenue, to which I have referred, you will find the figures set out, and the nearest they have ever come was seven hundred and ninety-six thousandths of one per cent. of the annual revenue. Why make our taxes so odious by penetrating inquisitorially into the secrets of every maiden lady and widow in the land, and inquiring whether she can conscientiously swear that her old carryall is not worth $300, for the sake of swelling in so slight a degree the surplus revenue?

Again, sir, it has occurred to me that the committee, believing many of these taxes to be inordinate, have hoped to enforce them by extreme penalties. Thus, in section sixty-nine it is provided:

"That if any distiller, rectifier, wholesale liquor dealer, compounder of liquors, distiller of oil, brewer, or manufacturer of tocacco or cigars, shall omit, neglect, or refuse to do or cause to be done any of the things required by law in the carrying on or conducting of his business, or shall do anything by this act prohibited, if there be no specific penalty or punishment imposed by any other section of this act for the neglecting, omitting, or refusing to do, or for the doing or causing to be done, the thing required or prohibited, he shall pay a penalty of $1000; and, if the person so offending be a distiller, rectifier, wholesale liquor dealer, or compounder of liquors, all distilled spirits or liquors owned by him, or in which he has any interest as owner, if he be a distiller of oil, all oil found in his distillery, and if he be a manufacturer of tobacco or cigars, all tobacco or cigars found in his manufactory, shall be forfeited to the United States."

What, sir! if his youngest errand boy commits an error of that kind, if some of his servants be suborned, if any of his agents do what ought not to be done, or omit to do what the law requires, are you to forfeit his whole stock? I trust the committee will at least insert the words "wilfully and designedly," so that for a mere accident the entire stock and business of a man may not be confiscated, or he be subjected to litigation.

Did my strength permit I would gladly consider some other provisions of the bill. But, sir, I have presented the main views that impress me. They are, in the first place, that the bill, even as modified by the suggestions of the chairman of the Committee of Ways and Means, and the reduction of the tax on whisky to seventy-five cents, offers a bribe of many million dollars to a ring organized throughout the country and knowing its men in every city, county, and State—a bribe of enormous amount to tempt bad men to perjury, conspiracy, and fraud; and I trust that the tax will be reduced to a point which will make it certain that molasses whisky cannot be made and sent to the West with profit.

Preclude the use of that imported ingredient, which may be distilled in any cellar or attic, and compel distillers to use grain, and you will secure to the officers of the revenue a chance to discover frauds, punish swindlers, and confiscate illegal goods. And I ask gentlemen while considering this bill to carry with them the proposition that the true standard of estimate for the receipts of the next year, and the true object at which to aim in making assessments, is simply to provide for the payment of the interest on the public debt and the current expenses. They may be assured that if they will make ample provision for these objects, they will provide the means to pay from forty to seventy millions of the principal of the public debt, as our receipts always largely exceed the Commissioner's and Secretary's estimates.

I have not the strength to stand while I analyze the figures I noted as they fell from the lips of the chairman of the committee. If I had I could, I think, make a perfect demonstration of my proposition from the materials he furnished. But, thanking the members of the committee for the attention they have given me, I leave the work in their hands with confidence that it will be faithfully done.

REPORT OF SPECIAL COMMISSIONER OF THE REVENUE.

Remarks Delivered in the House of Representatives, February 4, 1869.

The House being in Committee of the Whole on the state of the Union on the President's annual message—

Mr. Kelley said:

Mr. Chairman: On the 19th of January, the Committee on Printing submitted a resolution to print twenty thousand copies of the report of the Special Commissioner of the Revenue for the use of the House, and one thousand bound copies for the use of the Treasury Department, and though I had no hope of preventing its adoption, I felt constrained to resist the motion and submit the reasons which impelled me thereto as fully as I could in the brief time allowed me by the courtesy of the gentleman from New Hampshire, [Mr. Ela,] who presented the resolution. I could not hope that the House would refuse to print a report the preparation of which had cost the Government so much money in the pay of the Commissioner and his clerical assistants. What I sought to do was in some measure accomplished; it was to send with the report a note of warning to the country. I then said:

"I hope the resolution reported by the committee will not be adopted. I do not think the report ought to receive such an endorsement. I do not see how Congress can consistently cast it broadcast over the country. It is a report full of figures, which are so ingeniously selected and marshaled that one might suppose it had been prepared specially to show the pestilent character of that most false and dangerous of all the aphorisms embodied in the English language, namely, that 'figures cannot lie.' They are so culled and marshaled in this report as to lead to conclusions false, delusive, and damaging to our country, and especially unjust to that Congress which has carried the country through the great struggle from which she has just emerged. I do not mean to say that the figures embodied in it are in themselves false; *upon that point I do not speak now;* but I do mean to say that they are so detached from their correlatives as to lead to conclusions utterly at variance with facts which are notorious and familiar to every gentleman on this floor."

. . . .

"The gentleman who is named in the report as having collected the statistics and made the calculations has, *so far as I know*, done his duty fairly; but the Commissioner who selected the material for this report, and prepared and marshaled it, has not done so with a view to let Congress and the country deduce conclusions from an impartial array of facts, but to sustain a foregone conclusion and advocate a favorite theory of his own, which is, in my judgment, at variance with the true interests of the country."

And again:

"The thesis of the report is that we have since 1860 so legislated that while wealth is accumulating more rapidly than it ever accumulated in any land or age, the poor are steadily growing poorer and the rich richer; that the yawning gulf between poverty and wealth is ever widening in this country, and that the laboring man and his family cannot live as well upon their earnings as they could in 1860.

"The report—and it is voluminous—devotes five or six pages only to the progress of wealth and productive power in this country, but they suffice to show that it is with constantly increasing velocity and momentum. If it be true in that respect, and the laboring people are really becoming poorer daily, we are on the eve of an aristocracy more potent than any that has preceded it, and of a social condition such as the world has never seen. I propose to inquire whether this startling proposition be true. The Commissioner, assuming that his array of facts has established it, says on page 21:

"'It has been well said that there can be no true theoretic conclusion which will not be proved by the facts whenever the theory can be applied. We have given the theory of the effects of inconvertible paper money, and we find that the facts prove it. The rich become richer and the poor poorer.'

"Not satisfied with this, he says:

"'The aggregate wealth of the country is increasing, probably, as rapidly as at any former period; * yet it does not follow that there is the same increase in general prosperity. The laborer, especially he who has a large family to support, is not as prosperous as he was in 1860. His wages have not increased in proportion to the increase in the cost of his living. There is, therefore, an inequality

* In 1868 when his sinister ends required him to array the poor against the rich, the workman against his employer, Commissioner Wells found it covenient to make this truthful admission. But a year later, when preparing his report for 1869, which was happily his final one, he found it necessary to array the farmers of the country against the manufacturers, both workmen and employers, he devoted pages to proving that the increase of the aggregate wealth had been but about half as rapid as during the preceding decade. He stated correctly the rate of increase between 1850 and 1860 to have been 129 per cent., and fixed the rate for the last decade at but 65 per cent. The final result for the latter period has not been ascertained, but enough is known to prove that the rate was, notwithstanding the war, equal to that of the preceding decade, 129 per cent., as the aggregate as far as ascertained is over $31,000,000,000.

in the distribution of our annual product which we must, in no small degree, refer to artificial causes. This inequality exists even among the working classes themselves. The single man or woman, working for his or her support alone, is in the receipt of a rate of wages from which savings may be made equal or greater than ever before, especially in the manufacturing towns, where the price of board is, to a certain extent, regulated artificially by the employer.'

And again, I ask gentlemen to listen to the Commissioner's statement of the condition to which their legislation has reduced our countrymen :

"'Unmarried operatives, therefore, gain; while those who are obliged to support their own families in hired tenements lose. Hence, deposits in savings-banks increase, while marriage is discouraged; and the forced employment of young children is made almost a necessity in order that the family may live.'"

If this be the condition of our country, do we not, as I have said, perpetrate a great fraud when we ask the laboring immigrant to come and dwell among us?

The gentleman from Ohio [Mr. Garfield] did me the honor to reply to me in a rejoinder which had been prepared for the occasion, as appears from his remark that, "hearing that this attack was to be made, I have asked information from two sources in order to test the correctness of the Commissioner's position." His reply would, I doubt not, have been more candid had it been prepared after he had heard what I had to say. His misrepresentation of my position was not intentional. It arose from his misconception of the point I would make when I should have an opportunity to express my convictions. In view of the passages from my remarks already quoted, especially of my announcement that I did not mean to examine the question whether the figures embodied in the report are, in themselves, false, but did "mean to say that they are so detached from their correlatives as to lead to conclusions utterly at variance with facts which are notorious and familiar to every gentleman on this floor," he was hardly justified in saying that I had admitted "in the first place that the facts stated are generally correct; that the statistics collected and arranged in tables are true and correctly stated." *I certainly did not admit the truth or correctness of that which the single purpose of my remarks was to deny, and which every fact I presented contradicted.* I am sure, from the gentleman's well-known character, that he would not have made this assertion had his remarks been prepared after he had heard me. After he had thus charged me with admitting all I had been denying and disproving, he said that it must be, then, that I refuse to print this report because its facts and deductions do not square with my theories and notions, and exultingly proclaimed my opposition to the printing a most damaging admission.*

I resume the discussion in pursuance of a promise made when the fall of the Speaker's gavel announced the expiration of the brief time allowed me, and in the hope of showing by an array of facts, many of which were not then in my possession, the dangerous fallacies the Commissioner has attempted to sustain by "doctored," "manipulated," "garbled," "marshaled," or in other words, artfully arranged figures. The correctness of the figures set forth in the report I am willing, as I then was, to admit for argument sake, but not in fact, as time has not yet permitted me to test them fully. They may in themselves be true; but there is a falsehood known as the *suppressio veri*—the statement of part of the truth in such a manner as to produce the effect of a positive falsehood; and of that I charge that the Commissioner has been guilty in almost every part of his voluminous report. He who denies the existence of Deity, and in support of the denial quotes the last four words of the exclamation "the fool hath said in his heart, there is no God," as a complete sentence, misrepresents the teachings of the Psalmist, though he correctly quotes that particular portion of his language. The falsehood is in the manner of the statement, and not in the thing stated. This illustration is not inapplicable to the document under consideration.

Gentlemen who read the report from pages 14 to 21 inclusive, will find an abundant array of tabular comparative statements which, if they be true and in themselves constitute the whole truth, prove most adequately its assertion:

> "That for the year 1867, and for the first half of 1868, the average increase of all the elements which constitute the food, clothing, and shelter of a family has been about seventy-eight per cent., as compared with the standard prices of 1860–61."

And that the rate of increase in wages for the year 1867 as compared with 1860–61, was but as follows:

---

* For an illustration of the ludicrous absurdity of some of Mr. Wells' positions and fabricated facts, which Mr. Garfield hastened to defend with such zeal, readers are referred to the tables of weekly earnings and expenditures of families, quoted from the Commissioner's report on pages 271, 272. They show the wonderful dexterity with which Mr. Wells subordinates the most palpable facts to the theories he embraced during his visit to England.

"For unskilled mechanical labor, fifty per cent.; for skilled mechanical labor, sixty per cent."

I pause for a moment to deny the correctness of these statements, and to assert that the price of the necessaries of life enumerated in these tables are, on an average, not more than fifty per cent. higher than in 1860, while labor is now immeasurably more fully employed at an advance of from eighty to one hundred per cent. over the wages of that year. But this is a point about which ingenuity may cavil, and is not essential to the support of my argument. To give Mr. Wells' figures any practical value they should have been accompanied by another column for each year, in which should have been stated the number of working people employed in each of the several branches of business referred to, and the number who, though skilled workmen at those branches, were unable to obtain employment of any kind by which to earn wages. The omission of these elements from the calculation vitiates the Commissioner's figures, even though they are in themselves true, and conceals the fraud this report was intended to perpetrate. Let the gentleman from Ohio glorify the memory of 1860 as he may, I confidently reiterate what I said in the former discussion:

"Eighteen hundred and sixty and 1861, and from 1857 to the autumn of the latter year, was one of the darkest periods ever seen by the laboring people of America. Not one out of five of the skilled workmen of the country was steadily employed. In Philadelphia, when they wanted to build a street railroad they advertised for two hundred and fifty hands at sixty cents a day, and more than five thousand offered, a majority of whom were skilled artizans who could find no other employment. In the neighborhood of one of the establishments, the statistics of which go into this report, a rolling-mill, the number of unemployed men was so great that the county authorities, to save its skilled workmen from open pauperism, determined to build a turnpike, and experienced hands from rolling-mills were employed at breaking stone and road-making at fifty cents a day rather than become paupers. For the comparatively few who had employment the wages are, I assume, honestly given in the report; but of the many who were picking up a precarious living by getting an occasional day's work at half wages or quarter wages no account is taken; and thus facts that may be true in themselves, by being separated from those which would have explained and interpreted them, are made to libel our country and the Congress that carried it through the war.

"Let me in this connection bring the attention of gentlemen to some facts:

"Look at the palatial buildings erected in this city during the last year and the comfortable dwellings for mechanics and laborers.

17

How many of them there are you have all seen. They are built by squares and blocks. I have endeavored to ascertain how many were built in 1860, and can hear of but four dwelling houses built in Washington in that year. In 1861, so far as I have been able to learn, but one dwelling house and one public school-house, the contract price for which was $3500, were erected. Leaving Washington, I go to to my own city, and by turning to the report of the building inspectors find that in 1860 twenty-four hundred and seventy-two houses were built. The decline had commenced, and in 1861 but sixteen hundred and seventy-three were built. In 1860 we enlarged five hundred and eighty-eight buildings; in 1861 but two hundred and four were enlarged. But in 1868, when the Commissioner tells us labor was not as prosperous as in 1860, we erected forty-seven hundred and ninety-six buildings and enlarged twelve hundred and fifteen. In 1868 there was an active demand for labor, and its price was high. It could determine its own wages. In 1860 labor was begging employment and wages were low. As a general thing mechanics had to accept whatever wages were offered, though in a few instances favored establishments were able to run continuously, and pay fair wages, and these exceptional cases have furnished the Commissioner data for what he announces as a general law.

"The low rate of wages that ruled in 1860 would have led a proficient in political economy to look for the facts I am now about to lay before you. It is a law of social science that when employment is scarce labor must accept low wages, and lose time; but when employment is quick and active, labor regulates its own wages and is constantly employed. The tables presented by the Commissioner ignore this law, and are consequently a fraud upon Congress and a slander upon our country, the working people of which were never so prosperous as now.

"Let me exhibit some other comparisons between 1860 and 1868 which bear upon the question at issue. In that blessed year, 1860, which the Commissioner eulogizes, the sheriff of Philadelphia received seventeen hundred and forty writs for the sale of real estate, while in 1868, the year he denounces as one of congressional wrong and pecuniary depression, the sheriff of that city received but seven hundred and six writs for the sale of real estate, a falling off of largely more than fifty per cent., though in the interval there had been an increase of forty per cent. in the population, and vastly more than that in the wealth of the city."

In connection with these statements I brought to the attention of the House on that occasion such figures drawn from the reports of the savings-banks of seven States as I happened to have at hand. Since then I have been able to add to my collection of that class of facts, some which I will proceed to exhibit. I have the official statement of the total amount of deposits in the savings-banks of Maine, New Hampshire, Massachusetts, and Rhode Island, of the Philadelphia Saving-Fund Society, which is allowed to receive but $200 from any one depositor in a year, and of the savings-banks of the city of Newark, New Jersey, for 1860 and 1861, and of these institutions, and a third at Newark, a dime savings-bank, which has since come into existence, for 1867 and 1868. I have also reports from other states, but as they do not cover the four years designated they could not be embraced in the table I have compiled. That I have not been wanting in diligence in my endeavors to procure such official information as would enable me to make a general comparative table for these years will be attested by gentlemen on this floor and in the Senate, of whom I have requested the names of the proper parties to whom to apply, and by Mr. Spofford, the Librarian of Congress, to whose industry and courtesy I am much indebted.

All the information obtained shall be fully presented, and I think the gentleman from Ohio, [Mr. Garfield,] though he may remember 1860 as a pleasant and prosperous year, will be persuaded that millions of his countrymen remember it as a year of agony, during which gaunt want entered their homes because the last dollar of their past earnings had been extorted from them by idleness enforced by a revenue or free trade tariff.

I have not been able to ascertain the number of depositors in all the institutions to which I am referring for each year, but have them from the Saving-Fund Society of Philadelphia and the savings-banks of New Hampshire, Massachusetts, and Rhode Island. These are, however, sufficent to indicate the general condition of the class of people who are depositors in such institutions, and whose alleged relative poverty in 1867 Mr. Wells so deplores. On the 1st day of January, 1860, there were twenty-one thousand two hundred and sixty-five depositors in the institution at Philadelphia, and on the 1st of January, 1861, there were but twelve thousand six hundred and sixty-two; and the total amount of deposits had gone down from $4,083,450 to $2,251,646, or little more than one half. In Massachusetts, as an official statement before me shows, the number of depositors has fallen off in but two years between 1834 and 1868, inclusive. In 1865 the total decrease was one hundred and twenty-eight, an almost incalculably small fraction of one per cent., but in the year 1861, in consequence of the want of employment in 1860, the number fell off five thousand and ten, or two and one-sixth per cent., and the deposits remaining at the close of the year were reduced $268,797.

The number of depositors in the savings-banks of Rhode Island has receded in but one year between 1855 and 1868 inclusive, which was 1861, when they fell off five hundred and ninety-eight, notwithstanding which the aggregate deposit increased $119,119 33.

The extreme force of the depression which, as the result of our adhesion to free trade and an exportable metallic currency, overtook the country in 1857, and terminated only with the issue of the currency known as greenbacks, and the passage of the protective tariff of 1861 seems to have fallen upon New Hampshire as early as 1858. From 1850 to 1868, inclusive, the number of depositors in savings-banks of that State has decreased in but two years, 1858 and 1866. In the latter year the number of depositors fell off about one per cent., notwithstanding which the deposits increased $26,265 31; but in 1858 the depositors fell off seven per cent., or thirteen hundred and twenty-three, and the deposits were reduced $159,627 40.

While recounting the manifold blessings that period brought to the working people of the country the gentleman from Ohio [Mr. Garfield] reminded me that the working people were docile in that year, and indulged in no strikes either for higher wages or against a reduction of their pay. He said:

> "It was a year of plenty, of great increase. I remember, moreover, that it was a year of light taxes. There was but one great people on the face of the globe so lightly taxed as the American people in 1860. Now we are the most heavily taxed people except one, perhaps, on the face of the globe; and the weight of nearly all our taxes falls at last on the laboring man. This is an element which the gentleman seems to have omitted from his calculation altogether.
>
> "The gentleman says that at the present time laborers are doing better than in 1860. I ask him how many strikes there were among laborers in 1860–61? Were there any at all? And how many were there in 1868? Will the gentleman deny that strikes exhibit the unsettled and unsatisfactory condition of labor in its relations to capital? In our mines, in our mills and furnaces, in our manufacturing establishments, are not the laborers every day joining in strikes for higher wages, and saying that they need them on account of the high price of provisions, or that the capitalists get too large a share of the profits?"

The gentleman has my thanks for bringing this significant fact, so destructive of his own argument and that of Mr. Wells, to my attention. He knows that it was not until Jeshurun waxed fat that he kicked; and he ought to know that unemployed workmen, who had drawn the last dollar from the savings-bank, and parted with furniture in exchange for food and fuel, were not in a condition to strike, and had no employers whose decrees they might resist. I need no more powerful illustration of the absurdity of the assertions of the Commissioner than the fact that the workingmen of to-day, in contrast with their abject condition in 1860, find so wide a market for their labor and are so comparatively easy in their condition that when their rights or interests are assailed they are able to offer resistance to the assailant.

Our positions are fairly taken, and as the condition of savings-banks furnishes the truest and most general index to the condition of the laboring people, the facts I am about to present will overthrow him who is in error. Be the judgment of the general public what it may, I am confident that the memory of every American workingman who remembers the experience of 1860 will sustain me in this controversy. Having shown the loss of depositors and deposits in the only banks from which I could obtain information on those points in or about 1860, let me show the increase of depositors and deposits in the same banks in 1867 and 1868:

State or City.	Year.	Increase in number of depositors.	Increase of deposits.
New Hampshire	1867	4,967	$2,672,150 05
" "	1868	7,476	2,705,242 01
Massachusetts.......	1867	31,740	12,699,319 40
"	1868	34,501	14,406,752 83
Rhode Island........	1867	6,845	3.651,934 11
" "	1868	4.429	2,984.988 81
Philadelphia........	1867	2,490	579,746 03
"	1868	2,234	761,901 00
		94,682	$40,462,034 24

The contrast these figures present to those of 1860 does not give the Commissioner's theory much support, and casts a shade of doubt over the accuracy of the position taken by the gentleman from Ohio. It may, however, be regarded as exceptional, and I therefore propose to present a broader range of facts, embracing the amount of deposits in the banks of Maine, New Hampshire, Massachusetts, Newark, New Jersey, and the only institution at Philadelphia from which I have been able to obtain this information for the years 1860-61 and 1867-68. I have sought for corresponding facts from the other New England States and New York, but have not been able to obtain them. These tables are, therefore, as complete as industry and the broadest research possible in so limited a period could make them. As, however, they present so perfect a correspondence for both periods it is fair to presume that they indicate the condition of the savings-banks and their depositors throughout the country. The total amount of deposits in these banks in 1860-61 was as follows:

	1860	1861
Maine	$1,466,457 56	$1,620,270 26
New Hampshire	4,860,024 86	5,590,652 18
Massachusetts	45,054,236 00	44,785,439 00
Rhode Island	9,163,760 41	9,282,879 74
Philadelphia	4,083,450 28	2,251,646 46
Newark	1,687,551 51	1,539,932 34
	253,826 72	269,182 67
	66,569,307 34	$65,330,002 65
	65,330,002 65	
Decrease	$1,239,304 69	

By this statement it is shown that the savings-banks in these four States and two cities in one year, during what the Commissioner and the gentleman from Ohio call a season of great prosperity for working people, lost deposits amounting to $1,239,304 69.

The total deposits for 1867 and 1868 in the banks of the same States, the same institution in Philadelphia, the same in Newark, with the addition already referred to of a dime savings institution which was not in existence in 1861, were as follows:

	1867.	1868.
Maine	$5,998,600 26	$8,132,246 71
New Hampshire	10,463,418 50	13,541,534 96
Massachusetts	80,431,583 74	94,838,336 54
Rhode Island	21,413,647 14	24,408,635 95
Philadelphia	5,003,379 42	5,765,280 63
Newark	4,405,726 46	5,430,874 60
	1,116,762 26	1,338,596 94
	325,920 57	468,160 74
	$128,759,038 32	153,823,667 07
		128,759,038 32
Increase		$25,064,628 75

This exhibit is as unfortunate for the Commissioner's facts and theories as that which preceded it, for it shows that in spite of all his rhetoric about the crudities and oppressive character of the legislation of Congress the deposits in these banks, which fell off so largely in his season of prosperity, have increased $25,064,628 75 during the last year, and that the aggregate deposit at the close of 1868, his disastrous period, is largely more than double that of 1860, which he says was so prosperous. In the pursuit of a complete comparative table for these four years I have obtained an amount of information which, though it does not relate to the particular years alluded to, will not be without interest to the House and the country, and I will therefore proceed to present the figures with as much method as I can.

Through the kind assistance of the honorable gentleman from the Troy district, New York, [Mr. Griswold,] I have authentic statistics from the savings-banks of his State; and though we were unable to obtain the figures for the years 1861 or 1868, I can present the number of depositors, the total amount of deposits, and the amount deposited during each year for the years 1860, 1866, and 1867. They were as follows:

Year.	Total number of depositors.	Total amount of deposits.	Total deposited during the year.
1860	300,693	$67,440,397	$34,934,271
1866	488,501	131,769,074	84,765,054
1867	537,466	151,127,562	99,147,321

From Vermont I have been able to obtain only the total amount of deposits for 1867 and 1868. They were as follows:

Year.	Total amount of deposits.
1867	$1,898,107 58
1868	2,128,641 52

From Connecticut I have been able to obtain but the total amount of deposits for 1860, 1861 and 1866. They are as follows:

Year.	Total amount of deposits.
1860	$18,132,820 00
1861	19,377 670 00
1866	31,224,464 25

Thus the figures derived from every quarter are consistent with each other, and the contrast between the condition of things that prevailed between 1857 and 1861—

for the return to which the Commissioner sighs—and that from 1861 to the close of 1868, which he so deprecates, is in itself sufficient to show the grotesque absurdity of his theory, that the head of every family could save money and make deposits in 1860 and that none but unmarried people could do so in 1867 and 1868. Let me repeat his language on this point:

> "Unmarried operatives, therefore, gain; while those who are obliged to support their own families in hired tenements lose. Hence deposits in savings-banks increase, while marriage is discouraged; and the forced employment of young children is made almost a necessity in order that the family may live."

The country will hardly believe that when every head of a family among the laboring people of New York could save money the whole number put at interest but $34,000,-000 per annum, and that when their condition had been so sadly impaired by the unwise legislation of Congress that people feared to marry because their wages would not enable them to support families they deposited $99,000,000 annually, or nearly three dollars for one, and that the number of depositors nearly doubled, and the total amount on deposit to their credit ran up one hundred and twenty-five per cent.

Thus, in defiance of the Commissioner's facts, heartily as they are indorsed by the gentleman from Ohio, the returns from savings-banks prove that, with our labor protected and a cheap and expanded currency, our small farmers and workingmen have been able to lay up hundreds of millions of capital for their support in age or adversity, and upon which they receive interest. These are happily corroborated by other facts, which in a striking manner prove the superiority of the present condition of the classes of people to which I allude over that to which the Special Commissioner of the Revenue would lead them back. While accumulating capital in savings-banks they have felt themselves able to make still more ample provision for their families after they shall have been called away by the dread summoner, death. In the course of the former discussion of this subject I invited your attention to the fact that in Massachusetts alone there were policies of life insurance outstanding on the 1st of January, 1868, for the enormous sum of $1,234,630,473. Through the further kindness of the gentleman from New York [Mr. Griswold]

I have been able to obtain the life-insurance statistics for that State for 1859, 1860, 1866, and 1867. The tables show the number of policies in force at the close of each of these years, the total amount of the policies, and the number of companies issuing them:

Year.	No of companies.	No of policies.	Amount of policies in force.
1859	14	49,617	$141,497,977 82
1860	17	56,046	163,703,455 31
Increase	3	6,429	$22,205,477 49
1866	39	305,390	$853,105,877 24
1867	43	401,140	1,161,729,776 27
Increase	4	95,750	$308,623,899 03

From this table it will be seen that the increase in the number of policies and the amount insured during 1867 was nearly a hundred per cent. in excess of the total number insured and the amount of insurance at the close of 1860, and that the percentage of policies for such small sums as small farmers or workingmen may maintain had increased, as the average value of policies in 1860 was $2,920 88, and had fallen to $2,896 07 in 1867.

I had hoped to present results from the life insurance companies of Connecticut, but have failed to receive them. I have, however, some facts from one company chartered by New Jersey whose office is at Newark and its principal branch at Philadelphia. Through the kindness of the gentleman from New Jersey [Mr. Halsey] I am able to present the number of policies issued by the Mutual Benefit Life Insurance Company, the Company referred to, on the 1st of January of four years. They are as follows:

Date.	No. of policies outstanding.
January, 1861	7,575
January, 1862	7,026
January, 1867	29,858
January, 1868	34,31

I have also been favored with the number of policies outstanding for substantially the same period by the American Life Insurance Company of Philadelphia, together with the number of its policies which were for $3000 or less. They are as follows:

Date.	No. of olicies.	Amount insured for.
December 31, 1860.............	991	$1,090,450 00
December 31, 1861.............	1,120	1,206,000 00
December 31, 1867.............	7,656	18,312,478 93
December 31, 1868.............	10,282	24,759,901 59

The number of these policies in each year, which were on the lives of people of limited or moderate means, and were for $3000 or less was as follows:

Year.	No. of policies.	Amount insured.
1860............................	827	$789.150 00
1861............................	938	920,600 00
1867............................	6,125	9,724,378 93
1868............................	6,689	13,021,878 93

The relative magnitude of our national debt disappears before these statistics; for if the policies existing be maintained the companies of Massachusetts and New York and the two referred to outside of those States will pay to the widows and children or creditors of the parties insured a sum vastly in excess of our total debt, and it is not unfair to assume that the greater portion of the whole amount will be paid to that class of people whom the Commissioner describes as so oppressed by a protective tariff and the cheap and abundant currency now in use. When in my former remarks on this subject I invited your attention to the figures relating to life insurance then in my possession, I said:

"When people in addition to laying up money at interest are insuring their lives, they are living well; but when, as in 1860, past accumulations in savings-banks are running down, and they are wasting their time in enforced idleness, they cannot live well and contribute freely to the support of the Government. Accept the recommendations of the Commissioner and you will paralyze industry, reduce wages, throw the producing classes upon their deposits for support, and deprive them of the power to keep up the insurance on their lives. Such facts as I have presented are sufficient to refute a thousand fine-spun theories. It may with the ingenuity that fashioned this report, be said that the policies to which I have referred are on the lives of wealthy people. But such is not the case; two hundred and sixty-five out of each thousand of them are for $1000 or less; five hundred and forty out of each thousand are for $2000 or less; seven hundred out of each thousand for $3000 or less. Only three hundred out of each thousand are for amounts over $3000. These policies are the precautions taken by well-paid industry to provide for widowhood and orphanage after the head of the family shall have paid mortality's last debt."

It is not improper, Mr. Chairman, that in concluding this

branch of my subject I should say that I have presented no statement which is not warranted by official indorsement, and that I hesitate not to assert that could the business of the savings-banks and life insurance companies of the whole country be investigated the results would conform to those I have produced. They are truly surprising, and should they through our widely diffused periodicals find their way across the waters, will prove an abundant antidote to the Commissioner's notice to those who have thought of emigrating to this country, but who desire to live in wedlock, that they may not hope to do so under the legislation of that Congress which has for several years been in such absolute government of the country as to render the veto power of the Executive nugatory. They are, in my judgment, important enough to produce some effect upon the credit of the country, for they show that our laboring people are saving and putting at interest hundreds of millions of dollars annually, and that the people at large are paying from their abundance more, largely more, than the interest on our national debt to life insurance companies, as a provision for their widows and orphans when they shall no longer be able to provide for and protect them.*

---

* The facts presented in the text, exhibit the condition of the workingmen of Protective America, and the following testimony of Wm. Hoyle, of Manchester, and R. Dudley Baxter, will show how it compares with that of those of Free Trade England. It is found on pages 38 to 42 of the 4th edition of *Our National Resources*, by Wm. Hoyle. London. 1870.

"The present population of the United Kingdom (1869) is 30,838,210; of these, 1,281,651 are returned as paupers, and 6692 as vagrants.

"The following table will show the gradual and continued increase in our pauperism. It gives the number of paupers in the United Kingdom from 1860 to 1870 inclusive:

	England and Wales.	Scotland.	Ireland.	Total.
1860	851,020	114,209	44,929	1,010,158
1861	890,423	117,113	50,683	1,058,219
1862	946,166	118,928	59,541	1,124,635
1863	1,142,624	120,284	66,228	1,329,136
1864	1,009,289	120,705	68,135	1,198,129
1865	971,433	121,394	69,217	1,162,044
1866	920,344	119,608	65,057	1,105,009
1867	958,824	121,169	68,650	1,148,643
1868	1,034,823	128,976	72,925	1,236,724
1869	1,039,549	128,339	74,745	1,242,633
1870	1,079,391		73,921	

"The Government returns as to pauperism and vagrancy do not, however, by any means represent the extent of these two evils. They give the number

The Commissioner's theory, that our legislation is making the rich richer and the poor poorer, is that which was hurled at us by every copperhead orator, from Horatio Seymour down, during the last canvass. We also encountered it in every rebel paper in the South, and there were those who feared that it might produce an effect upon the popular mind. I was not one of them. The American people are intelligent enough to know when they have the toothache, or are involved in a lawsuit, or are being stripped of property through the medium of a sheriff's sale, and remembering the disasters of the last free-trade and hard-money era of the country, I contrasted it with their present condition and relied confidently upon their judgment. In order to test the accuracy of my memory and judgment on this point, I appealed during the canvass to the statistics of my own city, and among other telling facts found, as I have already told you, that in 1860 the sheriff of Philadelphia had received seventeen hundred and forty writs for the sale of real estate, and that in 1867 he had

---

of paupers on the books on the 1st day of January, and the number of vagrants who apply for lodging or casual relief on the same day; but this, but very imperfectly portrays the pauperism, etc. of the country. According to this method of reckoning, if a man becomes chargeable to the union on the 2d of January, and comes off again on the 31st of December, he is not counted, though he has been receiving relief during the whole year, except two days. The statistics of the Poor Law Board, give the number of paupers and vagrants relieved on one day, (which is what they profess to do), but it does not give the number of persons who get relief as paupers and vagrants during the year. This is the idea generally received, but it is erroneous.

"In order to get the number of persons who received relief during 1869, we must multiply 1,281,651 by 3½, which gives 4,485,778. This, then, is the real number of persons who were chargeable as paupers, at one time or another, during that year, or nearly one in seven of the entire population. Admitting that a considerable number of these might be persons who applied twice or three times over during the year, it would still leave us about one in every ten of the population as having been paupers during the course of the year."

"In reference to this subject, Mr. R. Dudley Baxter, in his work on *National Income*, remarks:—

"'The average number of paupers at one time in receipt of relief in 1866, was 916,000, being less than for any of the four preceding years. The total number relieved during 1866 may, on the authority of a return of 1867, given in the Appendix, be calculated at three and a half times that number, or 3,000,000. All these may be considered as belonging to the 16,000,000 of the manual labor classes, being as nearly as possible, twenty per cent. on their number; but the actual cases of relief give a very imperfect idea of the loss of work and wages. A large proportion of the poor submit to great hardships, and are many weeks, and even months, out of work before they will apply to the guardians. They exhaust their savings; they try to the utmost, their trade unions or benefit societies; they pawn little by little all their furniture; and at last are driven to ask relief.'

"But even the figures which have been given do not by any means represent adequately the pressure of our poverty. There are a very large number of persons who are dependent upon their friends and relations; and there are a num-

received but seven hundred and six—a decrease of more than sixty per cent., although the population of the city had increased more than forty per cent. What makes this fact more significant is, that under our system of selling land under ground rents the purchase of a homestead is the savings-bank of the Philadelphia workingman. I also ascertained the number of suits that were instituted in the years 1857-58-59 and 1865-66 and 1867, respectively, in our local courts. The evidence from this source is not less significant than any that has preceded it. The court of common pleas is emphatically the poor man's court. It obtains jurisdiction by appeal from the judgments of magistrates, and the amount at issue before its juries is for sums less than $100. The result of my investigation showed that the number of suits brought in the latter years, notwithstanding the increase of population which had taken place, was but little more than one-half the num-

---

ber who, as Dudley Baxter says, submit to great hardships sooner than apply for relief. If all who are thus situated be summed up, it cannot amount to much less than one-third of the entire population of the manual labor class, or from fifteen to twenty per cent. of the entire population.

"The Government returns in reference to vagrancy are even more imperfect and unsatisfactory than the pauper returns. I have not been able to obtain any national figures to illustrate this, but it will be sufficiently manifest if I give the statistics in reference to one union—the Bury Union, in which I reside.

"The following table gives the number of paupers and vagrants returned to the Poor-Law Board, January 1st, 1870, and published in their report as representing the pauperism and vagrancy in the Bury Union, the population of which, in 1861, was 101,142.

Paupers	4,372
Vagrants	11

"The actual number of cases of pauperism and vagrancy during the year ending March, 1870, in the Bury Union was as follows:

No. of cases of Paupers relieved	15,012
" " Vagrants "	15,474

"These returns corroborate the figures given by Mr. Purdy, in reference to the pauperism of the country; and they show that if the total cases of vagrancy during the year were given, it would numerically be equal to, or greater than the number of paupers.

"No doubt a very large number of the vagrant cases are from among the paupers, and in a large proportion of the cases, the same parties apply several times over in the same Union, and also at different Unions; still, it shows that there is a very large class of our population who have no fixed dwelling-place; they move about getting a living, by begging or stealing, or by imposition upon the public, as may be most convenient. Adding this class to the pauper class, it reveals an amount of destitution and demoralization in the country that is perfectly appalling, and that is a lasting disgrace to our civilization and christianity."

ber instituted in the former period. The figures are as follows:

SUITS IN COMMON PLEAS.

1857		2,503
1858		2,651
1859		3,041
		8,195
1865	1,500	
1866	1,461	
1867	1,672	
		4,633
Decrease of cases		3,562

The jurisdiction of the district court extends to all cases involving more than $100. Its records are consistent with those of the common pleas. The figures from its records are as follows:

DISTRICT COURT.

1857		9,894
1858		9,702
1859		7,262
		26,858
1865	4,977	
1866	5,716	
1867	6,674	
		17,367
Decrease		9,491

I am sure I do Mr. Wells no injustice when I complain of his palpable negligence in omitting to appeal to such sources of information as I have indicated, and attempting to deduce general laws by which to guide our legislation from the lame and impotent array of facts he has digested. We pay him a salary which he deems adequate. His traveling expenses are at the cost of the Treasury, and he is surrounded by a competent clerical force, and that he should have rested all his theories upon an array of facts so meagre and so easily disproved is, to say the least, not creditable to his industry or judgment.

The gentleman from Ohio [Mr. Garfield] told us that hearing of my intended attack he had asked information from two sources in order to test the correctness of the Commissioner's position. That was an idle waste of time. Had he spent it in examining Mr. Wells' figures, he would have discovered from their own manifest incongruity that no two or two hundred authorities could give them a character for respectability or the weight of authority. The gentleman is an arithmetician and knows that $111,000 are not twenty-one and forty-nine hundredths per cent. of $5,164,500, and that $37,000 are not seven and twenty-six hundredths per cent. of $5,053,500. Yet the Commissioner tells us they are, and so impairs the value of the important table on page 111 of his report. I invite the gentleman's attention to the two elaborate tables to be found on page 16 of the report, the first purporting to show in parallel columns the "average weekly expenditures for provisions, house-rent," etc.; the second, "average weekly earnings," and the third "surplus for clothing, housekeeping goods," etc., of families in 1867; the other in corresponding columns purporting to show "average weekly expenditures of families of varying numbers in the manufacturing towns of the United States for the years 1860 and 1867, respectively."

More remarkable tables than these never were prepared by statistician. I had supposed that Mr. Delmar, late chief of the Bureau of Statistics, was a paragon in his way; but he must look out for his honors, for in these tables the Special Commissioner of Revenue has beaten him roundly in his own department. Unhappy Delmar! Happy Commissioner Wells! For Delmar's report Congress had nothing but an indignant vote requiring its suppression, though it lay ready printed and bound; but for Wells' budget of more egregious blunders it has such admiration and approval, that no love of economy could restrain it from voting to print it for the widest possible circulation. The tables to which I refer must speak for themselves, for no man can describe or characterize them. They are as follows:

Average aggregate weekly earnings and expenses of families for 1867.

Size of families.	Average weekly expenditures for provisions, house-rent, etc.	Average weekly earnings.	Surplus for clothing, housekeeping goods, etc.
Parents and one child	$10 24	$17 00	$6 76
Three adults	8 35	17 52	9 17
Parents and two children	12 26	18 75	6 49
Parents and three children	15 02	19 50	4 48
Parents and four children	17 79	23 33	5 54
Parents and five children	15 23	17 11	1 88
Parents and six children	11 67	13 50	1 83
Parents and seven children	23 78	25 00	1 22
General average of the above	$14 29	$18 96	$4 67

Table showing the average weekly expenditures of families of varying numbers in the manufacturing towns of the United States for the years 1860 and 1867, respectively.

Size of families.	Average weekly wages.		Average weekly expenditures for provisions, house-rent, clothing, etc.		Surplus in 1860.
	In 1867.	In 1860.	In 1867.	In 1860.	
Parents and one child	$17 00	$12 17	$17 00	$9 96	$2 21
Three adults	17 52	12 00	17 52	10 31	1 69
Parents and two children	18 75	11 50	18 75	10 79	71
Parents and three children	19 50	12 41	19 50	11 33	1 08
Parents and four children	23 33	14 15	23 33	13 18	97
Parents and five children	17 11	10 37	17 11	9 46	91
Parents and six children	13 50	9 50	13 50	7 67	1 83
Parents and seven children	25 00	15 17	25 00	14 09	1 08
General average of the above	$18 96	$12 16	$18 96	$10 85	$1 31

I hope the gentleman from Ohio will give these tables a reasonable amount of consideration, and if he still thinks they may be correct refer them to another authority—the ancient matrons of his district. But before making this reference, I beg him to advise the ladies of the fact that he draws his question from an official document; for if he fails to take this precaution they will hold him guilty of perpetrating a practical joke at their expense, by submitting to their judgment so absurd a proposition. They will doubtless admit that parents with two children cannot live so well on the same money as parents with but one, and that as a general rule it costs more to maintain parents and three children than is required for the support of those with but two or one, and that the same is true with reference to parents and four children; but they will probably doubt his sincerity when he asks whether parents with five children can live as well on less money than is required to support parents with but three, and will laugh at the proposition that parents with six children can live as well on less money than parents with but two; and I think I hear them crying out, "Why, sir, what do you mean by asking us whether parents with six children can live for less than parents with two, and yet in the same breath telling us that if they happen to have a seventh, be it boy or girl, it will more than double the expenses of the whole family?" Unwelcome seventh child! According to Wells you come into the family of every laboring man to double the household expenses though all your six predecessors be still sheltered by the paternal roof! Lucky children numbers five and six!—henceforth you will be welcomed everywhere; for the Special Commissioner of Revenue has proved that in all instances your coming reduces the expenses of the family to less than they were when the household flock consisted of but two! According to the Commissioner this law of social life, hitherto undiscovered, is absolute, and prevailed alike in 1860 and 1867.

To invite attention to these tables is to subject them to ridicule; and yet, Mr. Chairman, they are the foundation-stone and the keystone of Mr. Wells' entire structure; upon them he rests all his argument, and from them he deduces his conclusion, that marriage is a luxury the laboring people of America cannot safely enjoy. Happily for the country they are so flagrantly and absurdly false, that Mr. Wells' deductions and conclusions will be received but as the vain imaginings of a dreamy and indolent theorist.*

In view of the unquestioned facts I have brought to the attention of the committee, and the urgency of the Commissioner for a return to the revenue tariff and contracted currency of 1860, I am forced to the conclusion that he regards poverty and idleness as supreme blessings to the laboring people of our country, and I rejoice that I succeeded in obtaining the floor upon the motion to print his report, and sounded an alarm to the masses of my countrymen by telling them that it is an insidious plea for their impoverishment.

In my judgment, the first duty of an American statesman is to watch and guard the rights of the laboring classes of the country. They produce its wealth, they fight its battles, and in their hands is its destiny; for at every election they cast a majority of the ballots, and upon their intelligence, integrity, and manly independence rest the welfare of the country. To make Republican government an enduring success, we must guard the productions of our laborers against competition with those of the ill-paid and oppressed laborers of Europe, so that each head of a family may by the wages he can earn maintain a home, and be able to support his children during the years required to

* The general judgment of Mr. Wells is less favorable than this. His sudden conversion to free trade is generally ascribed to something more tangible than dreams.

give them the advantages of our common school system. If the Commissioner's report proves anything to those who are able to detect its fallacies, and test the fulness and accuracy of its comparative tables, it is that under the influence of the cheap and abundant currency we now have, and the system of protection which the war forced us to adopt, the American people are consuming more of the necessaries and comforts of life than they were ever before able to consume; are producing more of what they consume than ever before, and in spite of the taxes imposed by the national debt and other incidents of the war, are coming to be commercially independent of other nations. Yes, sir, under the influence of a tariff which, though it levies duties on raw materials and commodities which we do not and cannot produce, is still in a measure protective, and an adequate amount of currency, we are slowly emerging from our commercial dependence upon England, as is shown by the fact that our imports have steadily diminished since 1865. Thus in 1866, 1867, and 1868, respectively, the amounts of foreign merchandise imported into the country were as follows:

Year ending 30th of June, 1866.............	$423,470,646
Year ending 30th of June, 1867.............	374,943,502
Year ending 30th of June, 1868.	344,873,433

Thus it appears that notwithstanding the facts that the increase of our wealth is unparalleled, and the natural increase of our population is very rapid, and that "from the 1st of July, 1865, to the 1st of December, 1868, about one million natives of foreign countries have sought a permanent home in the United States," our purchases of foreign commodities are steadily diminishing. The sapient deduction of the Special Commissioner of the Revenue from these facts is, that we are unable to trade with foreign nations, and that to stimulate foreign trade we must reduce the wages of our laborers, and diminish the amount of currency now profitably employed in the development of our productive power. His theory is that "all commerce is in the nature of barter or exchange," and his complaint is that:

"We have so raised the cost of all domestic products that exchange in kind with all foreign nations is almost impossible. The majority of what foreign nations have to sell us, as already shown, we must or will have. What foreign nations want and we produce, cotton and a few other articles excepted, they can buy elsewhere cheaper. We are, therefore, obliged to pay in no small part for such foreign productions as we need or will have, either in the precious metals or, what is worse, in unduly depreciated promises of national payment."

The Commissioner's exception of "cotton and a few other articles" leaves Hamlet out of the play, and surrenders his whole case, for we can raise enough of the articles he excepts, and of which we have a natural monopoly, to pay for every foreign production "we must or will have."

The beneficent results of free labor in the former slave States are an agreeable surprise to its most sanguine friends. The South is abundantly rich in mineral and agricultural resources, but she is suffering from the want of currency to develop them. Were she adequately supplied with currency, and the season should be a favorable one, her production of cotton, and the few other articles excepted by the Commissioner, would more than double that of 1868, and as other nations must have her cotton, tobacco, rice, and other semi-tropical productions which they cannot procure elsewhere, it seems to me that the true way to stop the flow of precious metals and Government bonds is to stimulate production by protecting the wages of labor and avoiding any contraction of the currency. In support of this view, let me call attention to the fact that we send from eighty to one hundred million dollars abroad annually for sugar. If capitalists will lend the planters of Florida, Louisiana, and Texas the means to cultivate their sugar-fields, they will produce crops that will save a large percentage of this vast sum to the country.*

I showed, in a former discussion of this subject, that we bought about forty-five per cent. of the entire amount of railroad iron exported by Great Britain during the first ten months of 1868, saying:

"I hold in my hand a circular which reads thus: 'Fifty-eight, Old Broad street, London, November 30, 1868, from S. W. Hopkins &

---

* Since my remarks were delivered, I have received from Messrs. McFarlan, Straight & Co., commission merchants of New Orleans, their trade circular of February 1st, from which I extract the following corroboration of my views:

"Receipts of the Louisiana sugar crop this season to 30th ultimo, inclusive, foot up 47,419 hogsheads sugar, and 109,518 barrels, 4692 half barrels, and 17 quarter barrels molasses. But for lack of promptness in commencing grinding early, and of adequate preparation on the part of the producers for securing a large yield, and the early severe frosts, succeeded by floods of rain, the Louisiana sugar crop of 1868 would probably have reached 115,000 hogsheads at least, or about three times the product of 1867. The yield of 1868 must have been re-

Co., exporters of railway iron. Monthly Report of Exports of Rails from Great Britain, extracted from the Government returns.' By this report it appears that in the ten months ending October 31, 1868, Great Britain exported 509,968 tons of rails. Gentlemen probably think that England's colonial dependencies took most of this iron; that British India, British North America, and Australia took it. No, gentlemen; we are her chief commercial dependency. She is our mistress, and we maintain her throne and aristocracy. No; the British dependencies took but 84,000 tons, and her Republican dependency, the United States, took 228,000 tons. Of the 509,968 tons of rails, we took 21,000 tons more than were taken by British India, Russia, British North America, Sweden, Prussia, France, Spain and the Canaries, Cuba, Brazil, Chili, and Australia."

The Commissioner makes no note of such facts as this, but finding some fortunately situated manufacturers of pig-iron guilty of making profits almost equal to those which merchants and bankers average, he holds them up to contempt and ridicule, and wonders—yes, in an official report, sneeringly expresses his surprise—that they have not petitioned Congress to legislate for the reduction of their profits! He probably does not know that the high rate at which pig-iron is now selling is stimulating the production of that primary article to an extent that promises an early home supply and such competition among our own people as must inevitably cheapen the price of iron and reduce the profits of those whose product is now in unusual request. In proof of this assertion, I not only point the Commissioner to the rapid increase of the means of producing pig-iron in Pennsylvania, but appeal to all the gentlemen on this floor from districts in or near which coal, iron ore, and limestone are found. Districts hitherto unknown to the iron trade are now producing large quantities of pig-iron; and I ask gentlemen from New York, New Jersey, Ohio, Indiana, southern Illinois, Missouri, Alabama, Georgia, Maryland, West Virginia, Kentucky, Tennessee,

---

duced by mere waste, caused by lack of wood, lateness in beginning to grind and the unfavorable weather during the latter part of the grinding season, say 25,000 hogsheads or more, leaving, perhaps, 90,000 hogsheads to be realized. This great waste from a bountiful crop is greatly to be regretted, and we may hope it will not be repeated.

"*The production of domestic cane-sweets, properly protected and encouraged, might be increased far beyond the ideas of many who are directly interested.* We believe the sugar lands of this State and Texas might be made to produce the entire 650,000 tons of sugar said to be required annually by the people of the United States, saving the $100,000,000 of specie paid yearly for foreign sweets, including charges and import duty, or perhaps fifty to sixty millions actually paid to foreign producers. We have space only to ask the genuine financier to consider this important instrumentality in aid of a return to the specie basis."—*Note to Pamphlet Edition.*

North Carolina, and Oregon, whether there are not more furnaces erecting in their States, respectively, than ever were in process of erection at one time before, and whether those already existing are not in full operation? Virginia has no voice on this floor with which to respond to my appeal, but it is within my knowledge that Pennsylvanians are constructing furnaces, forges, and rolling-mills in various parts of that State. If we would turn the balance of trade in our favor, and put our bonds at par, and stop the outflowing of gold interest by receiving them in the hands of immigrants, or in pay for our cotton, rice, tobacco, provisions, etc., we must avoid the Commissioner's nostrums, free trade, and hard money, and promote the development of the boundless natural resources of the country. By no other means can we arrest the export of specie and bonds in exchange for foreign commodities.

There are many points in the Commissioner's report that I would gladly review, but having addressed myself to a single one, I will leave them for the consideration of others. Meanwhile I congratulate the country that it is so strong, and the currents of its prosperity are so broad, and moving with such increasing volume, that no official report or the vagaries of no theorist can impair or arrest its progress.

THE EIGHT-HOUR SYSTEM.

LETTER TO THE OPERATIVES IN THE WORKSHOPS AND FACTORIES OF THE FOURTH CONGRESSIONAL DISTRICT OF PENNSYLVANIA.

THE duties with which Congress, by special resolution, charged the Committee of Ways and Means, of which I am a member, will probably consume the vacation, and require me to be absent from my district and laboriously engaged, while my colleagues are enjoying the rest and recreation which with my impaired health I so much need.

I cannot, under the circumstances, give the time to conference and correspondence with my constituents to which their interest in public affairs entitles them, and therefore address you thus publicly on topics which many communications from you show me you deem to be of primary importance at this time, viz: the practicability of the eight-hour system, and the propriety of the order of the Secretary of the Navy, which apportions the pay of workmen in the Navy Yards to the number of hours' service performed.

Though your letters differ in form, the substance is about the same: and by replying to two questions, I think I can answer most of your communications. You really ask but two questions, and I hope that each of you who has written to me on this subject will accept this as a reply. Your questions are:

First:—Are you in favor of the eight-hour system? Second:—Do you sustain the order of the Secretary of the Navy prohibiting the payment of the same wages for eight hours' work in a Navy Yard that are paid for ten hours' work in private establishments?

The first question I answer in the affirmative. I am in favor of the eight-hour system, and am not a recent convert to the doctrine. It is more than 35 years since, as an apprentice in a jewelry establishment, I united with the journeymen of that and other trades in promoting the recognition of the ten-hour system. There are some of my co-laborers who, at this distant day, can testify that in support of the reform we proposed, I then asserted that the laborer's day should be divided into three equal divisions, inasmuch as he could by eight hours of honest labor produce enough to entitle him to eight hours for rest, and eight hours for recreation or study. At that time a mechanic's day's work, at indoors employment, from September to April, ended at eight o'clock in the evening; and I never lighted my lamp for night-work without feeling that humanity was outraged by the fact that the millions whose toil produced all the wealth were compelled at the cost of sight and health to labor thus, while those who only bought and sold their productions were free from such exactions. Those early convictions abide with me, and have controlled my votes as your representative.

It is true that I have not proposed to establish the eight-hour system by Act of Congress. That would have been to attempt an impossibility; but that I have sedulously and courageously labored to remove all hindrances, and prepare the way for its establishment is also true. Much has been done; and that the time is near when the working people of the United States, if they will take a comprehensive view of their position, and firmly maintain their interests, can establish the eight-hour system, I conscientiously believe. One of the principal obstacles to this just reform has been to some extent removed, and another, which seemed to be beyond human control, has been wholly obliterated during the nine years through which I have been your representative. I, of course, allude to free trade and slavery.

Our country is so extended, its resources are so vast and diversified, and the sources of profitable employment for our people are so manifold, that we may establish our own industrial system, and maintain it against all opposition, without abridging the quantity or quality of the food, clothing, or culture of any of our people.

We can live and prosper, and expand while maintaining a system of absolute commercial independence. Then the eight-hour system will be practicable, but until this be effected, and while our markets are freely opened to the productions of Belgium, France, Germany, and England, our labor system must conform more or less closely to those of these competing nations. They produce every result of mechanical skill and labor that we can, but they do not pay the same price for any kind of labor. Belgium and France pay for a day's work by a skilled hand with francs worth twenty cents gold; England with shillings worth twenty-five cents gold; and America with dollars worth about seventy cents gold at this time;* and the American receives for almost every variety of work as many dollars as the Englishman does shillings, or the Belgian or Frenchman francs. It is, therefore, obvious that we cannot sell our productions in those countries, and that, in the absence of a tariff that will protect your wages, and which will equal the difference between the wages which workmen in those countries are compelled to accept, and those which you receive for ten hours', and hope to get for eight hours' labor, they can undersell us in our own markets, and deprive you of work and wages by closing our workshops and factories. Though politically independent, we are commercially dependent. We endured a long war as the price of our political independence, but have hitherto consented to be held in commercial dependence, and to allow Belgium, France, Germany, and England to determine what wages the American workman shall receive and how many hours he shall work each day to support his family. To promote our commercial independence and secure our labor market to our own people and those who may become such by immigration, have been the constant objects of my labors as your representative.

When these objects shall be attained, the eight-hour system can and will be established. But till then, you cannot enjoy it. To my mind nothing is more apparent than this.

A word, now, as to the prospect. In 1857, we had a revenue tariff. Free trade prevailed. What was your condition? A large portion of you were without employment. The price of goods was low, but you had no work by which you could earn money to buy them, cheap as they were. Banks and savings banks failed: the constable and sheriff were busy; immigration was arrested, and large numbers of immigrants, discouraged by the hopeless prospect, returned to their native countries convinced that

* Worth eighty-seven cents, July 10th, 1871.

the American Republic was not a happy home for the working man. Free trade is the subordination of the immense productive interests of our country to the demands of the few who are engaged in foreign commerce, and such were its natural results. We now have a protective tariff, and the circumstances are widely different. We are mining more coal, making more iron, planting more grain, and building more locomotives, houses, factories and workshops than ever before. Labor is in demand, and immigration increasing marvellously. The prospect of steady work and American wages, is bringing to our shores workmen skilled in every craft, and the assurance of a home market for their crops is bringing farmers from all the countries of Europe to settle among us. From the number that have already arrived, the Commissioners of Emigration predict that we will receive this year 400,000 European emigrants, an increase of 70,000 over any previous year. I submit to you the question, whether this is not a significant proof of the happy effect of the protective tariff which the exigences of the war compelled us to adopt. Under its influence labor is in demand, and the laborer is steadily becoming more independent; and if we perfect and maintain a system of thorough protection, you will be able to establish and maintain the eight-hour system. This will compel other nations to follow our benificent example, or behold their best workmen and most enterprising farmers leave their shores and come to swell the power of the great Republic. To ascertain how the existing tariff may be improved is the duty with which the Committee of Ways and Means is charged, and to which my colleagues and I expect to devote the entire vacation. The results of our labor must promote your objects. It is already apparent to the Committee that the administration of the law can be much improved, and that many articles, especially of tropical growth, which we do not produce, but which enter as raw material into many of our manufactures, and upon which duties are now collected, should be admitted free.

Four millions of laboring people, who, from the foundations of our government, have been used to antagonize your interests, are now free to co-operate with you. They were slaves, and their emancipation has not only enabled them to assert their right to just wages for their labor, but opened as a new field to free labor that portion of our country which is richest in combined agricultural and mineral resources, but from which trade societies and free schools for the children of working people have always been excluded. The results of this great change must soon be widely felt. Slaves, could not without danger to slavery, be trained to skilled labor. Therefore the South produced only raw materials, and her statesmen, desiring the markets of the world in which to sell their cotton and tobacco, and to buy their supply of manufactured goods, always supported free trade at the cost of the commercial independence of the country, and the interests of the working people of the North. The war against slavery was waged not more for the enslaved negro than for the rights of free labor.

To the second question I reply, that, inasmuch as I believe that public officers are bound to obey the law, I am compelled to sustain the order of the Secretary of the Navy. The law of 1862 provides "that the hours of labor and the rate of wages of the employees in the Navy Yards shall conform, as nearly as is consistent with the public interests, with those of private establishments in the immediate vicinity of the respective yards." This act is still in force, and the Solicitor of the Navy and the Attorney-General, to whom the question has been referred, have advised the Secretary and President Grant, that under its provisions the Government cannot legally pay for eight hours' work the same wages that are paid for ten hours by private establishments in the immediate vicinity of the yards respectively. If, therefore, men who work in Navy Yards are to receive 25 per cent. more than they would get for the same work in private establishments, the act of 1862 must be repealed. That can only be done by Congress. Neither the Secretary of the Navy, nor the President, has the power to repeal a law or the right to disregard one.

Though none of you have put the question to me directly, some of you will now ask, will you vote for the repeal of this act? I regret that I do not feel able to answer this question definitely. As at present advised, my judgment is against its repeal; but on either of two conditions, I will vote for it. The first of these conditions is, that it shall be made apparent to me that the tax-payers of my district, including the women and children, who labor in factories ten hours or more to the day, believe that the men who work in Navy Yards are entitled to 25 per cent. more wages for the same work than the same class of workmen receive in private establishments in Philadelphia

The other condition is, that I shall be convinced that the repeal of the act in question will promote the acceptance of the eight-hour system in private shops or yards. Private establishments compete with each other and with those of other countries in the sale of their productions. But the Government does not manufacture for a market, and, therefore, could not be cited as an example of the successful working of the system.

If the Government adopts this rule in advance of individual employers, you will find that all work that can be done in private shops will be sent there, and the number of hands employed in Navy Yards will be very limited. Congress, while struggling to reduce our colossal debt, will not require much work to be done at League Island, or any other station, if 25 per cent. above the average market rate is to be paid for every day's work.

But neither time nor printer's space will permit me to present all the considerations touching this question with which my mind is laboring. To such as I have set forth I invite your candid consideration. The destinies of the working people of our country are in their own keeping. I have not sought to flatter or propitiate you. While I remain your representative, you are entitled to know my views on questions which many of you regard as of vital importance; and I have written frankly, withholding no word that candor requires me to utter. I address you as a grateful friend, and not as a supplicant for further honors: for, if I am permitted to consult my own wishes, my connection with public office will terminate with the XLIst Congress.

Yours, very truly,

WM. D. KELLEY.

NEW YORK, *May* 19th, 1869.

MR. WELLS' REPORT.

SPEECH DELIVERED IN THE HOUSE OF REPRESENTATIVES, JANUARY 11, 1870.

The House being in the Committee of the Whole on the state of the Union—

Mr. Kelley said:

Mr. Chairman: I have more than once endeavored to impress upon Congress the fact that fire is the material force or nervous power, and iron and steel are the muscles of our more modern civilization. The trip-hammer, with its wonderful power and more wonderful precision and delicacy of stroke, has supplanted the sledge-hammer, and circular and gang-saws do in a day the work at which the hand-saw labored for months. Machine tools, such as lathes, drills, planers, and shaping machines, impelled like the trip-hammer and saws by the unwearying steam engine, itself a mere embodiment of coal and iron ore, increase the perfection and amount of the artisan's productions and relieve him of the exhausting toil which shortened the life of his father and made him prematurely old.

Nations, too, are subject to these new conditions. However free their institutions may be, a people who cannot supply their own demand for iron and steel, but purchase it from foreigners, are not independent; nor is their dependence merely commercial; they are politically dependent; and if the nation on which they depend for these essential elements of modern warfare be arrogant and treacherous, as England proved herself during our late civil war, they must endure contumely and outrage with unresisting humility. Commerce and war both demand iron ships; we tell the weight of our guns, whether of steel or iron, by the ton, and that of our steel-pointed shot by the hundred weight; and while we depend upon her for the material of which to construct ships, guns, and shot, the statesmen of England know they can trifle with and postpone the settlement of the Alabama claims. Able as we were to crush with irresistible power a gigantic rebellion, they know that until we shall have enough furnaces, forges, rolling-mills, machine-shops, and skilled artisans to produce and fashion a supply of iron and steel sufficient for our wants in peace and war, we cannot engage in war with England because we must depend on her for these primary essentials to successful modern warfare.*

I am impelled to renew these suggestions by the report of David A. Wells, Esq., Special Commissioner of Revenue, which abounds in propositions inimical to the best interests of the country, which if adopted by Congress will compel us to occupy a subordinate position among nations, though our population may equal that of all Europe, as our territory already does that of the whole family of European Powers. As I read page after page of this extraordinary paper I became more earnestly anxious to detect the full force of its suggestions, and, if possible, to divine the motive or spirit that prompted them. As an expression of the opinions of Mr. Wells this paper can do but little harm, but its circulation in Europe under the sanction of Congress may impair our credit and arrest the tide of immigration now flowing in upon us in unprecedented volume. It is in the nature of a notice to the capitalists of Europe that as a people, notwithstanding the amazing

---

* "The great mind of Washington was not too slow to make this discovery. And what did we also discover in our war of 1812, but that we had nothing to equip the war? Having no woolen manufacture, we could not clothe our soldiers; we could not even make a blanket. We had been free-traders, buying all such things because we could buy them cheaper; but we now discovered, that we might better have been making blankets at double the cost for the last fifty years. The same was true of saltpetre for gunpowder; of guns, and cannon and swords; and iron and steel out of which to make them. A nation that is to be a power must have at least a sufficient supply of iron made at home, no matter what the cost, to arm itself for war. We began also to make the discovery, shortly, that the very insignificant article of salt, coming in short supply, was nearly a dead necessity—one of the munitions of war—and that manufacturing it for ourselves at double the cost would have been a true advantage. . . . .

"Protection, though it be a losing bargain, as in trade, is generally necessary in States that are young, in order to their full organized development. We were a young nation in the war of 1812, and we very soon discovered in facts already referred to, the lowness of our organization, and the very incomplete scope of our industrial equipments. Our products were not various enough to make us a complete nation. It is often urged as the special advantage of young nations, that they can have the benefits of free trade, without trouble from the shock that must be given to old artificial investments; but we had another kind of shock to bear that was far more perilous, from the scant equipment in which our previous free-trade practice had left us. Perhaps we were gaining in wealth by such trade, but we were miserably unprepared by it for the stress of our great public trial."—*Rev. Horace Bushnell, D. D.*, "Free Trade and Protection." (*Scribner's Magazine*, for July, 1871.)

expansion of our country, we are tending toward bankruptcy; and to the oppressed laborers of other lands, that our working people are becoming from year to year, not only relatively but absolutely poorer, and that this is therefore not the country to which poor but aspiring men should emigrate. It demonstrates to the satisfaction of Mr. Wells' admirers and clients that though our wealth increased during the last decade one hundred and twenty-six per cent., its utmost increase during this decade can be but sixty-five and eight hundreths per cent.; and that the grand total of our real and personal property cannot be over $23,400,000,000.*

Time will not permit me to point out the fallacies in this portion of his report, as I would gladly do; and I proceed at once to invite the attention of the committee to points which seem to require more special animadversion. But, before turning to these, let me request gentlemen from Massachusetts, Ohio, Indiana, and New York, if they have not already done so, to turn to pages 24 *et seq.*, and learn how rapidly their respective States are sinking into poverty, and how much poorer their people are *per capita* than they were in 1860. The suggestion will doubtless surprise them; yet so cunningly does Mr. Wells present it

---

* Mr. Wells is the oracle of revenue reformers, and this furnishes an apt illustration of his accuracy, as his statement of the rate of increase was not much more than 50 per cent. out of the way.

"Deducting the value of the then slave property, the real and personal estate of this country, as shown by the census of 1860, amounted in round numbers to $14,000,000,000, being about $8,000,000,000 in excess of the valuation of 1850. 'Much, however, of this large increase,' as we have since been told by Commissioner Wells, 'is known to have been due to more accurate methods of enumeration, and to the inclusion of many elements previously left unnoticed.' Allowing for this, the increase of the decade could scarcely have exceeded $6,000,000, and is, indeed, estimated by the Commissioner at even less than this amount.

"Thus far the Census Bureau has given us no estimate of the property of 1870; but from a valuable document just now published by the Bureau of Statistics, and for which we are indebted to the labors of its head, Mr. Edward Young, we learn that it will be shown to be about $800 per head, giving, of course, thirty-one thousand millions as the total amount, and exhibiting an increase of probably seventeen thousand millions in a decade, nearly one-half of which had been years of war, accompanied by a waste of life and property such as had been rarely ever equalled.

"Through the decade 1850–60, there was none of the waste of war. Peace prevailing, eight millions were added to the numbers of our people, and yet the addition to our wealth amounted to but six thousand millions, or about $750 per head of the then added population.

"Throughout the last decade there was a waste of war estimated by Commissioner Wells at no less than nine thousand millions. The addition to our numbers proves to be but seven millions, and yet the growth of wealth has been seventeen hundred millions, or about $2500 for each head of the added population."—*Forney's Press*, June 15th, 1871.

that foreigners who are not familiar with the truth so patent to every observer will be deceived by it and feel they had better—

> "Bear those ills they have,
> Than fly to others that they know not of."

One of the processes by which Mr. Wells sustains his theory, though not wanting in ingenuity, is very simple. It is to assume that everything is now worth from thirty-five to thirty-nine per cent. less than it was at the time with which he proposes his comparison. We know that wheat and flour and every variety of cotton and woolen goods are cheaper now than they were in 1860. But Mr. Wells' theory is, that as there is a difference in the market value of gold and greenbacks, commodities of domestic production ought to be dearer; and applying his theory to such facts as he sees fit to present, he assumes that they are dearer, and so establishes the melancholy warning to all persons proposing to emigrate that this is not the country to which they should come. No demonstration of the falsity of his theory or of its absurdity induces him to halt, but in spite of these he presses onward and applies it in every case. When examining his last annual report I confronted him with the large accumulation of deposits in the savings-banks as evidence that the workingmen of the country were not then, as he asserted, "growing poorer, while the rich were growing richer," and, after a year's reflection, he answers my array of facts in this wise:

"Again, the returns of savings-banks are often referred to as showing a highly prosperous condition of the masses. Properly considered, however, they indicate a very different state of things. Thus, the first and almost the only fact which attracts the attention of a mere superficial observer in examining these statistics is a large apparent increase in deposits from 1860 to 1868 or 1869. But an intelligent examination will at once show that a very great part of the apparent accumulation referred to is mere inflation. For example, let us take the case of Massachusetts, where the conditions for increase would seem to be most favorable:

In 1860 the savings-banks deposits in this State were, in round numbers	$45,000,000
In January, 1869, in currency, $95,000,000, or in gold at 133	71,000,000
Increase in eight years	$26,000,000

or $6,000,000 less than the aggregate deposits of 1860 would have amounted to in the same time at a compound interest of seven per cent.; or in other words, the deposits of 1860 were not made good in 1869, without reference to the increase of population, even if we reckon only their natural increase at compound interest. It is evident, therefore, that some cause has eaten into the accumulation which existed eight years previously, and has occasioned the withdrawal of a portion of that accumulation."

If this statement be fair the deposits in the savings-banks of the country fluctuated fearfully on the 24th of September last, when gold ranged from 123 to 165 in an hour, and such of the depositors as were in that end of the New York gold-room where it was selling at 135 were vastly richer than those who were at the same moment in the other end at which Albert Spires was buying it for 160. A story told in connection with Mr. Spires' operations on that occasion seems to me to illustrate the value of Mr. Wells' theory. It is said that a young man without capital who had found his way to membership of the gold exchange, but had been bankrupted even of credit by the operations of the preceding day or two, stood near Mr. Spires, and as that gentleman cried "One sixty for one million," tapped him on the shoulder and said, "Taken." "Same price for two millions more," cried Spires. "Taken," said the young bankrupt; and so until Spires had bid, and he taken his bids for $13,000,000. They then separated, and the young bankrupt drawing aside, with a pencil calculated upon the back of a letter his profits, and turning to a friend triumphantly exclaimed "I have just made $750,000 out of old Spires." "Why," said a by-stander, "you do not expect to get any of it, do you?" "No; certainly not," said he, "but, blast him, I thought I would give him gold enough." This operation between a lunatic and a bankrupt, neither of whom owned a dollar of gold, and by which neither forfeited a cent, had about as much relation to their fortunes as the market price of gold has upon the price of domestic commodities, or deposits in the banks to which Mr. Wells applies it.

In further proof of its absurdity I invite attention to the fact that if his theory be correct the depositors in the savings-banks of Massachusetts have by no effort of their own, without increase of industry or unusual economy on their part, but by his magic power, acquired, since the preparation of his report, more than $9,000,000, as gold is now not at 133 but at 120; and that they will, if they do not make haste and withdraw their deposits, and we go on as we have gone for the last two or three months under the financial management of Grant and Boutwell, soon make $15,000,000 more in the same easy, and, I fear, unhallowed way; for when gold comes to par even Mr. Wells, with all his ingenious effrontery, will not deny that having been able to maintain a deposit of but $45,000,000 in 1860, they have in eight years become able to maintain one of $95,000,000, which amount they may draw in gold or redeemable currency, though they deposited greenbacks when gold was at more than 200. Before parting with this subject I beg leave to inform the committee and Commissioner Wells that at the close of 1869 the aggregate deposits at rest in the savings-banks of Massachusetts were not as he states $95,000,000, but $112,000,000, showing that the laboring people of that State, who he says are eating up their former savings so rapidly, have added $17,000,000 to their interest bearing investment during the last year.

The prominent characteristics of Mr. Wells' report are audacity and devotion to the interests of England and her American colonies. That it is ingenious and plausible cannot be denied; but that it is so does not in my judgment furnish proof of the Commissioner's ability or evidence of his possession of well-grounded convictions on industrial questions. Indeed, the fact that many of the suggestions which are most earnestly pressed contravene those embodied in his former reports, and his avowal that in offering them "he has placed himself in antagonism to many with whom he was formerly in close agreement," afford ample ground for doubt on both points.

"Remember, gentlemen," said the experienced merchant who now so ably fills the office of collector of the port of New York, when conferring with the Committee of Ways and Means, "that the legal ability of England and the continent is constantly retained by foreign manufacturers to indicate the means by which your tariffs may be evaded." Mr. Wells visited our transatlantic rivals in his official capacity, and while among them doubtless availed himself of the ability of their large array of able and well-paid counsel. Whether he also was retained is for the present the subject of conjecture. But that he enforces as "opinions and recommendations which have been forced upon him by conviction," the wishes of the English manufacturers, there is abundant evidence in his report, as I propose to show.

The most audacious of Mr. Wells' assertions, and one that pervades the whole report, is that customs duties are always a tax on the consumer, increasing the price of the imported article on which they are levied, and enabling the home producer to realize undue profits by keeping production steadily below the current demand for the commodity he produces. Were Mr. Wells a tyro, and this report his first publication, charity would deem this a blunder and ascribe it to ignorance; but he is a man of large experience, and has written much, and reference to any of the publications which led to his appointment to the commissionership, or to his preceding reports, will convict him of basing this official paper on a principle, the falsity of which he has time and again demonstrated. His bad faith in this is proven, I think, by a single extract from his report made December, 1867, in which, speaking of the higher duties he then advised Congress to put on steel, he said:*

"On steel much higher rates of duty than those recommended upon iron are submitted. Although these rates seem much higher, and are protested against by not a few American consumers of steel, yet the evidence presented to the Commissioner tends to establish the fact that if any less are granted, the development of a most important and desirable branch of domestic industry will, owing to the present currency derangement and the high price and scarcity of skilled labor, be arrested, if not entirely prostrated. This is claimed to be more especially true in regard to steel of the higher grades or qualities. It is also represented to the Commissioner that, since the introduction of the manufacture of these grades of steel in the United States, or since 1859, *the price of foreign steel of similar qualities has been very considerably reduced through the effect of the American competition, and that the whole country in this way has gained more than sufficient to counterbalance the tax levied as a protection for the American steel manufacture, which has grown up under its influence.*"

---

* Mr. Wells' recommendation of increased duties, in his report for 1867, was not confined to steel, but embraced almost every article we produce. And in his report for 1868, he did but point out the results of the system of protection, which, since his visit to England, he assails and endeavors to betray, when he said:

"More cotton spindles have been put in operation, more iron furnaces erected, more iron smelted, more bars rolled, more steel made, more coal and copper mined, more lumber sawed and hewn, more houses and shops constructed, more manufactories of different kinds started, and more petroleum collected, refined, and exported, than during any equal period in the history of the country; and this increase has been great both as regards *quality* and quantity, and greater than the legitimate increase to be expected from the normal increase of wealth and population."

Mr. Wells can dispute none of the facts asserted in the extract just read, which prove that he knows that prior to the close of 1867, highly protective duties on steel had not been a tax on, but a boon to the consumer; so great a boon, indeed, that, by enlarging the supply and increasing competition, they had so far reduced the price of steel that, to quote his words again, "the whole country in this way has gained more than sufficient to counterbalance the tax levied as a protection for the American steel manufacture, which has grown up under its influence."

You, Mr. Chairman, and many of our co-laborers on this floor, are interested in the extension and improvement of our magnificent railroad system, and I propose to illustrate the treachery of the Commissioner by briefly referring to the effect of high protective duties on Bessemer steel rails. In 1864, there was no establishment in the United States for the manufacture of such rails. The lowest price at which an American company could buy them in England was $150 per ton cash, gold, including freight to New York or Philadelphia. No English maker would sell them at less. Agents of the Pennsylvania Central, and Philadelphia, Wilmington and Baltimore roads, went abroad and canvassed the market, and having been assured that such rails could not be produced and sold at a living profit for a lower price than this, purchased a small quantity for each company. The duty was then, as now, an *ad valorem* duty of forty-five per cent., which at that price was equivalent to about three cents a pound. Gold was then above 200, and each ton of rails had cost when laid on the wharf in Philadelphia, $390, currency.

Our country abounds in the materials from which to make not only Bessemer rails, but every quality of steel, and the wages paid to American workmen are high enough to tempt skilled workmen from England and Germany; and in view of these facts, several enterprising railroad men determined to establish Bessemer rail works. This was not to be done in a day. It required the selection of a judicious site, the erection of extensive buildings, and the construction of a large amount of machinery, which consumed considerably more than a year. During all this time the price of English rails remained at $150 cash, gold, per ton delivered on the wharf in America. But at length the Freedom Works, at Harrisburg, Pennsylvania, so-called in commemoration of our partial enfranchisement from the grasp of foreign monopolists, were ready to take orders, and another establishment for their production was erecting at Troy, New York, when lo! the same English manufacturers, who had been unable to sell at less than $150 per ton, canvassed our market to find buyers at $130. What wrought this great change? Had the Commissioner's English friends been making profits off our railroad companies greater than he ascribes to our producers of salt, pig-iron, lumber, and other things essential to national independence; or were they willing to sacrifice the profit on a small part of their product in order to crush an infant rival, whose development they feared? Be this as it may, in less than four years competition has brought the price of Bessemer rails down so rapidly, that orders are now taken in England at eleven pounds sterling, or about fifty-five dollars, deliverable at Liverpool or Hull. Meanwhile, mills for their production at Troy, New York, Chester, Pennsylvania, Cleveland, Ohio, and Detroit, Michigan, have been completed; and the plans have been adopted for others at Mott Haven, New York; Pittsburg, Johnstown, and Bethlehem, Pennsylvania; and at Baltimore, Cincinnati, and St. Louis: but their construction awaits and is dependent on the action of Congress on the tariff. These facts are known to Mr. Wells, yet he endeavors to persuade the country that a protective duty is always a tax on the consumer, and labors to induce Congress to reduce a duty which was at the rate of three cents to one of one and a half cent per pound; a change which he well knows would close all our Bessemer rail works, and restore to his English friends the monopoly of our market, at such prices as they might demand. What can have brought him to such a conclusion? What is to be his reward for such a consummation?

If gentlemen will turn to page 125 of the report, they will find a schedule presenting a classification of steel, and proposed rates of duty on each class. It purports to be Mr. Wells' own suggestion, and is submitted with all the emphasis that the abundant resort to italics can give. I hope gentlemen will examine it, for I think that, with its private history, it furnishes a clew to his change of views on the question as to whether a protective duty that develops a great industry is a tax, and his Saul-like conversion on the steel question. For nearly a quarter of a century our duties on cast-steel have been assessed upon the value of the commodity, or *ad valorem*; and recent investigation by an agent of the Government has shown that throughout the whole of the period the steel-makers of Sheffield, by refusing to sell directly to American purchasers and consigning their goods to agents in this country for sale, by which cunning arrangement they could successfully practice a system of undervaluation, have been defrauding the Government of a large portion of its dues.

The Sheffield steel-makers are men of wealth and social position, and this discovery of their long-continued and systematic fraud upon our Government has not been a pleasant thing for them. The charge is distasteful to them. A combination to cheat and defraud has an ugly sound. They squirm under it, and admit that steel has been invoiced to the United States at lower rates than those at which they sell in England or to the people of the Continent, but assert that, low as the invoice prices have been, they are the prices at which they sell in this country. Good, kind-hearted, benevolent people! How they do love the Yankees! To be willing to sell them their wares cheaper than they will to their own countrymen or to any of the people of Europe! Have they any reason for doing so, or do they pretend to have any? Yes; they are not without a show of reason. They say—and their letters are on file in the Treasury Department, and their agents have appeared there to enforce the statement—*that our market is essential to the maintenance of their works, and that such is the competition they encounter from our steel-makers, that they are forced to sell to us at lower rates than they do to the English or any other people.* In a letter to our consul at that city, dated July 10th, 1869, Thomas Firth & Son, of Sheffield, say:

"We have a very large steel trade in America, amounting to a large proportion of our whole business, and in that market there is, from various circumstances, much competition; and these two causes—large trade and competition combined—have induced us to be satisfied with a smaller average profit there than we have realized on the average in our other markets."

Mr. Wells has seen the report referred to, that of Mr. Farwell, the Treasury agent, and has examined, or ought to have examined, all the papers in this controversy, and might have cited them as proof of the assertion in his former report, that the reduction in the price of steel has more than compensated the American people for all the duty paid on that article since the establishment of our first successful steel works in 1859. But I have been led into a digression.

I had said that the discovery of their systematic frauds was not a pleasant thing to the English steel-makers, and was proceeding to say that, foreseeing that it would probably lead to the abandonment of *ad valorem* and the levying of specific duties on steel, they overwhelmed the Secretary of the Treasury and other official personages with unsolicited, and, of course, disinterested advice. That we should not suffer for want of their experience, the draft of a bill providing a scale of duties on steel, was prepared, as I am informed and verily believe, by or in consultation with a member of one of the leading firms of steel-makers of Sheffield, and sent over to a gentleman specially connected with legislation on financial subjects. I have examined the original draft as it came from Sheffield, and have a copy of it before me. It is a proposition by the vulture to protect the dove. It is plausible in its minute classification. It would, had it been honestly named, have been entitled a bill to prohibit the manufacture of steel in the United States. It is, however, entitled, "A bill to amend an act entitled 'An act to increase duties on imports, and for other purposes,' approved June 30, 1864." It furnished Mr. Wells his schedule; and that gentlemen may see how completely he has adopted it, how entirely his views on this important subject are in accord with those of the steel monopolists of England, whose interest it is to hold us in commercial and maritime dependence, I will ask the reporters to put the two schedules in parallel columns. It is, perhaps, due to Mr. Wells, in this connection, that I should mention the fact that he so far exercised his own judgment in making this recommendation, as to modify two or three unimportant rates, and to change the order from that in which the items stand in the English draft of the bill; and that to make the comparison easy for the readers of the Globe, I have arranged them in the order chosen by Mr. Wells:

WELLS' SCHEDULE.	SHEFFIELD BILL.
On scrap steel, $\frac{1}{4}$ cent per pound.	On scrap steel, $\frac{1}{4}$ cent per pound.
On blister steel in bars broken up for melting, $1\frac{1}{2}$ cents per pound.	On blister steel in bars broken up for melting, $1\frac{1}{2}$ cents per pound.
On German steel in bars, 2 cents per pound.	On German steel in bars, 2 cents per pound.

Wells' Schedule.	Sheffield Bill.
On shear steel in bars, 2½ cents per pound.	On shear steel in bars, 2½ cents per pound.
On cast-steel ingots and on all rough and unfinished castings in steel, 1 cent per pound.	On cast-steel ingots, 1 cent per pound.
On castings in steel, drilled, bored, or *hammered cold,* 1¼ cents per pound.	On castings in steel with holes drilled or bored, hammered or turned or planed in parts, but *in no case hammered or worked hot,* 1¼ cents per pound.
On cast-steel in bars, 2½ cents per pound.	On cast-steel in bars, 2½ cents per pound.
On cast or German steel in plates to 16 wire gauge, inclusive, 2 cents per pound; from 17 to 24, 2½ cents per pound; above 24, 3 cents per pound.	On cast or German steel in sheets or plates to No. 23 wire gauge, 2½ cents per pound.
On cast or German steel in form of wire and sheets which are drawn or rolled cold to 16 wire gauge, 3 cents per pound.	On cast or German steel in form of wire or strips which are drawn or rolled cold to 16 wire gauge, 3 cents per pound.
Thinner than 16 wire gauge, 3½ cents per pound.	When drawn or rolled smaller than 16 wire gauge, 3½ cents per pound.
On cast-steel tires for rolling-stock for railroads, 2 cents per pound.	On cast-steel tires for rolling stock for railroads, 2 cents per pound.
On cast-steel straight axles, shafts, piston-rods, and general forgings to pattern, 1 cent per pound.	On cast-steel straight axles, piston, connecting and coupling-rods, crank-pins, slide-bars, and general forgings to pattern only, 1¼ cents per pound.
Do. do. rough-turned, 1½ cents per pound.	If forged to shape and rough-turned or planed, 1½ cents per pound.
Do. do. finished ready for use, 2 cents per pound.	If finished ready for use, 2 cents per pound.
On cast-steel crank axles forged to shape only, 1¼ cents per pound.	On cast-steel crank-shafts, if forged to shape only, 1¼ cents per pound.
On cast-steel crank axles forged to shape, rough-turned, planed, and slotted, 1½ cents per pound.	On cast-steel crank-shafts, if forged to shape, rough-turned, planed, and slotted, 1½ cents per pound.
Do. do. finished ready for use, 2 cents per pound.	On cast-steel crank-shafts, if forged to shape, finished ready for use, 2½ cents per pound.
On cast-steel rails 1½ cents per pound.	On cast-steel rails, 1 cent per pound.
On steel not otherwise provided for, 2 cents per pound.	On steel or manufactures of steel, not otherwise provided for, 2½ cents per pound.

It will be observed that the foregoing schedules are, as I intimated, not absolutely identical, but they are so nearly so as to prevent Mr. Wells from denying that they sprang from the same brain, and pleading the possibility of coincidence—I do not say the probability, but the possibility of coincidence—on so many points of rate and general and technical phraseology. And it will be further noticed that where the slightest departure in rate occurs in any one item, as is the case in two or three unimportant instances, it is immediately compensated for in the next item by a corresponding change the other way. Thus, Mr. Wells is more generous to his countrymen in the matter of Bessemer rails than their Sheffield rival would be. He proposes to kill them instantly by putting the rate at one cent per pound; while Mr. Wells is willing to give them breathing time in which to put their houses in order by letting them die slowly at one and a half cents. And in the next item the Englishman proves the more generous; for he proposes two and a half cents on all steel and manufactures of steel not provided for, and Mr. Wells would crush his countrymen instantly by making the duty on those articles but two cents.

I cannot leave this branch of the subject without saying that I believe gentlemen generally who compare these schedules will agree with me in thinking that Mr. Wells' Sheffield employers have treated him badly, scurvily. Having induced him to father their project, so predjudicial to his country and so destructive to the business of many of his countrymen, they violated faith with him when they made their paternity of the scheme known by sending a copy of the bill to official quarters in this country in advance of the publication of his report.

PIG-IRON.

With all the zeal of a new cónvert or counsel laboring to secure a contingent fee, Mr. Wells applies to pig-iron his assumption that a protective duty is necessarily a tax on the consumer, and by the plausibility of his argument would make innocent and inexperienced people believe that he really hoped to secure cheap pig-iron by reducing the duty on that article from nine dollars a ton to three. Could he close our steel works, as the acceptance of the Sheffield schedule recommended by him would do in three months, and arrest the progress we are making in the increased production of pig-iron, he would do more to retard the progress of his country toward commercial prosperity and national supremacy than Davis, Lee, and all the heads of the rebellion accomplished. I cannot conceive the single cause that would do more to depress and impoverish our people and retard the growth of our country than the sudden prostration of these great interests at a time when the English or continental manufacturer will purchase none of our grain for which he has to pay a penny in advance of the price for which he can buy from the peasants of Austria, Hungary and Russia.

But this recommendation with reference to pig-iron is consistent with the rest of the report, throughout which the desire is manifest to make the United States as commercially dependent on and tributary to England as though they were still part of her North American colonies. He cites pig-iron, coal, salt, and lumber as illustrations of a class of cases where excessive and unnecessary duties have been imposed and maintained "*with a view of enhancing the cost of articles indispensable to many other branches of production*;" and elsewhere says that the only reply offered to his assaults upon this great and essential interest "is that a continuance of the present duty on pig-iron is necessary to insure employment to American labor."

I pause to notice his assertion, that Congress in the midst of a great war imposed unnecessary exactions in order to increase the cost of an article so essential as iron to the life of the nation, simply to remark that such an intimation is worthy the man who can sap and mine the great interests of his country as Commissioner Wells is doing. The present duty on pig-iron was imposed for two purposes, both of which were patriotic. The first was to raise additional revenue, and the other to stimulate the conversion of ore, coal, and limestone, of which in almost every part of the country we have inexhaustible supplies, into a material the increased production of which was a prerequisite to the general extension of our industries and the maintenance of the dignity and rights of the nation, which were then being violated by the armed cruisers of the country to which we looked for a supply of pig-iron and Bessemer rails. And, sir, I am happy in being able to show that it has accomplished both these objects, and that if permitted to stand for five years it will, while contributing largely to the reduction of our debt, insure us not only a home supply of pig-iron, but such ample means of producing it as will enable us to enter the markets of the world in competition with England.

What has it done as a revenue measure? During the year that ended on the 30th of June, 1868, we derived from this duty $1,011,109 96; in the succeeding year, closing on the 30th of June, 1869, $1,199,762 55; and in the current fiscal year it will give us a still larger income, without in the slightest degree impairing the revenue derived from our consumption of foreign iron in more advanced condition. This is shown by the following statement of the quantities of the various kinds of iron and steel exported from Great Britain to the United States during the ten months ending October 31st, of the years 1868-69, in tons of 2000 pounds:

	1868.	1869.
Iron, pig and puddled	84,564	132,491
Iron, bar, angle, bolt, and rod	38,200	51,738
Iron, railroad, of all sorts	255,462	294,368
Iron castings	1,213	1,677
Iron hoops, sheets, and boiler plates	15,999	31,292
Iron, wrought of all sorts	4,020	7,364
Total	399,458	518,930
Steel, unwrought	14,847	15,612

Has not the duty of nine dollars per ton on pig-iron been eminently successful as a revenue measure? I think it has; but its most abundant success has been in its power to increase the supply, improve the quality, and lessen the cost of domestic pig-iron. The Commissioner raises no question as to the relative quality of British and American iron, and does not state the quantity of our annual production, except that in one of his hypothetical calculations of the values realized from different departments of industry, he places the annual product for 1869 at 1,725,000 tons, or about 175,000 tons below the ascertained production of that year. That the average quality of American pig, bar, and railroad iron is superior to the average of the same descriptions of English iron is an almost universally-conceded fact; but to blazon this to the world would not serve the interest of the Commissioner's British friends, and he is therefore silent upon this aspect of the question also, though he tells us with much elaboration what he has been told has been the cost of production per ton at several points in this country, and the market price per ton during the year in England and here.

But though his report abounds in hypotheses and calculations based on estimates and suppositions, he nowhere tells or attempts to tell us what we would have been made to pay the British iron master for his inferior pig, bar, sheet, and rails if the American production of pig-iron had not been more than doubled since the establishment of this duty, and if the manufacture of cast-steel and Bessemer rails had not also been established at so many points within our limits since the exigencies of the war compelled us to adopt protective duties. He is not ignorant of the fact that in little more than a year past sixty-five new blast furnaces have been erected, and that they are to employ a portion of the people of fifteen States. Six of them are in New York, one in New Jersey, nineteen in Pennsylvania, one in Maryland, four in Virginia, six in Ohio, five in Indiana, three in Illinois, five in Michigan, two in Wisconsin, six in Missouri, three in Kentucky, one in Georgia, two in Alabama, and one in Tennessee. These furnaces have increased our productive power to nearly two million five hundred thousand tons per annum. Arrangements are also making for the erection of more than fifty other furnaces during the year upon which we have just entered, many of which have been commenced. The estimated product of pig-iron for this year is two million two hundred and twenty-five thousand tons, or about fifty per cent. of the annual average production of Great Britain.

These facts are, I repeat, known to the Commissioner; and he knows also that by a law as inevitable as that of gravitation domestic competition increasing in such a ratio must at an early day bring down the price of iron as it has that of wheat and flour, and of knit and other cotton and woolen goods, to a point beyond danger from foreign competition; and that by thus relieving us from dependence on England for the first essential in a great war, it will also make us her competitor in the markets of the world in a field her supremacy in which has hitherto made her the commercial mistress of the world.

I will not offer an estimate of what would have been the price of pig-iron had not the necessities of the Government compelled Congress to impose duties that were protective and which justified men of enterprise in opening coal mines and ore-beds and erecting furnaces; but to enable gentlemen to judge for themselves, I submit the following. On page 85 of the report I am considering the Commissioner says:

"How great the demand of the future is likely to prove may be inferred from the circumstance that while the *per capita* consumption of Great Britain and Belgium, after allowing for exportation, has reached one hundred and eighty-nine pounds per annum, the present annual consumption of the United States is not in excess of one hundred pounds *per capita*. No nation, furthermore, at the present time, with the exception of Great Britain, is producing pig-iron in sufficient excess of its needs to allow of a surplus for exportation; and in Great Britain the prospect of any future increase is entirely dependent upon the uncertain condition of her being able to supply coal on a scale of consumption that is already in excess of one hundred and four million tons per annum."

On page 3 of his report made January, 1869, he tells us that—

"In France the annual product of pig-iron was in 1866, 1,253,100 tons, and in 1867, 1,142,800 tons, showing a decline of 110,300 tons.

"In Austria the official returns of the iron trade show a diminution of forty-two per cent. in 1866 as compared with 1860, and of sixty per cent. as compared with 1862."

In that valuable paper, the report of A. S. Hewitt, Esq., United States Commissioner to the Paris Exposition, we learn that ours is almost the only country in the world that can largely expand its production of iron. Mr. Hewitt agrees with Mr. Wells that it is problematical as to whether England can for the present increase her production materially. He thinks she may maintain her present position among continental producers; but beyond this he does not think she can go, by reason of the depth of her mines and the "intrinsic difficulties of producing the required supply of materials and labor, without an enormous increase of cost."

The iron production of the world for 1866, as stated by Mr. Hewitt, was as follows:

Countries.	Pig-iron. Tons.	Wrought iron. Tons.
England	4,530,051	3,500,000
France	1,200,320	844,734
Belgium	500,000	400,000
Prussia	800,000	400,000
Austria	312,000	200,000
Sweden	226,676	148,292
Russia	408,000	350,000
Spain	75,000	50,000
Italy	30,000	20,000
Switzerland	15,000	10,000
Zollverein	250,000	200,000
United States	1,175,900	882,000
Total	9,322,047	7,205,026

Thus it appears that with a production of less than ten million tons for the world's supply no other country than ours is in a position to make a large and immediate addition to its annual production. The difficulties in the way may be briefly stated thus: Sweden possesses exhaustless supplies of the richest primitive ores, but she has no coal, and her annual production of charcoal-iron is believed to have reached its limit. Her function will henceforth be to mine and export ore. Russia has ample supplies of ore, but so far as exploration has yet discovered is deficient in coal. She can, however, for some time somewhat augment her production of charcoal-iron. Austria, Italy, Spain, and the States of the Zollverein have ore, but little or no coal available for iron making, and are unable to extend, if they can maintain, their present production of charcoal-iron. France has neither coal nor ore sufficient to supply her wants; England furnishes her with one third the coal she now consumes in the manufacture of iron. Little Belgium has both coal and ore, and they are advantageously situated, but the field is so contracted that she cannot increase her production beyond her own wants, and Prussia is a large importer of coal and pig-iron from England. So much for the prospective increase of supplies; while, as illustrative of the growing demand, I need only allude to the gigantic systems of railroads building in America, Russia, and India, the latter at immense cost by England, in the hope of impairing our supremacy as producers of cotton.*

Had we continued to rely upon England for pig-iron in excess of our capacity to produce it at the time of fixing nine dollars as the duty, and also to draw our supplies of bar iron, cast-steel, and Bessemer rails from her, the extension of our railroad system must have been checked and the *per capita* consumption of iron in this country been much restricted. For nine years before the imposition of that duty our annual production had been less than 800,000 tons, and that of England had not increased at the rate of 100,000 tons per annum. Our demand increases at the rate of from 170;000 to 200,000 tons per annum. Whence but from our own ore beds and coal mines could the sup-

* There were in operation in the United States on the 1st of January, 1871, 53,399 miles of railroad, 4999 miles of which were completed during 1869, and 6199 during 1870. Could England have furnished the iron required for this extension?

ply have been drawn? The production of pig-iron in England and the United States from 1854 to 1862 inclusive, was as follows:

	England.	United States.
1854	3,069,838	716,674
1855	3,218,154	754,178
1856	3,586,377	874,428
1857	3,659,447	798,157
1858	3,456,064	705,094
1859	3,712,904	840,427
1860	3,826,752	913,774
1861	3,712,390	731,564
1862	3,943,469	787,662

These figures show that the two great iron-producing countries of the world, England and the United States, increased their joint production less than one hundred thousand tons per annum for nine consecutive years, while we alone demand an increase of at least one hundred and seventy thousand tons, and prove the assertion that but for the application of an incentive to the production of iron in this country the expansion of our railroad system and our general material progress must have been impossible. Was there any charm by which an increased supply could be evoked? Was there any means by which the disparity between the wages of English laborers in iron works and such as were essential to the support of American citizens who might engage in the production of iron could be counterbalanced? Yes, Mr. Chairman, there was one, and that was applied. It was to impose such a duty as would give capitalists and men of enterprise a guarantee that if they paid workmen fair American wages for building furnaces, digging and hauling coal, ore, and limestone, and converting them into pig-iron they should not be undersold in our own markets by the productions of underpaid British workmen. Nine dollars per ton it was believed would give them that guarantee, and yet leave our markets so largely open to English competition that we should derive more duty from pig-iron than we had done under lower duties.

I have spoken of the difference between the wages of English and American workmen. Let me show how great it is. The English shilling is twenty-five cents of our money. Commercial men know this; there are, however, many of our people not familiar with the details of commerce and the exchangeable value of money to whom it may be proper to state the fact. Turning again to the report of Mr. Hewitt, which I recur to frequently and always with a renewed sense of obligation, I find the rates of wages paid in England in 1866 to have been as follows:

WAGES PAID IN SOUTH STAFFORDSHIRE, ENGLAND, IN 1866.

	Per Day.				
Common laborers	2*s*.	6*d*.	to	3*s*.	0*d*.
Puddlers	7	6	to	7	10
Puddlers' helpers	2	6	to	2	11
Puddle rollers	9	0		......	
Heaters	7	0		......	
Heater helpers	3	6		......	
Finishing rollers	11	0		......	
Shinglers	9	0	to	15	0
Machinists	4	0	to	16	0
Blacksmiths	4	0	to	5	0
Masons	7	6	to	8	6

The average price of skilled and unskilled labor at the iron works in England does not exceed 4*s*. a day.

At the coal and iron works of Creed & Williams, in Belgium, the wages paid in 1866 were as follows:

	Per Day.				
Common laborers	1*s*.	2*d*.	to	3*s*.	6*d*.
Loaders of coal	2	6	to	2	11
Wood-cutters	2	6	to	2	11
Wood or tree-setters	3	1	to	5	0
Miners	2	11	to	4	2
Exceptional men	5	0	to	6	0
AT THE BLAST FURNACES.					
Fillers	1	1	to	2	1
Box fillers	1	4	to	1	8
Common laborers	1	5	to	1	8
Furnace-keepers	2	1	to	2	11
IN THE ROLLING-MILL.					
Puddlers	4	2	to	5	0
Helpers	2	3	to	3	1
Rollers	4	2	to	5	10
Helpers	3	4	to	4	2
Shearers	1	10	to	2	6
Common laborers	1	5	to	2	1

In all other European countries wages are lower than in England.

These figures are worthy of the study of the working men of this country, whom Mr. Commissioner Wells is striving to array in hostility against those whose interests are identical with their own—the men who have embarked their capital in an attempt to make the United States commercially and politically independent of Great Britain, and who, if sustained in good faith, will not only accomplish this, but enable us to meet her in the markets of the world with pig, bar, and sheet-iron, with steel in all its forms, including cutlery, and with iron ships carrying a commerce as extended as her own upon every sea.

Having shown that the experiment of nine dollars per ton has been successful as a revenue measure, now let us see what effect it has had in stimulating production. When it was adopted English iron-masters saw that with our inexhaustible fields and rich varieties of coal and ore we must soon become competitors with them for our home market, and at no distant day a formidable rival in the general markets of this continent. This it was their interest to prevent if possible, and though their increase of production had been less than 100,000 tons per annum for the preceding nine years, they added 500,000 tons the next year, and in 1865 produced nearly 900,000 tons more than they had ever done before. I have shown the production of the two countries from 1854 to 1862. The Morrill tariff, which raised the duty to $6, went into effect in 1861. In 1864 the duty was raised to $9. The results have been as follows:

	England.	United States.
1863	4,510,040	947,604
1864	4,767,951	1,135,497
1865	4,819,254	931,582
1866	4,523,897	1,350,943
1867	4,761,028	1,461,626
1868	....	1,603,000
1869	....	1,900,000

I regret my inability to ascertain the English production for 1868 and 1869; but in view of the average of the five years quoted, and the fact that the production of 1865 exceeds so largely the years that succeeded as well as those that preceded it, it is fair to assume that it has not been in excess of that year in either of these. These figures confirm the impression that England has attained her maximum production; for while her increase since 1863 has been scarcely appreciable, ours has been about one hundred and ten per cent. In view of all these facts, I think that it appears again in the matter of pig-iron, as it did in that of cast-steel and Bessemer rails, that a protective duty has not been, as Mr. Wells asserts, a tax on, but is a boon to the American consumer.

COAL AND THE BRITISH NORTH AMERICAN COLONIES.

I have said that the report is devoted to the promotion of the interests of England and her North American colonies, and have, I think, shown that if its suggestions were carried into effect it would arrest the rapid increase we are making in the production of iron and steel, and remand us to commercial and political dependence on our haughty and faithless rival. I propose now to illustrate Mr. Wells' palpable desire to promote the interests of England's North American colonies—the new dominion, that asylum of our foes in war and base of illicit operations against our revenue system in peace.

The sea-board provinces, whether on the Atlantic or Pacific ocean, are suffering discontent that is rapidly becoming chronic. From 1854 to 1866 the colonists were more than contented, they were proud and joyous, and immigrants flowed in and settled among them. They contrasted their condition with ours, and plumed themselves upon their superior prosperity. Their clip of wool and crops of cereals increased annually, their fisheries were increasingly profitable, and their coal mines yielded unparalleled profits—in one year one Nova Scotia coal company having paid its stockholders the almost fabulous profit of one hundred and seventy-five per cent. They were more than hopeful of the future; they were confident and arrogant. With them the southern confederacy was a foregone conclusion, and with it as an ally, and England as their sponsor, they saw the near approach of the day when this new triple alliance should hold the Yankee States as in a vice, and crush or strangle them at pleasure. This was in 1864. Their tone is less joyous now. Indeed, it is sad unto wailing. Listen to one of them, a Nova Scotian, as he pours the story of their wrongs and sufferings through the columns of Lippincott's Magazine for July last:

"But the petition of three hundred thousand good subjects was treated with indifference, and even an inquiry into their grievances was refused. Then it was, in the bitter sorrow and indignation that filled us at that time, that we turned our eyes to the great nation beside us for assistance. But even there no help was to be had. The reciprocity treaty had been abrogated in return for the sympathy and assistance which Canada had given to the South; and the only thing which could support our commerce and encourage our industries under the heavier duties of Canada was thus denied us, and continues to be denied us.* At the present moment we are in a sad case. The duties and taxes of the Canadian administration bear heavily upon us; our commerce is languishing, our industries are all but paralyzed. The markets which nature intended for us, and which commerce had marked out for her own, are closed to us, *and in consequence we fish less, mine less, manufacture less, export less.* Our political position is as bad as perplexing. We will not continue in our present union with Canada if we can help it. We have laid our grievances before England. England refers us to Canada; Canada refers us to England. England trusts to our loyalty, Canada to our cupidity or our fear, to keep us in the union. If even we succeed in getting repeal *we cannot stand alone without a treaty with the United States. If that is denied us—and who can doubt it?*—we must even seek our own good in transferring our allegiance."

This is a faithful portraiture of the condition of the British provinces on the Atlantic coast; and that of British Columbia on the Pacific and Puget Sound is quite as hopeless. It was once the base of an extended system of smuggling over our borders, but the provincial Government, being unable to support itself by internal taxes, was compelled to raise revenue by a tariff almost as heavy as our own, though there are no manufactures to protect. This destroyed the profitable business of smuggling across our borders, and brought Victoria, the city which it had been fondly hoped would be the commercial rival of San Francisco, to absolute despair. It is a deserted city. In July last, as my colleagues on the Committee of Ways and Means can attest, more than half the buildings within its limits were tenantless and for rent or sale, and at high noon its streets were as deserted as though pestilence had scourged it.

Let me pause, Mr. Speaker, to ask what has wrought this wondrous change, and why more than one hundred thousand of the people of the provinces during the last year came to dwell among us and share the burdens of our great war debt? These results are the legitimate consequences of wise and patriotic legislation by Congress. Commissioner Wells understands it as well as the rest of us. He knows as well as the Nova Scotian I have just

* The Reciprocity Treaty expired March, 1866.

quoted that the repeal of the Reciprocity Treaty wrought the ruin of the provinces. That treaty, which was forced upon us by our old southern masters, was designed especially to promote the prosperity of the British North American provinces at the cost of the northern States of the Union. *It was specially designed by the planters of the South as a blow at the prosperity of the farmers and stock-breeders of the northwest.* It went into effect in June, 1854, and expired, or I may properly say was rescinded by Congress, in March, 1866. It was admirably adapted to accomplish its purpose, and the period of its duration was that of the greatest growth of Britain's power along our borders. That gentlemen who represent the grain-growing States may not suspect me of misstating the object of the reciprocity movement, I beg leave to again invite their attention to a few words from pages 95 and 96 of that remarkable book, "Cotton is King," the politico-economical text-book of the authors of the late rebellion:

"This is the present aspect (1858) of the provision question as it regards slavery extension. Prices are approximating the maximum point beyond which our provisions cannot be fed to slaves unless there is a corresponding increase in the price of cotton. Such a result was not anticipated by southern statesmen when they had succeeded in overthrowing the protective policy, destroying the United States Bank, and establishing the sub-Treasury system.

"And why has this occurred? The mines of California prevented both the free-trade tariff and the sub-Treasury scheme from exhausting the country of the precious metals, extinguishing the circulation of bank notes, *and reducing the prices of agricultural products to the specie value.* At the date of the passage of the Nebraska bill *the multiplication of provisions by their more extended cultivation was the only measure left that could produce a reduction of prices,* and meet the wants of the planters. The Canadian Reciprocity Treaty, since secured, will bring the products of the British North American colonies, *free of duty, into competition with those of the United States* when prices with us rule high, and tend to diminish their cost."

But this treaty has been rescinded. Why refer to it? Does the Commissioner propose to renew it? No, sir; that would be frank, and not in accordance with his practice. He moves stealthily toward his sinister objects. He is a protective free-trader, a free-trade protectionist, a disciple of Henry Clay, but an advocate of the free-trade dogmas of John C. Calhoun. He does not propose a renewal of the Reciprocity Treaty; but asserting that all customs duties are taxes, and increase the price of the article on which they are levied, he demands cheap fuel, food, and beer, and proposes to secure these desirable objects by removing all duties from articles the production of the North American provinces. Nor does he do this in terms. Taking the leading staples of the provinces separately, he submits specious, but false reasons for the removal of all duties from each of them. He would give the people of the provinces the benefits they derived from the Reciprocity Treaty without stipulating for any of the few benefits it brought his countrymen. To adopt his recommendations in this behalf would be to pay from the Treasury of the United States annually to the colonists from six million to ten million dollars as a consideration for their continued submission to British legislation and colonial policy. They are tending toward the Union. They were alien enemies during the war, but millions of them now desire to be friends and fellow-countrymen, and the way to promote this consummation, so devoutly to be wished, is to let them know that the avenue to free trade with us is through annexation. This accomplished, they would share our prosperity and our responsibilities, and their country would cease to be a base of hostilities as it now is in peace and war.

Let me not be suspected of misrepresenting the position of Mr. Wells. The principal articles the provinces export are lumber, wool, coal, barley, and the other cereals, and from these he would remove all duties, though they yielded during the year which ended June 30, 1868, $4,352,770 49 in gold, or about six millions in currency. It is true some of the wool which contributed to this amount came from other countries, and some of the coal from England; but in order to restore prosperity to the trade of the provinces, he would admit their staples free, even though other countries might share the advantage.

Though very urgent that the duty should be taken off Canadian barley, he makes no specific recommendation as to the removal of duties from the other cereals. He merely speaks of the "extreme emergency" that can "justify a tax on the breadstuffs and food of a nation." His argument in favor of free grain and provisions from the provinces is enforced in this wise:

"Coal is a necessity of life next in importance to food; indeed, as both are in our climate absolutely indispensable, it cannot be said that either is more or less needful than the other, for life cannot be sustained without both. The universally recognized principle of taxation that a tax should be taken from what can be spared forbids the laying of a tax upon that which is indispensable to rich and poor alike."

A free translation of all which is, that as New England has no coal, and cannot raise her own supply of grain and provisions, and can get both cheaper from the British colonies than she can from the prairies of the northwest or the coal-fields of Pennsylvania, Maryland, Virginia, or North Carolina, it is a crime against nature and the British Government to lay duties on the grain and provisions of the provinces.

Leaving the question of the propriety of retaining duties on grain, live stock, and provisions to the consideration of gentlemen from the West, I propose to examine what the Commissioner has to say on the subject of coal. But before entering more fully upon this subject, let me apply to grain and provisions the argument he makes for free provincial coal, associating them with it in his text, that we may see whether his argument does not apply to them with greater force in proportion as Wisconsin, Iowa, Minnesota, and Kansas are more remote from "the northeastern sea-board" than the coal-fields of Virginia, North Carolina, Maryland, and Pennsylvania:

"'If the enhanced price paid by the consumer for his coal,' wheat, corn, or provisions, 'in consequence of the existence of this duty, were all paid to the Pennsylvania miner' or western farmer, 'it would be, of course, great injustice; but the country would be none the poorer because the law took money from one man and gave it to another. But it happens that while the consumer pays the increase, the immediate producer is not benefited, inasmuch as the whole enhanced price is expended in paying for the transportation of the coal,' grain, or provision, 'to a greater distance; in other words, the payment is for unnecessary transportation, *i. e.*, useless labor. Now, no acquisition of skill can change this. It is fixed by the laws of nature. To the end of time it will cost more; *i. e.*, it will take more labor to bring every ton of coal,' grain, or provisions 'from western Pennsylvania,' Wisconsin, Iowa, Minnesota, Missouri, or Kansas 'across the Alleghany mountains' or the lakes 'to the northeastern sea-board than to bring it from Nova Scotia. So long as a duty makes it possible to bring coal,' grain, or provisions 'from the former source, so long that unnecessary work will be done; but the price does not represent a profit, but the cost of useless labor.'"

Is not this argument conclusive? Does it not prove that her Britannic Majesty's liege subjects of the new Dominion should grow our grain and stock, and grind our flour, as well as mine our coal as long as their freedom from our war debt will enable them to do it more cheaply than we can? If this be not the conclusion to which it leads, I hope some gentleman from a grain-growing or cattle-raising district will show us why.

Mr. Wells does not like Pennsylvania, and throughout his report ignores the essential facts that Virginia and North Carolina have tide-water coal-fields of better quality and greater extent than those of Nova Scotia, from which New England can be more cheaply supplied than from the provinces; and that Maryland sends more bituminous coal from her mountains to the "northern sea-board" than Pennsylvania does or ever did. In this, however, he is as frank and truthful as in other respects. I do not wonder that he dislikes the people of Pennsylvania. By their persistent energy, as the letter of Thomas Firth & Son shows, they have so increased the supply and reduced the price of cast-steel as to seriously affect the profits of his Sheffield clients; and by the large increase they are making of blast furnaces they threaten to enter the markets of the world at an early day against all England with pig-iron. Nor do I forget that it was Pennsylvania Representatives and economists that hastened to bring to the attention of the country the equivocations, duplicity, and falsehoods with which his last annual report abounded.

Speaking of the duty on coal, he says, "it is urged as a protective measure," and refers to it as a "tax on fuel." This involves but two misstatements of fact, namely, that the duty is urged or levied for protection, and that it is a tax on any American consumer of coal. Neither of these allegations is true. The protectionists of the country do not regard the question of the duty on coal as a politico-economical question, and the New York Tribune, knowing that the price of coal would not be affected by the abolition of the duty, advocates its repeal as a means of proving the absurdity of the free trade argument. They do not urge it as a protective, but as a revenue measure, and, in view of the present condition of the provinces, as eminently a political question. As a political question it has great significance, as every provincial exporter of coal knows experimentally that the duty is not paid by the American consumer, but is deducted from the extraordinary profits he would realize if the duty were removed, and which he did realize during the continuance of the Reciprocity Treaty. As an economical or protective measure, it is not worth consideration; as a revenue measure, it involves the receipt by the Treasury of about five hundred thousand dollars gold annually, a comparatively small matter, but of some importance; but it is as a political question that it is most worthy of consideration. As Mr. Wells and the free-trade league have industriously promoted a general misapprehension of this subject, I propose, as I have said, to devote a few minutes to its elucidation.

I propose to show, first, that as an economical question it is not of sufficient importance to deserve consideration. This can be done by inviting attention to the relation of the total amount of foreign coal imported from all sources to the amount consumed in the northern Atlantic States alone. Were the whole amount involved it would not be sufficient to affect the supply or price, as the grand total imported from all countries on both coasts has exceeded 600,000 tons in but three years, and 500,000 in but three others, and the consumption of coal east of the Alleghany mountains and north of the Potomac will be about 20,000,000 tons this year. What the consumption is on the Pacific, where coal from British Columbia was until within a few years the sole dependence, I have no data for an accurate estimate. Whatever the amount is it should be deducted from the total in estimating the percentage of supply derived by New England from Nova Scotia and England; the residue, whatever it may be, is assuredly not sufficient to affect either the price or supply.

But the question does not relate to the whole of this residue, but only to so much as would be the amount imported if the duty were off in excess of that brought in under duty. As English coal has always been subject to duty, we have no means of ascertaining how much the repeal of the duty might increase importation from that country; but as her scientific men have admonished her of the danger of exhausting her supplies of coal—and even Mr. Wells agrees with recognized authorities in believing that her production has reached its maximum—and as she has more advantageous markets nearer home, the repeal of the duty would not probably affect perceptibly the importation from that quarter.

How much the imposition of the duty on provincial coal has affected the total amount imported we can ascertain, but, unfortunately, the Treasury reports do not enable us to distinguish between the amount imported on either coast. The Pacific States, as I have said, formerly depended on British Columbia; but since the opening of the mines at Mont Diablo, Seattle, and other points within our territory, the quantity of provincial coal imported is said to be diminishing. But assuming that the whole amount received on both coasts came from Nova Scotia, and was consumed in New England, the repeal of the treaty and imposition of the duty cannot have had an appreciable effect on the price or supply in the markets of that section, as will appear from the facts I am about to submit.

The amount of provincial coal imported into the country, on both coasts, has exceeded 400,000 tons in but two years; and the largest amount imported in any one year was 465,194 tons, which was in 1865. With one other exception, that of 1866, when the amount reached 404,254 tons, the total import on both coasts never reached 340,000. It is to be regretted that the proportion of these amounts that went into California and Oregon cannot be ascertained. Could this be done it would make the pretence that the duty on Nova Scotia coal affects either the price or supply of coal in New England so supremely absurd that Mr. Wells himself would abandon it. But the sum in controversy is less than this; it is the difference between the average amount annually imported free under the treaty and the amount which comes to our markets and pays a duty of $1 25 per ton.

The duty, as I have said, came into effect on the expiration of the treaty in March, 1866, so that the year in which the largest amount was imported was that immediately preceding its repeal. I propose to ascertain the amount about which this wide-spread controversy has been raised, by contrasting the average importation for the three last years of free coal under the treaty, including that which so far exceeded all others, with the three years immediately succeeding the repeal of the treaty, during which it paid $1 25 duty. During the last three years in which it was free from duty the average annual importation was 355,490 tons, and during the three succeeding years in which it paid duty the average annual importation has been 326,626, showing an annual difference of but 31,864 tons. Surely no man with less effrontery than Mr. Wells will say that the deduction of 31,864 tons from one of many sources from which a supply ranging at about 20,000,000 tons are derived can have affected either the supply or price of the commodity. But if we assume that one-third of the importation of provincial coal is upon the Pacific coast—which, I think, we may safely do—we will see how utterly inappreciable must be the effect of the maintenance or repeal of the duty on provincial coal.

Thus, Mr. Chairman, it must become apparent that the maintenance of the duty is not, as Mr. Wells asserts, "urged as a protective measure." Surely those who have the machinery to bring 20,000,000 tons to market annually need not shrink from the effect of a cause which increases or diminishes the total amount twenty or thirty thousand tons per annum.

I propose next to show the falsity of Mr. Wells' other proposition, namely, that this duty is a tax on the consumer. Happily, this is susceptible of demonstration. The Pictou coal is of a lower grade, and consequently of less value than the Cumberland coal of Maryland, or the tide-water coal of Virginia. Its price is always lower than these in any market. The average price of Nova Scotia coal by cargo at Boston per ton of 2240 pounds during 1861, the first year of the war, as shown by weekly quotations in the Boston shipping-list and price-current, was $4 67. It was then duty free, and so continued for more than five years. The war did not inflict greenbacks and an inflated currency upon the coal operators of Nova Scotia. It did not create an enormous system of internal taxation to oppress them. Their laborers were not tempted by patriotism or offers of bounty, or taken by draft to the battle-field to bleed and die for their country, as were those of the American operator. Nor did all these causes combine to make an increase of wages necessary to the support of the laborer and his family. No, sir; their wages remained as before, or were reduced by the fact that thousands of able-bodied sympathizers with the rebellion sought safety and employment in the provinces; and British emigration, that but for the war would have come to us, flowed in upon them. Our immigration, which for the six years preceding the war had exceeded an average of 140,000, fell off to less than 92,000 in each of the years 1861 and 1862, although the emigration from Liverpool to America was not diminished during these years: while therefore we suffered for the want of labor, it was from these causes for a time redundant in the provinces. All the conditions were such as to enable the provincial operators to produce and sell coal cheaper during the war than they had done before. But was the price in Boston regulated by its cost? No, prices never are; it depended on our necessities, and followed the price of American coal. Thus the average price in 1862, as shown by the authority I have already quoted, was $5 60; in 1863, $7 40; in 1864, $10 40; 1865, $9 60. In March of the next year the treaty expired, and it became subject to duty, and, according to Mr. Wells' theory, must have gone up $1 25, or to $10 85 per ton. But in this case his theory is in conflict with the facts, as it is so frequently, for in that year coal sold, duty paid, at $8 54, netting the exporter and foreign carrier but $7 29, and in 1869 it gave them forty-four cents less, having averaged but $8 10; and in 1868 it averaged $8 16, so that in each and every year it bore the same relation to Cumberland coal that it has always borne since the latter was introduced to the New England market about twenty years ago, and sold at about a dollar a ton lower.

These facts, in my judgment, prove two things; one of which is that the Acadian coal operators do not send us coal as a benevolent, but as a commercial operation, out of which they make all they can at the prices current in our market; and the other is, that they can afford to pay the duty and make a living profit by selling us the very limited amount they can mine at the rates current in our markets. In this they obey the law which is now teaching our western producers of grain, by a painful experience, the importance of a home market; that law, and it is universal in its application, is, that he who has to carry his commodities to a distant market must pay all the charges thereon, while he whose goods are sought by customers fixes his own prices and makes the purchaser pay all charges.

It thus becomes apparent that the repeal of the duty on coal would not reduce the price of that article in New England one cent. per ton or increase the amount brought to market appreciably; its only effect would be to take from the Treasury an average of from four to five hundred thousand dollars in gold annually and give it to the colonists as a reward for remaining contented subjects of her Britannic Majesty; a proposition at which my patriotism revolts, though it be ever so earnestly recommended by Mr. Commissioner Wells.

HOW THE SOUTH SHOULD DIVERSIFY ITS INDUSTRY.

I think I have sufficiently disclosed the devotion of our Special Commissioner of Revenue to the interests of England; but I cannot refrain from inviting the attention of gentlemen from the South to the treacherous suggestions he offers them on the subject of the proper means of diversifying their industry. On this subject he says:

"The large amount of capital thus becoming annually available at the South will undoubtedly seek in great part investment in domestic and local enterprises and speedily lead to the establishment of manufactures on an extensive scale. The true diversity of employment which results from freedom has now, therefore, become to the South for the first time possible; and southern capital can soon be advantageously applied to the manufacture of agricultural tools and implements, leather, wagons, wooden-ware, soap, starch, clothing, and similar articles. These are manufactures in which iron, steel and cloth are raw materials. They employ the largest amount of labor in proportion to product and capital, and warrant the payment of high wages. *On the other hand, what are commonly called manufactures, namely, iron and steel, and cotton and woolen cloth, are examples of concentration. They require large capital, employ but few hands, and would naturally come much later.* We already have in the United States an excess of cotton and woolen spindles, and to invest capital in more would be simply a waste when there are vast needs at the South requiring far less capital, and warranting much greater compensation for labor than can be paid in textile fabrics.*"

Most of the southern States abound in coal, varieties of iron ore of very high quality, limestone, and water-power. Inaccessible as their interior districts are from the sea-board, freight adds heavily to the cost of iron purchased either from the Atlantic States or England. They need preëminently among the States of the Union an extension of railroads and the establishment of founderies, rolling-mills, locomotive works, and machine-shops. The primary prerequisite to the ample development of the great resources of the southern States is an adequate supply of cheap iron and the means of shaping it for use.

---

* The people of Virginia, Tennessee and Georgia have wisely shown their contempt for Mr. Wells' suggestion that they should postpone efforts to make iron. Staunton, Atlanta and Chattanooga have already become celebrated for the quality and quantity of iron they produce, and the work done by their rolling-mills. This may be bad for Mr. Wells' English friends, but it is certainly well for us.

They have few skilled laborers, and the manufacture of pig-iron and the rolling of rails require but comparatively few skilled men. The digging and hauling of coal, ore, and limestone require no special preparation. It is work for the unskilled laborer at which freedmen can succeed, and they are therefore in a condition to engage in the production of this article of primary importance, though they may not have the trained artisans for the introduction of simpler branches of mechanics.

The cotton growing portion of the United States is the proper locality for cotton factories. The South can spin yarn and produce unbleached fabrics at from fifteen to twenty per cent. less than the same work can be done in New England, and cheaper even than it can be done by the underpaid laborers of Great Britain. Will gentlemen from the South consider that what the picking-room is to the English or northern factory the gin-room is to the factory near the cotton-field, and that all charges incurred between the two would be saved by the southern manufacturer? Before cotton reaches either New or Old England it must be pressed and baled and hooped and marked and transported, losing interest and paying freight and commission at each stage of the transportation; and when it has arrived at the threshold of the distant factory it must be freed from its hoops, stripped of its bagging, and put through the processes of the picking-room to restore it with as little damage as possible to the condition in which it was when it left the gin. From all these charges the manufacturer in the cotton district is free; and together they amount to what would be a fair profit, which in connection with the improved quality that would result from the use of the unbroken fiber he would use would enable him to spin yarns for all the northern States and England too.

But this would hurt the English cotton-spinner; this would advance the interests of the United States to the detriment of England, as would the establishment in the midst of the coal and iron fields of Virginia, Tennessee, Arkansas, Alabama, and Georgia of furnaces, founderies, rolling-mills, and steel-works. Fortunately, the people of the South are deeply impressed with the importance of the early introduction of these branches of manufactures; and among the sixty-five furnaces erected during the last year four are in Virginia, six in Missouri, three in Kentucky, one in Georgia, two in Alabama, and one in Tennessee. It is not, therefore, probable that very general heed will be given by the people of the South to the advice offered by Mr. Wells, or that they will abandon the hope of exporting their cotton in yarn and fabrics, the manufacture of which will give employment to and improve the condition of their now unemployed men, women, and children, or will forego the privilege of an adequate supply of good and cheap iron manufactured in their midst, in order to turn their attention to making "wooden-ware, soap, starch, clothing and similar articles." They will not, I apprehend, be willing to forego their greatest source of profit in order to oblige him by permitting England still to retain her supremacy as the cotton-spinner and principal iron manufacturer of the world.

WHAT TAXES SHOULD BE REPEALED.

Mr. Chairman, permit me to repeat the fact that duties which serve to develop the resources of a country and cheapen commodities, by inducing home competition, the diversification of labor and the opening of new sources of employment, and increase the general stock produced, are not taxes even though they fail to reduce immediately the price of the commodity on which they are imposed, as adequate duties on cast-steel and Bessemer rails have done. They are during the interim the price paid for establishing the commercial and political independence of the country; or may rather be regarded as a temporary advance to be reimbursed in the near future by producing a sense of national security, a wider field of profitable employment for the people at large, and an adequate and cheaper supply of better goods through the long future.* But such is not the case with all duties. There are duties that are taxes and must remain so forever, or into that far future whose possibilities we cannot foresee. Such are duties imposed on commodities which we do not

* The proposition is, or may be, to raise the price of a manufactured article for a time, in the expectation that advances in skill and machinery, and a more secure place in the market—where conspiracies abroad cannot break in to crush out the capital invested—will by and by, or perhaps in a very short time, afford us the same articles at prices greatly reduced. Even Adam Smith saw this; conceding that "a particular manufacture may sometimes be acquired sooner than it could have been otherwise, and after a certain time may be made at home as cheap, or cheaper than in the foreign country." ("Wealth of Nations," vol. i. p. 448.) And what have we ourselves discovered, in hundreds of ins-

and cannot produce, but which enter into the daily life of the people, either directly as food, or as the raw material of articles we are producing in competition with countries whose laborers receive not a moiety of the wages paid for the same work in this country, and which are necessary for the support of a family whose children are to be educated for future citizenship. We raise no tea or coffee, and the duty of twenty-five cents a pound on tea, which is at the rate of seventy-eight and a half per cent. on the cost of our whole importation for 1868, and of five cents a pound on coffee, or at the rate of forty-seven and a half per cent. on the importation of 1868, are taxes —purely and simply taxes. Yet the Commissioner does not propose to repeal or abate these, and why should he? Neither England nor her North American colonies produce tea or coffee. Not only does he not propose to repeal these taxes now, but in his "schedule of a tariff constructed with a view of obtaining from the smallest number of imported articles an annual revenue of $150,000,000" he retains them both and proposes to raise $22,000,000 a year from them, namely, $12,000,000 from coffee and $10,000,000 from tea. We now impose a duty of fifteen cents a pound on pepper. As we grow no pepper, this is a tax—a tax at the rate of two hundred and ninety-seven per cent. on the entire importation for 1868, and which extracted from the people in that year $792,490 45. The like duty on allspice is a tax. It is at the rate of three hundred and seventy-six and a half per cent., and drew from the people in 1868 $142,981 50. These duties and many scores of such that I could indicate are all taxes, as they stimulate no industry, but tax the food of the farmer and laborer; but they do not move the sympathies of the Commissioner. He does not propose to repeal them, for the articles they burden are not produced in England or her North American colonies. They were imposed as revenue measures during a great war, and have been

---

tances, but exactly this, that the losses or taxation prices we expected did not come, but that the articles protected have been cheapened, some of them, too, from the very first. Who could have imagined that our rough-handed, half-trained mechanics would be able to hold successful competition with the skilled workmen of Europe in the manufacture of an article as delicate as the watch? And yet we are getting our watches now at scarcely more than half the former price, and are even selling watches at a profit in the open market of the world. We consented to make a loss, but the gain came along too soon to let us distinctly see it.—*Bushnell, "Free Trade and Protection."*

cheerfully endured by a patriotic people, but they increase the cost of living, operate as a burden on our laboring people, and should be repealed at the earliest day the financial condition of the country will permit.

Mr. Chairman, there are other taxes, of some of which the people justly complain—taxes that burden our labor, consume the profits of capital, and paralyze the energy of the most enterprising among us. They add to the cost of our gas and our travel, whether by railroad, stage, or steamboat. We cannot draw our own money from bank or make a payment to our creditor without feeling them. They touch and prick us at all points. Their enforcement requires the maintenance of a special department of the Government, the agents of which penetrate inquisitorially every home and workshop in the land. They increase the cost of all our productions and restrict the limits of our commerce by shutting our overtaxed goods out of markets in which but for them we might compete with our foreign rivals. They, too, were the product of the war. The necessities in which it involved us gave rise to the system of internal taxes with its Commissioner, assessors, collectors, supervisors, detectives, and thousands of subordinates; and sound policy requires that those duties which, while they protect the wages of the laboring man and develop the resources of the country, supply the Treasury with large amounts of revenue should be retained, and that these direct and inquisitorial taxes which so oppress and annoy us should be removed as rapidly as possible. The repeal of these would animate all our industries; but the repeal of the duties recommended by the Commissioner would flood our country with the productions of the underpaid laborers of Europe, silence countless looms and spindles, close our factories, extinguish the fires in our furnaces and rolling-mills, and leave the grain of the husbandmen, for which there is now no market in Europe, to rot in the field or granary, while their countrymen and former customers starve. However ardently Mr. Commissioner Wells may desire this consummation, I trust that Congress, by protecting the wages of the American laborer, will forever avert it.

PERSONAL EXPLANATION.

SPEECH DELIVERED IN THE HOUSE OF REPRESENTATIVES, JANUARY 20TH, 1870.

The House being in session—

Mr. Kelley said:

I ask unanimous consent to make a brief personal explanation.

The Speaker. For how long?

Mr. Kelley. Five minutes.

There was no objection, and it was ordered accordingly.

Mr. Kelley. Mr. Speaker: I send to the Clerk's desk the St. Louis *Democrat* of January 17th, 1870, and ask the Clerk to read the paragraph I have marked.

The Clerk read as follows:

"This cheap cry of British gold is about played out. There are a great many more men in Congress and out of it, who are bribed to advocate what they know to be against the public interest by American gold than by British. We might easily retort on Mr. Kelley. It would be easy to say that his personal interest. to the extent of $100,000, in iron works in Irondale, Ohio, bribes him to cast a vote against the public welfare. But that sort of argument may well be left altogether to those who have no better at command."

Mr. Kelley. Mr. Speaker: I have called the attention of the House to this paragraph, not by reason of its own importance, but because I have from time to time seen articles in the papers, speaking of my great pecuniary interest in pig-iron. I did not know how to account for them until within a few days one of the gentlemen from Ohio, [Mr. Garfield,] or his colleague, [Mr. Wilson,] handed me a letter, the printed heading of which informed me that "William D. Kelley & Sons are the proprietors of Grant Furnace, Ironton, Ohio." I saw, then, that those who made this intimation had, at least, a reasonable basis of fact. I want to say that I do not know my namesake, but was pleased to hear that he is a worthy and prosperous man, with a large family of sons about him, who are laboriously aiding him in his business, while I, less fortunate, happen to have but one son, who is not yet fifteen years of age. I am not interested in a foot of land in the state of Ohio. I never had means enough, having been a lawyer whose services were not liberally requited, to embark in manufacturing pig-iron or any other commodity. Nor do I own, directly or indirectly, one dollar of capital or stock in any mining or manufacturing interest in the world. God knows that, as I feel years creeping over me, I regret my past indifference to pecuniary matters, and wish that I had been able to acquire some such property

FARMERS, MECHANICS, AND LABORERS NEED PROTECTION—CAPITAL CAN TAKE CARE OF ITSELF.

SPEECH DELIVERED IN THE HOUSE OF REPRESENTATIVES, MARCH 25, 1870.

The House being in the Committee of the Whole, and having under consideration the bill (H. R. No. 1068) to amend existing laws relating to the duties on imports, and for other purposes—

Mr. Kelley said:

Mr. Chairman: I presume that gentlemen who have listened to the course of this debate expect me to apologize for having been born in Pennsylvania and adhering to my native State. From what has been said it seems that her people are regarded by free traders as a discreditable community, and she, in her corporate capacity, as an object of odium.

Sir, I am proud of dear old Pennsylvania, my native State. She was the first to adopt the Federal Constitution, and was in fact the key-stone of the Federal arch, holding together the young Union when it consisted of but thirteen States, and she is to-day preëminently the representative State of the Union. You cannot strike her so that her industries shall bleed without those of other States feeling it, and feeling it vitally. She has no cotton, or sugar, or rice fields; but apart from these she is identified with every interest represented upon this floor.

Gentlemen from the rocky coast of New England and those from the more fertile and hospitable shores of the Pacific, especially the gentlemen from the beautifully wooded shores of Puget Sound, complain that their ship-yards are idle. Hers, alas! are also idle, although they are the yards in which were built the largest wooden ship the Government ever put afloat, and the largest sailing iron-clad it ever owned. She has her commerce and sympathizes with young San Francisco and our great commercial metropolis, New York. She was for long years the leading port of entry in the country. She still maintains a respectable direct commerce and imports very largely through New York, for the same reasons that London does through Liverpool, and Paris through Havre.

Are you interested in the production of fabrics, whether of silk, wool, flax, or cotton? If so her interests are identical with yours, for she employs as many spindles and looms as any New England State, and their productions are as various and as valuable. Are your interests in the commerce upon the lakes? Then go with me to her beautiful city of Erie and behold how Pennsylvania sympathizes with all your interests there. Are your interests identified with the navigation of the Mississippi and seeking markets for your products at the mouth of that river and on the Gulf? I pray you to remember that two of the navigable sources of the American "Father of Waters" take their rise in the bosom of her mountains, and that for many decades her enterprising and industrious people have been plucking from her hills bituminous coal and floating it past the coal-fields of Ohio, Kentucky, Indiana, Illinois, Missouri, and other coal-bearing States, to meet that of England in the market of New Orleans and try to drive it thence. Gentlemen from the gold regions, where were the miners trained who first brought to light, with any measure of science and experience, the vast resources in gold and silver-bearing quartz of the Pacific slope? They went to you from the coal, iron, and zinc mines of Pennsylvania. There they had learned to sink the shaft, run the drift, handle ore, and crush or smelt it. It was experience acquired in her mines that brought out the wealth of California almost as magically as we were taught in childhood to believe that Aladdin's lamp could convert base articles into gold.

Nor, sir, are the interests of Pennsylvania at variance with those of the great agricultural States? Before her Representatives in the two Houses of Congress had united their voices with those of gentlemen from the West to make magnificent land grants for the purpose of constructing railroads in different directions across the treeless but luxuriously fertile prairies, Pennsylvania was first among the great agricultural States. And to-day her products of the field, the garden, the orchard, and the dairy equal in value those of any other State. Gentlemen from Ohio, notwithstanding the statement of the gentleman from Iowa [Mr. Allison] that you alone manufacture Scotch pig-iron and suffer from its importation, as you alone have the black band ore from which it is made, is it not true that when Pennsylvania demands a tariff that will protect the wages of her laborers in the mine, the quarry, and the furnace, she does but defend the interests and rights of your laborers and those of every other iron-bearing State in the Union? Gentlemen from Virginia, Maryland, and North Carolina, Pennsylvania is denounced because she pleads for a duty on bituminous coal that will enable you to develop your magnificent coal-fields in competition with Nova Scotia. The coal of your tide-water fields is far more available than that of the inland fields of Pennsylvania, which depend on railroads for transportation. On the banks of the James, the Dan, and other navigable rivers, lie coal-beds to within a few hundred feet of which the vessels which are to carry the coal may come, and they lie nearer to the markets of New England than those of your colonial rivals at Nova Scotia; and when you were not here and Virginia and North Carolina were voiceless on this floor, I pleaded with the Thirty-Ninth Congress to retain the duty of $1 25 per ton in order that Virginia and North Carolina, soon to be reconstructed, should be able to produce fuel for New England better and cheaper than Nova Scotia does, and that it should be carried in New England built vessels, so that the thousands of people employed in producing and transporting it should create a market for the grain of the western farmer and the productions of American workshops. I might, Mr. Chairman, extend the illustration of the identity of the interests of Pennsylvania with those of the people of every other State, but will not detain the committee longer on that subject. In leaving it I however reiterate my assertion that you cannnot strike a blow at her industries without the people of at least half a score of other States feeling it as keenly as she will. She asks no boon from Congress. Her people, whether they depend for subsistence upon their daily toil, or have been so fortunate as to inherit or acquire capital, seek no special privileges from the Government. They demand that we shall legislate for the promotion of the equal welfare of all. They know that they must share the common fate, and that their prosperity depends upon that of their countrymen at large.

PROTECTION CHEAPENS COMMODITIES.

Mr. Chairman, many gentlemen have spoken since this bill was made a special order, and a great deal has been said upon the general subject of free trade and protection, and but little about the provisions embodied in the bill before the committee. I am probably expected to proceed at once to reply to the remarks of my colleague on the Committee of Ways and Means, from Iowa [Mr. Allison], who has just closed his remarks. But I may as well before proceeding to do so take a shot into the flock generally. The birds have all sung the same song. My colleague has gone more fully into the details of the bill than any of the others. But his statements are all in harmony with those of the several gentlemen who have given us the doctrines of the chief of the Bureau of Statistics, D. A. Wells, in their own admirable way. I propose to allude to some of their remarks.

The gentleman from New York [Mr. Brooks] in opening the debate promised to mount a peddler's wagon and ride through the agricultural districts of the country, exhibiting hoes, shovels, axes, chains, knives and forks, cottons, and woolens, and demonstrate to the people the unjust and enormous taxation imposed on them by the existing tariff. If he will redeem this promise, making candid statements of facts to the people, I will contribute toward his expenses and pray for the success of his mission.

Mr. Brooks, of New York. How much?

Mr. Kelley. I will contribute 25 per cent., and what may be more effective, will try to make an arrangement by which the proprietors of Flagg's Pain Exterminator will give the gentleman a seat in one of their wagons while going through the country. By no other means could he so perfectly demonstrate the fact that duties which are really protective are never a tax, and that protection invariably cheapens commodities. So invariably is this true that protective America, France, and Germany are crowding free-trade England out of the markets of the world with the articles named by the gentleman while purchasing from her the materials of which they are made, and paying protective duties on every pound of them. This is not mere declamation. It is truth demonstrated by experience.* The starving mechanics of England know it, and have at length succeeded in bringing it officially to the knowledge of Parliament. I have before me the report of a parliamentary commission which proves, that notwithstanding our duties on iron and steel, our knives and forks, horseshoe nails, etc., are crowding England out of general markets, that our hoes, shovels,

---

* A New York correspondent of the Sheffield *Independent* recently wrote to that paper as follows:

"*There will be no legislation this session on the tariff, which means no change in actual operation until 1873, at nearest. The opposition, therefore, which Sheffield manufacturers have to encounter from native and protected industry will not be abated for two, if not three years to come. This is not encouraging for such Sheffield trades as the saw trade, for instance, which is now nearly wholly driven from this market. It is no use denying, either, that during the respite which such trades here as the spring knife and table knife trade will have, their opposition will become more formidable. It is true that the manufacturers of table knives here seem to have gone as low as they can in price, and that Sheffield goods can just compete and that is all, and more than that no one pretends that American table knife concerns are making money. But there they stand, gigantic establishments. each with its little world of workmen round it, the representatives of much labor and capital invested under legal sanction, and, therefore, claiming tender consideration in any future financial adjustment.* The American-made one and two blade pocket knives are beginning to push out similar goods made in Sheffield all over the West and Northwest. They run chiefly on such styles, in one blade, as cost from three to six shillings per dozen in Sheffield, and such two blades as cost from six to ten shillings. In price they are about the same for the same pattern, but in fitting, finish and style, very much superior. The steel used, as a rule, is good, and the blades above complaint. Their patterns are not numerous. Indeed, they adopt precisely the same tactics as those used by the table knife manufacturers when they first commenced that competition with Sheffield which has ended, practically, in the transference of that business to this country. They choose a few good popular styles, they invent and use machinery for every process possible, they put in good blades, neatly ground, splendidly marked, and turn out every knife the precise duplicate of every other. Hence the uniformity, reliability, and general style which is found in *no* Sheffield goods, except those of standard makers. I regard it as absolutely certain that the Sheffield spring-knife trade has, so far as this market is concerned, to pass through precisely the same stages as those through which the table-knife trade has passed. Gradually, the methods used here will push out all medium and common imported goods; then will come a time of utter stagnation and bewilderment among the masters and men usually working for the United States trade; then none but goods with a name will remain saleable here; and, finally, it is to be hoped, as in the sister business, enterprising manufacturers will arise in Sheffield who, adopting machinery, will speedily regain the lost ground and bring back employment. There is no excuse, however, after past experience, for such a crisis arising. The machinery and processes used here are inexpensive, though effective—so effective, indeed, that one of the oldest and most energetic and successful of the Sheffield manufacturers, after investigating them on the spot here last year, could lay no more consolation to his heart than the old system 'would last *his* time out.' If the 'trade' would send out, at their expense, two intelligent practical men, and let them spend a month here and probe the subject to the bottom, they could, at an outlay of £150 or £200, save their fellowworkmen from a world of coming want and perplexity. Why not do it?"

and axes are bought by the people of all her colonies; and that our locks, sewing-machines, and other productions of iron and steel are underselling hers in the streets of London and Birmingham. Here is the "report from the select committee on scientific instruction, together with the proceedings of the committee, minutes of evidence, and appendix," ordered by the House of Commons to be printed 15th July, 1868. It is a ponderous volume and replete with instruction.

I find on page 479 a paper handed in by Mr. Field, containing a "list of some articles made in Birmingham and the hardware districts, which are largely replaced in common markets of the world by the productions of other countries." The author states that "this list might be immensely extended by further investigation, which the shortness of time has not permitted." Among the articles enumerated are hoes—and I ask the attention of the gentleman from New York [Mr. Brooks]—

"Hoes: for cotton and other purposes, an article of large consumption."

On this article the report remarks:

"The United States compete with us, for their own use and, to some extent, for export."

Then we have the following:

"Axes: for felling trees, etc., an article of large consumption. The United States supply our colonies and the world with the best article."

Then there are:

"Carpenters' broad-axes; carpenters' and coopers' adzes; coopers' tools, various sorts; shoemakers' hammers and tools."

With regard to these, "Germany and the United States" are mentioned as the countries "whose products are believed to have replaced those of England."

Speaking of cut nails, the report says:

"The United States export to South America and our colonies."

And, with regard to horseshoe nails, which we protect by a duty of 5 cents per pound, and the manufacture of which under that ample protection has been cheapened and so perfected, that this parliamentary report announces that they exclude the English from common markets, because they are—

"Beautifully made by machinery in the United States."

Mr. Winans. Will the gentleman allow me to ask him a question?

Mr. Kelley. Not at present. I will be glad, when I have got a little further into my subject, to answer, but not at this point.

Mr. Winans. My question comes in properly here

Mr. Kelley. I will hear the gentleman.

Mr. Winans. I understand that the purport of what the gentleman has been reading is to show that the United States, notwithstanding the high tariff—

Mr. Kelley. I do not yield to the gentleman for a speech. If he has a question to put, let him put it squarely.

Mr. Winans. I merely wished to make a preliminary remark. But, without any preliminaries, my question is this: If, under the operation of our tariff, American manufacturers could compete with British manufacturers in British markets, why should the high tariff be maintained to oppress our own people? *

Mr. Kelley. The gentleman's question will be abundantly answered as I proceed. But I may remark here, that, if by protection you secure to your capital and industry a certain market, capitalists will invest in the erection of workshops, and purchase of machinery, and by high wages will induce skilled and ingenious workmen to leave their

* Such a tariff is the only means of protecting our industries from overthrow by foreign conspirators. The British Government applauds such conspiracies, and the American Government should defend its people against them. Though the following extract from the report of a Parliamentary commission made in 1854 appears on page 41, I cite it here as a conclusive, though not the only answer to the question of Judge Winans:

"I believe that the laboring classes generally, in the manufacturing districts of this country, and especially in the iron and coal districts, are very little aware of the extent to which they are often indebted for their being employed at all to *the immense losses which their employers voluntarily incur in bad times, in order to destroy foreign competition, and to gain and keep possession of foreign markets.* Authentic instances are well known of employers having, in such times, carried on their work at a loss amounting, in the aggregate, to three or four hundred thousand pounds in the course of as many years. If the efforts of those who encourage the combinations to restrict the amount of labor, and to produce strikes, were to be successful for any length of time, *the great accumulations of capital could no longer be made, which enable a few of the most wealthy capitalists to overwhelm all foreign competition in times of great depression,* and thus to clear the way for the whole trade to step in when prices revive, and to carry on a great business before foreign capital can again accumulate to such an extent as to be able to establish a competition in prices with any chance of success. *The large capitals of this country are the great instruments of warfare against the competing capitalists of foreign countries,* and are the most essential instruments now remaining by which our manufacturing supremacy can be maintained; the other elements—cheap labor, abundance of raw materials, means of communication, and skilled labor—being rapidly in process of being realized."

homes and accept employment on better terms among strangers. Thus, under protection, capital has been invested, and skilled laborers gathered, and our inventive genius has improved the methods of production, until we have come to be able to make the articles mentioned in this list cheaper than free-trade England. But withdraw this protection, and you will enable foreigners, with the immense accumulations of capital they possess, to combine and undersell our home manufacturers for a few years, and thus destroy them. The purpose of a protective tariff is that of the fence around an orchard in a district where cattle are permitted to run at large. I believe I have answered the question of the gentleman.

The gentleman from New York [Mr. Brooks] said that his heart glowed with pride when, in a distant foreign land, he saw a camel robed in American muslin. The value of the kind of muslin used for such a purpose is almost all in the cost of the raw material; it is woven of the coarsest yarn. I wish he had been in Abyssinia in 1867; how his pulse would have quickened and his heart expanded as he saw that while England was wreathing the latest glory around her brow by moving an army into the heart of Abyssinia for the relief of a few of her subjects, the ingenuity and protected industry of the United States was from day to day providing that army with water.

For proof of this I turn again to the Parliamentary report. It says: "Pumps of various sorts largely exported from the United States." To this announcement is added the following note: "an American pump finding water for the Abyssinian expedition." Those pumps, unlike the coarse cotton, the sight of which so rejoiced the gentleman, involved a preponderant percentage of labor—labor for the digging and carrying of the coal, ore, and limestone, and on through successive grades of labor to their completion, so that probably 90 per cent. of their cost was labor. But I submit the list entire for the gentleman's consideration:

Appendix No. 22 to the report from the select Committee on Scientific Instruction, together with the proceedings of the committee, minutes of evidence, and appendix.

[Ordered by the House of Commons to be printed, 15th July, 1868.]

PAPER HANDED IN BY MR. FIELD.

List of some articles made in Birmingham and the hardware district, which are largely replaced in common markets of the world by the productions of other countries:

Articles or class of articles.	Country whose products are believed to have replaced those of this district, in whole or in part.
Carpenters' tools:	
As hammers, plyers, pincers, compasses, hand and bench vices.	Germany chiefly.
Chains:	
Of light description, where the cost is more in labor than in material, as halter chains and bow-ties, and such like.	Germany.
Frying-pans of fine finish......	France.
Wood-handled spades and shovels, an article of very large consumption.	United States exports them to all our colonies.
Hoes:	
For cotton and other purposes, an article of large consumption.	United States compete with us for their own use, and, to some extent, for export.
Axes:	
For felling trees, etc., an article of large consumption.	United States supply our colonies and the world with the best article.
Carpenters' broadaxes. Carpenters' and coopers' adzes. Coopers' tools, various sorts. Shoemakers' hammers and tools.	Germany and the United States.
Machetes:	
For cutting sugar canes, an important article.	Believed to be now Germany.
Nails:	
Cut........................	United States export to South America and our colonies.
Wrought......................	Belgium.
Point de Paris (wire nails.)....	French and Belgian largely supersede English.
Horse-nails	Beautifully made by machinery in the United States.
Pumps:	
Of various sorts..............	Largely exported by United States. NOTE.—An American pump finding water for the Abyssinian expedition.

LIST.—*Continued.*

Articles or class of articles.	Country whose products are believed to have replaced those of this district, in whole or in part.
Agricultural implements:	
Plows, cotton-gins, cultivators, kibbling machines, corn-crushers, churns, rice-hullers, mowing-machines, hay rakes.	Many articles similar to these are exported by United States to common markets.
Sewing machines	United States.
Lamps:	
For use with petroleum, now an article of very large consumption.	The United States petroleum lamps supplant the English in India and China.
Lamps for the table	French even imported to England.
Tin-ware:	
Tinned spoons, cooks' ladles, and various culinary articles of fine manufacture and finish.	France.
Locks:	
Door locks, chest locks, drawer locks, cupboard locks in great variety.	United States, France, and Germany.
Door latches in great variety.	United States exports to Canada.
Curry-combs	United States and France.
Traps:	
Rat, beaver, and fox	United States export to Canada.
Gimlets and augers (twisted)	United States export to Canada and probably elsewhere.
Brass-foundery, cast:	
As hinges, brass hooks, and castors, in great variety; door buttons, sash fasteners, and a great variety of other articles.	These articles in great variety, are now extensively exported from France and Germany.
Brass-foundery, stamped:	
As curtain pins and bands, cornices, gilt beading, and a great variety of other brass-foundery.	These articles, in great variety, are now extensively exported from Germany and France.
Needles:	
An article of large consumption.	Mostly Germany, (Rhenish Prussia,) even imported to England,
Fish-hooks	Believed Germany.
Guns:	
A great variety of sporting guns, articles of large consumption, formerly entirely from Birmingham.	Now exported largely from Liege, Belgium, and Etienne, France.
Breech-loading muskets and revolver pistols.	United States.

LIST.—*Continued.*

Articles or class of articles.	Country whose products are believed to have replaced those of this district, in whole or in part.
Watches and clocks..........	Switzerland and France import into England, United States, and France. [NOTE.—Watches made in the United States interchangeable, by machinery.]
Iron........................	Belgium.
Glass:	
For windows, an article of large consumption; spectacle and all other glass.	Belgium supplants ours in our own colonies.
Table glass..................	Believed to be Belgium and France.
Swords......................	Prussia and Belgium.
Jewelry:	
Gold, gilt, and fancy steel, in very great variety.	France and Germany. These articles are even imported into England.
Small steel trinkets:	
As bag and purse clasps, steel buttons, chains, key rings, and other fastenings, and many others in great variety.	France and Germany. Many of these even imported into England.
Leather bags, with clasps, purses, and courier bags, etc.	Austria, France, and Russia. We believe about all these articles sold in England are imported.
Buttons:	
Mother of pearl..............	Vienna, imported to England.
Horn	France, imported to England.
Porcelain (formerly Minton's of Stoke).	France entirely superseded English, and imported to England largely.
Steel buttons (formerly Bolton & Watt's).	France.
Florentine or lasting boot-buttons.	Germany.
Steel pens, pen-holders, brass scales and weights.	France.
Iron gas-tubing.............	Germany
Elastic belts with metal fastenings.	Germany.
Brass chandeliers and gas-fittings. Harness buckles and furniture.	France and Prussia.
German-silver spoons, forks, etc.	France, Austria, and Prussia.
Locks:	
Best trunk, door, and cabinet locks.	Prussia and France.

LIST.—*Continued.*

Articles or class of articles.	Country whose products are believed to have replaced those of this district, in whole or in part.
Umbrella furniture	France and Prussia.
Horn Combs	Prussia.
Pearl and tortoise shell articles.	France and Austria.
Iron wire	Prussia and Belgium.
Iron and brass hooks and eyes.	Prussia and France.
Bronzed articles	Prussia and France.
Hollow wares, enameled	France and Prussia.
Optical instruments. Mathematical instruments.	France, Austria, and Bavaria.
Japanned wares	Germany and France.
Bits and stirrups	Belgium and France.
Coach springs and axle-trees	France.
Electro-plated wares; (customers preferring French goods.)	France.
Gas-fittings	United States.
Weighing machines	United States.
Plumbers' brass-foundery	United States.
Table glass-ware	United States.
Door locks	United States.
Machines for domestic purposes, as sausage machines, coffee-mills, and washing-machines.	United States.
Nuts and bolts	United States.
Penknives and scissors	United States.
Stamped brass ware (certain kinds).	United States.
American "notions," as buckets, clothes-pegs, washing and agricultural machines.	United States.
Cutlery:	
In great variety: scissors, light-edge tools, such as chisels, etc.	Germany.
Pins for piano-strings and other small fittings for pianos. Silver wire for binding the bars, strings of pianos, etc.	France.

This list might be immensely extended by further investigation, which the shortness of time has not permitted.

THE INTERNAL REVENUE SYSTEM—IT IS EXPENSIVE AND INQUISITORIAL, AND SHOULD BE ABOLISHED AT THE EARLIEST POSSIBLE DAY.

At a later stage of the debate the gentleman from Ohio [Mr. Stevenson] presented his views on the general subject.

He had previously denounced the protectionists of the House as a faction, and now deplores the fact that "the beautiful idea," free trade, "cannot be wholly realized until the commercial millennium." He will, however, do all he can to hasten its triumph. In this direction he goes further than Calhoun or any southern leader ever went. His is a manufacturing and agricultural district, yet he not only echoes the demand of the gentleman from the free-trade commercial city of New York for free coal, iron, salt, and lumber, and a general reduction of the tariff, but leaps beyond him, and proposes to give permanence to the system of internal taxes, which was established as a temporary war measure, and which costs annually over $8,000,000, maintains an army of tens of thousands of office-holders, and makes inquisition into the private affairs of every citizen, and would simply remove from it "irritating, petty, useless, and vexatious elements." Sir, the gentleman cannot be ignorant of the fact that every dollar drawn from the people by these taxes is so much added to the cost of the productions of the farm and workshop, and operates as a bonus to the foreign competitors of our farmers and mechanics in common markets. But even this will not content him. He grieves that other and more onerous taxes cannot constitutionally be levied on the farms, workshops, and homes of the people of Ohio and the rest of the country. On this point he gives forth no uncertain sound. He hopes the Constitution will yet be so amended as to constrain every owner of a farm or cross-roads blacksmith's shop to make the acquaintance of a collector of United States taxes. On this point he said:

"In fact, I incline to the opinion that one of the errors committed by our forefathers in framing the Constitution—and since we have amended it in such material matters lately, we can afford to say that they did commit some errors in framing it—was in not permitting direct taxation upon property according to its value. And some day I trust the Constitution will permit the Government to levy taxes upon property according to its value. But until that day, as long as the debt remains a material burden, we must, in my judgment, retain the less objectionable and burdensome parts of both systems of taxation."

Mr. Stevenson. I want to know whether the gentleman does not consider that the material part of the internal revenue taxes must be continued while the debt remains?

Mr. Kelley. No, sir. I believe that if gentlemen will adopt the tariff bill now under consideration, extended as is its free list and great as are the reductions in rates of duties, we can take the internal taxes off all but eight articles by a law of this session, and go still further in that direction during the next session.

Mr. Stevenson. What articles are they?

Mr. Kelley. I will come to that in the course of my remarks. I have a note of them. While on this subject let me say that I believe further, that in the interest of the farmers of the country we should hasten the day when we can take the tax off distilled spirits.

Sir, the West has grain for which she can find no market. The Governments of Great Britain and France, coöperating with our internal tax system, deprive them of what would be a generous market. Take the tax of 65 cents a gallon off whisky, and the grain now stored in the granaries of the West would be distilled into alcohol and shipped to the countries of South America, the West India Islands, Turkey, and elsewhere.* I have now answered the gentleman as far as I propose to at present. I have, however, not yet done with him.

Mr. Stevenson. The gentleman is criticising what was drawn out of me by a question from himself. I ask him in fairness to permit me to put a question to him.

Mr. Kelley. Well, go on.

Mr. Stevenson. I want to know whether the gentleman is not in favor, before reducing the tariff on coal and iron, of taking the internal revenue tax off whisky and abolishing the tax on incomes entirely?

Mr. Kelley. I am in favor of abolishing at the earliest possible day a system that makes inquisition into the private affairs of every man and woman in the country, and has cost us for the three last years an average of $8,509,532 77 per annum, and taken probably 10,000 persons from industrial employments and fastened them as vampires upon the people. This is what I am in favor of. But I hold the floor for another purpose than a mere controversy with the gentleman.

Mr. Stevenson. Then the gentleman declines to answer my question.

---

* The tax on spirits not only restricts the market for grain, but taxes the farmer by the addition it makes to the cost of many articles he consumes. It adds about 15 cents to the cost of producing an ounce of quinine, and more largely to the cost of chloroform, collodion, and many other drugs, and almost every variety of perfumery. Before it was imposed, we exported such articles to many countries. Now we import them largely.

Mr. Kelley. I have answered the gentleman's question, and every gentleman present will, I think, say I have answered it frankly.

FREE TRADE MEANS LOW WAGES AND A LIMITED MARKET FOR GRAIN.

Mr. Chairman, I am not specially familiar with the gentleman's district. Though I have visited Cincinnati several times and ridden through Hamilton county, I have but few acquaintances within their limits; yet I know something about them. The last annual report of the Cincinnati Board of Trade informs us that during the year ending March 31, 1869, there were produced in the gentleman's district and the adjoining one, in about 3000 separate establishments, 187 distinct classes of manufactured articles, of an aggregate value of $104,657,612. The cash capital invested in these establishments, the report says, is $49,824,124, and they give employment to 55,275 hands.

Mr. Chairman, I venture the remark that there is not among these 55,275 working people one who will indorse the opinions advanced by the gentleman.

Mr. Stevenson. Will the gentleman yield to me for a moment?

Mr. Kelley. No, sir; I must decline.

Mr. Stevenson. The gentleman holds the floor without restriction by the courtesy of the House.

Mr. Kelley. I will yield further to the gentleman during the course of my remarks, but not at present.

Many of the laboring people of his district are immigrants and know how small are the wages of workmen on the other side of the Atlantic, and the fare on which they live. They know that free trade means low wages. Buy labor where you can buy it cheapest is the cardinal maxim of the free trader. More than 85 per cent. of the cost of every ton of coal, salt, and pig-iron is in the wages of labor, and when the gentleman shall have stricken the duties off these articles, the 1,500,000 people who are now earning good wages in their production must compete with the cheap labor of Turk's Island, England, Wales, and Germany. Thrown out of remunerative employment in the trades to which they have devoted their lives, as they will be, they must compete with workmen in other pursuits, even though they glut the market and bring down the general rate of wages throughout the land. He who advocates protective duties pleads the cause of the American laborer. I will not amplify this proposition. I regard it as a truism, and beg leave to illustrate it by inviting the attention of my colleague from Iowa, [Mr. Allison,] and the gentleman from Ohio, to a statement of the wages and subsistence of families of laborers in Europe, on page 179 of the monthly report of the Deputy Special Commissioner of the Revenue, No. 4 of the series 1869–70. It refers specially to Germany, and was translated and compiled from Nos. 10–12 of the publications of the Royal Prussian Statistical Bureau, Berlin, 1868.

This paper, gentlemen will remark, was not prepared for or by American politicians, or by a faithless officer of this Government, or by any representative of a free trade or protective league. Its facts are most significant.

The wheat-growers of Iowa and the West are suffering from the want of a market for their grain. Too large a proportion of our people are raising wheat. We want more miners, railroad men, and mechanics, and our present rates of wages are inducing them to come to us. Nearly half a million people tempted by these wages will come this year. Our working people are free consumers of wheat, beef, pork, and mutton. But could they be, under free trade or reduced duties? These articles are luxuries rarely enjoyed by the working people of England or the continent, with whom anti-protectionists would compel them to compete. The official paper to which I refer tells us that "rye and potatoes form the chief food of the laboring classes; that the wives and daughters of brick-makers, coal and iron miners, and furnace and rolling-mill men aid them in their rough employments; that the regular wages of workingmen average in summer and winter from 16$\frac{3}{10}$ to 24 cents per day, and those of females from 8½ to 14½ cents per day; that miners at tunneling are sometimes paid as much as 72 cents (1 thaler) per day, and that a brick-maker, aided by his wife, averages 80 cents per day; that wages for female labor are more uniform, and that 18 cents per day can be earned by a skillful hand; that juvenile laborers in factories begin with 48 cents per week for ten hours daily, and rise to 72 cents per week; that the general average of daily wages is as follows: males, for twelve hours' work per day in the country, 19¼ cents; in cities 24 cents; and that the wages of master-workmen, overseers, etc., are at least $172 per year." That gentlemen and their constituents may study this instructive paper I beg leave to submit it to the reporters entire.

Wages and subsistence of families of laborers in Europe.

GERMANY.

Lower Silesia, translated and compiled from No. 10–12 of the publications of the Royal Prussian Statistical Bureau, Berlin, 1868.

The regular wages of workingmen average in summer and winter from 16.8 cents to 24 cents (gold) per day; of females, from 08.4 to 14.4 cents per day, more nearly approaching the higher rate. During the short winter days workingmen receive for 8 hours' labor from 10 to 14.4 cents; the females, 7.2 cents; while in summer, for 12 to 13 hours' labor the relative wages are from 19.2 to 28.8 cents, and from 14.4 to 19.2 cents, respectively. The wages of those working in the royal forests are so regulated as to average 24 cents per day for males, and 14.4 cents per day for females; in some mountain countries the latter receive but 12 cents.

In larger cities wages rise above these rates, especially for skilled labor. Men working on railroads receive in summer from 28.8 to 36 cents per day; and women from 16.8 to 26.4 cents. In the larger cities ordinary female help in housekeeping is paid from 24 to 26.4 cents.

Work done by the piece or by contract is paid about one-third more than the customary wages. A common laborer expects in contract work from 36 to 48 cents; at railroad work even more.

When work is scarce the wages often fall to about 16.8 cents per day for males, and 9.6 cents for females.

Labor is often paid by the hour, at from 01.4 to 3 cents for males, and 0.4 to 2 cents for females; 2.4 cents per hour are the wages of an able field laborer in the mountains.

During the summer especially, opportunities for work are offered to children, who receive from 6.11 to 7.2 cents per day, and in winter about 4.8 cents.

Wherever the work rises above mere manual labor in a trade or factory, the daily wages of men are from 30 to 48 cents, and often rise to 60 cents. Miners at tunneling are frequently paid 72 cents (1 thaler); in the district of Görlitz, a brick-maker aided by his wife, averages 80 cents per day;* in the district of Fauer from $5 76 to $7 20 per week. Skilled workmen of large experience receive from $360 to $432 per annum. The wages of the molders and

---

* To compete with this "cheap and nasty" system England employs women, children and infants to make her bricks. "IN OUR BRICK-FIELDS AND BRICK-YARDS, THERE ARE FROM TWENTY TO THIRTY THOUSAND CHILDREN—FROM AS LOW AS 3 AND 4 UP TO 16 AND 17—UNDERGOING A BONDAGE OF TOIL AND A HORROR OF EVIL TRAINING THAT CARRIES PERIL IN IT."—*The Cry of the Children from the Brick-yards of England. By George Smith.* London: 1871, p. 7.

"But there are often phases of evil connected with work in brick-yards and clay-yards, generally, which I must not overlook, especially the demoralizing results ever accruing from the mixed employment of the sexes. A flippancy and familiarity of manners with boys and men, grows daily on the young girls. Then, the want of respect and delicacy toward females exhibits itself in every act, word, and look; for the lads grow so precocious, and the girls so coarse in their language and manners from close companionship at work, that in most

enamelers in iron founderies, of the locksmiths and joiners in machine-works, in piano factories, amount to from 72 cents to $1 08 per day; the same in manufactories of glass, silverware, watches, and hat factories. The highest wages paid to a very skillful joiner in a pianoforte factory were $12 24 per week.

Wages for female labor are more uniform throughout; 18 cents per day can be earned by a skillful hand, 24 cents per day very rarely.

Juvenile laborers in factories begin with wages of 48 cents per week, for 10 hours' work daily, and rise to 72 cents per week. The law prohibits the employment of children under 12 years of age; from 12 to 14 years it permits 6 hours', and from 14 to 16 years, 10 hours' daily labor.

The general average of daily wages is as follows: Males, for 12 hours' work per day, in the country, 19.2 cents; in cities 24 cents; harder labor, 30 cents; in cities, 36 cents; skilled labor, 60 cents.

The wages of master workmen, overseers, &c., are not included in the above average, but are at least $172 per annum.

In regard to the time of work, laborers in factories are employed 11 to 12 hours per day, (exclusive of time for meals;) where work is continued day and night, the hours for the day are from 6 to 12 a. m., and 1 to 7 p. m.; for the night, from 7 p. m. to 6 a. m., with ¼ hour recess; in a few districts 10 hours constitute a day's work. In many cloth factories and wool spinneries, males and females work 12 to 13 hours, and some even 16 hours per day. As an example, a cloth factory employs firemen and machinists 16 hours, spinners and dyers 14 hours, all others 12 hours, exclusive of time for meals. In glass-works, the nature of the work requires from 16 to 18 hours for melters, 13 to 15 hours for blowers; but then one party rests while the other works. Rye and potatoes form the chief food of the laboring classes.

Savings.

Although but few workingmen can save any portion of their earnings, still there are some who purchase a little piece of land, a house, or a cow, and the latest accounts from fifteen districts in Lower

---

cases, the modesty of female life gradually becomes a byeword instead of a reality, and they sing unblushingly before all, whilst at work, the lewdest and most disgusting songs, till oftentimes stopped short by the entrance of the master or foreman. The overtime work is still more objectionable because boys and girls, men and women, are less under the watchful eye of the master, nor looked upon by the eye of day. All these things, the criminality, levity, coarse phrases, sinful oaths, lewd gestures, and conduct of the adults and youths, exercise a terrible influence for evil on the young children. Hence a generation full of evil phrases, manners, and thoughts is daily growing up in our midst without the knowledge of better things. It is quite common for girls employed in brick-yards to have illegitimate children. Of the thousands whom I have met with, or know as working, I should say that one in every four who had arrived at the age of twenty had had an illegitimate child. Several had had three or four, and it is a deplorable fact that as a rule brick manufacturers do not trouble themselves to inquire into the moral character of either women or children, when they employ them. I have found myself often looked upon as an oddity when I have asked, 'is she of good character?' and have been subjected to sharp criticism when I have discharged a single woman, because she was palpably *enceinte*." —*A Brickmaster, quoted by Geo. Smith*, p. 22.

Silesia show deposits in savings-banks, from house servants of $428,-455; of apprentices and mechanical workmen of $124,522. No statistics of savings of factory workers were obtained. In some factories the workmen have established savings-banks, some of which have deposits of from $8000 to $10,000.

DETAILED STATEMENTS OF THE WAGES AND COST OF LIVING IN DIFFERENT DISTRICTS OF LOWER SILESIA.

1. *District of Bolkenhain.*

The annual expenses of a family of about 5 persons, (3 children,) belonging to the working class, were as follows:

Provisions, (per day, 0.144 to 0.168,) per year		$60 00
Rent, (8 thalers,)		5 76
Fuel		3 60
Clothing, linen, etc.		14 40
Furniture, tools, etc.		7 20
Taxes: State 0.72; church 12; commune 36,	$1 20	
School for 2 children	2 50	
		3 70
Total		$94 66

The expenses of a laborer's family being 24 to 26.4 cents per day, the earnings should be 28 to 30.8 cents per day, which the head of the family cannot earn. While his earnings are from 17 to 19 cents, the wife earns 8 to 10 cents, and the children must help as soon as old enough. Miners in this district have 24 to 29 cents daily wages; factory men from 19 to 29 cents; mechanics receive 48 to 54 cents per week, besides board; male house servants $17 to $30, and female $12 per annum, exclusive of board and lodging.

2. *District of Landeshut.*

Expenses of a family:

	In the country.	In a city.
Rent per annum	$5 76	$10 72
Provisions, (per week, 90 cents,) per annum	46 80*	56 10
Fuel and light per annum	14 40	16 42
Taxes, etc., per annum	3 60	4 32
Clothing, etc., per annum	8 56	10 00
Other expenses per annum	7 20	8 57
Total	$86 32	$106 13

The income of laborers' (weavers') families does generally not reach these amounts. Many are permitted to gather their wood from the royal forests, and spend little for clothing, which they beg from charitable neighbors. A weaver earns here from 48 to 72 cents, $1 and $1 50 per week; most weavers have 2 looms in operation, and together with their wives earn from $1 50 to $2 16 per week. The average earnings of weavers are given at 96 cents per week, or about $50 per annum.

* Per week, $1 08.

3. *District of Hirschberg.*

The lowest cost of living for a laborer's family is given at $64 80 to $72 per annum, of which are expended for provisions $43 30, for clothing $17, taxes $3 16, fuel $3 60, rent $4, etc. In the summer the wages for 12 hours' daily work, for males, are from 15 to 39 cents; for females 5 to 17 cents per day; in winter from 3 to 7 cents less. A male farm hand receives $12 to $22 per year; a boy $9 to $14; a maid-servant $12 to $18 per annum, with board.

The annual expenses of a laborer's family, living in a comfortable manner, without luxuries, would be nearly double the amount actually expended above.

The following is an estimate:

Rent, (one room, alcove, and bed-room,).......	$ 8 64
Fuel and light..................................	14 40
Provisions, (breakfast, coffee; at noon, potatoes, dumpling—10 cents; evening, bread, a little brandy—5 cents; supper, soup, bread, vegetables—6 cents,)........................	75 00
Clothing, (husband $6 48, wife $5 76, children $7 20; soap 72 cents,)....................	20 16
Taxes, etc..................................	2 16
Schooling of children, (2½ cents per week per child,).....................................	3 60
School books..................................	72
To lay by for sickness, etc....................	8 58
Unforeseen expenses..........................	8 58
Total....................................	$141 84

4. *District of Schönau.*

The ordinary yearly wages, in addition to board, paid to servants in this rural district, were as follows: Man-servant, $14 40 to $21 60; boys, $8 64 to $12 96; maid-servants, $8 64 to $17 28; children's nurses, $5 76 to $12 96.

During the harvest the daily wages for 14 hours' work are as follows: Mowers, from 19.2 to 28.8 cents; laborers, (males,) from 19.2 to 24 cents; females, from 14.4 to 17 cents.

In other seasons males receive for 10 hours' daily labor from 14.4 to 19.2 cents, and females 12 to 14.4 cents per day; and in winter males receive 12 cents, and females 7.4 to 9.6 cents. A laborer in the cities receives 24 to 28.8 cents per day; the "fellows" (journeymen) of trades receive from 60 cents to $1 20 per week, and board.

A laborer's family of 5 persons requires for its subsistence during the year the following amount: For provisions, $72 to $85 72; rent of 1 room and 3 bedrooms, $4 32; clothing, etc., $10 80; fuel, etc., $3 60; taxes, etc., $3 60. Total $108 04.

5. *District of Goldberg.*

The cost of living of a laborer's family, (husband, wife, and two children,) in this district is thus given: Provisions, $75 60; rent, $4 32; fuel, $7 20; clothing, $10 02; furniture, tools, etc., 72 cents; taxes, etc., $2 28. Total, $100 14. In less expensive times provisions have been estimated at $20 less.

In the rural portion men receive 21.6 cents, women 14.4 cents for a day's work; this average includes higher wages for skilled labor.

On a farm a man-servant receives $17 20 per year, in addition to board, etc., which may be estimated at $43 20; a maid-servant receives $14 40, besides board.

Laborers in stone-quarries earn from 24 to 43.2 cents per day; in cloth factories 1.8 to 2.2 cents per hour, while the daily wages of carpenters are from 33.6 to 38.4 cents; masons, 33.6 to 45.6 cents; roof-slaters, 33.6 to 45.6.

Shoemakers and tailors receive from 9 to 10 cents, besides their board and lodging, which is valued at 12 cents.

6. *District of Löwenberg.*

The yearly expenses of a family with 3 children are estimated at from $93 60 to $108, namely:

	In city.	*In country.*
Rent	$10 60	$ 4 32
Provisions, ($1 20 per week,)	62 40	55 72
Fuel and light	12 66	10 80
Taxes, school, etc	3 60	3 60
Clothing, etc	12 85	12 85
Other expenses	5 76	5 76
Total	$107 87	$93 05

Wages are as follows:

Men, day laborers, from 14.4 to 28.8 cents per day; women 12 to 18 cents per day; men, with board, 9.6 to 14.4 cents per day; women, with board, 7.2 to 12 cents per day. From 10 to 14 hours constitute a day's labor; more hours, and harder work secure higher wages.

Male servants per year, $14 40 to $36, and board; female per year, $8 57 to $21 60, and board.

Journeymen in trades obtain the following:

Wages per week (with board and lodging).	In cities.		In the country.	
	Minimum.	Maximum.	Minimum.	Maximum.
	Cents.	*Cents.*	*Cents.*	*Cents.*
Smiths	54	72	42	72
Wheelwrights	54	72	42	72
Shoemakers	54	60	42	72
Tailors	54	72	30	60
Cabinet-makers	54	72	42	72

7. *City of Greifenberg.*

The subsistence of a workingman's family, consisting of 5—man, wife, and 3 children—is thus given:

Income.

A mason receives 33.6 cents per day, regular work, 32 weeks in a year	$64 52
Weaving or other work, 4 months, at 48 to 60 cents per week, say	8 00
Yearly earnings of wife	7 20
Total	$79 72

A day laborer receives 24 cents per day, or $1 44 per week, regular work 40 weeks............	$57 60
During the rest of the year he and his wife may earn..	14 40
Total..................................	$72 00

A carpenter earns a little more than a mason, his chances for winter labor being better. A weaver, working at home, makes less than the day laborer; those in the factory earn per year $72.

Expenses of a family.

Rent, $8 64; clothing, $14 40, (shoes being a large item;) light, $1 44; fuel, $5 04; repairing tools, 72 cents; taxes, $1 44; school for three children, $1 44. Total, $33 12.

Provisions.—The meals consist of patatoes and bread, their means not being sufficient to allow meat; potatoes, 20 bushels, $10 08; bread, (6 cents per day,) $21 90; coffee, (chiccory 4 pounds per day,) $2 88; butter, (½ pound per week,) lard, herring, salt, (24 cents per week,) $12 48. Total, $47 26. Aggregate expenses, $80 38.

Note.—If the work is not regular, the demands of the family must be curtailed, and suffering often takes place.

8. *District of Görlitz.*

Here the condition of the laborer appears more comfortable, since work can be found throughout the year.

Masons and carpenters earn 36 to 43.4 cents per day; railroad laborers, 26.4 to 28.8; field laborers, 21.6 to 28.8 and females 14.5 to 24 cents.

The lowest expenses for a family consisting of 4 or 5 persons are thus computed:

Provisions........................	$57 60	to	$85 72
Rent, lights, and fuel...............	11 52	to	21 10
Clothing..........................	13 57	to	18 00
Tools, etc.........................	1 44	to	2 88
School............................	1 44	to	2 88
Taxes	72	to	1 44
Total.........................	$86 29	to	$132 02

By careful inquiries it has been reliably ascertained that a family can earn from $93 60 to $144 a year, so that some lay up small savings.

For the city of Görlitz the average income of a laborer's family is estimated at $95 to $144 a year; the expenses for 4 or 5 persons, from $115 to $172 80, namely:

Rent, light, and fuel................	$22 72	to	$32 15
Clothing, etc......................	14 40	to	21 60
Tools, furniture, etc................	1 44	to	5 76
School............................	4 32	to	5 04
Provisions.........................	72 00	to	108 25
Total.........................	$114 88	to	$172 80

9. *District of Glogau.*

Farm laborers' income:

Males—6 weeks in harvest, at 30 cents per day	$10 80
14 weeks, (sowing and haymaking,) at 24 cents per day	20 16
15 weeks, fall and spring, at 18 cents per day	16 20
15 weeks, winter, at 14.4 per day	12 96
Total, 50 weeks	$60 12
Females—6 weeks, at 12 cents per day (5 days per week) $3 60	
14 weeks, at 9.6 cents per day 6 72	
15 weeks, at 8.4 per day 6 30	
15 weeks, at 7.2 per day 5 40	
	22 02
Total, 50 weeks	$82 14

Expenses of a family with 3 children:

16 sheffels* rye, at $1 32	$21 12
sheffels wheat, at $1 80	3 60
2 sheffels barley, at $1 20	2 40
2 sheffels peas, at $1 44	2 88
2 sheffels millet, at $1 44	2 88
24 bags potatoes, at 38.4 cents	9 22
52 pounds butter, at 19.2 cents	9 98
18 quarts milk, at 24 cents	4 40
Meat, (2 quarters mutton, $3 60, 1 pig, $10 80)	14 40
52 pounds salt, at .024	1 25
Rent, $5 76; light, $1 52	7 28
Fuel, (wood, $9 72, coal, $3 18)	12 90
Clothing	18 72
Taxes, and other expenses	8 00
Total	$119 03

As, according to these statistics a man and wife can earn but $82 14 per year, a deficiency of $36 89 must be made up by the work of the children or by extra labor in the summer, especially at harvest time.

15. *District of Leignitz.*

Expenses of a family with three children:

Provisions—	
Bread, 1 pound flour per head daily	$26 52
Potatoes, $\frac{1}{2}$ bag or 75 pounds per week, at 18 cents	9 36
Barley, 2 sheffels, at 96 cents	0 96
Peas, 1 sheffel, at $1 08	1 08
Butter, 1 to $1\frac{3}{4}$ pound per week, $71\frac{1}{2}$ pounds per year, at 19 cents	13 73
Carried over	$51 65

* 1 sheffel equals 1·56 bushel, United States.

Brought over			$51 65
Milk, 4 quarts daily, at 4 cents			5 84
Meat, 1 swine for fattening, or 1 pound per week			5 56
Salt, 1 pound per week, at 2.4 cents			1 25
Coffee, chiccory, sugar			4 32
Wheat flour for cake on holidays			1 32
Beer			90
Rent, for a room, a garret-room and small space, per annum			7 20
Light, oil for 26 to 39 weeks, ½ to ¾ pound at 6 cents			2 34
Fuel, during 6 winter months 20 cents, summer 10 cents per week			8 00
Clothing—			
Husband: 2 shirts, at 72 cents		$1 44	
1 pair boots		2 88	
Pantaloons, (3 pairs in 2 years)		72	
Coat, etc		72	
		5 76	
Wife: 2 chemises	$1 44		
1 pair shoes	1 20		
Dress, etc	2 64		
		5 28	
Children: 2 shirts, at 36 cents each	2 16		
3 pairs shoes	2 16		
Clothing	2 16		
		6 48	
Soap for washing		1 20	
			18 72
Tools, for repair of			1 43
Taxes—income, 72 cents; communal, .384 cents; school, including books, $2.556			3 60
Total expenses			$112 13

Income of a family with two children:		
Husband averages 305 days, at 21.6 cents		$65 88
Wife averages 250 days, at 10.4 cents		26 00
Oldest child averages 60 days, at 7.2 cents		4 32
Every married workman receives:		
1 sheffel wheat	$1 80	
2 sheffels rye	2 16	
2 sheffels barley	1 92	
1 sheffel peas	1 08	
		6 96
He can raise on a patch of land 10 bags potatoes, valued at		2 88
And glean at harvest 3 sheffels of rye or barley		3 06
For extra work through the year		8 64
For a fat pig		5 76
Total income		$123 50

In the city of Leignitz the average expense of a laborer's family s estimated at $141 84 per year.

TABLE SHOWING THE RATES OF WAGES PAID FOR FACTORY AND OTHER LABOR IN LOWER SILESIA DURING THE YEAR 1868.

[*Rates expressed in cents, (gold,) United States.*]

Branches and occupations.	Wages per day.		
	Males.	Females.	Children.
Bleaching presses:			
Ordinary hands	18 to 36	14½ to 18	....
Bleachers	27 to 33	....	....
Manglers	36 to 42	....	....
Foremen	48 to 60	....	....
Brewers	24 to 36	....	....
Brickyards:			
Ordinary work	20 to 24	....	....
Molders	29 to 39	....	....
Chamotte-moulders	33 to 48	....	....
Contract work	36 to 60	14 to 20	10 to 17
Average summer wages	24 to 42	16 to 18	10 to 18
Cane factories:			
Turners	36 to 66	....	....
Engravers	36 to 60	....	....
Joiners	48	....	....
Laborers	28 to 42	....	....
Chemical works:			
Average wages	31½	....	....
Fireworks	24 to 36	8 to 15	4 to 6
Cigar factories:			
Foremen	44	....	....
Strippers	....	16 to 18	6 to 10
Skilled hands	$1 to $2	24 to 40	....
Box-makers	12	....	....
Wrappers	....	18 to 24	....
Rollers	24 to 72	....	....
Assorters	72 to $1.08	....	....
Packers	36 to 48	....	....
Foremen	$1 50	....	....
Distillers	18 to 36	....	....
Dyeing establishments:			
Carders	20 to 54	14 to 18	....
Fullers	24	15	....
Shearers	29 to 36	....	....
Foremen	$1 08	....	....
Earthenware, etc.:			
Pottery, molders	60 to 72	....	....
Ordinary work	24 to 60	14 to 22	....
Stoneware, ordinary work	18 to 24	....	....
Turners	24 to 48	....	....
Painters	24 to 42	....	....
Porcelain, glazing makers	30 to 36	18 to 24	....
Burners	30 to 42	....	....
Gilders	36 to 42	12 to 18	....

TABLE.—*Continued.*

Branches and occupations.	Wages per day.		
	Males.	Females.	Children.
Earthenware, etc.:			
Potter-turners	48	....	....
Foremen	96	....	....
Glass-works, polishers	....	10 to 24	....
Melters	60	....	....
Painters and gilders	40 to 72	18 to 36	....
Skilled hands	60 to 96	....	....
Bottle-makers	48 to 60	....	....
Ordinary hands	24 to 36	12 to 18	12
Flour mills:			
Laborers	22 to 29	....	....
Assistant millers	36 to 60	....	....
Firemen	24 to 29	....	....
Machinists	33	....	....
Foremen	72	....	....
Gas-works, laborers	24 to 36	....	....
Hatters:			
Ordinary hands	48 to $1	24 to 36	....
Skilled hands	$1 66 to $2	....	....
Iron-works:			
Laborers	18 to 28	....	....
Locksmiths	24 to 60	....	....
Machine-builders	60 to $1 08	....	....
Molders	42 to 72	....	12 to 20
Turners	52	....	....
Machinists	40 to 72	....	....
Foremen	72	....	....
Watchmen	48	....	....
Enamelers	36 to 72	....	....
Cutters	60 to 72	....	....
Lime kilns:			
Laborers, in winter	20 to 30	....	....
in summer	24 to 36	....	....
Mining:			
Ordinary labor	18 to 24	12	16 to 20
Miners	48 to 60	....	....
Drivers	36	....	....
Oil refiners	18 to 42	16	....
Paper mills:			
Ordinary laborers	21 to 48	10 to 24	8 to 16
Cutters	24	....	....
Holland-miller	30	....	....
Foremen	36 to 50	....	....
Machinists	36	....	....
Bookbinders	32 to 58	....	....
Printers	42 to 48	12 to 24	....
Railroad-car shop:			
Smiths	40 to 72	....	....
Locksmiths	36 to 96	....	......

TABLE.—*Continued.*

Branches and occupations.	Wages per day.		
	Males.	Females.	Children.
Railroad-car shop:			
Turners	42 to $1 08	....	....
Screw-cutters	30 to 60	....	....
Tinners	42 to 60	....	....
File-cutters	48 to 72	....	....
Wheelwrights	48 to 96	....	....
Carpenters	42 to 66	....	....
Painters	48 to 66	....	....
Upholsterers	36 to 60	....	....
Laborers	34	....	....
Starch factories	18 to 36	12 to 17	....
Foremen	36	....	....
Silversmiths	60 to 84	24 to 60	12 to 15
Watch-factory workmen	24 to 72	....	15
Saw-mills:			
Laborers	26 to 48	....	....
Machinists	36 to 60	....	....
Foremen	48	....	....
Spinning flax	24 to 42	12 to 30	12 to 24
cotton	20 to 42	12 to 18	9 to 12
wool	18 to 48	14 to 24	6 to 18
Sugar Refiners	14 to 36	9 to 15	....
Tanners	36 to 60	12 to 15	....
Toy factories:			
Ordinary laborers	18 to 36	10 to 24	....
Turners	36 to 48	....	....
Sculptors	36 to $1 08	....	....

The wages of journeymen in the following trades, including board and lodging, are as follows:

	Per Week.
Bakers	$0 92
Butchers	0 72
Smiths	1 08
Tinners	2 52
Wheelwrights	2 16
Furriers	2 16
Saddlers	0 72
Locksmiths	2 52
Tailors	2 52
Shoemakers	1 44
Fresco-painters	3 42
Cabinet-makers	2 88 to 3 60
Cloth-weavers	1 44 to 2 16

From the reports of the chambers of commerce of Germany the following labor statistics are collected:

In the coal mines of Rhenish-Prussia, average daily wages of 3661 laborers, with families of 8572 persons, males.......... $0 64

Iron foundery, (Duisburg,) average wages per day:

Founders	$0 65 to $0 72
Other skilled workmen	0 54
Laborers	0 43
Machinists and locksmiths	0 58
In two iron founderies, same district, average daily wages, respectively	0 58 to 0 65
Iron-bridge establishment	0 55
Safe factory, average yearly earnings	182 80
Zinc establishments, average wages, first-class hands	0 94
Second-class hands	0 72
Other laborers	0 53
Cotton factories, average wages per hand, including children	0 41
Cotton spinning, average wages per hand (mostly young persons)	0 36

Average weekly wages paid in the coal mines of Plauen, Saxony:

To miners	$3 10
To laborers	1 98
To boys	0 40

[From report of Chamber of Commerce of Chemnitz for 1868.]

SAXONY.

TABLE—*Showing the average Weekly Wages of Labor paid in the district of Chemnitz, Saxony, in the respective Years* 1860 *and* 1864 *to* 1868. *Rates expressed in United States gold values.*

TRADES.	MALES.						FEMALES OR (‡) CHILDREN.					
	1860.	1864.	1865.	1866.	1867.	1868.	1860.	1864.	1865.	1866.	1867.	1868.
Accordeon-makers	$2.16	$3.60	$2.52	$2.52	$2.52	$2.52	$1.08	$1.08	$0.96	$0.96	$0.96	$0.96
Artificial-flower makers	...	...	2.40	2.40	2.52	2.52	...	1.08	87	87	87	87
Bakers	1.08	1.44	2.16	2.16	2.52	2.88	...	...	...	...	...	...
Barbers	1.17	72	48	48	1.44	1.44	...	...	...	...	...	...
Basket-makers	1.80	2.52	1.92	1.92	2.16	2.16	...	...	...	...	...	...
Barrel-makers	...	...	3.60	3.60	3.60	3.60	...	...	...	...	...	...
Beer-brewers	3.24	3.60	2.16	2.88	2.88	3.24	...	...	...	...	...	...
Belt-makers, workers in bronze,	1.08	1.44	2.88	2.88	2.88	4.32	...	...	...	...	...	...
Bleachers	2.28	2.52	2.52	...	...	2.88	1.20	1.44	1.44	1.44	1.44	1.44
Bookbinders	2.04	2.52	2.40	2.40	2.64	2.88	1.08	1.44	...	...	...	...
Brass-founders	2.52	3.24	3.12	...	...	4.56	...	...	...	...	...	...
Brushmakers	1.80	2.16	72	72	72	72	...	...	...	...	...	...
Bricklayers	2.52	2.52	2.88	2.88	2.88	2.88	...	...	...	...	...	...
Brickmakers	2.52	2.52	3.24	3.24	3.60	3.60	...	...	...	...	...	...
Butchers	1.92	2.52	2.33	2.33	2.33	2.88	...	...	...	...	...	...
Button-makers	1.08	1.20	2.16	2.16	2.88	2.88	...	...	1.08	1.08	1.08	1.08
Card (playing) makers	2.88	3.24	2.88	2.88	2.88	2.88	1.08	1.20	...	...	...	...
Card (carding) makers	2.16	3.72	2.52	2.52	2.88	2.88	68	1.20	...	...	...	...
Cabinet-makers	2.16	2.88	2.16	2.16	2.16	2.16	...	...	...	...	...	...
Carpenters	2.64	2.76	2.70	2.79	2.88	3.24	...	...	...	...	...	...
Cartoon-makers	3.24	3.24	2.52	2.52	3.24	3.24	1.20	1.44	1.08	1.08	1.20	1.20
Cigar-makers	2.78	2.78	2.16	2.16	2.16	2.40	90	1.08	72	72	48	2.16
Chair-framers	2.16	2.16	2.52	2.52	2.88	2.88	...	...	...	...	...	...
Chemical manufacturers	1.62	1.98	2.40	2.40	2.40	2.40	72	96	...	...	...	...
Chimney sweeps	1.92	1.92	72	72	72	72	...	...	...	...	...	...
Cloth-finishers	2.37	2.37	3.24	3.24	3.24	3.24	90	1.08	‡96	‡96	‡96	‡96
Cloth-weavers	2.04	2.40	2.88	2.88	3.12	3.60	72	72	84	84	84	84
Cloth-shearers	1.80	2.52	2.88	2.88	2.88	2.88	...	...	...	...	...	...
Cloth-printers	3.24	2.16	3.24	3.24	...	3.60	1.44	1.62	‡48	...	...	‡58
Comb-makers	1.08	1.20	1.44	1.44	1.44	1.44	...	...	...	...	...	...
Confectioners	2.16	2.88	1.44	1.44	1.80	1.80	...	...	...	...	...	...

TABLE—*Continued.*

TRADES.	MALES.						FEMALES OR (‡) CHILDREN.					
	1860.	1864.	1865.	1866.	1867.	1868.	1860.	1864.	1865.	1866.	1867.	1868.
Coopers	2.40	2.88	3.60	3.60	3.60	3.60	...	...	...	...	...	...
Cotton-spinners	2.16	2.88	2.88	...	...	3.60	1.08	1.20	1.08	...	...	1.80
Crockeryware artists	4.32	5.04	4.32	5.04	5.04	5.04	...	...	...	...	...	...
Crockeryware workmen	2.88	2.88	...	...	...	...	...	...	...	...	...	...
Day laborers	1.68	1.92	2.04	2.07	2.16	2.34	...	...	...	...	...	...
Distillers	3.18	3.18	1.44	1.44	1.44	1.44	...	...	...	...	...	...
Dyers of silk and wool	1.44	1.80	2.88	2.88	2.88	2.88	...	...	...	...	...	...
Engravers	3.96	2.88	3.60	3.60	3.60	3.60	...	...	...	...	...	...
File-cutters	2.16	2.88	2.88	2.88	2.88	2.88	...	...	...	...	...	...
Fringe-makers	1.92	2.16	2.16	2.16	2.16	2.40	...	...	...	...	...	...
Furriers	1.56	1.80	2.42	2.42	...	3.60	...	...	...	...	...	...
Gardeners	1.80	2.16	1.44	1.44	1.44	1.44	...	...	...	...	...	...
Glaziers	1.08	1.26	2.64	2.64	2.88	2.88	...	...	...	...	...	...
Glass-workers	2.16	2.88	2.88	2.88	2.12	2.96	...	...	...	...	...	...
Glove-sewers	2.52	3.60	2.88	...	...	1.44	96	1.02	1.08	1.08	1.08	1.08
Goldsmiths	...	3.12	3.24	3.24	3.24	3.24	...	...	...	...	...	...
Gunsmiths	2.16	2.40	1.68	...	...	1.68	...	...	...	...	...	...
Hatters	1.68	2.16	2.16	2.16	2.52	2.52	...	...	...	...	...	...
Harness-makers	2.16	2.34	96	96	1.08	1.08	...	...	...	...	...	...
Iron and steel workers:												
Iron-founders	2.52	2.16 3.60	2.88	...	...	3.12 4.32	...	...	...	...	...	...
Machine-builders	3.24	3.24	3.12	3.12	3.17	3.24	...	...	...	...	...	...
Locksmiths	2.16	2.88	2.88	2.88	3.60	4.32	...	...	...	...	...	...
Cutlers	1.20	1.44	2.16	2.16	2.16	2.40	...	...	...	...	...	...
Nailmakers	...	2.52	2.40	2.40	2.40	2.40	...	...	...	...	...	...
Blacksmiths	1.08	1.20	96	96	1.08	1.08	...	...	...	...	...	...
Screw-makers	...	2.52	2.88	2.88	3.60	4.32	...	...	...	...	...	...
Lithographers	3.96	3.96	4.12	...	...	4.32	...	...	...	...	...	...
Loom-builders	2.16	2.88	2.52	2.52	2.52	2.52	...	...	...	...	...	...
Millers	2.05	2.15	1.92	1.92	1.92	1.92	...	...	...	...	...	...
Milliners	...	...	...	...	...	...	1.26	1.44	1.44	1.44	1.80	1.44
Mining:												
Carpenters	4.32	5.04	...	...	...	...	...	...	...	...	...	...
Miners	4.68	4.68	...	...	...	...	...	...	...	...	...	...
Drawers	2.52	2·52	...	...	...	...	...	...	...	...	...	...
Day laborers	2.30	2.50	...	...	...	...	...	...	...	...	...	...
Needlemakers	2.16	3.60	72	72	96	96	...	...	...	...	...	...
Oil-cloth makers	1.80	1.92	2.04	2.16	2.28	2.40	...	...	...	...	...	...
Potters	2.16	2.88	2.40	2.40	2.40	2.40	...	...	...	...	...	...
Printers:												
Compositors	3.60	3.60	3.24	3.24	3.60	3.60	...	...	...	...	...	...
Boys	1.06	1.04	72	...	...	96	...	...	‡24	...	...	‡30
Rope-makers	1.08	1.08	96	96	96	96	...	...	...	...	...	...
Saddlers	84	96	96	96	96	96	...	...	...	...	...	...
Saw-mill laborers	2.16	2.52	2.52	2.70	2.88	2.88	...	...	...	...	...	...
Slaters	1.80	1.80	1.92	1.92	1.92	1.92	...	...	...	...	...	...
Shoemakers	1.20	1.44	1.68	1.68	1.68	1.68	...	...	...	...	...	...
Shoemakers' tools	1.20	1.44	2.88	2.88	2.88	2.88	...	...	...	...	...	...
Soap-makers	1.80	2.12	2.52	2.52	...	2.88	...	...	...	...	...	...
Stocking-weavers (machine) ...	3.96	3.96	3.96	...	...	5.04	...	...	...	...	...	...
Stonemasons	2.16	2.64	2.64	...	...	3.60	...	...	...	...	...	...
Stonecutters	3.36	3.36	5.76	...	6.48	7.20	...	...	...	...	...	...
Stone quarrymen	1.98	2.16	2.16	2 16	2.16	2.16	...	...	...	...	...	...
Tailors	1.20	1.68	2.88	2.88	2.88	2.88	...	...	...	...	...	...
Tanners	1.08	1.20	1.08	1.08	1.08	1.44	...	...	...	...	...	...
Turners	96	1·08	96	96	1.08	1.08	...	...	...	...	...	...
Tapestry-makers	2.52	2.88	2.40	2.40	2.40	2.40	...	...	...	...	...	...
Watchmakers	1.08	1.08	2.16	2.16	2.40	2.88	...	...	...	...	...	...
Wheelwrights	2.16	2.52	2.28	2.40	2.52	2.88	...	...	...	...	...	...
Worsted work	...	...	1.44	1.68	1.68	1.68	60	48	48	48	60	60
Wire-cloth makers	2.52	2.88	2.16	2.16	2.16	2.16	...	...	...	...	...	...
Weavers (silk)	2.16	2.16	2.16	2.16	2.40	2.40	...	...	...	...	...	...
Wool combers	2.88	3.24	2.52	2.52	2.70	2.88	1.08	1.08	1.08	1.08	1.08	1.20

My colleague [Mr. Townsend] hands me a letter containing a statement of American wages in some of the same branches of labor. That gentleman may contrast them with the wages of Germany, as set forth by the Statistical Bureau of Prussia, I will also hand the letter to the reporters:

PHŒNIXVILLE, PENNSYLVANIA, *March* 21, 1870.

Dear Sir: Your favor of the 16th is before me.

Below I give you the prices paid per day to our principal workmen, as follows:

Rolling-mill on rails and beams.

	Per day.
Heaters	$4 50
Helpers	1 70
Extra helpers	1 60
Finishing rollerman	6 75
Roughing rollerman	2 70
Catchers	2 25
Hooks	1 80
Hot straighteners	2 50
Cold straighteners	3 60
Stochers	2 35
Pilers	1 50
Laborers	1 50
Engineers	2 10

Merchant iron.

Heaters	4 37
Helpers	1 70
Extra helpers	1 60
Finishing roller	4 05
Roughing roller	2 12
Catchers	1 60
Roughing catcher	1 30
Straightener	1 90
Engineers	2 80

Bar mill.

	Per day.
Heaters	$3 87
Helpers	1 70
Rollers	2 12
Catchers	1 55
Hooks	1 60

Heavy merchant iron.

Heaters	4 37
Helpers	1 70
Finishing roller	5 00
Roughers	2 35
Catchers	1 50
Straightener	1 50
Mauler	1 50
Engineer	1 90

Puddling.

Puddler	3 00
Puddler's helpers	2 00

Labor.

Common labor	1 40

I am unable to give the wages paid for the above classes of work either in England, France, or Belgium, but I am satisfied from the prices, as we have had them from time to time from these, that their present pay is not over an average of 40 per cent. of above.

Respectfully, JOHN GRIFFIN,
General Superintendent.

HON. WASHINGTON TOWNSEND.

Mr. Allison. Will the gentleman yield to me for a question?

Mr. Kelley. Yes, sir.

Mr. Allison. I will ask the gentleman whether that is not a report of wages paid by a company that manufactures what are known as iron beams for vessels and bridges?

Mr. Kelley. They manufacture beams, rails, and other heavy forms of iron.

Mr. Allison. And is it not a company which with three others has agreed upon an established list of prices for that class of articles, which prices embrace the prices abroad, together with the tariff duty and a profit on the cost of manufacture?

Mr. Kelley. I cannot answer the question, because I do not know. I can, however, say that I have never heard such an allegation. But, my dear sir, I do not care what they have agreed to do, if they are thereby enabling American workingmen to keep their children at school, well fed and comfortably clad, to maintain their seats in church, and to lay by something for old age and a rainy day, and not compelling them, as German workmen in like employments are compelled to do, to take their wives and daughters as colaborers into iron and coal mines and furnaces and rolling-mills, so that they may together earn enough to eke out a miserable subsistence.

Mr. Allison. I do not take issue with the gentleman upon that question, but merely desire to call his attention to the fact that this is one of four establishments that have a monopoly in this business.

Mr. Kelley. A monopoly! A workman a monopolist! A poor workman for wages a monopolist! A man who is earning daily wages by hard work in a mine, a furnace, or a rolling-mill will hardly be regarded as a monopolist, though his pay may be ten times what he could get in his native town. No, sir; such men are not monopolists, though free traders constantly denounce them as such.

CINCINNATI—HER WORKSHOPS AND WORKMEN.

Mr. Chairman, 90 per cent. of the cost of iron in all its forms is the wages of labor, and the money paid for this labor goes very largely to pay for wheat and pork and mutton and beef that are eaten, and woolen clothes that are worn by the workmen and their families. The wages of well-paid laborers thus find their way to the pockets of the farmer and the wool-grower.

Mr. Stevenson. Will the gentleman yield to me now for a question?

Mr. Kelley. Yes, sir.

Mr. Stevenson. It seems that the gentleman has just discovered that there are some manufacturers in Cincinnati. I want to know whether he has not also discovered that more than half of the capital and labor and production of those manufactories are in the articles of wood, iron, leather, and paper, upon which I want the duties reduced, and whether it is not to the interest of those producers to have cheap raw material?

Mr. Kelley. It is the interest of the working people of Cincinnati that the general rate of wages shall be maintained at the highest point. It is not for the interest of any mechanical producer in this country to have the duties on his productions, or others which involve much labor, so reduced that the cheap labor of France, Belgium, Germany, and Britain can come in competition with them in our home market. And thus I fully answer the gentleman's question.

The gentleman is mistaken. I have not just discovered that there are manufactories in Cincinnati, for as I heard the gentleman pleading for a law which would inevitably check their prosperity and progress and reduce the wages of labor I thought of old Charles Cist, and wondered whether his bones were not rattling in his coffin. From almost the birth of Cincinnati he was a champion of protection, and did more than any other man to build up her workshops and manufactories, and more than twenty years ago devoted a day to conducting me through many of the largest of them.

But I want to allude further to the remarks of the gentleman from Ohio [Mr. Stevenson]. Speaking of Pennsylvania, he said:

"Ah! she is shrewd! New England heretofore has had the reputation of great adroitness in taking care of her own interest, but Pennsylvania carries off the palm. Quietly she sits looking out for herself, we giving bounty, she appropriating it. And now, what is the result? If we suppose, for the sake of argument, that the tariff on iron and coal is added to the cost, then Pennsylvania received a premium on her production of iron and coal in 1868 of $14,859,168."

Has the gentleman a settled opinion on the question, Is a protective duty a tax or bounty? Or is he, like Bunsby, unable to give an opinion for want of premises on which to base it? "If so be," said Bunsby, on a memorable occasion, "as he's dead, my opinion is he won't come back no more; if so be as he's alive, my opinion is he will. Do I say he will? No. Why not? Because the bearings of this observation lays in the application on it." [Laughter.] "If we suppose for the sake of argument." A teacher of political economy that has not yet made up his mind whether a protecting duty is a tax or not comes here and arraigns Pennsylvania, and holds her up to ridicule as a cormorant fattening upon public bounty or plunder. But let me go on.

Mr. Stevenson. Will the gentleman give us his opinion upon that subject?

Mr. Kelley. I have given it, and will give it again.

PROTECTIVE DUTIES NOT A TAX.

Mr. Chairman, I apprehended that no enlightened student of political economy regards a protective duty as a tax.* Even the gentleman from Iowa [Mr. Allison] admitted that in most cases it is not; yet influenced, as I think, by a clever story which the chairman of our committee, who is somewhat of a wag, tells, he does not think the principle applies to pig-iron. I hope our chairman, who I see does me the honor to listen, will pardon me for referring to the anecdote. It runs thus: Some years ago, during the days of the Whig party, when the chairman of the committee [Mr. Schenck] was here as a Representative of that party and a friend of protection, he met as a member of this House a worthy old German from Reading, Pennsylvania, a staunch Democrat, but strongly in favor of protection on iron. The gentleman from Ohio,

---

* In a country whose resources, embracing every known mineral substance, are undeveloped, and which, though capable of producing boundless supplies of silk, cotton, flax, and wool, depends on foreigners for a large part of the fabrics in which to clothe its people, the question whether a protective duty is a tax touches but one and that a subordinate aspect of the problem a statesman must consider. This is well put by Dr. Bushnell in his recent article in *Scribner's Monthly*. He says:

"How then is it that free-trade science is going, as we hear, to settle peremptorily all the great questions of public economy? For if we set ourselves down to it as the test of economy, and say it is final, we are by and by obliged to ask, is there nothing to be done or thought of in the world that is out of economy, and rightly spurns it? May not the worst economy sometimes be the best? To be fostering modes of production, where the trade-scale balance shows only disadvantage, wears a bad look certainly, as respects the matter of economy. *But how many and vast supplies are wanted that must not be left to the uncertainties of trade; where to higgle over the expense would be even a contemptible weakness?* This is true in particular of all the supplies that are needed for the equipment of the state of public war. Without these no people is a proper nation, or at least by any possibility a strong one. *Therefore these we must not only have, but must have the way of making ourselves, at any cost.*"

who is fond of a joke, said to him one day, "Mr. R., I think I shall go with the free-traders on the iron sections of the tariff bill, especially on pig-iron." "Why will you do that?" was the response. "Well, my people want cheap plows, nails, horseshoes, etc." "But," replied the old German, "we make iron in Pennsylvania; and if you want to keep up the supply and keep the price down you ought to encourage the manufacture." "But you know," said our chairman, "that a protective duty is a tax, and adds just that much to the cost of the article." "Yes, I suppose it does generally increase the cost of the thing just so much as the duty is; all the leaders of our party say so, and we say so in our convention platforms and our public meeting resolutions; but, Mr. Schenck, somehow or other I think it don't work just that way mit pig-iron." [Laughter.]

The gentleman, while admitting that protective duties do not always, or even generally, increase the price of the manufactured article, thinks "that somehow or other it don't work that way mit pig-iron." Now, I think that iron in all its forms is subject to every general law, and that the duty of $9 per ton on pig-iron has reduced the price measured in wheat, wool, and other agricultural commodities, and increased the supply to such an extent as to prove that the duty has been a boon and not a tax. On nothing else produced in this country has the influence of protection been so broadly and beneficently felt by the people of the country at large.

On the 11th of January I submitted to the House some remarks in the nature of a review of the last report of Commissioner D. A. Wells, and showed that after the production of American pig-iron had been without increase for a decade, under the stimulus of this duty we more than doubled it in six years. The authentic figures I exhibited were as follows:

Production of pig-iron in England and the United States from 1854 to 1862, inclusive.

	England.	United States.
1854	3,069,838	716,674
1855	3,218,154	754,178
1856	3,586,377	874,428
1857	3,659,447	798,157
1858	3,456,064	705,094
1859	3,712,904	840,427
1860	3,826,752	913,774
1861	3,712,390	731,564
1862	3,943,469	787,662

The Morrill tariff, which raised the duty to $6, went into effect in 1861. In 1864 the duty was raised to $9. The results have been as follows:

	England.	United States.
1863	4,510,040	947,604
1864	4,767,951	1,135,497
1865	4,819,254	931,582
1866	4,523,897	1,350.943
1867	4,761,028	1,461,626
1868	....	1,603.000
1869	....	1,900,000

In connection with these figures I then invited the attention of the House to the fact that we built last year sixty-five furnaces in fifteen States of the Union, and that fifty-eight more had been begun. A few years more of such wonderful progress and we will produce from our own coal and iron our entire supply of iron and steel, and compete with England in supplying the demands of the world. The vast demand created by the extension of our railroad system, and those of Russia and India, are exceeding the capacity of England. She cannot largely increase her production without largely increasing its cost. The gentleman from Iowa was yesterday constrained to admit that the price of English iron has gone up steadily during the last year, because the demand is in excess of her capacity to produce; yet the price of American pig-iron has fallen at least $6 per ton on all grades within the last ten months. What is the cause of this reduction? Not British competition—and that is the only possible foreign competition—for the price of British iron has risen. No, sir; the price of American iron has gone down under domestic competition and the general depreciation of prices. Keep your duty high enough to induce other men to build furnaces and rolling-mills, and before five years you will find American iron cheapened to the level of the markets of the world, and that without a reduction of wages, but probably with an advance

HOW THE INTERNAL REVENUE CAN BE DISPENSED WITH.

But I return to my subject. The gentleman from Ohio asked from what eight sources $130,000,000 of revenue can be derived. I find I overstated the number required; but six articles are necessary to give us all the income we need this year from internal taxes. Let me state the receipts from these six sources during the last year. They were as follows:

From distilled spirits....................	$45,026,401
From tobacco..............................	23,430,709
From fermented liquors....................	6,099,879
From banks and bankers....................	3,335,516
From incomes..............................	34,791,855
From stamps...............................	16,420,710
	$129,104,068

Sir, month by month, since the close of the last fiscal year, the receipts from each of these sources have been larger than those of the corresponding month of last year. There is a regular monthly increase in every item. Retaining but these six sources of internal revenue we can mitigate their exactions at least by increasing the exemption from the income tax or reducing the rate, and still obtain an excess over the amount that is absolutely required. I am in favor of adopting this course, and believe that in three years more, or in, at most, five years, we can wipe out all our internal taxes except stamps and tobacco.

Mr. Schenck. And spirits.

Mr. Kelley. No. I am anxious to make spirits free as soon as we can. I would make this change in the interests of the farmers of the country. But I do not wish to run into a digression, and will recur to this point. I proceed to invite the attention of the committee to the cost of collecting the internal revenue. In 1867 it was $8,982,-686; in 1868, $9,327,301; and in 1869, $7,218,610, requiring for the three years the expenditure of $25,528,597. Why, sir, its abolition would be equal to the payment of $133,000,000 of the public debt. We hope to fund our interest-bearing debt at an average of 4½ per cent. This will save $18,000,000. Before the end of this fiscal year there will be in the Treasury $100,000,000 of our bonds, the interest on which is $6,000,000 per annum, which, with the other sum and the cost of collecting the internal revenue, would make a reduction of $32,500,000 in the annual expenses of the Government. If the bill under discussion shall become a law we will, I believe, although it lightens the burdens of the people at least $20,000,000 per annum, be able in five years to make even distilled spirits free, and rely on stamps and the tax on tobacco.

THE EFFECT OF PROTECTION ON PRICES AGAIN.

The gentleman from Iowa said that pig-iron sells at $40 a ton, and yields at least $15 profit. I have *The Iron Age*, a paper of the highest authority among dealers in iron and hardware, and I do not find it puts it at the price named by the gentleman. March 12 it quotes prices at Philadelphia of American pig-iron, No. 1, for foundery use, as $33 50 to $34; No. 2, foundery, $31 50 to $32; gray forge, $30 to $31; white and mottled, $28 50 to $29. There is some difference between these prices and $40; and if the gentleman was as far out of the way in the profits of iron-makers as in the current price of iron he has shown clearly enough that there is no profit in making pig-iron at this time. The gentleman from Ohio [Mr. Garfield] hands me a still later paper, showing a further reduction. But every business man knows that the price is receding under the rapid increase of domestic competition.

The English people know what would be the effect of the reduction of our duty. I hold in my hand the annual circular of a leading iron firm in London advising the English iron-makers of the state of the trade, and the prospect for this year. Let me read from this circular, which, I may remark, was evidently not intended for American consumption:

"No. 58 Old Broad Street,
"London, *December* 31, 1869.

"Sir: This has been a prosperous year for the iron-masters. Our monthly advice of exports will have revealed the cause. Three countries alone—Russia, India, and the United States—have purchased 940,000 tons of British rails. Under these unprecedented exports the price has ruled firm, and good Erie rails are now worth £6 15*s*. net.

"Coal and pig-iron.—Over-production has kept down the price; but at length the demand for pigs appears to have overtaken the supply, and they are firm at an advance of 5*s*. upon the year.

"Old rails have been largely used by rail-mills, and have advanced 10*s*. also during the year.

"Wages have advanced over the whole mining district. At a meeting in London this week the Welsh iron-masters voted an advance of 10 per cent.

"Cost of the finished rails to the manufacturer is thus settled. The buyer is, however, more interested in the relation of supply to demand.

"The supply of railway bars has greatly increased; many merchant bar-mills have taken to rails, and all the mills have increased their make. This increased product has, however, found ready sale, and will not probably decrease.

"The demand for next year promises to be good. Most of the mills have orders for three, and some for six months. Home railways must buy more largely than in 1869. India will also take more rails. Russia is not so eager a buyer as at this time last year. The Government, however, continues to build roads for commercial and military purposes, and while the English investors retain their present partiality for Russian securities there will be no lack of money. *Yet with the present out-turn a material reduction of the American duty, or something equally significant, is necessary to advance the price above £7.*"

Yes, Mr. Chairman, a material reduction of the American duty, or something equally significant, is necessary to enable the British iron-master to advance his price beyond £7; and the day the telegraph announces that we have reduced our duty on pig and railroad iron will be the day on which the price of British iron will go up. I pray gentlemen to be admonished by this circular.

I have also an article from the Manchester *Examiner* and *Times* of January 3, 1870, relating to cotton, as compared with the year preceding; and from what I shall read it will be seen that iron is not the only English interest which will be improved by the reduction of our duties. The organ of the cotton-spinners of Manchester says:

"As compared with the years preceding the American war, this country has received during the past few years £7,000,000 to £8,000,000 less per annum for the cost of manufacturing cotton, and there can be no question that in comparison with the cost of cotton this country has marketed the cheapest cloth ever made; *and if cotton manufacturers on the continent of Europe had not been protected by high tariffs they would have been swept from the field.*"

Yes, say the *Examiner* and *Times* of Manchester and the free-trade league, repeal the protective duties on cotton, which are so abhorrent to the gentleman from Iowa, and the cotton manufactures of the country will be swept from the field.

THE TARIFFS OF ENGLAND AND FRANCE DISCRIMINATE AGAINST AMERICAN FARMERS.

The gentleman from New York [Mr. Brooks] held up the English tariff to our view. Some may have been surprised to hear me say that I was very anxious to hasten the day when the tax on distilled spirits should be repealed. But gentlemen from the agricultural districts, do you know that France and England discriminate specially against you and your constituents in their tariffs, and that

England derives nearly half her customs from inordinate duties on the productions of the American farmer, or from agricultural products with which this country could supply her? Let us look at the facts. The gentleman from New York holding up the tariff of England, said it yields £21,602,414 sterling, or $108,000,000; but he did not invite your attention to the fact that she raises over $54,-000,000, or more than one half, by duties that discriminate against our farmers. Yet such is the case. She raises from tobacco and snuff, one of our leading agricultural staples and its immediate product, £6,542,460, or $32,-712,300. The friends of free trade say we do not import enough English iron; we do not import enough English cotton goods; we do not import enough English woolen goods, considering how cheap we can buy them all. If we are to reduce our duties and import more I beg the Representatives of the farming States of the West to demand something like reciprocity on behalf of their constituents, for whose grain there will be no market. Every yard of cotton and woolen goods and every ton of iron represent the grain and meat consumed by the families of the men who produce it; and while our grain goes to waste for the want of purchasers, the friends of protection protest against importing that grown in other countries, even when converted into cloth or iron. The cloth and iron would be as good if made where well-paid laborers eat freely of American wheat, butter, and meat; and to those who cannot sell their crop at any price a neighboring furnace, factory, or rolling-mill would be a blessing, even though they could not buy cloth or iron at English prices.* But I must proceed.

---

* Those only who know how large a number of horses, mules, and oxen are required to haul the ore, coal, and limestone, from the ore bed, mine and quarry to the furnace and the pig-iron thence to the point of shipment or use, and how many men are required to produce a thousand tons of pig-iron, can form an idea of the market for corn, oats, hay, straw, wheat, vegetables, and animal food, the development of the Marquette mines has created. How rapid this has been under a protective tariff, the following article from a Western paper shows:

IRON-MAKING IN THE WEST. PROGRESS OF THE MARQUETTE DISTRICT.

"The Marquette (Michigan) iron district is invested with special interest as one of the most recently developed iron-producing regions, and as the source whence the ore is received for one-fifth of all the iron manufactured in the United States. The history and statistics of this region, which lies on the shores of Lake Superior, have been recently compiled by Mr. A. P. Swineford, and present some gratifying facts. The following statement of the production of ore and iron,

I have shown that of the $108,000,000 England raises by her tariff she gets $32,712,300 by duties on one of our agricultural staples. Her duties on tobacco are taxes, for England has no tobacco-fields to develop. They are, therefore, not protective duties. Like our duties on tea, coffee, pepper, and spices, they are taxes purely. But let us go a little further into this matter. England raises $21,667,565 on spirits. This is an absolute discrimination

---

from 1856 to 1870, inclusive, together with the aggregate value, shows surprising progress, and affords conclusive evidence of the value of our tariff legislation:

Year.	Iron Ore.	Pig-Iron.	Value.
1856	7,000	....	$28,000
1857	21,000	....	60,000
1858	31,035	1,629	249,202
1859	65,679	7,258	575,529
1860	116,908	5,600	736,496
1861	45,430	7,970	419,501
1862	115,721	8,590	984,977
1863	185,257	9,813	1,416,935
1864	235,123	13,832	1,867,215
1865	196,256	12,883	1,590,430
1866	286,972	18,437	2,405,960
1867	466,076	30,911	3,475,820
1868	507,813	38,246	3,992,413
1869	633,238	39,003	4,968,435
1870	856,471	49,298	6,300,170
Total	3,771,989	243,460	$29,069,883

"The product of 1870 was from 16 mines. The pig-iron finds a market in all parts of the country. The largest portion of the ore is sent to Cleveland, whence it is re-shipped to the coal-fields of the Mahoning and Shenango Valleys by railroad. About 100 furnaces in Ohio and Pennsylvania use Lake Superior ore, while nearly all the charcoal furnaces in the Northwest are supplied with it. The number of furnaces is rapidly multiplying—the new ones built in 1869 increasing the demand for Lake Superior ore by at least 100,000 tons. The cost of producing a ton of pig iron in the Marquette district and of placing it in the Chicago market is estimated at $27 50, resulting from the following items: 1½ tons ore at $5 per ton, $7 50; 2 tons coal, $6 per ton, $12; flux, $1; labor, $3; incidentals, $1; freight to Chicago, $3. The cost of producing merchant iron and delivering it in Chicago is estimated at $58 62, which is made up of the following items: 1¼ tons pig metal, $24 50 per ton, $30 62; 2 tons coal, at $5 per ton, $10; labor, $15; freight to Chicago, $3. The average cost of mining and delivering ore in the cars at the mines is estimated at $2. The cost of transportation to Cleveland via Marquette, was, last year, $4 25, though in many instances better figures were obtained. At these rates the ore is put upon the dock at Cleveland, at a cost of $6 25, where it is sold at $8 and upward, leaving a net profit of $1 75 per ton; but this return is on the average considerably reduced by other expenses. The iron ores of this district are generally found in hills, rising from 100 to 500 feet above the level of the surrounding country. These hills are simply immense deposits of iron ore, though partially or wholly covered by layers of earth and rock. It is true they are also found in the valleys, but where so found are usually covered with a deep drift, and consequently cannot be so easily mined. Heavy losses were suffered in the early development of the mines, but all the mines now working are paying dividends, and liberal profits have been realized during late years."

against our grain. Were that duty removed the American farmer and distiller would be working together, and instead of exporting wheat and corn at prices that will not cover the cost of production and transportation their produce would be manufactured into alcohol, pork, and lard oil; and while our own laboring people would have cheaper provisions, the farmer would greatly reduce the cost of transportation and have an ample market for his grain in these advanced products or manufactures. Yet gentlemen representing agricultural districts plead with us to admit British goods at lower rates, while she gathers $54,599,865 in a single year by imposing such duties on tobacco as greatly diminish its consumption; and such on spirits as preclude the importation of our grain in the only forms in which it can be profitably exported.

ENGLAND A HIDEOUS MONOPOLY—FREE TRADE SUPPORTS IT.

Mr. Brooks of New York. Let me state that our great agricultural products—cotton, which is an immense product, and wheat, corn, etc.—are admitted duty free.

Mr. Kelley. To that I reply that they take our cotton because they cannot live without it, and our wheat and corn when they cannot buy cereals cheaper elsewhere. France has a duty on wheat and flour even when imported in French vessels. Our great wheat fields are too far from the sea-board, and the cost of transportation is too great for us to send them grain in bulk at present prices. The cheapest way of transporting corn is in the form of alcohol. In this form we could send it profitably were their duties not prohibitory. England will take raw materials from countries from which she can buy cheapest. But her much lauded free trade does not offer any advantage to the American farmer. Gentlemen talk about monopolists, and aver that protection fosters monopolies. Sir, the world has never seen another so heartless, so unrelenting, and so gigantic a monopoly as the British Government and the manufacturing power that sustains it. It is a monopoly which has desolated Ireland and swept her factories from the face of the earth. Ireland, less than a century ago, before the union, the home of a contented people, and the seat of busy and prosperous industries, is now a land whose people are born only to be watched and hunted as felons, or exiled from the land they love so well. The manufacturing and landed monopoly of England but a few years ago huddled into their graves the decaying bodies of more than 1,000,000 of the people of Ireland, who died of starvation in a single year.*

It is a monopoly which has inflicted on British India wrongs even greater than these. Three years ago the air of the whole wide district of Orissa was fetid with the stench rising from the decaying bodies of more than 1,000,000 people who had starved in one of the richest agricultural regions in the world, because under England's enlightened free trade they were not permitted to diversify their industries, and when their single crop failed they were permitted to starve, as the Irish were when the rot assailed their only crop, the potato. This English monopoly is so absolute and selfish that it will not allow provinces and colonies to diversify their industry. It binds them to the culture of one product—India, cotton, and Ireland, men for exportation. Shall she also hold the people of the Northwest as her commercial subjects and doom them to raise wheat and wheat alone? We can break its power and overthrow this monstrous monopoly. Yes, by peaceful arts, without the clash of arms, we can emancipate the hundreds of millions of people England now oppresses. The source of her power is her commercial and manufacturing supremacy, and this we can and should undermine, as we are its chief support. With our cotton-fields, our widespread and inexhaustible deposits of all the metals, and our immense sheep-walks, we should supply all our wants. When we do this our commerce will revive, for populous nations that supply their own markets always produce a surplus which they can export at low prices. But now England properly regards us as a dependency more profitable than "all the English-speaking dependencies of the empire." On this point the London *Times* of February 25, when discussing the bill now under consideration, says:

* Ireland with a population of 5,500,000 has 15,500,000 acres of arable land, most of it naturally rich; while Belgium, with a population of 4,894,000, has but 6,428,000 acres, generally by nature poor. Yet Ireland it is which, according to the "dismal philosopher," is "over populated," and it certainly is the country from which men flee to escape beggary and starvation,—that starvation which has within a quarter of a century carried off many hundreds of thousands of their fellow countrymen. Belgium on the contrary is one of the most prosperous countries of Europe—its people steadily advancing in material wealth as well as in intelligence and happiness.

"The fiscal policy of the United States is for us a subject of no remote or transient interest. Although statistics may be adduced to prove that in proportion to population the colonies are our best customers, yet in the mass our trade with republican America is by far the largest item in the balance-sheet of our exports to foreign countries, and is nearly equal to that with all the English-speaking dependencies of the empire."

A HOME MARKET—A PREDICTION FULFILLED.

Gentlemen sneer at the idea of a home market. Sir, on the 1st of June, 1868, we had under consideration a proposition to permit table whisky to remain in bond under certain conditions. In the course of the discussion I urged upon gentlemen from the West who were opposing it the propriety of giving effect to that proposition. I pressed upon the attention of the House the fact that age quadrupled the value by improving the quality of fine whisky, and that whisky distilled from American grain was superseding French brandy in general use. I urged the importance of this to the grain-growing States. Turning to my remarks I find the following prediction, the fulfilment of which has occurred even before I expected it:

"The people of the Northwest, it seems to me, are specially interested in this question. They will find that they cannot afford to expel from their inland section of the country any branch of manufactures. They need the opportunity to export their grain concentrated in the form of whisky, high-wines, or other manufactures. I am no Cassandra and they will not believe me, but I tell them they are entering upon a competition that will exclude them from the markets of the world if they depend upon the export of their grain in bulk as food or mere raw material. Do you mark, gentlemen of Missouri, Illinois, and Wisconsin, that California is loud in the expression of her gratitude for the fact that 130 vessels have been added to the fleet for carrying her grain to New York and transatlantic ports? They can send grain in bulk 23,000 miles to the seaboard of New England or Old England at less cost for transportation than you can send yours to the sea-board by rail. Oregon is groaning under her crop of wheat, and her people are fearing that means of its transportation to market may not be at hand. But this distant competition is not what you have most cause to dread. The South, no longer your customer for food for man and beast, looms up your competitor. Her advantages over you are mainfold as they are manifest. She lies between you and the ocean. Her grain-fields are upon the banks of navigable rivers which flow to the Gulf or the ocean, and at or near the mouth of each is a sea-port. From Norfolk around to Galveston, Texas, the grain of the farmers of the several States may be floated to the sea-board upon rafts and there find shipping. England and western Europe are not the countries to which we chiefly export grain and flour. Our chief markets for these are Central and South America, and the islands to which the Southern States are neighbors; and I tell you that if the people of the far Northwest do not take heed, and by diversifying their industry convert their raw materials into more compact productions, the day is not three years distant when their crops will waste in the fields for the want of a market to which they will pay the cost of transportation."*

Not two years have gone by, and you are crying out that you have raised wheat in vain, that there is no market for it; that the cost of getting it to a market consumes it. Ay, and the gentleman from Iowa [Mr. Allison] says that in the face of these facts we are offering inducements to thousands to go at wheat-growing, that the homestead law is tempting immigrants to engage in wheat-growing and add to the unsalable and unavailable stock. That is true; and how would he improve matters? He agrees with me that the homestead law is beneficent and should not be repealed. What, then, is his proposition. It is identical with those we have heard from so many gentlemen—repeal the duties on coal, and salt, and reduce those on hides, lumber, iron, and woolen goods.

This is the burden and refrain of all the sweet singers trained in the musical academy of D. A. Wells, Commissioner of Revenue, and let us right here test its merit. Lower the duties on coal, salt, lumber, hides, iron, and woolen goods. Well, how will this increase the number of consumers of American grain or diminish the number of grain-growers? There are more than 1,500,000 of our people engaged in or dependent on the labor of producing these articles. What will become of them? They cannot live on "rye and potatoes," as German workmen in the

---

* The prices of grain in Philadelphia, July 1st, 1868, and July 1st, 1871, were as follows:

1868.		1871.	
Wheat	$2.30 @ $2.37	Wheat	$1.40 @ 1.54
Corn	1.10 @ 1.13	Corn	.73 @ .76
Oats	.85 @ .89	Oats	.61 @ .66

But even at these reduced rates there is, as I know by observation and intercourse with many of their people, while traversing each State during July and August, 1871, no market for the immense crops with which the farmers of Missouri, Iowa, Kansas and Nebraska have been, shall I say, blessed or cursed. As they cannot sell their grain and provisions, they are of course without money with which to pay for manufactured articles whether foreign or American. A few additional forges, furnaces, rolling-mills, and woolen factories would have developed the coal-fields of each State and given the farmers a renumerative home market for every bushel of corn and wheat, and saved the cost of transportation on the small amount for which they may find a market.

same trades do. They will not even be content to get meat once a week, as the workmen of England are; and if they be not, work must stop. And I ask gentlemen from the grain country what they suppose these people will do with themselves when the fire has gone out in the forge and furnace, and the loom and spindle stand still, and the salt-kettle rusts, and there is no work in the coal mine because the manufactures that made a market for it have been transferred to foreign countries in which wages are low and where the "working people live on rye and potatoes"?

Thank God, we cannot doom them to this fate. The homestead law is their protection. In a cabin on 120 acres of public land they can raise wheat, potatoes, and a few sheep and pigs; the old-fashioned spinning-wheel and loom, easily made by skilled mechanics, will convert their home-grown wool into fabrics, and they can thus live till wiser legislators succeed us and reanimate the general industries of the country by restoring the protective system now in force.

Is theirs the true remedy? Is free trade a specific for all or any of our ills? No, sir, it is sheer quackery, charlatanism. The only cure for the evil of which western grain-growers complain, is to increase the number of consumers and relatively decrease the number of growers of wheat and corn; raise, if possible, the wages of workmen so as to make mechanical employments attractive; say to the farmers' sons, "There is work and good wages for you in the machine-shop, the forge, the furnace, or the mill;" say to the men whose capital is unproductive on farms, "Build mills, sink shafts to the coal-bed which underlies your farm; avail yourselves of the limestone quarry and the ore-bed, whether of iron, lead, copper, zinc, or nickel; employ your industry and capital so that it shall be profitable to you, your country, and mankind;" and in a little while you will cheapen iron and steel and make an adequate market for all the grain of the country. The gentleman's remedy is the theory of the homeopathic physician, that like cures like, which though it may be correct in physics, is not an approved maxim in social science.

Mr. Allison. I would like the gentleman to state how long it will be before that happy period will arrive?

Mr. Kelley. Well, sir, I cannot tell exactly. It will

depend upon the degree of promptness with which the remedy is applied. But if the Clerk will do me the kindness to give me a little rest by reading a letter from an Irish patriot, one who knew England's tenderness for her laboring people experimentally at home in Ireland, and who laid one of his limbs away in the service of our country during the war, and now lives in Quincy, Illinois, I will endeavor to give the gentleman some idea.

The Clerk read as follows:

"We have a population of 35,000 or 40,000, and our citizens are just commencing to awake to the necessity of encouraging local manufacturing. We have 2 paper mills, 10 flour mills, 5 tobacco factories; sales $1,300,000; 9 machine-shops; sales $1,050,000; 5 machine founderies; 5 stove founderies turned out last year 36,400 stoves, amounting to $473,200 cash sales; 2 boiler shops, turning out $216,000 per year; 15 wagon and plow shops, with a capital of $260,000; 4 planing mills, capital $180,000; 14 manufacturers of saddles and harness, capital $233,400; and numerous others too tedious to mention. There is a company at present engaged in boring for coal, with fine prospects of success. If we can only get coal here manufacturing will spring up all around us. I have thought some of organizing a stock company to build factories and supply funds to encourage skilled workmen to enter into what is called the coöperative system. I shall shortly test the matter to see if it can be made to work.

"If the friends of protection can hold their own till after the taking of the census the crisis will be passed, for that will show such progress in the material wealth of the nation that it will require a bold man indeed to attack our system of labor. It is useless for us to talk of competing with England while she keeps as many of her people in her poor-houses as she does in her public schools—a country that expends seven-eighths more to keep up her poor-houses than she does to support her schools. England and Scotland have a population of 24,599,277, for the education of which she has 14,591 schools, with 12,832 teachers, costing annually $4,212,500, while she expends for her poor-houses annually $32,595,000. Compare her with Illinois, a State sixty years ago in possession of the savages, but now possessing a population of about 2,500,000, with 11,000 schools and 20,000 teachers, costing $6,500,000 annually, more than 50 per cent. greater than England, with a population ten times larger than us. The free-trader says that pauperism is growing less in England under her free-trade system; but I find, from Purdy's Report in 1866, she had 842,860; and I see by the American Cyclopedia of 1868 for that year 1,034,832 paupers are reported. These are facts for the American people to profit by. It is reported that there are now in London more than 80,000 skilled workmen out of employment. We hear much about English liberty, but I have been of the opinion that the kind of liberty they are enjoying is that the wolf accords the lamb, or the strong the weak in all nations—a liberty which, I trust, will never find a place among our institutions.

"The sympathizers or advocates of this English system say that free trade will give us a market for our surplus produce in Europe. But I find the more we ship the less we receive. In 1868 we exported to England 4,414,230 hundred weight of wheat, receiving therefor $17,952,850; in 1869, for the same period, 7,938,818 hundred weight, receiving therefrom only $17,740,770, or $211,000 less than we received for half the amount the previous year. If we were to change our policy, and instead of sending our wheat to England induce those 80,000 skilled workmen to come to us we would not then be compelled to look to England for a market. They will be compelled to come to us for our cotton and tobacco; but there is no need of us going to them for manufactured goods. We can take their surplus labor, transfer it to this country, which would ultimately tend to the welfare of both, and thereby accomplish more than the sentimental philanthropists of Europe and America can ever do by preaching 'free trade.' We are influenced too much by the polical economists of Europe, who write to tickle the fancy of the wealthy few without any regard to the rights of the laboring millions."

Mr. Kelley. I desire in this connection, and before turning to other topics, to present a brief extract from a speech made in the United States Senate by the experienced merchant and enligtened statesman who represents New Jersey in that body, Hon. Alexander G. Cattell. In the course of his remarks on the 22d of January, 1867, he said:

"But, Mr. President, the harmony of interests which exists between agriculture and manufactures, and the truth of the position I have taken, are clearly shown by actual results. I am sure the Senate will excuse me if I draw an illustration from personal observation in my own mercantile life. Twenty years ago last autumn I embarked in the trade in breadstuffs in the city of Philadelphia. At that time, and for some succeeding years, the entire volume of my business was made up of consignments of agricultural products from the valleys of the Susquehanna, the Juniata, and the Lehigh. I have not the figures at command, but I am sure I speak within bounds when I say that my own house and the four or five others doing business from the same points must have received from this quarter 4,000,000 to 5,000,000 bushels of cereals per annum. Philadelphia is still the natural market for the surplus product of this territory, but for some years past there have not been consignments enough received from that entire section to realize commissions sufficient to pay the salary of a receiving clerk.

"Do you ask, has production fallen off? I answer, no; on the contrary, it has increased, but the whole line of these valleys has been dotted with furnaces and forges, and rolling-mills and saw-mills and factories and workshops, filled with operatives, and the consumer of agricultural products has been brought to the farmer's doors. He now finds a readier market for his products at home at prices equal to those ruling on the sea-board, of which he avails himself and thus saves all the cost of transportation and factorage, equal at average prices to about 20 per cent. Nay, more, sir, my own firm has frequently within the past few years sold and shipped to the millers in one of these valleys, that in which the iron interest has been most developed, the Lehigh, wheat drawn from Michigan, Illinois, Wisconsin, and Iowa to supply the deficiency in the consumptive want. And these products of the prairies of the West were sold, too, at a price far in excess of what could have been realized by exportation to any country on the face of the globe. As a consequence of this state of things land has risen in value through all this section, and farms that could have been bought fifteen or twenty years ago at $40 or $50 per acre are now saleable at $150 or $200 per acre. Villages have grown to be towns, and towns have grown to be cities, agriculture and manufactures have clasped hands and prosperity reigns."

PROTECTION STIMULATES IMMIGRATION.

Sir, the gentleman from Iowa asked how long it would take if we shut up our machine-shops and mills, and closed our coal-mines, to turn 100,000 men into agriculturists. It would take one season.

Mr. Allison. Oh no; that was not my question.

Mr. Kelley. That was what I was stating when you interrupted me.

Mr. Allison. I wanted to know how long it would be before iron and steel would be produced at a cheaper rate than it is now imported. That was my question.

Mr. Kelley. I do not think I said cheaper than it is now imported, but cheaper than it can then be imported. As the price goes down here it is going up in England; and under the present duty we will soon be able to supply our own demand, and meet England in common markets at equal prices. Sir, I want to show gentlemen from the West what effect the tariff has on immigration. I have before me the tariffs from the organization of the Government down to the present time, given in *ad valorem* percentages, and a statement of the number of immigrants that arrived in each year, from 1856 to 1869 inclusive. By comparing them I find that whenever our duties have been low immigration has fallen off, and whenever our duties have been high the volume of immigration has increased. This seems to be a fixed law.

Both papers are taken from the immaculate report of David A. Wells, Special Commissioner of Internal Revenue, and I therefore present them with some hesitancy, and with the remark that if they are incorrect it is not my fault.

I find by these tables that in the nine years from 1856 to 1864, inclusive, we received 1,403,497 immigrants; and in the four years of the protective tariff, of which so many gentlemen from the West whose States are not overcrowded complain, we have received 1,514,816, or over 111,000 more in the four years of protection than in the nine preceding years of free trade and low tariff. But I had better let the statement speak for itself. In introducing it Mr. Wells says:

"The following is a revised and the most accurate attainable statement of the course of alien immigration into the United States since and including the year 1856:

Year	Number
1856	200,436
1857	251,306
1858	123,126
1859	121,282
1860	153,640
1861	91,920
1862	91,987
1863	176,282
1864	193,418
1865	248,120
1866	318,554
1867	298,358
1868	297,215
1869	352,569
Total in fourteen years	2,918,213

"Total from July 1, 1865, to June 30, 1869, five years, 1,514,816."

In 1856 the rate of duty on the aggregate of our imports was 20.3, and the number of immigrants were 200,436; in 1859 the rate of duties had been reduced to 14.6, and the number of immigrants fell to 121,282. In 1861, by the Acts of March 2, August 5, and December 24, the rate of duties was further reduced to 11.2. This broke the camel's back. So many men were thrown out of employment and wages sunk so low that none but agriculturists could come to us with any prospect of improving their condition, and immigration sunk to a point lower than it had been since the ever-to-be-remembered free-trade crisis of 1837–40. In 1861 but 91,920 immigrants arrived, and the depression continued through 1862, during which the number of immigrants was but 91,987. By the Act of July 14, 1862, the duties were raised, so that in 1863 they were up to 23.7, and the immigration nearly equaled that of the two preceding years, having gone up 176,282. By the several Acts of 1864, 1865, and 1866 the duties were so increased, that they averaged on the importations of 1866 40.2 per cent., and immigration went up to 318,554. Last year, when the West was further oppressed by the increase of duties on wool and copper, they averaged 41.2, and the number of immigrants went up to 352,569; and the commissioners of immigration assure us that this year the number will exceed 400,000.

It is thus historically demonstrated that precisely as we make our duties protective of high wages for labor, do we bring skilled workmen from Germany, Belgium, France, and England to work in our mines, forges, furnaces, rolling-mills, cotton and woolen factories, and create a home market for the grain of Iowa, Illinois, and other States, whose farmers complain that they have no market for their crops.

SKILLED WORKMEN THE MOST VALUABLE COMMODITY WE CAN IMPORT.

Mr. Schenck. We have free trade in men.

Mr. Kelley. The chairman of the Committee of Ways and Means suggests in this connection that we have free trade in men. Yes, men are on the free list. They cost us not even freight. Yet how they swell the revenues and help to pay the debt of the country! They are raised from helpless infancy, through tender childhood, and trained to skilled labor in youth in other lands, and in manhood, allured by higher wages and freer institutions, they come to us and are welcomed to citizenship. In this way we have maintained a balance of trade that has enabled us to resist without bankruptcy the ordinary commercial balance that has been so heavily against us. We promote free trade in men, and it is the only free trade I am prepared to promote.

FRENCH FREE TRAD

The French tariff is as inimical to us as that of England. It is replete with prohibitory duties and absolute prohibitions. Yet France is spoken of by the English journals and in the rhapsodies of gentlemen as a free trade nation. Why, sir, on every article mentioned in the French tariff, unless it is absolutely free, the duty is so much if imported in French vessels, and so much more if imported in vessels of other nations. Every head of a column of the rates of duty established by the French tariff shows that you cannot import dutiable articles into France at the same rate in the vessel of another nation that you can in a French one. They read thus:

Articles.	General tariff.		Import tariff in treaty with Great Britain and other countries.	
	Imports.			
	In French vessels.	In other vessels.	In French and treaty vessels.	In other vessels.

Mr. Allison. Are you in favor of that rule?

Mr. Kelley. I am.

Mr. Allison. So am I.

Mr. Kelley. I am in favor of imposing duties so as to discriminate in favor of American shipping. I am for every form of protection to American industry and enterprise.

In the French tariff tobacco is classed as a colonial product, and its importation on private account is prohibited. It is a Government monopoly. American-grown tobacco, even in the leaf, is admitted into France only when the colonial supply fails; and then if it is carried in other than a French vessel it is made to pay an extra duty of nearly one cent on the pound, which is imposed in order to tax foreign shipping.

The gentleman from Iowa objects to the schedule under which duties are to be assessed under the committee's bill, and especially to that of sugar. Let me invite his attention to some of the provisions of the French tariff on sugar: Sugar from other than French possessions; sugar similar to refined powdered, above No. 20, from foreign countries, etc.; and sugar, refined, from other possessions, are prohibited. Thus all sugars refined or advanced in other than French possessions are prohibited, as is also molasses.

Mr. Schenck. That has built up their beet-sugar manufacture.

Mr. Kelley. Yes; and it is an industry we can and should build up in the West by adequately protective duties. I want to run cursorily through this French tariff. The importation of cast-iron into France is prohibited. Wrought-iron in plates is prohibited. Manufactures of iron of certain kinds are prohibited. All chemical products not enumerated are prohibited. All extracts of dye-woods are prohibited. Dye-woods are admitted free; but if American or other labor has been expended in making extracts from dye-woods the extracts are prohibited. Gentlemen of the free trade school generally and the gentlemen from New York [Mr. Brooks] and from Iowa [Mr. Allison] assail vehemently, and, as I think, most unfairly, the iron schedule and duties on steel proposed by the committee's bill. How differently France estimates the importance of these vital industries. Her tariff prohibits all manufactures of zinc and other metals not specially named and the following articles of iron and steel, in the production of which we excel both her and England in quality and cheapness:

"Castings, not polished: chairs for railroads, plates, etc., cast in open air; cylindric tubes, plain or grooved columns, gas-retorts, etc., and other articles without ornament or finish; hollow-ware not included above; castings, polished or turned; the same, tinned, varnished, etc.; household utensils and other articles not enumerated, of iron or sheet-iron, polished or painted; same, enameled or varnished; all articles of steel; iron, blacksmiths' work; locksmiths' work; nails, by machine; nails, by hand; wood-screws, bolts, screw-nuts."

France prohibits and excludes these articles that her poorly paid workmen may be protected against the productions of those of Belgium and Germany, who receive even less than they. All tissues of cotton, except nankeens, the produce of India, lace, manufactured by hand or otherwise, and tulle, with lace-work, are also prohibited. Cotton and woolen yarns are also prohibited by the general tariff, though admitted at high and most scientifically rated protective duties from England under the import tariff treaty with that country.

Yes, sir, if you spin our cotton into yarn, or weave it into a tissue or fabric, it is excluded from the broad empire of France. If you carry it there raw, with no labor in it save that of the slave or the freedman, you can take it in, but as yarn or a tissue it is prohibited.

THE PURPOSE OF THE FREE LIST.

The committee in proposing the extended free list embraced in the second section of the bill hoped to accomplish two important objects, one of which was to promote direct commerce between us and those non-manufacturing countries which require the productions of our shops and mills, and whose raw materials we require; and the other was to give our manufacturers and mechanics, free of duty, those essentials which France, England, and Belgium admit free. A majority of the committee believe that the adoption of this will do much to revive our commerce, and not only quicken established industries, but lead to the introduction of new ones, and thus increase the market for the productions of the farm and reduce the cost and price of a large range of manufactured goods. We think it is sound policy to let raw materials that we cannot produce in free, and collect our revenue from articles in the production of which much labor has been expended. This is the theory of the bill we reported. It has the sanction of the sagacity and experience of France and England, and was framed regardless of the teachings of mere theorists and schoolmen.

DUTIES ON WOOL AND WOOLENS.

Mr. Chairman, although I had made some preparation for its illustration, I had not expected to go into so general a discussion of the effect of protection upon the interests of the farmer. The wide range the discussion has taken must be my apology for presenting one other view of the subject. The gentleman from Iowa told us that the wool interest is suffering from the excessive duties imposed on woolen cloths by the existing tariff, and that the committee proposes to continue them. Sir, I may be very dull, but after hearing the gentleman it still seems to me that the wool interest must have been benefited by the bill increasing the duties on wool and woolens. We certainly have more people wearing wool now than we had in 1860. We have, as I have shown, received over 2,000,000 immigrants since then, and our natural increase is at least 1,000,000 per annum; yet I find by the thirteenth report of the commissioners of her Britannic Majesty's customs that the declared value of woolen manufactures exported to the United States was, in 1860, £3,414,050, while in 1868, nearly a decade thereafter, it was £3,658,432—an increase of but £234,382 in eight years.

Who has grown the wool that clothes our increased

population? Our freedmen now wear ordinary woolen clothes. The "poor whites" of the South now wear what they call "store goods," but to which they were unused before the rebellion. The cold Northwest, whose people wear woolen goods all the year, has increased its population so largely that it is demanding enlarged representation on this floor without waiting for the census.

Our wool-wearing population has nearly doubled; yet the amount of wool imported is scarcely greater than it was eight years ago. Where does the wool come from? Does it drop gently from the heavens, like the dew, or is it grown upon the sheep of western and southern farmers?

THE WAY TO REDUCE THE TAXES.

Sir, I am as anxious to reduce taxes as rapidly as it can be done consistently with the maintenance of the public credit and the gradual extinguishment of the debt as any man on this floor. I do not make this declaration now for the first time. On the 31st of January, 1866, I saw that, the war being over, the freedmen must be provided with the means of making a living by other labor than that of the plantation hand; that the women of the South must have employment; that there must be a diversification of our industry; that the Northwest would be shut out from her markets if she did not diversify her industries; and in the course of some remarks I made that day in favor of remitting taxes, both internal and external, I described the bill now under consideration. In stating how I would reduce the burdens of the people, I said:

"I have never been able to believe that a national debt is a national blessing. I have seen how good might be interwoven with or educed from evil, or how a great evil might, under certain conditions, be turned to good account; but beyond this I have never been able to regard debt, individual or national, as a blessing. It may be that, as in the inscrutable providence of God it required nearly five years of war to extirpate the national crime of slavery, and anguish and grief found their way to nearly every hearth-side in the country before we would recognize the manhood of the race we had so long oppressed, it was also necessary that we should be involved in a debt of unparalleled magnitude that we might be compelled to avail ourselves of the wealth that lies so freely around us, and by opening markets for well-rewarded industry make our land, what in theory it has ever been, the refuge of the oppressed of all climes. England, if supreme selfishness be consistent with sagacity, has been eminently sagacious in preventing us from becoming a manufacturing people; for with our enterprise, our ingenuity, our freer institutions, the extent of our country, the cheapness of our land, the diversity of our resources, the grandeur of our seas, lakes, and rivers, we should long ago have been able to offer her best workmen such inducements as would have brought them by millions to help bear our burdens and fight our battles. We can thus raise the standard of British and continental wages and protect American workmen against ill-paid competition. This we must do if we mean to maintain the national honor. The fields now under culture, the houses now existing, the mines now being worked, the men we now employ, cannot pay our debt. To meet its annual interest by taxing our present population and developed resources would be to continue an ever-enduring burden.

"The principal of the debt must be paid; but as it was contracted for posterity its extinguishment should not impoverish those who sustained the burdens of the war. I am not anxious to reduce the total of our debt, and would in this respect follow the example of England, and as its amount has been fixed, would not for the present trouble myself about its aggregate except to prevent its increase. *My anxiety is that the taxes it involves shall be as little oppressive as possible, and be so adjusted that while defending our industry against foreign assault, they may add nothing to the cost of those necessaries of life which we cannot produce, and for which we must therefore look to other lands. The raw materials entering into our manufactures, which we are yet unable to produce, but on which we unwisely impose duties, I would put into the free list with tea, coffee, and other such purely foreign essentials of life, and would impose duties on commodities that compete with American productions, so as to protect every feeble or infant branch of industry and quicken those that are robust. I would thus cheapen the elements of life and enable those whose capital is embarked in any branch of production to offer such wages to the skilled workmen of all lands as would steadily and rapidly increase our numbers, and, as is always the case in the neighborhood of growing cities or towns of considerable extent, increase the return for farm labor;* this policy would open new mines and quarries, build new furnaces, forges, and factories, and rapidly increase the taxable property and taxable inhabitants of the country.

"Let us pursue for twenty years the sound national policy of protection, and we will double our population and more than quadruple our capital and reduce our indebtedness *per capita* and per acre to little more than a nominal sum. Thus each man can 'without moneys' pay the bulk of his portion of the debt by blessing others with the ability to bear an honorable burden."

My views on these points have undergone no change, and I cannot more aptly describe the bill before the committee, in general terms, than I thus did more than four years ago.

THE DEFECTS OF THE PRESENT TARIFF, AND THE REMEDIES SUGGESTED BY THE NEW BILL.

Why not maintain the existing tariff, and wherein does the bill submitted by the Committee of Ways and Means differ from it? Several gentlemen have propounded these questions, and I now propose to answer them briefly and rapidly. The existing law is crude and contains many incongruous provisions. It is not in accord with the theory of the free-trader or the protectionist. It imposes the heaviest duties on articles of common consumption that we cannot produce. Thus, on chalk, not a cubic inch of which has, so far as I have heard, been discovered in our country, it imposes a duty of 833¼ per cent. It is bought at from 75 cents to $1 50 per ton, and the duty is $10. This onerous duty is not protective. We have no chalk-fields, and produce no substitute for it. It is therefore simply a tax, and one that everybody feels; the boy at his game of marbles, or before the blackboard in school, the housewife when she cleans her silver or britannia ware, and the farmer in the cost of putty for his windows. The new bill puts chalk on the free list.

Mr. Allison. Have we not increased the duty on putty, which enters into use in the house of every citizen in the land?

Mr. Kelley. Yes, sir; and why did we do it? All our western farmers are raising wheat, and many of them can find no market for their crop, and this bill, it is hoped, will, if it become a law, induce some of them to produce other things. We import immense amounts of linseed and castor-oil, and the majority of the committee hoped that by raising the duty on these oils, and those which may be substituted for them, it would induce some of them to raise flax and manufacture the oil. Again, we import great quantities of goods made of flax and substitutes for it, and we hoped that better duties on the oil and on these fabrics might lead to the establishment of linen and other mills in the interior. And as linseed-oil is the ingredient of chief value in putty, we raised the duty on it to correspond with that on oil. We hope thus to secure to every citizen good and cheap putty, made of free chalk and American-grown oil.

THE ALLEGATION THAT WE PROTECT OUR MANUFACTURES BY DUTIES AVERAGING FORTY PER CENT. IS NOT TRUE.

Mr. Chairman, I desire to call attention to the unfairness, unintentional of course, of the statement of the gentleman from New York [Mr. Brooks] that the existing tariff gives protection equal to an average of 41.2 per cent. That is the percentage of duties on the aggregate of our imports, and he will hardly claim that the duty of over 833 per cent. on chalk is protective of any of our industries.

Again, we collect a duty of 300 per cent. on pepper. Why should black pepper pay 300 per cent? Do we grow it anywhere in this country? Is this duty protective of any of our industries? You pay 5 cents a pound for pepper and the tariff imposes a duty of 15 cents, gold, equal to 300 per cent., and the gentleman includes this in his average of protective duties. Do we grow cloves or clove-stems in any part of the country? Is the duty on them protective? It is on cloves 355 per cent. and on clove-stems 386 per cent., and yet the gentleman also includes these with his protective duties. I think gentlemen perceive by this time what I meant when I said that many of the provisions of the present tariff are incongruous. While many of them are high enough for protection they are countervailed by higher duties on raw materials that we cannot produce, and which rival nations admit free or under very low duties.

I shall not attempt to bring all such incongruities to the attention of the committee, but beg leave to allude to a few more. On cayenne pepper, the duty is 303 per cent.; on allspice, 376½ per cent.; on nutmegs, 188½ per cent.; on crude camphor, 113 per cent.; on saltpetre, 77¾ per cent.; on varnish gums, none of which are produced in this country, 80 per cent.; on tea, the farmer's and laborer's refreshing drink, 78½ per cent.; on coffee, 47½ per cent. I could largely extend this list of duties, each of which is a tax on some article of common consumption not produced in the country, and to that extent a bonus to our competitors. I am in favor of making all such articles free; and the committee has reduced the duties on them or put them on the free list. When these provisions shall be enacted into law the gentleman from New York can calculate the percentage and find that our duties will compare favorably with those imposed by any manufacturing nation except England; whose brief trial of free trade has cost her her supremacy.*

* "The operatives have seen other classes of the community profiting by this policy and increasing in wealth, whilst they have been going steadily down hill: they have seen the operatives of Belgium, France, Germany, Switzerland, America advance in prosperity, in intelligence, in technical education, far more

DUTIES WHICH NEED READJUSTMENT.

Another serious fault of the existing law is that so many of its duties are *ad valorem.* Dishonest men take advantage of this and have goods invoiced below the proper value, and thus not only defraud the Government, but do wrong to both the home manufacturer and the honest importer. This system of duties has much to do with the decline of American commerce. The large temptation to defraud the Government by undervaluation has caused great houses abroad to establish agencies here and to refuse to sell directly to an American purchaser. This is so with all the Sheffield steel-makers and most of the continental silk houses. In this way the frauds of the steel-makers and silk manufacturers have been enormous, amounting to many millions of dollars. The new bill substitutes specific duties wherever it is practicable.

The duties now collected on alcoholic preparations, and those in the production of which spirits are used, such as quinine, chloroform, collodion, etc., are now much too high, having been adjusted to the tax of $2 per gallon on distilled spirits. The new bill adjusts them to the lower tax now collected.

Many of the existing duties are so high as to defeat all their legitimate objects and deprive the Government of all revenue. This is especially true of spices. It was in evidence from many sources that these are imported into New York or San Francisco and immediately shipped in

---

under a closely Protective Policy, than they have done under what is called Free Trade. They find that far from having maintained the lead that they had twenty years ago, in a vast number of manufactures, they have lost it, and been distanced by those whom their advisers told them were withering under the cold shade of protection.

"Twenty years ago free trade was the cure propounded for all the diseases the country suffered from; want of work, pauperism, crime, drunkenness, ignorance, were all to diminish under the new era; they have all increased; when we look at the result of the cure we have tried, can it be a matter of surprise if many of us still prefer the disease! We are told free trade principles are spreading; why, in Prussia, Austria, Belgium, Switzerland, the idea even of opening their ports and markets, and inviting competition with their own industrial population, has never yet been mooted; whilst in America, the operative's paradise, the duties on many British manufactures have been doubled during the last few years, and France, the promised land of free trade, is already trying to withdraw the nominal facilities doled out to us in the commercial treaty. The only man in France who is at heart a free trader, is the Emperor himself. Is this hopeful for the operative classes in England? Does the direction of public opinion in one single country on this subject afford the slightest hope that any one of them will admit our manufactures duty free? On the contrary, protection to native industry is more firmly established as a great universal rule of internal polity than any other, and wherever democratic principles extend this principle will intensify."—*Sir Edward Sullivan.*

bond to the British provinces, whence they are smuggled back. The bill of the committee proposes such reductions of the duties as will probably give the Government a handsome revenue while cheapening them to the consumer.

The value to the country of the changes proposed cannot fail to be very great.

THE PRESENT LAW SHOULD BE REVISED, NOT OVERTHROWN.

Would that I could impress upon the House my estimate of the value to the country of these proposed changes.

I am discussing the bill in no spirit of partisanship. In urging its acceptance I am pleading the cause of the farmer and laborer, as I conscientiously believe that it will, if adopted, increase the purchasing power, the exchangeable value of every bushel of grain grown and hour of labor performed in our country. I have no general condemnation for the existing law. It needs revision, but should not be overthrown. As a revenue measure it has exceeded the anticipations of its friends and the most earnest friends of the Government. It yielded for the year ending June 30, 1867, $176,417,810; for that ending June 30, 1868, $164,464,599 56; and for that ending June 30, 1869, $180,084,456 63; and no preceding tariff produced results comparable to these.

And, sir, notwithstanding its faults it has been of great value as a protective measure. By its protective influence it has added much to the power of the country and the prosperity of the people. Under it our production of pig-iron has, as I have already shown, been more than doubled, and its production has been extended into new and large fields in States where it was previously unknown. Thus has increased value been given to all the land in those States; the increase being equal to the addition of the value of the mineral lands to that of the agricultural surface; and more than that, it has provided a market in the neighborhood of each furnace, in which articles can be sold which would not bear transportation to distant points or foreign lands. The farmers of Iowa and Minnesota now produce for sale little of anything else than wheat and wool for exportation to the seaboard States. When manufactories are built or mines opened, villages spring up and create a market for roots, as potatoes and turnips, the productions of the garden and the orchard, and for hay, by which the western farmer will be relieved from the necessity of growing successive crops of wheat to the exhaustion of the soil. These villages also afford a market for lamb, veal, eggs, and all the thousand things that come in as subsidiary sources of income even to those who farm on a great scale. Thus have many farmers felt the protective influence of the existing tariff, as well as in the stimulus it has given to immigration, and the addition of the mineral to the agricultural value of immense bodies of land in almost every State; and while endeavoring to improve it I renew my protest against its repeal or overthrow.

THE CAREFUL CONSIDERATION THAT HAS BEEN BESTOWED UPON THE BILL BY THE COMMITTEE.

Mr. Chairman and gentlemen of the committee, your Committee of Ways and Means have devoted the earnest labor of a year to the consideration of the revision of the tariff, a duty you committed to them by special resolution of the House. In the discharge of that duty we have traveled in great part at our own proper cost, relieved largely by the hospitality of railroad, steamship, and other transportation companies, from the rocky coasts of Massachusetts, and the waters of its bay, along the long coast of California and Oregon, and over the beautiful waters of Puget Sound, the Willamette and the Columbia rivers; we have listened to merchants, manufacturers, farmers, and men of enterprise, representing all the interests of every section of the country; and we have been in all respects painstaking and deliberate in our efforts to ascertain how the existing provisions of the tariff can be so modified as to yield the Government adequate revenue, lighten the burdens of the people, and stimulate all their industries with equal hand. And I conscientiously believe that if the bill we have reported should be adopted without an amendment, except those the committee is prepared to suggest, its quickening influence would be felt in every department of the productive and commercial industries of the country. It would do much to revivify the languishing shipping interest. It would give new and grander proportions to the market for your agricultural products. It would maintain in a healthy condition your manufacturing and mechanical establishments, and it would say to capitalists here and abroad, "The protective policy of the country is confirmed; you may safely embark in new enterprises and develop new elements of the illimitable store and varieties of wealth now lying dormant within the country."

HOW IT WILL STIMULATE THE SHIPPING INTEREST.

Do gentlemen ask how it will quicken commerce? Let them turn to its free list. Our commerce is now with manufacturing nations inhabiting the grain-growing and metalliferous regions of Europe. They produce everything we do except cotton, rice, tobacco, and petroleum; other than these they want but little from us, unless war or drought or excessive rain prevails over so large a section as to materially diminish the grain crop. We should cultivate an exchange of products with the non-manufacturing tropical or semi-tropical countries. We want their gums, spices, barks, ivory, dye-woods, drugs, and other productions which they would gladly exchange for our grain, spirits, cotton fabrics, axes, hoes, shovels, and an infinite variety of our productions. These countries are our natural markets, but we have excluded ourselves from them by those provisions of our tariff laws which impose duties on their exports which we need as raw materials. All other manufacturing countries admit their productions free, while we impose duties on them which, as I have shown, are taxes upon ourselves in their consumption. But this does a further wrong to the shipping interest in this wise: the London merchant gets their productions in exchange for the shoddy cloth, low-grade iron, and general "Brumagen" wares of England, and imports them free of duty. He ships them to us in English steamers, and adds freight to his many other profits. This trade of right belongs to us, and under the committee's bill we will enjoy it.

Let me illustrate by a single example. The cost of saltpetre is a question of importance to every railroad builder, quarryman, and miner, and we ought to import the raw material for it from two countries remote from each other and manufacture it more cheaply than we now import it through London from India. The duties on this article are higher than they should be, and so apportioned as to discriminate against our labor. That on the crude article is 25 per cent. higher than that on the partially refined, and is at the rate of 77¾ per cent. They are as follows: on partially refined saltpetre, 2 cents per pound; on crude, 2½ cents, and on refined, 3 cents. The new bill removes the discrimination against ourselves and makes but two grades of duty. It reduces that on the crude article to 1½ cent, and on the refined to 2½ cents.

But while thus reducing the duty on this important article the bill of the committee invites the establishment of its cheaper manufacture in our midst and the employment of many ships in bringing us the raw material in equal proportions from Peru and Germany.

If gentlemen will examine the free list they will find that it embraces muriate of potassa and nitrate of soda. The latter is a natural product of Peru, and the former of Germany, and from 1000 tons of each we can produce 1000 tons of saltpetre cheaper than we can import it from India. This would double the tonnage required for the carrying of this article. I have thus presented to the committee but one of many illustrations with which I might detain them of the influence the bill will if it becomes a law exercise upon our commerce.

STEEL AD VALOREM.

I have said that one of the defects of the present law is its frequent application of *ad valorems,* which open the door to great frauds. I turn for an illustration to what seems to be a favorite topic of the gentleman from Iowa, [Mr. Allison]—the article of steel. The gentleman said the duty on steel in ingots, bars, sheets, and wire above a certain thickness is 2¼ cents, and that we had raised it to 3¼ cents, while reducing the duty a little on less important classes of steel. Let me state the case fairly. The present duty on ingots, bars, sheet, and wire not less than one quarter of an inch in diameter, valued at 7 cents per pound or less, is 2¼ cents per pound; value 7 and not above 11 cents per pound, 3 cents per pound; valued above 11 cents per pound, 3½ cents per pound and 10 per cent. *ad valorem.* The gentlemen attempted to discredit the evidence which proves the magnitude of the frauds which have been persistently perpetrated by the Sheffield steel makers for the last twenty years under this system; but the Secretary of the treasury is acting upon it, and is largely increasing the revenues of the country from steel by requiring it to be honestly invoiced.

Much evidence, confirmed by the admission of one of the firms engaged in it, establishes the fact that a combination has existed among these wealthy Englishmen to sell no steel to Americans in England, but to send it to agents in this country for sale, and to so undervalue it that that which should pay 3½ cents and 10 per cent. *ad valorem* has, to the extent of 9 pounds out of every 10, been brought in at 3 cents, and by the same fraudulent device and conspiracy the greater part of that which was subject to a duty of 3 cents has come in at 2¼.

Thus the Government has been defrauded of many millions of revenue. Now, what has the committee done in the premises? We have agreed to put all steel—that which was below and that which was above, that which paid 2¼ cents a pound and that which paid 5½ cents a pound, or 3½ cents and 10 per cent. *ad valorem*—under a duty of 3¼ cents per pound. We had importers and manufacturers of steel and experts before us, and they agreed that there was no conceivable test by which examiners and inspectors of customs could distinguish between steel worth from 4 to 7 cents and that worth more than 11 cents a pound; so that though we may by the proposed change for a brief time do some injustice to those who use low-priced steel and those who produce high qualities of steel, we have made a single duty, which will give us the revenue honestly due and enable our steel manufacturers to live and extend their works.

In my recent remarks on Mr. Wells' report I quoted the language of the senior partner of a steel-making firm in Sheffield, England, in which he admitted the fact of undervaluation, and declared that while the law remains as it is the Government will be defrauded and cannot prevent it. Thus the honest men among the English steelmakers implore us to close the door against fraud in which they must participate, or surrender our market to their less honest neighbors. Yet, for our well-devised effort to do justice to the Government and honest importers, we are denounced as taxing the people to build up monopolies!

The gentleman from Iowa will I am sure pardon me for correcting a statement of his, on which he amplified somewhat to-day touching steel-manufacturing in Pittsburg. The statement he read yesterday was not that her steel-makers were able to compete with England in 1859; it was that steel-making in that city first became an assured success in that year. Her enterprising men of capital had been for many years and with great loss renewing the yet fruitless experiment. Man after man and firm after firm had failed. Steel-works depreciated in value and new firms bought the stock and premises of old ones at reduced values, till, in 1859, "an assured success was attained." This was the phrase the gentleman from Iowa used yesterday when he had the paper before him.

STEPHEN COLWELL.

I am quite sure that the gentleman from Iowa would not intentionally misstate a fact. Nobody values him more highly than I do. He is as earnest on his side of this great question as I am on mine, and we are both of a temperament that requires us to have the figures before us to prevent a certain measure of exaggeration in our statements. There is, however, one point on which I am disposed to quarrel with him, and that is that he should have assumed to have found an ally in my venerable friend, Stephen Colwell, and by a perversion of his language made him seem to plead against protection for American labor when the very words he quoted were written in its behalf. Sir, Stephen Colwell's life has been devoted to his country. It has been a life-long labor of love with him to promote the development of her vast stores of wealth and the prosperity of her farmers and laborers. He was the friend and companion of Frederick List, the founder of the German Zollverein, who was for a few years an exile from his native land and a dweller in the then undeveloped coal regions of Pennsylvania. After his death Mr. Colwell collected his writings and found pleasure in editing them; he has also written and published much in defence of protection as a sure means of promoting national greatness, cheap commodities, and the prosperity of the people; and I confess that I was both astonished and grieved that a portion of an article of Mr. Colwell's demanding the repeal of internal taxes, and showing that they are a bonus to foreign manufacturers and a burden upon our home producers, should be quoted by the gentleman from Iowa against the tariff bill, and to prove that protective duties add to the cost of commodities. I know my friend did not think of the wrong he was doing, but it is not just to my venerable friend, whose life is drawing to a close, that his language should be thus perverted before the nation whose interests he has done so much to promote.

THE CLASSIFICATION OF IRON NOT NEW.

But the gentleman from Iowa asks why the classification of iron found in the bill was adopted by the committee. I will tell him why. Sir, so far as the classification of iron has been modified, and the changes are but few, we adopted the expressed opinion of the Senate and a former Committee of Ways and Means.

The Senate of the United States, on the 31st of January, 1867, passed a tariff bill. On the 18th of February of that year the Committee of Ways and Means reported it to this House with certain amendments; and your committee, finding a classification indorsed by the Senate and former Committee of Ways and Means, followed it, except where they thought change necessary or judicious. This is the classification of which the gentleman complains as novel and artful.

I am too weary, and too much exhausted, and your patience is too far gone for me to proceed further with the discussion at present. There are points I would like to consider; but I must draw rapidly to a conclusion.

PROOF THAT PROTECTION CHEAPENS GOODS.

The gentleman from Indiana [Mr. Kerr], speaking of my argument on Bessemer rails, said that as America produced but 30,000 tons per annum, the establishment of her works could have had no influence upon the price of English rails, because the quantity produced was relatively so small. I propose to illustrate the fallacy of that argument by the contents of the little box I hold in my hand. So long as America was unprepared to make Bessemer steel no Englishman would sell a ton of rails for less than $150. I have told the story to the committee once, and will not now repeat the details. But when in 1865 the works of Griswold & Co., at Troy, New York, and the Freedom Works, at Harrisburg, Pennsylvania, were ready to deliver Bessemer rails, Englishmen who had been swearing that they could not sell them at less than $150 a ton immediately offered them at $130. And when our works increased from two to six they dropped their price down to $100, and if necessary they will drop it to $50, or until they force the owners of our establishments to abandon the production and apply their premises and machinery to some other use.

Their policy is to crowd out our works; or, as Lord Brougham advised in 1815, just after the close of our war, "to spend any amount of money to strangle in the cradle the infant industries, the exigencies of the war had called into existence in the United States." They will spend any amount of money to crowd out these five or six Bessemer rail-works, and then put the price up to figures that will be satisfactory to themselves.

I said I would illustrate the argument by the contents

of a small box I hold in my hand. It contains a few very small articles and specimens of the material of which they are made. They are gas-tips of a kind that till quite lately were made exclusively in Germany. They then sold in our market at from $6 to $12 per gross. I cannot tell you whether this afforded so grand a profit as Bessemer rails did at $150 gold per ton. But, as recent events prove, it must have paid splendidly. Since the close of the war there has been found in the interior of Tennessee a deposit of talc, of which these are specimens [holding up small pieces]. This is carried not in foreign ships, but by our transportation companies, to Boston, giving business to our railroad companies between the heart of Tennessee and Massachusetts. There Yankee ingenuity converts the talc into gas-tips such as the Germans make, which will not corrode, and for which they had the monopoly of our market. These American men have embarked a large capital in this enterprise, and employ many people in Tennessee and Massachusetts. They are busy making these little gas-tips and creating a market for western grain, and converting newly-arrived laborers from Europe into well-paid American workingmen.

What effect has their enterprise had on the price of porcelain gas-tips? The German manufacturers who could not sell them for less than $6 to $12 a gross, now suddenly drop their price and are flooding the market with them at $2 a gross. At this price they will soon destroy their Yankee rival and regain their old monopoly.

Now, are we wrong when we say that if anybody makes a profit out of us we prefer that it shall be those who feed on American wheat, wear American wool, give good wages to American workmen, and pay American taxes,—are, in a word, Americans? The little gas-tip illustrates the truth that American competition cheapens small foreign commodities quite as well as the weightier article of steel rails.

SILK POPLINS.

Cases of this kind are continually occurring. Let me tell you of another from away up in the mountain counties of New York, at Schoharie. A quiet, unpretending citizen, seeing that there were a large number of unemployed girls in and about the village, made the experiment of manufacturing an article in great demand for ladies' dresses, known as silk poplins. He equaled the foreign goods in quality, was underselling them, and to the extent of his capacity to produce was driving them out of the market, when by a change in the wool tariff the duty on his goods was unintentionally reduced, and the foreigners have him at a disadvantage; and if we do not pass this bill, or give him other relief, he must close his factory, lose the capital he has invested in it, and scatter the formerly idle girls he now employs at good wages.

These are the facts of the case. The wool bill, in order to let coarse woolen goods in at a low rate, provides that when they are over a certain number of ounces to the square yard they shall come in at 40 per cent. Poplins are in considerable part of silk; they are finer and more valuable than any heavy woolen goods, but the silk adds to their weight, and it has been held that the duty on them has been reduced from 60 to 40 per cent. Unless the relief proposed in this bill be given, Mr. Baar is likely to be ruined and his factory closed.

TIN AND NICKEL.

The present law puts a duty of 15 per cent. on tin in pigs or bars. We produce no tin, though I believe they have recently discovered a bed of ore in California, and it is thought to exist in Missouri. I hope it does, and that both deposits may soon be developed. We cannot make tin-plates by reason of the duties on block tin and palm-oil. This bill of the committee proposes to put palm-oil, an African product, and block tin on the free list; so that we may begin the manufacture of sheet-tin, for which we export annually $8,000,000 in gold.

While we have no well-ascertained deposits of tin ore the country abounds in deposits of nickel. Missouri, Kentucky, Virginia, Pennsylvania, New Jersey, and Connecticut have large deposits of it; yet when the law of 1861 was passed its manufacture had not been attempted; and a duty of 15 per cent., the same as that on block tin, was put on nickel. Our bill proposes to enable the men of Missouri to work the vast deposits of mine La Motte; the men of Kentucky to work the large deposits in that State, and the people of Connecticut to establish nickel works in the immediate vicinity of their great factories of Britannia and other white-metal wares by putting the same rate of duty on nickel that we have on copper, zinc, lead, iron, and other metals.

THE EFFECT OF PROTECTING NICKEL.

Now let me show you what will be the effect of this measure. I hold in my hand a letter from Evans & Askin, the great nickel manufacturers of England. They tell us how they will punish us if we increase the tariff on nickel; and I hope you will join me in invoking their punishment. But let them speak for themselves, as they do in this letter. It reads thus:

BIRMINGHAM, *March* 18, 1868.

DEAR SIR: Although it is now some time since we had the pleasure of corresponding we hear from time to time of the progress you are making in the nickel trade in America, and we trust you find the business a renumerative and successful one.

We hear that attempts are being made to influence Congress to increase largely the import duties on refined nickel, and although perhaps we might at first regret that the duties should be raised, we are not quite sure it would not ultimately be to our advantage; for, if the duties are so raised as to render the import of nickel almost prohibitory we shall at once adopt measures to send out one of the junior members of our firm and erect a nickel refinery in the States. In fact, from the large quantities of nickel and cobalt ores offered to us by mine La Motte, the Haley Smelting Company, and several others, we are almost disposed to do so at once, as we think it might answer our purpose better than forwarding the refined article from this country. We are not, of course, selfish enough to wish a monopoly of the nickel trade in America, but we hope and intend to have a share of it, either by shipment to or refining in the States.

Should we decide upon erecting works in your country may we reckon on any supply of ore from your mine, in addition to other sources?

We are, dear sir, yours, faithfully, EVANS & ASKIN.

Mr. JOSEPH WHARTON.

Let them come on with their skilled nickel-makers; let them bring their capital by millions; let them, if they can, bring 100,000 people to consume the grain of Missouri; and we will give them all welcome.* By increasing the duty on nickel from 15 to 40 per cent. mine La Motte will

* Capital owned in this country is seeking investment in America. Our capitalists are lending largely to the United States, and enabling workmen to do that in the country to which they have emigrated which was wont to be done in this country. If labor in this land keeps the incubus of which we have spoken still hanging on its neck, it is perfectly certain that it will not be able to compete with younger nations in their ports; and accumulated wealth, as capital is, really will find its way out of the country. Keep up an expenditure of one hundred and fifty millions a year, at the same time lessen production, and it will follow, with unerring sureness, that we shall be left dying of starvation in the rear of other peoples. The ruin of a nation is not a result which shows itself all at once. It is the issue generally of a comparatively slow process; but it is not the less surely, because it is slowly, that a people who send off their most industrious workmen to increase the forces of other nations who are already competing with them for the world's trade, do come to ruin by such a course. It should not be forgotten that just the more favorable the conditions of labor are in the countries to which we send out our workmen, just so much the sooner will our adversity come to us from their competition.—*Social Politics: Kirk.*

thus become a great manufacturing centre, and there will be a new market, not dependent on long lines of railroad or ocean transportation, for the grain and wool of the valley of the Mississippi.

Now, Mr. Chairman, in conclusion, I plead with the gentlemen of the committee to forget their sectional feelings, to put aside party strife, to remember that the glory and the power of their country depend on the prosperity, intelligence, and inspiring hopes of the laboring people and their children. I beg them, as I know they all love their country, to stand by her industries, and to aid the poor and oppressed laborers of other lands to escape from a diet of "rye and potatoes," to a land of free schools and liberal wages, in which the daily fare of the family will be of wheat, mutton, beef, or pork, with the vegetables and fruits of all the States of our broad and then assuredly prosperous country.

APPENDIX.

THE TARIFFS OF THE UNITED STATES.

STATEMENT—Showing the revenue collected each year, from 1789 to 1868, the amount of dutiable imports and free goods imported annually, and the average rate of duty on imports annually. It was one of the appendices of the last annual report of the Special Commissioner of the Revenue. It is very suggestive, and to those who remember the financial condition of the country from 1837 to 1842, and from 1856 to 1861, the price of grain and the suffering endured by the laboring people at all commercial and manufacturing centres during those periods, will prove conclusive on many points:

DATES.	TARIFFS.	CUSTOMS.	IMPORTS.			Per ct. on dutiable.	Per ct. on aggregate.
			FREE.	DUTIABLE.	TOTAL.		
From March 4, 1789, to Dec. 31, 1790—Aug. 10...	General...........	....	....	....	....	......	.....
1791—March 3..	Spirits	$4,399,473 09	....	....	$52,200,000	....	8½
1792—May 2.....	General...........	3,443,070 85	....	....	31,500,000	....	11
1793	....	4,255,306 56	....	....	31,100,000	....	13½
1794—June 7....	General...........	4,801,065 28	....	....	34,600,000	....	14
1795—Jan. 29...	Supplementary.	5,588,461 26	....	....	69,756,268	....	9
1796	....	6,567,987 94	....	....	81,436,164	....	8½
1797—March 3..	General...........	7,549,649 65	....	....	75,379,406	....	10
1798	....	7,106,061 93	....	....	68,551,700	....	10½
1799	....	6,610,449 31	....	....	79,069,148	....	8½
1800—March 13	Sugar and wines	9,080,932 73	....	....	91,252,768	....	9¼
1801	....	10,750,778 93	....	....	111,363,511	....	9
1802	....	12,458,235 74	....	....	76,333,333	....	16
1803	....	10,479,417 61	....	....	64,666,666	....	16
1804—March 26	Mediterranean fund	11,098,565 33	....	....	85,000,000	....	14
1805—March 27	Light money	12,936,487 04	....	....	120,600,000	....	10½
1806	....	14,667,698 17	....	....	129,410,000	....	11⅓
1807	....	15,845,521 61	....	....	138,500,000	....	11½
1808	....	16,363,550 58	....	....	56,990,000	....	30
1809	....	7,296,020 58	....	....	59,400,000	....	12
1810	....	8,583,309 31	....	....	85,400,000	....	10
1811	....	13,313,222 73	....	....	53,400,000	....	25
1812—July 1....	War, double duties	8,958,777 53	....	....	77,030,000	....	11½

TABLE—*Continued.*

DATES.	TARIFFS.	CUSTOMS.	IMPORTS.			Per ct. on dutiable.	Per ct. on aggregate.
			FREE.	DUTIABLE.	TOTAL.		
1813—July 13...	Salt	$13,224,624 25	....	....	$22,005,000	....	60
1814	....	5,998,772 08	....	....	12,965,000	....	47
1815	....	7,282,942 22	....	....	13,041,274	....	55
1816—April 27..	Min. for protection	36,306,874 88	....	....	147,103,000	....	25
1817	....	26,283,348 49	....	....	99,250,000	....	27
1818—April 20..	Iron and alum..	17,176,385 00	....	....	121,750,000	....	14
1819—March 3..	Wines........	20,283,608 76	....	....	87,125,000	....	23
1820	....	15,006,612 15	....	....	74,450,000	....	20½
1821	....	18,475,703 57	$10,082,313	$52,503,411	62,585,724	35.6	29.5
1822	....	24,066,066 43	7,298,708	75,242,833	83,241,541	31.7	28.9
1823	....	22,402,024 29	9,048,288	68,530,979	77,579,267	32.7	28.8
1824—May 22...	General rise......	25,486,817 86	12,563,773	67,985,234	80,549,007	37.5	31.6
1825	....	31,653,871 50	10,947,510	85,392,565	96,340,075	37.1	32.8
1826	....	26,033,861 97	12,567,769	72,406,708	84,974,477	34.6	30.7
1827	....	27,948,956 57	11,855,104	67,628,964	79,484,068	41.3	35.1
1828—May 19...	Min. extended...	29,951,251 90	12,379,176	76,130,648	88,509,824	39.3	33.8
1829	....	27,688,701 11	11,805,501	62,687,026	74,492,527	44.3	37.1
1830—May 20...	Coffee, tea, molasses	28,389,505 05	12,746,245	58,130,675	70,876,920	48.8	40
1831	....	36,596,118 19	13,456,625	89,734,499	103,191,124	40.8	35.4
1832—July 14...	Modifications....	29,341,175 65	14,249,453	86,779,813	101,029,266	33.8	29
1833—March 2..	Compromise......	24,177,578 52	32,447,950	75,670,361	108,118,311	31.9	22.4
1834	....	18,960,705 96	68,393,180	58,128,152	126,521,332	32.6	15
1835	....	25,890,726 66	77,940,493	71,955,249	149,895,742	36.0	17.2
1836	....	30,818,327 67	92,056,481	97,923,554	189,980,035	31.6	16.2
1837	....	18,134,131 01	69,250,031	71,739,186	140,989,217	25.3	12.4
1838	....	19,702,825 45	60,860,005	52,857,399	113,717,404	37.8	17.3
1839	....	25,554,533 96	76,401,792	85,690,340	162,092,132	29.9	15.8
1840	....	15,104,790 63	57,196,204	49,945,315	107,141,519	30.4	14.1
1841—Sept. 11...	Free list tax.....	19,919,492 17	66,019,731	61,926,446	127,946,177	32.2	15.6
1842—Aug. 30...	General rise......	16,662,746 84	30,627,486	69,534,601	100,162,087	23.1	16.6
1843	....	10,208,000 43	35,574,584	29,179,215	64,753,799	35.7	15.7
1844	....	29,236,357 38	24,766,881	83,668,154	108,435,035	35.1	26.9
1845	....	30,952,416 21	22,147,840	95,106,724	117,254,564	32.5	26.4
1846—Aug 6....	Revenue tariff...	26,712,668 00	24,767,730	96,924,058	121,691,797	26½	21.9
1847	....	23,747,865 00	41,772,636	104,773,002	146,545,638	22½	16.2
1848	....	31,757,071 00	22,716,665	132,282,325	154,998,928	24	20.4
1849	....	28,346,739 00	22,377,614	125,479,774	147,857,439	23	19.2
1850	....	39,668,686 00	22,710,382	155,427,936	178,138,318	25.2	22.3
1851	....	49,017,568 00	25,106,587	191,118,345	216,224,932	26	22.6
1852	....	47,339,326 00	29,692,934	183,252,508	212,945,442	26	22.2
1853	....	58,931,865 00	31,383,534	236,595,113	267,978,647	25	22
1854	....	64,224,190 00	33,285,821	271,276,560	304,562,381	23.5	21.1
1855	....	53,025,794 00	40,090,336	221,378,184	261,468,520	23	20.3
1856	....	64,022,863 00	56,955,706	257,684,236	314,639,942	25	20.3
1857—March 3..	General	63,875,905 00	66,729,306	294,160,835	360,890,141	21.5	17.7
1858	....	41,789,621 00	80,319,275	202,293,875	282,613,150	20	14.8
1859	....	49,565,824 00	79,721,116	259,047,014	338,768,130	19	14.6
1860	....	53,187,511 00	90,841,749	279,872,327	362,166,254	19	14.7
1861 { Mar. 2, Aug. 5, Dec. 24 }	....	39,582,186 00	*134,559,196	218,180,191	352,739,387	18.1	11.2
1862—July 14...	General	49,056,398 00	*91,603,491	183,843,458	275,446,939	26.7	17.7
1863—March 3..	....	69,059,642 00	44,826,629	208,093,891	252,919,920	33.2	23.7
1864—June 30..	General	102,316,153 00	*54,244,183	275,320,951	329,565,134	37.2	31
1865—March 3..	....	84,928,260 00	54,329,588	194,226,064	248,555,652	43.7	34.2
1866 { Mar. 14, May 16, July 28 }	....	179,046,630 00	69,728,618	375,783,540	445,512,158	47.06	40.2
1867—March 2..	Wool and woollens	176,417,811 00	39,105,708	372,627,601	411,733,309	47.34	42 8
1868	....	164,464,599 56	29,804,147	343,605,301	373,409,448	47.86	44
1869—Feb. 24...	Copper increas'd	180,048,426 63	41,179,172	395,847,369	437,026,541	45.48	41.2

* In these amounts are included imports into the southern ports during the war, from which no revenue was derived, namely, in 1861, $17,089,234 ; in 1862, $90,789 ; and in 1864, $2220.

THE VALUE OF AN INEXPORTABLE CURRENCY.

SPEECH DELIVERED IN THE HOUSE OF REPRESENTATIVES, JUNE 8TH, 1870.

The House being in session—

Mr. Kelley said:

The fifteen minutes allotted me will not be sufficient to enable me to examine in detail the bill before the House. But I beg leave to offer a few general suggestions on the subject. In the first place, permit me to say that the South and West need and ought to have increased banking facilities and more bank currency. The Southern States have, if my memory is not at fault, but about two per cent., and the Southwestern States but about two and three-quarters per cent. of the national banking capital. They are entitled to more; and, in my judgment, it would be vastly to the benefit of the country if they could have considerably more.

Banks are found to be a convenience in New England, New York, Pennsylvania, and elsewhere, and their increase would promote the convenience of the people of the Western and Southern States. They would facilitate the development of the country, and promote its local trade and the forwarding of the crops. If the bill before the House contained but the first section, providing for the creation of $95,000,000 of banking capital in addition to the amount the country now possesses, with provisions subjecting it to the general banking law, and requiring it to have as its basis a deposit of the bonds of the Government now extant or those hereafter to be issued, and limiting its distribution to those States which have not a proper proportion, I would vote for it.

But I cannot sustain this bill; it proposes to construct an inverted pyramid; and I do not believe a thing of that form can be made to stand. The base ought to be broader than the apex and not narrower. The bill proposes to withdraw from the existing reserve of the banks the three per cent. certificates held by them and nearly fifty million dollars of greenbacks, and to issue $95,000,000 more national bank notes. This in itself would be a perceptible contraction. But the new banks in cities are required to hold a reserve equal to twenty-five per cent. of their circulation, and in the country fifteen per cent. These must necessarily consist of greenbacks. The effect would therefore be a contraction that would be felt by every bank and business man in the country.

Now, let me say with emphasis, in reply to gentlemen who maintain the opposite theory, that contraction is not the road to resumption, but rather to bankruptcy. Every $100,000 of your currency that you contract restrains the business, retards the development of the resources and diminishes the profits of the country. Gentlemen ask, how will you achieve resumption if you permit an expansion of bank paper? Sir, I do not wish to attempt the impossible. I am not anxious to resume specie payments until the commercial relations of our country shall have improved. Few greater misfortunes could happen us than that under some impulse we should attempt resumption before the balance of trade shall be in favor of our country and large amounts of our bonds shall have been brought home from abroad.

We owe $1,000,000,000 of overdue debt to Europe. It is not overdue from the Government, but from the people of the country. Our five-twenty bonds have not yet matured. But if we should resume specie payments, and tempt the caprice or the cupidity of bankers, merchants, or manufacturers abroad to bring us to bankruptcy, all they would have to do would be to send ten, fifteen or twenty million dollars of bonds home, to be sold at market rates, by which they would make a profit on their original investment and draw the purchase-money from us in gold.

Sir, in view of our vast foreign indebtedness, our safety is in the fact that we conduct our domestic exchanges with a non-exportable currency. The gentleman from Illinois [Mr. Ingersoll] reminded us this morning of the fact that in 1857, when our banks were on a specie basis and conducted their business by specie payments, the draft of $7,000,000 of gold for Europe was the proximate cause of the great financial crisis of that year. And if, with our immense debt abroad and the balance of trade against us heavily as it is, we were to resume, the unexpected draft by our creditors of from seven to ten million dollars would bring us to suspension and widespread commercial bankruptcy.*

Let me contrast the financial history of 1866 with that of 1857. In 1866 gold did not enter into our currency; it was a commodity. We were using a kind of money which you could not, according to the idea of the gentleman from Ohio [Mr. Garfield], put into the melting pot and after heating it to red heat find that it retained its original value. We were dealing exclusively with paper money. The precious metals constituted no part of our circulating medium. Yet in the month of May in that year England drew from us more than three times the sum that had produced the suspension in 1857. She took from us in the month of May, 1866, $23,744,194; in June, $15,890,956 more; and in July, $5,821,459 more. Yet we sustained the draft in three successive months—one quarter of the year 1866—of $45,456,609 in gold, and it created not a ripple in our immense, complicated and profitable domestic trade.† No bank failed, no leading house suspended, no railroad company was embarrassed. The business of the country went on growing and prospering as though no collapse had occurred in England, and no draft had been made on us. Why was it? It was, as I have said, because our money was non-exportable; and unable to cripple us by contracting our currency, our creditor satisfied himself with taking a supply of one of the productions of the country. It was, as the gentleman from Ohio [Mr. Garfield], the learned chairman of the committee, has said, because our money is as national as our flag. It is money wherever that flag floats supreme; it is money for all the purposes of the countless domestic exchanges between our citizens over all our broad land and in no other.

Mr. Garfield, of Ohio. How is it when it floats on the sea?

Mr. Kelley. It is still money. When it floats under our flag on the sea it settles the seamen's wages and the pay of the officers. Beyond the sea, in foreign lands, it fortunately is not money: but, sir, when have we had such a long and unbroken career of prosperity in business as since we adopted this non-exportable currency? When we were paying specie we had, at almost regular intervals of about seven

* This would have been accomplished, beyond a peradventure, within the sixty days immediately following the utterance of these words, by reason of a net loss of the precious metals, by export, in July 1870, of $17,313,763 consequent upon the declaration of war between France and Germany.

† See statement in regard to the exports of the precious metals for the fiscal year 1870–71, note, p. 132, *ante*.

years, crises that extended from one end of the country to the other, prostrating every branch of our internal trade and productive industry, and affecting our foreign commerce. These financial revulsions were brought about whenever the debtor nation needed money, as was the case in 1857. So it would be again with $1,000,000,000 of over-due indebtedness and the balance of trade heavily against us every year, if we should be tempted or forced by artificial means into the resumption of specie payments. Resumption, under existing circumstances, would be sheer madness. It would doom many of the enterprising men of this generation who by their energy are adding to the wealth and power of the country to struggle for the remainder of their lives in poverty, or to escape from harassing creditors through the provisions of the bankrupt law.

I am not an expansionist, but I do not fear a slight expansion. The volume of currency does not, as is so often asserted, regulate the price of commodities. We have as much currency to-day as we had in 1866. It is true that some compound-interest notes were then held by the banks as reserve; it is true that more of the three per cent. certificates were then held as reserve, which have been extinguished. But let me also call attention to the fact that during last year and the latter part of the preceding year and the months that have passed of the present year, our receipt of foreign gold has increased, our production has been large, and the shipments of specie have been much diminished; and that as this also enters into the bank reserve we have probably as great or a greater volume of currency than we had in 1866.

But how have prices been affected? Are they as high as they then were? No, sir. I ask gentlemen from the West how the price of wheat compares to-day with the price in 1866? I ask gentlemen from New England how the prices of cotton and woolen goods compare with those of 1866? You can now buy cotton and woolen goods of almost every form and character for currency at as low prices as you could buy them for gold in 1860, and for much less than you could in 1866. You can buy wheat at prices corresponding with those of the period before the war. But in 1866 wheat commanded double its present price; and the special Commissioner of Revenue delighted in holding up the high price of cotton and woolen goods and attributing it to the expanded condition of the currency. It was also the delight of Secretary McCullough to set forth in his annual reports the effect of the inflated currency upon the prices of various commodities. There is scarcely an American product save beef and pork that is not as cheap now as it was in 1860, and which is not vastly lower in price than it was under the same volume of currency in 1866, and the price of beef and pork comes down each year, as the destruction the war made of breeding stock is repaired.

I hope that this bill will be recommitted, with instructions to the committee to report a bill extending the banking system through the South and West, to the extent of from seventy-five to ninety million dollars, under the general provisions of the banking law, and providing that the bonds deposited as the basis of the circulation shall be those already in existence or hereafter to be issued by the Government. I believe such a measure would stimulate every industry, and that with such a measure carried out, some of the banks east of the Hudson might be willing to surrender either their charters or their currency. It would accomplish at any rate an equalization of banking facilities without a sudden or violent disturbance. It could injure no section of the country; it would benefit all its parts and people.

Sir, look at the present condition of California. I hold her up as an illustration of the point I am making, that an adequate volume of currency is essential to the employment of the people and the development of the country. With all the resources of that region, the like of which are not to be found upon the face of the earth, her working people, to the number of thousands, are idle. They congregate in the streets of San Francisco and other cities in want and idleness. Why? Not because there are not adequate and profitable fields for their employment, but because there is not currency enough in California, which rejects paper money, to enable men of enterprise to engage in new undertakings. Using nothing but gold as a currency, they restrain in equal degree their enterprise and the development of the resources of their State. As well might gentlemen maintain that no more than a fixed number of pound weights or yard sticks should be used as that no more than a fixed number of dollars should be permitted to exist. Each of them is but a convenient instrument of trade, for the want of an adequate supply of which the public must suffer.

JUDGE KELLEY'S ACCEPTANCE

OF THE NOMINATION FOR CONGRESS.

On Saturday, July 2d, 1870, Messrs. James Niell, William Sellers, A. M. Eastwick, John Dobson, A. Hanline, B. T. Roberts, and William Matthews, the committee appointed at the late Republican Congressional Convention of the Fourth District, visited Judge Kelley at his residence, and informed him of his renomination to Congress.

Mr. Niell, Chairman of the committee, addressed him as follows:

"We meet you to discharge a duty committed to us by the Convention of Congressional Delegates of the Fourth District, held June 15, that of tendering to you (now for the sixth time) the nomination as their representative in Congress, and also of presenting a series of resolutions, which not only convey the high estimate your constituents put upon your public services, but endorse the manly position assumed by you in your letter of March 8th, now known throughout the country.*

"In making you this tender we frankly confess to have been governed by selfish motives. To decline it, we are well aware, would be to secure to yourself more ease, larger remuneration for your valuable labors, as well as exemption from a thousand perplexities incident to your present position, but for your constituents it would be an irreparable loss. To you they look, as heretofore, for

* The letter referred to was a protest against certain evils which from long practice had the apparent sanction of law. Its substance is contained in the following extract:

"If, therefore, the acceptance of a renomination is to be understood as implying a willingness on my part to be longer regarded as an employment agent, I must beg leave to decline the honor, grateful as I would be to receive it freed from this condition, and tendered in so complimentary a manner. I assure you, my dear sirs, I appreciate most profoundly the honor done me by your letter. I regard the frequent re-election of a citizen to Congress by the people among whom his life has passed as intrinsically the highest honor that can be conferred under our Government, and would be willing to make great personal sacrifices to be its recipient. Permit me, therefore, to suggest that it may be possible that the Republican voters of the Fourth district, having had this great and growing evil brought to their attention, will condemn and endeavor to extirpate it. This could be done by electing a nominating convention which would approve a proper civil service bill, and instruct the candidate nominated to make its principles his rule of action if elected; or would adopt a resolution deprecating the interference of Representatives in the selection of subordinate employes in the public offices and workshops. If this can be done, and the Representative can be permitted to devote his time to the study of the important questions now at issue, and the support of the great interests at stake, I will waive all personal objections, and gratefully comply with your request by placing myself in your hands as a candidate for renomination."

the successful defence of that system of protection to American industry which has made your district one of the most prosperous in the country. We regard the next Congress as among the most important ever held, when great questions of national policy will be discussed and settled, and your services having been of the highest value in the past, they will be more so in the immediate future.

"You were never so well qualified to grapple with the difficulties before us as now; you never occupied a prouder position than now; and we never needed you more than at present. As Mr. Lincoln said to the people on his second election, so we say to you—we have no disposition to trade horses in the middle of the stream; and when you have borne your burden to the other shore, we have no disposition to trade even there. We hope, therefore, you will accept the nomination, pledging ourselves to use our best efforts to give you a triumphant return to your seat in Congress."

Judge Kelley said in reply:

Mr. Chairman and Gentlemen of the Committee: Permit me to thank you for the generous expressions you have been pleased to use toward me in performing the duty confided to you by the convention. You but do me justice in assuming that if I could have retired from public life at the close of the present Congress, without ingratitude or indifference to the wishes of a constituency that, through more than twenty-seven years has, by its many expressions of confidence, sustained me in the discharge of the duties of high public trusts, I would gladly have done so. It seemed to me to be a fitting time to retire. But I should indeed be wanting in sensibility were I not profoundly gratified by the manner in which my renomination was made, and by the unanimous adoption by the convention of the resolution approving the position I assumed in my letter of March 8th. While, therefore, I cannot say that I gladly accept the honor you tender me, I would be wanting in candor if I did not assure you that I do it with just pride and a renewed determination to prove myself worthy of the confidence of so generous a constituency.

The decade with which I entered Congress has been well rounded. The momentous issues which then overshadowed the country have been settled. The Union, cemented by the blood of thousands of the country's bravest and best men, remains united and indivisible. They who were then slaves now enjoy the rights and exercise the prerogatives of citizenship. The importance of this change is not generally appreciated. Good men hail its accomplishment as a grand act of justice, and economical science will soon establish its value as a measure of policy. Slavery excluded free paid labor from the fields and mines of the South, to which freedom welcomes them, and, by the complete enfranchisement of the slaves, several hundred thousand votes have been added to those of the producing classes, by which they may so much the better guard their rights in legislative halls. The workingmen of the country will appreciate the importance of this change in the near future.

New issues have arisen, and they are almost as grave as were those we have thus happily settled. The great question with which we have to deal is not a national but an international one. The parties are not to be summoned by bugle-call, or marched to the music of the rolling drum and ear-piercing fife. Their movements will be determined by the average rates of wages for labor, and the measure of education and chances in life offered to the children of laborers. The historian of the current decade will dwell less upon armies, navies, and ministerial changes, than upon the apportionment of taxes and impost duties, the ebb and flow of immigration, and the relative development of the mineral resources of the countries of which he shall write. The contest is for the commercial independence of the United States or the supremacy of England. *The imminent question for the statesman is how to cheapen all that contributes to the support of human life, while enhancing the value of life by increasing the rewards of labor.* This will, in my judgment, be best accomplished by that nation which, by the well-paid labor of its people produces most of its supplies from raw materials found within its limits; or which, in the language of a quaint old English writer, "sets at work all the poor of the country with the growth of its own lands." Controlled by this theory, I have labored to reduce the schedule of internal taxes with which our industry, enterprise and capital are burdened; to reduce the duties on tea, coffee and spices, which we all consume but none produce, and to put on the free list every species of raw material for manufactures which we do not produce. Much of this has been done. The Senate is still engaged upon the bill, but it has gone far enough to justify me in assuring you that you will, by the legislation of this session, be relieved of at least $70,000,000 of taxes.*

---

* The bill, as it was adopted, repeals taxes which yielded over $80,000,000 revenue during their last year.

The recent experience of England is giving new and startling confirmation to the theories I maintain. Till within a quarter of a century she was the most protective of nations, and enjoyed the proud titles of "Mistress of the Sea," and "Workshop of the World." Keeping her people employed on her raw material, she found in every land a market for her coal, limestone, iron ore, wool, and the labor that had wrought them into articles of utility. But captivated by the glittering sophisms of free traders, she repealed her protective duties, and subjected her industries to competition with those of France, Belgium, Prussia and Austria, whose workmen are paid little more than half the wages received even by the underpaid British artizan. The experiment has been fatal to many of her industries. Observe this pile of recent books and pamphlets, each of which bears the imprint of London or Manchester. They are eight distinct and intelligent protests against a system which, in twenty-five years, has reduced England from her commanding position to that of a mere carrier, and *exporter of skilled workmen,* raw wool, and coal, and manufactures but little advanced, such as yarn and pig-iron. There are men who would force free trade upon this country, and compel our mechanics to compete with those whose inadequate wages have enabled their employers to undermine almost every branch of industry in England, low as her wages are in comparison with those received by the American workman. I cannot refrain from detaining you by citing brief passages from two of these books. Sir Edward Sullivan, in his "Protection to Native Industry," published in February last, says :

"France, Belgium, Switzerland, Prussia and America have increased materially in wealth and prosperity during the last twenty years: capital has flowed steadily and with increased rapidity into them; new manufactures have sprung up, existing industries have increased, trade has flourished, speculation and enterprise have taken the place of apathy and want of confidence. All this has taken place under a system of rigid protection. During the same period England, under a half and half system of free trade, has also increased her commerce, but not in any degree in the same proportion. Our industries are everywhere depressed; many of them have left us, or are fast doing so; trade and manufactures that we once monopolized, are springing up elsewhere under the fostering care of protection; the confidence of our manufacturers is shaken; a spirit of discontent and uneasiness depresses the operative. Now, is this decline of manufacturing prosperity in England, as compared with the increasing prosperity of manufacturing industries throughout the rest of Europe and America, a natural consequence of the spread of capital and communication, or is it the result of our throwing open our ports to foreign competition, removing all protection from our native industries, and bringing into competition with our extravagant workmen and dear labor the cheaper productions of more economical communities?"

In this book, "Home Politics, or the Growth of Trade, considered in its Relations to Labor, Pauperism, and Emigration," which appeared in March last, Mr. Daniel Grant in confirmation of Sir Edward's allegations, says:

"At the outset of this book the question was asked, 'How are the people to find work and food?' And this question is forced upward from the condition in which England stands to-day. We have an enormous pauper population, and a population still greater just above pauperism. We have an export trade that is stationary; a limitation in the demand for labor through the introduction of machinery; a decrease of employment through the force of foreign competition; and, to intensify all these, we have a population whose increase is at least six hundred per day. How are these conditions to be dealt with? It is idle and weak to speak of the great wealth of England as a panacea for our present evils, while starvation exists in our streets, and pauperism and destitution threaten to overwhelm us. The weight of our present position is beginning to produce its natural effect, and men who are usually removed from the impulses which guide public life, are looking around them and saying 'Where is this to end?' It is known that manufacturers are wasting the fortunes which they had amassed in the past, in the endeavor to keep on their mills at half time. It is known that every kind and every class of employment are not only filled to overflowing, but the applicants are hopeless in their endeavors to obtain work. In the streets of London men are to be found by thousands, who are ready to toil and cannot find the work to do, and as week passes week fresh circumstances continually crop up, showing that underneath all this there are states of destitution still more terrible; and it is thus that the question comes fairly home, how is this to end?"

So regardless of the rights of our laboring people are the free-traders, or revenue reformers, as they call themselves in this country, that, in full view of the effect of free trade upon the laboring classes of England, they would prostrate flourishing and leading industries by repealing the duties on coal, salt, lumber, pig-iron, etc. They would do this, they say, to give the workman cheap coal, salt, and other commodities. To the unemployed workman whose rent is due, and who has not the means to buy a meal, it is of not much importance whether the price of a ton of coal or salt is a few cents more or less. What he wants is steady work and fair wages. Without these his life is a waste and his family a burden, though he loves them ever so tenderly.

Let me, as an illustration, consider the coal question for a moment. We have more coal than all other civilized nations combined. Its measures stretch across the continent from Rhode Island and North Carolina to Mount Diablo, near the Bay of San Francisco, and around the extended shores of Puget Sound. It also abounds in the British Provinces on both coasts. Its production and transportation are among the great industries of our country, and give employment to many thousands of men and support to their families and the villages in which they dwell. They feed on American grain and meat, and are clad in American wool, spun and woven by American labor. Their product is carried over our railroads and canals, and when transported by sea, gives employment to American-built vessels. There is a duty of $1.25 per ton on foreign coal imported into this country. The wages paid in the British Provinces do not equal ours by one half, nor are the provinces burdened by our war debt and taxes; and we derive every year about $500,000 duty in gold from the importation of foreign coal. It is mined by men who feed on provincial grain, and wear English cloth, hats, and shoes, and is brought to our ports by vessels built with the cheap labor of the Provinces. What benefit could possibly accrue to any of our laboring people by removing the duty on coal, stimulating its importation, and robbing the treasury of half a million dollars annually? I freely confess that I am too dull to see it.

But I detain you too long. As I have said, I accept with pride the nomination you so handsomely tender me, and pledge myself to continued endeavors to prove myself worthy of the confidence you and those you represent so generously bestow.

LETTER ON THE CHINESE QUESTION.

JOHN C. LIBE, ESQ., *Recording Secretary of Science Council of the Order of United American Mechanics:*

Dear Sir: Your favor covering the circular which you inform me you were instructed by your Council to transmit to me, with the request that I would "favor the members of the Council with my views upon the questions embodied therein," is at hand.

It is to be regretted that neither your note nor the circular propounds a question. The latter, however, embraces the preamble and resolutions adopted by the Council on the 5th of July last, which have reference to a question of great public and private interest. Having bestowed much consideration upon the subject to which they relate, I am grateful to the members of your Council for the opportunity thus afforded me of expressing my views thereon to so numerous and intelligent a body of my fellow-citizens as the members of the Order of United American Mechanics.

The preamble and resolutions assert that "a movement has been inaugurated in neighboring States to introduce Chinese labor on an extensive scale into this country, and that such movement, if successful, must operate to the great disadvantage of the American mechanic and laboring man," and that "the time has arrived" when the members of your order should "use every exertion and exercise all the influence in their power to prevent the carrying out of this iniquitous and unjust measure." These propositions, I believe, involve the questions on which you request an expression of my views.

It is proper that, before proceeding to the consideration of details, I should say that I believe that humanity and the true interests of all the people of our broad, richly endowed and diversified, but thinly settled country, require us to welcome such of the people of all other countries as may, in pursuance of their own choice, come to dwell among us, adopt our language and habits, and help us to develop our dormant resources and maintain our republican institutions.

But this proposition, broad as it is, does not cover those who may be brought hither by force or decoyed by false representation, for the purpose of being used, without regard to their rights or those of the people at large. For instance, it does not embrace such as may be found to have been brought as slaves were in the early days of the Republic from Africa, or coolies were from India prior to the Act of February 19, 1862, entitled "An Act to prohibit the coolie trade by American citizens in American vessels," the text of which may be found on page 145 of 2d Brightly's Digest. Though but a new member at the date of its passage by the House of Representatives, it was my privilege to co-operate with its distinguished author, the late Hon. T. Dawes Eliot, in procuring the enactment of this humane law. Nor, again, does my proposition apply to those who, being ignorant of our language and of the ordinary rate of wages paid for labor and the cost of living in this country, are seduced into coming here under a contract for years of labor for wages which, though in advance of those they might earn at home, are insufficient for the support of an American mechanic and the maintenance of his children while obtaining the education due to them in our common schools. Our laws should secure to the victims of such wrongs the amplest means of redress, and, at least, enable them to return to their native land at the cost of the wrong-doer.

The coolie trade was suppressed by law because it was a system of violence and robbery; and as the system by which Koopmanschap and others are attempting to induce hordes of Chinese laborers to come to this country, under contract to work for wages upon which they cannot live as American workingmen should live, is an organized system of deception and fraud, it should be reprobated by our laws as sternly as the other has been.

You will observe that my opposition to organized efforts to stimulate Chinese emigration to this country is not based on hostility to the Chinese, but that it arises from their ignorance of the value and current price of the services they contract to render, of the habits of our working people, and of the general cost of living in this country; and that, coming as mere sojourners, to return at the expiration of a contract, they will be unencumbered by the expense of a family, or civic or social duties, and can afford to work for wages that will not enable an American citizen to maintain a home and educate his children as republican institutions require.

The constant aim of American statesmanship should be to secure to labor such a share of its production as may enable each laborer to make provision for age or adversity. Our country is so broad, and embraces such an infinite variety of soil, climate and resources that, had we the population and skill to convert every description of our raw material and avail ourselves of the diversities of our soil and climate, we might supply our own wants and maintain a rate of wages independent of those of other countries. But so long as part of our workshops are beyond the seas, and we depend on foreign shops for a large part of our manufactured goods, our rates of wages must be affected by those of other countries.*

Chinese wages are, I believe, lower than those paid in any other civilized country. American wages are the highest, and the two rates cannot be maintained in the same community. The attempt on an extended scale to commingle them would be as disastrous to the capital as it would to the labor of the country. It would unsettle prices and cause anarchy in trade. A little reflection will satisfy any experienced business man on this point, as the

---

* How thoroughly British capitalists understand the effect of our higher wages upon the prices of commodities, and the inadequacy of the existing tariff, especially on iron, to counter-balance this difference, is shown by the following extract from Ryland's *Iron Trade Circular* (Birmingham, England), of July 1st, 1871:

"Notwithstanding the efforts which many of our foreign customers are making to develop their own iron trade, we as yet do not seem to suffer. The most important of these efforts is that made by the United States of America. We have often called attention to the remarkable development of the American iron trade, and the possibility of the people of that great country supplying themselves entirely with their own iron. America teems with the raw material, and it only waits the hand of man to dig the ore, to smelt and puddle the iron, and to turn it into all the varieties of the finished article. So far America, no doubt, could supply the world with the whole of its requirements, and could thus close the English trade altogether. But as long as the labor market in the United States remains in its present condition, so long will the English iron trade maintain its hold upon that country. American capitalists are not at all anxious to invest in the iron trade, notwithstanding its strong protective tariff, and while labor forms ninety per cent. of every ton of manufactured iron, and when this item is of far greater value in the States than it is in our own country, it is quite impossible for the Americans to compete with us even with such a highly protective tariff as they now enjoy."

employer who paid Chinese wages could always undersell those in the same business who sought to enable their workmen to live as American citizens should live, by paying them our customary wages for their work.

Sir Edward Sullivan, in his recent noble appeal for the working people of England, entitled "Protection to Native Industry," says:

> "Wages in France, Belgium, Prussia, Austria, and Switzerland are from thirty to fifty per cent. lower than in England; rent, clothing, food, beer, taxes and general charges are all in the same proportion; the habits of the people are economical in the extreme; the manufacturers have as much capital, science and enterprise, and the operatives as much skill and intelligence and technical education and industry as we have; they get their raw materials very nearly at the same price as we do. The question is, Can our manufacturers, with higher wages, higher rates and taxes, higher general charges, and our operatives, with dearer food, dearer clothing, dearer house rent and extravagant habits, produce as cheaply as they can?"

Let us press Sir Edward's point a little further, and apply it to the question under consideration. A report just made to the Treasury Department, by Mr. Edward Young, Chief of the Bureau of Statistics, shows that English wages are as far below ours as those of continental States are below those of England. The report appears to have been compiled from ample data and with great care, and makes due allowance for the difference between gold and our currency and the number of hours of labor required for a week's pay. Without detaining you with too many examples, let me say that this official report shows that operatives in cotton mills in the New England and Middle States, exclusive of overseers, receive 39.9 per cent. more than in England, and that in the case of overseers the excess is 74.3 per cent.

The comparison of the wages paid in woolen mills is made from a wider field, as this branch of industry is growing rapidly in the West. It embraces the mills of Virginia, Indiana, Wisconsin, Iowa, and Kansas, as well as those of the Middle and New England States, and shows that the "average advance of wages paid in the United States in 1869 over those of England in 1867–68 (both in gold) was 24.36 per cent." The rates paid in American paper mills, including those to boys and females, as ascertained from the mills of New England, Pennsylvania, Ohio, Illinois and Wisconsin, are 82 per cent. greater than in England. And, as the last illustration drawn from Mr. Young's report with which I will detain you, workmen in iron founderies and in machine shops throughout New England, the Middle and Western States, and California receive for their labor 86 per cent. more than is paid in England.

Thus it appears that though the average English operative receives for his work nearly double the wages paid his continental competitor, he gets on an average little more than half as much as he would for the same work in this country. The welfare of our country, both present and ultimate, requires the maintenance of our scale of wages, and its advance whenever and wherever it is practicable. But how is this to be accomplished? How can the present rates be defended against competition with the productions of the underpaid laborers of England and the continent? I believe that a protective tariff is the only possible defence of our rate of wages. While the underpaid labor is performed in foreign countries, we may defend the wages of the American mechanic against competition by imposing upon its productions, when imported into this country, duties equal to the difference between our wages and the lowest rates paid in competing countries.

An adequately protective tariff is the American workman's sole defence against ruinous competition by the underpaid workmen of foreign countries. But if French, Belgian, German, Austrian or English mechanics could be brought to this country under contract to work for three, five or seven years for such wages as they receive at home, how could the wages of the American workman be defended against the destructive competition? I freely admit that I cannot see how it might be done. Can you or any member of your council show me? No tariff or other law can protect wages against home competition, and I am, therefore, opposed to permitting the importation of men who have contracted to work in our midst for a term of years at such wages as are paid in China, Austria, Belgium, Germany or England. The prevalence of such a system would, as your resolutions assert, "greatly reduce the pay for skilled labor, and thereby lessen the family comforts of the great body of the American people."

"Buy where you can buy cheapest," is a cardinal maxim of free traders and revenue reformers. It is plausible, but delusive. If applied to labor, it would bring Chinese workmen to us by the million. Yet the free trade agitators, both in and out of Congress, when vindicating this maxim, assert that the tariff which protects his wages and his chances for steady work, injures the workingman by increasing the price of the commodities he consumes. They also say that in addition to cheapening what he consumes, the laborer's market would be increased by a reduction of his wages, as we could then increase our commerce and ship our goods to foreign countries in competition with European manufacturers. To the thoughtless and inexperienced this is all very plausible. But with your experience and observation, you must perceive that to reduce the price of our goods low enough to accomplish this would require us to reduce our wages below the English standard, as the cheaper labor of France, Belgium, Switzerland, Germany and Austria is restricting her exports and driving the productions of England out of common markets. "Buy where you can buy the cheapest," the only doctrine by which the employment of coolie labor in this country can be justified, is not only ruining the working people of England, but uprooting many of her industries which were believed to be established on impregnable foundations, and thus involving the laborer and capitalist in a common ruin. To attain cheapness she repealed, not only the duties imposed on food, but those which protected her labor against the competition of the lower wages of the continent. She entered enthusiastically upon the experiment of free trade, and has persisted in it for about a quarter of a century. What has been the result of this race for cheap labor and cheap goods? Its consequences have been such as I hope our country may long escape. British exports are not only stationary, but declining, and poverty and pauperism have increased so rapidly that the people of Great Britain are no longer able to consume their own productions as freely as they formerly could, and the demand for labor falls off under the double influence of both declining export trade and home consumption.*

* A correspondent of the *N. Y. Tribune* writing from London, March 11th, 1871, said:

"It is stated that M. Thiers declined M. Bismarck's proposals for a treaty of commerce between France and Germany on the ground 'that France would be compelled to restore the equilibrium of her finances by a high tariff.' In making this declaration, the distinguished French statesman was not only foreshadow-

In his recent work, "Home Politics, or the Growth of Trade Considered in its Relation to Labor, Pauperism and Emigration," Mr. Daniel Grant demonstrates the correctness of these assertions by presenting from the highest official sources the number of England's paupers, and the value of her exports for the three latest years for which the figures had been compiled. They are as follows:

	Paupers.	Exports.
1866	920,344	£188,917,536
1867	958,824	181,183,971
1868	1,004,823	179,463,644

---

ing a commercial policy in harmony with his antecedents as a strong Protectionist, but one absolutely forced upon his country by the exigencies of her position. To obtain the revenue which France now finds herself compelled to raise, she must resort to the most stringent measures; and there is no form of impost at once so productive and so little burdensome to the mass of the people as a high tariff. The remark is trite; but no man feels an indirect tax as he does a direct one. A moderate, or even a considerable enhancement in the price of various commodities, will be borne with far more patience than a house, property, or income-tax, which must be paid, at stated intervals, in hard cash.

"It is a curious fact; but, when France has reversed her commercial policy, as she proposes to do, England will be the only great manufacturing country in Europe—I might say in the world—which still adheres to Free Trade. Even her own colonies—those at least, in which the people are allowed self-government, such as Canada and Australia—have deliberately adopted a Protective Tariff. As to England herself, she has now tried Free Trade for several years, and with what result? In the opinion of Cobden and the Manchester school of political economists, it was to be a panacea for every ill. The loom was to be ever busy; the workshop ever full! Well! such an utter prostration of business as has existed in this country for the last five years has not been known since 1840. It is true this state of things cannot be exclusively attributed to Free Trade. But if Free Trade be not altogether responsible for the stagnation of business, it has certainly not in any way modified, but, on the contrary, in a considerable degree intensified the distress which has arisen from it. Numerous branches of industry have been seriously affected, while some, like the paper and silk manufactures, have been all but completely ruined by the present commercial policy of Great Britain. The cheapness of labor on the continent—notably in Belgium—has induced English capitalists in many instances to enter into contracts with firms there to execute orders for machinery and iron work of all kinds, both of which have hitherto been specialties of this country. In some cases, indeed, iron manufacturers have closed their factories here and established others in Belgium, simply on account of the difference in the price of labor. Not only the locomotives, but a very considerable portion of the other rolling-stock of English railways, is now manufactured in that country or in Denmark. The very cars on the Brixton and Kensington Tramway, by which I travel daily, have—with the exception of the pattern cars, which were built in New York—been made in Copenhagen. And it is a fact within my knowledge that the contract for the whole of the wood-work on the new St. Thomas's Hospital was executed in Norway; even the window-sashes and frames were fitted and put together there, and sent over finished and ready to be inserted in the brick-work.

"The middle, or trading, class is not altogether dissatisfied with the present state of things. So long as they can buy and sell, they care not whose labor has prepared the article for the market, whether the article be domestic or foreign. But this narrow, short-sighted policy would, if persisted in, ultimately defeat itself. At present, there is an enormous amount of accumulated wealth in England, and the evil of the mass of non-workers (for pauperism is frightfully on the increase), who have to be supported by the workers, is only partially felt by the community at large; and scarcely at all by the law-making class."

After commenting upon the fact that more than one thousand paupers are each week added to the already terrible list, Mr. Grant says:

> "Even this large increase does not indicate the exact extent of poverty—it points to the still wider field of misery that exists among the classes from which pauperism is fed. Let any one think what is the state of destitution through which a man passes before he is willing to accept relief and allow himself to be branded as a pauper. Those who know the working classes best know the profound abhorrence they entertain of the workhouse. Any privation, any sorrow, any destitution rather than that; and the natural inference is that the pressure of want is not only severe, but has been long enough sustained to have swept away all articles of clothing, as well as all household goods, before the sufferers bend to their fate."

Thus deplorable has been the effect upon the laboring classes of England of the determination of her people to accept the glittering fallacies of the free trade school of economists, and buy labor and its products where they can buy them cheapest. Let us now glance for a moment at the effect it has had upon capital invested in special industries. It was soon discovered that the surface ores of the copper mines of Peru, which are dug by peons—another name for slaves—were cheaper than those of the deep mines of Cornwall and Devonshire. These latter, with all their machinery, have consequently been abandoned, and such of the miners employed in them as had saved sufficient to pay their passage have emigrated, and the balance with their families have gone to the workhouse. The manufacture of silk had made prosperous towns of Coventry and Macclesfield, but Lyons and Paris could undersell them, and regardless of the interests of their toiling countrymen, "the nobility and gentry" of England, looking only to the interests of the consumer, bought where they could buy cheapest, and the silk-mills of Coventry and Macclesfield, with their expensive machinery, became worthless, and many of the people who had found employment in them went to the workhouse also. I could refer to scores of such instances, but they will occur to your own mind, and I will proceed to an illustration of a more general character.

Having heard that the home consumption of British cottons had, within a few years, fallen off thirty-five per cent., I wrote to a friend who has resided in England for some years to learn whether the statement was based on a mere estimate or was an ascertained fact. I could not credit the assertion. My correspondent, however, sent me copies of elaborate tables from a paper prepared and read before the Manchester Statistical Society by Mr. Elijah Helms, which was printed by the society. By comparing the home consumption of British cottons during the years 1866–7–8 with that during 1859–60–61, Mr. Helms shows that the decrease in that brief period had been equal to 211,933,000 pounds of raw cotton, or thirty-five per cent. I have also before me an able pamphlet, by a Cotton Manufacturer, entitled "An Inquiry into the Cause of the long-continued Depression of the Cotton Trade," which was published in London and Manchester in the latter part of last year, in which the fact is again proven. After spreading before his readers a large array of official figures the author says:

"The case stands as follows: Our entire exports of cotton goods to all countries have increased six per cent.; to India they have decreased thirteen per cent.; to the four principal continental countries they have increased forty-five per cent.; while the imports from these four countries have fallen off two and a half per cent. At the same time our home trade, *which should have been our principal support*, has fallen off thirty-five per cent."

The facts I have thus hastily thrown together address themselves not only to the artisan and laborer, but to the farmer and him whose capital is employed in any branch of productive industry. What each wants is a steady and remunerative market for that which he has to sell, and this cannot be had when that great mass of consumers who live by toil are compelled, as they are in other countries, to labor for the least amount of compensation that will serve to keep body and soul together, without an aspiration or a hope that is to be realized this side of the grave. No amount of foreign trade would compensate the farmers and manufacturers of the United States for the curtailment of their home market that would inevitably follow the reduction of our wages even to the English standard. To whose industry, enterprise or capital can the more than one million English paupers give profitable employment? Or, who can sell his goods to that more numerous class from which Mr. Grant says "pauperism is fed," and who are selling "all articles of clothing, as well as household goods" in the vain hope of escaping the workhouse? Do you think that they know much about the color and quality of American wheat, or even of the flavor of the beef or mutton of "Merrie England," or are liberal patrons of any branch of industry?

The apostles of free trade regard the value of a nation's exports as the test of its prosperity. They worship foreign trade and commerce. From this test I dissent. *That nation is most truly prosperous which has fewest paupers, the freest domestic commerce, and whose people are able to enjoy most largely the comforts and luxuries of life as the rewards of their labor, even though it have no foreign trade.* To promote foreign trade free traders would cheapen goods, although it is apparent that to cheapen them sufficiently to enable us to take her customers from England, and so increase our trade, we must reduce our wages to a point below those she pays, as we must underbid her in order to induce them to buy from us. Regarding protective duties as an obstruction to commerce, they resist their enactment and strive to repeal or reduce those imposed by existing laws, although to effect either their repeal or reduction would inevitably compel a general reduction of the rate of wages; for were we to repeal the duties which now defend and protect the wages of the American mechanic, and secure to him our generous home market for his labor, our stores and warehouses would soon be gorged with the cheaper productions of the ill-paid labor of Europe, and the proprietors of our mines, mills, factories and workshops would be forced, by the want of a market for their higher priced goods, to discharge their hands and close their establishments. Nothing can be clearer than this. And in three years from our abandonment of the protective system the workingmen of the country would suffer again the agonies endured in 1837, and 1857, and British statesmen would be able, as they then were, to comment upon the depression of American labor, and show that poverty and pauperism were increasing as rapidly in the industrial centres of the United States as they now are in those of England. Indeed, such action on our part would be an unspeakable blessing to England. It would revive her trade and some of the leading branches of her languishing industry. She has natural advantages, which counterbalance the lower wages of the continent in the production of many articles, among which I may name salt, coal, pig and bar iron, rails, both of iron and Bessemer steel, cast steel, and iron steamships, with all of which she would supply our market in the absence of protective duties and the venerable law which prohibits the granting of an American register to a foreign-built vessel.

But you may ask what has all this to do with the question upon which Science Council directed you to request an expression of my views? A moment's reflection will show you its pertinence. The danger you would ward off is the competition of underpaid labor; and if it be true that low wages, even in distant countries, against which a protective tariff can defend you, may in the event of the withdrawal of such defence by Congress, overwhelm and destroy you, how much more destructive would be the effect of the importation of hordes of men bound by contract to work in your midst at Chinese, French, Belgian, German, Austrian or English wages? If once established in your midst, no law could protect you against their competition; and I assure you and the members of your council that I have too just a sense of the rights and dignity of labor, and have toiled too long and hard to secure compensation even to the slave for his work in the shop, or cotton, sugar, or rice field, to permit myself to approve of such an arrangement, let it promise what incidental advantages it may.

In conclusion, permit me to say again that I am not opposed to the voluntary immigration of the people of China into this country. If left to their own impulses, and to pay the cost of the voyage, those only will come who are of the better class and have by energy and thrift been able to accumulate a sum sufficient to bring them here and start them in their new home; but under a system by which each man's passage is paid and his subsistence while here assured, we shall probably get the most abject and possibly only the most degraded denizens of the populous cities of China. Those who come voluntarily and at their own cost will take an interest in their adopted country and its institutions, acquire our language, and adopt our habits. Such an immigration would, like that from other countries, stimulate our general industries while increasing our productive power; it would, by peopling our vast territories that now lie waste and unproductive, enhance the demand for labor by increasing our home market and the carrying trade in which so much of our capital and so many of our people are engaged. But it may do more than this. It is in the power of the Chinese to establish new and profitable industries among us. Let me mention two, the introduction of which would injure none of us but benefit all. I allude to tea and silk. For tea we send abroad about $10,000,000 annually, and for silk, about $20,000,000. We produce no tea, and are but experimenting in the production of raw silk, of which we import $2,500,000 per annum for the use of our infant silk manufactories at Paterson, Hartford, and Philadelphia, in some of which I may remark, machinery is now used that was once profitably employed in Coventry and Macclesfield. We have immense natural fields for the cultivation of both tea and silk besides those of California and Arkansas, and the Chinese, the earliest and most successful cultivators of both, would benefit us immensely by transferring their experience and patient industry to our country. I would not, therefore, exclude them by legal enactment. But to protect the right even of foreigners to fair wages for work done in this country, and to avert the dangers threatened to American mechanics by the importation of hordes of coolies, I would provide by statute that any contract made in a foreign country by which a person proposing to emigrate to any State or territory within the United States shall bind himself to labor for any term of years or months, at a rate of wages specified therein, shall be null and void.

Believing that a law embodying these provisions will be enacted by Congress at its next session, I remain,

Yours, very truly,

WM. D. KELLEY.

PHILADELPHIA, *August* 22, 1870.

CENTENNIAL CELEBRATION AND INTERNATIONAL EXPOSITION.

Speech Delivered in the House of Representatives, January 10th, 1871.

The House having under consideration the bill (H. R. No. 1478) to provide for celebrating the one hundredth anniversary of American independence by holding an international exhibition of arts, manufactures, and products of the soil and mine, in the city of Philadelphia and State of Pennsylvania, in the year 1876—

Mr. Kelley said:

Mr. Speaker: This bill has been treated by its opponents as though its object were a purely local one. It is not so. The city of Philadelphia, the State of Pennsylvania, and the Franklin Institute of Pennsylvania originated the movement for the centennial celebration of the Declaration of Independence, and are willing to take, under the auspices of the Government of the United States, the responsibility of its preparation and management. And to that end the bill does little more than ordain that such a celebration shall be had at Philadelphia, and provide for the appointment by the President of one commissioner from each State and Territory upon the nomination of the Governor thereof.

The proposed exhibition is to celebrate events that are not merely of national but of world-wide interest. It is to commemorate not a day, but an epoch in universal history; not an event, but a series of events that occurred in rapid succession, gave birth to republican liberty, and organized a nation that stands to-day, when measured by the number of its population, the extent and geographical position of its territory, the intelligence and enterprise of its people, and the variety and volume of its resources and productions first and proudest, though but an infant among the nations of the world. London and Paris were venerable cities when the American continent was discovered, and this bill proposes to invite the people of London,

Paris, and the world at large to behold the results of one century of republican liberty in a country, whose people are the offspring of those of every land and clime, and to challenge them to present the best results of their genius, experience, and labor in comparison with those of this young and heterogeneous but free people.

The proposed celebration, sir, will prove to be of national importance by its relation to the business of the country. I hold in my hand one of the most instructive politico-economic works of the last year. "Home Politics; or, the Growth of Trade considered in its Relation to Labor, Pauperism, and Emigration," by Daniel Grant, published in London. I request the attention of the House to a passage from this work with respect to the influence of the first and second expositions on the trade of England. It is as follows:

> "In an early part of this chapter it was pointed out that the personal knowledge of buyer and seller forms an important link in the growth of trade, and in one sense the first exhibition aided this. Men who for years had known each other by name came to know each other as a matter of fact, and thus built up relations that produced a mutual good. The mere prestige of the 'world's bazaar' brought men from every quarter of the habitable world, and they carried away with them to their distant homes the memory of English productions, that bore fruit then and has borne fruit since. At the time, among the whole of our manufacturers, it was recognized as an unchallengable fact that the exhibition had stimulated trade, that orders were plentiful, and that its success was great.
>
> "The statistics do more than bear this point out; the bound in our exports is both clear and decisive. It will be necessary to notice here that the direct results of the exhibition would not be manifest until the year after it closed, and would most probably extend twelve months beyond. The exhibition did not close until the end of the year; the orders given during the time would be delivered partly in the year 1851, and partly in 1852, and the return orders some months later, so that the effects would appear in the following years. The statistics here given show very markedly the growth of our exports at the particular epochs.
>
> "Our exports in 1851, were £74,448,722, in 1852, £78,076,854, and in 1853, £98,933,780; showing an advance in the two years of £24,485,050.
>
> "The same results are apparent in the two years after our second exhibition.
>
> "Our exports in 1862, were £123,992,264; in 1863, £146,602,342; and in 1864, £160,444,053; showing an advance in the two years of £36,456,789."

No one can consider these figures and the reflections of Mr. Grant without conceding that such an exhibition, held in one of our great cities, would largely expand the trade of the entire country, and would attract an enormous flow of immigration, especially of skilled mechanics, artists, and men of enterprise whose capital though too limited to produce a competence in Europe, might enable them to amass fortunes in this country of cheap land and undeveloped resources.

The question, therefore, is one of national importance, and should not be treated as a local one, because it is proposed that the commemorative exhibition shall be held in the city in which the events which it is to commemorate occurred. I regret exceedingly that the gentleman from New Jersey [Mr. Cleveland] is not in his seat. He proposed to hold such a celebration in New York, and, in support of his strange proposition, invited the attention of the House to the fact that for forty years New York has had an association for the promotion of the mechanic arts, known as the American Institute. Sir, forty-five years ago, I was a copy-reader in a printing office, and I remember well that among the copy which most puzzled me was that of Dr. Jones, who was then at the head of the Patent Office and editor of the journal of the Franklin Institute, an institution which had then been publishing its proceedings for several years. This was five years before the organization of the American Institute. The Franklin Institute of Pennsylvania hailed the organization of and has rejoiced in the prosperity of the American Institute, and recognizes it as its most successful offspring and as one of its most influential co-workers in developing our manufacturing and mining resources and promoting the general interests of our country.

The gentleman from New York [Mr. Brooks], in opposing the bill, spoke of. the inconsequential character of the preamble and resolutions. Regarding the proposed exposition as a commemoration only of the Declaration of Independence, he said that document had nothing to do with the progress of manufactures and the arts. In this opinion he dissents from that of Thomas Jefferson, as he will discover by turning to volume one of Jefferson's Works, page 129. He will there find that Mr. Jefferson assigns the attempt by England to suppress manufactures and prevent their establishment as a potent cause of the revolt of the Colonies. He says:

"That to heighten still the idea of parliamentary justice, and to show with what moderation they are like to exercise power where themselves are to feel no part of its weight, we take leave to mention to his Majesty certain other acts of the British Parliament by which we were prohibited from manufacturing for our own use the articles we raise on our own lands with our own labor. By an act passed in the fifth year of the reign of his late Majesty, King George II., an American subject is forbidden to make a hat for himself of the fur which he has taken perhaps on his own soil; an instance of despotism to which no parallel can be produced in the most arbitrary ages of British history. By one other act, passed in the twenty-third year of the same reign, the iron which we make we are forbidden to manufacture; and heavy as that article is, and necessary in every branch of husbandry, besides commission and insurance, we are to pay freight for it to Great Britain, and freight for it back again, for the purpose of supporting, not men, but machines, in the island of Great Britain."*

That gentlemen may perceive how well founded these complaints of the colonists were, let me 'quote a portion of the two laws to which Mr. Jefferson refers. I might cite many kindred acts, but parts of these will suffice. Let me read the fourth section of chapter twenty-two of the fifth year (1732) of George II. It is as follows:

"Whereas the art and mystery of making hats in Great Britain hath arrived to great perfection, and considerable quantities of hats manufactured in this kingdom have heretofore been exported to his Majesty's plantations or Colonies in America, who have been wholly supplied with hats from Great Britain; and whereas great quantities of hats have of late years been made, and the said manufacture is daily increasing in the British plantations in America, and is from thence exported to foreign markets, which were heretofore supplied from Great Britain, and the hat-makers in the said plantations take many apprentices for small terms, to the discouragement of the said trade, and debasing the said mannfacture; wherefore, for preventing the said ill practices for the future, and for promoting and encouraging the trade of making hats in Great Britain,

"*Be it enacted by the king's most excellent majesty, by and with the advice and consent of the Lords spiritual and temporal and Commons in this present Parliament assembled, and by the authority of the same,* That from and after the 29th day of September, A. D. 1732, no hats or felts whatsoever, dyed or undyed, finished or unfinished, shall be shipped, laden, or put on board any ship, or vessel in any place or ports within any of the British plantations, upon any pretence whatsoever, by any person or persons whatsoever; and also, that no hats or felts, either dyed or undyed, finished or unfinished, shall be laden upon any horse, cart, or other carriage, to the intent or purpose to be exported, transported, shipped off, carried, or conveyed out of any of the said British plantations to any other of the British plantations, or to any other place whatsoever, by any person or persons whatsoever."

---

* See Jefferson's letter of January 9, 1816—*ante*, page 51.

The ninth and tenth sections of the other act referred to, chapter twenty-eight of the twenty-third year (1750) of George II., are as follows:

"IX. That from and after the 24th day of June, 1750, no mill or other engine for slitting or rolling of iron, or any plating forge to work with a tilt-hammer, or any furnace for making steel, shall be erected, or after such erection, continued in any of his Majesty's colonies in America; and if any person or persons shall erect, or cause to be erected, or after such erection continue, or cause to be continued, in any of the said Colonies, any such mill, engine, forge, or furnace, every person or persons so offending shall, for every such mill, engine, forge, or furnace, forfeit the sum of £200 of lawful money of Great Britain.

"X. *And it is hereby further enacted by the authority aforesaid*, That every such mill, engine, forge, or furnace so erected or continued, contrary to the directions of this act, shall be deemed a common nuisance; and that every Governor, Lieutenant-Governor, or Commander-in-chief of his Majesty's colonies in America, where any such mill, engine, forge, or furnace shall be erected or continued, shall, upon information to him made and given, upon the oath of any two or more credible witnesses, that any such mill, engine, forge, or furnace hath been so erected or continued, (which oath such Governor, Lieutenant-Governor, or Commander-in-chief is hereby authorized and required to administer,) order and cause every such mill, engine, forge or furnace to be abated within the space of thirty days next after such information given and made as aforesaid; and if any Governor, Lieutenant-Governor, or Commander-in-chief shall neglect or refuse to do so within the time herein before limited for that purpose, every such Governor, Lieutenant-Governor, or Commander-in-chief so offending shall, for every such offense, forfeit the sum of £500 of lawful money of Great Britain, and shall from thenceforth be disabled to hold or enjoy any office of trust or profit under his Majesty, his heirs or successors."

Thus, sir, the history of the Colonies, the laws of England, and the express assertion of the author of the Declaration of Independence assure us that no character of celebration of the events we propose to commemorate could be more appropriate than one which would exhibit to the world the results of the mining, manufacturing, and artistic skill of a people who, one hundred years ago, were not permitted to manufacture a felt hat or a plow or nail from the productions of their own soil. Certainly no celebration could be more apposite or more fitting.

Then comes the question, "Where should it be held?" Why, sir, it should, in the judgment of the country, be held where the Continental Congress assembled, deliberated, and acted, and where Carpenters' Hall still stands, as it did when the first prayer for Congress was uttered. It should be in the vicinity of Independence Hall, where the Declaration of Independence was signed and proclaimed to the people, and where may be seen the old bell, whose peals summoned them, now shattered, but still perfect in form, and bearing the prophetic inscription, cast upon it about a century before the great event it announced. "Proclaim liberty throughout all the land unto all the inhabitants thereof." It should be near to the hall in which the Constitution was framed and adopted, and to that in which the first Congress of the United States assembled; and these are all in Philadelphia. Were the celebration of the centennial anniversary of this great epoch, embracing this series of grand historical events, to be held in any other city it would be out of place, and the people who might attend it would wander from its precincts to Philadelphia, in search of the scenes and halls amid which and in which the men whose deeds they would commemorate had consummated their great designs.

Can Philadelphia accommodate it? Sir, many of the members of this House, including members of the Committee on Foreign Affairs and the Committee on Manufactures, have visited our city with reference to this question. They spent delightful hours in our park, unequaled in the world, either in extent or beauty, through which flow the beautiful Schuylkill and the romantic Wissahickon, and which contains more than twenty-six hundred acres of undulating land, embracing both banks of these beautiful streams. When Miss Frances Anne Kemble first visited us she was fresh from Italy and Switzerland, among whose mountains and lakes she had passed years; yet familiar as she was with the wondrous beauty of their scenery she found its equal within the limits of Philadelphia's park. Listen to what she said on the subject:

To the Wissahickon.

My feet shall tread no more thy mossy side,
  When once they turn away, thou pleasant water,
Nor ever more, reflected in thy tide,
  Will shine the eyes of the white island's daughter.
But often in my dreams, when I am gone
  Beyond the sea that parts thy home and mine,
  Upon thy banks the evening sun will shine,
And I shall hear thy low, still flowing on.
And when the burden of existence lies
  Upon my soul darkly and heavily,
I'll clasp my hands over my weary eyes,
  Thou pleasant water, and thy clear waves see.

Bright be thy course, forever and forever—
  Child of pure mountain springs and mountain snow
And as thou wanderest on to meet the river,
  Oh, still in light and music may'st thou flow!
I never shall come back to thee again,
When once my sail is shadowed on the main;
Nor ever shall I hear thy laughing voice,
As on their rippling way thy waves rejoice;
Nor ever see the dark green cedar throw
Its gloomy shade o'er the clear depths below.
Never, from stony rifts of granite gray,
Sparkling like diamond rocks in the sun's ray,
Shall I look down on thee, thou pleasant stream,
Beneath whose crystal folds the gold sands gleam.
Wherefore, farewell! but whensoe'er again
  The wintry spell melts from the earth and air;
And the young spring comes dancing through thy glen,
  With fragrant, flowery breath, and sunny hair;
When through the snow the scarlet berries gleam,
Like jewels strewn upon thy banks, fair stream,
My spirit shall through many a summer's day
Return among thy peaceful woods to stray.

Here, sir, amidst these scenes of beauty, and in the midst of a collection of American trees and foliage such as is nowhere else to be found within the limits of a city, we ask that this exposition shall be held. Sir, we make this request not with reference to the beauty of the site alone, but to its utility and fitness also.

Through the Philadelphia park passes the junction railway, by which goods shipped for exhibition from any part of the continent of America, which is connected with a through line of railway, may be delivered at the ground proposed to be set apart for the exhibition without transfer or breaking bulk.

Again, the great thing that the people of Europe would learn by visiting us, would be the effect of free institutions upon the masses of the people, and that which they would most admire, and which they could see nowhere else in such numbers and perfection, would be the homes of our working people. I repeat, sir, that by nothing that they would see in this country would the workingmen or the capitalists of Europe be more instructed than in looking at the homes of the workmen of Philadelphia. No tenement houses there. Each laborer who has a family dwells under a separate roof, which is most frequently his own; in a house lighted by gas, supplied with an abundance of pure hydrant water. In every house there is a bath-room, into which there run streams, warm and cold, of the pure water provided by the public. This is a startling contrast to the homes of the workingmen of England,* France, Belgium, Prussia, or any other land. To thus bring the people of Europe to a knowledge of how laborers live in our free Republic would give an upward impulse to the temporal condition of humanity everywhere.

Sir, the gentleman from New York [Mr. Brooks] said he was not hostile to Philadelphia, inasmuch as he regarded her as one of the principal suburbs of New York. I do not wonder at that, for in truth the two cities are each the other's principal suburb. They are so near each other, their population is so nearly equal, and each is so thoroughly the complement of the other, that each may, without affectation, so regard the other. They are but little more than two hours apart, and the road that connects them is the one to which I have alluded that runs through the park.

London imports through Liverpool, Paris through Havre, and our merchants receive most of their importations through New York for precisely the same reasons that control those of London and Paris. They do it for greater convenience, and our imports thus swell the volume of New York's apparent greatness. In her we find one of our principal customers, and she is largely our factor and distributing agent.

We have no rivalry with New York. Her field of operations is with foreign countries; ours is at home. We convert the raw material of our own and other lands into utilities and matters of taste and *vertu.* We are a producing people; they are a trading people. Our roots are fixed in the soil of our country; they move with the

---

* Toil as they may, our working-classes (and I do not limit the term to our manual-labor class), even under favorable circumstances, have a hard task in providing for their old age—for that night of life when no man can work. They have brought up families, and the family should do its duty so far as it can to the parent—the bread-winner, who supported its members in helpless infancy, and even, it may be, at no small cost to himself, started them in life. Yet in many cases, if not in all, the most a working man can do, is by contributing to sick-societies and others, to lay by so much as will keep himself during transient illness, or when temporarily out of employment. We regret to say it, but it really seems to us impossible for the working-classes as a body to lay by enough to keep them during the impotence of old age.—*The State, the Poor, and the Country,—Patterson.*

House rent in our larger towns has risen, till anything like a wholesome dwelling is beyond the reach of the average workmen.—*Social Politics,—Kirk.*

changes of commerce. And New York, but for the possibility of increasing her manufactures, which local taxation and excessive prices for real estate and high rents must retard, may one day follow the great cities that have, from time to time, been reared on the commercial routes of the past, and are now known only to history. A city depending exclusively upon trade may be regarded as possibly transitory, so long as the routes of commerce are liable to change.

Sir, in comparing the two cities (I have no idea of contrasting them, for, as an American, I rejoice in the growth and progress of each) let me tell you something of the people of Philadelphia and their products. The census just taken is incomplete. General Walker, the Superintendent of the Census Bureau, assured me to-day that the statement which I hold in my hand is from twenty to twenty-five per cent. too low in its aggregate of her manufacturing products. The total of imports into the country during the last fiscal year, not into New York, but into the country; not on the Atlantic coast, but on the Atlantic and Pacific coasts, amounted to a little more than four hundred and sixty-two million dollars. That was the value of our entire import of manufactured articles, and of raw material, whether for food or manufacture. The entire imports were, I say, but $462,377,587, while the products of industry, as far as ascertained, in Philadelphia alone were $251,663,921. Add to this, as I am authorized by the Superintendent of the Census to add, twenty per cent., and it will be found that her productions alone were far greater than the manufactured imports of the country, and equal to more than two-thirds of the entire imports of raw materials and manufactured articles.

Philadelphia has, far as ascertained (and the numbers will be greatly increased by the revision now making), 6090 establishments, employing a capital of $205,564,238; employing in horse-power, of steam, 31,582, and of water, 2226; employing 88,631 males above sixteen years of age, 23,545 females above that age, 7356 children and youth; paying wages annually to the amount of $52,236,026; using materials to the value of $132,618,873; and yielding manufactured products, as I have already said, to the value of $251,663,921. And the Superintendent of the Census, from information already in his posssession, justifies me in swelling this amount to $300,000,000.* But for the further information of the House I will at this point incorporate in my remarks the table in detail imperfect as it is. (See next page.)

Here, then, among these appliances for the conversion of raw materials into the comforts and luxuries of life; here among these busy mechanicians; here, in the home of Franklin, whose old printing press will furnish a striking contrast when put beside the "Hoe's last fast" or the latest patent press that will be operating in those days; here, where Jefferson and his compatriots consulted upon the problem of independence, where Washington presided over the Convention which framed the Constitution, where, under that Constitution, he dwelt as Chief Magistrate of the country, surrounded by the great men of that day from all the then States; here, where, in a park embracing more than twenty-six hundred acres of land, the dimensions of the exhibition may spread to a hundred or five hundred acres, from every point of which the eye shall be filled with natural beauty; here, at a spot accessible from every part of the country, blessed with a railroad, should this commemorative exhibition be held.

I am asked what it will cost. The amendment submitted by my colleague [Mr. Morrell] proposes to limit the amount that may be expended by the Government to $50,000 a year until 1876, when the sum may be increased to $250,000, making a total expenditure of $500,000. Sir, I have no idea that under the provisions of this bill the first year's expenses of the commissioners will be

---

* The following is an approximate summary of the Industrial Establishments of Philadelphia, their machinery and production for the census of 1870: as corrected (at Philadelphia) up to September 1st, 1871.

No. of Establishments		8,119
Capital employed, (not including value of land)		$172,079,754
No. of Factories driven by steam		1,668
Horse power of these		45,101
No. of Looms		15,692
" Spindles		189,757
" Machines driven by steam		51,152
" Men employed	86,939	
" Females (over 16 years)	34,728	
" Boys and girls (under 16 years)	9,202	
Total persons employed	130,869	
Aggregate wages paid		$ 58,997,010
" cost of raw material		174,139,094
" value of manufactures		325,371,943

GENERAL ABSTRACT—SCHEDULE FOUR— RECAPITULATION—CITY OF PHILADELPHIA, PENNSYLVANIA.

TITLES, (not revised.*)	No. of establishments.	CAPITAL.	Horse-power		Hands employed.			WAGES.	MATERIALS.	PRODUCTS.
			Steam.	Water.	Males above 16.	Females above 16.	Children and youth.			
Boots and shoes...	674	$2,274,636	42	...	4,620	1,380	215	$2,478,082	$3,279,548	$7,724,809
Boot and shoe fitters..............	17	57,150	...	...	88	114	6	67,743	61,411	150,657
Brick-makers	80	1,814,500	395	...	2,332	...	437	1,151,647	356,984	2,703,148
Breweries	53	3,221,450	445	...	485	4	7	327,440	1,706,106	4,182,050
Bakeries	391	768,075	119	...	1,091	27	86	298,981	1,714,462	3,004,189
Bread, cake, ice-cream, etc.......	10	44,700	...	...	45	16	1	25,040	64,016	116,340
Blacksmiths	139	200,685	22	...	505	...	8	217,664	154,890	587,776
Brass founderies..	23	383,750	96	...	275	...	12	134,438	170,548	532,067
Cigars	345	986,040	34	...	1,213	160	113	524,168	791,851	2,014,058
Carriages............	118	1,707,497	181	...	1,502	3	15	865,880	660,264	2,103,884
" (children's)	4	59,100	20	...	45	...	14	32,452	28,070	83,922
Carpets	205	2,363,650	500	...	3,464	872	379	1,700,436	4,798,253	7,397,636
Confectionery......	81	266,750	20	...	271	53	28	99,438	282,258	601,452
Cabinet-makers...	138	1,767,955	402	...	1,682	18	53	1,006,190	1,097,080	3,004,873
Coopers	59	409,487	125	...	526	...	5	275,278	338,982	896,284
Clothing	310	4,369,114	...	...	4,038	4,464	73	2,032,639	6,546,731	10,707,008
Carpenters and builders	87	1,110,500	...	...	1,337	15	18	753,863	1,647,475	4,180,643
Carpenters..........	148	383,050	1	...	658	...	10	438,664	917,141	1,691,401
Cotton-mills........	21	2,682,000	1,015	690	1,034	1,445	469	898,662	2,122,354	3,476,454
Drugs and chemicals	24	2,579,500	501	...	589	114	34	384,008	2,562,190	3,877,180
Founderies (iron).	71	4,240,420	675	...	2,480	...	115	1,414,227	2,213,004	5,295,072
Grist-mills..........	21	597,500	1,017	131	157	...	1	107,060	3,827,085	4,835,593
Glass-works	9	1,226,016	170	...	727	28	560	552,610	482,792	1,560,643
Hosiery..............	50	1,627,700	469	...	797	1,664	557	834,870	1,921,546	3,265,807
Jewelers.............	84	811,800	39	...	630	74	42	389,980	744,643	1,515,476
Machinists	90	5,107,245	1,541	...	3,194	5	31	1,675,711	1,618,060	4,605,312
Machinery and tubing.............	1	5,000,000	800	...	1,300	...	...	750,000	2,528,000	5,000,000
Plumbers & gas-fitters	97	293,400	35	...	478	...	21	211,426	421,188	876,434
Printers	123	4,974,200	762	...	2,119	239	190	1,820,285	2,559,485	6,301,397
Paper-mills.........	5	2,560,000	435	767	691	141	3	352,200	1,524,379	2,444,000
Painters	107	228,625	...	...	547	9	9	286,322	348,824	893,161
Pianos	8	493,000	121	...	278	2	3	173,250	111,200	431,800
Paints, lead and linseed oil........	13	1,466,750	467	...	326	...	...	181,622	1,316,374	3,216,410
Patent medicines	27	1,405,774	43	...	158	105	8	126,045	2,681,502	5,591,832
Planing-mills	28	907,800	700	8	387	...	15	221,369	1,001,994	1,833,316
Sashes, doors, and blinds	41	829,735	820	...	537	1	17	395,592	709,886	1,451,804
Sewing-machines.	5	700,000	59	...	312	2	3	195,440	182,380	671,000
Soap and candles.	33	787,600	499	...	329	31	32	176,129	827,031	1,625,981
Sugar refiners	11	3,494,000	1,796	...	942	...	1	373,308	18,206,062	19,581,374
Tinsmiths	130	598,750	...	...	545	53	51	237,671	429,288	930,755
Woolen-mills.......	54	7,149,000	2,558	155	1,903	3,183	724	1,793,163	6,728,516	11,204,802
Yarns	44	2,255,000	1,237	225	779	581	375	536,084	3,226,851	4,952,904
	3,979	74,203,904	18,161	1,975	45,317	14,803	4,741	26,617,077	82,910,704	147,120,704
All others..........	2,111	131,360,334	13,421	250	43,314	8,742	2,615	25,618,949	49,708,169	104,543,217
Total	6,090	$205,564,238	31,582	2,226	88,631	23,545	7,356	$52,236,026	$132,618,873	$251,663,921

An abstract from the manufacturing returns of Philadelphia, as received from the assistant marshals—correspondence not completed—respectfully furnished for the information of Hon. William D. Kelley, U. S. House of Representatives. FRANCIS A. WALKER, *Superintendent Census.*

* I have not adopted a classification.—F. A. W.

anything like that amount. But, assuming that they will, we appropriated the same sum to send a few articles to the Paris Exposition.* Here we invite the people of every State and Territory to present in brilliant array among and in comparison with the best productions of other countries their best productions of field, mine, workshop, or studio. And the appropriation is asked for the benefit of the people of the more remote and poorer States, to whose borders many an immigrant would be attracted by a generous exhibition of the many and various elements of wealth, in which every part of the country abounds in such marvelous profusion.

---

* These provisions were stricken from the bill. The U. S. Government is not to be responsible for any part of the cost of the exhibition.

DOMINICA.

SPEECH DELIVERED IN THE HOUSE OF REPRESENTATIVES. JANUARY 27, 1871.

The house having under consideration the joint resolution (S. R. No. 262) authorizing the appointment of commissioners in relation to the republic of Dominica—

Mr. Kelley said:

Mr. Speaker: The desire of President Grant to acquire direct trade with and a footing upon San Domingo, the richest of the West India islands, is inspired by a keen perception of the commercial requirements of the country, and sanctioned by the action of Washington and his most illustrious successors in the presidental office. On the 14th of October, 1789, less than six months after his inauguration, Washington addressed an autograph letter to Mr. Gouverneur Morris, who was then representing us in Europe, in which he said:

"Let it be strongly impressed on your mind that the privilege of carrying our productions in our own vessels to their islands, and bringing in return the productions of those islands to our ports and markets, is regarded here as of the greatest importance."

Time and observation increased Washington's appreciation of the importance of this trade to our country. He adhered to the point with the tenacity which characterizes the efforts of President Grant. And in his letter of instructions to Mr. Jay, our minister to England, nearly five years after his letter to Mr. Morris, in May, 1794, he said:

"If to the actual footing of our commerce and navigation in the British European dominions could be added the privilege of carrying directly from the United States to the British West Indies, *in our bottoms generally, or of certain specified burdens, the articles which by the act of Parliament,* (28 *Geo. III., chap.* 6,) *may be carried thither in British bottoms, and of bringing others thence directly to the United States in American bottoms*, this would afford an acceptable basis of treaty for a term not exceeding fifteen years."

It was not, however, permitted the Father of his Country to secure to its people this important commercial privilege, even as to a few articles and in vessels of limited tonnage. Presidents Adams, Jefferson, Madison, Monroe, and John Quincy Adams made the same object a leading feature of their respective administrations, but with like want of success. It is possible that the younger Adams might have succeeded but for the fact that what Washington and the others had sued for as a privilege he demanded as a right. By thus placing the negotiation upon a new footing he failed as the others had done. At the end of more than forty years, however, President Jackson succeeded in accomplishing this most desirable object; and to his administration belongs the glory of its consummation and the immense and immediate expansion of our commerce that ensued.

Let me pause for a moment to ask why the fathers of the country were so anxious for the privilege of direct trade with the West Indies, and why the European powers who had dominion over the archipelago so persistently refused to accord us the privilege of direct communication with our neighbors, of whose productions we have ever been such large consumers? It was because those Governments saw, as clearly as the statesmen of our country, the importance to the American Republic of unrestricted trade with the islands of the Caribbean sea, whose waters wash our shores.

The fathers of the country having been forced into armed rebellion by the restrictions imposed by Great Britain upon the development of our natural resources and manufacturing and commercial power, had learned that international trade conducted exclusively along parallels of latitude, and between nations producing the same commodities, could not be generally profitable to the people of both countries, and must, if left to the government of the laws of trade, uninfluenced by a tariff of compensatory duties, be ultimately beneficial only to those countries whose mines had been opened, industries established, tools and machinery paid for, by past profits, and who, with skilled and disciplined laborers and artisans, were also in the enjoyment of capital; and must prevent or restrict the progress in the arts of the younger competitor, whose mines were to be opened, factories built, machinery acquired, industries organized; and all this with inadequate capital, as was the case with the United States.

The only commerce in which our fathers could hope to engage with advantage was with non-manufacturing and tropical countries, from which they could obtain those articles of food and raw material for manufacture which we do not produce, and whose people would require the productions of the fields and workshops of our colder country. To prevent the young Republic from carrying to and from the West Indies was to deprive it of the power to establish a commercial marine, such as might provide and man a navy in time of war; and to add to the price of tropical food and raw material its people might require for consumption as food or in the arts the cost of transportation, first to the mother country and thence to our ports, with profits and commissions to foreign merchants and bankers. Hence it was that every American patriot saw that direct and even unrestricted trade with the West India islands would be a blessing to the country, and every European statesman perceived with equal clearness that our maritime and manufacturing power must be greatly restricted, and we continue to be producers of raw materials only, so long as this boon could be withheld from us.

Nor, sir, are these considerations less potent to-day than they were in the infancy of the country. The treachery of our great commercial rival has swept that part of our commercial marine which was engaged in foreign commerce from the sea, and her ships are largely engaged in bringing the productions of the West Indies to our ports. Meanwhile the export duties laid by the Governments of the islands, including the Dominican republic, upon mahogany, fustic, logwood, satin-wood, lance-wood, coffee, cocoa, and other articles, and the import duties which, although they do not compete with our industries, but enter into our food or are consumed in our manufactures, we absurdly impose upon them, are taxes upon our industry, handicapping it in its race with the manufacturing nations of Europe.

The fathers also saw the incompatibility of maintaining, under the simple Government they had founded, a large standing army and navy. They perceived the necessity of preparing for war in time of peace, but they felt themselves unable to bear the cost, and clearly perceived the danger to republican institutions of maintaining great armies or a great navy during peace, and wisely determined to rely upon the militia for the exigencies of war. As to land forces, there was no difficulty in executing this purpose; but if they were to rely upon the people for ships, officers, and sailors in war, they must establish and maintain a commerce sufficiently extended to make ships profitable and create a constantly augmenting commercial marine. Looking at our extended coast, they saw that if we were to be prepared to defend it and to maintain our flag upon the sea we must have ship-yards at many points along the coast, skill and capital to use them to advantage, and the trade in which to profitably engage the vessels they would construct. They believed in the constitutional right to promote these great national objects by special legislation, and did it promptly and successfully. Denied the privilege of trading with the West Indies they secured to American built ships, owned by American citizens domiciled within the country, the entire carrying-trade between the ports of the United States by the provisions of the act of September 1, 1789, for regulating the coasting trade, and for other purposes.

This beneficent act, preceding which but ten laws had been signed by Washington, and which British ship-builders are imploring us to repeal, limits the carrying between any ports of the United States to vessels bearing an American register, and denies such register to any vessel not built within the States, and belonging wholly to a citizen or citizens thereof, and, by section five, denies any part of our domestic carrying-trade even to a "ship or vessel owned in whole or in part by any citizen of the United States usually residing in any foreign country, unless he be an agent for or a partner in some house or copartnership consisting of citizens of the United States actually carrying on trade in the said States."

We have to thank the prescience which ordained these wise provisions in the earliest days of our national existence for the magnificent results achieved upon the ocean and lakes by our Navy in the war of 1812, for the commanding proportions our commercial marine had assumed when the unhappy rebellion enabled England to drive it from the sea, and for the ability of our merchants to furnish the Government promptly with adequate transportation for troops and munitions of war and to maintain a substantial blockade of more than two thousand miles of coast.*

The acquisition of San Domingo would bring the territory of that republic within the influence of this venerable and wholesome law, and thus do more to stimulate ship-building and expand the commerce of the country than could be done by giving effect to the wisest suggestions upon the subject that have been brought before the House by bill or report since the close of the rebellion.

No gentleman who has not given special attention to this question can have any idea of the proportion our trade with the West India islands bears to our entire foreign commerce. Whether tested by the amount we import from each country, or by the total of our imports and exports to and from each country, our trade with the West India islands stands second; that with the United Kingdoms of England, Scotland, and Ireland alone exceeding it. It is true that our exports to France exceed our exports to the West Indies; but our imports from the islands are more than fifty per cent. in advance of those from France. The countries having dominion over these islands are careful to so regulate their trade that while the American people may be the chief consumers of the raw materials produced by their colonies, their own fields, factories and workshops, and not ours, shall supply them with cereals and the productions of agricultural and manu-

* The wisdom of this law is receiving a new illustration: notwithstanding the immense amount of cotton and other bulky products, formerly dependent on water transportation that are now carried by rail, and our exclusion by England's protective system of subsidies, from equal chances in foreign commerce, ship building and the production of marine enginery are reviving. In his report to the Secretary of the Treasury, January 10th, 1871, Mr. Joseph Nimmo, jr., Chief of Tonnage Division, says:

"Our coastwise, or home commerce, is confined exclusively to American vessels by the law of 1817, [which renews and extends the provisions of the act of 1789] a similiar policy in regard to home commerce being maintained by almost every other commercial nation on the globe. In this branch of our shipping we enjoy a fair degree of prosperity, and to-day our coastwise marine is larger and more prosperous than that of any other nation. Our entire steam tonnage, embracing the Atlantic and Pacific coasts, the Mississippi river and its tributaries, and the northern lakes, exceeds the total steam marine of Great Britain, home and foreign combined."

The facts reported by Mr. Nimmo show that protection by inducing the rapid development of our resources, and quickening and augmenting our home trade, has increased the demand for tonnage. Under the lowest rate of duties we have had since July, 1812, the tonnage built in each year, as appears by his report, was as follows:

In 1857, 182,841; in 1858, 145,827; in 1859, 75,081; in 1860, 115,841. While under the highest tariff we have ever had, the tonnage built in each year has been as follows: in 1867, 196,343; in 1868, 196,962; in 1869, 164,388; in 1870, 185,851. Average under the low tariff 129,897½ tons, under the high tariff, 185,886 tons.

facturing skill and industry. In order that gentlemen may have the subject fairly and fully before them, I present a statement of the commerce of the United States with all other countries for the year ending June 30, 1870, as shown by the report of the Secretary of the Treasury on commerce and navigation. It is as follows.

Countries.	Imports.	Exports.	Total.
England	$147,352,493	$262,288,129	$409,640,622
Scotland	7,444,304	8,283,207	15,727,511
Ireland	247,075	8,593,531	8,840,606
West Indies	71,620,106	35,075,591	106,695,697
France	48,087,410	54,834,609	102,922,019
Mexico, Central and South America	57,430,749	28,688,550	86,119,299
Hamburg, Bremen, Prussia, and North Germany	27,397,958	42,747,854	70,145,812
Dominion of Canada and other British possessions in North America	41,089,801	26,849,324	67,939,125
China	14,628,487	9,040,066	23,668,553
Spain	3,638,345	9,782,403	13,420,748
Italy	6,641,664	6,474,653	13,116,317
British East Indies	10,050,834	243,648	10,294,482
Belgium	3,141,074	7,055,634	10,196,708
Holland	1,344,922	6,399,835	7,744,757
Spanish possessions not named above.	6,685,686	221,799	6,907,485
Russia	1,581,637	4,194,360	5,775,997
Japan	4,183,365	1,529,714	5,713,079
Gibraltar	48,535	4,071,293	4,119,828
Australia	278,964	3,466,575	3,745,539
Turkey	678,718	2,578,314	3,257,032
British possessions in Africa	1,836,070	1,378,691	3,214,761
Dutch East Indies	2,550,692	158,636	2,709,328
Sandwich Islands	1,144,248	868,416	2,012,664
Austria	371,409	1,208,697	1,580,106
Portugal	303,997	1,565,963	1,869,960
Sweden and Norway	1,180,741	105,532	1,286,273
French possessions not above named.	200,929	377,667	578,596
Liberia	104,605	154,442	259,047
British possessions not named above.	191,378	64,237	255,715
Portuguese possessions do. do.	42,477	200,816	243,293
Greece	80,001	......	80,001
All other countries and ports	798,913	1,017,016	1,815,929
Total	$462,377,587	$529,519,302	$991,896,889

EFFECT OF THE ACQUISITION UPON SLAVERY.

Some of my friends who remember the energy with which I have hitherto opposed the acquisition of southern territory may deem me inconsistent in advocating earnestly, as I do, the acquisition of San Domingo; but if they will listen for a moment they will, I think, perceive that I could not maintain my consistency and do otherwise. Believing, as I have long done, that commerce, to be generally and enduringly profitable to both parties, must cross parallels of latitude and not run upon them, I have believed that it would add to the completeness of our country to acquire tropical or semi-tropical territory with the people of which we might exchange, under our own revenue system, without the interposition of duties, the products of our northern fields and workshops for the many commodities which they produce but which we cannot, and of which we are large consumers. But, sir, notwithstanding these convictions, and the fact that I was a member of the Democratic party, I opposed the annexation of Texas, was hostile to the armed occupation of Yucatan, as suggested by President Polk in his message of April 29, 1848, and regarded the Ostend manifesto and other efforts to acquire Cuba, as outrages upon humanity and our republican institutions.

I did not stop to consider the constitutionality of these measures. They were projected in pursuance of precedents which, though confessedly indefensible on constitutional grounds, had vindicated themselves to the judgment of the country, the acquisition of the Louisiana territory and the Floridas. My hostility to them did not, therefore, rest on constitutional scruples, but upon the fact that they were efforts to extend the area of slavery and to perpetuate that accursed institution. They were all favorite measures of the Democratic party, whose degenerate leaders array themselves against the acquisition of San Domingo, and have resisted with all their power the ordering of a commission to inquire into the propriety of accepting dominion over it. Absurdly—I had almost said impiously—they claim to be the successors of Jefferson and Jackson, but do not believe in the expansion of our country and its manifest destiny. They are purblind and without faith in the capacity of man for self-government, and I apprehend that they and I have changed grounds on this question for the same reason. They resist the acquisition of San Domingo because it will extend the area of freedom and give republican institutions, common schools, a free press, our laws, language, literature, and all the appliances of modern civilization to a tropical people, most of whom are of African descent, while I give it my support for this as chief among a thousand reasons, each one of which is, in my judgment, conclusive.

The people of the United States have waded through a sea of blood and encumbered themselves and their posterity with mountains of debt in abolishing human slavery and making our institutions throughout our broad limits homogeneous and harmonious with the fundamental principles that underlie them. And yet, sir, we are to-day the support and buttress of slavery wherever it exists upon the continent or islands of America, as we must continue to be until we shall acquire tropical territory, on which to grow coffee and sugar, and tobacco equal to that of Cuba. By the acquisition of San Domingo, and by no other peaceable means, we can overthrow both slavery and Spanish supremacy in Cuba, for we consume fully seventy per cent. of her exports, every pound of which might be produced by free labor in San Domingo.

Few gentlemen have probably considered the question in this connection, and I beg leave to invite attention to a few facts illustrative of its importance. But before doing so, permit me to suggest that San Domingo produces large-grained white coffee equal to that of Java, and vastly superior to the green coffee of Brazil, with sugars, molasses, and melada equal in quality to those of Cuba, and tobacco which compares favorably with the best smoking tobacco from the finest fields of that island; and that were the production of these articles stimulated by the sense of security that would be imparted by our acquisition of her territory and by the admission of her productions to our ports free of duty, it would cause the transfer of the American and other foreign capital now employed in Cuba to San Domingo, and thereby people the latter and increase her productions and deprive Cuba of the power to support the Spanish army, which holds her in subjection, or to make the contributions toward the support of the Spanish monarchy, which now regards her as its most profitable appendage. Cuba owes its commercial importance to the fact that San Domingo has been distracted and desolated by war and oppression from the year of its discovery to the present date. Hispaniola, as San Domingo was first called, was once the most fertile, most highly cultivated, and most productive of all the West India islands; but she has relapsed into a wilderness and would present to the enterprise that would seek her fields, under the sense of security imparted by American law and administration, as fertile and virgin a soil as she did to the followers of Columbus nearly four centuries ago.

The population of the entire island in 1492–93 was believed to exceed a million, but such were the cruelty and rapacity of the Spaniards that an enumeration made in 1507 showed that the native population had been reduced by the exhausting labors demanded from the enslaved natives in the unventilated gold mines, and the barbarous means by which their labor was enforced, to sixty thousand. Another enumeration, made by an officer known as the distributor of Indians, in 1514, showed that the number had been reduced to fourteen thousand; and the history of the island from these early dates to the close of the war between Hayti and Dominica is but a continuous story of wrong, outrage, and desolation. After consulting the best authorities to which I have access, I estimate the entire population of the island at this time at from one million to twelve hundred thousand, of which number not more than twenty per cent. are within the limits of San Domingo.

The natives welcomed Columbus on his return from Spain with presents, consisting chiefly of great quantities of gold, and in the course of his progress through the island, in 1495, in grateful return he imposed tribute on all of them above the age of fourteen, requiring each one to pay quarterly a certain quantity of gold or twenty-five pounds of cotton. It is recorded by Captain James Birney, in his History of the Buccaneers of America, that to prevent evasion of paying this tribute Columbus caused "rings or tokens to be produced, in the nature of receipts, which were given to the islanders on their paying the tribute, and any islander found without such a mark in his possession was deemed not to have paid, and was proceeded against."

In a recent conversation with an intelligent merchant of Philadelphia, who has spent many years in Cuba and San Domingo, I said to him, "What would be the effect of American occupation of San Domingo, or its acquisition by us, upon the productions and commerce of the island?" To which he replied:

"In five years from the occurrence of such an event San Domingo will have resumed her former station among the producing and commercial countries of the world, and will have become the wealthiest and most prosperous island in the Archipelago. Under such new circumstances it will far exceed the Cuba of to-day. San

Domingo is in my judgment worth five times what Cuba is worth. Prior to the revolution of 1789 and 1790, San Domingo was the wealthiest American colonial possession owned by any nation. The French part was immensely prosperous, although the French had kept it but a few years. I have not the figures at hand, but, having examined them, assure you that the exports of coffee, tobacco, sugar, indigo, cocoa, and other productions sustain my assertion. The Spanish side was also very prosperous. In fact, the whole island was in a prosperous condition, and the mines were yielding large quantities of gold. Since the revolution of 1790, when the blacks expelled the French from San Domingo, the condition of the country has retrograded, and very little progress has since been made in Hayti."

In view of these facts we may certainly regard the soil of Dominica as virgin, and by embracing it under our jurisdiction do for the wealth and commerce of the world what Columbus and their Catholic majesties might have done could they have founded a liberal republic whose affairs should be so administered as to promote the welfare of all the inhabitants of the island.

The march of our prosperity has marked and measured the prosperity of the ruling classes in Cuba. In 1820 she produced but fifty thousand tons of sugar, and in 1868, to meet our increased wants, she produced nine hundred thousand tons. The increase has always been in proportion to the increasing market our country afforded. It was to supply our market that she maintained the slave trade with Africa, and still patronizes the equally inhuman and murderous traffic in coolies. Enriched by our patronage she employs to-day both of these execrable agencies in our service. Let me prove this. She ships her sugar in the following proportions: seventy per cent. directly to the United States; twenty-two per cent. to Great Britain direct, and to Falmouth or a market; two per cent. to Spain, (a large estimate); and six per cent. to other countries of Europe and to South America.

I have said, sir, that Cuba has maintained and does maintain the slave trade and the coolie trade in order to supply our wants. More and worse than this, prior to 1861 she imported her victims chiefly under our flag, though our law declared the slave trade to be piracy. Spain had bound herself by treaty with England to abolish the slave trade, for doing which she received what she deemed ample compensation; yet slaves continued to be introduced clandestinely under the Spanish flag, under the administration of every captain general; but the favorite flag of the slave-trader was the stars and stripes, because vessels bearing it were exempt from search by British cruisers on the coast of Africa. The execution of the slave-trader, Gordon, at New York, in 1861, put a stop to the use of our flag to cover this unholy traffic. Since then comparatively few slaves have been introduced into Cuba, but the number of coolies imported annually has greatly increased.

OUR RESPONSIBILITY, AND HOW WE MAY AVOID IT.

Such are our responsibilities; and it is now in our power to control the whole subject, not by ravishing Naboth's vineyard, but by confirming his title thereto and enabling him to enjoy in serene confidence his vine and fig-tree.

The duty of two cents a pound imposed by our laws on raw sugar with those on molasses, melada, tobacco, and other productions common to both islands would make it so much more profitable to produce them in San Domingo than in Cuba that the Spanish despots and native slaveholders who govern that island would have no need for new victims, but would find a steadily diminishing market for the crops grown by those they now hold in bondage.

The duties on imports from Cuba into this country during the fiscal year ending June 30, 1870, all of which could have been raised by free labor in San Domingo, amounted to $32,268,750, and the value of the imports were $52,964,225. This statement embraces only sugar, molasses, melada, tobacco, and cigars, which, though the principal, are not our only imports from Cuba. The whole could have been grown in San Domingo, together with immense quantities of coffee, cocoa, indigo, and the valuable woods of the island. The following table shows the amount of each of the commodities named that we imported from Cuba during the last fiscal year, the value thereof, and the duty to which they were subject at three cents per pound of sugar, eight cents per gallon on molasses, and three cents per pound on melada:

	Quantity.	Value.	Duty.
Sugar, lbs....	801,633,343	$38,086,448	$24,049,000
Molasses, gals.	45,084,152	9,696,783	3,606,732
Melada, lbs...	35,828,771	1,247,249	1,074,863
Tobacco and cigars......		3,933,745	3,538,155
		$52,964,225	$32,268,750

I need not further elaborate this point to merchant or philanthropist, for every man who will dispassionately consider the facts presented will admit that, were San Domingo free, and her people strengthened by the sense of security that would be derived from American protection against Haytian or other invasion, and were her savannas and hill-sides cultivated, as they then might be, with modern appliances and American energy, slavery would cease to be valuable to Cuba, and Spain would be divested of interest in her as a colony. This is the age of commerce, and the laws of trade are invincible. By accepting San Domingo we can peaceably emancipate the whole archipelago, and secure to those of our people whose constitution fits them for tropical homes possession and the peaceable enjoyment of the most productive island of the world.

EXTENT TO WHICH WE SUPPORT SLAVERY IN FOREIGN COUNTRIES.

I have said that, notwithstanding the sacrifices we made in abolishing slavery, we are its support and buttress throughout the world. We cannot ascertain precisely the total amount of slave products imported into this country during the last fiscal year, but I find enough in the four leading articles mentioned, together with coffee, to demonstrate the truth of my proposition, and to show, by the amount of duties collected from these articles, that if we could produce them within the limits of our revenue system, as San Domingo would be if accepted by us, we could overthrow slavery on every island of the archipelago, and so far impair its value in Brazil as to make emancipation probable. The value of slave-grown productions imported from Cuba, Porto Rico, and Brazil during that year was $79,414,049, being seventeen per cent. of the entire imports of the country, and the amount of duties on them $45,930,374, or nearly twenty-four per cent. of the total duties collected for the year.

The following statement exhibits the amount and value of the articles named which we imported from slave-labor countries during the last fiscal year, and the amount of duties collected thereon. Of those from Cuba, which I have already given in detail, I refer but to the value and amount of duties:

		Value.	Duty.
Cuba:			
Total		$52,964,225	$32,268,750
Porto Rico:			
Sugar, lbs	130,706,182	6,081,072	3,921,185
Molasses, gals	7,119,928	2,046,172	569,594
Brazil:			
Coffee, lbs	183,413 456	18,322,580	9,170,672
		$79,414,049	$45,930,201

As I have said, Mr. Speaker, San Domingo is capable of producing an equal amount of all the commodities embraced in this statement; and she can do this without impairing her capacity to export mahogany, satin, and other woods for furniture, indigo, and a considerable list of dyewoods. That portion of the island which belongs to the Dominican Republic could support a population of five million people and an immense export trade, yet the exports of the entire island, embracing Hayti and San Domingo, to this country for the last year were but $979,655 of which $419,700, or about four-ninths, came to us in foreign vessels. The people of Dominica are not only without machinery, but without the simplest tools for agriculture or the arts. There is not an iron plow within the limits of the republic nor the simplest form of a saw-mill, though among the leading exports are mahogany, lignum-vitæ, fustic, logwood, lance, satin, and other woods; and it is impossible to estimate what would be the value and extent of the productions of the country under the application of modern improvements in science, agricultural machinery, and the processes for manufacturing sugar and reducing fine woods to slab and veneer, or the stimulus that would be given to American ship-building, the production of agricultural and other implements, and to our carrying trade and commerce, by the development of the resources of this island by American intelligence and enterprise.

FALSE POSITION OF THE DEMOCRACY ON THIS SUBJECT.

Those who lead the Democratic party and claim to have inherited the patriotism and wisdom of Jefferson and Jackson cannot see that any advantage is to result to the country from the acquisition of San Domingo. They cannot even tolerate inquiry into the propriety thereof. They dread territorial expansion, and would rather let our ocean commerce perish and the country remain tributary to Spain and Brazil than incur the risk of accepting San Domingo from a people who seek peace and security by adopting our institutions and identifying their fortunes and fate with ours. Could anything be more absurd than the pretentious claim of these timid and purblind beings to be inspired by the spirit of Jefferson and Jackson?

There was never a day in the life of the Democratic party, before slavery was abolished, on which it would not gladly have availed itself of an opportunity to secure unrestricted and direct trade with the West India islands, and to plant upon the grandest of them an outpost of our country as a matter of convenience and safety in time of war. Worthy and respected as was General Lewis Cass, he was never regarded as among the far-sighted and courageous leaders of his party. There were always those who would gladly have elevated him to the Presidency, yet few regarded him as preeminently qualified to lead public opinion or shape the destinies of a nation. He was characterized by a broad measure of good practical sense, but not by keen foresight; yet he foresaw more of the results of the last quarter of a century than these men, who have lived through it and witnessed all its stirring events, are even now able to see.

The influence that steam was to exercise in ocean commerce and naval warfare had been but dimly foreshadowed in 1848; yet, on the 10th of May, in that year, General Cass addressed the Senate of the United States in support of Mr. Polk's proposition to take armed occupation of Yucatan, in order, as was their theory, to prevent England from getting possession thereof, and to countervail her influence in setting up the Mosquito king. There had then been no contest between Ericsson's Monitor and the Merrimac. France and England had no navy of ponderous iron ships. The bulky commerce of the world was still carried in wooden vessels, under sail. Yet General Cass foresaw what, as I have said, the blind leaders of the Democratic party are incapable of perceiving to-day. They have not yet discovered that depots for fuel are a paramount necessity for commercial nations, and that without them steam navigation must be circumscribed and inefficient; but in the speech to which I have referred General Cass said:

"The application of steam-power to armed vessels has introduced an improvement which may occasion an entire change in naval warfare. It is difficult to foresee its consequences, or the effect it may hereafter produce. One thing, however, is certain, that armed steam vessels, of a size and draught suitable to the navigation they are designed to encounter, will take a decisive part in naval operations. Depots for fuel become, therefore, of paramount necessity for commercial nations. Without them their steam navigation will be circumscribed and inefficient. With them, to furnish the supplies required to vessels as they call for them, the world may be circumnavigated, and steam-power everywhere used. Now, sir, we have no places of deposit anywhere but at home, and England has them everywhere. She has selected her positions for that purpose with that foresight which marks her character, and she will keep them at all times supplied with abundance of necessary fuel. The advantages she will derive from this system of policy are sufficiently obvious, and we must depend upon our energy to meet them as best we can when the proper time comes."

Mr. Speaker, the acquisition of San Domingo would not only increase our ocean commerce and enable us to rely mainly upon a volunteer navy for war purposes, but it would give us such a depot and coaling station as could be established on no other island in the Caribbean sea. The Bay of Samana is unequaled in extent, beauty, and safety, and if we may rely on the report of General McClellan, the hills around it are filled with coal suitable for the purposes of the workshop and the generation of steam, and crowned with wood fit for naval purposes. Man's experience discloses no want for which nature has not made ample provision; and the Bay of Samana, in its extent and safety and the mineral deposits and forests of timber which surround it, seems to have been preordained for a great naval station, and one, too, that would give the nation to which it might belong control of the passages through the archipelago, of our southern coast and of the shores of Central and the northern part of South America.

The scheme of the pro-slavery Democracy of 1848 for the armed occupation of Yucatan having failed, and the necessity for a station for supplies and repairs having pressed itself upon the attention of successive Administrations, President Pierce ordered then Captain since General George B. McClellan to repair to the Dominican republic, inquire into and report upon the fitness of its bays and harbors for such a station. A copy of his report is before me. It is dated August 27, 1854. He says he found three good harbors, of which Samana was the best, the others being Mansanilla and Ocoa. He found excellent oak and yellow pine fit for use in naval construction, and palm and other trees adequate for the construction of durable wharves in a tropical sea. One of these, the name of which escaped his memory before he made his report, he learned was peculiarly free from liability to attack by worms, the special foe to timber when exposed to salt water at tropical temperature. He also found bituminous coal in many places, and certifies that specimens thereof that had been exposed to the weather for three years burned well.* As to the fitness of Samana for such a station, he says:

"The best harbors in the republic of Dominica are those of Samana, Mansanilla, and Ocoa.

"Ocoa, nearly in the middle of the southern coast of the island, is entirely out of the usual track of navigation, and commands nothing. Mansanilla, on the northern coast, about two-thirds of its length to the westward, is too far from the Mona passage, is somewhat out of the way from the passage between Cuba and Hayti, and is badly situated with regard to the line of reefs extending eastward from the Inagua islands, besides having dangerous reefs near its entrance.

"The harbor of Samana is almost directly in the route of all vessels using the Mona passage, and gives complete command of that very important thoroughfare, which is the most safely approached, and most advantageous in its position with regard to the Spanish main and Caribbean sea of all the frequented passages.

"Having reason to believe that it possessed all the requisite properties, and great advantages over the others with regard to health and defense, I devoted all my time and attention to its examination. The bay of Samana, extending some thirty miles from east to west, and from nine to twelve north and south, is formed by the narrow peninsula of the same name. The entrance for vessels drawing more than eight feet is contracted into two thousand yards by a broad coral reef extending from the southern shore of the bay. At the north point of the reef are five keys, the largest containing about one hundred acres, the smallest a mere sand-bank; the passage for vessels lies between the most northern key and the peninsula. The largest ships of the line can enter this bay with the utmost ease, and find secure anchorage within, entirely out of cannon range from vessels outside the keys.

"The anchorages and small harbors on the northern side of the bay near the entrance are very good, and have excellent holding-ground. The only objection to this bay arises from the rareness of land breezes at certain seasons of the year at least; so that it is difficult for large vessels to sail out, as the channel is somewhat narrow for them to beat through. This difficulty can be remedied by the use of a steam-tug, by kedging, or warping. Were the channel well 'buoyed out,' it is probable that a ship of the line could, in case of necessity, beat out. With respect to steamers, there is no obstacle

* This coal must have been carried there, as subsequent examination disproves the existence of a natural deposit thereof

in the way of their entering or leaving at any time in the day or night. The peninsula of Samana is almost an island; for at its base the land is low and swampy, much cut up by inlets, and overgrown with mangrove bushes. The approach from the mainland is for a league and a half over a narrow, winding path, practicable for only one man at a time, partly under water to the armpits, and in many places overhead in mud and water on either side.

"The peninsula itself is high and broken; the hills ranging from a few hundred to two thousand feet in altitude, exceedingly steep, very irregular in direction, and interspersed with narrow, sloping valleys, the whole covered with a dense growth of underbush, vines, and timber. It is well watered by small mountain streams. The predominant rock is a limestone, generally porous, but often occurring of such a quality as to form a good building-stone in that climate, and in localities convenient for working."

But General McClellan's report is not the only evidence furnished by Democratic Administrations while statesmen of sagacity were at the head of that party of the wisdom and patriotism of President Grant's effort to acquire San Domingo. It apears that Yucatan was not sufficient to satisfy the ambitious desires of Mr. Polk and his administration. In February, 1845, he sent Mr. John Hogan as "the special agent and commissioner of the United States to the island of San Domingo or Hayti." The duties enjoined on him were "particularly to inquire into and report upon the present condition, capacity, and resources of the new republic of Dominica." Mr. Hogan having performed his duties made a much more elaborate and intelligent report than General McClellan submitted to President Pierce, nine years later. Let me quote his description of the island and its probable future relation to the international affairs of the world. In opening his report he said:

"The island known under the several names of Hispaniola, San Domingo, and Hayti is, as is well known, in extent among the largest, and in fertility of soil, character, and quantity of its productions, one of the most important of the islands of the West Indies. The central position which it occupies in that archipelago, separated from Cuba by a channel of only forty miles, intermediate between Jamaica on the west and Porto Rico on the east, its vicinity to the commercial ports of the United States; the provinces of Honduras and Yucatan, and what has been long known as the Spanish main of South America, confer upon it a political importance second only to its commercial. *In the hands of a powerful and enterprising nation its influence would be felt in all the ramifications of human concerns.*

"This island is again peculiar from the number and capacity of its harbors. The entire coast is studded with deep and valuable ports, and intersected with rivers penetrating far into the interior, which render all its resources, natural and industrial, available in augmenting the power and extending the commerce of the nation which might either acquire the power of sovereignty over it or become connected with it in the relations of mutual independence. A glance at the map will exhibit at once to your eye the inestimable value of this island, and its commanding position in a military and commercial point of view. Independently of its own internal resources, mineral and agricultural, its position renders this magnificent island one of the most admirable positions which the world can exhibit for a commercial emporium. Its vast and secure bays would afford shelter for the congregated navies of the world. Its situation renders it accessible to the most important marts of this continent."

If, as Mr. Hogan predicts, the influence of San Domingo is to be felt in all the ramifications of human concerns, had it not better be under the inspiration of American republicanism than as the colony of any of the despotic or reactionary Governments of Europe? That she may put forth her influence wisely and for the good of mankind I would give her our literature, laws, and institutions, and through her common schools begin the work of making our language that of the people of the entire archipelago.

But let us hear further from President Polk's commissioner, Mr. Hogan, as to the importance of the geographical position and the grandeur and variety of her material resources. Recurring to the subject, and speaking first of the whole island, he says:

"The island, which has of late years resumed in the hands of the blacks its original name of Haiti, or Hayti, was usually known as San Domingo by the English and French, and as Hispaniola by the Spaniards. It lies about southeast of the island of Cuba, from which it is separated by a channel of about forty miles in width; eastwardly from Jamaica, which is at the distance of one hundred miles; westwardly from Porto Rico, distant thirty miles. It is directly south from the city of New York, which is about fifteen hundred miles removed; from Charleston and Savannah, about nine hundred miles; within a few days' sail of Nicaragua, Yucatan, and Honduras, and equally convenient to Trinidad and the northern shores of the South American continent. This commanding position, in both a political and commercial point of view, is materially strengthened by the number and capacity of its harbors. The Bay of Samana, on the eastern extremity of the island, trends into the interior for a depth of eight leagues, with a proportionate width, and is capable of holding all the navies of the world. The character of the shores of this bay and the noble timber which covers the adjacent country furnish inexhaustible means for repairing or even building ships of every dimension. This island extends, in its greatest length, nearly, from east to west, a distance of about three hundred miles, and from north to south its greatest breadth is about one hundred and fifty miles, with a superficial area of thirty thousand square miles. Its Indian name, Hayti, meaning mountainous, indicates the most striking feature in its physical conformation, the most elevated points rising to the height of about six thousand feet above the surrounding ocean. The hilly region is, however, intersected with numerous valleys, where the fertile character of the soil and a genial climate produce an exuberance of the most valuable and diversified vegetation. In other parts of the island extensive natural meadows or savannahs appear, which furnish an abundant provision for large quantities of cattle and horses. San Domingo is, in general, well watered by numerous rivers, which penetrate into the interior and add to the productive capacities of a soil of unsurpassed fertility. The irregular character of the surface and the greater or less distance from the ocean occasion considerable diversities of climate, varying from the oppressive tropical heat, which, combined with a humid atmosphere, renders some parts peculiarly obnoxious to the vomito or yellow fever, to the elevated mountain ridges, where the cold is sometimes found to be unpleasant to those habituated to the more enervating influences of the tropics. The excessive heat, which would otherwise be insupportable, of the sea-board is, however, delightfully tempered by the sea breeze, which regularly, at ten o'clock a. m., lends its refreshing influences to the weary and exhausted sufferers.

"Under such propitious circumstances, as may readily be supposed, the vegetable products of the island are as abundant as they are diversified in character. Almost all the productions of the tropical and temperate zones find a genial soil and climate in some part of its various regions. The sugar-cane, cotton, tobacco, rice, and cocoa are grown in great abundance; while the plantain, vanilla, potato, and other minor articles are indigenous to the soil. The mountains are covered with valuable timber, among which are especially to be noticed the mahogany, satin-wood, live-oak, and other useful descriptions of tree.

"Nor are the mineral riches of this island less important. It is well known that from the period of its discovery by the Spaniards large quantities of gold have been extracted from the soil, chiefly, however, by washing from the hills. It is known that there also exist the most copious supplies of copper, coal, rock-salt, iron ore, nitre, and other valuable minerals. These, however, owing to the distracted state of the country, have been imperfectly developed.

"This magnificent island, upon which nature has lavished her choicest treasures with a profuse hand, has, however, been the victim of all the misery which man can inflict upon his brother man. It was occupied by the divided authority of France and Spain, the former possessing the western portion and the latter the eastern part of the island, while the line of demarcation between them was irregular, extending in a northerly and southwardly course across it. The part belonging to Spain extended over rather a greater extent of superfices than that which appertained to France.

"About the year 1789 the island had perhaps attained its highest condition of prosperity, and its exports were then deemed more abundant and more valuable than those of Cuba. At that period broke out those devastating intestine commotions which spread horror and misery over this unfortunate region, marked by traits of ferocity and a depth of human suffering rarely equaled and never surpassed. The black population of the French moiety of the island rose in insurrection against their masters; a servile war raged with all its terrors. Armies, the pride and boast of France, were annihilated by the combined influences of war and climate; the negroes established their ascendency, and the independency of the Haytian republic was finally recognized by the French monarch in 1825, in consideration of a large pecuniary indemnity, payable to the former proprietors of the soil.

"It is, however, to be remarked, what cannot indeed be readily understood and has not been satisfactorily explained, so far as my information extends, that although the political authority of the blacks had been extended as early as 1821 over the Spanish portion of the island, so that it was wholly subjugated to their sway, yet this recognition of independence by France is in terms restricted to the French part of the island.

"This extension of the black authority continued without intermission until the opening of the year 1844, when the inhabitants of the Spanish portion o the island raised the standard of revolt, threw off the ignominious yoke which had been imposed by the authorities of Hayti, and declared their independence. The republic of Dominica was then constituted. Since that period the war between the two parties has been continued, but the new community has thus far successfully maintained its independence, has organized a regular form of government, established a written fundamental constitution based upon republican principles, and holds out the best founded prospects of triumphing in the contest, even to the extent of extending its authority throughout the entire island.

"Such was the origin, and in brief such the present position of the new republic, to which I have had the honor of being commissioned.

"The territories of the republic are those which formerly belonged to Spain, and constitute about a moiety of the island, whether we estimate the extent of country, the character of the soil, and generally the sources of wealth. The population consists of about two hundred and thirty thousand, of whom forty thousand are blacks, and over one hundred thousand are whites."

Such, Mr. Speaker, is San Domingo, the true Queen of the Antilles, and such is the sad story of her people. Her natural wealth is boundless, and infinite in its variety. It is also exhaustless, for its sources are perennial; yet her impoverished and decimated people live in dread uncertainty, which, like the shadow of impending death, precludes exertion for the future. In view of her resources and her many capacious bays and harbors, she should be the centre of a world-wide and busy commerce; but her bays and harbors are rarely shadowed by a sail, and a single steamer, the Tybee, visiting her ports but once a month, suffices for the greater part of her regular trade and communication with the great commercial Republic whose immediate neighbor she is. From the depths of their despair the people of the republic of Dominica implore us to remove the dread shadow under which they live, expose her wealth to view, and cause it to be applied to the uses of mankind. Moved by their appeal, and instructed by the action of all his really great predecessors, the President proposes to the country to bless them and the world by granting their prayer; and for this he is assailed by the puny and short-sighted leaders of the Democratic party. Against their assaults I will not pause to defend him. He has vindicated to the world and history the singleness and rectitude of his purposes by the selection of Benjamin F. Wade, Andrew D. White, and Samuel G. Howe, as commissioners to make the inquiries ordered by Congress. Truer men than these he could not have named, nor men more free from the suspicion of liability to corrupt or sinister influences; and President Grant may well express a willingness to abide the issue of their investigations, confident that it will justify all he has done, and result in adding the tropical wealth of San Domingo to the mighty resources of the United States, and in the revival and expansion of our languishing Ocean commerce.

REVENUE REFORM.

SPEECH DELIVERED IN THE HOUSE OF REPRESENTATIVES, APRIL 18th, 1871.

The House being in session—

The Speaker said: The committees having been called through, the regular order is the consideration of the resolution offered yesterday by the gentleman from New Hampshire [Mr. Bell] in regard to public expenditures and taxation, which went over under the rule, and comes up this morning for discussion.

After speaking some time in support of the resolution, *Mr. Cox* said: I yield to the gentleman from Pennsylvania [Mr. Kelley].

Mr. Kelley. Mr. Speaker, in the preamble of the resolution of the gentleman from New York * there are abstract propositions with which I cordially concur. But I desire to bring to the attention of the House, and, if possible, of the country, one proposition contained in the resolution which seems to be in accordance with a popular delusion. It declares that "this House disapproves of inordinate taxation to pay off immense amounts of the public debt as heretofore practiced by the Secretary of the Treasury."

I believe this side of the House disapproves of inordinate taxation for the sake of the speedy payment of the debt; I certainly do. But, sir, we are older in legislation than the gentleman from New York, and have more experience in the management of affairs, and know that the Secretary of the Treasury has imposed no taxes upon the people. The taxes of which he complains are imposed by law, and not by order of the Secretary of the Treasury, who has had nothing to do with them, except

* Though submitted by the gentleman from New Hampshire, the resolution was understood to be that of the gentleman from New York.

to see that they are efficiently collected and that the funds derived thereby are faithfully applied.

Let me call the attention of the House to the history of this question. For the six months preceding the inauguration of General Grant and the installation of Secretary Boutwell the revenues of the country were inadequate to meet its current expenditures. Each month for six months showed a declining balance in the Treasury. After the 4th of March, 1869, however, it was found that this was reversed. The same tariff and tax laws prevailed. No increase of duty, no increase of internal taxes; yet it was found that taxes which had been insufficient for the current expenses of the Government were, under Republican administration, not only adequate for that purpose, but sufficient to justify the Government in beginning to pay the public debt. Sir, in addition to paying the current expenses, Secretary Boutwell has out of these taxes paid $204,000,000 of the public debt and reduced the annual payment of gold interest more than twelve million dollars.

More than that, sir. Congress, at its last session, repealed internal taxes which yielded $55,000,000 annually and duties upon imports which yielded $23,000,000. The total repeal of duties was $26,000,000; but by increase of duty on certain articles it is believed $3,000,000 additional revenue will be derived, whereby the reduction will be diminished, thus making a total reduction of $78,000,000 on the annual income of the Government. And yet, with that reduction of the sources of revenue, the Secretary of the Treasury goes on paying the public debt and reducing the annual interest so rapidly that the gentleman and many Republicans find fault with him. To what use would he have the Secretary apply the money thus collected? Would he have it lie dead in the Treasury? Would he thus withdraw from circulation the money collected and produce embarrassment and a commercial crisis? By buying bonds and restoring these funds to circulation the Secretary of the Treasury has not only reduced our debt and annual interest, but given us a steadiness in financial affairs such as is unparalleled in the history of our country for twenty-five years. Gold has stood for months between 110 and 111. Domestic commerce, foreign trade and the manufacturing industries of the country have gone on more steadily and even-handedly than they have for the same period of time in a quarter of a century preceding it.

Now, sir, I agree heartily with the gentleman that there may and should be a great reduction of taxes; that the income of the Government should be largely reduced. I insisted during the last Congress that the reduction should be $100,000,000, instead of $80,000,000, at which the Committee of Ways and Means aimed, and I believe that with judicious legislation, to be devised by the Committee of Ways and Means, we can repeal from seventy-five to eighty million dollars of taxes during the next session and still go on paying the debt.

Let me assure the gentleman from New York that I am "in dead earnest" for the abolition of the internal revenue system at the earliest day compatible with the maintenance of the faith and credit of the Government. I am for freeing the American people from the system of supervision, inquisition, and espionage it necessarily involves, and which is so disagreeable to them. It was called into life by the contingencies of the war, and should be abolished as soon as possible.

Mr. Brooks, of New York. With the gentleman's permission, I will ask him a question. Admitting the fact that we are receiving now from taxes an income which can and ought to be reduced seventy-five or eighty million dollars, why not do it now, now, now, instead of putting it off to January, 1873?

Mr. Kelley. Because we are in the last day of the session and without committees. If the Committee of Ways and Means were appointed I should favor charging it with an investigation and revision such as were required of the committee of the last Congress, of which the gentleman from New York and I were members, and to the fidelity of which I am confident he will bear testimony, although he did not agree in the conclusions reported.

Mr. Cox. I wish to ask a question.

Mr. Kelley. I am speaking in your time.

Mr. Cox. In your resolution abolishing internal taxes did you not except out of it spirits and tobacco?

Mr. Kelley. No, sir. I merely indicated that they should be retained as subjects of taxation so long as any internal taxes were required for the maintenance of the Government.

Mr. Cox. And by what machinery did the gentleman propose to collect the tax on spirits and tobacco?

Mr. Kelley. Why, so long as any internal taxes are required, I would collect them by appropriate machinery; but I would, at the earliest possible day compatible with the maintenance of the faith and credit of the Government, abolish the whole system.*

Mr. Cox. Then the gentleman would break down the internal taxation on tobacco and on whisky, which are always regarded as proper subjects of taxation; and all the machinery of the inquisition, all the odium belonging to the internal revenue system, he would keep up until the very last moment—and what for?

Mr. Kelley. What last moment?

Mr. Cox. Well, the gentleman does not explain himself clearly, or else I would not interrogate him.

Mr. Kelley. I would, as I have said, retain these taxes as long as any internal taxes are necessary to the maintenance of the faith and credit of the Government, and not one moment longer.

Mr. Cox. The gentleman did not intend, therefore, so long as he cared for the credit of the Government, to abolish the internal revenue tax on tobacco and on spirits; and everybody knows that nearly all the frauds on the internal revenue are in regard to these two articles.

Mr. Kelley. You cannot strike down a system which yields $150,000,000, as the internal revenue system pro-

---

* INTERNAL TAXES—REVENUE REFORM.—*Mr. Kelley.* I move that the rules be so suspended as to adopt the following resolution:

Resolved, That this House reaffirms the resolution adopted on the 12th of December, 1870, by the House of Representatives of the Fortieth Congress, declaring that the true principle of revenue reform points to the abolition of the internal revenue system, which was created as a war measure to provide for extraordinary expenses, and the continuance of which involves the employment, at a cost of millions of dollars annually, of an army of assessors, collectors, supervisors, detectives, and other officers previously unknown, and requires the repeal at the earliest day consistent with the maintenance of the faith and credit of the Government of all stamp and other internal taxes; and that properly adjusted rates shall be retained on distilled spirits, tobacco, and malt liquors so long as the legitimate expenses of the Government require the collection of any sum from internal taxes.

Mr. Cox. I object to that pig-iron resolution.

The Speaker. The question is upon suspending the rules and passing the resolution.

Mr. Kelley. And on that question I call for the yeas and nays.

The yeas and nays were ordered.

The question was than taken; and there were—yeas 130, nays 21, not voting 76. —*The Globe, April 11th,* 1871.

bably will this year, one-third of which at least is absolutely required to meet the expenditures of the Government; you cannot strike that system down, I say, all at once. And therefore I indicated in my resolution the subjects of taxation which I would retain to the last.*

Mr. Finkelnburg. Will the gentleman yield to me for a question?

Mr. Kelley. Certainly.

Mr. Finkelnburg. I desire to ask the gentleman from Pennsylvania a question for the purpose of understanding the position he occupies on the question of taxation. Would he take off the internal taxes upon such articles as tobacco and whisky before commencing to reduce the customs duties upon such articles of necessity as coal, salt, and woolen goods and other articles?

Mr. Cox. That is the question I wanted to get at. Will the gentleman answer that?

Mr. Kelley. I will answer that question fairly and very fully if not cut short by the gentleman from New York, in whose time I am speaking. I would not repeal those taxes before commencing to revise many of the provisions of the tariff. On salt I have already declared myself as believing that a reduction of fifty per cent. of the duty would be judicious. On the question of coal I am thoroughly satisfied that the existence of that duty does not add one farthing to the cost of a ton of coal to any American consumer. It brings to the Treasury nearly half a million of dollars per annum, and if we were to repeal it, that half million dollars would go to provincial and English coal producers to the detriment of the American tax-payers. I am satisfied of that, sir, from a careful examination and analysis of the prices of

---

* The effect the internal tax on spirits or tax on whisky, as Mr. Cox phrases it, has on the grain-growing interest has been shown elsewhere, and the following paragraph from the *Pittsburgh Commercial* shows how prejudicially it has operated on the shipping interest of the country and the foreign trade of Mr. Cox's district:

"The merchants of New York formerly conducted a thriving business in the exportation of alcohol. Large quantities were carried to Mediterranean ports in American ships, and fruit was brought in return from Smyrna and other places. Now these vessels, it is asserted, are idle, or have been transferred to other or less lucrative branches of trade. Vessels trading to ports along the Mediterranean, it is asserted, will not take freights to the United States, because they are not sure of back cargoes. Consequently fruits go to Liverpool, and are transhipped at that port in British craft sailing for New York. The regular trade in alcohol, from New York, it is asserted, should amount to ten millions of dollars a year."

coal in the city of Boston for years before the reciprocity treaty, for the ten years or more that the reciprocity treaty existed, and for the years that have succeeded the repeal of the treaty. Such an examination of facts taken from the Boston Shipping List will settle in the mind of any candid man the fact that to repeal this duty is to take from our Treasury half a million dollars in gold per annum, and bestow it upon the people of Nova Scotia as a bribe to them to remain English subjects and free from our system of internal taxes. That is the whole of the coal question.

Mr. Cox. I must resume the floor.

Mr. Kelley. I thank the gentleman for his indulgence. I would be glad to go on for an hour answering any questions that revenue reformers or free-traders might put to me. While grieving that I cannot be further catechised, I again thank the gentleman from New York for his courtesy.

THE NEW NORTHWEST.

AN ADDRESS ON THE NORTH PACIFIC RAILWAY, IN ITS RELATIONS TO THE DEVELOPMENT OF THE NORTHWESTERN SECTION OF THE UNITED STATES, AND TO THE INDUSTRIAL AND COMMERCIAL INTERESTS OF THE NATION. DELIVERED IN THE ACADEMY OF MUSIC, PHILADELPHIA, JUNE, 12TH, 1871. REPORTED BY D. WOLFE BROWN, PHONOGRAPHER.

Hon. William. D. Kelley, who was received with hearty and long-continued applause, said:

I thank you, ladies and gentlemen, for this very cordial reception, and beg leave to express my gratitude to the gentlemen who, by their invitation, have afforded me an opportunity to contribute, however humbly, towards the completion of a work which, for more than a quarter of a century, I have regarded as of prime importance to the country, and of special value to my native city and State, and for the promotion of which, during that period, I have labored as opportunity offered. I do not expect the statement of facts I shall make to be accepted without many grains of allowance by those of my hearers who have not visited the trans-Missouri portion of our country; and shall not be surprised if many of you leave the hall with the opinion that I have dealt largely in exaggeration. Yet it is my purpose to speak within the limits of truth, and to make no statement that is not justified by my personal observation, authorities that all are bound to recognize, or the concurrent statements of numbers of inhabitants of, and travellers through, the country of which I am to speak.

The truth is, that however well-informed a man may be and however large the grasp of his mind, if his life has been passed between the Atlantic and the Mississippi river, he cannot fully conceive the strange contrasts between the characteristics of the Atlantic and Pacific portions of our country. The difference in topography is marked, and recognized by all; but as to the subtle differences of climate, soil, temperature and atmosphere, experience, alone, can impart conviction.

About two years ago, it was my privilege, in connection with my colleagues on the Committee of Ways and Means of the National House of Representatives, to traverse the entire route of the Union and Central Pacific Road by daylight, and to visit Salt Lake City, which was, as all know, located in the heart of the "Great Desert," that it might be the centre of a Mormon empire that would be guarded by the forces of Nature against Gentile intrusion. After having somewhat studied California, with San Francisco as our head-quarters, we passed up the coast to the mouth of the Columbia river, along that beautiful stream to its confluence with the Willamette, and up the Willamette to Portland, Oregon, as a new point of departure for observation, visiting thence on one line of steamers, Oregon city, with its immense flouring and woolen mills, and on another, the grandeur (for beauty does not express it) of the Columbia river beyond the Cascades and onward to the Dalles. Though that region had so long been a matter of interest to me, the study of which had afforded so much pleasure, each day revealed new and strange conditions, and imbued me with a fresh sense, not only of the extent of our country, but of the grandeur and infinite variety of its resources and the beneficence and power of the Almighty, in adapting all parts of it to the sustenance and comfort of man. But of this hereafter.

Let me first invite your attention to facts within the memory of some of my auditors, which show that the resources of the new northwest and its adaptability to railroad purposes are not, as is sometimes intimated, of recent discovery, but have long been known, and that the route of the Northern Pacific Railroad is that which was originally proposed, because it is the shortest and best by which to connect the seaboard at Baltimore, Philadelphia, New York, Boston, and Portland, Me., with the waters of Puget Sound and the commerce of the ancient East, which is now the West, the march towards which, of American ideas is illustrating again the truth that,

"Westward the course of empire takes its way."

Pacific Railroad History.

During the summer of 1845, twenty six years ago, Asa Whitney, of New York, who had spent many years in China, and sought by all such agencies as were at the command of private enterprise, information about the country lying between Lake Michigan and Puget Sound, did me the honor to seek my acquaintance and bring to my attention the subject of a railroad from the base of the lake to some point in Oregon, on the waters of Puget Sound or the Columbia River, or to a point on each. The whole subject was new to me; but Mr. Whitney came prepared to enlighten those who were ignorant, and to inspire with faith those who doubted. His general views were in print, and embodied columns of statistics, obtained from official sources, and many facts reported by persons who had traveled more or less through the region which the proposed road was to traverse. The magnitude of the subject inspired me, and my enthusiasm for his great project induced Mr. Whitney, despite the disparity in our years, to favor me with frequent conferences, and to bring to my attention whatever information relating to the subject he obtained. Early in the year 1846, I felt justified, by the growth of sentiment in its favor, in undertaking to secure him an opportunity to present his project to a public meeting of the citizens of Philadelphia. To induce a sufficient number of gentlemen to act as officers of the meeting was the work of time. I found few who took an interest in, or believed in the feasibility of, the project. Some said that a railroad so far north would not be available for as many months in the year as the Pennsylvania canals were; that it would be buried in snow more than half the year. Others cried, "What madness to talk of a railroad more than two thousand miles long through that wilderness, when it is impossible to build one over the Alleghanies!" (Laughter and applause.)

As I went from man to man with Mr. Whitney's invaluable collection of facts and figures, I discovered that the doubts with which the work must contend were infinite in number, and it was not until six months had elapsed that a sufficient number of well-known citizens to constitute the officers of a meeting had consented to sign the call for one and act as such. But patience and perseverance accomplish a good deal in this world. The cause had gained adherents, and, as I find by reference to the papers of that day, the meeting for which I had so long labored was held in the Chinese Museum, on the evening of December 23d, 1846. Some of these my venerable friends who sit around me probably remember the occasion, as I see among them some who acted as officers. His honor, John Swift, then Mayor of the city, presided. Col. James Page, Hons. Richard Vaux, William M. Meredith and John F. Belsterling, with Mr. David S. Brown and Mr. Charles B. Trego (all of whom still survive) were among the vice-presidents; and Senator Wm. A. Crabb, since deceased, and William D. Kelley served as secretaries. The speakers were Messrs. Whitney, Josiah Randall, Peter A. Browne and William D. Kelley.

Mayor Swift, with a few cautious words commendatory of his great enterprise, introduced Mr. Whitney, who stated, with great clearness, his project, and the advantages that would result from its execution. It was, he said, to be a railroad from the base of Lake Michigan to a point on navigable water in Oregon. He believed that it could be constructed on a line about 2400 miles in length; and he and his associates hoped to be able to build it in twenty years, if the Government would grant sixty miles' breadth of land for the whole distance. When asked how he would make land in that remote northern wilderness available for the building of a road, he described the character of the climate, and showed that north of the forty-ninth degree of north latitude, and in valleys extending up to the fifty-sixth degree, the climate was in summer as genial as that of southern Pennsylvania; and asserted emphatically that a railroad through that section would be less obstructed by snow than one through Central New York or Pennsylvania.

His scheme was to organize a vast system of immigration from the cities of the Eastern States and from Europe; the workmen were to be paid in part in land, and a corps was to be detailed to prepare a part of each farm for cultivation the next year, so that when the laborers of the second year should go forward they would leave behind them those of the first as farmers and guardsmen of the road; by this process many millions of poor and oppressed people would be lifted to the dignity of free-holding American citizens, and the great route for the commerce of the world would be established amid the development of the boundless resources of the yet new Northwest. (Applause.)

At the close of an eloquent address, the late Josiah Randall, Esq., submitted a series of resolutions, from which I quote the following, which were heartily adopted:

"Whereas, the completion of a railroad from Lake Michigan to the Pacific would secure the carrying of the greater portion of the commerce of the world to American enterprise, and open to it the markets of Japan and the vast empire of China, of all India, and of all the islands of the Pacific and Indian Oceans, together with those of the Western Coast of Mexico and South America;

And, whereas, we have in our public lands a fund sufficient for and appropriate to the construction of so great and beneficent a work; and the proposition of Asa Whitney, Esq., of New York, to construct a railroad from Lake Michigan to the Pacific for the grant of a strip of land 60 miles wide, offers a feasible and cheap, if not the only plan for the early completion of an avenue from ocean to ocean; therefore,

"*Resolved*, That we cordially approve of the project of Asa Whitney, Esq., for the construction of a railroad to the Pacific, and respectfully petition Congress to grant or set apart, before the close of the present session, the lands prayed for by Mr. Whitney for this purpose."

It was also resolved to send copies of the resolutions and proceedings of the meeting to our senators and members of Congress, and to the Governor of the Commonwealth, with the request that he would bring the subject to the attention of the Legislature.

Encouraged by this success, Mr. Whitney visited other cities, and brought his plans before the people. On the 4th of January, 1847, he addressed an immense meeting in the Tabernacle, New York, which was presided over by the mayor and participated in by the leading men of that city. His remarks were listened to, but at their close a mob took possession of the hall and denounced the project as a swindle, declaring that it was an attempt on the part of a band of conspirators to defraud the people by inducing the Government to make an immense grant of land for an impracticable project.

This was the initial movement of a powerful and organized opposition, before which Mr. Whitney retired, silenced in his effort to promote one of the grandest works ever conceived by an American citizen. (Applause.) But his labors had not been in vain. On the 23d of June, 1848, Hon. James Pollock, the present Director of the United States Mint, who does me the honor to listen to me, and who was then in Congress from this State, as chairman of a special committee appointed in accordance with a resolution he had offered, presented a favorable report on the project of a Pacific Railroad, recommending that steps be taken to secure adequate explorations and surveys of the trans-Mississippi country. The "madness" of the project was still laughed at by "grave and reverend" senators; and it was not until the 3d of March, 1853, that the President signed an act authorizing the Secretary of War, under his direction, "to employ such portion of the corps of topographical engineers and such other persons as he may deem necessary to make such explorations and surveys as he may deem advisable, to ascertain the most practicable and economical route for a railroad from the Mississippi river to the Pacific ocean." Effect was given to this resolution at the earliest day, but it was not until the 27th of February, 1855, that the Secretary of War was able to submit to the President, for communication to Congress, the reports of the several surveying parties. The first of these reports were given to the public by order of Congress in the latter part of that year. They fill thirteen large quarto volumes, and I shall have occasion to refer to them hereafter.

THE PENNSYLVANIA CENTRAL ROAD.

As experience is a trusted teacher it may be well to pause and examine the condition of the railroad interests of the country at that time. At the close of 1846, we had 4930 miles of road in operation, 297 of which had been completed during that year. A system of continuous railroad had not been proposed. Until about that time the function of railroads had been assumed to be to connect water-courses Thus the Columbia Railroad, constructed by our State authorities, connected the waters of the Pennsylvania canals with those of the Delaware river; the Camden and Amboy road connected the waters of the Delaware with those of the Raritan; from Philadelphia to Baltimore, until 1838, communication was by steamboat from Philadelphia to Newcastle, thence by rail to Frenchtown, thence by steamboat to Baltimore. The route from Boston to New York was by railroad from Boston to Providence, and by steamboat thence to New York. These connecting links of road soon developed a commerce, not equal to their capacity but beyond that of available water conveyance, and thus demonstrated the necessity of a more general resort to roads. Hence the subject of the expansion of our system was attracting attention. The construction of the Pennsylvania Central road was under consideration. On the 3d of April, 1846, the Legislature, after much and violent controversy, had consented to give the madcaps, who were willing to engage in such a project, a charter; but to prevent them from practising fraud, by peddling the franchise or holding it for sinister purposes, the act required that $2,500,000 of stock should be subscribed, and that the enormous sum of $250,000 should be paid in before the issuing of letters patent. Most of you, doubtless, suppose that the requisite subscription was obtained at once. No; nearly twelve months were required to induce the enterprising men of Philadelphia to risk two millions and a half of dollars in building a road over the Alleghanies. "The grades on the road," it was said, "would be impracticable; the heavy snows and long winter would render the road unavailable; the project was a mad one." Those only who remember the efforts required to induce the people of Pennsylvania to make that small subscription would believe the story, could it be faithfully told. The active young men of this day would regard it as a pungent satire.

Town meetings were held, and "block-committees" were appointed, by whom citizens were solicited to subscribe for five shares or three or one, for the sake of the experiment, even though the investment might be unproductive. Meetings of draymen and porters were held, and they were shown that if each would take a share, it would help the enterprise; that if the road should prove a success they would get good interest on their money with great increase of business; and if not, it would have been wisely spent in promoting an enterprise which, in the judgment of many good men, promised great benefit to the City and State.

I have spoken of the business men of Philadelphia, but the appeal was not to them alone; it was to the people of Pennsylvania. This was to be a Pennsylvania road, and by the act of incorporation the commissioners for receiving subscriptions were required to open books at Pittsburg, Hollidaysburg, Harrisburg, and all the chief towns along the line of the road, as well as in Philadelphia; and the energy, enterprise, and capital of the whole State stood appaled at the magnitude and doubtful character of an undertaking to build a continuous line of railroad from Philadelphia to Pittsburg.

It was not until the 30th of March, 1847, but three days less than one year from the granting of the charter, that the petty subscription required was obtained, letters patent issued, and a board of directors organized. And it remained for some time thereafter a grave question whether capital could be obtained by subscription or loan to complete the road.

But by the middle of October, 1850, a single track was completed from Harrisburg, its then point of departure, to Altoona, at the foot of the Alleghany mountains. The triumph was immense; and on the 18th of October, 1850, the event was celebrated by an excursion, which was enjoyed by many prominent business men and other friends of the road. In the evening a meeting was held over a pleasant dinner, at which I remember my friend, General Patterson (pointing to the General, who sat on the stage in company with Governor Geary), and his friend, old General Riley, were speakers. The late President Buchanan and Joseph R. Ingersoll, Esq., also deceased, spoke. At the close of a very brilliant speech, my friend, Morton McMichael, Esq., did me the honor to introduce me as one who had been an early and efficient friend of the road.

From a musty copy of the *North American* now before me, I find that, among other things, I expressed my pride "in the fact that I was a Philadelphian, a member of that community which, with aid from but a single township—that of Allegheny—had, in the face of a host of discouragements, embarked their capital, enterprise, energy and skill in the construction of the magnificent road over which we had travelled that day, and which, though not yet completed, was sufficiently advanced to earn in a few years the means for its completion, should they not be supplied from other sources." And, alluding to what was then my favorite project, I said:

> "The English mail for Calcutta will yet travel over our Pennsylvania Railroad, and its iron ribs will groan under the weight of commodities passing to and fro between the 250,000,000 of people east of the Atlantic and the 750,000,000 west of the Pacific. The discovery of our Continent by Columbus was accidental; but the builders of this road and its several continuations through the Western States are vindicating his sagacity. He sailed due west from Europe to find a shorter route to the wealth of India. He was

right; the fact that he encountered a continent did not increase the distance between the points; it did but demonstrate the necessity for a new mode of conveyance. This the railroad and locomotive supply. The passage of the two oceans by steam and the crossing of our country on a railroad will reduce the time requisite for a voyage from London to Canton to less than thirty days.

"Columbus was no enthusiast. He looked calmly and gravely at facts, and spoke the words of sober wisdom; and so, let folly sneer as it may, do those who speak of the Pennsylvania road as a link in a chain of commercial facilities which is to girdle the earth." (Applause.)

And again:

"The Mississippi Valley is not our Western country, nor is the Pacific coast of our country the 'far West' we look to. Columbus would go west to the Indies; and we will do it. The riches of our West, now the world's East, will lade our road, stimulate our agriculture, develop our vast mineral resources, quicken and expand our enterprise, and drop their fatness throughout our borders." * (Applause.)

I find that, when somewhat laughed at for this outburst of subdued enthusiasm, I replied by saying:

"Why, you can find in Philadelphia to-day more men clamorous for a road from St. Louis to San Francisco than you could who believed in the possibility of constructing a continuous road over the mountains hence to Pittsburg six years ago."

This, you will remember, was after the acquisition of California and the discovery of her gold-fields.

A QUARTER OF A CENTURY.

But to return to 1846, a quarter of a century ago. Let no man think that the Pacific Railroad then projected was to run to San Francisco, or elsewhere than to the heart of the unorganized Territory of Oregon, which extended from the 42d to the 49th parallel of laditude, and embraced what is now the State of Oregon and Washington Territory, into which no settlers had yet gone.

There was then no San Francisco. Not a cabin or a hut stood within the now corporate limits of that beautiful and

---

* On the 16th of August, 1871, I was a passenger on the Union Pacific Railroad. While breakfasting at Grand Island, Nebraska, I was shown by C. P. Huntington, Esq., Vice President of the Central Pacific Co., a telegram informing him that his company had on the 15th contracted for the carriage from San Francisco of 930 tons—93 car loads—of tea, much of which was to go to New York, via the Pennsylvania Central Road. The largest preceding engagement had been for 570 tons.

prosperous city. California, Nevada, Arizona and New Mexico, were still Mexican territory. Neither science nor observation had detected the deposits of gold and silver, or the agricultural capabilities of that vast region of country. The great railroad centre of the West, Chicago, had not yet come into public view. The less than 10,000 people who had gathered at the confluence of the Chicago river with Lake Michigan had no presentiment that the swamp in which they dwelt would, in less than twenty years, be filled up and raised nearly twenty feet, to provide drainage for the streets of the most enterprising and remarkable city of its age in the world. Michigan then had a population of less than 250,000, and Wisconsin and Iowa each but 100,000; and civilization had not yet penetrated the wild region then known as Minnesota Territory, where the census takers, four years later, found but 6038 people. Four years later there were but 91,635 people in California, which had then been ceded to us by Mexico, and admitted to the Union as a State, and whose recently discovered deposits of gold had attracted immigrants from every clime. There was no Government in Kansas and Nebraska, that whole fertile region being in possession of the Indian and the buffalo. The name of that busy centre of river and railroad commerce, Omaha, had not been heard by English-speaking people, and the vast mineral, grazing and agricultural region through which the Union and Central Pacific railroad is now doing a profitable and rapidly increasing business, was noted by geographers as the "Great American Desert." Philadelphia had no railroad connection with Pittsburg, Pittsburg none with Cincinnati or Chicago, nor any of these with St. Louis. The northwestern part of our State was known as the "wild-cat country," in which it was regarded as a misfortune to own land unless it was timbered and on the banks of a mountain stream; and properties in that wide section in which coal and petroleum have since been discovered were sold every few years for taxes, because people could not afford to own land in such a cold, mountainous, unproductive and inaccessible country. (Laughter and applause.)

Surely the world moves and time does work wonders. What railroads we have you know; what railroads we are to have you only begin to suspect. In Europe, during this quarter of a century, dynasties and the boundaries of empires have changed, but the increase of population has been scarcely perceptible. The oppressions of the feudal past linger there, and cannot be shaken off. But here, where man is free, and nature offers boundless returns to enterprise, broad empires have risen, embracing towns, cities, and states; and millions of people born in many lands with poverty and oppression as their only birthright, are now, as American citizens, enjoying all the comforts and refinements of civilization, and with capital rivaling that of European princes, originating and pressing forward great enterprises which are in the next quarter of a century to work more marvellous changes than any I have alluded to. Yes, ladies and gentlemen, were supernal power to unfold to our view our country as it shall be a quarter of a century hence, the most far-seeing and sanguine of us would regard the reality as a magnificent delusion. Our extension of territory and law, great as it has been, is of small consequence in comparison with the achievements of mind in the empire of science and art, whereby man is enabled to produce ten-fold, and in many departments of productive industry a hundred-fold as much as he could twenty-five years ago by the same amount of labor. New roads are to be built; new towns, cities and states to be created; new resources developed; and the sluggish people of the Orient are to be awakened to their own interests and induced to contribute their vast share to the progress and commerce of the world. The vision that filled the soul of Columbus was a grand one; but that which opens to our view, and should possess and animate us, is as much grander and more beneficent as the civilization and arts of the close of the 19th are superior to those of the dawning days of the 14th century.

THE NORTHERN PACIFIC RAILROAD.

I regard the construction of the Northern Pacific Railroad as chief among the great works of the future, and believe that while it will be a magnificent monument to its builders and promoters, and abundantly reward their enterprise and labor, its construction will add inconceivably to the wealth, power and influence of the nation. It will open to settlement, under the homestead and pre-emption laws, a territory that would accommodate all the peasantry of Europe, and, by the development of its boundless and varied mineral and agricultural resources, lift millions of men from poverty to wealth, and enable many who are burdens upon society to bless it by their prosperity. (Applause.)

These are well considered convictions. If I am mistaken, I have, as I have shown you, cherished the delusion through the greater part of my manhood; and the study of many authorities, much intercourse with men, and extended travel have only served to confirm it. Nor do I now express them for the first time. On the 26th of April, 1866, a bill proposing to authorize the Government to aid in the construction of the Northern Pacific Railroad was under consideration by Congress, and I participated in the discussion. By reference to the *Globe*, I find, that after having characterized the construction of the road as a matter of not only National but world-wide importance I said:

"From Lake Superior to Puget Sound! A railroad stretching from Lake Superior to Puget Sound, a distance of 1800 miles! To open to civilization an empire longer and broader than Western Europe, from the southern vinelands of sunny Spain on the one hand to the Hyperborean forests of Norway on the other! Yes, sir; an empire equal in extent to England, Ireland, Scotland, France, Belgium, the German States, Austria, Holland, Italy, Switzerland, Denmark, Sweden, Norway, Spain and Portugal.

"We fail, Mr. Speaker, to understand our relations to the age in which we live and our duties to mankind, because we fail to appreciate the grand dimensions and unimagined resources of our country. We would regard ourselves as giants did we estimate ourselves in proportion to possessions so grand in a country so abounding in multiform resources, so undeveloped, and so sparsely settled.

"The region through which it is proposed to construct this road, exceeding in extent all the countries I have named, also embodies more mineral wealth than they all combined ever possessed. But what is its condition? It is a wilderness. Almost every acre of it is still innocent of the tread of a tax collector. It yields the Government no revenue. Along the Pacific coast a few thriving villages dot it. Some of them will be one day great cities, but thy are now on the borders of a vast wilderness."

COMPARED WITH OTHER ROUTES.

But there are those who, while admitting the vast extent and wonderful resources of the country, assert that it is unfit for occupancy by communities by reason of its high latitude and the altitude of its mountains. They present all the objections that were made to the construction of the Pennsylvania Railroad. "The mountains are too high," "the snows are too deep, and lie too long!" Are not these objections as groundless in this case as they were in that? Let us see. Government surveys and other observations show, beyond reasonable question, that a railroad between the 47th and 49th parallels will have a better route than any other road north of the 32d degree, which line has the drawback of a summer climate that is so nearly tropical as to interfere with travel and the general transit of goods. I am convinced that the country through which the Northern Pacific Railroad is to pass will, twenty-five years hence, contain double the population that will then be found along the line of the road which connects Omaha and Sacramento. Indeed I believe I would be within the bounds of reasonable prediction if I made my proposition embrace the continuation of the road from the city of Sacramento to San Francisco, notwithstanding the wondrous attractions California presents to those who are seeking a new home and a more profitable field for enterprise.

The Central route must create its way traffic; none awaited its construction. From Omaha to Sacramento not a navigable stream crosses the route of the Union and Central road; nor does one approach it. Let me not be understood as disparaging the value of this road, or as intimating that it is not already doing a profitable business, or that it will not, as every other railroad in this country has done, create a constantly increasing volume of business that will enable it to rapidly decrease its rates for freight and travel, while increasing its income and net profits. Indeed it is already doing this, and its present charges for freight and travel compare very favorably with those of 1869.

Yes, it has its way business to create, and is doing it rapidly. Witness the two branch roads already constructed, one from Denver to Cheyenne, and the other from Salt Lake City to Ogden. Before the main line was built, who dreamed of railroads along either of those valleys? Behold, also, the enormous development of the coal and iron fields at Evanston, 500 miles west of Cheyenne, and more than 1000 miles west of Omaha. Two years ago the fact was proudly announced that both coal and iron had been discovered at Evanston; and now the place is marked by the smoke and din of forges, furnaces, rolling-mills, machine shops, and preparations are making for the manufacture of Bessemer steel rails, the construction of the works having been commenced. (Applause.)

Look, too, at the mavellous development by "gentile" hands of the silver mines in southern Utah, to which the Mormons, Brigham Young having driven the first spike about a fortnight ago, are extending their branch road in order to carry silver ore, the transportation of which from the mines to Swansea, England, taxes it $40 a ton.* This tax will be saved when Americans shall be enterprising enough to put up adequate smelting works in a country in which coal and rich ores abound. Yes, British vessels coming to New York and Philadelphia with salt or iron return freighted with the ores of southern Utah, because we have not the enterprise to smelt them.

Look, again, at the development of the wool trade. In many of the valleys along the line of the Central and Union road there are flocks numbering not thirty, not fifty, not a hundred sheep, as in the old States, but thousands; and some flocks numbering more than ten thousand head now range valleys in the very heart of the "Great American Desert," where it was supposed civilization would never find an abode.

What a field for genius, enterprise and industry! It will, at no distant day, swarm with men of grit. There are thousands of young men in this city filling small offices, or in some other way picking up a precarious living, getting through the world somehow, never knowing whether both ends will meet at the end of any month, who, were they to go to this country, carrying with them the knowledge gained in our furnaces, machine shops or factories, would in a few years find themselves at the head of large establishments and commanding hundreds of employees. (Applause.) I rejoice in the fact that the Grand Army of the Republic is organizing one-armed and one-legged soldiers to go and settle in colonies upon the public lands, on the theory that their wives and children will share their labors in securing a homestead and honest independence. The scheme is as judicious as it is noble, and the poor disabled fellows will, I doubt not, in a few years write back to their

---

* The proprietors of the Emma Mine, which is about twenty miles south of Salt Lake City, have a contract with the Union Pacific Company to carry 100 tons of argentiferous Galena ore per day. This requires ten cars, but does not dispose of all the ore yielded by this mine. The remainder with ore from other mines is reduced to matt at Stockton and Salt Lake City. Ingots weighing hundreds of pounds, of which gold is the element of chief value, silver the next, and lead the least, though chief in bulk, are always to be found in great stacks upon the side-walks of the business street of Salt Lake City awaiting purchasers.

less energetic but unmutilated comrades to come and work for and be fed and clothed by them. (Laughter and applause.)

These branch roads and expanding industries are but some of the many precursors and sure pledges of the immense sources of traffic that are to rise along a road, the drinking water for many of whose agents, as well as for the supply of many of its engines, is brought in tanks over alkaline plains for hundreds of miles, and one of the summits of which, at Sherman, is a mile and a-half above the topmost spire of Philadelphia, and 3285 feet higher than the most elevated summit on the Northern road,—that at Deer Lodge Pass.

GROWTH OF RAILROAD TRAFFIC.

That this road will create business for itself, and speedily return the capital embarked in its construction, I am abundantly persuaded. This opinion is confirmed by the highest authority on such questions known to railroad men in this country, H. V. Poor, Esq., who in his admirable sketch of the railroads of the United States, published last year, says:

"It is safe to estimate that the railroad tonnage of the country would dulplicate itself as often as once in ten years, were there no increase of line or population, from the progress made in its industries and in the mechanic arts."

Mr. Poor amply sustains this proposition by facts deduced from the railroad history of the country, and says:

"Our means will increase just in the degree in which we render available the wealth that now lies dormant in our soil." *

---

* PHILADELPHIA, June 30, 1871.

DEAR SIR: There is, in my opinion, no portion of our community whose future is more, if even so much, dependent upon the maintenance of a protective policy as is the railroad one. When the domestic commerce thrives, then do railroad stocks pay dividends. When that commerce is sacrificed at the shrine of foreign trade, then do stockholders suffer. Look to the closing years of the last free-trade period, say 1859–60, and you will see that $400,000,000 would have bought the whole $1,000,000,000 that had then been spent on roads. That the reverse of this is now the case is due to the fact, that for the last ten years the policy of the country has looked to the development of our great mineral resources, and to the emancipation of our roads from dependence on a mere through trade for which competition is at all times so great that it is carried on at the lowest possible rate of profit, even when not at an absolute loss. Let that dependence be re-established and our railroad companies will find themselves

Speaking of the year 1869, he says:

"The tonnage traffic of the railroads constructed the past year, at only one thousand tons to the mile, will equal five million tons, having a value of $750,000,000! Every road constructed adds five times its value to the aggregate value of the property of the country. The cost of the works constructed the past year will equal at least $150,000,000. The increased value, consequently, of property due to the construction will equal $600,000,000."

These observations of Mr. Poor are specially applicable to the Northen Pacific road, the construction of which will not only create an immense volume of through travel, but develop a region not exceeded in native wealth by any equal area on the face of the globe; which abounds in the precious and other metals, in wheat-lands and lumber forests, and embraces the natural home of the sheep and goat, and grazing fields in which herds of cattle large enough to supply our entire market, may graze throughout the year, growing and fattening upon natural grasses, which in the dry atmosphere of the country do not decompose as

---

again in the position from which they had been rescued by the passage of the Morrill tariff of 1861.

How wonderful has been the growth of our domestic commerce under the protective system then established, is shown in the brief statement of facts, derived from Mr. Poor's excellent "Manual of the Railroads of the United States," that will now be given, as follows:—

Ten years since, say in 1860, the net tonnage of more than 30,000 miles of road was but 18,500,000, the growth of ten years of peace at home and war from abroad on all our industries under the British free-trade system then existing, having been but 14,000,000; this, too, notwithstanding an increase of population amounting to more than 8,000,000. Last year, at the close of another ten years' period nearly half of which had been attended with great destruction of property, and with such waste of life that the increase of population had been but 7,000,000, or two-thirds of what had been anticipated, the net tonnage of 50,000 miles of road—exclusive of coal, ore, and other low-priced freights, exceeding 20,000,000 tons—had reached 72,500,000, giving an increase of no less than 54,000,000 tons.

In the first or free-trade decade, the tonnage added was but 1¾ tons to each added head of population. In the last, or protective one, it has proved to be but little short of 8 tons to each of the added population.

In the first, the increase in the value carried, per head of our total population, was but $55. In the second, it has been nearly thrice that, or $141.

In the first or free-trade one, the earnings remained precisely where they had stood in 1850, at but $4000 per mile. In the second, or protective one, with a decrease rather than an increase in the rates of freight, they have more than doubled, having risen to more than $9000 per mile.

In the first, our policy had looked towards subjecting the country to British influence, and hence was it that our railroad owners had been so nearly ruined. In the second, it has looked to the establishment of industrial and commercial independence, and hence it is that all our railroad owners have so largely profited.

That the extraordinary increase here exhibited of railroad transportation has not only not been attended with any diminution of shipping employed in domestic

ours do when exposed to the weather, but cure where they grow, and feed herds of buffalo, elk, antelope and mountain sheep the year round.

THE NEW NORTHWEST.

Minnesota, through which the road will be completed by October, from Lake Superior to the Red River, 266 miles, is the great wheat field of our country. It is a land of lakes and rivers, of forest and prairie. Its farmers are prosperous and contented. Its population numbered 6077 in 1850; had swollen to 172,022 by 1860; and was found to be 436,057 in 1870. The value of its farm products as reported by the census of 1870 was $33,350,923; the cash value of its farms $97,621,691; and its production of wheat during 1869 was about 19,000,000 bushels. It contains (listen young men who are working for wages,) 53,459,840 acres, of which but 3,637,671 are occupied. The remaining 50,000,000 await your coming for their development. (Applause.) It is not yet fourteen years since the lumbermen

---

commerce, but that, on the contrary, this last, after having been paralyzed under British free-trade, has grown, under protection, with extraordinary rapidity, is proved by facts derived from Mr. Nimmo's valuable report on our foreign commerce, and here given, as follows:

In 1850, the home shipping built amounted to 114,000 tons. In the last three years of the free-trade system, say 1858–60, notwithstanding a growth of population unusually large in its proportions, the average was but 112,000.

In 1870, after nine years of protection, it has been 185,000, and the average of the three last years has been 182,000, showing an increase of more than 60 per cent.

With an increase of numbers in the last decade of less than 25 per cent. there has been an increase of domestic commerce, by land and water, of more than 300 per cent.—thus nearly proving the accuracy of Commissioner Wells's assertion, made in 1868, that its growth had been sixteen times more rapid than that of the population.

Of the enormous increase thus exhibited, not even the fiftieth part has been due to our trade with the manufacturing countries of Europe; and yet, there are men, intelligent men too, connected with railroads, who are even now disposed once again to sacrifice the great domestic commerce in the hope of augmenting the insignificant foreign one.

Whether or not this shall be done will be determined at the presidential election in 1872. As that goes, so will it be settled as to whether we are to go forward in the direction of industrial and political independence, or return to the state of subjection to British traders and British bankers that existed in the free-trade days of the tariff of 1857. In the one case, railroad owners will find their property improve from year to year; whereas, in the other, they, or such of them at least as had given their influence in the free-trade direction, will find that they had been killing the goose that had given the golden eggs.

Hoping that your patriotic efforts may be crowned with success, I remain,

Very respectfully, yours,

H. C. CAREY.

GEO. S. BOWEN, Esq.,
President American Association Home Industries, Chicago, Ill.

of Minnesota were fed on wheat imported from other States. Yet the wheat crop raised during 1870, from the small part of the State then occupied, is believed to have been not less than 30,000,000 bushels. Time will not permit me even to indicate the immense resources of this State in lumber, iron, slate, and other commodities, that bear transportation; and I leave Minnesota with the remark that when the winter traveler westward on the Northern Pacific Railroad, shall leave her limits and cross the Red River of the North, he will leave behind him the coldest part of the road, and that most liable to obstruction by snow. The only other point at which he will, even under exceptional circumstances, meet with as great a depression of the mercury will be in the neighborhood of Fort Stevenson, in Central Dakota.

A GENIAL CLIMATE.

How, ladies and gentlemen, shall I help you to understand something about the climate of the country west of Minnesota? To us of the East it seems incredible that the temperature of the mountains, along a line running between the 47th and 49th parallels should be so mild; yet so it is; and the climate of Washington Territory, along the 49th parallel, is more equable the year round, and milder in winter than that of Philadelphia or Baltimore. Indeed, the mean temperature at Olympia, at the head of Puget Sound, is that of Norfolk, Va., but the dwellers on the Sound are strangers alike to the extreme heat of a Virginia summer and the extreme cold of its winter. There cattle are not housed at any season, and thrive upon the grasses they find on the plains. In the western valleys of Washington Territory, winter is unknown. Snow comes occasionally to remind settlers of what they used to see in the States of the East; but it never lies. But once since 1847, when the first settlements were made, have cattle been deprived by snow for three consecutive days, of the natural pasture furnished throughout the winter months west of the mountains in Washington Territory and Oregon.

The winter climate upon the mountains of Idaho, Montana and Dakota, is more severe; but in their valleys the buffalo, elk and antelope have been accustomed to winter; and domestic cattle, worn by labor in the service of exploring expeditions and transportation companies, are turned into the valleys and herded, and come out in the spring fat and ready for another tour of duty. This is so inconsistent with our experience, that I beg leave to fortify the statement with a single authority, the equal to which I could produce by scores. I will, however, content myself with a brief extract from the report of explorations of the Yellowstone, made by Gen. Raynolds, of the Engineer Corps of the U. S. Army, who wintered, in 1860, in the valley of Deer Creek, in which the Northern Pacific Road will attain its greatest elevation and cross the Rocky Mountains. On this subject he says:

"Throughout the whole of the season's march, the subsistence of our animals had been obtained by grazing after we had reached camp in the afternoon, and for an hour or two between the dawn of day and our time of starting. The consequence was that when we reached our winter quarters there were but few animals in the train that were in a condition to have continued the march without a generous grain diet. Poorer and more broken down creatures it would be difficult to find. In the spring all were in as fine condition for commencing another season's work as could be desired. A greater change in their appearance could not have been produced, even if they had been grain-fed and stable-housed all winter. *Only one was lost*, the furious storm of December coming on before it had gained sufficient strength to endure it. *This fact, that seventy exhausted animals turned out to winter on the plains on the first of November came out in the best condition, and with the loss of but one, is the most forcible commentary I can make on the quality of the grass and the character of the winter.*"

This seems incredible, but many degrees to the north of our territories are immense valleys, which, if the testimony of British officers, civil and military, and of missionaries and settlers who have dwelt there for years, may be believed, rival Minnesota in wheat-producing capacity, and eastern Oregon and Washington Territory in the mildness of their mean temperature. Exploration and settlement have abolished the "The Great American Desert," of which these territories formed a conspicuous part, and it no longer finds a place on maps. And the Mormons have demonstrated that by conducting the melting snow of the mountains to the foot-hills and valleys, the whole region can be made to bloom as the rose, and bear crops of cereals, roots and fruit equal to those yielded by the best farms in the choice valleys of Pennsylvania.

WOOL AND BEET-ROOT SUGAR.

Since these apparently inhospitable regions have been penetrated by railroads, and mining adventure has created settlements up even to the northern boundary of Dakota, Montana and Idaho, we are discovering why we have not succeeded in raising wool, and why we are still, while boasting of our agricultural productions, dependent for our supply of wool, upon non-manufacturing countries which are not famed for their agricultural resources or skill. The reason is found in the fact that we have not carried flocks to those portions of our country which are pre-eminently adapted to the support of wool-bearing animals.

Mountainous and volcanic as are our territories, which extend from the 32d to the 49th parallel, they are peculiarly adapted to sheep culture. With their settlement we shall become the greatest wool-producing country of the world, though our present production gives but small promise of such a result. The sources and amount of the wool-clip of 1868 were in round figures about as follows:

	Pounds.
British North American Provinces...	10,000,000
Australia, South America, and Africa.	76,000,000
United States......................	100,000,000
Spain, Portugal and Italy............	119,000,000
France............................	123,000,000
European Russia.....................	125,000,000
Germany..........................	200,000,000
Great Britain......................	260,000,000
Asia	470,000,000

Thus it appears that Asia, Australia, Africa and South America, which furnish no such markets for mutton as the commercial and manufacturing centres of Europe and this country, and where sheep must be raised for the wool alone, are its great producers. Why is wool chief among the staple exports of South America? Because her pampas present the same conditions as our territories. Why has Australia built up a great city more by its wool trade than by its gold? It is because her sheep walks are dry and covered with bunch grass, which is cured naturally in the field as is the case in our Territories. Why does Asia produce more wool than Great Britain and Germany together, and almost as much as Great Britain, Germany and the United States? It is because the grasses of the elevated plains on which her countless flocks of sheep and goats range are the same nutritious, aromatic grasses upon which the elk, the buffalo and the mountain sheep have fed through all time upon "The Great American Desert." (Applause.)

Under the impulse given to this interest by the Union and Central road, flocks numbering thousands, collected in Illinois, Wisconsin, Iowa, and more eastern States have been transferred to such plains and valleys as are accessible by the road, and where the expense of raising sheep is but the cost of the first flock and of herding. There the finest wool may be produced, and with increasing railroad facilities, mining, manufacturing, and commercial centres will furnish markets for mutton, and add to the wool grower's profits. To say that the wool-clip of the United States, as shown by the census of 1880, will exceed that of Great Britain is not to offer a prediction, but to assert a foregone conclusion; and it is also safe to say that the clip of that year will embrace not only wool of all grades of sheep, but of the Cashmere, Angora, and other goats, the value of whose hair is so well known to manufacturers and merchants. But more than this, remembering the rapidity with which flocks increase, I predict that at an early day our wool clip will equal that of Asia,* which

* On the day after the delivery of the text, my attention was invited to the following striking confirmation of my views furnished by M. Alcan, Professor of Spinning and Weaving at the Conservatoire Impérial des Arts, &c.

APPROXIMATE PRODUCTION OF WOOLS IN 1866.

[Translated from Alcan's "Etudes sur les Arts Textile à l'Exposition Universelle de 1867" for the April number of the Bulletin of the National Association of Wool Manufacturers.]

"The quantity of the production of wools in weight may be reckoned approximately by the number of sheep in each country. We estimate the sheep at the numbers indicated in the following table:

	No. of Sheep.
France	30,000,000
Algeria	10,000,000
Russia	54,000,000
England	26,376,000
Austria	27,000,000
Prussia, Zollverein	24,000,000
Ottoman Empire	32,000,000
Australia	35,000,000
Cape of Good Hope	12,000,000
New Zealand	15,000,000
The Equator or La Plata	30,000,000
Spain	20,000,000
Italy	8,500,000
Belgium	3,000,000
The Low Countries	1,500,000
Portugal	2,417,000
Total,	330,783,000

"*Remarks upon the numbers of the preceding table.*—If we compare the present

will insure us supremacy in the manufacture of the entire range of woolen and worsted goods.

And with this increased production of wool, will come another great industry. You will question my judgment when I tell you that the territory along the 46th, 47th, 48th and 49th degrees of latitude high up the mountain sides is to be a great sugar-producing country. Yet as sure as the world moves and science helps man to supply his wants cheaply, the country along the routes of the Union and Central and the Northern Pacific Railroads will in a few years produce immense quantities of sugar. Of course, I speak of beet-root sugar, the manufacture of which will thrive not only along our northern boundary, but in the more northern settlements of the Assineboine and Saskatchewan valleys as it does in Russia, Sweden and Norway; as it is already doing in California, Illinois and Wisconsin, and will do in all the States of the Northwest. Many causes conspire to make the introduction of this industry into our country a necessity; and in the region of cheap land, abundant fuel and pure water from the mountain snows, and in which the cost of transportation more than doubles the price of cane sugar, it must find an early and extensive development.

To show that these views are not new or strained, permit me to bring to your notice a letter I had the honor to address to Dr. Latham, a cultivated and intelligent gentleman, who, after spending years in the Territories, devoted last winter to bringing their resources to the attention of the wool-growers and woolen manufacturers of the Eastern States.

"HOUSE OF REPRESENTATIVES,
Washington, D. C., Dec. 18, 1870.

"DR. H. LATHAM,
"LARAMIE,
"*Wyoming Territory.*

"DEAR SIR.—I must admit that I thought some of the statements you made when I met you at Laramie, and you were kind enough

---

number of sheep as indicated in the preceding table with the numbers heretofore given by us, it will not be difficult to recognize that while the production of sheep has decreased or remained stationary in Europe, it has prodigiously developed itself in the new countries beyond the ocean. Thus, for example, the number of wool-bearing animals has diminished in England, in Spain, and even in France, if we do not include Algeria; and it has remained nearly stationary in the different parts of Germany. On the contrary, the development exhibits an enormous progression at the Cape, in Australia, and, above all, in La Plata. In seven years, from 1860 to 1867, the production has been raised nearly 108 per cent. for the first of these countries, nearly 100 per cent. for the second, and 268 per cent. for the third."

to accompany us eastward, were exaggerated; but subsequent observation and study have satisfied me that you did not fully indicate the capacity of the territories for varied production and the sustenance of a numerous and prosperous population.*

"Two industries, each of primary importance to the country, should be introduced at an early day, because both will find there the conditions under which they may be brought almost immediately to absolute perfection. I mean the growth of wool, both from the Angora and Cashmere goats and sheep, and the production of beet-root sugar. For the latter, Grant, in his admirable little book, says the primary essentials are cheap land and fuel and pure water. All these you have wherever the melting snow of the mountains can be carried for irrigation, and in the neighborhood of all your mountain streams. Your natural grasses and aromatic herbage are identical with those of the great sheep-fields of Asia and Australia; and should you establish the production of the beet, and the manufacture of sugar on a large scale, you will find, as it has been found everywhere else, that three tons of the refuse beet, from which the saccharine matter has been expressed, will be equivalent to two tons of the best hay in sustaining and fattening sheep and cattle. It, therefore, seems to me that you will render a very important service, not only to your own section, but to the country at large, if, by making known these peculiar resources you promote the establishment of two such vital industries. Either of them will doubtless succeed if undertaken by proper hands; but both should be established, as each will contribute to the success of the other.

"Again thanking you for the important information you have given me, and wishing you abundant success in your efforts to promote the development of this extended and interesting portion of our country, I remain

"Yours, very truly,

"WM. D. KELLEY."

MONTANA—LIEUT. DOANE'S REPORT.

Thanks to the admirable scientific training given our army officers at West Point, and the desire of that distinguished soldier and son of Pennsylvania, Gen. Winfield S. Hancock, (applause,) to ascertain and disclose the resources of the district of which he is in command, we have a recent official report on the characteristics of a hitherto unexplored section of Montana, the wonders of

* Leaving Philadelphia on the 20th of July, I passed about in four weeks Colorado, Wyoming and Utah; most of the time in the Laramie valley, Wyoming. Much of each day was passed on horseback, or in open wagon; and I am satisfied that when the population of our country shall number hundreds of millions, the slopes and valleys of the Rocky Mountains will be the great source from which will be drawn cattle, sheep, tallow, hides, wool, butter, cheese and condensed milk. On one estate near Laramie, that of Mr. Hutton, are more than 8000 cattle, 6000 sheep, and 500 horses and breeding mares. My friend Dr. Latham's stock embraces more than 4500 cattle and 3000 sheep.

which not only exceed those of Niagara and the geysers of California, but rival in magnitude and extraordinary combination those of the Yo Semite, the canons of Colorado and the geysers of Iceland. But I cannot pause even to allude to these. Tourists and men of science will give the world many a description of them. My purpose is to illustrate the climate and the fertility not only of the valleys but of the mountains, which bear trees rising beyond one hundred feet in height at an elevation which in New York or New England would mark the region of perpetual snow.

I have here Executive Document No. 51, of the Third Session, Forty-first Congress. It is the report (and you will see that it is quite brief) of Lieut. Gustavus C. Doane, upon the so-called Yellowstone expedition of 1870. It is Lieut. Doane's account of a brief tour made by the Surveyor General of Montana, whose duty it was to survey the yet hidden region of his district, and who applied to Gen. Hancock for an escort to enable him to do so with safety. The General promptly complied with the request, and put the escort under the charge of Lieut. Doane, with instructions to keep a record, noting the condition of the barometer and thermometer, and the elevation of each day's camp, and to report these and such other facts as might in his opinion be of general interest.

The party were out thirty-four days. Their point of departure was Fort Ellis, which is at an elevation of 4911 feet, and at which the thermometer at noon, on the day of their departure, August 22d, 1870, stood at 92°. On the morning of the third day they found themselves at an elevation of 4837 feet, the barometer standing at 25.10, the thermometer 40°. In noting that day's experience, Lieut. Doane says:

"Throughout the forenoon it rained occasional showers, but before 12 o'clock the clouds rolled away in heavy masses along the mountain sides, the sun came out and the atmosphere was clear again. From this point a beautiful view is obtained. The mining camp of Emigrant Gulch is nearly opposite, on a small stream coming down from the mountains on the opposite side of the river. A few settlements have been made in this vicinity, and small herds of cattle range at will over the broad extent of the valley. Our camp was situated at the base of the foot-hills, near a small grove, from which flowed several large springs of clear water, capable of irrigating the whole bottom in front. The soil here is very fertile, and lies favorably for irrigation; timber is convenient, water everywhere abundant, and the climate for this region remarkably mild. Residents informed me that snow seldom fell in the valley. Stock of every kind subsist through winter without being fed or sheltered. Excepting the Judith Basin, I have seen no district in the western territories so eligible for settlement as the upper valley of the Yellowstone. Several of the party were very successful during the morning in fishing for trout, of which we afterward had an abundant and continued supply. The Yellowstone here is from 50 to 100 yards wide, and at the lowest stage four feet deep on the riffles, running over a bed of drift boulders and gravel with a very rapid current. The flow of water is fully equal to that of the Missouri at Fort Benton, owing to the rapidity of the current, though the channel is much more narrow."

By the fifth day the party had attained an elevation of 7331 feet, where the thermometer at noon marked 72°. Here they found themselves in the midst of indescribable volcanic wonders. They were, however, notwithstanding their great elevation, in the midst of groves of pine and aspen.

In his notes of the eighth day Lieut. Doane says:

"Barometer, 23°; thermometer, 50°; elevation, 7270 feet.

"Coming into camp in advance, passing through a grove of pine——"

Can one who has not visited the pampas of South America, Australia, the elevated plains of Asia, or our own sheep-growing territory, imagine a forest of pines at 48° north latitude, rising from an elevation of 7270 feet above the level of the sea?

"Coming into camp in advance, passing through a grove of pine, on the margin of a little creek, I was met face to face on the path, by two magnificent buck elk, one of which I wounded, but lost in the woods. Mr. Smith started up a small bear, which also got away. The ground was everywhere tracked by the passage of herds of elk and mountain sheep; and bear sign was everywhere visible."

The tenth day found the party at an elevation of 7697 feet, with the thermometer at 46° in the morning. Describing the high hills, (one of which, Langford's Peak, rises abruptly to the height of 10,327 feet,) by which they were surrounded, and through which the waters of the Yellowstone poured in one of the grandest cataracts of the world, Lieut. Doane says:

"On the caps of these dizzy heights, mountain sheep and elk rest during the night. I followed down the stream on horseback, to where it breaks through the range, threading my way through the forest on game trails with little difficulty. Selecting the channel of a small creek and leaving the horses, I followed it down on foot, wading in the bed of the stream, which fell off at an angle of about 30° between walls of gypsum. Private McConnell accompanied me. On entering the ravine we came at once to hot springs of sulphur, sulphate of copper, alum, steam jets, etc., in endless variety, some of them of very peculiar form. One of them in particular of sulphur had built up a tall spire from the slope of the wall, standing out like an enormous horn, with hot water trickling down its sides. The creek ran on a bed of solid rock, in many places smooth and slippery, in others obstructed by masses of débris formed from the overhanging cliffs of the sulphuretted limestone above. After descending for three miles in the channel we came to a sort of bench or terrace, the same one seen previously in following down the creek from our first camp in the basin. Here we found a large flock of mountain sheep, very tame, and greatly astonished, no doubt, at our sudden appearance. McConnell killed one and wounded another, whereupon the rest disappeared, clambering up the steep walls with a celerity truly astonishing."

On the twelfth day, at an elevation of 7487 feet, they discovered a recent volcano, throwing steam and mud to the height of 300 feet. I refer to this, not to dwell upon this wonder (for it was but one among a myriad), but as evidence of the condition of vegetation and the capacity of the country to sustain flocks at that elevation. Lieut. Doane says:

"The distances to which this mud has been thrown, are truly astonishing. Directly above the crater rises a steep bank, a hundred feet in height, *on the apex of which the tallest tree near is* 110 *feet high.* The topmost branches of this tree were loaded with mud 200 feet above and 50 feet laterally away from the crater. The ground and fallen trees near by, were splashed at a horizontal distance of 200 feet. The trees below were either broken down or their branches festooned with dry mud, which appeared in the tops of trees growing on the side hill from the same level with the crater, 50 feet in height, and at a distance of 180 feet from the volcano."

Certainly vegetation is not stunted by climate when in this elevated and volcanic region upon the apex of the hills, trees attain the height of 110 feet!

But Lieut. Doane's report is replete with evidence that the valleys are capable of sheltering sheep and cattle from the severity of climate that prevails upon the greater elevations during the winter.

But the route of the Northern Pacific Railroad is not obstructed by mountains like these; the highest point it attains being the Deer Lodge Pass through the Rocky Mountains, which is 4950 feet, being 3285 feet below the grade of the Union Pacific Road at Sherman, where, two years ago, I gathered a bouquet composed of the wild flowers common to Eastern Pennsylvania.

SETTLEMENTS ALONG THE LINE.

It must be admitted that a portion of the land in Dakota, Montana, and Idaho, through which this road will run, is unsuited to cultivation, but the proportion is much less than will be found on the line of any more southern road. The alkali plains alone which the Union and Central road traverses are broader than the breadth of all the bad lands along the line of the Northern route. Governor Stevens, who superintended the original government survey of this line, and frequently crossed the country, said, that "not more than one-fifth of the land from Red River to Puget Sound is unsuited to cultivation, and this fifth is largely made up of mountains covered with bunch grass and valuable timber, and filled with precious metals." But, ladies and gentlemen, were it true that but one-fifth instead of four-fifths of the land granted to the Northern Pacific Company between the western boundary of Minnesota and the eastern boundary of Washington and Oregon, is presently available for the purposes of settlement, the grant would, in my judgment, be adequate for the construction of the road. Indeed, I believe that the lands granted in Minnesota, Oregon and Washington Territory, would build and equip the road.

COMMERCIAL ADVANTAGES.

No part of the capital employed in constructing this road will be long unproductive, as a remunerative business awaits the completion of each section. From the Missouri at Omaha to the Sacramento no navigable stream crosses or approaches the Union and Central road, while the route of this road is traversed, at intervals of about two hundred miles, along its whole extent by navigable streams upon which there are considerable settlements. One eastern terminus of the road is the westernmost point of our magnificent system of Lake navigation—the other is the head of navigation on the Mississippi river at St. Paul, a city whose population numbers about 25,000. Duluth, its lake terminus, is rising into commercial importance more rapidly than did Chicago, and with the promise of continuous growth. It is the port through which the people of Minnesota and the entire new Northwest will exchange commodities not only with all the lake ports of the United States and British America, but with Europe, and the commercial cities of the Atlantic seaboard. It will be the chief outlet for the increasing tens of millions of bushels of wheat and feet of lumber, produced by the farmers and lumbermen of Minnesota. Though Duluth is not yet four years old, her foreign commerce is large enough to command the attention of the Treasury Department, and require the appointment of a deputy collector and several minor officers of customs.

THE NORTHERN RIVER SYSTEM.

The settlements on the Red River of the North, the western boundary of Minnesota, are numerous, and the trade of the extended and fertile valleys it drains will await the completion of the road to that river, which will be accomplished by the 1st of September. Beyond Minnesota, the line crosses or runs upon the banks of the Dakota, Missouri and Yellowstone, which are east of the Rocky Mountains, and navigable for hundreds or thousands of miles; and beyond the Rocky Mountains, the Snake, the Cowlitz and the Columbia rivers, will prove immediate and valuable tributaries to its business. Its western termini are at Portland on the Willamette, twelve miles above its confluence with the Columbia, which is already an important commercial centre, and a point yet to be determined on the waters of Puget Sound, which are the predestined field of a commerce that, at an early day, will exceed that of San Francisco, and, in the not very distant future, equal the present commerce of New York. I cannot give the figures to show the extent of the trade of the Columbia river and its confluents, but am able to assure you from actual observation that it has been large and profitable enough to give the original stockholders of the *Oregon Steam Navigation Co.* prominent places in the roll of heavy capitalists on the Pacific Coast.

THE FUTURE PACIFIC METROPOLIS.

That the commercial metropolis of the Pacific coast will be south of Puget Sound I have never believed. Observation confirmed the conviction with which Mr. Whitney had impressed me. And early in August, 1869, just after my return from the Pacific coast, at the request of Col. John W. Forney, I held a protracted conversation with Mr. Joseph I. Gilbert, an experienced phonographic reporter, who, on the 27th of that month, presented to the readers of the *Press* the substance of the interview. Recurring to the *Press* of that date, I find that, speaking on this point, I said:

"Allow me to state one conclusion from personal observation. It is that San Francisco will, in the course of time, cease to be the great city of the Pacific coast. Her location constitutes her for the present the *entrepot* for all the commerce of the coast, embracing the trade from the South American coast, from the Sandwich Islands, from China, Japan, British Columbia, and our territory north of that city. The Bay of San Francisco, too, is quite capable of accommodating the commerce of the world. It is, I think, unequalled as a bay, in extent, beauty and safety. The city has made most magnificent strides. She has her dry-dock, her ample wharves, her steam-tugs, her coast defences, and has made very considerable progress in manufactures. But notwithstanding all these advantages, my firm impression is that the great city of the Pacific coast will have its location on or near the waters of Puget Sound.

. . . .

"Here are to be found in abundance timber, coal, iron, fish, wheat, all domestic grasses, the potato, apple, pear, plum, and during more than half the year, all the fruits known to our own tables. Here, in my judgment, will be located the great city of the Pacific coast, as, owing to the peculiar conformation of the Sound, communication may easily be had between distant parts of this territory by water.

"Another consideration is that a city located here would be practically nearer to China than is San Francisco; because vessels leaving San Francisco for China, notwithstanding the point for which they are destined is south of their point of departure, are compelled on account of the prevailing winds, to make what sailors call a "northing," quite up to the Straits of Fuca; in consequence of which a vessel starting from the latter point for the same destination would have an advantage of three or four days over her San Francisco competitor."

SOME OFFICIAL TESTIMONY.

But, ladies and gentlemen, let me hasten on and show you by official testimony the advantages presented by this route to the Pacific over any other north of the 32d parallel, on which, as I have said, the almost tropical climate would prove an obstacle to general travel and commerce. In pursuance of the act of Congress of March 3, 1853, the Topographical Engineers designated by the Secretary of War, surveyed seven routes extending from the line of the Northern Pacific southward to the 32d parallel. Their reports were referred by the Secretary of War for examination to Captain A. A. Humphreys and Lieut. G. K. Warren, both of whom are well known to the country for the distinguished services they rendered as commanding generals during the late war, and the former of whom is now at the head of the Engineer Department of the United States Army. On the 5th of February 1855, these officers submitted the results of their analysis and comparisons in an elaborate report, in which speaking of the route near the 47th and 49th parallel they say:

"The advantages of this route are—its low profile, which is important in relation to climate; its easy grades, and small amount of ascents and descents, both important if the road should be developed, to its full working power; the great extension west of the prairie lands; in the supplies of timber over the western half of the route; the facilities which the Columbia River and its tributaries, and the Missouri, will afford to the construction of the road; in the short distance from the Missisippi to a seaport of the Pacific; in the western terminus of the road on Puget Sound being nearer to the ports of Asia than the termini of the other routes; in the proximity of the eastern terminus to Lake Superior, from which a continuous navigation for sea-going vessels extends to the Atlantic Ocean; and in the existence of coal on Puget Sound."

The explorations had been but preliminary and had not disclosed the important fact that an abundant supply of coal is distributed at easy points along the whole route.*

On page 107 of the first volume of the report, to which I refer for a moment, is found a tabular statement, showing the relative distance by each of the seven routes surveyed; the sum of ascents and descents: the length of level route of equal working expense; the comparative cost of different routes; the number of miles of route through arable land; the number of miles of route through lands generally uncultivated, arable soil being found in small areas; number of square miles of sums of areas of largest bodies of arable land in uncultivable region; number of miles at an elevation less than 1000 feet; number at an elevation greater than 1000 and less than 2000; greater than 2000 and less than 3000; greater than 3000 and less than 4000; greater than 4000 and less than 5000; greater than 5000 and less than 6000, at which point the Northern route disappears from the table, while two of the routes have each twenty miles at grades above 10,000 feet, and both of which it would be necessary to tunnel at an eleva-

* San Francisco and her ocean steamers are now supplied with coal mined on Puget Sound, near the western terminus of the Northern Pacific Railroad. Twenty-five thousand tons were shipped for this purpose in 1870.

tion of 9540 feet, which is 4590 feet above the highest summit the Northern road will cross.

GRADES—A NATURAL PATHWAY.

In each of these respects the Northern route is shown to compare favorably with all of its competitors. But its most remarkable advantage appears under the head of the sum of ascents and descents. High rates under this head indicate increased percentages of danger and current expense. The lower the rate of ascent and descent the safer and more economical is travel. And while the Northern route is charged under this head with but 19,100 feet, the route comparing most favorably with it in this respect is that on the 41st and 42d parallels, in which the sum is 29,120, an increase of more than fifty per cent.; and the extreme contrast is that of the route on the 38th and 39th parallels, in which the sum reaches 56,514.

The study of these voluminous reports will satisfy any reasonable man that from Duluth to a point on Puget Sound is nature's own route for a Pacific railroad. So startling indeed were the advantages presented by this route, that the then Secretary of War, Jefferson Davis, struck from the report of Governor Stevens, since so distinguished as a soldier and engineer, the estimate he presented of the cost, which was $117,121,000, and inserted in lieu thereof $130,781,000. Davis' keen foresight showed him that the development of the then almost unknown Northwest, by the construction of a road upon easy gradients through a region of such wonderful resources, would, in a few years, place his beloved South and slavery at the mercy of a free people, overwhelmingly outnumbering those of the plantation States. How reckless and unjust this action was, is proven by the fact that all of the more recent estimates fix the cost at but little more than sixty-six per cent. of that of Governor Stevens, or $77,000,000 for the road and original equipment.

EFFECT ON AMERICAN COMMERCE.

The effect the completion of this road, with its immense advantages of position and grades, is to have upon our commerce cannot be predicted. I reiterate the assertion that the trade of the Pacific Ocean must find its chief *entrepot* on Puget Sound; and as evidence of my appreciation of the future extent and value of this commerce let me again refer to the remarks I made in Congress on the 26th of April, 1866. Replying to a distinguished representative from Chicago, Ill., who had reminded members who were disposed to vote for aid to the Northern Pacific Road, that a Congressional election was at hand, I said:

"I appeal from the constituents of the gentleman from Chicago [Mr. Wentworth], on the eve of an election, to posterity, and ask gentlemen to view the proposed enterprise in the light in which future generations will behold it. They will look beyond the vast and undeveloped empire I have indicated; for beyond it lies the broad Pacific, capable of bearing a commerce a thousand times heavier than has ever chafed the waters of the Atlantic, but on which our flag is seen floating only from the masts of coasting craft or whalers wending their slow way to the Northern seas in quest of hard earned wealth. So slight is our power on this ocean that the recently pardoned rebel Semmes, with a single vessel, destroyed nearly a hundred of our peaceable whalers, giving their cargoes, gathered by years of dangerous toil, to the flames or the waves. It bounds our country for more than a thousand miles, and our maritime power, which could not now protect a mile of it, should be seen and felt upon it, and our flag and white sails or the curling smoke of our steamers should shadow its every wave.

"The commerce of the Pacific Ocean belongs to us; and we should confirm our title by the right of occupancy; for when we cast our eyes beyond its placid surface, we behold what is to be our next conquest. The Old World is to be awakened by American ideas. Its unnumbered people are to be quickened, instructed, and redeemed by American enterprise. Some statisticians tell us that there are 750,000,000 people in the ancient theocratic countries of the East, which is the West to which the star of our commercial empire will next take its way. Others put the population at 1,000,000,000; and others at 1,300,000,000. There, where civilization dawned and the drowsy past yet lingers, the first impulses of a new cycle begin to be felt. Japan is yielding to the impulses of our age. The Chinese wall is crumbling away. It was but yesterday that I had a letter informing me that our countryman, Dr. Martin, interpreter of the American Legation at Pekin, under the employment of the Chinese Government, had rendered into that language our Wheaton's Law of Nations. Thus, that vast and long isolated Power is preparing to enter into commercial connections with the world. The ancient civilization of Asia is giving way, the doctrine of sacred castes is about to yield to the sublimer creed of man's freedom and equality. Muscular labor will soon be done there by the potent agents we now employ—coal and iron—and the genius of the buried dead, embodied in mechanism, will soon relieve their toiling millions as it now does ours. Their whole life is to be quickened by modern enterprise, and they will swell the numbers of the people on our Pacific slope."

When it is asserted that these roads will give us the control of the commerce of China, purblind philosophers point to the small portion of that trade that is carried by the Central and Union road as proof that that commerce will never cross our country. It is not two years since that road was completed. Commerce follows cheap and rapid lines of transit, and railroad fares are regulated by the amount of business done. Thus in 1850, by the average rate of fares on American roads, it cost $20 to transport a ton of wheat 100 miles; in 1870, a ton of wheat was transported the same distance for $1.25. (Applause.)

With increase of business the Central and Union Pacific Road will be able, while increasing its profits, to reduce its rates for freight and travel. It is doing it already. Its present rates for passengers and freight compare, as I have said, most favorably with those of 1869; and when twenty or thirty other branches, like those to Denver and Salt Lake City, shall throw their business upon the trunk line, and when other Evanstons and Cheyennes shall have sprung up, when Omaha shall be a city like San Francisco, and San Francisco a city like Philadelphia, all of which may occur within the next quarter of a century, who shall say how small will be the charge for carrying a chest of tea or a case of silk across the continent? It will be very small, and when railroads shall be able to carry this freight as cheaply and more quickly than it can be moved by steamers, the trade of China and Japan will cross our continent, and my prophecies of 1846 and 1850 will be more than fulfilled, as the Pennsylvania road will carry the freight of two Pacific roads—one from San Francisco and the other from the Columbia and Puget Sound. (Applause.)

PACIFIC COAST HARBORS.—PUGET SOUND.

Among the strange contrasts presented by our two coasts, few are more impressive than the coast line itself. Harbors are numerous along the Atlantic coast. No seaboard State is without one or more good harbors. Count them, from Galveston northward and eastward to Portland, Maine, and the number will surprise you. The agricultural and mineral productions of almost every State could be floated to the sea, while our long Pacific coast, south of Alaska, presents but four harbors or fair points for commercial centres, the Bays of San Diego and San Francisco, the Columbia River and Puget Sound, the entrance to which is the Straits of Fuca. The Alleghanies are inland mountains; but the "coast range," as their name indicates, lie along the coast of the Pacific, leaving harbors only where the great waters have forced their way through the rocks.

As I have said, the commerce of China and Japan must near our coast north of the Bay of San Francisco, north even of the mouth of the Columbia, and at a point near to the Straits of Fuca. While, therefore, the commerce of the Pacific must to some extent be shared by San Diego, San Francisco, Portland, and Astoria, a city yet to arise on Puget Sound will be its great centre.

PRODUCTIONS, RESOURCES AND SEASONS.

Would that I could convey to your minds a moderate conception of the wealth and climate of this far Northwestern country and of the body of water called the Straits of Fuca and Puget Sound—so calm, so deep, so guarded by forests such as no man who has not visited them has ever seen. The Straits of Fuca run in an almost direct course more than ninety miles, at an average width of more than ten miles. The shore-line of Puget Sound extends nearly 1900 miles, but, such is its conformation, that the points at greatest distance from each other are not four hundred miles apart. The Sound is a series of canals, bays, inlets and harbors. Gov. Stevens, who lived on its shores for a number of years, likened it to a tree, with a very recognizable body called Admiralty Inlet, and innumerable side-branches, the trunk and branches filling a region seventy nautical miles in length from north to south, and thirty in breath from east to west. In speaking of it again, he said:

"On the whole west coast, from San Diego to the north, nothing like this is met. All the water channels of which Admiralty Inlet is composed, are comparatively narrow and long. They have more or less bold shores and are throughout very deep and abrupt, so much so that in many places a ship's side will strike the shore before the keel will touch the ground. Even in the interior and hidden parts, depths of 50 and 100 fathoms occur as broad as De Fuca Strait itself. Vancouver found 60 fathoms near the Vashon Island within a cable length of the shore, and in Possesion Sound he found no soundings with a line of 110 fathoms. Our modern, more extensive soundings prove that this depth diminishes toward the extremities of the inlets and basins. Nothing can exceed the beauty and safety of these waters for navigation. Not a shoal exists within them; not a hidden rock; no sudden overfalls of the water or the air; no such strong flaws of the wind as in other narrow waters, for instance as in those of Magellan's Straits. And there are in this region so many excellent and most secure ports that the commercial marine of the Pacific Ocean may be here easily accommodated."

There is but little waste land in Oregon and Washington Territory. Oregon embraces 60,975,360 acres, and its population in 1870 was but 90,933. Washington Territory contains 112,730,240 acres, and the census takers found but 23,955 civilized people dwelling upon them. This State and Territory are among the most fertile and productive sections of our country. The wheat of Oregon and Washington, as you may ascertain by consulting the commercial papers of San Francisco, commands, in the markets of that city, ten cents per bushel more than the wheat of California; and oats from the Territory are worth fifteen cents per cental more than the best California oats. As we get the wheat of the entire Pacific slope through California, we know it only as California wheat; but in the home market the difference I have indicated is constantly maintained by reason of the superiority of the more northern grain.

The forests that shelter these waters are composed of trees running up from 250 to 350 feet, with a diameter of from 8 to 12 feet, and throwing out their first arms at from 60 to 100 feet above the ground. In these glorious solitudes, upon the waters of Puget Sound there are in operation saw mills that will this year ship largely over 200,000,000 feet of superior lumber to San Francisco, Callao, Valparaiso, the Sandwich Islands, Australia and China. These forests, an inexhaustible store of wealth in themselves, are underlaid by rich deposits of coal, iron, gold and silver. The beds of iron and coal are already utilized to some extent; and the existence of the precious metals is established by the fact that the washings of the water-courses furnish traces of gold and other metals. Of the fish with which these waters teem, I dare not tax your credulity by speaking.

Though bounded by the 49th degree of latitude, the climate is genial throughout the year. So mild are the winters—indeed, I may say, so free is the country from winter—that, notwithstanding the moisture of the climate, west of the Coast Range, no provision is made for housing cattle at any season of the year. In the month of July, 1869, within the limits of Astor's old fort, near the mouth of the Columbia River, I picked from the orchard of a farmer who had gone thither from Bedford County, Pa., a variety of delicious apples, pears and plums; and from vines near the trunks of the trees, raspberries, strawberries and blackberries—a combination of fruits that could not be found in the month of July upon the best cultivated and most fortunately situated farm in Pennsylvania. And a week before, our party had found Indian women and children vending these fruits and the apricot in the streets of Victoria, the capital of British Columbia.

At Olympia, the capital of Washington Territory, situated at the head of Puget Sound, it was my pleasure to pass the greater part of a day with my young friend Elwood Evans, Esq., son of Chas. Evans, the press manufacturer of this city (whom I recognize among my auditors), and to gather luscious fruit from tree and vine in the gardens attached to his comfortable home and his law-office hard by upon the same street.

THE WORK OF DEVELOPMENT.

Do you ask, as others have done, why with such stores of wealth, waiting to respond with such boundless generosity to the demands of man, the population does not equal one man, woman or child to each square mile? If you do, the answer is ready. It is because the people and Government of the United States did not promptly respond to the suggestion of Asa Whitney, and either by the means proposed by him, or those they should select, connect our Pacific territory with the great lakes by a railway. Had that been done, and the way then been opened to immigrants, Washington Territory would long since have been divided into two or more States, California and Oregon would be great commercial rivals, and the population of our Pacific States would equal or exceed that of busy and blessed New England.

To reach the golden lands of the Pacific coast has been a matter of too much time and expense for the poor man, and too full of trials for families. The fact that in spite of these almost insuperable difficulties, so many intelligent people have found their way thither is a testimonial to the wonderful attractions of the country, and the immense rewards it offers to industry and enterprise.

Build this road, open these multiform and exhaustless resources to the poor but enterprising people of the Eastern States and Europe, and population will flow into them so rapidly that they who shall a few years hence hear the story of the doubts of to-day about the Northern Pacific

Railroad will experience wonder similar to that which you feel at the want of forecast that characterized the people of Pennsylvania twenty-five years ago, when they shrank from embarking so small a percentage of their capital in building the Pennsylvania Central road; and in a few years the trunk line of this great thoroughfare will carry the trade of innumerable lateral branches, penetrating not only our valleys but those of the British Provinces to the North, whose people will thus be made tributary to us forever, or induced to unite their destinies with ours, under a common constitution and flag. This is not declamation or prophecy. It is the announcement of conclusions that flow irresistibly from an ample store of unquestioned facts.

Do you ask whence the population would have come to effect the changes I have indicated? By the construction of the road, the character of the climate and resources of the country would have been disclosed long years ago, and the sheep-growers of the States from Vermont to Iowa would have transferred their flocks to the Asiatic and Australian fields that slope the Rocky Mountains. The hardy lumbermen from the forests of New England and northern Pennsylvania would have found their way to these richer forests in more genial climes. Nor would we then have suffered the decline in our ship-building so much and so justly bemoaned; for difficult of access as the country is, and slender as is its population and commerce, we found along these woody shores ship-yards, having on the stocks first-class ships, the outer planks of which were without a joint, having been cut sheer from one of the monarchs of the forest on the shores of the Sound. The increased coast trade of the Pacific and commerce between our Atlantic and Pacific ports would have kept alive this decaying branch of business, which with the completion of the Northern Pacific Railroad, must revive with grander proportions than it ever assumed in the past.

Where will the people come from to make this wealth available, to build cities at the points along this road at which railroad and river traffic shall intersect, to raise provisions for the mining camps, and to build up commerce on Puget Sound and the Columbia River? What American, whose memory is good for a quarter of a century, asks this question? Where have the people come from who, since we discussed the propriety of building the Pennsylvania Railroad, and Asa Whitney submitted the project of a Pacific road, have settled Iowa and Wisconsin, whose joint population, though then but 200,000, now numbers two millions and a quarter, each having over a million? Where did the people come from who, within a brief quarter of a century have doubled the population of the Northern States of the Union? Where have the people come from who have meanwhile populated so many of the gold and silver-producing sections of our vast territories, and built up the States of Texas, California, Minnesota and Oregon? Let Edward Young, Esq., Chief of the Bureau of Statistics, answer these questions. I hold in my hand a recent report of his—a document that should be circulated by millions through the Eastern States and Europe. It is entitled, "Special Report on Immigration, accompanying Information for Immigrants relative to the Prices and Rentals of Lands, the Staple Products, Facilities of Access to Market, Cost of Farm Stock, Kind of Labor in Demand in the Western and Southern States, etc." This report shows that during the 8 years terminating with the 31st of December, 1846, we received 736,887 immigrants, of whom 416,950 came from the British Isles. But, Mr. Doubter, you interrupt me to ask whether this tide of immigration will continue? whether it has not reached its climax? The Chief of the Bureau of Statistics shall answer you again; for his report shows that during the like period of 8 years, terminating the 31st of last December, we received 2,307,554 immigrants, of whom there came from the British Isles 1,015,517, or more than 33 per cent. more than the entire immigration during the former 8 years.

Yes, the tide of immigration will continue, and for many years it will increase. Each year will see its volume rolling in, until regenerated Europe shall give the laborer ample remuneration, political power and social consideration. (Applause.) Our cheap land and democratic institutions will bring her bone and sinew and enterprise to develop the resources and add to the wealth and power of our country. (Loud applause.) And nothing will do more to promote the movement than the advertisement to all the world of the vast resources of the region through which this road is to run and the wonderful field for labor, enterprise and adventure at its Pacific termini.

PHILADELPHIA INTERESTS.

But what will be the effect of the road upon Philadelphia? What relations has all this to our city and State? These questions, which you propounded to me in your invitation, have, I think, been answered by what I have said. What State or city shares more largely than ours in the general prosperity or depression of the country? Who will be more benefited by the cheapening of freight on raw materials and manufactured articles than we? What American city produces so many of the comforts and luxuries which the people along the line of this road will consume as Philadelphia? Their demands will stimulate our industry, and their abounding means will enable them to reward it abundantly. The construction of one railroad bridge—that over the Mississippi River at St. Louis—gave to one Philadelphia firm, the Wm. Butcher Steel Works, a contract for $500,000 worth of steel. And even now, hundreds of Philadelphia mechanics are busy building locomotives and passenger and freight cars for the Northern Pacific Railroad.

I need not elaborate this point. We are a community of working people. (The mass of the citizens of Philadelphia absolutely live by manual labor.) The prosperity of the capitalists of this city is dependent upon the steady employment and liberal wages of her working people. (Applause.) When labor is idle, capital is idle, or employed at little profit; when the laborer earns no wages, the landlord is not always sure of his rent. (Laughter and applause.) The effect that the construction of this road will have upon the employment and wages of laboring people was discussed by me in the Congressional remarks to which I have already referred. Let me read a paragraph or two from what I then said:

"But the inviting field of the ocean, and the vast field of enterprise and reward open to us in Asia are not the only considerations that induce me to support this bill. The laboring people of every eastern city have an intense interest in this question. The safety of our country depends upon the intelligence, the virtue, the stability of our laboring people. He legislates not wisely for a democratic republic who does not make it the aim of all his acts to improve the material condition of the great laboring masses of the country. If we would perpetuate our institutions, we must see that the wages of labor are so maintained that the children of the working man shall grow up amid the endearments of home, and with the expectation that their children shall find more elegance and refinement in their homes than their parents were familiar with in childhood.

"The construction of a road through our northern gold region will open a field that will be a constant refuge for any unemployed labor of our eastern States. There will be a refuge for those masses of ingenious workmen who are jostled each year by lack of adjustment of their numbers to the demand for their branch of labor, or are deprived of the advantage of the skill they acquired in youth by the invention of labor-saving machinery; and instead of finding themselves, as age gathers on their brow, without the means of livelihood, rich fields of enterprise, easily reached, will cheer their declining years.

"But, again, the depression of our laboring people springs not alone or chiefly from local causes. Beyond the Atlantic Ocean there are 250,000,000 people, in every community of which laboring men are held as raw material; and under the grasping influence of capital, and the oppression of despotic government are held in such bondage, that they are made to subsist, even when they toil most assiduously, upon a modicum of the elements of life, upon a minimum of the amount that will keep the soul in a tolerably sound body. Escaping from this subjection, they are borne to our shores by tens and hundreds of thousands each year. They are strangers in a strange land, many of them unacquainted with our language and habits, and are unconsciously and unwillingly the means of depressing wages. But if we give the company the means to inaugurate work on this road, we will not only relieve the laboring masses of our crowded eastern cities, but furnish employment for more than the annual influx of those whom we gladly welcome, because they strengthen and enrich us by their toil. Could we drain Europe of its surplus laborers we would raise her wages as she now too often depresses ours.

"What will be the true policy of the builders of this road? Will it not be to employ as laborers the heads of families, and to pay them with land and money, and settle the families along the line of the road, so that the laborer of one year will in the next farm his land and supply fresh laborers with bread? Thus will he who enters into an engagement with the company a pauper, or little better, find himself at the end of a year or two an independent farmer upon the world's great commercial highway. The managers of the road must pursue this policy, and will thus create business for and guard their road; thus, too, they will quicken the mineral and agricultural resources of the country, and give to the tax collector, whether at a port of entry or in the service of the internal revenue department, more money each year than this bill is likely to cause to be taken from the treasury.

"I ask gentlemen in considering this question to rise to its dignity and grandeur. I am, sir, a devotee to freedom, but would make every country in the world tributary to my own. I delight in every manifestation of my country's power, and glow with pride as I contemplate its gigantic proportions, and see how rapidly its people subdue the wilderness, and would, as I have said, make every nation tributary to its power. But I would do this, not by oppressing any people, not by war with any government, but by improving the condition of the masses of my countrymen and those who may become such by immigration, and showing the rulers and people of the world how speedily free institutions exalt the poor and oppressed of all nations into free, self-sustaining and self-governing citizens. It is in our power to do this, and by no other means can we do it so well or so quickly as by passing this supplement and vivifying the charter granted to the Northern Pacific Railroad Company."

But, ladies and gentlemen, I have detained you too long, and must close. Not, however, until I shall have reminded you that the grades and snows of the Alleghanies have not interfered with the prosperity of the Pennsylvania Railroad Company. That road has not been a failure. It has done something for the improvement of Philadelphia. It is the most profitable railroad, and most powerful corporation in the United States. (Applause.) It has stretched its controlling influence clear across the Continent. Its vice-president, our esteemed townsman, Thomas A. Scott, Esq., is the master-spirit of the Union Pacific Company, and of more than one line connecting it with Philadelphia. (Applause.) Roads owned or managed by the Pennsylvania Company await the business of the Northern Pacific road, both at St. Paul and Duluth. It has built a road to Erie, our beautiful City of the Lakes, where vessels charged with freight at Duluth will in the early spring and later autumn of each year discharge cargo for New York and Boston, and throughout the season of Lake navigation, for Philadelphia and Baltimore; and it requires but little power of the imagination to behold Erie expanding into generous rivalry with Buffalo, Cleveland and Detroit.

Though the great characteristics of Philadelphia will always be those of a manufacturing city, her commerce is to revive. She will have not *a* line but numerous lines of steamships; and many of the men who now hear me will see the day when her existing wharf line will be wholly inadequate for her commerce. Indeed the completion of the Northern Pacific road, with the steadily increasing trade of the Central route, will settle the now vexed question of a railroad along the entire river front, and require the construction of docks from Greenwich Point to Richmond. But familiar as you are with the resources of our city and State, and the advanced condition of our industries, I leave you to estimate the impulse that will be given to every interest and industry of our people by the early completion of the Northern Pacific Railroad. (Amid earnest and prolonged applause the speaker retired.)

INDEX.

CATALOGUE

OF

PRACTICAL AND SCIENTIFIC BOOKS,

PUBLISHED BY

HENRY CAREY BAIRD,

INDUSTRIAL PUBLISHER,

No. 406 WALNUT STREET,

PHILADELPHIA.

☞ Any of the Books comprised in this Catalogue will be sent by mail, free of postage, at the publication price.

☞ My New and Enlarged Catalogue, 95 pages 8vo., with full descriptions of Books, will be sent, free of postage, to any one who will favor me with his address.

ARMENGAUD, AMOUROUX, AND JOHNSON.—THE PRACTICAL DRAUGHTSMAN'S BOOK OF INDUSTRIAL DESIGN, AND MACHINIST'S AND ENGINEER'S DRAWING COMPANION: Forming a complete course of Mechanical Engineering and Architectural Drawing. From the French of M. Armengaud the elder, Prof. of Design in the Conservatoire of Arts and Industry, Paris, and MM. Armengaud the younger and Amouroux, Civil Engineers. Rewritten and arranged, with additional matter and plates, selections from and examples of the most useful and generally employed mechanism of the day. By William Johnson, Assoc. Inst. C. E., Editor of "The Practical Mechanic's Journal." Illustrated by 50 folio steel plates and 50 wood-cuts. A new edition, 4to. . $10 00

ARLOT.—A COMPLETE GUIDE FOR COACH PAINTERS. Translated from the French of M. Arlot, Coach Painter; late Master Painter for eleven years with M. Ehrler, Coach Manufacturer, Paris. With important American additions . . $1 25

ARROWSMITH.—PAPER-HANGER'S COMPANION: A Treatise in which the Practical Operations of the Trade are Systematically laid down: with Copious Directions Preparatory to Papering; Preventives against the Effect of Damp on Walls; the Various Cements and Pastes adapted to the Several Purposes of the Trade; Observations and Directions for the Panelling and Ornamenting of Rooms, &c. By James Arrowsmith. 12mo., cloth $1 25

BAIRD.—THE AMERICAN COTTON SPINNER, AND MANAGER'S AND CARDER'S GUIDE:

A Practical Treatise on Cotton Spinning; giving the Dimensions and Speed of Machinery, Draught and Twist Calculations, etc.; with notices of recent Improvements: together with Rules and Examples for making changes in the sizes and numbers of Roving and Yarn. Compiled from the papers of the late ROBERT H. BAIRD. 12mo. . . . $1 50

BAKER.—LONG-SPAN RAILWAY BRIDGES:

Comprising Investigations of the Comparative Theoretical and Practical Advantages of the various Adopted or Proposed Type Systems of Construction; with numerous Formulæ and Tables. By B. Baker. 12mo. $2 00

BAKEWELL.—A MANUAL OF ELECTRICITY—PRACTICAL AND THEORETICAL:

By F. C. BAKEWELL, Inventor of the Copying Telegraph. Second Edition. Revised and enlarged. Illustrated by numerous engravings. 12mo. Cloth . . . .

BEANS.—A TREATISE ON RAILROAD CURVES AND THE LOCATION OF RAILROADS:

By E. W. BEANS, C. E. 12mo. . . . $2 00

BLENKARN.—PRACTICAL SPECIFICATIONS OF WORKS EXECUTED IN ARCHITECTURE, CIVIL AND MECHANICAL ENGINEERING, AND IN ROAD MAKING AND SEWERING:

To which are added a series of practically useful Agreements and Reports. By JOHN BLENKARN. Illustrated by fifteen large folding plates. 8vo. $9 00

BLINN.—A PRACTICAL WORKSHOP COMPANION FOR TIN, SHEET-IRON, AND COPPER-PLATE WORKERS:

Containing Rules for Describing various kinds of Patterns used by Tin, Sheet-iron, and Copper-plate Workers; Practical Geometry; Mensuration of Surfaces and Solids; Tables of the Weight of Metals, Lead Pipe, etc.; Tables of Areas and Circumferences of Circles; Japans, Varnishes, Lackers, Cements, Compositions, etc. etc. By LEROY J. BLINN, Master Mechanic. With over One Hundred Illustrations. 12mo. $2 50

BOOTH.—MARBLE WORKER'S MANUAL:

Containing Practical Information respecting Marbles in general, their Cutting, Working, and Polishing; Veneering of Marble; Mosaics; Composition and Use of Artificial Marble, Stuccos, Cements, Receipts, Secrets, etc. etc. Translated from the French by M. L. Booth. With an Appendix concerning American Marbles. 12mo., cloth . . $1 50

BOOTH AND MORFIT.—THE ENCYCLOPEDIA OF CHEMISTRY, PRACTICAL AND THEORETICAL:

Embracing its application to the Arts, Metallurgy, Mineralogy, Geology, Medicine, and Pharmacy. By James C. Booth, Melter and Refiner in the United States Mint, Professor of Applied Chemistry in the Franklin Institute, etc., assisted by Campbell Morfit, author of "Chemical Manipulations," etc. Seventh edition. Complete in one volume, royal 8vo., 978 pages, with numerous wood-cuts and other illustrations. $5 00

BOWDITCH.—ANALYSIS, TECHNICAL VALUATION, PURIFICATION, AND USE OF COAL GAS:

By Rev. W. R. Bowditch. Illustrated with wood engravings. 8vo. $6 50

BOX.—PRACTICAL HYDRAULICS:

A Series of Rules and Tables for the use of Engineers, etc. By Thomas Box. 12mo. $2 50

BUCKMASTER.—THE ELEMENTS OF MECHANICAL PHYSICS:

By J. C. Buckmaster, late Student in the Government School of Mines; Certified Teacher of Science by the Department of Science and Art; Examiner in Chemistry and Physics in the Royal College of Preceptors; and late Lecturer in Chemistry and Physics of the Royal Polytechnic Institute. Illustrated with numerous engravings. In one vol. 12mo. . $1 50

BULLOCK.—THE AMERICAN COTTAGE BUILDER:

A Series of Designs, Plans, and Specifications, from $200 to to $20,000 for Homes for the People; together with Warming, Ventilation, Drainage, Painting, and Landscape Gardening. By John Bullock, Architect, Civil Engineer, Mechanician, and Editor of "The Rudiments of Architecture and Building," etc. Illustrated by 75 engravings. In one vol. 8vo. $3 50

BULLOCK. — THE RUDIMENTS OF ARCHITECTURE AND BUILDING:

For the use of Architects, Builders, Draughtsmen, Machinists, Engineers, and Mechanics. Edited by JOHN BULLOCK, author of "The American Cottage Builder." Illustrated by 250 engravings. In one volume 8vo. $3 50

BURGH.—PRACTICAL ILLUSTRATIONS OF LAND AND MARINE ENGINES:

Showing in detail the Modern Improvements of High and Low Pressure, Surface Condensation, and Super-heating, together with Land and Marine Boilers. By N. P. BURGH, Engineer. Illustrated by twenty plates, double elephant folio, with text. $21 00

BURGH.—PRACTICAL RULES FOR THE PROPORTIONS OF MODERN ENGINES AND BOILERS FOR LAND AND MARINE PURPOSES.

By N. P. BURGH, Engineer. 12mo. $2 00

BURGH.—THE SLIDE-VALVE PRACTICALLY CONSIDERED:

By N. P. BURGH, author of "A Treatise on Sugar Machinery," "Practical Illustrations of Land and Marine Engines," "A Pocket-Book of Practical Rules for Designing Land and Marine Engines, Boilers," etc. etc. etc. Completely illustrated. 12mo. $2 00

BYRN.—THE COMPLETE PRACTICAL BREWER:

Or, Plain, Accurate, and Thorough Instructions in the Art of Brewing Beer, Ale, Porter, including the Process of making Bavarian Beer, all the Small Beers, such as Root-beer, Ginger-pop, Sarsaparilla-beer, Mead, Spruce beer, etc. etc. Adapted to the use of Public Brewers and Private Families. By M. LA FAYETTE BYRN, M. D. With illustrations. 12mo. $1 25

BYRN.—THE COMPLETE PRACTICAL DISTILLER:

Comprising the most perfect and exact Theoretical and Practical Description of the Art of Distillation and Rectification; including all of the most recent improvements in distilling apparatus; instructions for preparing spirits from the numerous vegetables, fruits, etc.; directions for the distillation and preparation of all kinds of brandies and other spirits, spirituous and other compounds, etc. etc.; all of which is so simplified that it is adapted not only to the use of extensive distillers, but for every farmer, or others who may wish to engage in the art of distilling. By M. LA FAYETTE BYRN, M. D. With numerous engravings. In one volume, 12mo. $1 50

BYRNE.—POCKET BOOK FOR RAILROAD AND CIVIL ENGINEERS:
Containing New, Exact, and Concise Methods for Laying out Railroad Curves, Switches, Frog Angles and Crossings; the Staking out of work; Levelling; the Calculation of Cuttings; Embankments; Earth-work, etc. By OLIVER BYRNE. Illustrated, 18mo., full bound $1 75

BYRNE.—THE HANDBOOK FOR THE ARTISAN, MECHANIC, AND ENGINEER:
By OLIVER BYRNE. Illustrated by 185 Wood Engravings. 8vo. $5 00

BYRNE.—THE ESSENTIAL ELEMENTS OF PRACTICAL MECHANICS:
For Engineering Students, based on the Principle of Work. By OLIVER BYRNE. Illustrated by Numerous Wood Engravings, 12mo. $3 63

BYRNE.—THE PRACTICAL METAL-WORKER'S ASSISTANT:
Comprising Metallurgic Chemistry; the Arts of Working all Metals and Alloys; Forging of Iron and Steel; Hardening and Tempering; Melting and Mixing; Casting and Founding; Works in Sheet Metal; the Processes Dependent on the Ductility of the Metals; Soldering; and the most Improved Processes and Tools employed by Metal-Workers. With the Application of the Art of Electro-Metallurgy to Manufacturing Processes; collected from Original Sources, and from the Works of Holtzapffel, Bergeron, Leupold, Plumier, Napier, and others. By OLIVER BYRNE. A New, Revised, and improved Edition, with Additions by John Scoffern, M. B , William Clay, Wm. Fairbairn, F. R. S., and James Napier. With Five Hundred and Ninety-two Engravings; Illustrating every Branch of the Subject. In one volume, 8vo. 652 pages . $7 00

BYRNE.—THE PRACTICAL MODEL CALCULATOR:
For the Engineer, Mechanic, Manufacturer of Engine Work, Naval Architect, Miner, and Millwright. By OLIVER BYRNE. 1 volume, 8vo., nearly 600 pages $4 50

BEMROSE.—MANUAL OF WOOD CARVING: With Practical Illustrations for Learners of the Art, and Original and Selected designs. By WILLIAM BEMROSE, Jr. With an Introduction by LLEWELLYN JEWITT, F. S. A., etc. With 128 Illustrations. 4to., cloth $3 00

BAIRD.—PROTECTION OF HOME LABOR AND HOME PRODUCTIONS NECESSARY TO THE PROSPERITY OF THE AMERICAN FARMER:

By HENRY CAREY BAIRD. 8vo., paper 10

BAIRD.—THE RIGHTS OF AMERICAN PRODUCERS, AND THE WRONGS OF BRITISH FREE TRADE REVENUE REFORM.

By HENRY CAREY BAIRD. (1870) 5

BAIRD.—SOME OF THE FALLACIES OF BRITISH-FREE-TRADE REVENUE-REFORM.

Two Letters to Prof. A. L. Perry, of Williams College, Mass. By HENRY CAREY BAIRD. (1871.) Paper 5

BAIRD.—STANDARD WAGES COMPUTING TABLES:

An Improvement in all former Methods of Computation, so arranged that wages for days, hours, or fractions of hours, at a specified rate per day or hour, may be ascertained at a glance. By T. SPANGLER BAIRD. Oblong folio $5 00

BAUERMAN.—TREATISE ON THE METALLURGY OF IRON.

Illustrated. 12mo. $2 50

BICKNELL'S VILLAGE BUILDER.

55 large plates. 4to. $10 00

BISHOP.—A HISTORY OF AMERICAN MANUFACTURES:

From 1608 to 1866; exhibiting the Origin and Growth of the Principal Mechanic Arts and Manufactures, from the Earliest Colonial Period to the Present Time; By J. LEANDER BISHOP, M. D., EDWARD YOUNG, and EDWIN T. FREEDLEY. Three vols. 8vo., $10 00

BOX.—A PRACTICAL TREATISE ON HEAT AS APPLIED TO THE USEFUL ARTS:

For the use of Engineers, Architects, etc. By THOMAS BOX, author of "Practical Hydraulics." Illustrated by 14 plates, containing 114 figures. 12mo. $4 25

CABINET MAKER'S ALBUM OF FURNITURE:

Comprising a Collection of Designs for the Newest and Most Elegant Styles of Furniture. Illustrated by Forty-eight Large and Beautifully Engraved Plates. In one volume, oblong $5 00

CHAPMAN.—A TREATISE ON ROPE-MAKING:

As practised in private and public Rope-yards, with a Description of the Manufacture, Rules, Tables of Weights, etc., adapted to the Trade; Shipping, Mining, Railways, Builders, etc. By ROBERT CHAPMAN. 24mo. $1 50

CRAIK.—THE PRACTICAL AMERICAN MILLWRIGHT AND MILLER.

Comprising the Elementary Principles of Mechanics, Mechanism, and Motive Power, Hydraulics and Hydraulic Motors, Mill-dams, Saw Mills, Grist Mills, the Oat Meal Mill, the Barley Mill, Wool Carding, and Cloth Fulling and Dressing, Wind Mills, Steam Power, &c. By DAVID CRAIK, Millwright. Illustrated by numerous wood engravings, and five folding plates. 1 vol. 8vo. $5 00

CAMPIN.—A PRACTICAL TREATISE ON MECHANICAL ENGINEERING:

Comprising Metallurgy, Moulding, Casting, Forging, Tools, Workshop Machinery, Mechanical Manipulation, Manufacture of Steam-engines, etc. etc. With an Appendix on the Analysis of Iron and Iron Ores. By FRANCIS CAMPIN, C. E. To which are added, Observations on the Construction of Steam Boilers, and Remarks upon Furnaces used for Smoke Prevention; with a Chapter on Explosions. By R. Armstrong, C. E., and John Bourne. Rules for Calculating the Change Wheels for Screws on a Turning Lathe, and for a Wheel-cutting Machine. By J. LA NICCA. Management of Steel, including Forging, Hardening, Tempering, Annealing, Shrinking, and Expansion. And the Case-hardening of Iron. By G. EDE. 8vo. Illustrated with 29 plates and 100 wood engravings. $6 00

CAMPIN.—THE PRACTICE OF HAND-TURNING IN WOOD, IVORY, SHELL, ETC.:

With Instructions for Turning such works in Metal as may be required in the Practice of Turning Wood, Ivory, etc. Also an Appendix on Ornamental Turning. By FRANCIS CAMPIN, with Numerous Illustrations, 12mo., cloth . . $3 00

CAPRON DE DOLE.—DUSSAUCE.—BLUES AND CARMINES OF INDIGO.

A Practical Treatise on the Fabrication of every Commercial Product derived from Indigo. By FELICIEN CAPRON DE DOLE. Translated, with important additions, by Professor H. DUSSAUCE. 12mo.

CAREY.—THE WORKS OF HENRY C. CAREY:

CONTRACTION OR EXPANSION? REPUDIATION OR RESUMPTION? Letters to Hon. Hugh McCulloch. 8vo. 38

FINANCIAL CRISES, their Causes and Effects. 8vo. paper 25

HARMONY OF INTERESTS; Agricultural, Manufacturing, and Commercial. 8vo., paper $1 00
Do. do. cloth $1 50

LETTERS TO THE PRESIDENT OF THE UNITED STATES. Paper $1 00

MANUAL OF SOCIAL SCIENCE. Condensed from Carey's "Principles of Social Science." By KATE MCKEAN. 1 vol. 12mo. $2 25

MISCELLANEOUS WORKS: comprising "Harmony of Interests," "Money," "Letters to the President," "French and American Tariffs," "Financial Crises," "The Way to Outdo England without Fighting Her," "Resources of the Union," "The Public Debt," "Contraction or Expansion," "Review of the Decade 1857—'67," "Reconstruction," etc. etc. 1 vol. 8vo., cloth $4 50

MONEY: A LECTURE before the N. Y. Geographical and Statistical Society. 8vo., paper 25

PAST, PRESENT, AND FUTURE. 8vo. $2 50

PRINCIPLES OF SOCIAL SCIENCE. 3 volumes 8vo., cloth $10 00

REVIEW OF THE DECADE 1857—'67. 8vo., paper 50

RECONSTRUCTION: INDUSTRIAL, FINANCIAL, AND POLITICAL. Letters to the Hon. Henry Wilson, U. S. S. 8vo. paper 50

THE PUBLIC DEBT, LOCAL AND NATIONAL. How to provide for its discharge while lessening the burden of Taxation. Letter to David A. Wells, Esq., U. S. Revenue Commission. 8vo., paper 25

THE RESOURCES OF THE UNION. A Lecture read, Dec. 1865, before the American Geographical and Statistical Society, N. Y., and before the American Association for the Advancement of Social Science, Boston 50

THE SLAVE TRADE, DOMESTIC AND FOREIGN; Why it Exists, and How it may be Extinguished. 12mo., cloth $1 50

LETTERS ON INTERNATIONAL COPYRIGHT. (1867.) Paper 50

REVIEW OF THE FARMERS' QUESTION. (1870.) Paper 25

RESUMPTION! HOW IT MAY PROFITABLY BE BROUGHT AROUT. (1869.) 8vo., paper 50

REVIEW OF THE REPORT OF HON. D. A. WELLS, Special Commissioner of the Revenue. (1869.) 8vo., paper 50

SHALL WE HAVE PEACE? Peace Financial and Peace Political. Letters to the President Elect. (1868.) 8vo., paper 50

THE FINANCE MINISTER AND THE CURRENCY, AND THE PUBLIC DEBT. (1868.) 8vo., paper . . 50

THE WAY TO OUTDO ENGLAND WITHOUT FIGHTING HER. Letters to Hon. Schuyler Colfax. (1865.) 8vo., paper $1 00

WEALTH! OF WHAT DOES IT CONSIST? (1870.) Paper 25

CAMUS.—A TREATISE ON THE TEETH OF WHEELS:

Demonstrating the best forms which can be given to them for the purposes of Machinery, such as Mill-work and Clock-work. Translated from the French of M. CAMUS. By JOHN I. HAWKINS. Illustrated by 40 plates. 8vo. $3 00

COXE.—MINING LEGISLATION.

A paper read before the Am. Social Science Association. By ECKLEY B. COXE. Paper 20

COLBURN.—THE GAS-WORKS OF LONDON:

Comprising a sketch of the Gas-works of the city, Process of Manufacture, Quantity Produced, Cost, Profit, etc. By ZERAH COLBURN. 8vo., cloth 75

COLBURN.—THE LOCOMOTIVE ENGINE:

Including a Description of its Structure, Rules for Estimating its Capabilities, and Practical Observations on its Construction and Management. By ZERAH COLBURN. Illustrated. A new edition. 12mo. $1 25

COLBURN AND MAW.—THE WATER-WORKS OF LONDON:

Together with a Series of Articles on various other Waterworks. By ZERAH COLBURN and W. MAW. Reprinted from "Engineering." In one volume, 8vo. . . $4 00

DAGUERREOTYPIST AND PHOTOGRAPHER'S COMPANION:

12mo., cloth $1 25

DIRCKS.—PERPETUAL MOTION:

Or Search for Self-Motive Power during the 17th, 18th, and 19th centuries. Illustrated from various authentic sources in Papers, Essays, Letters, Paragraphs, and numerous Patent Specifications, with an Introductory Essay by HENRY DIRCKS, C. E. Illustrated by numerous engravings of machines. 12mo., cloth $3 50

DIXON.—THE PRACTICAL MILLWRIGHT'S AND ENGINEER'S GUIDE:

Or Tables for Finding the Diameter and Power of Cogwheels; Diameter, Weight, and Power of Shafts; Diameter and Strength of Bolts, etc. etc. By THOMAS DIXON. 12mo., cloth. $1 50

DUNCAN.—PRACTICAL SURVEYOR'S GUIDE:

Containing the necessary information to make any person, of common capacity, a finished land surveyor without the aid of a teacher. By ANDREW DUNCAN. Illustrated. 12mo., cloth. $1 25

DUSSAUCE.—A NEW AND COMPLETE TREATISE ON THE ARTS OF TANNING, CURRYING, AND LEATHER DRESSING:

Comprising all the Discoveries and Improvements made in France, Great Britain, and the United States. Edited from Notes and Documents of Messrs. Sallerou, Grouvelle, Duval, Dessables, Labarraque, Payen, René, De Fontenelle, Malapeyre, etc. etc. By Prof. H. DUSSAUCE, Chemist. Illustrated by 212 wood engravings. 8vo. $10 00

DUSSAUCE.—A GENERAL TREATISE ON THE MANUFACTURE OF SOAP, THEORETICAL AND PRACTICAL:

Comprising the Chemistry of the Art, a Description of all the Raw Materials and their Uses. Directions for the Establishment of a Soap Factory, with the necessary Apparatus, Instructions in the Manufacture of every variety of Soap, the Assay and Determination of the Value of Alkalies, Fatty Substances, Soaps, etc. etc. By PROFESSOR H. DUSSAUCE. With an Appendix, containing Extracts from the Reports of the International Jury on Soaps, as exhibited in the Paris Universal Exposition, 1867, numerous Tables, etc. etc. Illustrated by engravings. In one volume 8vo. of over 800 pages $10 00

DUSSAUCE.—PRACTICAL TREATISE ON THE FABRICATION OF MATCHES, GUN COTTON, AND FULMINATING POWDERS.

By Professor H. DUSSAUCE. 12mo. $3 00

DUSSAUCE.—A PRACTICAL GUIDE FOR THE PERFUMER:
Being a New Treatise on Perfumery the most favorable to the Beauty without being injurious to the Health, comprising a Description of the substances used in Perfumery, the Formulæ of more than one thousand Preparations, such as Cosmetics, Perfumed Oils, Tooth Powders, Waters, Extracts, Tinctures, Infusions, Vinaigres, Essential Oils, Pastels, Creams, Soaps, and many new Hygienic Products not hitherto described. Edited from Notes and Documents of Messrs. Debay, Lunel, etc. With additions by Professor H. DUSSAUCE, Chemist. 12mo. $3 00

DUSSAUCE.—A GENERAL TREATISE ON THE MANUFACTURE OF VINEGAR, THEORETICAL AND PRACTICAL.
Comprising the various methods, by the slow and the quick processes, with Alcohol, Wine, Grain, Cider, and Molasses, as well as the Fabrication of Wood Vinegar, etc. By Prof. H. DUSSAUCE. 12mo. $5 00

DUPLAIS.—A COMPLETE TREATISE ON THE DISTILLATION AND MANUFACTURE OF ALCOHOLIC LIQUORS:
From the French of M. DUPLAIS. Translated and Edited by M. MCKENNIE, M D. Illustrated by numerous large plates and wood engravings of the best apparatus calculated for producing the finest products. In one vol. royal 8vo. $10 00

☞ This is a treatise of the highest scientific merit and of the greatest practical value, surpassing in these respects, as well as in the variety of its contents, any similar volume in the English language.

DE GRAFF.—THE GEOMETRICAL STAIR-BUILDERS' GUIDE:
Being a Plain Practical System of Hand-Railing, embracing all its necessary Details, and Geometrically Illustrated by 22 Steel Engravings; together with the use of the most approved principles of Practical Geometry. By SIMON DE GRAFF, Architect. 4to. $5 00

DYER AND COLOR-MAKER'S COMPANION:
Containing upwards of two hundred Receipts for making Colors, on the most approved principles, for all the various styles and fabrics now in existence; with the Scouring Process, and plain Directions for Preparing, Washing-off, and Finishing the Goods. In one vol. 12mo. $1 25

EASTON.—A PRACTICAL TREATISE ON STREET OR HORSE-POWER RAILWAYS:

Their Location, Construction, and Management; with General Plans and Rules for their Organization and Operation; together with Examinations as to their Comparative Advantages over the Omnibus System, and Inquiries as to their Value for Investment; including Copies of Municipal Ordinances relating thereto. By ALEXANDER EASTON, C. E. Illustrated by 23 plates, 8vo., cloth $2 00

FORSYTH.—BOOK OF DESIGNS FOR HEAD-STONES, MURAL, AND OTHER MONUMENTS:

Containing 78 Elaborate and Exquisite Designs. By FORSYTH. 4to., cloth $5 00

*** This volume, for the beauty and variety of its designs, has never been surpassed by any publication of the kind, and should be in the hands of every marble-worker who does fine monumental work.

FAIRBAIRN.—THE PRINCIPLES OF MECHANISM AND MACHINERY OF TRANSMISSION:

Comprising the Principles of Mechanism, Wheels, and Pulleys, Strength and Proportions of Shafts, Couplings of Shafts, and Engaging and Disengaging Gear. By WILLIAM FAIRBAIRN, Esq., C. E., LL. D., F. R. S., F. G. S., Corresponding Member of the National Institute of France, and of the Royal Academy of Turin; Chevalier of the Legion of Honor, etc. etc. Beautifully illustrated by over 150 wood-cuts. In one volume 12mo. $2 50

FAIRBAIRN.—PRIME-MOVERS:

Comprising the Accumulation of Water-power; the Construction of Water-wheels and Turbines; the Properties of Steam; the Varieties of Steam-engines and Boilers and Wind-mills. By WILLIAM FAIRBAIRN, C. E., LL. D., F. R. S., F. G. S. Author of "Principles of Mechanism and the Machinery of Transmission." With Numerous Illustrations. In one volume. (In press.)

GILBART.—A PRACTICAL TREATISE ON BANKING:

By JAMES WILLIAM GILBART. To which is added: THE NATIONAL BANK ACT AS NOW IN FORCE. 8vo. . . . $4 50

GESNER.—A PRACTICAL TREATISE ON COAL, PETROLEUM, AND OTHER DISTILLED OILS.

By ABRAHAM GESNER, M. D., F. G. S. Second edition, revised and enlarged. By GEORGE WELTDEN GESNER, Consulting Chemist and Engineer. Illustrated. 8vo. . . . $3 50

GOTHIC ALBUM FOR CABINET MAKERS:
Comprising a Collection of Designs for Gothic Furniture. Illustrated by twenty-three large and beautifully engraved plates. Oblong $3 00

GRANT.—BEET-ROOT SUGAR AND CULTIVATION OF THE BEET:
By E. B. GRANT. 12mo. $1 25

GREGORY.—MATHEMATICS FOR PRACTICAL MEN:
Adapted to the Pursuits of Surveyors, Architects, Mechanics, and Civil Engineers. By OLINTHUS GREGORY. 8vo., plates, cloth $3 00

GRISWOLD.—RAILROAD ENGINEER'S POCKET COMPANION.
Comprising Rules for Calculating Deflection Distances and Angles, Tangential Distances and Angles, and all Necessary Tables for Engineers; also the art of Levelling from Preliminary Survey to the Construction of Railroads, intended Expressly for the Young Engineer, together with Numerous Valuable Rules and Examples. By W. GRISWOLD. 12mo., tucks. $1 75

GUETTIER.—METALLIC ALLOYS:
Being a Practical Guide to their Chemical and Physical Properties, their Preparation, Composition, and Uses. Translated from the French of A. GUETTIER, Engineer and Director of Founderies, author of "La Fouderie en France," etc. etc. By A. A. FESQUET, Chemist and Engineer. In one volume, 12mo. $3 00

HATS AND FELTING:
A Practical Treatise on their Manufacture. By a Practical Hatter. Illustrated by Drawings of Machinery, &c., 8vo. $1 25

HAY.—THE INTERIOR DECORATOR:
The Laws of Harmonious Coloring adapted to Interior Decorations: with a Practical Treatise on House-Painting. By D. R. HAY, House-Painter and Decorator. Illustrated by a Diagram of the Primary, Secondary, and Tertiary Colors. 12mo. $2 25

HUGHES.—AMERICAN MILLER AND MILLWRIGHT'S ASSISTANT:
By WM. CARTER HUGHES. A new edition. In one volume, 12mo. $1 50

HUNT.—THE PRACTICE OF PHOTOGRAPHY.

By Robert Hunt, Vice-President of the Photographic Society, London. With numerous illustrations. 12mo., cloth . 75

HURST.—A HAND-BOOK FOR ARCHITECTURAL SURVEYORS:

Comprising Formulæ useful in Designing Builders' work, Table of Weights, of the materials used in Building, Memoranda connected with Builders' work, Mensuration, the Practice of Builders' Measurement, Contracts of Labor, Valuation of Property, Summary of the Practice in Dilapidation, etc. etc. By J. F. Hurst, C. E. 2d edition, pocket-book form, full bound $2 50

JERVIS.—RAILWAY PROPERTY:

A Treatise on the Construction and Management of Railways; designed to afford useful knowledge, in the popular style, to the holders of this class of property; as well as Railway Managers, Officers, and Agents. By John B. Jervis, late Chief Engineer of the Hudson River Railroad, Croton Aqueduct, &c. One vol. 12mo., cloth $2 00

JOHNSON.—A REPORT TO THE NAVY DEPARTMENT OF THE UNITED STATES ON AMERICAN COALS:

Applicable to Steam Navigation and to other purposes. By Walter R. Johnson. With numerous illustrations. 607 pp. 8vo., ... $10 00

JOHNSTON.—INSTRUCTIONS FOR THE ANALYSIS OF SOILS, LIMESTONES, AND MANURES.

By J. W. F. Johnston. 12mo. 35

KEENE.—A HAND-BOOK OF PRACTICAL GAUGING,

For the Use of Beginners, to which is added a Chapter on Distillation, describing the process in operation at the Custom House for ascertaining the strength of wines. By James B. Keene, of H. M. Customs. 8vo. . . . $1 25

KENTISH.—A TREATISE ON A BOX OF INSTRUMENTS,

And the Slide Rule; with the Theory of Trigonometry and Logarithms, including Practical Geometry, Surveying, Measuring of Timber, Cask and Malt Gauging, Heights, and Distances. By THOMAS KENTISH. In one volume. 12mo. . . $1 25

KOBELL.—ERNI.—MINERALOGY SIMPLIFIED:

A short method of Determining and Classifying Minerals, by means of simple Chemical Experiments in the Wet Way. Translated from the last German Edition of F. VON KOBELL, with an Introduction to Blowpipe Analysis and other additions. By HENRI ERNI, M. D., Chief Chemist, Department of Agriculture, author of "Coal Oil and Petroleum." In one volume. 12mo. $2 50

LANDRIN.—A TREATISE ON STEEL:

Comprising its Theory, Metallurgy, Properties, Practical Working, and Use. By M. H. C. LANDRIN, Jr., Civil Engineer. Translated from the French, with Notes, by A. A. FESQUET, Chemist and Engineer. With an Appendix on the Bessemer and the Martin Processes for Manufacturing Steel, from the Report of ABRAM S. HEWITT, United States Commissioner to the Universal Exposition, Paris, 1867. 12mo. . . $3 00

LARKIN.—THE PRACTICAL BRASS AND IRON FOUNDER'S GUIDE.

A Concise Treatise on Brass Founding, Moulding, the Metals and their Alloys, etc.; to which are added Recent Improvements in the Manufacture of Iron, Steel by the Bessemer Process, etc. etc. By JAMES LARKIN, late Conductor of the Brass Foundry Department in Reany, Neafie & Co.'s Penn Works, Philadelphia. Fifth edition, revised, with extensive Additions. In one volume. 12mo. $2 25

LEAVITT.—FACTS ABOUT PEAT AS AN ARTICLE OF FUEL:
With Remarks upon its Origin and Composition, the Localities in which it is found, the Methods of Preparation and Manufacture, and the various Uses to which it is applicable; together with many other matters of Practical and Scientific Interest. To which is added a chapter on the Utilization of Coal Dust with Peat for the Production of an Excellent Fuel at Moderate Cost, especially adapted for Steam Service. By H. T. Leavitt. Third edition. 12mo. $1 75

LEROUX.—A PRACTICAL TREATISE ON THE MANUFACTURE OF WORSTEDS AND CARDED YARNS:
Translated from the French of Charles Leroux, Mechanical Engineer, and Superintendent of a Spinning Mill. By Dr. H. Paine, and A. A. Fesquet. Illustrated by 12 large plates. In one volume 8vo. $5 00

LESLIE (MISS).—COMPLETE COOKERY:
Directions for Cookery in its Various Branches. By Miss Leslie. 60th edition. Thoroughly revised, with the addition of New Receipts. In 1 vol. 12mo., cloth . . $1 50

LESLIE (MISS). LADIES' HOUSE BOOK:
a Manual of Domestic Economy. 20th revised edition. 12mo., cloth $1 25

LESLIE (MISS).—TWO HUNDRED RECEIPTS IN FRENCH COOKERY.
12mo. 50

LIEBER.—ASSAYER'S GUIDE:
Or, Practical Directions to Assayers, Miners, and Smelters, for the Tests and Assays, by Heat and by Wet Processes, for the Ores of all the principal Metals, of Gold and Silver Coins and Alloys, and of Coal, etc. By Oscar M. Lieber. 12mo., cloth $1 25

LOVE.—THE ART OF DYEING, CLEANING, SCOURING, AND FINISHING:
On the most approved English and French methods; being Practical Instructions in Dyeing Silks, Woollens, and Cottons, Feathers, Chips, Straw, etc.; Scouring and Cleaning Bed and Window Curtains, Carpets, Rugs, etc.; French and English Cleaning, etc. By Thomas Love. Second American Edition, to which are added General Instructions for the Use of Aniline Colors. 8vo. 5 00

MAIN AND BROWN.—QUESTIONS ON SUBJECTS CONNECTED WITH THE MARINE STEAM-ENGINE:

And Examination Papers; with Hints for their Solution. By THOMAS J. MAIN, Professor of Mathematics, Royal Naval College, and THOMAS BROWN, Chief Engineer, R. N. 12mo., cloth $1 50

MAIN AND BROWN.—THE INDICATOR AND DYNAMOMETER:

With their Practical Applications to the Steam-Engine. By THOMAS J. MAIN, M. A. F. R., Ass't Prof. Royal Naval College, Portsmouth, and THOMAS BROWN, Assoc. Inst. C. E., Chief Engineer, R. N., attached to the R. N. College. Illustrated. From the Fourth London Edition. 8vo. $1 50

MAIN AND BROWN.—THE MARINE STEAM-ENGINE.

By THOMAS J. MAIN, F. R. Ass't S. Mathematical Professor at Royal Naval College, and THOMAS BROWN, Assoc. Inst. C. E. Chief Engineer, R. N. Attached to the Royal Naval College. Authors of "Questions Connected with the Marine Steam-Engine," and the "Indicator and Dynamometer." With numerous Illustrations. In one volume 8vo. $5 00

MARTIN.—SCREW-CUTTING TABLES, FOR THE USE OF MECHANICAL ENGINEERS:

Showing the Proper Arrangement of Wheels for Cutting the Threads of Screws of any required Pitch; with a Table for Making the Universal Gas-Pipe Thread and Taps. By W. A. MARTIN, Engineer. 8vo. 50

MILES—A PLAIN TREATISE ON HORSE-SHOEING.

With Illustrations. By WILLIAM MILES, author of "The Horse's Foot"

MOLESWORTH.—POCKET-BOOK OF USEFUL FORMULÆ AND MEMORANDA FOR CIVIL AND MECHANICAL ENGINEERS.

By GUILFORD L. MOLESWORTH, Member of the Institution of Civil Engineers, Chief Resident Engineer of the Ceylon Railway. Second American from the Tenth London Edition. In one volume, full bound in pocket-book form $2 00

MOORE.—THE INVENTOR'S GUIDE:

Patent Office and Patent Laws: or, a Guide to Inventors, and a Book of Reference for Judges, Lawyers, Magistrates, and others. By J. G. MOORE. 12mo., cloth $1 25

NAPIER.—A MANUAL OF ELECTRO-METALLURGY:

Including the Application of the Art to Manufacturing Processes. By JAMES NAPIER. Fourth American, from the Fourth London edition, revised and enlarged. Illustrated by engravings. In one volume, 8vo. $2 00

NAPIER.—A SYSTEM OF CHEMISTRY APPLIED TO DYEING:
By JAMES NAPIER, F. C. S. A New and Thoroughly Revised Edition, completely brought up to the present state of the Science, including the Chemistry of Coal Tar Colors. By A. A. FESQUET, Chemist and Engineer. With an Appendix on Dyeing and Calico Printing, as shown at the Paris Universal Exposition of 1867, from the Reports of the International Jury, etc. Illustrated. In one volume 8vo., 400 pages $5 00

NEWBERY.—GLEANINGS FROM ORNAMENTAL ART OF EVERY STYLE;
Drawn from Examples in the British, South Kensington, Indian, Crystal Palace, and other Museums, the Exhibitions of 1851 and 1862, and the best English and Foreign works. In a series of one hundred exquisitely drawn Plates, containing many hundred examples. By ROBERT NEWBERY. 4to. $15 00

NICHOLSON.—A MANUAL OF THE ART OF BOOK-BINDING:
Containing full instructions in the different Branches of Forwarding, Gilding, and Finishing. Also, the Art of Marbling Book-edges and Paper. By JAMES B. NICHOLSON. Illustrated. 12mo. cloth $2 25

NORRIS.—A HAND-BOOK FOR LOCOMOTIVE ENGINEERS AND MACHINISTS:
Comprising the Proportions and Calculations for Constructing Locomotives; Manner of Setting Valves; Tables of Squares, Cubes, Areas, etc. etc. By SEPTIMUS NORRIS, Civil and Mechanical Engineer. New edition. Illustrated, 12mo., cloth $2 00

NYSTROM.—ON TECHNOLOGICAL EDUCATION AND THE CONSTRUCTION OF SHIPS AND SCREW PROPELLERS:
For Naval and Marine Engineers. By JOHN W. NYSTROM, late Acting Chief Engineer U. S. N. Second edition, revised with additional matter. Illustrated by seven engravings. 12mo. $2 50

O'NEILL.—A DICTIONARY OF DYEING AND CALICO PRINTING:
Containing a brief account of all the Substances and Processes in use in the Art of Dyeing and Printing Textile Fabrics: with Practical Receipts and Scientific Information. By CHARLES O'NEILL, Analytical Chemist; Fellow of the Chemical Society of London; Member of the Literary and Philosophical Society of Manchester; Author of "Chemistry of Calico Printing and Dyeing." To which is added An Essay on Coal Tar Colors and their Application to

Dyeing and Calico Printing. By A. A. FESQUET, Chemist and Engineer. With an Appendix on Dyeing and Calico Printing, as shown at the Exposition of 1867, from the Reports of the International Jury, etc. In one volume 8vo., 491 pages . . $6 00

OSBORN.—THE METALLURGY OF IRON AND STEEL:

Theoretical and Practical: In all its Branches; With Special Reference to American Materials and Processes. By H. S. OSBORN, LL. D., Professor of Mining and Metallurgy in Lafayette College, Easton, Pa. Illustrated by 230 Engravings on Wood, and 6 Folding Plates. 8vo., 972 pages $10 00

OSBORN.—AMERICAN MINES AND MINING:

Theoretically and Practically Considered. By Prof. H. S. OSBORN, Illustrated by numerous engravings. 8vo. (*In preparation.*)

PAINTER, GILDER, AND VARNISHER'S COMPANION:

Containing Rules and Regulations in everything relating to the Arts of Painting, Gilding, Varnishing, and Glass Staining, with numerous useful and valuable Receipts; Tests for the Detection of Adulterations in Oils and Colors, and a statement of the Diseases and Accidents to which Painters, Gilders, and Varnishers are particularly liable, with the simplest methods of Prevention and Remedy. With Directions for Graining, Marbling, Sign Writing, and Gilding on Glass. To which are added COMPLETE INSTRUCTIONS FOR COACH PAINTING AND VARNISHING. 12mo., cloth, $1 50

PALLETT.—THE MILLER'S, MILLWRIGHT'S, AND ENGINEER'S GUIDE.

By HENRY PALLETT. Illustrated. In one vol. 12mo. . $3 00

PERKINS.—GAS AND VENTILATION.

Practical Treatise on Gas and Ventilation. With Special Relation to Illuminating, Heating, and Cooking by Gas. Including Scientific Helps to Engineer-students and others. With illustrated Diagrams. By E. E. PERKINS. 12mo., cloth . . . $1 25

PERKINS AND STOWE.—A NEW GUIDE TO THE SHEET-IRON AND BOILER PLATE ROLLER:

Containing a Series of Tables showing the Weight of Slabs and Piles to Produce Boiler Plates, and of the Weight of Piles and the Sizes of Bars to Produce Sheet-iron; the Thickness of the Bar Gauge in Decimals; the Weight per foot, and the Thickness on the Bar or Wire Gauge of the fractional parts of an inch; the Weight per sheet, and the Thickness on the Wire Gauge of Sheet-iron of various dimensions to weigh 112 lbs. per bundle; and the conversion of Short Weight into Long Weight, and Long Weight into Short. Estimated and collected by G. H. PERKINS and J. G. STOWE $2 50

PHILLIPS AND DARLINGTON.—RECORDS OF MINING AND METALLURGY:

Or, Facts and Memoranda for the use of the Mine Agent and Smelter. By J. ARTHUR PHILLIPS, Mining Engineer, Graduate of the Imperial School of Mines, France, etc., and JOHN DARLINGTON. Illustrated by numerous engravings. In one vol. 12mo. . $2 00

PRADAL, MALEPEYRE, AND DUSSAUCE.—A COMPLETE TREATISE ON PERFUMERY:

Containing notices of the Raw Material used in the Art, and the Best Formulæ. According to the most approved Methods followed in France, England, and the United States. By M. P. PRADAL, Perfumer-Chemist, and M. F. MALEPEYRE. Translated from the French, with extensive additions, by Prof. H. DUSSAUCE. 8vo. $10

PROTEAUX.—PRACTICAL GUIDE FOR THE MANUFACTURE OF PAPER AND BOARDS.

By A. PROTEAUX, Civil Engineer, and Graduate of the School of Arts and Manufactures, Director of Thiers's Paper Mill, 'Puy-de-Dômé. With additions, by L. S. LE NORMAND. Translated from the French, with Notes, by HORATIO PAINE, A. B., M. D. To which is added a Chapter on the Manufacture of Paper from Wood in the United States, by HENRY T. BROWN, of the "American Artisan." Illustrated by six plates, containing Drawings of Raw Materials, Machinery, Plans of Paper-Mills, etc. etc. 8vo. $5 00

REGNAULT.—ELEMENTS OF CHEMISTRY.

By M. V. REGNAULT. Translated from the French by T. FORREST BENTON, M. D., and edited, with notes, by JAMES C. BOOTH, Melter and Refiner U. S. Mint, and WM. L. FABER, Metallurgist and Mining Engineer. Illustrated by nearly 700 wood engravings. Comprising nearly 1500 pages. In two vols. 8vo., cloth $10 00

REID.—A PRACTICAL TREATISE ON THE MANUFACTURE OF PORTLAND CEMENT:

By HENRY REID, C. E. To which is added a Translation of M. A. Lipowitz's Work, describing a new method adopted in Germany of Manufacturing that Cement. By W. F. REID. Illustrated by plates and wood engravings. 8vo. $7 00

RIFFAULT, VERGNAUD, AND TOUSSAINT.—A PRACTICAL TREATISE ON THE MANUFACTURE OF COLORS FOR PAINTING:

Containing the best Formulæ and the Processes the Newest and in most General Use. By MM. RIFFAULT, VERGNAUD, and TOUSSAINT. Revised and Edited by M. F. MALEPEYRE and Dr. EMIL WINCKLER. Illustrated by Engravings. In one vol. 8vo. *(In preparation.)*

RIFFAULT, VERGNAUD, AND TOUSSAINT.—A PRACTICAL TREATISE ON THE MANUFACTURE OF VARNISHES:
By MM. RIFFAULT, VERGNAUD, and TOUSSAINT. Revised and Edited by M. F. MALEPEYRE and Dr. EMIL WINCKLER. Illustrated. In one vol. 8vo. (*In preparation.*)

SHUNK.—A PRACTICAL TREATISE ON RAILWAY CURVES AND LOCATION, FOR YOUNG ENGINEERS.
By WM. F. SHUNK, Civil Engineer. 12mo., tucks . . $2 00

SMEATON.—BUILDER'S POCKET COMPANION:
Containing the Elements of Building, Surveying, and Architecture; with Practical Rules and Instructions connected with the subject. By A. C. SMEATON, Civil Engineer, etc. In one volume, 12mo. $1 50

SMITH.—THE DYER'S INSTRUCTOR:
Comprising Practical Instructions in the Art of Dyeing Silk, Cotton, Wool, and Worsted, and Woollen Goods: containing nearly 800 Receipts. To which is added a Treatise on the Art of Padding; and the Printing of Silk Warps, Skeins, and Handkerchiefs, and the various Mordants and Colors for the different styles of such work. By DAVID SMITH, Pattern Dyer, 12mo., cloth $3 00

SMITH.—THE PRACTICAL DYER'S GUIDE:
Comprising Practical Instructions in the Dyeing of Shot Cobourgs, Silk Striped Orleans, Colored Orleans from Black Warps, ditto from White Warps, Colored Cobourgs from White Warps, Merinos, Yarns, Woollen Cloths, etc. Containing nearly 300 Receipts, to most of which a Dyed Pattern is annexed. Also, a Treatise on the Art of Padding. By DAVID SMITH. In one vol. 8vo. $25 00

SHAW.—CIVIL ARCHITECTURE:
Being a Complete Theoretical and Practical System of Building, containing the Fundamental Principles of the Art. By EDWARD SHAW, Architect. To which is added a Treatise on Gothic Architecture, &c. By THOMAS W. SILLOWAY and GEORGE M. HARDING, Architects. The whole illustrated by 102 quarto plates finely engraved on copper. Eleventh Edition. 4to. Cloth. $10 00

SLOAN.—AMERICAN HOUSES:
A variety of Original Designs for Rural Buildings. Illustrated by 26 colored Engravings, with Descriptive References. By SAMUEL SLOAN, Architect, author of the "Model Architect," etc. etc. 8vo. $2 50

SCHINZ.—RESEARCHES ON THE ACTION OF THE BLAST-FURNACE.
By CHAS. SCHINZ. Seven plates. 12mo. . . . $4 25

SMITH.—PARKS AND PLEASURE GROUNDS:

Or, Practical Notes on Country Residences, Villas, Public Parks, and Gardens. By CHARLES H. J. SMITH, Landscape Gardener and Garden Architect, etc. etc. 12mo. $2 25

STOKES.—CABINET-MAKER'S AND UPHOLSTERER'S COMPANION:

Comprising the Rudiments and Principles of Cabinet-making and Upholstery, with Familiar Instructions, Illustrated by Examples for attaining a Proficiency in the Art of Drawing, as applicable to Cabinet-work; The Processes of Veneering, Inlaying, and Buhl-work; the Art of Dyeing and Staining Wood, Bone, Tortoise Shell, etc. Directions for Lackering, Japanning, and Varnishing; to make French Polish; to prepare the Best Glues, Cements, and Compositions, and a number of Receipts, particularly for workmen generally. By J. STOKES. In one vol. 12mo. With illustrations $1 25

STRENGTH AND OTHER PROPERTIES OF METALS.

Reports of Experiments on the Strength and other Properties of Metals for Cannon. With a Description of the Machines for Testing Metals, and of the Classification of Cannon in service. By Officers of the Ordnance Department U. S. Army. By authority of the Secretary of War. Illustrated by 25 large steel plates. In 1 vol. quarto $10 00

SULLIVAN.—PROTECTION TO NATIVE INDUSTRY.

By Sir EDWARD SULLIVAN, Baronet. (1870.) 8vo. . $1 50

TABLES SHOWING THE WEIGHT OF ROUND, SQUARE, AND FLAT BAR IRON, STEEL, ETC.

By Measurement. Cloth 63

TAYLOR.—STATISTICS OF COAL:

Including Mineral Bituminous Substances employed in Arts and Manufactures; with their Geographical, Geological, and Commercial Distribution and amount of Production and Consumption on the American Continent. With Incidental Statistics of the Iron Manufacture. By R. C. TAYLOR. Second edition, revised by S. S. HALDEMAN. Illustrated by five Maps and many wood engravings. 8vo., cloth $6 00

TEMPLETON.—THE PRACTICAL EXAMINATOR ON STEAM AND THE STEAM-ENGINE:

With Instructive References relative thereto, for the Use of Engineers, Students, and others. By WM. TEMPLETON, Engineer. 12mo. $1 25

THOMAS.—THE MODERN PRACTICE OF PHOTOGRAPHY.
By R. W. THOMAS, F. C. S. 8vo., cloth 75

THOMSON.—FREIGHT CHARGES CALCULATOR.
By ANDREW THOMSON, Freight Agent $1 25

TURNING: SPECIMENS OF FANCY TURNING EXECUTED ON THE HAND OR FOOT LATHE:
With Geometric, Oval, and Eccentric Chucks, and Elliptical Cutting Frame. By an Amateur. Illustrated by 30 exquisite Photographs. 4to. $3 00

TURNER'S (THE) COMPANION:
Containing Instructions in Concentric, Elliptic, and Eccentric Turning; also various Plates of Chucks, Tools, and Instruments; and Directions for using the Eccentric Cutter, Drill, Vertical Cutter, and Circular Rest; with Patterns and Instructions for working them. A new edition in 1 vol. 12mo. $1 50

URBIN—BRULL.—A PRACTICAL GUIDE FOR PUDDLING IRON AND STEEL.
By ED. URBIN, Engineer of Arts and Manufactures. A Prize Essay read before the Association of Engineers, Graduate of the School of Mines, of Liege, Belgium, at the Meeting of 1865–6. To which is added a COMPARISON OF THE RESISTING PROPERTIES OF IRON AND STEEL. By A. BRULL. Translated from the French by A. A. FESQUET, Chemist and Engineer. In one volume, 8vo. $1 00

VOGDES.—THE ARCHITECT'S AND BUILDER'S POCKET COMPANION AND PRICE BOOK.
By F. W. VOGDES, Architect. Illustrated. Full bound in pocket-book form. $2 00
In book form, 18mo., muslin 1 50

WARN.—THE SHEET METAL WORKER'S INSTRUCTOR, FOR ZINC, SHEET-IRON, COPPER AND TIN PLATE WORKERS, &c.
By REUBEN HENRY WARN, Practical Tin Plate Worker. Illustrated by 32 plates and 37 wood engravings. 8vo. . . $3 00

WATSON.—A MANUAL OF THE HAND-LATHE.
By EGBERT P. WATSON, Late of the "Scientific American," Author of "Modern Practice of American Machinists and Engineers," In one volume, 12mo. $1 50

WATSON.—THE MODERN PRACTICE OF AMERICAN MACHINISTS AND ENGINEERS:

Including the Construction, Application, and Use of Drills, Lathe Tools, Cutters for Boring Cylinders, and Hollow Work Generally, with the most Economical Speed of the same, the Results verified by Actual Practice at the Lathe, the Vice, and on the Floor. Together with Workshop management, Economy of Manufacture, the Steam-Engine, Boilers, Gears, Belting, etc. etc. By EGBERT P. WATSON, late of the "Scientific American." Illustrated by eighty-six engravings. 12mo. $2 50

WATSON.—THE THEORY AND PRACTICE OF THE ART OF WEAVING BY HAND AND POWER:

With Calculations and Tables for the use of those connected with the Trade. By JOHN WATSON, Manufacturer and Practical Machine Maker. Illustrated by large drawings of the best Power-Looms. 8vo. $10 00

WEATHERLY.—TREATISE ON THE ART OF BOILING SUGAR, CRYSTALLIZING, LOZENGE-MAKING, COMFITS, GUM GOODS,

And other processes for Confectionery, &c. In which are explained, in an easy and familiar manner, the various Methods of Manufacturing every description of Raw and Refined Sugar Goods, as sold by Confectioners and others $2 00

WILL.—TABLES FOR QUALITATIVE CHEMICAL ANALYSIS.

By Prof. HEINRICH WILL, of Giessen, Germany. Seventh edition. Translated by CHARLES F. HIMES, Ph. D., Professor of Natural Science, Dickinson College, Carlisle, Pa. . . $1 25

WILLIAMS.—ON HEAT AND STEAM:

Embracing New Views of Vaporization, Condensation, and Expansion. By CHARLES WYE WILLIAMS, A. I. C. E. Illustrated. 8vo. $3 50

WORSSAM.—ON MECHANICAL SAWS:

From the Transactions of the Society of Engineers, 1867. By S. W. WORSSAM, Jr. Illustrated by 18 large folding plates. 8vo. $5 00

WÖHLER.—A HAND-BOOK OF MINERAL ANALYSIS.

By F. WÖHLER. Edited by H. B. NASON, Professor of Chemistry, Rensselaer Institute, Troy, N. Y. With numerous Illustrations. 12mo. $3 00

www.ingramcontent.com/pod-product-compliance
Lightning Source LLC
LaVergne TN
LVHW021235110826
845150LV00002B/339

* 9 7 8 1 4 2 5 5 6 2 6 1 8 *